Contents

ILLUSTRATIONS vii
ACKNOWLEDGEMENTS ix

Part I 'Youth in Feeling'

1 A Blessed Boy 1840–1862 3
2 Venus Discovered 1862–1866 31
3 Vita Nova 1866–1869 55
4 'What Have We Done to Death?' 1870–1875 78
5 'Carnival of Folly' and Founding of the Stud 1875–1878 108
6 The Children of Shem 1877–1880 136

Part II 'Manhood in Battle'

7 Egypt, Arise! 1880–1882 167
8 Wind and Whirlwind, 1882 179
9 A Passage through India 1883–1884 193
10 'Am I a Tory Democrat?' 1884–1885 207
11 A New Pilgrimage 1886–1887 224
12 'Balfour's Criminal' 1887 239
13 In Chains for Ireland 1888 254
14 Disentanglement 1888–1890 270
15 The Amorist 1891–1894 286
16 *Grande Passion* 1895–1896 309

Part III 'Old Age in Meditation'

17 'Poor Wicked Century, Farewell!' 1897–1900 327
18 The Shame of the Twentieth Century 1901–1906 345
19 The Parting 1906–1909 362
20 'Pilgrim of Distress' 1910–1913 381
21 Peacocks and Prophets 1914–1917 393
22 The Unconquered Flame 1918–1922 412

BIBLIOGRAPHY 433
REFERENCES 437
INDEX 449

Elizabeth Longford

A Pilgrimage of Passion

The Life of Wilfrid Scawen Blunt

A PANTHER BOOK

GRANADA
London Toronto Sydney New York

Published by Granada Publishing Limited in 1982

ISBN 0 586 05307 7

First published in Great Britain by
Weidenfeld and Nicolson 1979

Granada Publishing Limited
Frogmore, St Albans, Herts AL2 2NF
and
36 Golden Square, London W1R 4AH
866 United Nations Plaza, New York, NY 10017, USA
117 York Street, Sydney, NSW 2000, Australia
100 Skyway Avenue, Rexdale, Ontario, M9W 3A6, Canada
61 Beach Road, Auckland, New Zealand

Printed and bound in Great Britain by
Cox & Wyman Ltd, Reading
Set in Monotype Bembo

To Frank

Illustrations

1 Self-portrait of Wilfrid, aged fourteen.
2 Wilfrid in diplomatic uniform.
3 Alice Blunt, Wilfrid's sister.
4 Newbuildings Place.
5 Crabbet Park.
6 Letter from Lady Anne Blunt to W.S.B. probably 1874.
7 Lady Anne Blunt with Kassida.
8 Catherine Walters ('Skittles').
9 Lady Anne Isabella (King-) Noel.
10 Margaret Maria Laprimaudaye, afterwards Mrs 'Minnie' Pollen.
11 'Georgie' Sumner.
12 Mrs Ella Baird.
13 Madeline Wyndham, 1873.
14 Mrs William Morris (Janey) at Kelmscott House, Hammersmith.
15 Lady Elcho (Countess of Wemyss).
16 Margaret Talbot.
17 Lady Mary Charteris about 1904.
18 Dorothy Carleton.
19 W.S.B. on Pharaoh, by Lady Anne Blunt, 1881.
20 Ahmed Arabi, 1882, drawn from a photograph in Cairo prison.
21 Lady Anne in Dublin, 1888. W.S.B. regarded this as her best photograph.
22 W.S.B. in prison clothes, 1888.
23 Lady Emily Lytton, 1892, wearing W.S.B.'s overcoat.
24 Judith and Neville Lytton and their spaniels at Crabbet.
25 Anne, Winnie and Anthony Lytton.
26 After the 'Peacock Dinner', January 1914. W. B. Yeats stands on the right of W.S.B., Ezra Pound on his left.
27 W.S.B. in old age by Neville Lytton.

Family of Wilfrid Scawen Blunt

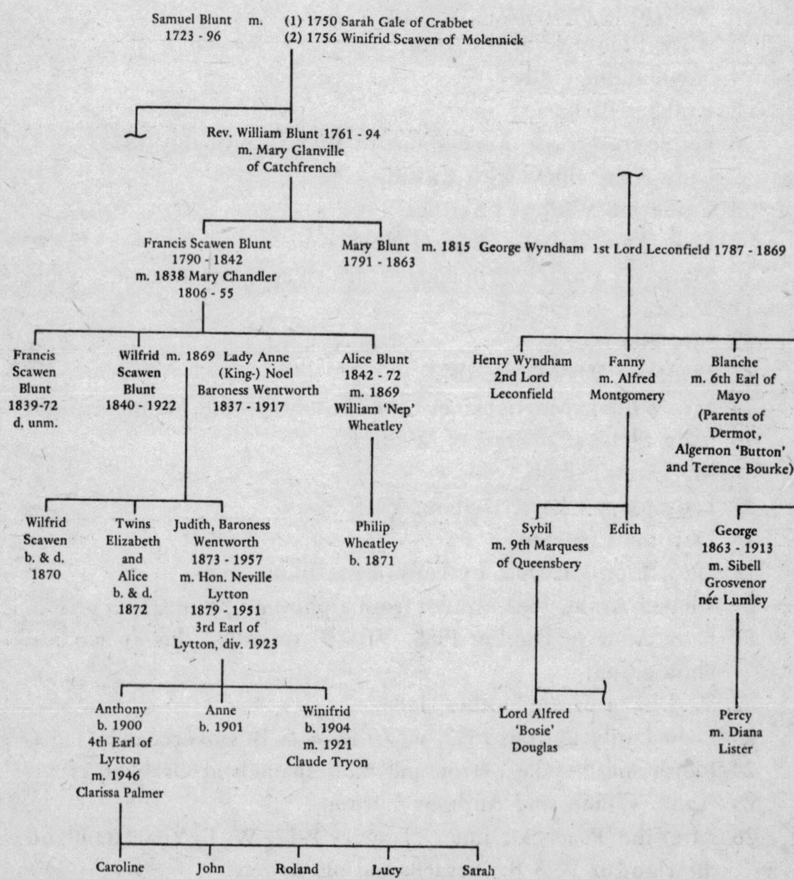

The countess of Longford, CBE, formerly Lady Pakenham, is one of the greatest living biographers. After taking her degree in literature at Oxford, she was a lecturer for the Workers' Educational Association in English, Economics and Politics. She has stood twice for Parliament as a Labour Party candidate. She has also appeared on numerous television and radio programmes, and is a Trustee of the National Portrait Gallery and a Member of the Royal Society of Literature.

During his lifetime Blunt published extracts from his diaries covering the years 1888 to 1914, but his 'Secret Memoirs', extending from his birth in 1840 to his death in 1922, have never been available before. For reasons of discretion and safety, they were lodged in the archives of the Fitzwilliam Museum, Cambridge, upon Blunt's death, with a ban on them for fifty years. Now, the Museum has commissioned Elizabeth Longford to write his official life based on his complete papers, both published and unpublished.

This biography of Wilfrid Scawen Blunt ranks for depth of interpretation, humour and originality with Elizabeth Longford's much acclaimed biographies of Queen Victoria, Byron and Wellington.

By the same author

Victoria R.I.
Wellington: The Years of the Sword
Wellington: Pillar of State
Piety in Queen Victoria's Reign
Byron's Greece
Life of Byron
The Royal House of Windsor
Winston Churchill

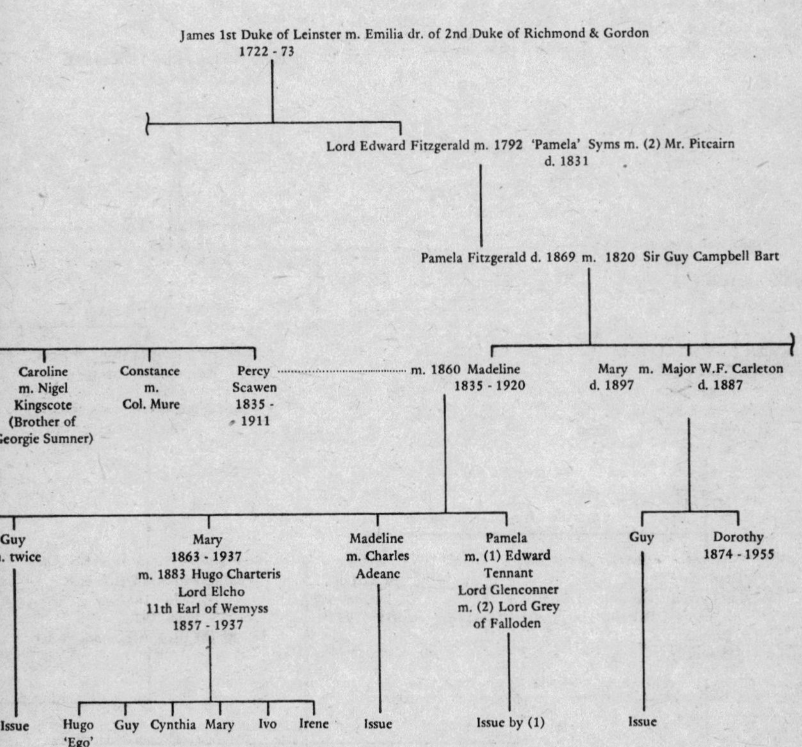

James 1st Duke of Leinster m. Emilia dr. of 2nd Duke of Richmond & Gordon
1722 - 73
Lord Edward Fitzgerald m. 1792 'Pamela' Syms m. (2) Mr. Pitcairn
d. 1831
Pamela Fitzgerald d. 1869 m. 1820 Sir Guy Campbell Bart
Caroline
m. Nigel
Kingscote
(Brother of
Georgie Sumner)
Constance
m.
Col. Mure
Percy
Scawen
1835 -
1911
m. 1860 Madeline
1835 - 1920
Mary m. Major W.F. Carleton
d. 1897
d. 1887
Guy
m. twice
Mary
1863 - 1937
m. 1883 Hugo Charteris
Lord Elcho
11th Earl of Wemyss
1857 - 1937
Madeline
m. Charles
Adeane
Pamela
m. (1) Edward
Tennant
Lord Glenconner
m. (2) Lord Grey
of Falloden
Guy
Dorothy
1874 - 1955
Issue
Hugo
'Ego'
Guy
Cynthia
Mary
Ivo
Irene
Issue
Issue by (1)
Issue

Family of Lady Anne Blunt

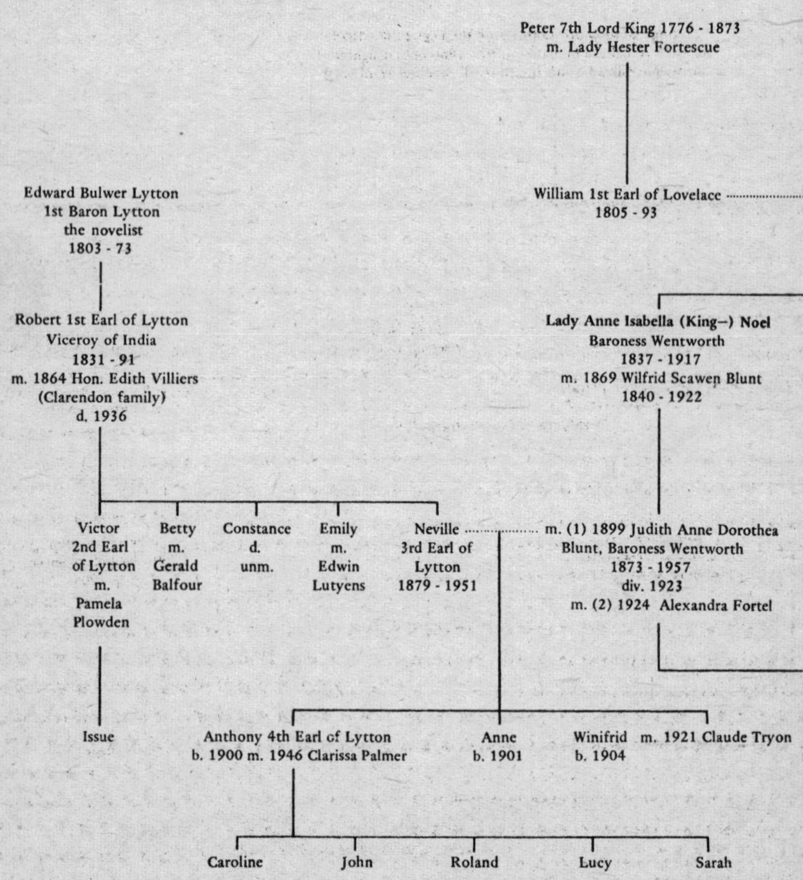

George Gordon 6th Lord Byron the Poet 1788 - 1824
m. 1815 Annabella Milbanke 1792 - 1860 only daughter of
Sir Ralph Milbanke and Judith Noel, Baroness Wentworth

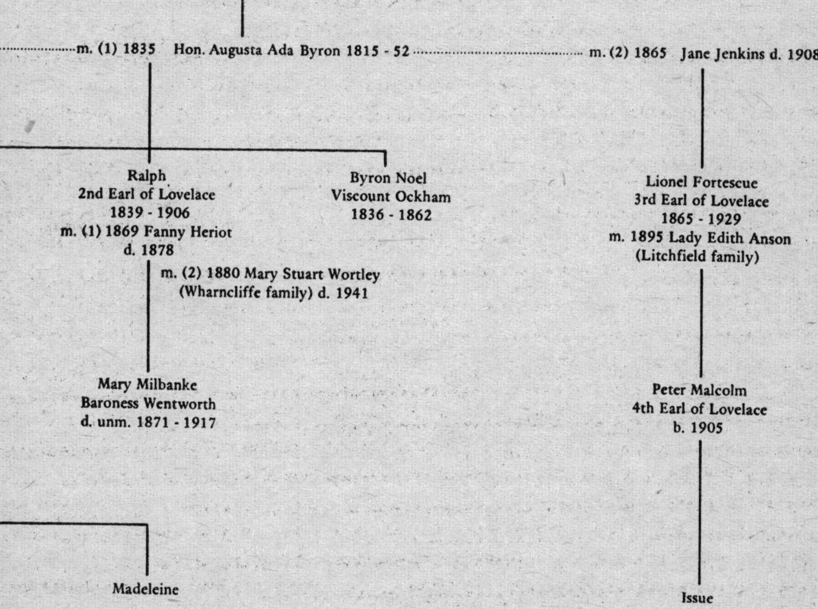

Acknowledgements

The sealed collection of Wilfrid Scawen Blunt's private papers at the Fitzwilliam Museum, Cambridge, was not finally opened until 1972, fifty years after his death. We are all, therefore, much beholden to those who have kept alive the memory of that extraordinary man through books based on their personal reminiscences or his own published works. First and foremost is his grandson Lord Lytton, whose *Wilfrid Scawen Blunt: A Memoir* is of unique importance. Lord Lytton's *The Desert and the Green* contains further memories, and his novel *Mickla Bendore* may be regarded in part as an imaginative re-creation of the brilliant but trying lady who was Blunt's daughter and Lord Lytton's mother, Judith Lady Wentworth. In Lady Wentworth's *Authentic Arabian* there is an extremely biased and unfair chapter on her father, which is nevertheless of value to his biographer. Edith Finch published in 1938 the only full-scale life of Blunt. She never met him, and Lady Wentworth regarded it as pedestrian and unjust to her mother Lady Anne Blunt; its thorough researches into Blunt's public life, however, deserve high praise.

Three of Blunt's young friends, Neville Lytton his son-in-law, Desmond MacCarthy and Sir Shane Leslie have contributed outstanding chapters on him in their respective collections of Victorian and Edwardian portraits. Among those who are writing today, I owe much to Peter Mansfield's *The British in Egypt*, Max Egremont's *The Cousins* and Wilfrid Blunt's *Cockerell*, where the author has found room for four splendid chapters on his distant cousin and his family. The books of Lady Emily Lutyens are full of fascination.

If it is asked why relatively few writers have concerned themselves biographically with a diarist so much quoted, a poet so much anthologized and a personality so colourful, there can be only one answer. The half-century ban on the material concerning his private life.

Coming to those to whom I owe a personal debt, I must begin by thanking the Syndicate of the Fitzwilliam Museum and its Director,

Professor Michael Jaffé, for commissioning this book. Professor Jaffé has performed many acts of special kindness and given continual encouragement and advice. I am greatly indebted to the Museum's archivist Paul Woudhuysen for untiring energy and patience; as also to Margaret Robertson, Hon. Keeper of Historical Mss. I must repeat my gratitude to Lord Lytton, this time for allowing me to use his unpublished papers, searching his memory and that of his friends on my behalf, arranging for me to see the Sussex haunts of his grandfather and furnishing me with data for tracing Blunt's tour of India and home in Egypt. With Lord Lytton I would like to associate Lady Lytton, their children, and his sisters Lady Anne Lytton and Lady Winifrid Tryon. To Lady Anne I am deeply grateful both for her incomparable knowledge of the Crabbet Arabian Stud and for harbouring me at Newbuildings Place. To Lady Winifrid I am equally indebted for her written and verbal impressions of the grandfather to whose memory she and her sister and brother are so movingly devoted. Their friends Peggy and Desmond Aldridge have been exceptionally kind and efficient in locating family material, including pictures and pedigrees, and in solving many problems.

I would like to thank the following for putting at my disposal or putting me in touch with valuable original sources: the late Miss Christabel Draper and Mr Gladstone Moore, executors of Lady Wentworth, for permission to read her private papers; Lady Armstrong, the Hon. Colin Tennant, Mr Wilfrid Blunt and Mr Christopher Blunt, Lady Fairfax-Lucy, Mr Charles Chevenix Trench, Mr H. Montgomery Hyde, the Hon. Mrs Arthur Pollen, Mary Lutyens (Mrs J. G. Links), Mrs Virginia Surtees, Mrs Elizabeth Hawkins of Greatham, Miss Brigid Boardman, Mrs Doris Langley Moore, the Rt Hon. Sir Patrick Browne, Lady Mander, Mr Anthony Curtis, Lord Egremont, Mrs Raymond Carr, Mr Christopher Howard, Mr Christopher Hibbert, Mr Kenneth Rose, Mr Alan Napier, Mr James Fleming, Mrs Rosemary Archer, Mrs Michael King and the Rev. R. G. Wickham of Twyford School.

I have benefited greatly from the specialized knowledge of Mr Peter Upton who has read and corrected the 'Arabian horse' parts of my manuscript, and to those who have answered particular questions: Mr Esmond Warner, Mrs Ruth Daniel, Sir Christopher Cockerell, the Rev. J. O'Brien, Mr Thomas Sobey, Mrs Humphrey, Mrs Joyce Barnard, Mr David Kensett and Mr Richard Lutyens. My warm thanks are due to Mr and Mrs Patrick Tritton for a conducted tour of Worth Forest, to Dr and Mrs Brookes and Mr and Mrs Morrison for showing me over Forest House (formerly Blunt's Forest Cottage) and to Mr C. T. H. Russell and Mr Brian Young for allowing me to see the mansion and stables of Crabbet Park.

Miss Janet Backhouse, Assistant Keeper in the Department of Manuscripts, British Library, has been of inestimable help, particularly through her knowledge of the Blunts' travels; and I am grateful to Mr G. R. Smith for his translations of Arabic. I would like to thank Dr R. J. Bingle, Mr B. C. Bloomfield and Mr D. M. Blake of the India Office Library and Records; and the ever-helpful staffs of the London Library, Kensington and Chelsea Library and Newspaper Library, Colindale.

I greatly appreciate the support of my publishers, especially Christopher Falkus, Linda Osband and Chris Warwick. To Victoria Glendinning I am immensely indebted, not only for her skill in essential pruning, but also for the time spent on someone else's book by a biographer of her distinction.

I thank Agnes Fenner for continuing to type my manuscripts with unabated zeal; and Flora Fraser for kind help.

My son Michael read and discussed the political chapters, and he, Thomas and Rachel generously organized my visits to India and Egypt. I cannot thank Frank and Antonia enough for as usual reading the whole manuscript chapter by chapter, particularly as they each had biographies of their own in the pipeline.

The author and publishers would like to thank the following for their kind permission to reproduce the photographs: The Earl and Countess of Lytton, Lady Anne Lytton, Lady Winifrid Tryon and Pearl Wheatley: 1, 2, 3, 4, 5, 6, 7, 9, 10, 19, 24; The Fitzwilliam Museum, 8, 11, 12, 13, 14, 16, 17, 18, 21, 22, 23, 25, 26, 27; BBC Hulton Picture Library, 15, 20. The family trees and the map on pages 124–5 were drawn by John Payne.

Hugh Chandler came for the day bringing his fiancée with him to show me. . . . They will have many children and be as happy as poverty will permit. I have given them my blessing and £100 to start them on their pilgrimage of passion.

From the Memoirs of W. S. Blunt,
22 October 1916.

No life is perfect that has not been lived – youth in feeling – manhood in battle – old age in meditation.

From the *Love Sonnets of Proteus*
by W. S. Blunt,
fourth edition.

PART I

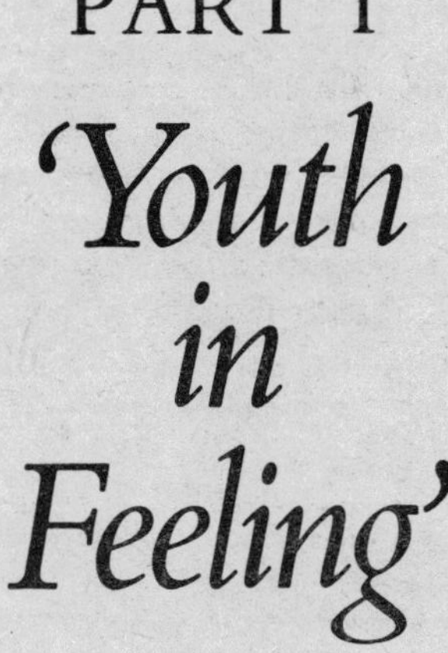

'Youth in Feeling'

[1]
A Blessed Boy
1840–1862

He was a poet in whose honour six young poets, including W. B. Yeats and Ezra Pound, initiated a Peacock Dinner in 1914; the peacock being there to eat, not as a symbol of the poet's beauty and vanity, though he was always beautiful and sometimes vain.

He was a traveller in the Middle East and an Arabist, whom T. E. Lawrence called a prophet.

He was a nationalist and anti-imperialist. Roger Casement, the Irish hero, wrote to him: 'I have often thought of you and wanted to meet you . . . and wondered how any Englishman could be brave enough and unselfish enough to attack the British Holy of Holies – their right to exploit weaker peoples.'[1] His many other friends in Ireland, India and Egypt would have said the same.

He was founder with his wife Anne, Byron's granddaughter, of the Crabbet Arabian Stud of pure Arab horses, which their daughter Judith Lady Wentworth continued.

He was an amorist whose morals were not as pure as his stud; but one who had the gift of changing a love relationship into a friendship and keeping it.

He was a born pilgrim, pursuing his varied goals with passionate intensity, and seeking all his life for that 'Religion of Happiness' which in the end he believed that he had found.

During his lusty middle age Wilfrid Scawen Blunt felt almost certain of posthumous fame. Posterity would surely read his poetry and remember him as a man of action. Posthumous fame was what he wanted, envying above all King David, whose psalms were read every day three thousand years after his death. Old age brought doubts. He began to lose faith in all but one of his achievements. His personal memoirs, bolstered by an intermittent diary, always seemed to him a unique piece of social history which could not fail to captivate the men and women of the future.

There is room for differences of opinion about Blunt as poet and politician. But as a social diarist he is on a par with Charles Greville. His memoirs cover the second half of Queen Victoria's reign (roughly where Greville left off), the whole Edwardian period and a sliver of George V's reign, enough to register the cataclysm of the Great War. Like Greville, Blunt mixed up scandalous gossip with serious commentary. They both larded their diaries with vows of abject repentance, Greville for his gambling, Blunt for his womanizing. Each of them had been long dead before his unexpurgated memoirs were read; indeed Blunt put a ban of fifty years on his 'Secret Memoirs'. Although he later reduced the ban to thirty years, on the ground that too long a gap would diminish the lessons they taught, nevertheless, one look at his papers in 1952 convinced their custodians that they must wait the full fifty years. It was therefore 1972 before the two tin boxes, which had been stored for security in the Fitzwilliam Museum, were opened and studied.

Blunt thought in terms of secrets. He published a *Secret History of Egypt*, and referred to his other historical works, on Gordon in Khartoum, Ireland and India as 'my secret histories'. By this he meant that they revealed secrets which had been kept from the public but ought to be known.

His personal memoirs were 'secret' in a different sense. Too valuable to be destroyed, he knew they were too hot for immediate publication. He never considered the story of his life as a paradigm of virtue or success. But it was the truth about eighty years of social history, seen through the eyes of a brilliant eccentric.

Born on 17 August 1840, no one ever considered he had a better start in life than Wilfrid Blunt. His memoirs began:

> I was born under circumstances peculiarly fortunate as I think for happiness. Those of an English country gentleman of the XIXth Century – my father a Sussex squire of fair estate, owning some four thousand acres of land mostly poor but very beautiful in the most beautiful of Southern counties – my mother of the same social rank, respectable both and locally respected. Such a position at such a date, 1840, was perhaps as good a starting point for a happy life as could well have been afforded me.

He found himself free from the two main obstacles in the path of high-spirited youth: the necessity of labouring with his hands and of asserting himself socially. 'England', he wrote, 'is the freest of all countries and the easiest to begin life in for those who can pay their way at once and have nothing to explain.'

That was all very well. But there were hidden drawbacks in this ideal prospect. It was Wilfrid's freedom at the age of thirty from the need to work for a living that was directly answerable for most of the things which he would later have to 'explain'.

He felt occasional qualms about his family's favoured position, even in the days of his father. When the Great War struck Sussex in September 1914, Wilfrid was asked to enrol his men-servants in a 'Civil Guard', for the protection of property in the case of bread riots. Wilfrid thought his men had better join the regular army. 'I certainly do not wish to be mixed up in active measures against hungry people, though my father took a lead in such in 1830 at Crabbet.' Crabbet Park was the Blunts' ancestral home. It had been threatened by the agricultural rising of 'Captain Swing', the English folk-hero. The political views of Wilfrid's father were crude. His tenants had the choice of ' "voting right" or going'. Nevertheless Wilfrid was devoted to his father's memory, and managed to recall a happier intervention by the squire of Crabbet. When his neighbour Sir Charles Burrell was confronted with a labourers' strike, Squire Blunt settled it by negotiating a rise in wages and a distribution of free beer; 'They were turned into Sir Charles's cellar.'

'In him I see reflected', wrote Wilfrid of his father, 'the better, more adventurous, happier side of my man's nature.' Born in 1790, Francis Scawen Blunt came of a long line of Sussex landowners, with a proud dash of West Country blood from the Glanvilles of Catchfrench and Scawens of Molennick, both in the Liskeard area of Cornwall. In Sussex there had been Blunts for over three hundred years. Wilfrid was to celebrate the earliest of them;

> This silent first forefather of the paternal woods reclaimed
> Holding his place beneath the sun with sullen desperate caution.[2]

Samuel Blunt, the great-grandfather of Francis, was of especial importance through his two marriages. The first was to Sarah Gale in 1750, an heiress who gave him three more Sussex estates; Crabbet, Newbuildings and Worth Forest, Newbuildings being Wilfrid's final home. The second marriage, in 1756, was to Winifrid Scawen, who gave Samuel three sons: Robert, William and Harry, William being Wilfrid's great-grandfather. He married Mary Glanville.

There was also a significant marriage of a Blunt with the powerful Wyndhams of Petworth House in West Sussex, when Francis Blunt's sister Mary married George Wyndham, afterwards 1st Lord Leconfield. The effect of this Wyndham connection and cousinship on Wilfrid cannot be exaggerated.

The Crabbet estate adjoined the Shelley property in Horsham parish, and the grandfathers of Francis Scawen Blunt and Percy Bysshe Shelley had sat together as Justices of the Peace on the Horsham bench. Francis found himself fagging at Harrow School for the young Lord Byron, the lame athlete who taught him to swim. The Byron connection was to feature as prominently as the Wyndham one in Wilfrid's life.

After Harrow Francis joined the crack Grenadier Guards, and was wounded at Corunna. He made the Grand Tour, spoke French, Spanish and Italian and, in his son's words, 'was emancipated from the grosser English prejudices' – as well as from the need to work. He was indeed a man of pleasure. The Prince Regent's set at Brighton absorbed him, with their cock fights, gambling, boxing and racing. Francis was forty-eight when he married at last on May Day 1838; four years later he died of a chill contracted while cub-hunting at Crabbet.

Wilfrid remembered his mother as a tall pale widow. From her he inherited more intellectual qualities, though of 'a less happy kind'. The daughter of a squire and rector of Witley in Surrey, Mary Chandler was thirty-two when she married. Brilliant, but not easily satisfied, she had rejected many earlier offers. She too was well connected, one uncle being the Dean of Chichester and another Henry Currie the banker. Again the Byron connection comes up. Henry Currie had lent Ada Lovelace, Byron's daughter, £500 in 1848, and Currie's home at West Horsley, where Wilfrid often spent his holidays, adjoined East Horsley, home of Lord Byron's son-in-law Lord Lovelace.

The account of his mother's qualities must be given in Wilfrid's own words:

> Religious, poetical, sceptically enquiring, passionate in affection, unsatisfied by any fortune, restless in action, grieving in repose; such was her character, and such too has been at periods my own.

Mary Blunt had her three children quickly, as if she knew time was short. Her elder son Francis Scawen was born at Crabbet on 14 June 1839, a year after the marriage. Her daughter Alice Mary also arrived at Crabbet, on 4 January 1842, less than a year before the squire died on 17 December. In between came Wilfrid Scawen.

But Wilfrid was born at Petworth, which he always described as a 'palace'.* He was christened in the Surrey parish church of Witley and spent the next two and a half years at Crabbet, until the family were forced to let it after the squire's sudden death. Then the forlorn Mrs Blunt with her three small children moved into Petworth Rectory, and it was from there that the three-year-old Wilfrid paid his earliest remembered visit to the 'palace', with its magnificent painted hall, the gigantic doll's house at the foot of the stair, the huge rooms and Turner pictures and Grinling Gibbons carvings, the troop of

*His mother's bedroom was at the top of the grand staircase, the first door on the right, her bed a four-poster with old green velvet hangings. (FM 216/1975, 20 February 1922, Constance Leconfield to Dorothy Carleton.)

Wyndham cousins, the deer and emus in the park, and the butterflies, always nature's masterpieces in Wilfrid's eyes – peacocks and red admirals in the immense kitchen gardens.

One tender memory of Petworth stayed with him. As a child of four he saw his cousin the beautiful Edith Montgomery lying in her cradle. He fell in love with her and presented her with his sole possession, a silver pencil case.

The first letter from his mother to her 'dear little Wilfrid' bears the same date as his earliest memory, 1843. She hopes that he is a very good boy – 'learning to hold your Fork like a Gentleman' – and that he will be glad to see Mama when she comes to Petworth. Wilfrid's recollection of 'seeing Mama' at this period was that it happened only once a week, when the children were brought in and offered her portrait-bracelet of their father to kiss. But at four or five she made the boys her 'companions'.

A closer companion was Archdeacon Manning from neighbouring Lavington. He would ride over to Petworth Rectory almost every afternoon. The Archdeacon had lost his wife as Mrs Blunt her husband, and Wilfrid always believed that their friendship was 'not wholly without sentiment'. Much later, as Cardinal-Archbishop of Westminster, Manning was to live in 'desolate state', needing the sympathy of a woman and never failing to remind Blunt that he was his mother's son. The Cardinal described Mary Blunt as the wittiest woman he had known. She in turn liked his High Church views (he was still an Anglican) and also liked teasing him about his social ambitions, nicknaming him 'Doctor of the Genteels'.

By the summer of 1844 the restless Mrs Blunt was ready to transfer herself and her family to another temporary home, Bury Lodge, Alverstoke, a rented red-brick eighteenth-century house on the junction of the roads to Gosport and Anglesey. It had a rookery and a large garden where Wilfrid remembered being dragged along the endless paths by his nursemaid Harriet. 'Hurry up, don't be lazy, you're getting under my feet.'

Mrs Blunt's heart was not in the garden but in the parish church and her work for the High Church movement of the 1840s; the rector at Alverstoke, Samuel Wilberforce, was destined to be an Anglican bishop, as, 'Soapy Sam'.

Less than two years later, in spring 1846, their pale slim mother told her children they were to leave Alverstoke and travel through France to the Pyrenees. They gathered it was for the sake of her health. Before they left for the Continent, their Crabbet tenants invited them to pay a visit to the gamekeeper's cottage in Worth Forest, to which her late husband's valet old Henry Selwood and his wife had retired as pensioners. This visit remained another of Wilfrid's first memories.

Forest Cottage stood inside the square mile of a lovely deciduous woodland on the edge of St Leonard's Forest. Wilfrid remembered getting out of the train at Balcombe Tunnel (considered dangerous) and driving in a fly up and down the Sussex lanes until they reached the tiny 'doll's palace' in the wood. It was a cool green place with great trees and a little stream running through an orchard. At night the dimity curtains were drawn and Wilfrid lay awake listening to the plates being washed up in the scullery. Old Selwood was a skilful ventriloquist. He would take the children down the forest path, making the growls and roars of wild beasts come out from the bushes on either side. Fortunately, when they reached the old-fashioned hutch trap at the end of the path, it had caught not a tiger but a leveret.

Then off they rumbled in their father's huge travelling chariot that he had bought for the Grand Tour in Boney's day. Coaches were still necessary in 1846, for it was just before the French railways arrived. Wilfrid and Francis sat on the box with the coachman Robert Moorey, one of their mother's old retainers from Witley who had volunteered to repel the threatened Napoleonic invasion of 1804. He talked all day to the boys of battles, telling them what monkeys those French were, good for nothing but fiddling and dancing. Wilfrid's mother would repeat a rhyme dating from the same period (she was born in 1804):

Says Boney to Johnny 'I'll soon be at Dover'.
Says Johnny to Boney 'That's doubted by some'
Says Boney 'But if I should really *come over*?'
'Why really you then will be *overcome*.'

In Pau the five-year-old Wilfrid committed 'the earliest and most pardonable piece of wickedness of a very corrupt life'. He picked some orange blossom, denied the deed and was whipped. And here also his guileless brother Francis committed his only wilful crime, the sin of Eve: he stole a forbidden cake, ate, 'and gave us to eat'.

Wilfrid loved the chestnut woods of the Pyrenees. But what fascinated him most were the terrible nets into which wild pigeons were driven by boys perched on long poles. As a man he decided that 'there is something instinctively attractive in a net, as though it conceals danger. Such is a spider's web, and such perhaps was later the fascination tennis had for me, with the mystery of its netted galleries.' Such also was surely his lifelong attraction to and repulsion from sin.

His first religious feelings were aroused in Bagnères de Bigorre where he was taken to see the clothing of a nun. Here again there was a conflict. Spiritual emotion fought in him with dread of Rome. For his nurse Grace Porter was a Scottish Presbyterian who taught him that to whistle on the Sabbath was a crime and that this world was 'a bad world, a preparation for a worse'. (One might be tempted to compare

Blunt's severe Grace Porter with Byron's odious May Gray, both Scottish Calvinist nursemaids.)

A Spanish family, the de Silvas, lodged above the Blunts in Pau. Their little daughter was not his first love, for Edith Montgomery in her cradle had got in first. But Edith was blue-eyed, and this Spanish child was Wilfrid's 'earliest child's romance for a creature with black eyes'. When he was presented with his first watch he called it after her – Inez.

Wilfrid was now about to be seven and Francis eight. The two boys were outwardly much alike, with dark chestnut hair and large brown eyes. Their mother loved them both passionately, but Wilfrid even more than his brother, probably because of his quite exceptional beauty and the spice of rebellion in his nature. Francis, wrote Wilfrid, was to pass through life without any of his own moral lapses or intellectual contradictions; he himself had inherited from their mother 'a certain restlessness of mood'. In youth it showed itself as vanity, in middle age as ambition. In the end it made of his life 'a chequer-work of bad and good'.

As for their mother, Blunt was to attribute many of her troubles to religion. On reading through a packet of her earliest letters to her husband, he was struck by their carefree happiness. After his parents fell for religion his mother's letters became noticeably less kind. He was reminded of Lady Byron's letters; the same religious dogmatism and pride. Blunt put it down partly to the ill effects of letter-writing itself – 'Letters I think show the worst of us' – but the genteel fashion of the day was also responsible for much of the censoriousness. The untimely death of Mrs Blunt's husband had convinced her that she would find only in heaven the happiness which could no longer be hers on earth. Her son believed that excessive church-going and fasting undermined her already frail health, and her incessant travelling to recover it merely increased the damage.

From his own point of view they should never have left Crabbet, he felt afterwards: 'for a life to be perfect should have for its beginning the strong and definite visual impression of a permanent home'. Nevertheless his first formative years had left him with a rich store of happiness. But, abruptly, five days before his seventh birthday, it all changed.

This was the last decade of what Wilfrid thought of as Wellington's half-century (he was to die in 1852) – 'an iron age for boys'. Blunt's father had been a devotee of Wellington. His elder son was to enter the army. It may therefore have been his widow's relations who advised her to send her two small boys to (in Wilfrid's phrase) the 'most hideous epitome of the world's wickedness, a private school'.

Twyford School, preparatory for nearby Winchester, was chosen in those days by many worthy men for the education of their sons. Changed out of all recognition, it still flourishes 130 years later and may not have been even in 1847 quite the cesspool of young Wilfrid's horror stories. It is safe to say, however, that Blunt drew a true picture of a normal English preparatory school in the 1840s as seen through the eyes of a sensitive child.

There were sixty boys of whom Wilfrid was the youngest and physically weakest. 'I became at once the slave, the football of them all', wrote Blunt, 'as one sees some unhappy captive beast tortured in a camp of savages.' His ears were boxed, his shins kicked, and he was insulted and pitilessly cross-questioned. In a matter of weeks he had lost all sense of right and wrong, cringing, flattering and deceiving simply to survive. His cousin, Frank Wyndham, afterwards a monsignor of the Church, sat next to him at the bottom of the class. Knowing each other at home, they were friends at Twyford. But during an epidemic of bullying, cousinship too went to the wall. Frank insisted on twisting Wilfrid's arm. 'I *must* do it. You are the only boy I am big enough to bully.'

The school had a reputation for scholarship of a medieval kind, and Wilfrid benefited to the extent of some slight knowledge of Latin grammar. Otherwise, outside the classroom with its three masters' thrones and 'breeching cupboards' for thrashing, it was nothing but 'a school for depravity'. Though none of the boys was over twelve, they were already old in vice. Not in the physical act as yet, but in talk picked up from older brothers and relaid with all the gusto of a London brothel in the nightly 'pandemonium of the bedrooms'. The miracle was that anyone escaped unscathed from this deluge of dirt. Yet afterwards many attained honourable positions, one of the worst boys becoming a bishop. Of himself Blunt wrote: 'I was too young to be permanently affected, only half understanding what I heard; yet it degraded me as the treatment of a prison degrades, revealing to me as in nightmare the possibilities of ugliness and cruelty and wrong.'

Wilfrid's courage, self-respect and health, physical and moral, all ebbed away. Always hungry, he and Francis would wander on their free afternoons like starved dogs over the Winchester downs, picking up edible scraps of orange peel, gingerbread or nuts which the crowd from race-meetings had thrown away. There was no such thing as sanitation. 'The privies were abominable pits, the approaches to them a mass of living filth never removed, the stench of them corruption.' No boy washed more than face, hands and feet once a week. They arrived home from each half-year's schooling black from the neck to ankles, their knees and elbows so caked with grime that it took several days of scrubbing to remove it.

Why did not the Blunt boys tell their mother? Because they were unaware that such misery could be changed. From this cruel fact Wilfrid Blunt was to draw his own more general conclusions:

> It is this ignorance and helplesness that keeps whole populations in barren wildernesses or on pestilential rivers, and other populations of Christian people in the hideous misery of great smoking towns.

Escape was not so much impossible as inconceivable. Blunt, after six months at Twyford, felt that he had been born a slave. His devotion in manhood to the liberation of oppressed nationalities he had no hesitation in deriving from his own bitter experience of slavery.

One consolation for the two waifs was building small grottoes and totems. On the downs they made secret collections of oyster shells, flowers, butterflies and chalk tablets bearing their names; and – personal to Wilfrid – a piece of knotted wood he called Damon, for which he built a shrine, crediting it with occult powers.[3] In the playground they kept a family of pet snails in a hollow tree, alas, soon to be found by the louts and destroyed. As time went on Wilfrid was in danger of becoming a lout himself. He got in with a set of big boys and would have learnt to tyrannize, as he had been tyrannized over. But at the nadir of his moral fortunes, in summer 1849, he fell seriously ill.

His mother was hurriedly sent for, to find him with acute pneumonia and being bled almost to death. A note from Twyford written by her to the children's nurse, Mrs Porter, shows how critical was the situation:

> Wilfrid is no better but worse. The inflammation has got to his lungs, and attacked them violently. His strength is sinking and cough increasing. Nevertheless while there is life there is hope, and we must pray God to spare him a while, if for his good, dear innocent thing that he now is. Try and make Alice pray for him.

The rescue of her beautiful innocent from death's doors may well have hastened Mrs Blunt towards the drastic religious step she was soon to take. The illness had lasting effects on Wilfrid also. His weak lungs, a hereditary failing, were permanently damaged. Yet his narrow escape from the next world meant that he could hardly escape in this one from spoiling. At home his ethereal beauty seemed to be an ever-fluttering danger signal. 'Master Wilfrid was "too beautiful to live"!' Master Wilfrid might (and did) turn the whole house upside down, reduce his brother and sister to tears, and the household to hysterics, but he was '"not to be thwarted" or he might fall ill and die!'[4]

Wilfrid was taken abroad for the winters of 1849 and 1850: to Marseilles, where he learnt to speak French and act in Shakespeare; and to Nîmes and Avignon, where he drew and painted the medieval walls and bridges. The backs of the finished pictures were covered with livelier sketches of Wilfrid's favourite knights in armour and wild galloping animals. A letter from him to Mrs 'Woodie' (Selwood) on the return from Marseilles, dated 28 March 1850, shows him to be a self-conscious young invalid. Mama, Francis and Alice, he says, have gone to church without him, 'but I have got for my companions some chicks a day old chirping and twittering in a basket with a handkerchief over them. I went out yesterday a little in the sun. I have got a picture of myself which I am going to sell by auction. Nursie bids 2/6 and she said that you would bid 5s.'[5]

On the slow return journey from France in 1851, everything possible went wrong; a fire lit in Wilfrid's room burnt through the floor, so that his bed fell with a 'volcanic crash' into the crater a few minutes after his mother had taken him downstairs; later 'poor Wilfs' got two attacks of fever, requiring special food, sal volatile and nursing on his mother's lap, while the rest of the family shared between them 'spring fever', the Nîmes 'epidemic' and the Lyons 'grippe'.[6]

His return to Twyford for two more years coincided with the advent of a new headmaster named Roberts, jollier but in some ways worse than his predecessor. In deference to Wilfrid's physical delicacy he would offer him special treats of food and drink – but would restore the balance with hideous floggings, the excuse being that the boy had fallen hopelessly behind in his school work. Blunt visited him once many years later, and was surprised to find the old schoolmaster quite unaware of any tension in their early relations. A fine old latitudinarian in religion – 'nearly the last of his school' – Roberts enjoyed a fat living, a big house and the care of a mere hundred souls. He talked to Blunt about the boys who had now become generals, ambassadors, deans; and told Blunt that Twyford was the origin of the private school in *Tom Brown's Schooldays*.

Despite Wilfrid's many humiliations at Twyford, there is some evidence that he secretly considered himself superior to his puny fellows. Whether by accident or design, he preserved a relic of Twyford, a red leather notebook dated 30 September 1848 and containing various school lists, among which are sketches of fish, sea birds and a boy leaning against a stone. The boy may be Wilfrid seeing himself as Gulliver, for tiny men are swarming up his legs.

Wilfrid's lifelong love of natural history had been given its conscious start by his mother, who in 1849 presented Francis with a book by Charles St John on wild life and sport in the Highlands. It became one of their two favourite books. The other favourite was *Silk and Scarlet* (about racing and hunting) by 'The Druid', in which Wilfrid read of the Godolphin and Darley Arabians, and a mare called Beeswing who could hardly make fifteen-two but always 'ran big, and had the sweetest head in the world'.

While Wilfrid was wrestling with Twyford his mother had a more complex problem on her hands. In 1849 she had exchanged the atmosphere of High Anglican curates for her own childhood home in Surrey, Witley Vicarage. Wilfrid painted it in water-colours with loving attention to the Gothic windows, front door fashioned like a church porch, and the grey church itself rising behind their home. Mrs Blunt was now free to follow the spiritual adventures of her closest ecclesiastical friend. The following year, 1850, Archdeacon Manning resigned from Lavington, having earlier refused preferment offered him by Queen Victoria on the advice of Samuel Wilberforce. On 6 April 1851 Manning was received into the Roman Catholic Church. That Easter Mrs Blunt was received also.

This was the heyday of the Tractarians or Puseyites, and their High Church 'Oxford Movement'. Henry Manning and Mary Blunt were only two among the stream of enthusiasts who went further, into Rome. Another was the Rev. Charles Laprimaudaye, Manning's curate. Yet another was John Hungerford Pollen, a young don at Merton College. The families of Pollen and Laprimaudaye were to have a powerful influence on Wilfrid's life.

It was many months before Mary Blunt broke the news of her conversion to her sons – a measure of the trepidation with which she regarded this inevitable step. Meanwhile at the end of the summer Wilfrid and Francis left Twyford. All their mother told them was that they were going abroad in the autumn, a not unpleasant prospect. At last, when they reached the French coast in November, she decided to drop her bombshell. Her roundabout approach, however, only heightened the drama.

Mr Manning, she began, had decided to change his whole life and become a Roman Catholic.

The boys were at first astonished but not upset. They thought their mother was tactfully disclosing to them the existence of a secret wickedness on the part of the archdeacon, into which even the best could occasionally fall, and warning them against similar dangers. This impression was quickly dispelled by the news that she herself had followed the archdeacon.

'We could hardly believe our ears. It filled us with unspeakable shame, and we both burst into tears.'

The boys, now eleven and twelve, had been looking forward to Harrow. As their father's old school it had its strong romance for them, and they already knew of his flattering association with Lord Byron. They had no doubt boasted to the Twyford boys of their glittering future. What would those boys think now? Wilfrid, in a tumult of hurt pride and fear, obstinately refused to accept his mother's new religion, although his sweet-tempered and docile brother quickly conformed.

To schoolboys, and even to the majority of adults in 1851, this seemingly freakish movement towards Roman Catholicism was an act of treason against national morality and common sense. Only the year before, in 1850, the so-called 'Papal Aggression', whereby the Roman hierarchy was restored in Britain, had raised a tremendous Protestant howl. London was placarded with exhortations: 'English men! Will you be governed by Queen Victoria or by Cardinal Wiseman?' There were enough sons of clergymen at Twyford School for the echoes of that howl to reach Wilfrid's ears. It is interesting that Blunt, writing in 1913, regarded the gulf between that date and 1851 to be vast, speaking of 'these days of tolerance and unbelief'.

There was one comfort for Wilfrid, despite the sudden collapse of his early hopes. He and his brother were to continue their education in Italy, under a young tutor. He was Edmund Coffin, a cheerful and 'muscular' Catholic, much beloved of Wilfrid and capable if anyone was of coaxing him away from what he was to call 'my wild goat's life outside the fold'.[7]

On the way through Paris Wilfrid stepped into history. It was Tuesday, 2 December. From the window of the Hotel Wagram they saw troops marching through the Tuileries gardens and, according to Mrs Blunt, 'thousands of idle Parisians passing and repassing in the most asinine way conceivable – nothing ferocious about them. Such gabies you can have no idea!' They hired a fiacre and drove about the streets, 'walking being scarcely safe', until they suddenly saw the French President, Prince Louis Napoleon, riding down the rue de Rivoli surrounded by his fellow 'conspirators'. The Blunt family were in fact witnessing the coup d'état of the man who had just declared himself to be the Emperor Napoleon III.

The family did not reach Italy until the spring of 1852; Blunt hints that the delay was due to his own intransigence. As he showed no signs of being converted, young Father Coffin and Mrs Blunt decided to spend January and February in France instead of Italy, at Aix-en-Provence, an old-fashioned town where the Church was much in evidence.

Mrs Blunt's letters to her brother suggest that the family's incessant illnesses were a contributory cause of delay. Writing from Aix on 12 January 1852 she informed her brother that all were down with a mixture of grippe and influenza. Not till March was Wilfrid 'very much better'. At last on Shrove Tuesday 1852 the three Blunt children were received into the Church at Aix with due pomp and publicity.

Wilfrid was still not quite happy with the change; nor was his health fully recovered from the rigours of Twyford. He frequently walked in his sleep, screaming.

Springtime in Italy should have been a foretaste of heaven. But when they reached Mentone, down they all went again with fever. The English doctor warned Mrs Blunt that her three children were extremely *'delicate'*; she had better turn northwards as soon as they had rested for a couple of months in Genoa.

Wilfrid remembered with affection the astute inmates of the Capuchin convent in Genoa, who discovered how to please this handsome but obstinate boy – not by mixing him in with the crowd but by picking him out. He was allowed to serve at Mass, swinging the censor before all eyes. Their rambling villa at Albaro became very dear to him, especially the terraces, rose gardens, rosemary bushes and the long avenue of cypresses that sheltered colonies of sparrows and beggars. They set off in the summer for leafy Bagni di Lucca. Mrs Blunt, with her usual contempt for doctors, had decided to go southwards instead of northwards.

The long slow journey was punctuated by religious observance in every town and village, where the fervent Mrs Blunt and her three children would join in all the street processions and 'cults of graven images'. The sudden vision of the Tuscan hills wiped out, for Wilfrid, past miseries of heat and tiredness. He was to call this wonderful sight his 'first positive happiness of boyhood'. A human vision of beauty was soon to enhance the splendour of a perfect summer.

On the upper ridges of the Apennines, wrote Blunt, but only at the very highest altitude, was to be found 'that glorious apparition the Apollo butterfly'. Such a butterfly was found also in Lucca. She was the sixteen-year-old daughter of the Rev. Charles Laprimaudaye, whose family were all pious and clever, and the daughters all beautiful. Along with the Mannings, nephews and nieces of Henry, these children became Blunt's inseparable companions.

To have companions at all was in itself a pleasure, for the widow had hitherto excluded the social world. Indeed the gregarious life of Lucca was not altogether to Mrs Blunt's liking. It was now that she wrote some of the censorious, Lady Byron-like letters to her brother which were to shock her son fifty years later. She liked their own villa chiefly because it was the last house in the bay, 'in fact the end of all things and therefore quite out of the way of visitors'. Charles Manning, Henry's brother, she had known before: 'rather a bore than otherwise – but NOTHING to what he is now – it is a *little* defect that increases by age!'

Annie Laprimaudaye was tall with almond eyes and cheeks of milk and roses. Both Francis and Wilfrid adored her, though they were three and four years younger than their goddess. Afterwards Blunt wondered why she had been so kind to him, a wild boy of not quite twelve, whose delight was to chase butterflies or ride rough, broken-kneed ponies and to dip in the green pool which had been dammed with boughs in the river, at the end of a mulberry alley leading to their house. Annie was later to become a nun, like her sister Catherine. Perhaps, thought Blunt, Annie had already decided on a religious vocation and was imitating the Virgin's maternal tenderness – besides being attracted by 'a beautiful boy's face, as yet unconscious of its beauty'. When it was time to go back to Genoa for the autumn, Wilfrid and Francis met Annie under the trees of their favourite chestnut wood by the river, to say a tearful farewell. As Wilfrid stammered out his love and gratitude, Anne stooped and kissed him. 'The kiss you gave me/at parting,/I yet can feel on my face.'[8]

> It was an elder sister's kiss – perhaps a little more. To me at least it had a supernatural significance, something of the divine, a sacramental rite transforming me with its all-efficient grace from the unmannered savage of the woods I was, into an aspiring being with a sentient soul. I date from it my earliest glimpse of the seraphic vision we speak of when we talk of happiness – a thing apart from the material gaiety of childhood and to which alone we rightly give the name of religion.

This vision tempered his boyhood uncouthness, wrote Blunt, during the next few years; for he was now in rude health. It also had a long-term effect of confusing religion and love inextricably in his heart. Where there was no 'seraphic vision' he could feel no ecstatic love. Conversely, where a religious emotion was present, love, however anti-religious or positively wicked it might seem, would flash into being.

Young Wilfrid discovered that their autumn villa in Albaro, the Palazzo Pagani, was only a stone's throw from Byron's Casa Saluzzo. Thirty years ago had not Byron plunged daily into this sea? Wilfrid bathed 'as he did', and learnt to swim. While Wilfrid thought of Byron, his mother entertained the 'Doctor of the Genteels', now Father Henry Manning. With him was Aubrey de Vere, the Irish poet, who had been received into the Church at Avignon. He and Manning were on their way to Rome where the dogma of the Immaculate Conception was about to be promulgated. According to this dogma, the Virgin Mary was exempted from original sin and born sinless.

By September Mrs Blunt had become well satisfied with her family's progress. 'The boys are such huge creatures that I have moved them out of round jackets and they now wear on Sundays and holidays a suit of dark snuff colour, coat of the same gamekeeper cut, horn buttons, waistcoat, and trousers!!' A strange outfit for the Italian September sun. At midwinter she arranged for them all to travel over the frozen Mont Cenis pass by sledge, so that the boys might be in time for their new English school. Even the casual Byron had hesitated and finally decided against taking his natural daughter Allegra across the Alps in winter.

Stonyhurst College, the famous Jesuit foundation in Lancashire which possessed relics of St Thomas More, introduced Wilfrid in 1853 to an entirely different type of education. His mother, who was now living in Mortlake, Surrey, had again chosen for her two sons the most strenuous discipline she could find. Wilfrid later applauded her choice and defended the Jesuit system, both in general and as applied to himself. If the Church really believed in her own infallibility, she was only being logical in exacting total obedience. He personally needed a period of strict discipline in order to cure his weaknesses: no ambition in work or play; self-indulgence and wilfulness; physical cowardice 'through my ill treatment at Twyford'. This last required a system of protection and encouragement such as the Jesuit fathers could also provide. Father Thomas Porter S. J., Wilfrid's form master, was a real father in every respect to his class of boys. Wilfrid immediately gave him his complete confidence.

If there was absolutely no freedom, that meant to Wilfrid no freedom for bigger boys to bully him. He was thankful to hear not a single word of profanity or rebellion during the six months he was at Stonyhurst. Night fears of every kind were eliminated, for a prefect went the rounds of the dormitories with a dark lantern. Twyford was blotted out. 'I felt myself born again.'

The strict surveyance of knowledge did not unduly worry him, even though a natural history book sent him by his mother was confiscated. It bore on the title-page the misleading motto 'Through the Contemplation of Created Things, by steps we may ascend to God'. However, having learnt that he must ascend to God through the sacraments, Wilfrid was encouraged to develop his interest in 'created things'. He and his friend John Gerard, afterwards a doughty Jesuit opponent of 'Darwinism', kept caterpillars in boxes pierced with pinholes in the shapes of the major constellations, Orion and the Great Bear, so that these humble beings also should make their ascent to God by imagining themselves outdoors under the stars. Wilfrid's devotion to butterflies had been stimulated by his visit to Italy. He now contributed 'A Few Words About Butterflies, Moths, Caterpillars and Chrysalises' to Father Porter's class magazine. Tiger moths, for instance, were beautiful when first out of the chrysalis 'but lose much of their brilliancy as they get older'. For the first and last time in his life he won a prize open to the whole Lower School. The subject was 'Death' and Wilfrid's views were conventionally Catholic.

His holiday excursions at Stonyhurst, led by Father Porter, were the best he could remember: skating, walking, damming the river for trout. Yet when the first half-year was completed and he was given the choice of continuing his education in his mother's house at Mortlake or returning for another term to Stonyhurst, he opted for Mortlake. If he had stayed at Stonyhurst, he felt, he would have followed his friend Father Gerard, and become a Jesuit. 'Even today (half a century later) I could find it in my heart to regret. It would have been a short cut to the happiness my life has found. But such a solution was not in my fate.'

At Mortlake Wilfrid was still under the direction of the beloved Father Edmund Coffin and meeting other young priests such as Father Faber, 'who was constantly crossing the line which separates the sublime from the ridiculous'.* He was also moving in the artistic society of Mortlake and Sheen. His mother, whose wit had always been of the Shandean variety, appealed strongly to that distinguished pair of neighbours, Sir Henry Taylor, the poet and civil servant, and Mrs Julia Margaret Cameron, the pioneer of photography whose two passions were for G. F. Watts the painter and the splendid, bearded Taylor himself. She combined the two in her possession of Taylor's portrait by Watts, for which she had constructed a shrine in her drawing-room with a lamp perpetually burning. One day she saw some of Wilfrid's drawings and in her enthusiastic way declared him an 'embryo genius'. It is probable that his striking beauty assisted her in forming this opinion. He should go as a pupil, she said, to the great Watts himself (despite the fact that Watts did not take pupils) and learn to draw in his studio at Little Holland House.

So the thirteen-year-old Wilfrid was introduced to Watts by Mrs Cameron, and for three days a week he would prepare for his final apotheosis as Watts's pupil by visiting a studio in Newman Street, where he made chalk drawings from casts or occasionally from a living model. How considerable his talents were is shown by a self-portrait he painted in oils at fourteen, a remarkably mature achievement in the romantic Watts style, wearing a Byronic collar.

But his burgeoning career was terminated in 1854, when Father Coffin decided that he, Coffin, must go abroad for his health. So the whole family removed to Carlsbad. Father Coffin's health was restored but Mrs Blunt caught a severe chill from overzealous church-going. She was never to recover completely; Wilfrid never returned to his studio life, and never worked under Watts.

* Frederick William Faber, 1833–1863, was the first Superior of the London Oratory and another of the young 'Oxford' converts. His temperamental exuberance often trapped him into becoming 'ridiculous by over-emphasis'. Raleigh Addington, *Faber* (1974), pp. 188, 312.

Back in England in 1855, the two Blunt boys found themselves from April to June at another Catholic boarding-school, St Mary's College, Oscott, while their mother, dying of consumption, bravely faced her last months in seaside lodging-houses. In a note written shortly before her death she informed the faithful Mrs Selwood that 'Doctor said yesterday I might live a week, a month or many months, which is just what doctors *always* say in a precarious case, as it gives them the certainty of being right *anyway*.'

Finally the boys were sent for to Grand Parade, St Leonards-on-Sea. It had still not crossed their pious young minds that their mother could die. Had they not made countless novenas for her recovery, even obtaining, on the advice of sympathetic nuns, some water from the miraculous fountain of La Salette? On 3 June they were ranged round their mother's chair by Father Coffin, waiting as they thought for the cure. Edmund Coffin had nursed her while the children were at school and now she clung to him. Gradually they fell asleep one by one. Suddenly around nine o'clock there was a commotion. They started up to hear her cry out 'Edmund'. Then she laid her head on the chair and was dead.

In those days Catholics were still buried in Protestant graveyards. Blunt remembered the old port-drinking parson at Worth reading the Anglican burial service over his mother. Father Coffin gave him a Catholic memorial card: 'Pray for the soul of Mary Blunt who died Trinity Sunday 1855 aged fifty.'

The only continuity that now remained between Wilfrid's old and new life was Oscott, to which it was arranged he should return in the autumn. Unlike Stonyhurst, the Oscott experience during his mother's last months had been thoroughly bad. Blunt describes this Midlands school as a 'Sleepy Hollow'. He particularly disliked its neo-Gothic architecture. It was close to the great industrial centre of Birmingham and had no excuse to be sleepy. John Henry Newman himself wrote to Wilfrid that November inviting him and Francis to visit the Birmingham Oratory, but no use seems to have been made of the invitation. A section of the boys was being trained for the priesthood. These 'coarse and rowdy' fellows stuck together, ostracizing Wilfrid and his lay friends, who in turn put on superior airs. Among the most superior was a dandy and bully whom Wilfrid intensely disliked, William O'Shea.

Painting occupied his mind in a desultory but nonetheless creative way. Blunt was later to resent the two years wasted at Oscott almost more than the Twyford purgatory. Possibly, in these bleak recollections he failed to allow for his reactions to his mother's death.

Wilfrid felt the death of their much prayed-for parent to be something 'amazing', 'confounding' and 'staggering'. She, poor lady, had done her best to assure her children a Catholic future. Under the influence of their confessor, Canon Wenham, she appointed as the boys' guardian the excellent Dr Grant, Catholic Bishop of Southwark. The Lord Chancellor, however, whose wards they were, overruled this choice in favour of the children's two nearest relations: Mrs Percy Wyndham, their father's sister and chatelaine of Petworth; and their mother's uncle, Henry Currie, the banker. Both guardians were Protestant, and though they did not take advantage of their position to tamper with the children's religion, the change could not but be felt. A 'thin diet' of Low Mass was provided for them on Sundays in the half-ruined east wing of lovely Sutton Place. Wilfrid enjoyed it aesthetically but devotionally it was colourless. Besides, there were a hundred distractions from religion in the joyous life at West Horsley Place, where the Blunts went for their summer holidays.

For the first time Wilfrid roamed the fields with a muzzle-loader, occasionally knocking down a pheasant on the land of their neighbour Lord Lovelace. There were girl cousins with whom a boy of fifteen could dance, play battledore, read poetry and fall in love; though Wilfrid was still so shy that if he accidentally caught a girl's eye his pale face would flush scarlet. Mary Currie, older than him, was as kind in response to his devotion as Annie Laprimaudaye had been. It was now that he first discovered the fact of his own good looks. All this was a far cry from the south coast boarding-houses of his mother's last months; there the only company had been Father Coffin and visiting priests, the only entertainment a quiet rubber of whist.

Though Wilfrid's guardians dropped the idea of painting as a profession for him, they were meticulous in sending him and Francis back to Oscott in the autumn, while Alice, now fourteen, went to the Sacred Heart Convent at Roehampton. Fortunately the year 1856 brought a dramatic change in Oscott. A new professor of philosophy arrived in the romantic shape of Dr Charles Meynell. This brilliant young priest was still under thirty. His wit and eloquence matched his good looks; he was dark-faced, Byronic, with piercing luminous eyes. He had just returned from the English College in Rome. A member of the Yorkshire family of Meynells,* he had Celtic blood and shared Wilfrid's love for field and river as well as encouraging Wilfrid's painting.

The English hierarchy had picked on him for what was almost a special mission. They felt the time had come when Catholic boys should know something of modern controversies. Metaphysicians such as Kant and Hegel or the popular Auguste Comte were totally

* No close connection with the Meynells of Sussex.

unknown; so was the historical and archaeological criticism of the Bible. As for physics and chemistry, the only sign that they were taught at all was an occasional dull explosion.

Dr Meynell was no modernist, in the sense of opposing the Vatican, but he was, as Blunt put it, 'a forerunner'. From him Blunt learnt to love the unorthodox poetry of Shelley and Keats. Oscott now provided teaching which appealed to his reason as well as to his heart. Father Meynell taught his boys, in Blunt's words, 'to ride Reason on a loose rein in perfect confidence that Reason and Faith were wholly and indissolubly one'.

Wilfrid and Francis left school in June 1857, Wilfrid with an interest in metaphysics that was never to desert him, and the ambition to become not a painter but a poet. This to him was the summit of 'romance'.

Oscott, it seemed, having been persuaded to face the devil and all his works, including biblical criticism, was sending out two young Catholics aged eighteen and nearly seventeen well equipped to survive any and every peril. Through no fault of Father Meynell's, however, they had not been able to renounce *all* the devil's works. The enemy had only half-revealed himself by 1857. It was to be another two years before the great nineteenth-century challenge was issued. Charles Darwin was to publish his *Origin of Species* in 1859, too late for Charles Meynell to read and discuss it with Wilfrid Blunt. Another two years and Blunt would hack his own path through the thickets of evolution. Nearly twenty years after he had left Oscott he turned at last for guidance to Father Meynell. Again too late.

The Blunt boys spent part of the next two summer holidays together. It was now that Wilfrid had to deal once and for all with a long-standing flaw in his character, physical cowardice. In 1857 the brothers went on a walking tour in the Highlands. Wilfrid looked at the hills of Skye but dared not climb them. Next summer their guardian Henry Currie took a party of boys into the High Alps. They scaled Monte Rosa in twelve hours, Wilfrid spending his eighteenth birthday, 17 August 1858, on the summit.

> All all that wilderness of rock and plain
> Rolled at my feet, and, when with heel fast set
> On Nature's neck I knew the giant slain
> I was transfigured.[9]

On the way down, Nature reasserted herself and there was almost a serious accident. Richard Lane Fox, son of the squire of Bramham, slipped, fell and was caught on a ledge just above a 2,000-foot drop. None was roped. All waited in trepidation while the guide laboriously cut steps. 'The discovery that I was proof against peril so prolonged', wrote Blunt, 'was to me a revelation of the possibility of manly action in the world.' He was later to attribute any moral courage he might possess to this early rout of physical fear. If the tremendous powers of nature could be conquered, why should he fear man?

Women were different. The holidays were still spent partly at West Horsley, and his charming cousin Mary Currie now read him Tennyson's *Maud*, telling Wilfrid that she was its heroine. One day she invited him to come into her bedroom, the shrine of her most sacred *arcana*: 'pictures, sacred texts, dressing table with combs and brushes, washing-stand, bed!'

Holidays at West Horsley were reinforced with a course of 'good society' in London. His Aunt Wyndham, infinitely kind and as completely conventional, allowed him to treat her house in fashionable Grosvenor Place as his home. Here the 'cousinship' that he had enjoyed long ago at Petworth moved on to a more adult plane, but still an innocent one. He thought he would die if he did not marry Constance Wyndham, but 'she married Willy Mure in 1859 and I did not die'. Sybil Montgomery, the sister of baby Edith whom he had kissed in her cradle, was another idol to whom he nearly proposed ten years later; she was to become Marchioness of Queensberry and mother of that thorn in Blunt's flesh, Lord Alfred Douglas.

The cousinship kept Wilfrid from 'more vagrant thoughts', as did his frequent visits to his sister Alice at the Sacred Heart. Though he rarely mentioned Alice in his first reminiscences, he insisted that she was his closest friend in childhood and in her early womanhood, and the being he loved most. Like Byron's Augusta, Wilfrid's Alice enchanted him because she was so much like himself: in looks, the same pale beautiful face and dark eyes; in temperament, the same emotional outbursts. Blunt even suggested that her poetry was as good or better than his own. In his own *Songs and Sonnets of Proteus*, first published anonymously, he was to include Alice's poem beginning with a lovely line,

> Spring of a sudden came to life one day....

But it was Wilfrid who had given beauty to the line, which Alice had originally written, less happily, as

> Warm Spring weather burst into life one day....

Another effective break on youthful escapades was Wilfrid's shortage of money. As a younger son depending on the interest from a capital of £7,500 and an allowance of £100 a year from Aunt Wyndham, he must enter one of the gentlemanly professions. His guardians had decided on the Indian Civil Service, now thrown open to public competition. Unfortunately his mathematics were inadequate. He was therefore sent to lodge with a well-known tutor, Edward Walford, at 28 Old Burlington Street. This man had married twice and in trying to provide for two large families had developed a vile temper. During Walford's quarrels with his second wife Wilfrid constantly took her part, until one day he found himself thrusting his carpet bag into Walford's face and knocking him down. Immediately the wife changed sides and joined her husband in hauling Wilfrid before the Marlborough Street magistrates. Wilfrid afterwards recalled this episode as his 'first lesson in the ways of the world' – if he had made Walford's wife his mistress she would have stuck to him.

Meanwhile the scandal was hushed up by the family lawyers and Wilfrid received some sympathy and advice from his friends. Father Edmund Coffin at Mortlake wrote 'My dear old Wilf, What a "rum-ti-tum with the chill off?" you have had! I found a *werry* strong letter from Walford on my table last evening.... I hope old fellow that when you get a chance you will make it up with Walford and apologize to him.'[10]

Dr Charles Meynell tactfully mingled congratulations on Wilfrid's escape from Walford – 'a queer sort of fellow' – with a facetious warning against rages. 'Thou must repress the insidious beginnings of that mania which the vulgar call a temper, a kind of mental, nay, bodily disease, akin to epilepsy, as may be seen by its symptoms viz. contortions of the countenance – rollings of the eyes – clenchings of the hands – and windmill action of the same.'

Unexpectedly in October 1858 Wilfrid found himself a candidate for the Diplomatic Service. His cousin Charlie Bourke, son of Lord Mayo, had failed in his Diplomatic examinations. Like all Bourkes, wrote Blunt, Charlie could not spell. Aunt Wyndham at once applied for the Bourke nomination to be transferred to Wilfrid; he was sent to Orleans to improve his French; he sat the examination and passed with credit. Shortly afterwards, however, an official note arrived to say that Mr Wilfrid Blunt's appointment had been dropped. What could have happened? Wilfrid neither drank, gambled, ran into debt nor ran after women. His redoubtable aunt promptly drove round in her yellow barouche to the Foreign Office and demanded to see Lord Malmesbury, who had given her nephew the nomination. Wilfrid meanwhile was being quizzed by two noted wags, the Foreign Office secretaries Drummond Wolff and John Bidwell, who wanted to know about his 'immoralities' and 'breaking up of families'. At last it dawned on Wilfrid that 'the little scribbler Walford' had taken his revenge by accusing him of having seduced his wife. Wilfrid was sent for by Malmesbury to defend himself, which he did by bursting into uncontrollable tears, 'a natural eloquence than which no words could have served me better'.

Lord Malmesbury was moved to pity, Lady Malmesbury invited Wilfrid and his aunt to luncheon; the priesthood – the President of Oscott, Dr Grant of Southwark, and Father Coffin – rallied round with glowing testimonials. Wilfrid was gazetted an unpaid attaché on 31 December 1858.

Among Wilfrid's farewell parties in London, one stands out as a signpost for the future. He records it in a fragmented diary, most of which he afterwards burnt because of its 'vulgarities', 'crude absurdities' and puerile taste. It is easy to see why he kept this extract after duly pruning it.[11]

1 March, 1859 In the evening came the Pollens. . . . I had no occasion for a good talk with Minnie, and she came late and left before we went to the drawing room. She did not look quite so pretty as she did the other night at the Wards,* but her manner is as different from what it used to be as a man could wish.

This entry suggests that the beautiful Maria Margaret (Minnie) Laprimaudaye of Lucca may have been less kind than her sister Annie. In that same year John Pollen had fallen in love with Minnie, aged fourteen, as she sat at a window in Rome watching the world go by. He married her at sixteen after her mother's death, he being thirty.

From 1856 onward the artistic young Pollens had lived in Hampstead and spent their Sundays at the home of Dante Gabriel Rossetti. Minnie's tender feelings for Rossetti and his for her may have been responsible for her later more relaxed attitude to Wilfrid.

Athens in 1859: Wilfrid's first posting. His diary registered a day of heavy rain clouds, and a desert between Piraeus and Athens, haunted only by crows and hawks. 'I will enjoy Athens. . . . I will not be set against it.' His subsequent list of picnics and parties showed that he succeeded. He bought a veteran half-Arab stallion which had allegedly seen service in the Greek War of Independence. He named it Apocalypse, after Shelley's 'white horse splashed with blood'. But as he galloped across the plains brandishing pistols against brigands, or curvetted about the narrow streets of Athens, it was of Byron that he was constantly reminded: 'half a dozen pallikars, among whose names Byron had counted those of his brethren in arms, stalked the streets in their national Albanian dress of fustanella and gold embroidery.'

Wilfrid fancied himself a Byronic hero, rejoicing in his new freedom. He wrote to his Aunt Wyndham (now Lady Leconfield) about a splendid ball he had given in the New Year 1860. She hoped, in reply,

* The Wards were converts to Catholicism through the Oxford Movement like the Mannings, Laprimaudayes, Pollens and Blunts.

that the floor had not collapsed and shrewdly observed that it was all 'to astonish your friends'.[12] Wilfrid's amusing illustration in his letter reminded her of 'your dear father's talent'. He was reading Carlyle's *Frederick the Great*, and had met General Church who had commanded a Greek army. He sat at the feet of George Finlay the historian of Greece, and once Byron's guest on Cephallonia. In the great heat of summer he would sail in a caïque to Sounion, lie in cool caves by day and by moonlight skim past the isles of Greece. He was soon writing a lyric highly imitative of Byron, in which 'Athens' hoary plain' vied in beauty with 'marble-footed mountains' whose strange furrows had been scored by centuries of 'pre-Adamite rain'.

Francis arrived in July and the brothers toured the Morea and afterwards visited Euboea. At Achmetaga they found the unkempt but romantic Edward Noel, one of the latest philhellenes to be connected by kinship with the Byron legend.* With his lifelong delight in girls of sixteen, Blunt fell in love with Noel's blue-eyed, bare-footed daughter Alice. A Swiss Protestant girl, Helen Leutwein, attracted him even more deeply; but before he could worry himself to death over the problem of a Catholic loving a Protestant, Helen herself died.

Wilfrid's life in the legation was still that of a boy; he enjoyed weekly paper-chases and his worst vices were 'noise and nonsense and occasional drunkenness'. He made the most of his £300 a year. His superiors seemed equally guileless, Lord Dufferin dancing 'the tight-rope and jigs' at Christmas; even Byron's 'Maid of Athens' had become a respectable elderly lady residing at Piraeus, Mrs Black.

A change came, as so often in Blunt's life, when he fell ill. Towards the end of summer 1860 a severe attack of fever caused the Foreign Office to allow him a long period of convalescence, including travel on the Continent, light work, and leave in London.

In Constantinople, where he copied despatches for Sir Henry Bulwer, the ambassador, on the proposed Suez Canal, Blunt became disturbingly aware of the contrast between Orthodox Christianity and the Mohammedan East. All the visible vice and squalor in the teeming city seemed to be Christian, while the beauty was of Islam. On the homeward journey across the great plain of the Dobruja he awoke to another disconcerting but seductive idea. Here was a world more ancient than Christendom or even Islam; the patriarchal life of the Old Testament. The level grasslands were pastured only by camels; only eagle owls marked the sites of ancient battles, as they brooded in pairs on the burial mounds. For the first time Blunt compared uncivilized nature with the ugliness created by modern man; and primitive with Christian races.

* Edward Noel's father was Tom Noel, natural son of Thomas Lord Wentworth, the uncle of Annabella Milbanke, Lady Byron.

On board the Danube steamer was Henry Stanley, who directed Blunt's thoughts still further from Christianity. Afterwards Lord Stanley of Alderley, he was on his way home from India, having abjured Christianity and embraced Islam. Blunt sprinkled Stanley with holy water in St Stephen's Cathedral at Vienna, half expecting his heretical friend to vanish in a puff of smoke.

On reaching home Blunt was invited by Stanley to his father's house in Dover Street, where he met the three Stanley sisters, Maude, Katherine and Rosalind. Blunt was dazzled by the girls, whom he described as 'enthusiastic iconoclasts'. Kate was to become Lady Amberley, mother of Bertrand Russell, and Rosalind, Lady Carlisle. He was soon a regular visitor at Dover Street, skirmishing with his new friends over every field human and divine.

His aunt Lady Leconfield had hoped that Francis would join one of the aristocratic Guards regiments (he was gazetted to the 60th Rifles that September), since a brother in the Guards would have helped Wilfrid's position in the Diplomatic Service. It was impossible to get on, she wrote, 'without being *known* in society' – unless of course one had extraordinary industry and talents. 'You have so much energy and character', she assured Wilfrid, 'that if you struggle against being carried away by the love of pleasure, I feel your success would be certain, humanly speaking – at any rate, *do try*.' The Wyndhams pulled strings to get Wilfrid transferred to Germany from Greece, since he still suffered from ague, and in September the good news came through. He was to go to Frankfurt, and his aunt would send an introduction to the ambassador, Sir Alexander Malet, who was a distant relation of the late Lord Egremont of Petworth. Diplomacy was a right little tight little world.

Early in 1861 Wilfrid travelled to Frankfurt. It proved to be a battle-ground for him not of diplomacy but of religion. Here in a frankly rationalist society all his previous puzzles were intensified. Lady Malet, the ambassadress, was the step-daughter, 'probably the real daughter', of Lord Brougham, an early evolutionist. At no table to which Blunt was invited did guests fail to discuss Darwin's *Origin of Species*. Yet Blunt had not read it. If Meynell allowed Kant in 1857 surely the Church would now permit Darwin? He wrote for permission to Canon Wenham, his boyhood confessor. The answer was no. Nevertheless Blunt did take and read. 'It was, I think, my first deliberate sin, and, as with Adam in the Garden of Eden, this eating of the fruit of the forbidden tree of knowledge was attended with the immediate ruin of my intellectual innocence.'

With scarcely a struggle the twenty-year-old Blunt lost his faith in the Bible and in God as Creator of the world. 'If we find an order in nature, is it necessary to assume an Orderer? Why should blind forces be necessarily a chaos?' The great battles of intellect which he had foreseen between himself and the rationalists simply never took place. Matter had quietly usurped God's throne and assumed his title. Matter itself was God, 'the Eternal, the Infinite, the Self-existent, the Thing that is, was and ever should be, world without end'.

Blunt's heart, however, could not follow his head. He was never quite to give up hope of finding some other solution to the great scientific problems of the age than this 'cruel logic'. Indeed even in Frankfurt, soon after his conversion to scepticism, he was already trying to have it both ways. He wrote a paper on philosophy in 1861 for Count Usedom, the liberal Prussian envoy to the German Federation, in reply to an article from *Die Ziet* which the Count had lent him. Blunt's thesis is that the existence of God cannot be proved from the order of nature. Nevertheless his last paragraph concludes with an appeal: 'In God's name and for the sake of His recognition among men let us avoid the *Natur-forscher* [Natural Philosophy] and hold fast by our internal unreasonable consciousness of a father who is in Heaven.'

Beyond Blunt's wish to believe – what he called 'an inherited instinct of my soul' – his closest friends and their innocent way of life helped keep agnosticism at bay. Lord Schomberg Kerr, a fellow Catholic attaché at the legation aged twenty-seven, was suffering similar though less violent doubts. Neither he nor Blunt had yet broken the sexual code; no sex outside marriage, no marriage outside the Catholic Church. That meant no sex. Their pastimes were still childish. They trundled hoops through the Frankfurt suburbs, to the amusement of their more sophisticated colleagues, and raced the trains as they crossed the bridge over the river. Countess Olympia Usedom, a Scots woman married to the Prussian envoy, would invite the friends into her home, where they could talk nonsense with her little daughter Hildegard and forget both the origins of species and of the Schleswig-Holstein dispute.

Fear of hell was yet another aid to the virtuous life. Blunt found that the demons of scripture were still almost as powerful as what he called 'the demon of materialism'. Hardly daring to ride across rough country 'for fear of breaking my fool's neck', he would still attend Mass and pray to a God in whom he did not quite believe. He might have halted longer on the border of irreligion but for a midsummer crisis at home.

It began on a March afternoon in 1861, when the English mail brought a letter from nineteen-year-old Alice to announce her return to the Sacred Heart at Roehampton as a postulant. Francis, Dr Grant, Canon Wenham and Henry Currie approved. Only their aunt, Lady Leconfield, was beside herself with disapproval. She wrote to Wilfrid:

'What shall I do, what shall I say, *where* shall I send her?!!!' If only Alice could travel abroad with some nice people for two years, 'but where *are* the people?'[13] Alice's entertainment had been reduced to evenings out with Mrs Henry Wilberforce, the convert sister of Cardinal Manning's late wife.

Wilfrid's immediate reaction was horror. He felt called upon to save his sister from sacrificing her young life to 'the dogmas of the old world, when she had not begun to enjoy the beauties of the earth'. He and his friend Kerr walked together in a lovely German forest discussing the news. Kerr also had 'lost a sister' behind a convent wall; he urged Blunt to do battle for his. Lady Malet counselled him to rush home and 'forbid the banns'. He did so, and his vehemence persuaded even Canon Wenham and Francis.

The latter's capitulation seemed the more surprising because Francis's own mind was set on endowing the Capuchin friary at Crawley, near Crabbet. He had promised his dying mother to do so when he came into his inheritance. Lady Leconfield, as a devout Protestant, of course backed Wilfrid. But she rejected Wilfrid's later suggestion that the problem of Alice should be settled by an arranged marriage. 'What *can* you mean', she wrote to him, 'about the eligible offer of Matrimony!! Do ladies' Mamas or Papas do such things for their daughters in Germany I wonder!'[14]

At last with many tears Alice consented to postpone her decision on taking the veil until she was twenty-one, and to live with her Protestant Chandler relations at Witley. Wilfrid was triumphant. But principally his triumph was over the Church. From now on he went no more to Mass. He had turned his back, as he said, on heaven.

The beginning of spring 1862 in Frankfurt was a time of secret restlessness and disappointment. Blunt could find no satisfying substitute for the religion he had lost. Love was still barred, and the interest of his diplomatic career was not powerful enough to fill the gap.

During the previous August, Sir Alexander Malet had had to send Blunt three peremptory notes. In the first he remarked on the absence of both Blunt and Kerr from the office, and ordered one or other to attend next day at 11 a.m., 'it being unbecoming that the whole work of the legation should be left to the Minister'. The next two notes were sent one after the other on the same day. The second explains the situation.

Dear Mr. Blunt, I sent to your house in the first place a little after 5, neither you or yr. Servt. were to be found. At 6½ I sent Note no. 1, with orders to look you up – the result was the same. I have now to instruct you to come to the Office at whatever *hour* you return to yr. Lodging and if you do not find me sitting up for you, you will find a Servt. and light, – and directions as to what you have to do.[15]

But if the office found fault with Wilfrid, the wives and daughters of the corps diplomatique knew better. He was frankly spoilt. When the time for Blunt's next transfer arrived Lady Malet wrote: 'As for me it has made me sorrowful to know I shall see you here in the old way no more!' As for Olympia Usedom, she referred to all the young secretaries as her 'Babies', but Wilfrid was her 'Dearest Baby Boy'. Her answer to a letter of his in 1862 was lyrically maternal; 'I have missed and do miss you dreadfully. I want your shaggy head and dreamy voice and no-one has yet supplied your lack!... Are you writing poetry? ... Write me something dear old Baby Blunt. You are a gt. darling and as I *could* be your mother there is no harm in my saying it.'

After a visit from Alice to Frankfurt in spring 1862, Wilfrid found she had made friends with 'intellectual society women'; Lady Burrell, Lady Kenmare, Madeline Wyndham, wife of young Percy, Georgie Sumner, married to a member of the Prince of Wales's set. There was also Maria Margaret Pollen, formerly the beautiful younger Laprimaudaye sister at Lucca. Wilfrid wondered whether he too could not find happiness in society, in the Court circles which milled around Château Rumpenheim and Frankfurt that summer.

He met Princess Mary Adelaide of Cambridge, cousin of Queen Victoria, Princess Alice of Hesse, the Queen's daughter, and the young Princesses Alexandra and Olga of Denmark. Was this to be his new heaven? Dancing with Mary Adelaide was quite the most delightful of his duties, for despite her 'huge bulk' she was light-footed. 'We became rather friends.' Olga had flowing hair and a pair of dark eyes 'of which she was beginning to make use'. She and her sister, however, struck Wilfrid as being so badly dressed that they might have passed in a crowd for two little German modistes not even in their Sunday best. Nevertheless the Frankfurt Legation received a confidential message that the Prince of Wales had proposed to Alexandra. Could not Wilfrid pursue his Court connection with an eye to his subsequent career?

Unfortunately, he discovered that his new vein of irreverent scepticism extended even to royalty.

In their company I was constantly reminded of the in-bred short-horned cattle we exhibit at our shows, high-pedigreed ruminants bred to fatten, kindly and complete in their digestive organs but of no other interest, gazing wide-eyed on a world they believe to be made for them and whose realities they do not understand.

In despair he decided to reverse the direction of the past two years. If there was no happiness outside the 'protective haven' of religion, he would make one last bid to get back. This was to be the first of many 'final attempts' to regain paradise.

He had been transferred from Frankfurt to Madrid. This allowed him to spend a few weeks at home on leave in between. It was June. A spiritual retreat at the house of the Redemptorists in Clapham should be his Rubicon. Either he would cross over into a life of full pleasure, however illicit, or turn back to positive obedience. He had chosen Clapham because the rector was his mother's confessor and friend, Father Coffin.

On the first day of the retreat Blunt poured out the story of his crisis, went to all the services and left the rest in Father Coffin's hands. Father Coffin, 'good man', argued little, trusting to prayer and the *Confessions of St. Augustine*, which Blunt was reading for the first time. Nothing could have moved him more than this story of the great 'sinner saint'. The days passed in study or walking with the community in the garden, where he listened expectantly for the voice Augustine had heard. Nevertheless, as the retreat drew to a close, he was still not completely at rest. Indeed on the last day he had come to differentiate between his two possible alternatives more drastically than before. If he were not to plunge into the pit, he must enter the Redemptorist novitiate then and there. He longed to choose Clapham. But 'cruel logic' remained unappeased. Not only logic, but a human obsession also: St Augustine had at least enjoyed the full experience of sin. 'Give me chastity . . . but not yet.' Blunt was still chaste. He wished to be able to pray likewise.

That evening he and Father Coffin were standing by a big tank from which a lay brother was drawing water for the garden. The priest discoursed on the ultimate end of humn life, heaven or hell. Then he bade Blunt look down into the dark water and observe how narrow a line divided time from eternity. 'It would be easy to drown there and in five minutes to stand before the judgment seat of God and know all. Shall I plunge in? If it would win you I would do it, though I should die thus in my sin. Say only the word.'

Blunt did not say it. That same night he was roused by the sound of chanting in the corridor and of flagellation on naked shoulders. He knew that it was the final appeal. The words of the Seven Penitential Psalms which the monks sang were to return to him during many a subsequent crisis. But he had made up his mind. Next morning he left; though not before he had threaded a daisy chain in the garden and hung it on a nail outside his bedroom window. Superstition, he knew; but there was a real wish that it might one day bind him and bring him back. Then, for the third time in two years, he announced that he 'went out like Adam' from the biblical Paradise. This time it was true.

[2]
Venus Discovered 1862–1866

The Frankfurt legation's 'Baby Boy' was in no hurry to take up his new post. Lady Malet wrote anxiously to her protégé on 18 October 1862: 'Dear Mr. Blunt, so I hear you are not yet gone to Madrid!!! How wrong of you.'[1] At length, however, Blunt said goodbye to Forest Cottage and the woods of Sussex and his kind old Aunt Leconfield whom he was never to see again.

Around Christmas 1862 he arrived in Madrid. It proved to be 'a dull old-fashiond form of society'. He had begun to feel a 'perverse' attraction for 'anything singular in my mode of life'. His duty, for instance, as a member of the corps diplomatique was to stand for interminable periods in the throne room watching the Spanish royal family having their fingers kissed by a procession of grandees and officers; Queen Isabella with great fat hands at the end of arms like 'rounds of raw beef', her husband small and stiff, the infanta an anaemic girl of thirteen, and the six-year-old Prince of the Asturias offering a limp hand as he slept soundly in his gilt chair.

As there was nothing serious to do, Blunt's young fellow attachés threw themselves into 'gambling madness'. He himself kept a drawer full of huge silver Spanish pieces with which he played until they were all lost. His slender resources were in no state to sustain heavy debts; and there was a moment when he and his friends were in grave danger. All desperately poor, they had 'borrowed' from a Church fund at the legation, each putting an IOU into the rifled box. When someone pointed out that the IOU would not save them if the theft were discovered, they managed to make good the deficit. For Blunt at least it was a salutary shock. 'Many a poor bank clerk had gone to prison for a less offence', he admitted; he confided his lapse in a letter to his aunt and never again gambled to excess.

The other occupation of these young diplomats was amorous adventure. Blunt began to be ashamed of his own 'virtue', which was no longer founded on conviction. But the high romance that he awaited did not come his way. At last he engaged a Spanish Irishman,

Guillermo O'Shea, to procure him a respectable mistress who would instruct him in her language and anything else he needed to know. 'The result was Lola.'

She was twenty-three, a little Madrilène who had been abandoned by her husband and lived with her mother by her needle. Their existence was meagre and Lola no astonishing beauty, though decorous in public and gay and witty in private. As for her religious conscience, it accused her of no more than venial sin, since her husband was to blame and her lover as a 'Cristiano' – a Catholic. Blunt found that Spanish opinion, 'which is really oriental', could be far from intolerant towards a man who helped a deserted young wife and her poor mother to get a supplement of pimientos with their daily bread.

Lola's lovemaking was simple and sincere, but it was not what Blunt had expected of the much vaunted 'passion'. The passion which Lola did convey to him, however, was for the bullfight. The Corrida was her one weekly festival. So faithfully did Blunt absorb his mistress's expertise that he himself would sometimes be invited to play the role of matador. There is a story of Sir William Gregory, a future ally of Blunt's in a tougher kind of fight – against John Bull himself – enquiring who was the young hero of the bullring. 'I wonder you were not afraid', said Sir William when they met later. Blunt replied, 'I was very much afraid indeed, but I would not give in.'*[2] His poem 'Sancho Sanchez' suggests that the prospect of death was still linked for him with hell, so that his courage in the bullring was both spectacular and 'perverse'. In swinging verses Blunt imagines a dying matador telling his comrades that their profession has deep meaning and is worth dying for. They should be filled with glorious pride

> Because the wicked Beast was death, and the horns
> of death were hell. . . .

Those who had faced the bull would not flinch when the devil himself came for them on their last day:

> And the boast of our profession was a bulwark against danger
> With its fearless expectation of what good or ill may come,
> For the very prince of darkness shall burst forth on us no
> stranger
> When the doors of death fly open to the rolling of the drum.

In Wilfrid's own case the doors of death indeed flew open and were closed again only with the greatest difficulty. But not to the rolling of any drum; rather to the whispers of the sick room.

* Strangely, I have found no account by Blunt of his own performance in the bullring, apart from his statement in 'Alms to Oblivion' Part II, that he once considered bullfighting as a profession.

He had been sitting in the Corrida one June afternoon in 1863 without a coat. A violent inflammation of the lungs struck him down. Within two days he was at death's door and remained so until the efficient acting-consul Captain Reginald Graham took charge. The Spanish surgeon's zeal for blistering was repressed, the papal nuncio and the evangelical Earl of Aberdeen (then touring Spain) were persuaded not to battle over Blunt's helpless body for his soul, two little French nursing Sisters of Hope were engaged, and Francis and Alice were summoned from England, bringing with them Canon Wenham. Wilfrid turned the corner, but his poor Aunt Leconfield, while visiting the Foreign Office for news of her favourite nephew, died of a heart attack.

She was over seventy. Blunt missed her love and her devoted advice if he did not always take it. In a small envelope dated 1859 and labelled M.W., he kept a curl of Mary Wyndham's hair, light brown with white threads in it.

Blunt was afterwards to feel that he owed his life and lungs to Graham and the Sisters of Hope, rather than to his sister's prayers. During the weeks of his physical exhaustion, however, he slipped back into his faith, joining in the daily prayers of his brother and sister, if only to please those who loved him.

It is a remarkable fact that one who was to live so long found himself again and again on the brink of the grave. In these moments of crisis either he himself or his friends, believing he had but a few weeks to live, would consent to courses of action which otherwise would have been ruled out. For good or ill, the turns and twists in Blunt's life were controlled by the terrible visitations upon himself and his family of that scourge of the nineteenth century, tuberculosis.

His reunion with Alice brought him exquisite happiness, for they had drifted apart since her convent episode and his loss of faith. Now, obedient to Alice's plans, he spent contented weeks at the Escurial, saying his prayers, wandering on the terraces between aromatic box hedges and in the ilex woods, or resting in the cool corridors where she read to him the children's books of their youth. As his strength returned they prepared for a long tour together on horseback without guides, and carrying their few necessities behind their horses in bags of the kind used by Arabs.

During the third week in July they set out in high spirits. Crossing and recrossing the western Pyrenees by deserted mule tracks, they visited Bagnères de Bigorre in France, familiar to their childhood, and rode into Pamplona in Spain over the wild passes of Roncevalles. 'Los Moros! Los Moros!' cried the delighted inhabitants, for Alice and Wilfrid, deeply sunburned in their white turbans and followed by a mule and their two dogs Rachel and George, looked like a Moorish troupe about to stage a show. This was the first but not the last time that Blunt was mistaken for an Arab.

Meanwhile Francis had dealt with Wilfrid's responsibilities in Madrid, paying off Lola and reporting her 'quite content'. In fact one of Wilfrid's young friends Frank Lascelles took her on, and Wilfrid received news of her from him during the following year. On being transferred to Paris, Frank wrote: 'Your furniture is not yet sold and Lola wants to keep your bed which I suppose I shall have to give her'. Six days later Frank's final advice to Wilfrid was 'practice Tennis and beware of women'.[3] Wilfrid ignored the advice. Lola, however, never again became his mistress, though he returned as attaché to Madrid in October 1863. For in the meantime he had risen above the Lolas of this world as a man does who has been walking 'cubits high' with a goddess.

During his last years, Blunt revised the unpublished memoir which he had entitled *Alms to Oblivion*. By February 1920 he had reached the end of Part II, called 'Esther', dealing with the period 1863–6. The result was not displeasing to him. 'I am surprised to find how well it is written. Indeed I doubt if any English memoir (I do not say French) was ever better than it is so far, for it is absolutely truthful and at the same time decent, though treating of the least decent period of my life.'

In telling the story of these same years, Blunt's biographer has the advantage of hindsight. Blunt himself was to find out much about 'Esther', the heroine of Part II, which he refrained from interpolating into the original memoir. In Part II, for instance, he never deviated from the pseudonym 'Esther', the name which he adopted for his remarkable narrative poem describing this episode. Later on he would call her 'Lady C' in his published *My Diaries*, or in his unpublished 'Secret Memoirs', 'XX', or in his letter file, 'Miss Walters'. They were all one and the same person: the most famous courtesan of the late Victorian age, Catherine Walters – the inimitable 'Skittles'.*

'My fate' was how Blunt described his first meeting with his first *grande passion*. The romance struck on 20 September 1863, the very day that Alice left him. He had seen her off on her ship for England at Bordeaux. Listless and dejected, he turned in at a wayside show advertised in scarlet letters as 'The Booth of Beauty'. Inside a brass band blared; in half-darkness were two female monsters, one a 'spotted girl with leopard lips', the other a woman seven feet high. There was also another woman in the booth, 'a little woman dressed in

* The two names by which Wilfrid Blunt never referred to Miss Walters were Skittles and Mrs Baillie; the first presumably because Skittles was the nickname invented by her earlier lovers; the second because Catherine herself never used the name she had acquired in a marriage still wrapped in some mystery. (See p. 419 below.) In later letters Catherine signed herself Katy, Katie or Kitty, addressing Blunt as Winny or even 'Darling Winny Boy'.

black', who stood on tiptoe and clutched Wilfrid's arm each time the monsters sent through the crowd a 'shiver of half fear, half merriment'. This was Esther.

Her brow was pale, but it was lit with light,
  And mirth flashed out of it, it seemed in rays.
A childish face, but wise in woman's wit,
  And something, too, pathetic in its gaze.

After being challenged by the huge monster to handle her knee, and in doing so inviting the 'inhuman' laughter of the crowd, Wilfrid fled from the booth. Fate next stationed him outside the local theatre reading a handbill which advertised 'Mademoiselle Esther' in *Manon Lescaut.* Suddenly a side door opened and Esther herself stepped out, the 'little woman of the Fair'. In a moment he found himself parading hand in hand with her through a maze of shops and stalls, listening to her 'fool's talk' as she bargained and bantered with the vendors. It seemed a mad dream and yet the only reality.

The past, the future, all of weal or woe
  In my old life was gone, forever gone.
And still to this I clung as one who clings
  To hope's last hencoop in the wreck of things.

She took him to her apartment, where a 'Madame', passing for Esther's dressmaker, was quickly asked to leave while Esther

Undid her jacket and anon her dress
  With the jet buttons of it one by one
And stood but clothed the more in loveliness,
  A sight sublime, a dream, a miracle,
A little goddess from some luminous field
  Brought down unconscious on our Earth to dwell.
And in an age of innocence revealed,
  Naked but not ashamed....

This story, as told in his *Esther*, seemed to Blunt 'too near the truth to be easily re-told'.*

Skittles was on her way from Paris to Biarritz to join the imperial circle of Napoleon III and his Empress Eugénie, then enjoying a long seaside fête at the fashionable Spanish resort. To Skittles, this beautiful youth with the face of a John the Baptist, as she put it, and the work-a-day rags of a shepherd boy, was a pleasant titillation for the holiday season. It was her habit now and then to roam the streets

* In the poem Lyons appears as a cover for Bordeaux, where Blunt first met Skittles, not in Biarritz as is always assumed; nor was Blunt a virgin, as is equally erroneously stated. See Henry Blyth, *Skittles* (1970), p. 152, for example. Though Mr Blyth has made a fine bonfire of many false legends surrounding his heroine, it was inevitable that many others should still remain, until the Blunt papers in the Fitzwilliam Museum were opened.

incognita. Next morning she had the black dress stowed away for another occasion. Now 'in the full glory of her demi-mondaine beauty', she popped Blunt into her splendid coach and rumbled into Biarritz. She took him to live with her, publicly displaying her exotic new prize.

'Sunburned and untamed', Blunt attracted all eyes, including those of the Emperor and Empress. The French Court could afford in Biarritz if nowhere else to look on odd romances with indulgence. The imperial family themselves had abandoned etiquette and returned to their old bohemian life. Eugénie looked kindly on Blunt, herself escorted by four laughing young Basques who boated with her daily and 'shared her bathings far out to sea'. A noisy group of local boys had been recruited for the young Prince Imperial. Even Napoleon III and his Chamberlain, Tascher La Pagerie, smiled protectingly as they walked slowly arm-in-arm on the plage each morning. Silent and self-possessed, with 'heavy sallow face and lack-lustre eyes', the Emperor seemed 'to conceal all secrets'. One of his secrets, Blunt discovered, was that he too paid addresses to Esther, under the name of Captain Jones.

Into this Vanity Fair Esther and her ragged John the Baptist plunged together. To Wilfrid had come at last the great romantic love for which he had almost ceased to hope. With the suddenness and completeness of a forest fire it changed the landscape of his mind overnight. Her whims became his ideals, her fancies his crusades, her desires his paradise regained.

> Esther's was a potent personality and dominated me to a degree for which I have long learned to be ashamed, but while it lasted it was absolute and held me captive to ideals of vanity and trivial pleasure not my own but which allured me as being hers. These at times still [after some forty years] affect me.

Esther's influence on him at the time was totally unpoetic, though he was later to write to her some of his best verse. Indeed he would no more have dreamt of telling her that he wrote poetry than of confessing to his religious doubts and solemnities. All serious subjects were as forgotten as if they had never been.

> For two years and more after my meeting with Esther I was convinced that the trifles that occupied her of dress and vanity were the things of most importance in the world and that its serious pursuits were a mere waste of time.

Up to the third week in his fool's paradise he had been blissfully unaware of Esther's past. In his besotted state he imagined that any moment he could take his 'phoenix of creation' into the nearest church and marry her. That he was penniless and living on her wealth never troubled him. Nor did Esther give him more than a hint (which in any case he refused to take) of how that wealth had been acquired. She had agreed to marry a very distinguished personage, she told him, but the engagement had been broken off, since which she had been living in Paris on an allowance made by him, enough to save her from the necessity of taking other lovers. Adorers she had in plenty, but when Wilfrid appeared she had long been without an accepted lover. 'Out of this thin texture of comparative virtue I had spun my cloud castle regarding her.' She had behaved to him with the munificence of a queen, and it was not her fault that he clothed her in 'a kind of supernatural innocence, impossible and absurd'.

After Skittles's death in 1920, a large packet of several hundred letters was handed over to Blunt for safe-keeping by her last and most devoted companion, the Hon. Gerald de Saumarez. Immured until now with Blunt's own papers in the Fitzwilliam Museum's tin boxes, they were written to Skittles by Lord Hartington, the 'very distinguished personage' of her partial revelations to Blunt in the early 1860s. They cover a good deal of what Skittles left out. Moreover Skittles herself was to tell Wilfrid more of her true story, and Wilfrid to write it down, four years after their first meeting.

Catherine Walters was born in 1839, the daughter of a Liverpool sea-captain by his Irish wife, who had her christened a Catholic. Her mother died when she was four; Catherine was sent to a convent in Chester, from which she ran away after beating up the nun in charge. Beautiful and wild, she had a passion for horses and was employed by the keeper of a livery-stable, where she displayed his animals (and herself) on the hunting field, receiving a percentage on sales. She rode chiefly with the Cheshire Hunt, soon acquiring a local reputation and the nickname 'Skittles' – from her skill in a Cheshire skittles alley, not in Paris, as has been said. Her loveliness was piquant rather than classical, though she had eyes of the classical grey-blue. Her complexion glowed with health and her delicate figure was strong and graceful from much exercise. Blunt and a French admirer both described her hair as 'fair', though a third admirer called it 'bright chestnut'.*

At sixteen she became the mistress of George, Lord Fitzwilliam, master of the Fitzwilliam hounds, but deserted him within a few years for Lord Cavendish ('Cav'), later Marquess of Hartington (Harty-Tarty) and eighth Duke of Devonshire. Her tales of these and other aristocrats on the hunting field were never less than salty. Both George and 'Cav', she told Blunt, were honourable men, George making her a

* Blunt's biographer, Edith Finch, follows this latter description. On the same page (43) she says that Skittles was 'not precisely beautiful', apparently following a misleading line in the poem *Esther*: 'I am not pretty.' In 1908 Skittles was to recall to Blunt that her hair had been 'auburn'. (20 April 1908. FM.)

parting settlement of £300 a year with £2,000 at the bank, and 'Cav' ready to marry her once he obtained his father's consent. But the consent was never forthcoming, despite the old Duke having got as far as kissing Skitsy himself.* Neverthless Hartington and Skittles wrote to each other almost every day and hunted together in Leicestershire. He settled on her £500 a year, hunters – 'my little Skits is rather expensive' – and a house, 34 Park Street. With characteristic generosity she gave him shirts, handkerchiefs, gloves, flowers, a cigar case.

In London Skittles rode in the Park, admired by all who saw her. In the words of young Alfred Austin, future poet laureate and friend of Blunt, 'With slackened rein swift Skittles rules the Row'. Skittles may have ruled the Row but she could not rule Hartington. She was packed off to Paris and, later, to Ems. Hartington continued to write to her. One letter from him, written in 1863 and addressed to Mrs Walters, Poste Restante, Ems, lamented that Skitsy's 'Madame' had given such a sad account of his darling's low spirits:

> Poor little Madame . . . she thought me a great brute I am sure. . . . I know you think me very hard and cruel to you Skitsy but you don't think as a brute I know Skitsy. I do care for you I think darling of you as much as ever. Post is just going and I must leave off.

His last dated letter to her in the series was written less than three months before Blunt met her. It was addressed to Madame de Walters, Württemberg:

> *2 July 1863* . . . what a long time it is now since I have seen you my darling, it makes me very sad when I think how much unhappiness my poor little darling has had all [torn paper] . . . times; but I do hope that now she is going to get better. . . .[4]

His little darling *was* going to get better – in the arms of another. When Hartington returned from a visit to America (packed off in his turn, by his father), he found that she and her 'little Madame' had agreed that she could not remain virtuous forever. Skittles graciously accepted a financial settlement of £500 a year. So relieved were the ducal family at her 'good feeling' that she was permitted to show herself when she pleased on the fringes of Chatsworth.

When Wilfrid first met her she was based in Paris, favoured by the Emperor but with no public lover. Now twenty-four years old, she had begun to create the atmosphere of mystery that was to surround her all her life and add greatly to her prestige. The mystery, wrote

* From the Hartington–Walters correspondence Blunt eventually learnt that among the old Duke's objections to the marriage was Skittles' health – 'The epileptic fits she was subject to, which were such a puzzle to me in those first days.' (FM 461/1975, 9 November 1920.)

Blunt, was founded on two principles; never to sell herself to the first comer, and never to have a woman friend. Thus she could 'keep her secrets close'. That Esther actually had any secrets only began to dawn on Wilfrid during the third week at Biarritz.

The first sting of suspicion came when Esther received a love-letter from a Russian prince, travelling beyond Moscow with her portrait on the seat opposite him. Blunt recollected his feelings of jealousy in one of the *Manon* sonnets called 'On Reading Certain Letters':

> I seem to hear some pagan chaunt of praise ...
> I shut my ears, yet hear it still, my eyes
> See not, yet see the unchaste the unlawful fire;
> ... then in my ire
> I rise up, as on Horeb, and I cry
> 'There is none other god, but only I!'*

That same afternoon they were romping for possession of a cushion:

> I as the stronger had held it just a second too long for her short patience when to my amazement I saw a look of anger in her beautiful eyes, a flash of passionate resentment, almost of hatred, as when playing with a panther it should turn without warning and strike one with an unsheathed claw. 'You would dare', she exclaimed, 'try strengths with me!' There was a note of scorn in her voice which filled me as I dropped the cushion with dismay. The whole was over in an instant but it left its sting. I seemed to see an abyss of possible disaster opened at my feet and I was giddy at the thought.

'And one in terror spells love's epitaph.'[5] Next day Esther was restless, avoiding his eyes. On the third day the crash came. She must leave for Paris. Wilfrid should have been back in Madrid. She did not want to get him into trouble.

Her coolness in planning their separation filled him with amazement and horror. His tears melted her to the extent that she allowed him to travel with her to Paris and say goodbye there. This clinging to her skirts like a child had a humiliating sequel. He was admitted to her hotel but no longer flaunted in public. Sent to an English tailor to be 'made respectable', he returned to her looking like an awkward peasant in the Sunday suit. His natural shyness was increased by the arrival of a tittering attaché from the Russian embassy with news of the love-sick prince. Tears flowed again and Wilfrid 'dared' to accuse her of inconstancy. Out came the claws again. Esther roundly scolded him for being a fool and sent him packing to Madrid – though not without a parting kiss, a lock of her fair hair and the prospect of meeting again

* Blunt's daughter Judith in early life adoring and later abusing her father as tyrant, tried to prove from the last two lines of this sonnet, quoted above, that he really did consider himself a latter-day Jehovah. She missed the point of the sonnet, in which Blunt mocked himself for having in his youthful arrogance expected to be Manon's only god.

when he was wiser. 'And so in a final cataract of tears, yet half consoled, the curtain fell upon my insane heart's paradise.'

It is impossible not to suspect that Wilfrid had been made to act out, for Skittles' consolation, her own suffering at the hands of Hartington. Blunt does not say this in his memoirs, putting the entire blame on himself and his ridiculous childishness; but some of the letters from Skittles to Wilfrid are highly suggestive. Even the language used by Skittles to her rejected lover faithfully echoes that of Hartington to his.

22 October 1863 Thursday. My little darling – How are you? . . . Poor little Child* I do hope you are happy, more so than me, for I am too wretched and miserable a creature to write to any so pray forgive me. I am just off for England so God Bless you yours Aff. K.W.

A second letter written by Skittles to Wilfrid seventeen months later again introduced the familiar Hartington tone: 'I pity you my poor child from the bottom of my heart. . . . We are so very different . . . now darling please try to be a good and sensible child you know I am not so thoroughly without a heart as the world makes me out to be. . . .'

Blunt calls his departure from Paris in 1863 the end of Act I of his 'first passionate affair'. The sequel was to come a year later and to result in a new enslavement to Esther – though ultimately he 'won free'. Nowhere does he blame Esther for the consequences. Nor does his own analysis of the disaster square with the two main legends which have grown up around him.

Some have believed that his consuming passion for Skittles burnt him out like a house gutted by fire. Never again, according to this theory, was he to be capable of loving with his whole heart. His biographer Edith Finch writes: 'In after life Blunt is said to have held that Skittles set his passion so fully ablaze that it burnt out once for all. No other woman could do more than stir the embers.'[6] Henry Blyth, the biographer of Skittles, follows Edith Finch: 'He [Blunt] never again committed himself fully to the conflict of deeply-felt physical passion . . . his mistresses sensed that it was not they of whom he dreamt but someone else in his life, and the knowledge of this piqued them, and his inaccessibility added greatly to his charm.'[7]

Blunt's daughter Judith Lady Wentworth advanced a variant of this theory, namely, that his future love-life became a long drawn-out revenge on other women for the wrong Skittles had done him. This is an ingenious idea based on Blunt's two sonnet sequences written about Skittles, called respectively *Esther* and *Manon*. Not surprisingly truth and fiction were mingled in these sonnets with a poet's usual licence. Judith, however, in her own unpublished memoir 'Myself and Others', takes all her father's lines as fact:

* Hartington often called Skittles his 'little child'.

I have loved too much, too loyally, too long,
Today I am a pirate of the sea.
Let others suffer. I have suffered wrong.
Let others love, and love as tenderly.
Oh, Manon, there are women yet unborn
Shall rue thy frailty, else am I foresworn.[8]

The 'locked box' containing her father's papers, Judith surmised, was the repository of love letters to Blunt from later victims on whom he had revenged 'Manon's' cruelty. In a semi-biographical book, *The Authentic Arabian*, Judith sums up her father's attitude to women as 'a life-long vendetta'.[9]

There is no support for either of these theories – the burnt-out case or the vendetta – in Blunt's own diaries and memoirs, which Judith incidentally never saw though she advised posterity to read them with a pinch of salt. Indeed if we accept the stories that Blunt tells of other romantic love affairs, we must believe that his heart was capable of a far more complete passion than the gifted but superficial Skittles inspired. 'Dear passionate Esther, soulless but how kind!'[10]

This is not to say that his first passion was not an indelible memory – as first passions often are. On the eve of a much later adventure, for example, he noted that the date was auspicious – 20 September 1893, the thirtieth anniversary of his unforgettable encounter in Bordeaux.

What then were the evil consequences of Blunt's 'summer adventure'? He emphasizes that they were not erotic. They went much deeper. The adventure had 'perverted and disturbed him' to the depths of his being, leaving him 'a pauper' both morally and intellectually for several years: 'From that moment life appeared to me in a wholly novel aspect with ambitions of a kind strange to my earlier imagination, and which more or less control me still.' Blunt's experience was to give him a permanent and energetic taste for Vanity Fair.

At the same time, he never ceased to look for (and often find) an 'ideal love'. These ideal loves were as remote from Biarritz as – on another level – his half-hearted diplomatic activities in Madrid were from the passionate political ideals he was later to follow in Egypt, India and Ireland.

His return to Madrid, indeed, in autumn 1863 proved a pitiful fiasco. Before his summer adventure he had sometimes been idle but more often 'an industrious good young man'. Afterwards he was lazy, self-willed and avid for further doses of his 'scandalous renown'. A severe letter from his well-wisher Lady Malet showed that his notoriety had spread to at least one other chancellery:

I heard you had amused yourself at Biarritz in a way which according to report was objectionable – and you must forgive me for saying that you ought to know better than to follow in the steps of Labouchere and others.*

The wanderings of heart and fancy are a man's own affair, but when his wanderings take an oblique direction, and he exhibits them in public, then he is to blame, for he sins against good feeling and good taste.... It is always so unnecessary besides.[11]

There spoke the woman of the world, the world of the 1860s. But Wilfrid was too far gone in 'oblique directions' to take Lady Malet's advice. His only worthwhile occupation during the following nine months was copying at the Madrid picture galleries with his Irish friend Molony – in himself a queer enough companion, if Judith Wentworth is to be believed: 'a wicked old atheist with the padded skin of a mummy and a pointed nose which twitched when he was angry'.

In August 1864 Blunt was moved from Madrid to Paris. This should have been a splendid step in his career; instead, he was to throw away his happiness and reputation in a series of what he frankly called blunders and stupidities. 'The next year of my life', he wrote in retrospect, 'is perhaps the most painful of all in memory.'

Wilfrid Blunt's first evening at the Paris Embassy was perilously auspicious. Paris was *en fête*. It was 15 August, no longer known as the Feast of the Assumption but of St Napoleon. Since the fashionable world had left, Blunt was invited to dine early with the ambassador, Earl Cowley. A table was set in the garden of that splendid mansion which Cowley's late uncle, the Iron Duke, had bought fifty years before from Napoleon's sister Pauline on behalf of the British Foreign Office. If Blunt found Lord Cowley burdened by the Wellesleys' heavy reserve – 'a curiously silent man stiff and awkward, typically British in his anti-social manners, and ill at ease even in the bosom of his family' – his women provided all the lightness and gaiety that Blunt could wish for. Lady Cowley was kindness itself, and there was an unmarried daughter, Lady Feodorowna (Feodore) Wellesley, with dancing blue eyes. After dinner Blunt, the two ladies and a secretary paraded slowly in their carriage through the crowded, brilliant streets. He felt again the vainglory he had enjoyed as the showpiece of 'Madame de Walters' in Biarritz. Or perhaps he was one of the Napoleons riding through his capital. Was Feodore to be his Josephine, his Eugénie? 'I found myself making a kind of love to her which was not ill received ... and our toes touched.'

This was the beginning of a promising intimacy. Throughout that winter Blunt went everywhere in the ambassadorial train, always

* Henry Dupré Labouchere, 1831–1912, one of the gay dogs in the diplomatic service who was also very rich; a Liberal M.P. from 1864 to 1905, editor of *Truth* and a political friend of Blunt.

dancing with Feodore and in fact receiving invitations as her accepted fiancé. Given a little consistency of conduct he knew he could have built on it a structure of ambition, even of happiness. 'All the more it torments me now how little I deserved the affection given and the chances thrown away. And for what an absurdity of folly!'

It was about Christmas when the call which John the Baptist had secretly been expecting came. The Cowleys were on holiday in England and the attachés idling in the chancellery. One morning a note was brought to Wilfrid by an old woman whom he recognized as Esther's *bonne* Julie. Madame had been ill and only just learnt of Monsieur's presence in Paris. Could he come to her? A fiacre was waiting at the door for him and he went without another word.

For a second time his dazzled eyes saw the prospect of paradise with Esther. But now it was to be a simple, holy paradise with old Julie buying their daily fowl from the rôtisseur's round the corner, making their pastry and coffee and having the entire care of their ménage. Esther was broke. A woebegone, pale beauty, she visited England 'to settle her affairs', vowing that she was through with luxury and only wanted to share a humble apartment with Wilfrid. Jubilantly he and Julie discovered four small rooms on the second floor of a suitable little house. 'To live in poverty with Esther! What fortune could be more sublime, what life more consonant with my noblest dreams!'

On Esther's return, he was badly shaken. No longer sad and subdued, she was smartly dressed and once more in the full radiance of her wonderful beauty. A new, lavishly furnished apartment was taken for her and her sister Eveline at 123 avenue des Champs Elysées near the Arc de Triomphe. But it was no triumph for Wilfrid. He was relegated to the original four poor rooms and allowed to visit Madame once a day only, at dawn; after breakfast they would walk or ride in the Bois. When he left for the embassy she would do – what? Naïvely he did not suspect a snake in his Eden, though he would glower at the crowds surrounding her, as she drove a pair of sleek ponies in the afternoon. He could still feel himself in Eden, for about once a week she would summon him of an evening and he would find her wrapped in the little black dress with a woollen veil over her head, ready to visit the bric-à-brac shops, haggle saucily with the vendors and return home with a fowl and chestnuts for Julie to cook for their supper.

The end of the Paris summer season brought two almost simultaneous crises in Blunt's life. Lady Cowley announced that she was taking Feodore to England to continue the season there. Blunt at once realized she wished to bring the affair to a head. Feodore was a year older than he, almost twenty-five. On a hot evening he was invited to a family dinner where love was in the air, Freddy Wellesley, Feodore's brother, being in love with Lady Dangan, the eldest son's wife. After dinner both couples wandered into the twilit garden, Wilfrid and Feodore choosing their favourite seat screened by lilac bushes, under the east wall where the garden was then a wilderness. 'I had it more than once upon my tongue to talk of marriage', wrote Blunt, for he loved Feodore and could not doubt that she loved him. Each time, however, that he tried to speak the image of Esther arose to 'forbid the banns' as Wilfrid himself had once forbidden the banns of Alice's marriage with the Church. Up to this moment he had felt scarcely affected in his relations with Feodore by his love for Esther, the two being on so different a footing. Now he knew the truth.

At the end of the hour the lovers *manqués* returned to the house and to the enquiring glances of the Wellesleys. After an embarrassed goodbye, 'I took my leave and so passed out from among them, never, as it was fated, to find myself with them again.' Six years later Feodore married Frank Bertie, later Sir Francis Bertie the ambassador, and found the happiness she would assuredly have missed with Wilfrid Scawen Blunt. For Blunt was honest enough to ask himself, when he came to write his memoirs, whether he and Feodore would have been happy together, and to reply: 'Being what I am I doubt it.'

Meanwhile his love for Esther was coming to a point of crisis as well. When Wilfrid had discovered in May that the owner of Esther's new finery – her white and gold salon with its satin upholstery and gilt mirrors – was actually established with her at 123 Champs Elysées, he could deceive himself no longer. Challenged, she retorted that the man was a childhood friend, a mere *amant en titre*, while Wilfrid was the *amant de coeur*. She followed this up by a sharp letter:

> *(May 1865) L'Avenue Champs Elysées* ... now darling what do you really mean by saying I *deceived* you? I have nothing I want to deceive you in, if I want to do anything dearest I do it. If you were to ask me I should tell you straightforwardly. It is very wicked dear to have such ideas as these.[12]

Waves of jealousy tortured Wilfrid nonetheless. There were constant quarrels, their evening rambles ceased and without Julie's reconciling role the end would have come even sooner than it did.

It came when Wilfrid, walking up the Champs Elysées, raised his eyes to Esther's corner house as he passed. There sat young Lord Dunmore in the window, an adventurous Apollo whom Wilfrid had known at Athens, his arm around Esther's waist, his face close to hers and his lips moving in what Wilfrid could guess was a lover's nonsense.

In a moment Wilfrid was back in his bare room dashing off a letter full of wild reproaches. Esther disdained to give any explanation, merely forbidding him to meddle. At once his stand collapsed and for three days, backed by Julie and his own tears, he implored forgiveness. Should he throw himself under her carriage wheels? He sat at his window all one afternoon, watching for her beautiful ponies to appear in that long line of magnificent equipages riding up and down the avenue four abreast. Her carriage did not come.

On the fourth day a great longing for Sussex and his sister Alice seized him. He fled from Paris, his retreat covered by some kind of informal leave. Lord Cowley, however, already not over-pleased by his newest attaché's record at the embassy, and now thoroughly aroused by the scandal which broke over Wilfrid's absent head, refused to have him back. The news reached Wilfrid at Worth Forest Cottage. He was to proceed immediately to Lisbon. So after a week with Alice he was again to be an exile. His anguish had not had time to lift and humiliation was added to grief. Nevertheless, Alice's ministrations were henceforth to dominate his imagination as the epitome of loving kindness, and Sussex as a haven of beauty and balm.

> Naught here may harm or hurt. This is a sanctuary
> For the world's weak hedged in with love and fenced
> and sealed....[13]

Blunt was within a month of his twenty-fifth birthday when he arrived in Portugal. For the past two years he had lived on his emotions; now he remembered that he had an intellectual life to save, if not a soul. He also discovered that he had a friend, 'a pure gift of the Gods', to help him save it.

Robert Lytton happened to be chargé d'affaires to the Lisbon legation.* Wilfrid had seen him for a moment when passing through Vienna five years earlier. Now just over thirty, Robert had married the well-born Edith Villiers the year before, whose long rippling hair and pathetic pre-Raphaelite beauty inspired the painter G. F. Watts. She was now awaiting her first child in England, while Robert lived in Cintra, the famous beauty-spot fifteen miles from Lisbon, at the picturesque Hotel Lawrence. Here Blunt providentially joined him on a miserably wet evening, to be welcomed by 'old Mother Lawrence', a clean, sturdy Welsh landlady.[14] It was the same hotel at which Byron had stayed over half a century before.

'The new Attaché Blunt seems a very nice fellow – great improvement on Eden', wrote Lytton to his wife on 15 July.[15] To Blunt, Lytton was 'a great improvement' on almost every man he had hitherto met. On that first evening Lytton had run out bareheaded in the rain to wring Blunt's hand and all night long the two talked until, as the candles burnt low, the younger man realized he was Bunyan's Pilrim

* Edward Robert Bulwer, 1st Earl of Lytton, 1831–91, son of Bulwer Lytton the novelist; poet, diplomat and statesman, Viceroy of India 1876–80.

who had reached the Delectable Mountains. His sins like Pilgrim's seemed to fall from his back. Lytton, though blissfully happy in his recent marriage, was also a man of the world and a poet, writing under the name of Owen Meredith; he could sympathize with Blunt's case. Not long after his first letter Lytton gave his wife a further picture of the newcomer.

> Blunt the new Secretary sleeps in my room like a tame cat, but he is a quite gentlemanlike fellow who does not snore or irritate me as much as anyone else would. He is tall, good looking, with eyes which remind me of Paget – large and brown – a manly pleasant manner. He writes poetry, I believe, which he does not show me, but has already consulted me about a plot of a story. . . . I think my present colleague has something on his mind, which I imagine to be a 'passion malheureuse'.[16]

Lytton then went on to give his new friend's version of the Lady Feodore affair, according to which Blunt had been removed from Paris because Lady Cowley thought he was getting 'too thick' with her daughter, Lady Cowley having at first encouraged him because she erroneously believed him to be rich. Did Feodore love him? Blunt 'humm'd and haa'd'. Did Blunt love her? Not in the least, as he was obsessed all the time with someone else. This is not quite the story Blunt was to tell in his memoirs, that version being less flattering to himself and showing more self-knowledge. By 29 July, the 'tame cat' had become almost too domesticated:

> Blunt, by the way, though very sympathetic is one of the coolest hands I ever met with. He uses everything that is mine as though it were his own, without your leave or by your leave – my tobacco, my wine, my beer, and even my money, observing with the utmost seriousness that agreeable intercourse in life is quite incompatible with the doctrines of meum and tuum.[17]

Edith Lytton replied to her husband's letter tartly on 4 August: 'What a queer chap Blunt must be. . . . I don't approve of young Mr. Blunt helping himself to all that belongs to you in that cool way either!' But by that time Lytton was getting to like the cool young man 'better and better'. Nor had Blunt really taken money; he had simply pocketed some of Lytton's change by mistake.

In his letter of 29 July Lytton had described Blunt's presentation to Don Fernando, the ex-King Consort of Portugal who was first cousin to both Queen Victoria and Prince Albert. The two diplomats were henceforth frequent visitors at the mock Scottish baronial castle, on the summit of the Peña high above Cintra; they would ride up on donkeys, Blunt with his butterfly net. Fernando's mixture of pomp and bohemianism greatly appealed to Blunt. Blunt was expected to 'fool about' with Fernando's stout, good-natured mistress, Elise Hensler, actress daughter of an American tailor, while Lytton entertained them all with his Gallic wit.

It was soon after their first visit to Peña that Lytton confirmed that 'Blunt is a poet, and really and truly so far as I can yet judge I think him a *genuine* poet. This discovery has given me great pleasure.' Three weeks later Lytton was sending Edith a sample of Blunt's lyrical style. 'Don't you think there is genuine merit in these lines? I was very much struck by them.'

> Red red gold, a Kingdom's ransom, child,
> To weave thy yellow hair she bade them spin,
> At early dawn the gossamer spiders toil'd
> And wove the sunrise in.[18]

No disciple ever felt more indebted to his master than Blunt did to Lytton. He regarded Lytton's as a 'mature mind' that had immediately perceived the literary potential of Blunt's last two fallow years, during which he had produced nothing but a 'wealth of undisciplined emotion'. Two things, Blunt believed, had hitherto frustrated him as a poet. First, neither Lola nor Esther could inspire him, the former sharing with him no common language, the latter too glorious in her physical beauty to be trifled with in the 'poor banalities' of his rhymes. Second, he was still bound by convention, believing that poetry might weave itself around a sleeping beauty, a damsel in distress, perhaps a fair beggar-maid, but never a prostitute.

> What Lytton achieved for me was little by little to free me from all such fetters of reticent timidity and point the way for truth as worthy of sole worship, truth even the nakedest so that it would be worthily enshrined in Art.

Blunt's gradual escape from traditional phrases into direct utterance, from conventional into 'alien' subject matter, was assisted by Lytton's choice of poets for reading aloud in the evenings. He introduced Blunt to the dramatic skill of Browning and the lyrics of Heine (in translation), Hugo and Musset. Blunt was to regard Lytton himself as the English Musset. Like Browning, Blunt was soon – or so he fancied – 'in full revolt against the smooth monotony of Tennyson's blank verse'.

Stability returned with this vigorous intellectual life. At high noon he would read and write under the Peña castle walls while the world had its siesta:

> For sleep cometh upon all,
> Rock and castle, flower and tree;
> And the turrets wave and quiver. . . .[19]

Or he would make a lair for himself against a warm rock in the cork woods among the aromatic herbs, and sketch the first idea of *Esther* –

in blank verse, for it would take more than a few weeks to replace Tennysonian smoothness by his own characteristic and irregular sonnet form. Lytton found him a more and more remarkable and versatile companion.

> He has a keen eye for Nature and love for all that is beautiful therein. A very rare talent form in design ... he models, draws and paints in oils – and understands what he does.... I think with all this that he is a man of heart and has a good deal of depth of feeling as well as thought.[20]

Lytton himself was a man of heart. During these months the foundations of the friendship that was to be all-important in Blunt's life were laid. This intimacy with a man was to be equalled only three times – with three cousins, George Wyndham, Francis Currie and Algernon Bourke.

One September afternoon the friends visited the beach at Cascais, watching the wild Atlantic waves break on the shore. Lytton's mood changed from that of the sage counsellor to the romantic poet, and both he and Blunt began recalling the passions of their past, how 'the tyranny of love' was worth all its price. They returned home in a state of high excitement that at one blow destroyed Blunt's new peace of mind. Next morning he wrote to Esther imploring forgiveness.

Her reply from London, though ominously reminscent of the note brought to him in Paris by Julie last year ('quite free' – 'in distress' – 'her one true friend' – 'come at once') set his heart ablaze. He rushed to Lytton, poured out the whole story of his 'passion malheureuse' and insisted on taking flight by the first ship to England.

Lytton was thunderstruck. 'Only fancy', he wrote to Edith, 'my just discovering that he's desperately in love with – whom do you suppose – Skittles.' Lytton determined to save his young friend from total disaster. He telegraphed to Lord John Russell and obtained leave of absence for Blunt, so that when his love-sick colleague boarded his ship for England his job was still relatively safe.

In the light of these deplorable events Lytton was for a time to revise his high opinion of Blunt. 'It is a thousand pities for B. is a very clever and very lovable creature – but as wild as a hawk, being reckless and rather selfish, and I fear he is born to get himself into trouble by pleasing himself too unconditionally on every occasion.'[21]

Lytton even began to suspect that Blunt's flirtations with Mme Hensler at Peña might eventually have got him into 'a very nasty scrape'. (Blunt in his memoirs says that Fernando egged him on, since such fooling was in keeping with Fernando's 'Wilhelm Meister scheme of life'.) But when Edith commiserated with her husband, Lytton leapt to Blunt's defence: 'Pray don't think he has treated me ill in any way – quite the contrary, and I like the boy but fear qu'il file un mauvais coton.'[22]

Meanwhile the boy was in England, spinning a very poor thread indeed.

Blunt found Esther at her pretty Park Lane house lapped in luxury. It was therefore a surprise, after two or three blissful days, to be suddenly asked for £2,000. Up till now she had never accepted from his slender purse more than flowers, bric-à-brac or a box at the opera. However, it was to free her finally from debt, she said, and in a spirit of high chivalry he hurried to Chandler, his family lawyer, who raised the loan on Blunt's small remaining capital. His mission accomplished, he laid the gift triumphantly at his enchantress' feet.

She received it almost ungraciously, 'with a strange ambiguous smile . . . the smile of a receiver who has many times received and who seeks already an issue from her obligation'. At the time he was unable to interpret the smile.

He was to describe this incident as 'ugly'. The final curtain fell on a less ugly but more theatrical débâcle – indeed one that he had often seen on the stage. He had called at Park Street to see her. She was out. Tired of waiting, he sat down to write a message. His eyes accidentally fell on the mirror opposite, in which he saw reflected a note she had written and blotted. It was dated that very morning and addressed to a Jewish banker well known for his liberality to the cocottes of Paris.*

Blunt was more revolted by this than by anything else she had made him suffer. 'What baser could there be than to share her with this Jew on the self-same terms of money payments? It was the worst that could befall.' He left a furious farewell note beside the tell-tale blotting-paper and departed with a curse for the woman who had destroyed his long dream:

> Accursed be the hour of that sad day
> The careless potter put his hand to thee. . . .

Then he fled as before to Worth Forest.

Once again when writing his memoir, Blunt contemplated the next part of his story with intense disgust. 'The months that followed this last bankruptcy of my heart are the most disreputable in my young man's life.' The episode may have left one particularly ugly scar; for his almost lifelong mockery of Jews seemed to go deeper than the

* Blunt gave the banker's name as 'Bamberger', perhaps a cover for Catherine Walters' Jewish patron Achille Fould.

normal upper-class aberrations of his era. The one Jew who bought Skittles over his head was to be punished in Blunt's writings by the flaying of a thousand scapegoats.

Neither Alice nor Francis were at Forest Cottage to comfort him, Alice being absorbed in her own love affair with Lord William Kerr and Francis hunting with his cousin Percy Wyndham at Coldstream. Old Mrs Selwood and his two dogs Rachel and George were his only companions. He seriously thought of suicide when, on a dark November afternoon, he found himself wandering in the forest with his gun. He sat on the root of a pollarded oak in Whitley Gill debating the question, while George ranged through the birch underwood. His religious faith had been set aside for happiness in human love. That was a grotesque thought now. His search for love had brought him to a dead wall of pain. Why should he hold back? Two arguments for continued life came to him: Lytton's belief in him as destined for great things; and the memory of a suicide's bloated corpse in a cornfield outside Hamburg. This second argument was the stronger, for Blunt had become proud of his physical beauty: how could he desecrate his face thus? A belated third argument supervened, the strongest of all: 'My dog's nose was pressing gently against my knee and I decided to live.'

In memory of his 'grim debate' he was later to have the infant river Mole banked across from side to side at Whitley Gill and made into 'Forest Pond', a poetic sheet of green water in the autumn, surrounded by yellowing birches, dark yews and tall papery reeds. In his poem *Worth Forest* he was to imagine a love-sick half-witted labourer named Marden drowning himself in this pool. Local legend contributed the story of an equally ill-fated novice from Crawley Monastery.

> Deep down and over-browed with sombre trees,
> Shutting its surface primly from the breeze,
> The landscape's innocent eye set open wide
> To watch the heavens – yet with homicide
> Steeped to the lids.[23]

Strangers still wonder at the pond's lonely beauty, imagining that it is an ancient hammer pond and has been for centuries in these deep Sussex woods. But as Wilfrid Blunt wrote in his memoir, 'this is the true story'.

In retrospect Blunt was able to persuade himself that the rage he vented during the next months was not against Skittles. Having discovered her 'worthlessness', he hated himself. It was part of himself he intended to destroy, tearing out his love with every form of savagery 'in the very shrine of its worship'. He would return to Paris and overwhelm that part of himself with 'immundities'.* Choosing the streets and cafés where he and Esther had been happiest, he profaned his sacred memories with the cheapest French prostitutes, those who sold themselves for 40 francs a night to the first customer. Esther had despised them; he chose them. There was also a notorious English prostitute of a different calibre, Cora Pearl, whom Esther had mocked for her gaudy displays of nakedness. Blunt gave his attention to Cora Pearl. The nights seemed as long as midwinter and he rarely faced daylight.

Two things brought this debauch to an end. he was ordered back to Frankfurt for the New Year; and on one of his rare morning appearances he ran into Zizi Arcos and her sister out for a walk. Mme Arcos was the wife of an absent Brazilian. Quickly disposing of the sister, she took Blunt home and confessed that she had often watched Esther in his company with envy. He and Zizi became lovers. Though the liaison lasted only for a brief while it was important for Blunt; Zizi became the second example (Skittles being the first) of a woman who had been his mistress remaining his friend for life. Few indeed of Blunt's affairs were to end in silence and tears; more often in afternoon visits, cups of tea, a bundle of affectionate letters and a nostalgic obituary by Blunt in his diary.† For he outlived most of them.

Zizi was also the first 'married woman of the world' who had wooed and won him, and in doing so had taught him 'how greatly of more value even as amusement was the love of a woman in respectable society than of one outside it'. By 'respectable society', Blunt seems to have meant something as far above the vicarage as the vicarage was above the brothel. Zizi was to become *lectrice* to the Empress Eugénie, while a titled lady who proposed an Irish 'honeymoon' with Blunt in 1864 turned out to be one of Queen Victoria's bedchamber women. At the time he had considered her too old, but later regretted the loss of an interesting connection with the Court.

The return to Frankfurt proved a bitter disappointment. Lord Schomberg Kerr had married; the Usedoms and their liberalism were politically out of favour and they had been relegated to Florence. Meanwhile the politics of Frankfurt were unable to fill the gap in Blunt's interest. While he was 'a diplomatist by trade' he felt at this date no interest in politics whatever, being 'a most unprofitable servant of the Foreign Office'. Only when he had left the profession did he busy himself in the world of great affairs. Though recognizing this paradox Blunt never diagnosed its cause: namely, that he was one of those rebels whose focus of inspiration is not in 'the collective'.

* Immund, a rare word meaning unclean or foul. Immundicities, impurities.

† 1 December 1913: 'I see in the paper that Madame Arcos is dead. Poor Zizi, the little episode of our love has been always a pleasant memory.'

His friend Lytton tried to revive Blunt's intellectual interests by criticizing his poetry. There were too many false rhymes (six in one 'exquisite sonnet on youth'), and a favourite noun, 'thing', was too often repeated throughout the sequence. Blunt's revolutionary use of false rhymes that so startled Lytton may have been one of the reasons why younger poets such as Yeats and Pound admired him. The six false rhymes in the sonnet on youth from *The Love Sonnets of Proteus* are the two words 'attribute' and 'flute' followed by the four words 'blood', 'wood', 'food' and 'renewed'. Lytton rightly calls the sonnet exquisite, for it contains one of the most perfect lines Blunt ever wrote: 'Clear as the pale green edge where dawn began. . . .'

Lytton went on to offer Blunt an optimistic way of looking at his misery: 'Those who plunge into the depths, if they escape the shark and the polypus, ought to ascend by and by with the pearl.' Lytton recommended to Blunt Victor Hugo's latest prescription for recovery:

> Pour chasser le spleen
> J'entrais dans un inn
> Où je bus du gin,
> God save the Queen.[24]

If gin never appealed to Blunt, the circles where gin was consumed now attracted him.

The neighbouring principality of Hesse Homburg, with its famous kursaal, seemed a more lively arena than Frankfurt. Though Blunt had foresworn gambling for high stakes, the sight of others in the throes of 'grim gaiety' fascinated him. So he moved his lodgings to Homburg, catching an early morning train to Frankfurt each day for the copy of despatches, but constantly being absent when wanted. He only got away with it, he suspected, because Sir Alexander Malet himself liked to slip over now and then to stake a louis at roulette. Blunt developed a novelist's interest in the characters whom he met at the tables; fraudulent cashiers, ruined gold-miners, unfrocked priests, a judge who had taken bribes, a blonde who claimed to have been Victor Hugo's mistress and an aristocratic Polish lady (with both of whom Blunt 'simulated love, not greatly less debased than they'), and a high-minded young curate from London's East End 'who had brought with him the contents of his alms box to gamble with, so he explained, "for his poor"'. Henry Labouchere was still around and still disreputable. It was springtime and Blunt soon found an Englishwoman ready to make love with him in the flowery Taunus woods, while her husband was pinned to the gaming tables.

In June a storm that even Blunt could not ignore descended upon the whole German world.

Otto von Bismarck had become Prussia's first minister shortly before Blunt went to Madrid in 1862. Blunt had met him in 1864 when Bismarck was over in England for the abortive Schleswig–Holstein conference; Lady Malet had invited the twenty-four-year old attaché and the statesman to the house of her step-father, Lord Brougham, in Dover Street. It said much for Lady Malet's faith in her young protégé that she should have accorded him this rare privilege notwithstanding the regular blotting of his copybook. Blunt had been impressed by Bismarck's taut figure and knowledge of English literature, but had not at that time been interested in German politics.

By the time of Blunt's second Frankfurt posting, in 1866, an imminent war between Prussia and Austria was the talk of the legations. Yet still Blunt lingered in Homburg, officially to drink the waters, in fact to woo his English lover. It was only when hostilities had actually broken out that an angry Sir Alexander Malet insisted that he took at least a bedroom in a Frankfurt hotel. Blunt was to look back on these months with self-reproach: 'In those days I was perverse for perversity's sake, abhorring all rules and regulations of an official kind.'

On returning at last to Frankfurt Blunt found it defended by 6,000 Bavarians and Hessians, drawn from the independent states which had decided to support Austria in the struggle against Prussia. Spurred on by the general excitement, Blunt started writing a fragmentary diary. One entry describes his being sent to Darmstadt to assist Malet in evacuating Princess Alice of Hesse's children to Windsor. The authorities still laboured under the delusion that the handsome young attaché was a natural for Court circles. An even odder entry, in view of Blunt's future, described the state of his political sympathies at the outbreak of war:

> First, I dislike the Italian Kingdom and should not be sorry to see it broken up. Secondly I sympathize with Austria and Germany, though I have no wish for the separate existence of the smaller German States. Thirdly, I dislike National Prussia and the national Verein [Union]; and fourthly, I have a deep personal sympathy with Bismarck, as the oldest political gambler of the age. His success will be a protest against the strength of 'progress' [Liberalism], which tramples man.

Lady Malet had done her work all too well in introducing the future hero of 'blood and iron' to the impressionable Blunt. It is alarming to think of Britain's diplomacy even minimally at the mercy of such confused thinking. Fortunately, however, Blunt's political concern was to subside as suddenly as it had arisen. As for Lady Malet, her interest in Bismarck was to have an ironical conclusion. With Bismarck's victory the 'free' city of Frankfurt disappeared as the centre of German constitutionalism, showing how right liberals like the Usedoms had been to detest Bismarck from the start. The end of

Frankfurt's political power spelled the end of Malet's job. The unlucky Sir Alexander found his position irreparably damaged, while even Lady Malet was forced to admit to Blunt, in a letter of 1 September 1866, 'The Prussians are like the Bull in the china shop – and stick at nothing – hit him when he is down – and have no friends in their rule!'[25] She was to throw her warm partisanship into the career of her son Edward, an up-and-coming young diplomat destined to clash violently with her former protégé Blunt.* And Blunt himself was to be the first to repudiate his predilection of 1866 for great empires, championing small nationalities in the 1880s with far more political vigour than had seemed possible in his youth.

But by the end of June 1866 it appeared doubtful whether Wilfrid Blunt was to have a future at all. On 26 June, while again in Homburg, he was struck down with a sudden fever. After a night of terrible dreams about the war, he staggered to his desk in Frankfurt hardly able to sit up, but in bad odour with his colleagues for having missed the day before. This forced him to keep going for another few days, until on 3 July he collapsed and was returned to Homburg with double pneumonia and pleurisy. His diary came to an abrupt end, and he lay in a coma while the German army marched and counter-marched under his windows. The news of Hanover's surrender meant nothing to him, nor was he conscious of Austria's defeat at the Battle of Sadowa (Königgrätz) on 13 July. For a month he lay between life and death, cared for by Skittles's *bonne* Julie, whom he had taken over, and 'that dearest of my cousins Percy Wyndham', who got through to him in mid-July. Alice and Francis were brought back from a tour of Denmark.

He was without a post and without one lung, when his brother and sister conveyed him by slow stages to Lausanne in the autumn. If he survived they were to winter in Italy.

> The old life of the last three years, with the nightmare of its passion for Esther, had been swept clean out of remembrance by my sickness and I was restored to sanity of soul if not of body. A great sadness had come upon me, but I was once more contented in my sister's hands to wait the thing that should be for me whether of evil or perhaps of good.

* Sir Edward Baldwin Malet, 1837–1908, diplomat. Served in Washington, Paris, Constantinople and Berlin (for the Congress), consul-general Egypt, 1879–83.

[3]
Vita Nova
1866–1869

Blunt first saw the Lake of Geneva on his twenty-sixth birthday, 17 August 1866. The lake's classical beauty seemed to him the 'purest in Europe'. They were to stay at Ouchy in the same little old-fashioned Anchor Inn that Byron and Shelley had patronized on their visit to Chillon fifty years before. Indeed Blunt was assigned Byron's traditional room, still provided with the same Empire furniture that had been new in his day. Blunt was reading Rousseau's *Confessions* just as Byron had read them. Years later he remembered that the effect of the *Confessions* had been to make him write his own life-story – and to have a more 'satisfactory' life to recall.

Wilfrid was still expected to die before the winter had passed. On warm evenings Alice would swathe him in shawls and allow him on the lake, but he himself hardly hoped to recover completely. His thoughts became harrowing when he remembered all his dreams and believed time would not be given to accomplish any of them. It was in this mood that he received permission during their second week at Ouchy to chaperone Alice at a dance given by the Bairds of Bellerive. Prominent among the Anglo-Swiss families of Ouchy were the Goffs and the Bairds, especially Robin Goff, with whom Wilfrid had been at school at Twyford, and his sister Mrs Ella Baird.

Alice had not long vacated her chair, placed by Wilfrid's sofa outside the ballroom, when a pretty young stranger took her place. The girl seemed to know him, and he longed to know her the moment he noticed the contrast between the 'strange pathetic cadence of her voice' and the gaiety of her blue eyes, pink and white Marie Antoinette dress and smiling red lips. She turned out to be his hostess, Mrs Baird, the acknowledged Lady of the Lake. She was to be the first 'Juliet' of his sonnets. There was no difficulty about getting to know her better, for she felt sorry for the beautiful youth who might be dying, and her garden gates were close to the Anchor. Blunt, still too weak to feel physical passion, did not yet recognize in his 'troubled' sensations the first sign of 'a great passion of the Soul'.

After Alice returned to England, Wilfrid became more dependent on the semi-maternal care of Mrs Baird, who was nearly thirty (he was twenty-six) and had several children. He had visited Vevey and undergone a cautery of his left side, relieving the lung and giving hope of ultimate recovery. When September turned into October they discussed his journey to Italy. They would have a last picnic at Roveray in the chestnut woods on her thirtieth birthday, with a paper-chase and a heap of cushions for Blunt to rest on. As he lay there in the sad autumn sunshine a wave of self-pity overwhelmed him. Tears began to trickle and he murmured to himself the words on the title-page of Goethe's *Sorrows of Werther*: 'I have tasted a little honey and behold I die!'

But behold he lived – for Juliet was there. She had stayed behind to be with him when he woke. The moment was 'ineffably sweet'. It seemed to tell him that he was loved. And the knowledge was strengthened when the others returned. Robin teased his sister for being so old, whereupon she pelted him with prickly chestnut cases, one of which accidentally hit Blunt. He flung it back at her with a cry of 'Wretch!' A word of such extraordinary familiarity used in a society ruled by strict verbal convention could mean only one thing: it proved to them both 'how dear to each other we physically were'. Yet still nothing had been said. Before leaving on 12 October he asked her for the rose in her dress, not daring to ask for more.

> There a rose lay curled
> It was the reddest rose in all the world.[1]

On 13 October he crossed the Simplon Pass with Mme de Staël's *Corinne* on his lap. It had been given him by Ella Baird to read on his way through the Bernese Oberland. Byron had met 'Corinne' herself at Coppet. But it was Ella's face that Blunt saw on every page.

A welcome very different from the unspoken intensities of Ouchy awaited him on Lake Maggiore. Here, near Stresa, Count Usedom and his wife were on holiday from official duties in Florence. Blunt was met uproariously by their strapping thirteen-year-old daughter Hildegard, and received as a prodigal son by her mother, the large-hearted, large-minded and altogether outsize Olympia. Their house, the Villa Caproni at Castel Solcio, was always crowded with guests, and the polyglot rattle of French, German, English and Italian livened him up despite himself, forcing him out of his hypochondriac sadness.

There was much music at the villa, but Blunt's fragile health gave him an excuse to take refuge in Hildegard's schoolroom. A mottled purple notebook dated 1866 contains a rough draft of *Esther* and some prose 'written at Castel Solcio' headed 'Not worth keeping'.

His love-affair with Ella Baird was languishing, mainly because her letters were so guarded. In November chill winds off the Alps drove the Usedoms back to their official residence in Florence, taking Blunt with them. His spirits were falling as fast as the thermometer. Rome was his next destination and there he had planned to meet his 'Juliet' again. But this prospect too was fading. It was thus at the nadir of Blunt's hopes that Mme Usedom unfolded her own 'intention' for him.

The controversial Olympia Usedom was the daughter of Sir John Malcolm, the Oriental scholar and British ambassador in Persia. She had married in Count Usedom an ardent liberal who was bound to clash with Bismarck and did so. Lady Malet disliked her for this reason at first, and later because she considered Olympia's influence on Blunt to be wholly bad. Olympia had fat Prussian admirers and kept a noisy drawing-room. 'Baby Boy' was not a title Lady Malet would have chosen for one of H.M.'s servants. Nor did she approve the way in which he was 'nourished and cherished and petted'. Did Lady Malet show misplaced jealousy? Or did she prophesy truly of Olympia when she wrote to Blunt, 'She will do no good to no one'?[2]

'I will find you a *nice rich wife*', Mme Usedom had written to her Baby Boy in July 1865,[3] and find one she did. Her large mind worked logically. *Here* was Blunt, forlorn, penniless and well-born – and in danger of ruining his life with an older woman (for he had told Olympia about Mrs Baird). *There* was an unmarried girl (only a year younger than Mrs Baird, but still . . .) travelling about Italy forlorn, rich and well-born.* They should be brought together.

Blunt listened to Olympia's proposition with curiosity. He had heard of Lady Annabella King-Noel, Lord Byron's granddaughter and only daughter of Byron's Ada. Who had not? This very Lady Annabella was expected to stay with the Usedoms in Florence on her way to Italian friends in Milan, the Trivulzios. Olympia had met her the year before and become in some sort her confidante. She was forced to lead a solitary, unprotected life, since her mother Ada and grandmother Lady Byron had died, and her father Lord Lovelace had married again. Her own marriage would be the 'best issue from a difficult position'. Olympia might be able to arrange it for Blunt, 'if only I would show the personal interest which such things required'.

Olympia then proceeded to enumerate the candidate's personal attractions. 'She was in every way one to make me happy; quiet and good and most distinguished with many gifts natural and acquired, a good musician and a better painter . . . it would be an ark of salvation

* According to Lady Annabella Blunt's daughter Judith, her mother was descended from the Royal Plantagenets, Alfred the Great, Charlemagne, and Charles Martel who defeated the Saracens.

for me I should be a fool to overlook.' As for Annabella herself, an English marriage would be better than an Italian one, 'in which her money would be sought more than her person, and such seldom turned out well'. Her father was opposed to any marriage for her, desiring the fortune she had inherited from Lady Byron for the son of his second marriage. Of her two brothers, the elder, Byron, had died estranged from the family; while the younger, Ralph, was eccentric and could give her no settled home. Blunt at least, said Olympia, had 'a position in the world to offer her, in return for what she had to give'.

With this mixture of worldliness and sentiment Olympia concluded her case. Blunt promised to make himself agreeable to her guest who, it transpired, was to arrive that very evening.

The appearance of Lady Annabella proved reassuring. Though twenty-nine years old on 22 September of that year,* she seemed both physically and mentally younger than she was. Blunt put down her youthful looks to her total lack of vanity.

> She thought herself plainer than she was, and had none of the ways of a pretty woman, though in truth she had that sort of prettiness that a bird has, a redbreast or a nightingale, agreeable to the eye if not aggressively attractive. Her colouring, indeed, I used to think was like a robin's, with its bright black eyes, its russet plumage and its tinge of crimson red. She had beautiful white teeth and complexion rather brown than fair, of the short-skulled west of England type she represented well [a reference to Byron's Cornish ancestry]. In stature less than tall, well poised and active, with a trim light figure set on a pair of small high-instepped feet.
>
> It is thus I see her in recollection, an unobtrusive quiet figure in Mme d'Usedom's noisy drawing-room, dressed in pale russet with a single crimson rose for ornament, rather behind the fashion of the day, but dignified and bright.

They danced together at Olympia's insistence, despite Blunt's shortness of breath; it was for the last as well as the first time in their lives. The next day and the day after passed equally successfully, Annabella showing them her excellent pen-and-ink sketches of Italy, and exchanging recollections with Wilfrid of life at the two Horsleys (where he and his cousins Emily and Mary Currie in the West had often speculated on the peculiar characters of those in the East). The youthful freshness of her mind he attributed to her unworldly upbringing, as related to him by Mme Usedom (the rounded and polished account of his first impressions in his 'Alms to Oblivion' has evidently been embellished by hindsight).

Annabella's mother had died when she was fifteen and her father

* Blunt wrongly said she was twenty-eight, either chivalrously or carelessly. He always called her two years older than himself, whereas she was three years older all but a month.

had withheld the indulgences common to girls of her rank; she was 'ill-fed, ill-clothed, suffering from winter cold in fireless rooms'. When taken to live with her grandmother, Lady Byron, 'it was to find herself in an intellectual bondage almost as severe', that of the Swiss Fellenberg educational system. As she grew older, her father took her with him on continental holidays, where she learned to speak not only French, German, Spanish, and Italian, but also Swiss patois. She possessed two Stradivarius violins and had been taught by Joachim, while her drawing-master had been John Ruskin. The moral code she received from Lady Byron had all the rigidity to be expected from that self-confident lady: no christening, no religious dogma, 'no basis of supernatural teaching' on which to rest her severe rules of conduct. Because Annabella was 'thorough and exact' as well as 'good and docile by nature', she had accepted all her grandmother's teaching without question. 'She neither prayed nor needed prayer', continued Blunt, 'and I feel sure she had never committed any act less than entirely conscientious and entirely honourable.'

At the same time, her imagination had been stunted by the lack of frivolity as a child, and of poetry and fiction as a girl. She had never been encouraged to play with words or develop wit and humour; 'and though able to talk well on almost any subject it was always according to the Evangelical rule of "Yea yea and nay nay", to which Lady Byron herself had always adhered. There was, however, nothing at all about Lady Annabella of her grandmother's censorious pride. She was humble-minded to an extreme about herself and correspondingly large-minded about others.'

Blunt's portrait is convincing – almost too convincing. He has left out all the human potentialities and inconsistencies in Annabella's character. Her often-recorded love of concerts and her many penetrating sketches suggest that her imaginative life was not atrophied. Many years later she was to insist that Lady Byron had not been the severe grandmother the world believed. She had always been ready to play children's games. Annabella's deprivation of poetry was due to Lady Byron's obsessive fear of the dead Byron's influence. It is possible, of course, that Olympia had exaggerated the rationalism of Annabella's upbringing, partly because she herself was a humanist, and partly to please Blunt, who had lost his faith. However, what Blunt says about Annabella's 'exactness' her diaries confirm. She kept incredibly neat and thorough accounts.

On the third morning of the visit Annabella and Wilfrid parted, Annabella echoing Wilfrid's hope that they should meet again. 'Nothing had, however, been as much as hinted between us in the direction of Mme Usedom's plan', he wrote. The impression left on his mind by the encounter was simply of 'a pleasant possibility, not really possible'. Her own pocket diary for 1866 made no reference to Wilfrid Blunt, though the Trivulzios were mentioned; but not the fact that she and Count Trivulzio had entered into some vague kind of understanding.

The conclusion of Blunt's 'cotton-wool' holiday in Florence and his plunge into the loneliness of Rome and Naples for the winter immediately sent his health and spirits into a new decline. He described these months as 'a dream of suffering I do not like to think of'. Ella Baird had not kept their tryst, and his only friends in Rome were English ecclesiastics, Monsignor Stonor and Cardinal Howard. The thought of Shelley was a consolation. He visited his grave in Rome, and in Naples recited his 'Stanzas written in Dejection':

> I could lie down like a tired child
> And weep away the life of care....

He had visited St Peter's in the spirit of a pilgrim, devoutly kissing the Apostle's toe in the mighty Basilica. One day, while walking on the Pincio, he saw a man in white cassock and cloak approaching him, the centre of a group of priests. 'It was the good Pope, Pio Nono, and I knelt on the gravel to receive his blessing which he gave me with a fatherly bright smile.' Blunt could always draw comfort from physical expressions of piety while his mind was in a state of suspended unbelief. A second contribution to his well-being came in a letter from Mrs Baird of 13 January. She seemed to show a certain pique at Mme d'Usedom's scheme for him and the Lady Annabella:

> I hope you will never do anything so dreadful for your happiness as to marry simply for money. I think there are some men who, if they married a woman only for her money would at last get to care about her, out of habit, or pity, but I am sure *you* never would, and though I should pity you I should pity the heiress still more.[4]

Mme Usedom, however, regarded Mrs Baird as a far greater danger to Blunt than any arranged marriage. She had news for him on Christmas Day and appended a final appeal to forget his 'ideal woman': 'Dear Blunt, this telegram arrived Friday for you. Wilfrid Blunt care of English Legation, Florence. Will you go out as Second Secretary to Buenos Ayres. Sandmore. Foreign Office.' To which she added: 'Think a hundred times of *my* plan & your own *folly*. Be a man & break at once. Ever yours O.'[5]

Before becoming a man in South America Blunt longed to be cosseted by some woman in Europe. Since 'Juliet' had failed him the answer must be old Julie. He would stop in Paris on his way home, get well and get news of Esther. His mind was finally made up by an invitation to share a hedonistic existence in the apartment at 11 rue de Beaujolais of his cousin Francis Gore Currie.

'Bitters' Currie seems today a character from fiction. In a sense Blunt too felt that his cousin had somehow opted out of the real world. Nevertheless, he had good reasons for devoting several pages of 'Alms to Oblivion' to the older man's portrait. One reason was that something like Bitters' crude attitude to life was needed at that moment, to shake Blunt out of his romantic melancholy; the other, that the 'philosophy of happiness' worked out by Bitters was to have a lasting effect on the younger man. Blunt's wife and daughter would sometimes blame all that went wrong in their family life on one or other of the Wyndhams. They would have been nearer the mark if they had found their scapegoat in Currie.

Service to his country in the Crimean war and Indian mutiny had seemed to Bitters all that patriotism required. He had retired to his quarters in Paris at scarcely more than twenty-five years old, to live in idleness on an income of £1,000 a year for the rest of his life. He was 'the handsomest man in Europe', but he was neither ambitious nor addicted to drink or gambling. Unhurried and content, he took his pleasures reasonably – and they were limited virtually to women. Men admired him for his wit, tolerance, and skill with the foil, even though he had no use for 'those schoolboy games all Englishmen adore'. Women found his intuitive knowledge of their thoughts and weaknesses irresistible. Always at their service, he was ready to amuse and make them happy, yet never allowed himself to be fooled or trapped into slavery; and for this they respected him. So did Blunt; worshipped him even. In contrast to his own restless, fruitless search for the ideal, Bitters' tranquil eroticism seemed wisdom itself.

While Blunt was staying with Bitters a sensible letter arrived from Lady Malet in Carlsruhe, advising him to endure philosophically the inevitable disenchantments of youth. Blunt, however, preferred the more cynical solution of Bitters. He was introduced to *Les Liaisons Dangereuses* and other 'seductive' French books, and taught to believe that he had spoiled his own happiness in love either by too much haste at the outset or by 'too little insistence on the essential element of fruition [with Juliet] or again by too long a clinging [to Esther] after love was dead'.

The first fruits of this discipleship was a new Bitters-type relationship with Skittles. Old Julie informed him that Madame wished for a visit. Blunt went to her house and again became her lover; but Juliet had driven Esther from her place in his imagination, and this episode in Paris banished the disturbing memory of her physical beauty even from his dreams. 'It cured my heart finally of its trouble in respect of her'; but as often as they were to meet in the future, the pleasant memory was to be renewed 'and is surviving still'.

Meanwhile the weeks with Bitters had had yet another important repercussion. Wilfrid's much admired cousin Madeline Wyndham was visiting Paris for the first time in May 1867. It was in July 1860 that Wilfrid had heard from his dear aunt, Lady Leconfield, that her son Percy Wyndham was to marry Madeline Campbell, daughter of Sir Guy Campbell who lived in Ireland. Madeline's 'mysterious beauty' was inherited from her grandmother, Lord Edward Fitzgerald's Pamela, said to be the daughter of Mme de Genlis, mistress of the Duke of Orleans.

Wilfrid was prepared for Madeline's beauty but not for her lack of chic. He took his lovely cousin in hand, sending her to Skittles' dressmaker so that she might be 'made a pretty woman of'. Then on one happy afternoon Wilfrid lured her to 11 rue de Beaujolais where he feasted her on strawberries, read her poetry, kissed her feet and told her he loved her. Madeline replied with a pleasant, half-mocking laugh that she loved him too, even though she was four years older than he. Meanwhile Percy had become 'terribly bored with Paris', if not with Wilfrid. Farewells were said in their hotel. 'I found her', wrote Wilfrid, 'sitting alone and reading in the dusk and asked her what her book was. "My Bible", she said sighing as she kissed me. "I have been too long away from my respectable life."'

According to Wilfrid, this Paris visit launched Madeline on her career as an acknowledged beauty and model for G. F. Watts in his two famous pictures 'The Three Graces' and 'Orpheus and Eurydice'. Moreover it inspired in Wilfrid some reflections on the lives of Victorian ladies which marked the beginning of his mission to 'liberate' women and contributed to the social purpose of his memoirs.

It was a new thing in the 1860s, he noted, for a married woman of thirty like Madeline Wyndham to go into the London streets without a servant, to dine at a restaurant or be seen at a theatre with a young man, even though he was a relation.

> None of these things could be done without remark, nor was it easy even for those who had serious love affairs to arrange matters to their liking without infinite trouble, risk and small vexations. As a consequence, such serious love affairs were rare in good society and where they were indulged in seldom led to much happiness. All the more for this reason was a trip abroad, especially a trip to Paris regarded as a licensed moment when . . . opinion, to a certain extent, excused irregularity of conduct. For English women, Paris was always somewhat in a state of Carnival, and pleasant incidents were . . . desired there which in London would not have been tolerated.

If Blunt felt that he had successfully handled his first serious love for a Wyndham cousin (though it was not then consummated, despite Bitters' advice), this affair was soon replaced by one 'less wisely dealt with'. He received an unexpected note from Mrs Baird announcing her arrival in Paris with her husband and daughter. Would Mr Blunt call? He flew to her and found that the love between them – never yet declared – was now unmistakable. She blushed scarlet, and yielded her hand to him. 'I thought I should have died of joy', he wrote. It was evening and her family were at church. As the room darkened he kissed her and held her in his arms, but their happiness was 'never quite complete'. She refused Wilfrid's plea for a secret assignation at the rue de Beaujolais, insisting that all their meetings should be accidental. An accident brought the romance temporarily to an end.

He took her and her husband to Sardou's play *Froufrou*, as a parting entertainment, its theme being the choice of a 'more or less virtuous woman' between her lover and her family. The effect on Mrs Baird was decisive. Next day she wrote saying their love must cease. This concluded what Blunt was to call the second act of their love.

Two factors had caused the intensity of Blunt's passion for Mrs Baird, her own goodness and the tragic element in their love. 'She was my first quite good woman to give me all her heart.* She remains the type with me of all that is most noble, tenderest, and best in womanhood.' Blunt's conviction that 'without tragedy love is hardly love' shows that he was not to be a modern poet, as he hoped, but one of the last romantics: 'The sweetest love of all were love in pain. . . .'[6] There was a good deal of Childe Harold in the young Blunt.

'Good springs sometimes out of evil and wisdom from despair.' This was to be Blunt's sententious comment on the ruin of his brief happiness with Ella Baird. For it threw him back on the idea of marriage. His daughter Judith would not have agreed that the result of his despair was 'wisdom'. She never ceased to blame him for contemplating marriage when he loved another (though she seems to have believed, wrongly, that the other woman was Catherine Walters). But the situation was not as simple as that. With his romantic temperament, he was bound always to set his heart on the unattainable and to love, in series, 'another'.

As he had done after the delirium of his passion for Skittles, he again took flight from Paris to his beloved Worth, where he found Alice. They had no secrets from one another. She told him that her hopes of Lord William Kerr had foundered; he had entered the Jesuit novitiate at Roehampton, close to the convent which she herself had once wished to enter. Wilfrid spoke to Alice of Juliet, and of Mme Usedom's plan for his marriage to Lady Annabella Noel. Just then a letter arrived from Olympia giving Annabella's address in London and telling him that she was still not engaged. 'A marriage, if it could be arranged, I was ready to make, but not to go out in chase of it.' After two days' fishing with Alice in the Alder meadows, he decided to angle for his heiress by letter.

* Blunt used 'quite' in the sense of 'absolutely'.

2nd July 1867. Worth. Dear Lady Annabella, Six months ago as I wished you goodbye at the door of the Villa Caproni I had it on my lips to ask you to marry me. But something held my tongue and then I thought we should meet again so soon. I have never done repenting.

There were obstacles, he continued, which had prevented him returning to Florence: 'And now when at last I can honestly and truly offer you my love, my heart misgives me that it is too late.' He explained that he realized she might have changed.

At least, we never used to disagree. . . . I have gone through a sea of anxieties and troubles since we parted, and you are the only pleasant thing with your bright eyes and your brown gown which never changes in my recollection. Can you venture to make sail with me in what has been such troubled water? I know that I could make you happy and I know that you have need of happiness – but it is weary work looking for it alone. . . .[7]

Alice personally took the letter, with flowers, to Annabella in London.

Wilfrid waited a week. No reply. He then wrote again on 9 July 'in terrible anxiety'. The reply from Annabella, dated five days later, apologized for the delay and explained that she ought to have answered 'no' at once. There were three reasons why she could not marry him: she was older than he thought – thirty in September; he would be disappointed in her 'doubting and hesitating character' which difficulties weakened instead of strengthening; and as proof, she had broken off a previous semi-engagement (to Count Trivulzio) 'in a kind of terror'. Would he answer to the Hotel Cavour, Milan?*[8]

Four days later, Annabella again wrote apologetically, but this time to her friend, Mme Usedom. She blamed herself over the Trivulzio affair. 'Then my visit to England and speaking with my father has, in spite of myself, discouraged me so much – he is so strongly persuaded, I have so difficult a disposition that I should not be able to contribute to anyone's happiness.'

Annabella's letter decided Wilfrid and Alice to follow her to Milan arriving, as if by accident, to stay with Olympia Usedom. Wilfrid had been almost as puzzled by Annabella's reply to his proposal as Byron had once been by Annabella Milbanke's. 'The writer in her conscientious regard for the exact truth', commented Wilfrid, 'had involved it in obscurities which might be interpreted in either fashion. It was not distinctly a "no" though at the same time it was hardly a "yes".' But, whereas Miss Milbanke's puzzle had been meant to

* Blunt's recollection of these letters was inaccurate. He thought Annabella had already left for Milan before his proposal arrived and that he had waited three weeks for an answer, because of forwarding, rather than as was the case, because of Annabella's 'doubting and hesitating character'. Judith Wentworth stated that her mother had hesitated because of Blunt's 'ill reputation'.

entrap, her granddaughter's obscurities, as Wilfrid recognized, were transparently honest in purpose.

When they reached Castel Solcio, Wilfrid and Annabella were sent out immediately on to Lake Maggiore. The proposal of marriage was renewed, gratitude was expressed – but again the nebulous 'other man' seemed to stand in the way. Annabella admitted that the Trevulzio affair had been 'arranged' and her heart was not involved. Nevertheless she was not free to consider Wilfrid.

Wilfrid 'felt it an adjournment, perhaps of victory, not an absolute defeat and in the meantime I was free'. Mme Usedom still felt in her bones that the marriage would come off some day. It was one of the 'remorses of my life', Wilfrid wrote, that he did not see Olympia or any of the Usedoms again. The large Wagnerian Hildegard wasted her girlhood in a vain romance for King Ludwig of Bavaria and never married. Olympia died a widow in the 1880s, her husband having been ruined by Bismarck. Shortly after his marriage, Blunt was to request repayment of a loan he had made to Count Usedom in 1864 of £500. A pathetic answer came from the Count's secretary asking if he could 'postpone the need owing to the Count's predicament'. One hopes that time was allowed for repayment – or was this too part of Wilfrid's 'remorses'?[9]

In that summer of 1867 the brother and sister set off together for England. They had both been lovelorn; now both were cheerful. Alice was to housekeep for Wilfrid in South America. They would drop in casually to Ouchy on their way.

If he wanted the symbol of a new life Blunt met it on the road to Stresa. A bearded man was standing by the shore of Lake Maggiore in a red shirt. The young Blunts had been given flowers on leaving Solcio. They bent down from their horses and handed the man their bunches. He did not say *Quo vadis?* but *Buon viaggio*. It was Garibaldi.

Alice had heard that Mrs Baird was away in the Bernese Oberland for her health. So, despite her partisanship of Annabella, she allowed her brother to peep inside the garden gate of Bellerive, like 'a sad Adam driven out of Paradise'. But Mrs Baird was there. They spent two days together. 'It was now agreed that our love should last for life' – a Vita Nova of which 'Juliet' should be the core. How often was Blunt to write those same words in his memoirs, but in other contexts. As his departure for Buenos Aires with Alice had already been fixed, the most they could really do was to 'arrange a life together on our return'. On 22 October 1867, a letter came from Annabella. She was glad to have seen him in England; he would be often in her thoughts. So that door too was still open.

An ever-open door was Skittles. She had taken rooms for herself and 'Winnie' in the village inn of Edensor at the park gates of Chatsworth; the Devonshires, in gratitude for her 'good feeling', had given her the free run of the estate. For once Blunt enjoyed sightseeing. Since the family were away, they had access at all hours to Chatsworth House. What did this extraordinary rendezvous signify? Not treachery to his Juliet, but freedom from the old thraldom to Esther 'and a new position of equality with my once enchantress'. Vita Nova.

At Southampton on 9 October, Mrs John Pollen, formerly Minnie Laprimaudaye, joined the family party to see them off. In the final confusion of the general leave-taking, Minnie kissed Wilfrid as well as Alice – 'being moved to it', as she told him afterwards, 'by a sudden impulse in contradiction to her matronly reserve and the decorum of her extremely pious life as an ultramontane Catholic'. Wilfrid thought of Annie's kiss at Lucca.

As they docked for a day at a coaling station in the Cape Verde Islands, Wilfrid saw scores of starving mothers holding up their hands in supplication with babies for sale. Wilfrid paid four shillings for little ten-year-old Pompey; as black as the coaling station and nothing on but a shirt. Pompey proved to be the best of all majordomos, following his adoptive family all over the world and becoming the head of Blunt's household in England. His life was relatively short, but Blunt arranged for him to achieve his highest ambition: to marry a white housemaid. This, in spite of Blunt's belief that neither black and white bodies nor black and white cultures should be mixed. Whether he acquired this theory from some of the writing on race coming out at this date, or from alleged experience, is not clear. Either way, Pompey was the one who first inspired Blunt's passionate interest in 'the coloured races of mankind'.

> I would not allow him to be taught his letters though Alice would have done so, but I believed then and I still think rightly that the negro is happier in life without them.

There was no point in assimilating, according to Blunt:

> What is valuable in the black man is that his race is a distinct one with instincts and ways of thought apart from ours and less divergent from the general animal type, and so much the happier. It is doing him no benefit to place him by education in our white groove of discontent and restless ambition.

Nevertheless, without letters, Pompey learned to speak English and Spanish; and he had his own 'white groove' with the housemaid.

The Spanish-Americans of Buenos Aires seemed to Wilfrid a marvellous race, with their courage, polished manners and love of horses. His little house at San Ysidro was kept to perfection by two strong

Irish girls, Catherine and Bridget, freshly arrived from Donegal. However, it was the notorious explorer Sir Richard Burton who really unlocked the gates of Blunt's youthful imagination, leaving him night after night in a state of fascinated horror. At the lowest ebb in his career, Burton was seldom sober, and when words failed him he would argue a point with a knife. He stuffed Blunt with fairy tales of anthropology and staggered from horizon to horizon of metaphysics, displaying his marvellous gift of tongues and offering to all takers his 'diabolical gipsy faith'. A constant companion of Burton's was Orton the butcher, better known as the Tichborne Claimant. Blunt found Orton 'heavy lump as he was, the more gentleman of the two'.*

Fortunately for Alice her brother was seldom tied to the legation desk. As usual in the sixties, there seemed to be nothing pending in the legation in-trays. Without applying for leave, Wilfrid set out with Alice after the March heats were over to cover 800 miles alone in a tiny two-wheeled carriage without springs and loaded with tents, a bullock trunk, blankets, waterproofs, and an ostrich-feather rug on the top of which they both sat. Wilfrid always carried a rifle upright in his hand so that even distant enemies might see and mark its silhouette. In all his journeys he was never attacked when in that posture.

One night a huge yellow mastiff that had been left loose in error sprang out at him when he was crossing the patio barefoot. Wilfrid gave himself up for lost but the animal stopped in his rush, lay down and licked his feet. Wilfrid bought Turco next day for a silver dollar – to become the most efficient member of their caravan and of all the dogs he would later love, the one to be loved best. 'He was an equal and a friend. I esteemed him because I had begun by fearing him and I loved him because he had suddenly loved me.' In this incident some of Wilfrid's deepest feelings were involved; fear, and fears of fear; and his craving for mastery. It may help to explain a story told with horror by his daughter, of her father holding up his spaniels by the ears to see how long they could endure. She knew nothing of his own debasement as a child at the hands of bullies.

A more terrifying experience was of a snow 'pampero'. They had lingered too many days watching the multiplicity of birds in the woodlands at the foot of the higher plateaux, between the Atlantic and the Andes. Winter overtook them on a plateau and a fierce black wind from the south, mingled with violent thunder and lightning, swept them to the ground, obliterating even their hands from before their faces. Had they not found a ruined posthouse just as the 'pampero' began, all would have been over.

He and Alice arrived back at Cordova to find their New Year's mail.

* Blunt was at school at Twyford with Sir Roger Tichborne's brother and noticed that Orton had black eyebrows meeting over the nose, just like Tichborne's brother.

Bitters Currie sent Wilfrid gossip from the rue de Beaujolais. He was now entangled with 'an English married lady, I have not yet crowned the edifice and I have received a severe check from the belle-mère of my object'.

From Paris to the hunting country of Yorkshire was a long and as it happened tragic leap. Francis had taken the field at Minley with his Wyndham cousins. Urgent news was sent in the New Year 1868 that he had burst a blood-vessel in his lungs. He would never be able to hunt again and might be an invalid for life. Alice must join him at once in San Remo – to whose kind climate the tuberculosis and cancer sufferers of prosperous Europe withdrew. Wilfrid was asked to think again about the future. He might become Head of the Family – H. F., as they were to call him forty years on.

Meanwhile, with Alice gone, he needed someone to look after him. He had not had a single woman in South America as long as he was living under his sister's care. As soon as she left, a little woman, half Indian, half English, took possession of him. They danced together all the evening, Wilfrid whispering and pressing her hand. In the confusion of the storm that broke towards midnight and continued all night, she left her husband's bed and came to Wilfrid.

He never forgot Anita, though she died in the great pestilence of the 1870s, along with Irish Catherine who had gone to work for her as a link with Wilfrid. Her husband was kind to her, but he could not give her a child; and Wilfrid regretted going home before he had accomplished that task. However, Anita found another 'donor' and had her baby before she died. Her letters to 'darling old Willie' sent out a stream of uncomplicated love for two years after he had gone. Because of Anita, Wilfrid evolved a theory about dark-eyed women that might have appealed to Queen Victoria, with her distrust of too many royal marriages with fair-haired, 'lymphatic' northerners:

> Anita was . . . a primitive woman such as in my experience dark-eyed women only are, the truest hearted and the best to love having the sexual instinct stronger and less selfishly maternal. Our fair-haired women of the north attract by their variety but are seldom as sincere; they know their minds less well and deceive themselves in what they wish and feel. It is less safe to count on them for happiness.

Another dark-eyed woman was more and more insistently recalled to Wilfrid's attention. Annabella, divested of the patient Count Trivulzio, had joined Francis and Alice at San Remo. In September 1868 Wilfrid wrote to her again, saying that his journeys in South America reminded him of travelling with her up from Italy – everything the same 'except you and the Alps'. He hoped to be home for Easter.[10] The last evening with Anita came and went. She and her friend Mrs Stuart sat in the window, Anita singing Schubert and Mrs Stuart strumming the guitar, while the thunder and the tears rolled. Catherine the maid ran howling away having presented Wilfrid with a gold pen and a pair of knitted open-work socks.

Blunt loitered on the way home, as one not over-eager to arrive. He and Turco the yellow mastiff got lost in the Organ Mountains above Rio, and spent a night alone together in the wild. 'It was the experience I had sought, a sense of solitude above the world, profound and menacing.' A letter from Francis, however, called him to heel:

> We have spent a very pleasant Christmas here [San Remo] the pleasantest that I have spent for many years. Lady Annabella has been staying with us now for a month and adds very much to our happiness. I had never met with anyone with whom it was so easy to live and who enters so thoroughly into all we do, riding and play-acting and the rest. I never met anyone half so clever. I live in hopes of having her some day as my sister. I really think she would suit you well.[11]

With Francis now entering the last stages of the illness from which their mother had died, the responsibility for steering Wilfrid into matrimony fell to Alice. For a family fitting as tightly and neatly into their soil as mushroom stalks, it was unthinkable that there should be no Blunt children springing up at Crabbet. Nevertheless Alice found it hard to face the loss of their travels together. She was engaged to marry William ('Nep') Wheatley, whom she had met in South America. The only thing, she wrote, to stick in her throat, 'is that I may never ride a cock horse in the wilds with you again'.[12] But there must be no more wailing by Wilfrid for his 'ideal lover'. Alice, with a little sleight of hand, had it all arranged.

When Wilfrid arrived at Marseilles from South America, a letter from Alice awaited him, telling him not to call at Ouchy. Nothing serious had happened; 'only Mrs B. [Baird] told me that she hoped you would not come there because she was sure if you did there would be a rumpus . . . That is really all . . . There – I think I have put it plainly.'[13] Plain as possible; particularly as Mrs B.'s apostacy had not actually taken place. Months afterwards Mrs Baird protested to Blunt that she had told Alice no such thing. Blunt never quite forgave his sister for her deception. Meanwhile he went straight to England without the Ouchy detour. By mid-March he was writing to tell Annabella how he had become 'so strong' in South America that he hardly felt the frightful English cold. When would she be home from Florence so that he could see her?[14]

Juliet's apparent defection had left him hurt and angry. 'In spite of my infidelities my heart still was hers, and had I found things as they had been with her we should have rushed together and all else would have been forgotten.' A protective barrier of old friends was formed around him in this vulnerable mood: Madeline Wyndham, Minnie Pollen, Henrietta Burrell, even Catherine Walters, all urging him to marry. For the first time in his life he went to parties with the idea of proposing to someone – 'an odd feeling of temptation', as when standing on a cliff-edge one had a double urge, to jump over and flee away. Lady Alice Kerr and Lady Mary Herbert were two sirens who seemed to beckon. Blunt believed that if a marriage with the latter had been 'arranged' she would not have refused him, 'nor do I doubt we should have been happy. She was of the very salt of the earth and I should have loved her.'* He would have proposed at the end of the season but for 'the other fate'.

The other fate seemed in retrospect to have been touch and go. Annabella had written noncommittally from Florence on 20 March that she was travelling, and so would regretfully miss him in England. Something brought her back early and he sent her a note. She replied next day with her usual forthrightness:

6 April 1869 Emily à Court has asked me to luncheon tomorrow and when I told her I was anxious to see you before you go to Lisbon she said she would write and ask you. I hope you will be able to come.[15]

The à Courts were another family of Blunt's cousins, and their names together with the Curries used to appear in Annabella's girlhood diaries. With Alice and Francis still away in Algiers, the great cousinship was doing its duty. Fate struck at the à Court's luncheon on 7 April. To his 'surprise' he wrote in his memoirs, Annabella was there at luncheon, just back from Italy:

It was with pleasure that we met. There was hardly a pretence of chance in our so doing, nor had I the trouble to make up my mind. When we were left together, the meal over, it was she not I that gathered up the threads of our past history. Simply and honestly she told me that she had not said 'yes' at Castel Solcio and was prepared if I would forgive to say it now. It needed no more words; and so it was arranged between us.

Slips of memory about a past that is forty years old are of no particular significance. The interest of Blunt's slips lies in their direction: all in the same direction, towards establishing his own passivity. He has forgotten his letter to Annabella, presumably of 5 April, and her reply to him, that she intended to get him invited. There could have been no element of surprise whatever in the lovers' meeting. Nevertheless there is no reason to doubt the basis of Blunt's story that Annabella took the lead after luncheon. It was like the plain 'Yea yea and nay nay' of her upbringing to do so. And in an *arranged* marriage – how often

* Lady Mary Herbert married Baron Frederic von Hügel.

does not that word come up in the Blunt memoirs? – it surely does not greatly matter who puts the final question.

Five days later he was writing to her as 'My darling child', and informing her that Lady Burrell had said he could honourably consent to children not being baptized Catholics, but 'not to talk about it'. Then Wilfrid went to Lisbon to meet Alice and Francis, leaving Annabella feeling lost. 'Dearest', she wrote to him on 19 April, 'I feel as if I had suddenly come into a great unknown world in which only you could guide me – and now you have gone away.' She signed another April letter 'your old-fashioned child'. And in answer to Wilfrid's plea that she must not judge him like other people, or it would be too hardly, Annabella replied that he was not like other people. From Lisbon on the twenty-seventh he wrote: 'This is perhaps the last letter I shall ever write you, at any rate for years', since they were about to meet; in a way he was sorry as he loved 'savouring all the joys of love and marriage'. But he wrote twice more, from Paris, to say he was kept in bed with an ague, and then with settling up a 'rather painful business', which he would tell her about some day, and how funny old Julie was about the marriage, regarding Annabella as a princess of the Arabian Nights. His princess wound up the series with a touching letter on 28 April: 'How strange it seems to me that the labyrinth of troubles I grew up in and through should have suddenly disappeared out of my life.'[16]

As the two wedding dates drew nearer – for Alice was to be married a week after Wilfrid – correspondence dwindled into notes. Wilfrid received notes from Annabella signed 'your Robin' and addressed to 'My tyrant!' He replied to 'Dicky'. Both Alice and Francis had chosen to call their sister-in-law 'Anne'; the name Annabella was dropped by general consent. Henceforth she is Anne.

Wilfrid was well satisfied with the two months of his engagement. At first he could think of nothing but the delightful contrast between the calm of 'an accepted courtship' and the fevers of 'illicit love' – the only kind of sexual love he had as yet known. Then through the gentle euphoric haze he began to sort out the finer points of his marriage. Because Anne was an inheritor of the Byron tradition, it was regarded as a 'great marriage', with Wilfrid called to share in intellectual fame. It was therefore a first step in Wilfrid's own poetic progress, and as such was welcomed by Lytton. It was a return of the prodigal son and a matter of rejoicing by all Wilfrid's relations. Financially he was now to be married to an income of £3,000 a year at a moment when his own younger son's capital had fallen to £700. 'It placed me', he wrote cheerfully, 'almost in the rank of the world's sublimities.' Anne's personal worth he had too much elegance to include in this numbered list. 'I speedily discovered', he added, 'that I had acquired in her a pearl of the greatest possible price, a heart entirely single in the devotion it was prepared to give.' How could he have made this conquest with so little effort? That was perhaps their tragedy. It was not unusual for a young man to have a beautiful mistress and then enjoy rapturous domesticity with his 'Towsy' or 'Stumpie' or 'Little Ugly' – as Alice and he called Anne. The rarity lay in the man himself being beautiful.

Anne's stance as his 'old-fashioned child', though much travelled and three years his senior, might seem defensive; an impression which her nickname for him of 'tyrant', even 'dearest tyrant', does nothing to diminish. Even if at the time of her marriage it was all in fun, her daughter Judith felt justified in arguing that Anne was frightened of him from the start.

Wilfrid himself was left in no doubt about the 'labyrinth of troubles', as Anne called it, that had entangled her youth. He met her father Lord Lovelace at East Horsley; he coveted her succession to the Wentworth (Milbanke) title for his son Lionel, but was mollified by Wilfrid's agreement that if he and Anne had no children, Lionel should succeed to the property. Anne told Wilfrid about the death of her full brother, Byron, in her arms at Woolwich dockyard from lung haemorrhage. But when these melancholy reminiscences were over, their wanderings together among the scenes of his youth became an enchantment: the Surrey Downs, Honeysuckle Bottom, Ranmore Common – nothing had changed except that for the first time in his life he was happy 'with a feeling of finality'. Her 'quiet affection' (she hardly ever kissed him) if not the exotic ideal of his turbulent youth, promised 'a practical romance'. 'Anne with her curious old world goodness and simplicity made love with her a wild flower new to me, and in her companionship I forgot the rest.'

Anne Isabella Noel was married to Wilfrid Scawen Blunt on Tuesday, 8 June 1869 at the smartest church in London, St George's, Hanover Square. According to Anne's diary, it would have been a Catholic church but for the unacceptable conditions of the 'authorities'. From a later diary of Wilfrid's it appears that he had been round to his old friend Father Coffin at Clapham, presumably to make a deal over the children's religion and ask for two religious ceremonies. But Cardinal Manning had recently forbidden this way out for Catholics.

Anne chose all her six bridesmaids from among relations, four of her own and two of Wilfrid's; Hester King, Mary Fortescue, Darea Curzon, Minnie Jenkins, Alice Noel, Mary Chandler and Mary Wyndham – the last being Madeline Wyndham's young daughter, a beautiful and baleful star on Anne's distant horizon. Their dresses, wrote Anne with a habitual touch of dryness, were adorned by the young ladies rather than vice versa, for at Lady Burrell's instigation they had been concocted on the premises of 'an artistick society' with no sense of fashion 'or anything'. The best man was Philip Currie, to whom Wilfrid gave a gold-headed cane 'well suited to his probable tendency to become an old bachelor'. (Here Anne was distinctly astray, for Philip Currie was not only to take a lady away from Wilfrid but later to marry her.) Percy Wyndham was Wilfrid's trustee and Sir Percy Burrell lent Wilfrid his house to be married from. Ralph Lord Wentworth, Anne's brother, gave her away. What Anne did not know and Wilfrid fortunately discovered only months later, was that Mrs Baird had sat in tears throughout the ceremony at the back of the church.

The first week of the honeymoon was to be spent at Worth Forest Cottage. Off they drove under a blazing sky and a shower of slippers, in an open carriage with four postilions. Rice was thrown when they changed horses at Croydon; 'the country of course seemed enchanted to me', wrote Anne in her diary. A triumphal arch had been erected outside Forest Cottage, and through it they could see a beaming Mrs Selwood: 'We both kissed Mrs Woodie.' The week was spent driving about the Forest in a pony carriage, and then it was time for Alice and Nep's wedding on the sixteenth, held with the authorities' blessing at the Catholic church of St Mary's, Chelsea. 'Towsy' was in some difficulty about a wedding hat to cover her rebellious hair. 'Couldn't you wear the bonnet I had at your wedding', wrote Alice on the eleventh, 'nobody would know it and I am going to wear a hat – mention this in your next letter. If not I will get one [for you] on Monday.'[17]

With Alice married, the Blunts resumed their honeymoon. Anne was attended by a lady's maid named Isabella Cowie, a Catholic girl from Hertfordshire who was to play a brilliantly tactful part in the marriage. Wilfrid engaged her for Anne on Waterloo Station:

> When I saw her, pretty as she was, on the platform I had it on the tip of my tongue to say 'you are far too pretty for the place'. But I did not say it, and from first to last I refrained from the least word of flattery or love. For this she was grateful, and we were throughout fast friends and possibly a little more, though always unacknowledged, for to a woman in her rank of life, silence is the sincerest homage.[18]

The case of Cowie shows that Wilfrid Blunt was not an uncontrollable amorist.

Lord Lovelace, Anne's embittered father, had insisted on their including in their honeymoon several weeks' visit to Ashley Combe, his romantically situated house in Somerset. But when they reached the moors and deep hanging woods above the sea, the house was empty – not even a cook or housekeeper.[19] A tour of Anne's grand relations in the West Country – Fortescues, Portsmouths, Devons – was broken by a visit to Wilfrid's ancient Aunt Bessie and Uncle Harry, the Glanvilles of Catchfrench. It was here in 1809 that Wilfrid's father had been nursed, after landing at Plymouth from the *Victory* with his Corunna wound. Wilfrid's grandfather William Blunt had been curate at St Germain's in 1788, the year of Byron's birth, and married Wilfrid's grandmother Mary Glanville there.

On 4 July Anne's brother Ralph announced his engagement to a Miss Fanny Herriot. On this note, which turned out to be a discordant one, the honeymoon ended.

Less than two months after the wedding Anne began to feel ill. She was pregnant and in Paris, on her way with Wilfrid to his new posting at Berne. They reached Berne in August where, on the sixth, Anne had a miscarriage. This was the beginning of a tragic pattern. Anne wrote in her diary: 'And thus we lost the hope of having a child soon.'[20] This first failure in her woman's function did nothing for her self-confidence. On Wilfrid's twenty-ninth birthday she noted: 'I gave him flowers and a little wooden screen with silly little pictures on it.' Birthday presents were soon to become an even sillier 'tease' between them.

Still not properly recovered by 19 August, she was carried by Wilfrid across a river when they went out 'trouting' on Lake Thun. At home she would paint, read Shelley and Charlotte Brontë and – provided Wilfrid was away at the legation – practise her violin. When their St Bernard pup chewed up one of Wilfrid's paintings it was Anne who pasted it together.

The Byron scandal was their main serious concern of the autumn. It had been resuscitated in *Macmillan's Magazine* by Mrs Beecher Stowe's article, in which the relations of Byron and his half-sister Mrs Augusta Leigh were said to have been incestuous. Anne was deeply distressed by 'the odious Stowe pamphlet', as she called it, not least because her beloved grandmother Lady Byron had been imprudent enough to take this woman into her confidence. Wilfrid wrote to Godfrey Lushington on Anne's behalf to see if his father, Dr Stephen Lushington, Lady Byron's legal adviser at the time of her separation, could throw light on Lady Byron's evidence. But Godfrey ducked the issue, replying to Wilfrid that his father would never reveal anything – 'he would be only hurt at *my* asking him'.[21] Godfrey suspected, however, that if his father believed the incest story to be 'a mere fabrication', he would have felt it his duty to Lord Byron to deny the charge. Godfrey was convinced there must be 'another valid cause' for the separation beyond incest, 'and there were plenty to choose from'. One was 'another crime'. (This may have been a hint at the bigamy myth.) Anne, having written to Dr Lushington herself and received no answer whatever, considered the possibility of her brother Ralph approaching old Lord Russell, the Prime Minister, and one of the few still alive to whom Thomas Moore had shown the lost Byron memoirs. Nothing can have come of this for Anne tackled instead Lord Lovelace: 'My father', she wrote to Francis, 'who would certainly know whether any proofs of [incest] existed even if he had not seen them has replied that it rests as far as he knows on one witness's assertion or belief – that witness being my grandmother.' And so Anne brought herself to criticize Lady Byron. 'Now her belief may, and must, I feel, have been a mistaken one. It is a great misfortune that she ever should have believed so dreadful a thing, or that believing it she should have told anyone.' More important than the individual was the family. Anne and Wilfrid were prepared to do anything to wipe out the Byron smear for the sake of his great-grandchild not yet born.*

Meanwhile Wilfrid's Vita Nova was to undergo an extraordinary change. He had come one day from Thun to Berne to look up some material for the legation. There in the Bernerhof reading-room he ran into Mrs Baird. 'It woke in me', wrote Blunt, 'the passionate longing which had slumbered for the past three years, with all the romance which had possessed my soul and which had never really been supplanted.' Blunt must needs now run his 'passionate romance' in harness with his 'practical romance'. On 19 September Mrs Baird was writing to Blunt from Ouchy that her husband Robert had taken rooms at the Anchor Inn for them, and Alice and her husband Nep would soon be joining them for their autumn holiday. To complete the party, Ralph Wentworth and 'his too-pretty wife' Fanny came too.

The October weather was as beautiful as in 1866 and they made the same excursions on the lake and in the hills. 'It was not quite love again between Juliet and me but a very near attachment which seemed to wait its time.' In the evenings Anne would embroider a cushion-cover when she was not mending Wilfrid's socks, or she and 'Juliet' would play the violin and piano together. 'Anne in her good contentment', wrote Wilfrid, 'cared not where her tent with me was set and though I did not explain to her all the reason, rejoiced with me because she saw the change had made he happier.' He described their extended family party in terms that today might be used of a commune. 'It was an atmosphere of honeymoon which I thought might be made to last forever, a new earthly Paradise, on such ideal lines as Shelley's had been at Lerici.† I did not look beyond the present, nor I think did Juliet.' A grievous piece of news brought the idyll to an end. A letter arrived for Wilfrid saying that the Wheatleys were not coming to

* The Blunts later came to believe that Lady Byron had not been mistaken.

† Two couples, Percy and Mary Shelley and Edward and Jane Williams, enjoyed cross-currents of romance at Lerici, until on 8 July 1822 Shelley and Williams were drowned.

Ouchy. Alice was in a decline, the fatal family illness having declared itself in her too, as a result of her first pregnancy. She was at Caldwell in North Britain where her husband Nep was in charge of the Renfrewshire militia. If Wilfrid wanted to see his sister again alive he must come at once.

From Caldwell Wilfrid sent an agonized note to Anne at Ouchy, where she had been left with the Bairds till he returned. 'I am in pain Dick and you must suffer it too because you love me – the bitterest pain I ever had to bear.'[22] He was convinced that Alice could not live. Not only that, but the towering form of Nep seemed to get between him and his sister's love. 'How good of you to come!' she had exclaimed, and then, pushing Wilfrid from her and examining him closely, 'What is it I find strange in you? How *small* you have become!' It was true. Nep, whom he had thought 'fairly' good-looking, was much the taller of the two. To his shame, Wilfrid realized he was jealous of Nep – and jealousy had no place in that kind of Vita Nova.

Despite the horror of his jealousy Wilfrid felt he must do his duty by the sister who had gone with him to the ends of the earth when *he* was ill. He moved her from Scotland to Torquay for the new year, 1870, having telegraphed Anne to find a house there for six months. Then, when Anne got home from Ouchy, they took council together.

There seemed to be good reasons, all connected with illness, why Wilfrid should quit the diplomatic service. His own constant applications for sick leave irked both him and the office. Francis had been vainly seeking health in Melbourne, Cape Town and now in Madeira, where he kept a gloomy diary about his more and more frequent haemorrhages and shorter and shorter expeditions in his litter. And now Alice. Wilfrid was necessary at home and his heiress 'yearned to have our lives more at our own disposal'. When the Foreign Office offered him a post at St Petersburg, he and Anne agreed that he should decline and leave the service. His retirement was gazetted on 31 December 1869, eleven years to the day after he joined.

Francis had offered to let them a seventeenth-century farmhouse on his Sussex estate, near Southwater and Dragons Green, called Newbuildings. This they now decided to accept as their future home.

The weeks at Torquay were a disaster. Only Anne and Alice remained on perfect terms, though Alice lost her baby and Anne could not be happy until she was sure of having started another one. She had her violin, however, and a carriage to make calls in. Wilfrid felt stranded. He disliked their windswept villa Glen-y-Mor, perched on the top of a cliff without the advantages of town or country. His jealousy of Nep crystallized sharply and was assuaged only when he painted a portrait of Alice with long loose hair.

But the real thing against Torquay was that it could never be

Ouchy. The breakup of that 'earthly Paradise' was of far more significance than his departure from the Foreign Office. Looking back, Blunt believed that the Ouchy set-up had been his one and only chance to keep his marriage permanently afloat; to keep the 'practical romance' and the 'ideal romance' of his life in balance.

Blunt's freedom henceforth from Foreign Office disciplines, such as they were, had two important effects. Positively, he was spurred on to fill the gaps in his time with writing. His friend Lytton congratulated him on escaping from 'this wretched profession' and hoped he would use his freedom in something congenial to his genius and worthy of its originality. The negative effect was no less apparent. Blunt would have nothing whatever to do except write poetry – and seek the environments in which poetry could be written. This did not sound like a blueprint for stable marriage. And here again Robert Lytton's remarks were relevant. Having politely expressed a wish to meet Wilfrid's charming wife, he went on:

> I hope you have not lost and never will lose your wondrous elasticity of life. Marriage is hardly favourable to the preservation of it. What little I ever had is gone and I long to bathe my sensations for a moment in the buoyancy of yours, as a tired traveller longs for a plunge in some mountain pool. I think you are very wise to give yourself occasional relaxations of the nuptial knot. Variety of sensation is the sole refuge from permament insensibility.[23]

Thus Lytton found it easy to approve of his friend's new blueprint for yet another version of the Vita Nova. 'I am curious to hear about your trip to Paris', he wrote, 'and whether you do not find the beatifications of domestic life refreshed by a temporary suspension of them.'

[4]
'What Have We Done to Death?'
1870–1875

The trip to Paris had been intended by Blunt simply as a brief morale-raiser. But he stayed with his cousin Francis 'Bitters' Currie, and soon the old bachelor magic began to work again. By February 1870 Blunt had made up his mind to find a semi-permanent apartment for himself and Anne in Paris. Apart from the magnetism of Bitters, he might somehow keep in touch with Juliet.

Anne had been much upset by his departure. A letter from Wilfrid dated 11 February accused her of being a goose. It was surely not so bad as all that to be separated for a mere fortnight from 'a tiresome teasing creature like me. . . .' And if she needed a break, so did he:

> If I never went away but dined at home every night of my life our love would be smothered to death. I have a horror of getting overgrown by habits which hide all the beauty of life and even you would regret it if I became a sleepy idiotical husband . . . I don't know Dick whether you imagine that I am unhappy with you. I am not so and perhaps I have never been so happy in my life – but happiness, sensual happiness, is not everything and we must be wise too.[1]

Anne felt there was nothing in life until Wilfrid once more put her in the family way. This he fortunately did in about March. But they had not learnt caution from Anne's previous miscarriage; off they went to Paris, which guaranteed excitement. Their new apartment, fine and central, was on the first floor of 204 rue de Rivoli, with all its memories for Blunt. But one of the memories was becoming blurred: that of Napoleon III riding up the street to power. The ageing Emperor had by now lost the faith of the masses, and though he appeared to face outside threats with confidence, there was no certainty that France would win in a conflict with Prussia. So impressed was Blunt by the early rumbles of war that he re-started his diary:

> *4 July* . . . news that Prim [the Spanish Minister] has offered the crown of Spain to one of the Hohenzollerns . . . and that the candidature is accepted. On this a general outcry from all sides. A Hohenzollern, it is said, at the Escurial

will complete the wild beast show of Europe. We have already seen a Bonaparte at Fontainebleau, a Savoy at Venice, a Hapsburg in Mexico. Today the rage is for German Kings, the most wonderful phenomenon of the age.

It was also the *casus belli.* Napoleon III protested to the King of Prussia at the invasion of the Spanish throne by a German. William withdrew his candidate, but the telegram with which he accompanied this act of peace – the notorious Ems telegram – was drafted by Bismarck in provocative terms so as to ensure hostilities between Prussia and France. Napoleon III tottered headlong into the trap and declared war on 15 July.

Just as the Franco-Prussian war was getting under way Wilfrid and Anne were invited by Robert and Edith Lytton to pay their first visit to Knebworth, the Lyttons' home in Hertfordshire. It was a relief for Anne, now pregnant again. The truth was that Wilfrid's letters from Paris, though frequent, had been demonstrably undemonstrative. They began with a plain 'Dick' and ended 'Your husband W.S.B.'. It was only Alice who petted Anne with 'dearest', 'little Anne', 'Towsy', 'Stumpy' and 'Dearan'. Wilfrid had already decided that Anne's own reticence meant she did not care for expressions of sentiment in others. He wrongly believed that her love for him would slip painlessly, like his own for her, into a 'practical romance'. But at Knebworth Anne was happy, appearing for the first time before Wilfrid's friends as the wife of this glorious being.

On 26 July the Blunts returned to a martial Paris. Here Blunt found the French public was being served with doctored news; their gallant soldiers were always winning but always retreating. Blunt was to remember these unreal bulletins of 1870 during the autumn of 1914, when the London press was allowed to publish only the roseate official reports from Paris. Old Julie, as a staunch Republican, harked back to the days when the people had saved France. But twenty years of Napoleon III and his Caesarism seemed to Blunt to have sapped the people's virtue. He wrote in his diary of 8 August:

It is well to talk of 1792, but the Republicans then were other men than now, and when their army was beaten, the people fought on. Today French patriotism is limited to killing the enemy. Nobody cares to be killed.
12 o'clock midnight. Dined on the Boulevard. Great crowds of people. Saw a carriage attacked by twenty or thirty people, a man standing up in it looking very pale and waving his arms. A troop of dragoons came down the Boulevard and people cried 'A la frontière!' This is because they think no troops should remain at Paris.

Next day (9 August) Blunt reported at the British Embassy to offer his services.

At the Embassy [wrote Blunt] they talk of a Republic under General Trochu. I confess I never heard of him before. The Chamber opens today. Great bands of blouses [workmen] have marched there, and a great band also of police. They say the Opposition will demand the immediate arming of all the citizens.... No one ever speaks of the Emperor now. He has either run away, or abdicated, or been shot.

At midnight Blunt began writing down his recollections of Napoleon III, including the Emperor's appearance at balls in the Tuileries while Blunt himself was still in the diplomatic service: 'a thick-set, coarsely made man (with legs too short for his body), and in his uniform might be taken for a sergeant. He has nothing remarkable in his face, except his cold green eyes which have a strangely fascinating, but repellent power.'

Anne meanwhile had been sent out of Paris to Deauville where other refugees were collecting. In Paris, Blunt sounds curiously elated:

17 August This is my birthday of thirty. It finds me healthy wealthy and wise, things I never thought to be. Anne has given me a silver coffee pot I have long coveted, a Louis XVI one of very beautiful French design. I have nothing left to wish for as a birthday gift, except the destruction of the German army.

Four days later he was taking Anne and her cousin Alice Noel to Caen. On the way there they stopped at Dives where a list was kept in the church of Norman knights who had followed William to England in 1066. Husband and wife were well satisfied to find their own family names along with the sixty-eight others that they knew still existed in England: the Byrons (de Buron), Glanvilles and Bluns or Blunts (le Blond). Picking up a Paris journal in Caen, Wilfrid saw mention of a quarrel between France and England. Suddenly he felt the position so serious that he decided to miss out Brittany and take Anne straight to the north. If there were a rupture he would be formally bound to his own country, though his sympathies would be with France. For the first time in seven years he entered a church and heard vespers. To pray for France somehow made sense.

He himself could not keep away from Paris. There was a decree to expel 'useless mouths', and a letter in *Le Figaro* enquiring whether ladies of pleasure should be properly so styled. The French government had corralled 2,000 of them in the Conciergerie, ready to be packed off as soon as they ate too much. There seemed to be little anxiety at the embassy. Blunt wrote a letter to *The Times* protesting at its pro-Prussian attitude but it was not published. He sent £100 to a fund for the French wounded. Every day he would visit Bitters and his circle of stimulating friends, where they would speculate endlessly about the war. Blunt would gladly have stayed and seen the drama out with Bitters – but there was Anne. It was with admiration and perhaps envy that he later recorded Bitters' war record: 'He remained quietly in his rooms in the Palais Royale through both siege and Commune, pursuing his philosophical occupation, the pursuit of pleasure, without disturbance, in spite of adverse circumstances.' So the ladies' mouths had not been officially deemed 'useless' after all.

Wilfrid left Paris, however reluctantly, on 26 August to join Anne and Alice Noel in Rouen. It was his last visit before German armies invested the city and the siege began. They drove to Dieppe on the twenty-eighth where they waited among the concourse of refugees until well after the German victory at Sedan, on 2 September. On the sixth Wilfrid sent Julie a 100 lb box of ship's biscuits, which got through just in time and stood her in good stead when others were down to dead cats.

Anne also had kept a war diary from 7 August until 10 September, when she and Wilfrid landed at Newhaven. How different was his from hers; nothing was conceded, in the way of heightened colour, to the general confusion.

6 September, Dieppe Breakfasted upstairs. Afterwards walked out with Alice. Went to bookshop – and ivory shop – and got a newspaper. Prussians approaching the capital. This had been telegraphed also and posted up in the town – and we had also seen numbers of all sorts of people going in the rain to be drilled. Dined at the table d'hôte. What a frightful panorama of people.[2]

On the opposite page Anne illustrated the frightful panorama: three women and two men all hangdog and hideous, entitled 'Pleasant vis-à-vis'. This was followed by a double spread of six more refugees (like themselves) labelled 'A fine family'. Anne's flat style of writing, applied regardless to flying rumours, torrential rains and storms that held them up for days on end, finally achieves its own dramatic effect.

It was a dreary homecoming to Forest Cottage. Francis was coughing away his time before embarking again in October for Madeira accompanied by Alice and Nep. Wilfrid brooded incessantly over the fate of Paris. A telegram from King William to Queen Augusta had made him feel sick and angry: 'May God who has hitherto befriended us continue his protection to our arms!' Everyone at home was 'crowing' over Sedan. Wilfrid refused to read a paper till peace was made. Even then he feared lest the destructive influence of Prussia should spread far beyond its own borders. 'The whole social fabric will probably have broken down before ten years are up.'

In mid-September they paid a visit to Anne's cousin Robert Curzon, Lord Zouche, the Oriental traveller who lived at beautiful Parham in West Sussex. They were filling in time, waiting for two things; for Newbuildings, which Francis would definitely let them at £120 a year with an option to buy for £5,000; and for Anne's baby. The birth was not due for some weeks; but Anne was already ailing at the beginning of November. It was, however, Wilfrid not Anne who on Friday 11 November began to feel and look terrible. Anne sent for Dr Black and Wilfrid was ordered to bed with jaundice. Shortly after Dr Black's visit Anne herself felt a 'little unwell'. Probably unwilling to compete with Wilfrid's illness, she minimized her own discomfort and dined downstairs. Her diary carried on in pencil:

> *Saturday November 12* Better. Stayed in bed. Wilfrid got up in the afternoon. I was in pain in the night – about ½ past 4 asked Wilfrid to send for the doctor. Mr. Smith from Crawley was sent for.
> *Sunday November 13* And Dr. Black telegraphed for. Dr. Smith came about 6 or 7. Dr. Black arrived by special train in the course of the morning. Dr. Martin too, came. At ½ past 4 on *Monday November 14* the boy was born. . . .
> *Tuesday November 15* Wilfrid baptized the little child. Mrs. Tullet held him. Cowie and Mrs. Selwood were present. In my room. He was baptized Wilfrid Scawen.
> *Wednesday November 16* Mrs. Brown the nurse came. I hated the sight of her.
> *Thursday November 17* Had the little child in bed with me. He died on Friday morning, at ½ past 2.
> *November 18th 1870* Wilfrid went to Crawley on Monday morning and on Tuesday November 22 the little child was buried with my little ring.
> *November 19* Warning given to Mrs. Brown.
> *November 20* Mrs. Brown had to go.[3]

Everything had gone – the little child and with him poor Anne's hope of pleasing her husband in the most obvious way.

The paternity that was snatched away so cruelly from Wilfrid had meant everything to him. He called a whole chapter of his memoirs 'Paternity', though his son had lived for only four days. It meant history. He had seen his family tree going back to those Bluns or Blonds on the Conqueror's roll-call in Normandy. It meant the old house in Sussex, Newbuildings. It was empty now but waiting to be lived in. Would it be empty again of Blunts after he was gone?

Wilfrid was determined to confer some reality on his lost son, describing him as 'a very beautiful child', though it was probably imagination that added beauty to the pathos of infant mortality. The christening of the child, whose survival was from the first uncertain, with his own name, gives further insight into Blunt's character. Holding no brief for an afterlife, he did believe with passion in family heritage. The cross he made on his child's forehead was not an act of faith but 'one of paternal piety towards a son who would not without it have had so much as a name in our pedigree. . . .' This lay baptism was to have its consequences. Parson Bankes of Worth parish church refused to bury the improperly christened little corpse in the family vault with Wilfrid's father and mother. In a rage, Wilfrid approached the Catholic friars of Crawley, who 'in all courtesy and with pomp of choral chanting, and by the light of many tapers' laid the child in the ground by night, where in a year's time Wilfrid's brother, sister and two more children were to be buried. 'I was the only mourner present', wrote Wilfrid, 'for this my only son. God rest his small soul.'

After this, Wilfrid took Anne for a riding holiday in Spain. The Spanish tour was, literally, a wild success, the first of many wild journeys to be made with Anne, 'and perhaps the happiest'. At one point they were threatened with death by brigands and released only because their guide intimated that Anne was first cousin of Queen Victoria. At Granada, a desperate entry appeared in Anne's diary. (Her diary was generally strictly factual, so that these rare *cris de coeur* stand out.)

> *April 13* Today is a dark day for me, a day on which all the world seems blank and every little thing gives me pain, no future seems at all hopeful – instead of a mirage, I see a dark deep hole – although the sun is blazing outside the house and there are flowers everywhere and a bright blue sea.[4]

It sounds like another disappointment of her hopes of a child.

In August they were again at the rue de Rivoli, the German invaders and French Communards having both been replaced by the Third Republic. Blunt saw this as the satisfactory end of a political chapter. Like most of his contemporaries he failed to draw the necessary deductions; namely, that the Prussian enemy would reappear, while no revolution like the Commune would ever again survive in face of a modern government resolved to quell it by force. The Franco-Prussian war and the Commune left him always half-expecting a social revolution in Western Europe which never came.

On his birthday, 17 August, there was no Louis Seize silver coffee-pot or indeed anything else for Wilfrid. In retaliation he gave Anne only a cherry-pie flower on 22 September – 'No nice present', she wrote, 'because he said he had had none on his birthday.'[5]

While in Granada, Wilfrid had heard of Anita's death. This had decided him to visit Juliet at Ouchy, leaving Anne in Paris. For the 'dark deep hole' had filled up and she was again pregnant. But the Ouchy visit was to be a disaster.

Blunt arrived on a sudden impulse for Juliet's birthday in October. The surprise alarmed her. They could not go on the lake for it was wrapped in autumn fog. She tried to pick him a red rose as before; they had all been gathered. Then she accepted the omens, bidding him go and leave her in peace. He did not wait to be ordered twice. He received a heart-broken letter from her:

> I shall *never* (when this dreadful time is passed) repent what I have done. I do not expect happiness. All *that* was not to be for me. I hope you may some

day find all you think you have lost now.... I am going back to my old life.[6]

This débâcle he contrasted with a recent chance encounter on the way from Worth to France. Rosalind Stanley that was, now Rosalind Howard, had been travelling with her husband George, a painter, to London. Ten years had passed since those battles of wit with the brilliant Rosalind and her sisters and brothers in Dover Street. Wilfrid felt a not altogether unwelcome pang of jealousy and entered with her into sentimental reminiscences. After his dismissal by Juliet, he at once wrote to Rosalind in romantic terms.

A new crisis, however, directed his thoughts temporarily elsewhere. An SOS arrived from his brother and sister in Madeira. Francis was alarmingly ill. Leaving Anne in the care of Cowie and Julie, Wilfrid reached Madeira at the end of November, and for the next four months was Francis' nurse, dedicating himself passionately to the prolongation of 'his poor life'. Four times a day he would give his brother an injection of morphia and for half an hour every evening rub his chest with oil, after his game of cards or dominoes. Macabre touches were added by Francis' engagement to Janey Hinton, a girl of the island (he had never been in love before except vaguely with Lucy Laprimaudaye, who later became a nun), and the fact that his chaplain was also dying of consumption.

It may have been the tensions inherent in this experience that drew from Wilfrid a counter-balancing burst of vitality. In the glowing afternoons, while Francis and Alice were carried in their hammocks across the hills above Funchal, Wilfrid would career on his pony as near to the perilous edge of a precipice as possible, or plunge through a paradise of shrubs, butterflies and wild canaries. In the warm nights, for just over a month, he risked the sensual pleasure of a sudden romance.

Arthur Sumner and his wife Georgie were family friends of the Blunts. Indeed Georgie was part of the great Wyndham nexus, for her brother Nigel Kingscote had married Wilfrid's cousin Caroline Wyndham. Wilfrid's already strong leaning towards anything that savoured of a family, almost a tribal link, had been strengthened recently in Paris, by a conversation with the French writer Joseph Arthur Comte de Gobineau.* The Sumners were both members of the Prince of Wales's fast set, but Georgie also belonged to the circle of artistic society women which Alice Blunt had joined in the early 1860s, with Madeline Wyndham as its centre and Lady Alice Kerr as its photographer. Rossetti drew Georgie, and Lady Paget devoted a

* This man was one of the smaller channels through whom theories of race were conducted around Europe, in the wake of Darwin's great splash. Gobineau persuaded Blunt that interbreeding within the race, far from being unfavourable to its longevity, was the best of all recipes.

paragraph to her in her memoirs, stressing her heroic stature, aquiline features and bright brown eyes, 'in which some red sparkled like precious stones'. (Her thick ripply hair, however, was lustreless, for she was one of the first to set a fashion of dyeing it red and so, according to Wilfrid, destroying its sheen.) In advance of her husband, Georgie had arrived on 5 December in Madeira with their two little girls. She was not consumptive, wrote Blunt; just suffering from her rackety life. The word 'rest-cure' had not yet been invented.

Blunt was a better cure. She was to write to her 'brown-eyed boy' four months later: 'It's not excitement you give, but strength, distinct from anyone else I've ever met. . . . I believe it was often you, not Madeira made me so well there.'[7] Francis was cheered by this splendid creature and persuaded her to stay in his *quinta*, rather than with Alice. Wilfrid was of course living there too. He had agreed with Anne to buy some furniture for Newbuildings while in Madeira. He found a beautiful carved Spanish bed, four feet wide, with spiralling posts and rows of smaller spirals at the head, about which he wrote triumphantly to Anne. But it had been bought 'as a new nuptial couch' – for Georgie.*

Anne lived for his letters, and kept their comparative scores in her diary – twelve from him and sixteen from her by 24 January 1872. Sixteen from him and twenty-two from her by 8 February. 'I feel like a beast', he wrote, 'enjoying myself out here as much as I do, when you are living alone in Paris'; but Heaven was performing a miracle, through his presence, in seeming to restore Francis. Nine days later he jokingly sent Anne a batch of 'poems without words' on the 'Seven Delights of Man' – the seventh of which was 'a love scene'. But the seventh delight came to an end when Georgie's husband arrived in March. By the eighth Wilfrid was getting restless and proposing that he and Anne should buy a very small house in London just for themselves, avoiding a 'team of servants'. They would live in England, not France, but visit Paris once a year.[8]

Meanwhile Anne was in dire trouble. Her diary had showed a complete blank for a month, and it was not till 9 March that she recorded in shaky pencil 'six weeks of a sort of agony', dosed by hateful Dr Campbell with laudanum and chlorodyne. The first night of March had been spent, she now wrote, 'under the shadow of death', followed by a night floating between hope and fear. On the third night she felt it was impossible to put off the birth any longer – though it was not due for three months. At 7.55 p.m. a child was born and baptized Elizabeth Cordelia Catherine by Dr Campbell, a Catholic. 'There is

* After Blunt's death in 1922 his daughter Judith Wentworth refused to sleep in it, saying it was haunted and gave her nightmares. She relegated it to the attic. I spent a most comfortable night in it at Newbuildings in 1976.

another to be born', he said. At 8.20 p.m. Alice Maria arrived and died at 10.30 p.m. She was taken away from the armchair where she had been lying in a bed of hot-water bottles with her sister. On the night of the seventh, the other twin was too weak to cry for food. Anne asked for the child to be given to her. 'It is better', she wrote, 'my own child should die in my arms if it must die.'

> I feel as if I could not bear anyone else to touch it. Oh, it was so lovely to me, it had feet and hands like its father and its voice went to my heart, and it opened its eyes and looked at me, how many times and the last time the eyes were open they saw me and I kissed the lids to shut them forever and I kissed my child's hands and feet and head. I kissed the mouth.[9]

Then she sent the news to her 'master'. He tried to cheer her: 'A later telegram says you are doing well. After all, that is what matters most, and of course there is a dismal satisfaction that the children were not boys.' (Anne surprisingly agreed.) He reminded her that human beings were in the hands of a 'blind fate' which might change its mind any moment, 'and you know in the fairy stories people always succeed the third time if they have failed twice'. They must get on their horses, 'and ride among the hills and forget all this'.[10]

As Wilfrid wrote in one of his early sonnets, 'The Two Highwaymen':

> What have we done to thee, thou monstrous Time?
> What have we done to Death that we must die?[11]

Wilfrid brought his brother Francis to England at the beginning of April fully expecting him to go home to Crabbet, after resting a few days at Radley's Hotel in Southampton. Leaving him in Minnie Pollen's care, he fetched Anne from Paris, and then with Madeline Wyndham to share his vigil returned to Francis' bedside. On 21 April Wilfrid was woken by the nurse at 5 a.m. He saw the signs of change, but gave the morphia to his brother as usual, fifteen drops. Francis' last coherent wish was for Wilfrid to read him something from Newman's *Dream of Gerontius*, followed by the Seven Penitential Psalms. They had reached only the fifth when the dying man's mind began to wander. 'Meet me as much as you can there', he murmured, 'but I shall be there long before you.'

Wilfrid asked Anne and Madeline to draw Francis on his deathbed; Madeline also arranged for a photographer to come. Wilfrid drew him too; but for him the death had been terrible as the smile that passed over Francis' face at the last. 'He looked', wrote Wilfrid, 'like Christ dying in his agony.' 'All the winter through', wrote Wilfrid afterwards in his diary, 'unbeliever as I am, I have had a secret hope that at the last moment when it came I might catch a glimpse of some other world revealed to me through his dying eyes.' But instead of seeing Heaven open for him, they had watched him being 'utterly extinguished'. Wilfrid asked himself, 'If this is the death of the righteous, what shall our own be?'

As always with Wilfrid, intensity of grief drove him to the consolations of love. His first reaction on arriving in England, while Minnie was in charge, had been to make a dash for the fascinating Rosalind Howard. When he saw her in her grand house at Palace Green he realized that she had dressed up specially for him. Her style was something that he had never seen before – a green serge gown copied from drawings of Marguerite in *Faust*, with slashed sleeves, a looped skirt and satchel hung on a chain from the waist. This, he later discovered, was the neo-pagan fancy of London town ladies, whose Bible was William Morris's *Earthly Paradise* and whose Book of Hours Rossetti's pre-Raphaelite preachings. Blunt found Rosalind's 'fantastic garb' unbecoming, but it excited him. He tried to kiss her after luncheon. She rebuffed him volubly – and then held out both hands in friendship. His head, however, had been turned in Madeira, and he left abruptly slamming her heavy front door behind him. They were not to meet again for ten years, when Blunt offered her a sonnet beginning,

> If I was angry once that you refused
> The bread I asked and offered me a stone ...
> Believe me now I would that wrong atone....[12]

The impetuous love that Rosalind had rejected was accepted by Minnie. Sitting together in Radley's Hotel while Francis slept his drugged sleep, they talked of their meeting in Southampton three years before and the first kiss she had given Wilfrid. In his present state it was impossible that he should not immediately demand another. And so began what Wilfrid called 'the longest love of my life, and perhaps the strongest'. If he liked best the forbidden fruit, this fruit was forbidden at least fifteen times – by the thought of her greatly esteemed husband, two sisters already nuns with two more to follow, and ten children of whom her eldest daughter Anne was to become a nun, with two sons Jesuits and one an Oratorian. Minnie herself had lived all her life in an atmosphere of piety. She was now thirty-five, but she belonged to the class of beautiful women in their thirties (Georgie was another) whom Blunt noticed were afraid of life slipping by without allowing them a *grande passion*. Minnie had not lost her faith, as he had. Her conscience, however, was partly silenced by the thought of bringing the wild goat back into the fold.

And indeed she partially succeeded. Though her love lit in him 'a perverse flame', the other side of his nature was touched at being thought worth saving. Her attraction for him is summed up in his own words:

> At that time of my youth and indeed throughout, it has been rather goodness than beauty that has attracted me.... The attraction lay in the forbidden character, in the sinfulness it involved for her if not for me, in the enormity of the perverseness of one almost a Saint, and above all in the strange revenge of time offered me with the sister of the object of my first boyish adoration in the hills of Lucca....

As soon as Madeline had taken Minnie's place at Francis' bedside Wilfrid's passion was almost automatically transferred to her. The element of sorrow that had been absent from their earlier Paris relationship was now poignantly present. He waited only for the right moment to 'crown' (his word) perhaps the richest of his Wyndham loves. Anne, his wife, also stood for life as against death:

> I found her now... recovered safely from her child-bearing, [he wrote] and consoled her as I could with the result of Judith's birth in the following year. In this way I never neglected her, not only through a duty of affection but through my desire of a son and heir, always a strong instinct in me and made stronger now by the mere prospect of my becoming the head of our house in Sussex.

Lastly there was Georgie. She did not return from Madeira until May, but Wilfrid already knew there was to be a child born in October. He saw a good deal of her that summer, where she lived in strict seclusion in Stafford House, the palatial home of the Duchess of Sutherland. Wilfrid believed that Georgie's secret was never suspected, except possibly by Madeline Wyndham who was the child's godmother. However, a story he tells of the Duchess hiding behind a screen one day to watch how Wilfrid and Georgie greeted one another, suggests that society was aware of what, after all, was not a rare event in those days when illicit love, like any other kind, meant children.

Wilfrid's idyll with Georgie came to an abrupt end in the summer, when she retired to Dunrobin Castle. There she met the Rev. Norman Macleod who had come over to preach to Queen Victoria, also a guest of the Sutherlands. 'The Queen's visit', wrote Georgie to Wilfrid on 19 September, 'was a great success. I fell in love with John Brown and almost made Her Majesty jealous.'[13] But it was Macleod and his eloquent Presbyterian faith with which she had really fallen in love. She handed Wilfrid back to Anne, describing her as a 'pal', 'good sort', 'trump' and 'brick'. Georgie's son was born at Berkeley Castle on 6 October and called after it. Lest someone should 'put Berkeley under the Jesuits', Blunt was not allowed to see his son until he was married and in the navy. Georgie allowed her former lover to say goodbye before he went abroad in 1873. It turned out to be goodbye virtually forever; they did not meet again for twenty years and then only by accident.

Minnie, Madeline, Anne, Georgie – it seems a surplus of love for one summer. But Wilfrid felt in need of every possible consolation. Soon after the death of Francis he realized that Alice also was mortally ill. He installed her in Forest Cottage to await the end.

Meanwhile, he was absorbed in creating an effigy of his brother, to be placed above the grave in the Crawley monastery. For weeks Wilfrid worked alone with feverish concentration on the clay, producing a more than life-size recumbent figure dressed in the Franciscan habit, to show that Francis had been a Tertiary of that order. When the clay model was finished, John Pollen found Wilfrid a skilled (though drunken) workman to help him with his chisel. With the memory of his brother's dead face and hands continually before him, Wilfrid achieved an extraordinary result – one that proved, as he said, what strong love could do without artistic training.

Every inch of the marble tells of Wilfrid's ordeal as well as his brother's. In its way it is a masterpiece, certainly a brilliant achievement by one who was never again to attempt the art of sculpture. A weakness of his statue, as also of some of his poetry, lies perhaps in a too direct reflection of his own personal experience. And so he is here more strikingly successful in portraying the stark suffering than in transcending it.

Wilfrid's other source of comfort lay in Crabbet. With Francis dead, he himself was now the squire – a position that suited him far better than his other-worldly brother. Wilfrid found the many farms, covering sixteen different parishes, flourishing. Not so the manor house. He had no hesitation in rebuilding the dilapidated Tudor house entirely, apart from a conservatory, some servants' rooms and the old library. Beside these old rooms rose the new Crabbet Park, owing its unique character to the combined genius of Wilfrid and Anne – its architects – a clerk of the works provided by John Pollen, and the builders and raw materials of Sussex. The bricks came from Wilfrid's own brickyards, the heavy slates for the roof from nearby Horsham. Only the white Portland stone for the facings was beyond Sussex to supply. Wilfrid felt he had watched the laying of every brick, having ensured good work by signing on the builders storey by storey, instead of for the whole, so that at each stage a contractor could be dismissed if he overran his estimates. When the cornerstone was laid, he placed inside it along with the date an appropriate curse. It was to bring damnation on the man who uncovered it, 'if he should be a German'. Wilfrid's wrath at the Prussian invasion of France still sizzled.

Solidity was its hallmark. Wilfrid utterly rejected any touch of the fashionable 'fantastics' associated with Victorian Gothic, adhering strictly to a William and Mary classicism. All was solid, from the large oblong windows, each with twenty-eight panes, right up to the balustrade round the roof and the central port-hole window surrounded by the stone sun-rays which symbolized Blunt's motto: 'By thy light I live'. Inside, the panelling and mouldings were copied by the old estate carpenter from the Wyndhams' 'palace' at Petworth. The Gobelins tapestries in the hall Wilfrid had picked up in Paris for a mere £200. The whole thing cost him under £5,000. (Anne may quietly have contributed more.)

He was the squire. This was his ancestral home. Now he only needed to become an ancestor himself.

For him Alice's death-bed was even bitterer than his brother's. Though he and Alice had promised to remain first in one another's hearts, despite their marriages, jealousy and estrangement had developed. Minnie Pollen again took over the death-chamber when the last day came on 11 August, praying and singing hymns ever more loudly to drown the delirium. Twice it became so agonizing that Anne had to lead Wilfrid out into the Forest. The first time she read aloud the wonderful *Dies Irae* from the Catholic burial service. The second time Wilfrid did what he and Alice used to do on their travels when something went wrong: read from a story-book, usually Jane Austen. Now he chose Admiral Byron's account of the *Wager*'s shipwreck off the coast of Patagonia. Soothed, he and Anne returned for the end. But when they prayed 'Thy will be done', he left the house for the third time, alone. 'Here again, as when Francis died', he wrote, 'I saw no sign of any passage into another life – only a terrible and ruthless crushing of the thing I loved.'

Alice Mary was buried on Wilfrid's thirty-second birthday, 17 August 1872, in the Capuchin church, along with Francis Scawen, little Wilfrid Scawen, Elizabeth Cordelia Catherine and little Alice Maria. It was hardly surprising that Wilfrid should have regarded as 'blind' the fate that had snatched from him in less than two years an only brother and sister, a son and twin daughters. He felt that the flowers placed on the coffins – cowslips, primroses and bluebells for Francis, water-lilies for Alice – had been desecrated for ever, and to the end of his life refused to allow any flowers but dried *immortelles* inside his house. Nor was it much more surprising that as he walked home with Minnie from Forest Cottage to Crabbet, day after day through that cruel summer, he should have grasped as if with drowning hands at life and warmth and beauty. When he had buried Alice he wrote: 'I bade a final farewell to my first youth, and having washed my face like

David I ceased to weep and set myself with an impatient ardour to enjoy that second youth which comes with perfect manhood.'

He and Minnie stayed during the autumn at West Grinstead Park, invited by Lady Burrell, who wanted to meet Alice's staunch friend. Wilfrid always found the autumn more provocative of passion than any other season. He and Minnie, watching the bucks fighting, discussed the loves of the deer. That evening he ran up to her room just before she came to bed and hid behind the window curtains. She began to unloose her hair; then suddenly sensed his presence and fled with muffled cries. 'She told me afterwards she had heard my heart beat.' Next morning he drove her to the station. At the crossroads where their ways parted, his to Newbuildings on the left, hers to London on the right, he asked her which she would take – the left with him or the right to her own family. 'I offer you the Kingdoms of the world and the glory of them, if you will fall down and worship me.' 'I *do* worship', she replied, 'but I must not fall down' – and she pointed to the right. 'And again', wrote Blunt, 'the glory was deferred.'

Three weeks later she appeared to him in the evening gloom at Newbuildings, ready, she said, to kneel down. 'And so that night it was, and we were happy in the old beloved home.'

One side of Blunt felt no compunction. Nor was he willing to 'accept as valid the fanciful lines women draw who are ready to excite their lover's passion and not to fulfil it'. Moreover, he passionately believed that fulfilment in this sense 'crowned' a woman also, and brought her 'glory'. The love between himself and Minnie he described as 'a blessing to us both'. In his Catholic moods, however, the glory would suddenly sink into sin.

He had taken a London house, 45 Lower Brook Street, for Anne's new confinement expected in March 1873. Here Minnie would come every morning before Christmas to help Anne and then take Wilfrid off to Mass at Farm Street. As he was to reflect afterwards, 'by one of those contradictions of the soul which have constantly accompanied my lifelong unbelief, this new connection, wicked though it was, proved the beginning of a more spiritual life'. In his diary for 24 December 1872 he noted that he had visited his old friend Father Coffin at Clapham. Never since just before his marriage had his mood been so tractable:

> Then my heart was very hard, but now the events of this year, Francis' death and Alice's, and this new love of Minnie, have softened me. . . . How happy I could be serving God with Minnie and sinning sins with her, for which we should both sit in sackcloth.

That same Christmas Eve he persuaded Minnie to go to Confession, even if it meant their separation. She did so; and in the New Year 1873 departed with her family for Germany, having decided to live away from temptation.*

The time was drawing near when Anne would make her third attempt to give a child to her husband. A good deal of superstition was attached to this third-time-lucky birth. 'Wilfrid said he should retire into a Convent, as soon as this child is born', Anne reported in her diary, 'to repent of his sins.' The unfortunate Anne had to listen to his prediction that the new year 1873 would be fatal to him and he would die on 31 October. Three weeks before the child's birth he was giving Anne written instructions in case of his death.

Just after Wilfrid came in from a game of real tennis on 4 February, Anne suddenly felt ill. A false alarm, said Dr Cumberbatch. But at 3.30 a.m. on 6 February 1873, at 45 Lower Brook Street, their child was born. Anne wrote that though a month premature it might live. 'Wilfrid gave me the chloroform and sat on the bed all night.'

Wilfrid's diary showed that he had expected something grim if not gruesome, and found instead poetry: 'The birth of a child is an easier matter than I have ever thought and the first cry of the infant is a touching sound. Anne when she heard it, cried out "Oh my little titty thing!" I confess tears came into my eyes.'

For most of the second day Anne had her frail infant in bed with her to keep it warm; the devoted maid Cowie also stayed in bed four days on end for the same purpose. It was not till 22 February that Anne heard from the doctor what she called a great saying: 'That child will do; that pulse will do for me – couldn't be better.'[14]

The christening had more magic than even Blunt expected. He had intended to baptize her himself, in order to keep out clergy and godparents. But Constance Mure, one of his favourite Wyndham cousins, was aghast. So to please her and in memory of her mother Lady Leconfield, he asked Monsignor Talbot, brother of Lady Lothian, to administer baptism on 7 February as if for an infant in danger of death. There were no sponsors and only Cowie was present with the parents. According to Anne's diary the names were drawn out of a hat: Judith Anne Dorothea. Judith was the name of Anne's great-grandmother Lady Noel, and Dorothea of the saint on whose feast the child was born.

Here again Wilfrid detected a miraculous influence, for Dorothea meant 'Gift of God' and they felt their daughter was just that. More mysterious still, they received a letter from Monsignor Stonor in Rome to say that the Pope had despatched a holy medal in answer to

* According to Anne Pollen's life of her father, *John Hungerford Pollen*, the family went to Germany as an economy move. None of them ever had the slightest suspicion of their mother's romance.

Wilfrid's request for a papal blessing, and Wilfrid worked out that it must have been sent precisely as Anne's labour pains started. Unfortunately the medal had fallen out of the packet. Wilfrid asked Father Edmund Coffin to complete the miracle by getting St Anthony to find the medal; after all, the Holy Father could have done even better over the birth; 'he might have made it a boy'.

With the seemingly miraculous birth, Wilfrid felt renewed need to put death behind him and seize life for himself in its most vivid and active form. His friend Lytton saw Blunt's 'second youth' as lying in the pursuit of poetry. But Blunt rejected this emphatically. To his friend's dismay he wrote the sonnet entitled 'He is not a Poet':

I would not, if I could, be called a poet,
I have no natural love of the 'chaste muse'...
In my hot youth I held it that a man
With heart to dare and stomach to enjoy
Had better work to his hand in any plan
Of any folly, so the thing were done,
Than in the noblest dreaming of mere dreams.[15]

His ambition was, as he said in his memoirs, 'to act my own part of hero in the world, not merely to be the bard of heroes'. Moreover, the world of great art seemed to him a matter of laborious dedication, rather than of inspiration. Only in music did he admit the possibility of 'supernatural inspiration' – because he did not understand it.

Among some sketches by Anne symbolizing his ambitions at the time, there were no references to literary fame but plenty to exploration and a journey through Central Asia. Indeed he and Anne had long been determined, as soon as the baby was born, to seek new adventure in Eastern lands. Then came his morbid premonitions of death, driving out the life force. At the same time Ralph Wentworth's marriage broke down and he divorced his unfaithful wife Fanny, shortly before she gave birth to a second child, a son, whom he announced was not his. As a parting shot she retorted, 'Nor was Mary.' (This was a cruel lie; but Ralph would never acknowledge poor Mary, though she lived to become Lady Wentworth.)

Throughout the spring of 1873 Blunt was waiting impatiently for Anne to be well enough to travel. He filled in time by leading the appropriate London social life. Minnie Pollen took him to the house of Leslie Stephen in Hammersmith to watch the Boat Race, and Wilfrid described it in terms of insect life (which incidentally he much preferred): boats shooting over the glittering mirror of the Thames like black gnats on a pond; the opposite bank an anthill black with spectators; and the trees everywhere hung with black clusters of boys like swarming bees.

Madeline Wyndham allowed Blunt to read Shelley to her until it was time to dress for the Queen's Drawing-Room; later he and Anne returned to see Madeline in a train of black and lavender, and to hear her solution of a woman's problem: 'Every woman as she grows old, ought to collect great pearls and hide herself under them.'

John Pollen, who was an assistant keeper at the South Kensington Museum (later the Victoria and Albert) took Blunt on a round of studios including those of Boehm and Millais. The latter struck Blunt as 'a great strong plethoric man of rather gross clay', despite his fine features. It may have been due to his daughter's birth that Blunt's diary contained at this time more than one reference to 'breeding' – a preoccupation which was soon to be intensified by his Eastern travels.

Ralph's disowned daughter Mary and little Judith Blunt, together with her wet nurse, were taken in by the Pollens when the Blunts at last found themselves ready to start. They left England on 10 April for Turkey. As they crossed the Alps Wilfrid wrote a sonnet:

This is the sublime
To be alone with eagles in the air....[16]

Anne let him transcribe it on the last page of her diary note-book. 'Perhaps it will still be there', she wrote, 'if this book exists a hundred years hence.* He let me read it – this is the greatest pleasure I could have, poetry is a sort of miracle to me, and I do love it. He who can write it should be happy.' Anne was Byron's granddaughter after all, despite her grandmother Lady Byron's fears of poetry.

This chapter of his 'Alms to Oblivion' Wilfrid entitled 'First Eastern Travels'. He felt it necessary afterwards to write an introduction, analysing the effect of their travels on his married life. His inner life in the 'old-fashioned East', he wrote, 'was sober and restrained'. Its romance lay in 'penetrating unknown regions of the earth' and getting to know the ways of its people, among whom women played a background part. The only woman in this life of romantic action was his wife.

My pleasures in the East were not those of the flesh and almost as little of the intellect. They were the pleasures of an outdoor life which is too soberly severe for folly, a life of bodily toil, of an abstemious habit in meat and drink, rough lying on the ground by night, endurance of sun wind and rain by day. There was little time for thought still less for passionate longings bred of idleness....

He and Anne discovered a new dignity by wearing the raiment of the East. And a new happiness through the perfect unison of their feelings

* It does exist (1978) in the British Library, bequeathed with the rest of Anne's diaries by Judith Wentworth on her death in 1957.

and interests while on their travels. Wilfrid gave up his journal on 13 May after writing the sonnet 'Roumeli Hissar':[17]

> I had no secrets to set down in one, what I thought she thought, what I did she did, what I felt she felt. These times were our true times of marriage, more than in Europe, and they were happy times.

To Anne their Turkish journey of spring 1873 was 'a new honeymoon'. For Wilfrid it was an interlude of saner pleasures, restoring his 'intellectual tone', despite his succumbing to one of his vicious attacks of pneumonia on the way down the Danube, which, as so often before, put his life in sudden jeopardy. As soon as he was able to leave his bed, he visited the horse-market at Stamboul with Anne. They bought some cheap country ponies and a half-Arab to carry their baggage. On their way home, in Smyrna, they made a more significant purchase. The valiant little grey horse, Turkeycock, if not a pure Kehailan was the first Eastern blood they possessed at Crabbet, where they established him as a forerunner of the Crabbet Arabian Stud.

Turkey itself was also a forerunner of the many Muslim lands with which the Blunts were later to identify themselves. Anne's high rank produced ready hospitality, for everywhere there was keen appreciation of breeding. And perhaps as a result of Blunt's healthier 'intellectual tone', he made a short excursion into sociology. The Turkish peasants he believed led a happier and freer life than their Sussex counterparts. Though the Turks had no civil rights they were not interfered with, apart from conscription. The accumulation of wealth might be prevented by exactions, but those who were content with a sufficiency had not much to fear – certainly not the 'petty regulations' of civilized Britain:

> They could wander where they would, work or not work at their choice, bring up their children as they pleased, being free of school boards and sanitary boards and all those restrictions and obligations which make our poor men's lives intolerable.

This was Wilfrid Blunt the Sussex squire, never averse to doing battle with parish councillors and local bye-laws. A deep vein of rebelliousness was always to be his, however much he might later hobnob with socialists and Fabians.

As soon as the Blunts returned to England in July, what Wilfrid called the European aspect of their marriage reasserted itself. Anne did not welcome it and longed to be back in their white tent with its dark brown lining and striped blanket hung over the entrance. 'I have been almost too happy, I suppose in our being alone', she wrote, 'and now everybody will be there, and if we never make another journey I shall never be happy any more (in that way).' Judith was no compensation to Anne for the loss of Wilfrid's exclusive company.

A bad cough caught from Pompey at first prevented her from holding Judith, 'my own little thing ... as if it were my bird or my dog'. But was it really fear of infection that inhibited her? Eight months later, after returning from a second long journey with Wilfrid, she wrote: 'I went to see the children but I am shy of my own child because I am in despair about her ever fancying me – it is of no use to try and alter my nature. I cannot manage very young children. I don't know how.'[18] She did not want to know. She had eyes only for her 'master'.

Meanwhile the master, who was also the 'tyrant', revelled in the Western romance of love that always followed headlong upon his Eastern romance of travel.

It was hard for his marriage to thrive, he admitted, in this Western context, devoted as it was to art, poetry and adventures with women. These affairs of the heart 'occupied almost all its foreground and were pursued by me with unscrupulous eagerness and in defiance of domestic ties'.

He was to describe 1873 as the year of Madeline Wyndham, in which their 'paganly aesthetic' needs were satisfied. On neither side was there 'a full devotion of the soul', and Blunt insisted that Madeline did no wrong to her husband or children, on whom her bountiful nature lavished the love of an earth-mother. He used the word 'heroic' of their tenderness for one another, but saw nothing else heroic in their romance. Its nature is described in the 'Juliet' sonnet of 1873:

> You ask my love. What shall my love then be?...
> The sweetest love of all were love in pain,
> And that I will not give.[19]

A different kind of love also found its renewal during the autumn. Minnie's second exile in Germany had 'exhausted her powers of abnegation and when she at last came home it was to throw off all restraint with me', wrote Blunt, 'and indulge our common passion without further let or hindrance'. But Minnie still prayed sincerely for her lover's conversion and the consequent end of their connection and her sin.

The connection can hardly be considered a 'blessing' for Minnie (as Blunt once called it), whichever way it is looked at; and indeed Minnie was probably prepared to save her lover's soul at the cost of her own, like Father Coffin when he offered to drown himself for Blunt in the pool at Clapham. Blunt was not unaware of the religious as well as sexual benefits to himself from his connection with Minnie. 'It was a link too for me and an ever-growing one with the Catholic faith of my boyhood.'

To a reader in the later twentieth century, the behaviour and reasoning described above is so unutterably strange as at first to cast doubts on the reliability of Blunt's account. Did he imagine these scenes of heroic self-damnation? I think not. He wanted to write the truth but often wrote it as he wanted it to be.

At the same time that Minnie prayed for Wilfrid she poured out kindnesses on Anne, who depended touchingly on her. She also made for Wilfrid and Judith what Wilfrid was to call 'a second home' at Newbuildings during the next fifteen years. Newbuildings was a lovely old Charles II house, with three priest-holes, a high-pitched stone roof of Horsham stone, gables, dormer windows, apricot brick walls and white curves of rococo stone decoration. It had been intended by Francis for Wilfrid, Anne and their family. Newbuildings needed a tenant, and Blunt let it rent free for fifteen years to the Pollen family, in return for Minnie's mothering of Judith and Ralph's daughter Mary, whenever the Blunts were abroad. The Pollen and Blunt families were almost merged, wrote Wilfrid, adding, 'I do not think in either household were the true relations existing between us suspected; not even when at last the quarrel came.'

The year 1874 was to be described by Wilfrid as an unsatisfactory one. The old year had ended glamorously for the Blunts with a visit to Madeline at Hyères, on their way to Algiers. Anne sketched placidly while Wilfrid romped with Madeline and Madeline with her children. In those classical olive groves Madeline seemed superbly at home, a 'peasant wench' loved by the gods, faultless in her marble beauty, 'but of no fastidious modesty'. Blunt realized that this chapter of his love would end for ever when they returned to England. Meanwhile, he and Anne were off for a first sight of the desert Arabs.

Their Algerian adventure had what Wilfrid called 'a tragical false start'. Anne found the Arab hospitality overwhelming. She was 'worn out' before she had reached the cous-cous and then had to taste four kinds of pastry and dates and listen to ballads about Abd-el-Kader, the great Algerian patriot now exiled to Damascus. Fleas in their rugs gave her little rest at night. Planning to visit the country beyond the Atlas mountains, they had hired mules from Boghar meaning to transfer to camels on the edge of the lesser desert and proceed to Biskra. The mule-ride across the hills was rough and exhausting. On the second day, 13 January, they pitched their tent on the desert plateau. That night Anne 'without more warning' miscarried of a two-months' boy. Anne blamed herself. She later tore the fatal page from her diary notebook, but recorded the catastrophe in her brief pocket-diary on 15 January:

> I was ill – could not go on and so we have lost both the chance for the future [of a male heir] and the journey now. I did not think I was doing a folly – but it seems to me I should have known I was trying the impossible.[20]

On the fourteenth she perked up, praising the comfort of a tent to be ill in, and the tea, coffee and soup made by Pompey and their Armenian guide Hadji. Her anxiety was now lest she should not dare make another journey for fear of being 'a clog on another people'.

Wilfrid's anxiety was sharper and more immediate. They were fifty miles from civilization in a poor tent with scant provisions and no medical aids. Wilfrid was nurse, guardian against 'intrusive' Arab women, and undertaker: 'In the silence of a moonlit night I went out alone and heaped with a bitter heart a cairn of stones over the spot where our hope lay buried.'

With any woman less courageous than Anne their journey would have ended after the sixteenth, when she was carried by twelve Arabs, four at a time, to Boughzoul.

> For me [continued Wilfrid] it was perhaps the blackest week of all my wandering life, a week of helplessness and self-reproach for having thus brought her into a wild land at such an untimely moment; of grief for what might have been to us both once more the joy of a male heir, not again to be granted.

They detected an incongruous figure on the horizon near Ain Mahdi, west of Laghouat. Swathed in coats and cloaks though with bare head, the newcomer had only a single guide and no luggage but a filter, a huge Bologna sausage and a violin. It was Ralph Wentworth, come to join them on the spur of the moment. After the first joy they were driven mad by his nightly practice of scales.

On their way home, they caught their first glimpse of true Bedouin life in the Sahara. Anne got out her paint-box again and sketched the receding desert in a frame of low arid hills; Wilfrid wrote a sonnet, bringing in the ever-present image of the 'net':

> Death last of all
> Spreads out his net and watches for our fall.[21]

It was sex as well as death, however, that spread its net for Wilfrid. 'The first news that greeted me', he wrote, 'on my return to England on the 22nd of April 1874 was that Minnie too like Anne had miscarried of a child, a five-months' boy some time in March.' When, on Minnie's urgent request, Blunt went round to see her, he found that she had told her intimate friend and fellow-Catholic, Lady Kenmare, 'how it had been between us'. While Minnie was recovering in

London, Blunt made her husband John Pollen his chief companion and friend – such are the complicated patterns which human beings can weave into their lives. When August came, Lady Kenmare invited Blunt to stay with her at Killarney, the Pollens to follow later. The invitation showed a lack of even minimal caution.

Lady Kenmare herself confessed to Minnie that the idea of a *'grande passion'* with this glorious lover was no mean temptation. However, she resisted it by stationing her chaplain in the room next to her own. In all other ways the days passed in the 'atmosphere of honeymoon', Blunt reading his verses to her on the many romantic promontories around the lake. The arrival of Minnie and her young daughter Anne – known as Pansy – found Blunt ravenous for the poetry of love, especially since Minnie informed him that Pansy was desperately shy and needed bringing out.

On an expedition to the Gap of Dunloe Minnie stayed behind and put Pansy in Blunt's care with the words, 'I leave her in your charge and you must flirt with her. I have told her you will, and you will not find it difficult, for she is in love with you already.' For four days the playful courtship went on, Blunt showering the pretty sixteen-year-old with wild flowers and 'nonsense', Minnie alternately encouraging and scolding, Pansy in tears at being 'made a fool of', but for just one afternoon, in love with him. He wrote for her the sonnet beginning 'If it were possible the fierce sun',[22] and also sent her a small ring for her birthday with a wild pansy on it and the motto, 'Pensez à moi'. Rings were to be his sign language. Pansy's mother had already received one in Germany saying 'Fare well and fare back', and his wife was to be given a consolation ring in four months' time. As for Pansy, she found herself despatched to Roehampton where her aunt Lucy Laprimaudaye was a nun. Pansy took the veil in due course. Blunt was to describe her as 'the most perfect of human beings . . . a thing apart from the world's wickedness'. For the next forty years she remained his ideal woman.

Blunt's political education began at Killarney, though he did not yet know it. Lady Kenmare confided to him her dream of a fairy palace built high above the old Killarney house, 'in the Land of the Sidhe'. The building of this new palace necessitated the raising of £100,000 through the rents by a hitherto kindly Catholic landlord, Lord Kenmare, and a popular agent – and this at the moment when Michael Davitt had started the Irish land war in Connaught and was 'sweeping down their way'. Lord Kenmare and his peasants were soon locked in struggle, his estate was bankrupted and his lady's life in her fairy palace rendered impossible. During the next decade Blunt himself was to enter the land war – on the opposite side to his ill-advised friends.

Anne had come home a little before her husband. She knew that she would be seeing him soon. 'Only I can't help writing, and wanting to write, for every moment of the day I miss him.' There had been a suggestion that he should publish his sonnets under her name, provided she could write a few herself for form's sake. But she couldn't. 'Oh, why can I neither speak nor sing – why can I find no words. I think of the desert which I have lived in, and loved, and the wonderful and happy life we have led, and am dumb.'[23]

In May there was one wonderful day at Crabbet, when she, Wilfrid and Minnie sat on the grass by the pond while Judith and Mary played. But by June Anne was apparently pregnant once more and had been forced by Dr Lewis – 'a fool' – to take to a wheelchair or even her bed, for 'absolute rest and opium'. She had been married five years, she noted on 8 June, 'and I am sad that in all this long time there is but one child to show – though there should have been six – and the new thing will be the seventh attempt'. She was ill again in August and rejoiced when she had passed 9 September, for on that day she was exactly the age at which her mother Ada Lovelace had died – thirteen days short of thirty-seven years. Ada had once told Anne, 'You will not pass forty.'

Wilfrid was away for part of the next month, staying at Monteviot with his friend Schomberg Kerr, now Lord Lothian, and railing in his diary against Schomberg's 'idle domestic happiness'. Blunt feared lest he too should become 'a waster of my days', and wrote the sonnet:

> If I could live without the thought of death . . .
> I could afford to wait, but for the hurt
> Of this dull tick of time which chides my ear.
> But now I dare not sit with loins ungirt
> And staff unlifted, for death stands too near.
> I must be up and doing – ay, each minute.
> The grave gives time for rest when we are in it.[24]

He longed to strike out in the direction of 'adventurous folly', rather than the idle domestic happiness of Schomberg. But he returned home in November to find, instead, a spell of domestic unhappiness, preceded by another bizarre moment of folly.

Ella Baird suddenly appeared in London and came to Crabbet for the night of 17 November. After Anne had gone to bed she crept down to Blunt in the library. He asked her to sleep with him. She refused. They both became angry and he pushed her out of the room. Neither slept. Next morning he told her to trouble him no more; but she returned to him after saying goodbye to Anne, and in a fury he took from his neck the little golden heart she had given him at the beginning of their love. She threw it into the fire, burst into tears and left the room. But back she came. 'You are a cruel woman, Ella.' She put her hand on his and he in turn burst into tears. The quarrel ended with one of Blunt's moments of euphoric fantasy: they 'agreed' to spend the winter together in Paris or Italy. 'Juliet still loves me', he wrote in his diary. 'Let the world do as it will. I care not.'

Two days later he developed a bad cold, telling Anne it was due to his being too much indoors. Anne indeed had been in bed for nearly six months and both were feeling the strain. 'I hope it won't last for more than a year longer', was Wilfrid's ironic comment, and Anne felt the same. It was intolerable, she wrote, to have to keep a journal entirely about other people's activities. The crisis of this seventh 'thing' began on 13 December when Dr Lewis suddenly announced there was no prospect of Anne ever having 'any child'. Something internal required treatment, though very likely it would prove incurable; he needed a second opinion.

Poor Anne. She would have to give this 'very disagreeable news' to Wilfrid when he came in. The humiliation and even fear come through in her diary. Her misery, however, was vented on the doctors. Why couldn't they have started the treatment earlier?

Dr Cumberbatch, who had delivered Judith, decided next day there was 'inflammation of the machinery within'. Immediately Anne sprang out of bed, resolved never to lie up again. For a week or so she walked about the house still carrying her child, despite 'the bad state of the machinery'. Then the end came, not mentioned by her but entered in Blunt's diary on 23 December: 'Anne has had another disappointment. I gave her a little ring to comfort her. One thing is clear. There is small chance now of her having more children, and I have no son.' He tramped for three hours through the snow that lay thick in Worth Forest, finishing at the very gill where he had sat nine years ago on an oak root deciding whether or not to shoot himself. He wrote in his diary: 'This spot attracts me and shall some day see the end of my tragi-comedy. But not yet. . . .'

Perhaps one of the factors in Blunt's 'not yet' was the birth of a real relationship with the only living child of his marriage. Until September of this year he had not remarked on her, except to observe that she was self-willed and had cerulean eyes, when they ought to have been brown. Then one morning at Crabbet she was standing with her nurse at the top of the four stairs leading from her mother's large bedroom to the nursery wing. Blunt looked up from below and the child, now just on his level, put out her arms. He reached up and she kissed him. Suddenly for the first time he felt paternal tenderness. A new epoch began that was to last for twenty years, during which the thought of his daughter would call him home from distant lands and alien loves.

Could the year 1875 begin well, asked Anne in her diary, since it was beginning on a *Friday*? Fridays apart, ill-health and idleness cast a gloom over both their diaries. Anne complained of 'doctors, doctors, doctors', prescribing iron pills and later quinine and port wine, and frightening her to death. When she asked Dr Cumberbatch if the disease of her 'machinery' would kill her, he replied blandly that cancers began in the same sort of way.

Wilfrid had nothing to do. He was waiting to take his wife abroad. Meanwhile he paid endless unsatisfying visits to women friends. Skittles was most affectionate, but only in proportion to his own reserve; Minnie sent Pansy out of the house whenever he called; and Madeline he knew forgot him the moment his back was turned. He was beginning to feel that Madeline's style might be too modern for him: 'a tall strong woman, such as are the fashion now; no porcelain figure like the beauties of the last century, nor yet the dull classic marble our fathers loved'. She was a 'pottery' goddess, human and barbarous. 'I do not think her beautiful, or wise, or good. Her beauty is too little refined, her wisdom too fantastic, her goodness too selfish. Yet I cannot say I do not love her. . . .' He turned instead to friends. Victoria Lothian, Schomberg's wife, left him with a pleasant sensation after a call: 'a dear little woman, nearly the only one of those I know well who does not expect me to make love to her'.

At last in February he got away to Paris where he met his friend Lord Lytton. They drank their morning coffee together at Voisin's and poured out their hearts – Wilfrid ruefully accepting Robert's quotation from Remusat, 'The best way of getting out of a bad situation is to remain in it.'

With Anne, he dawdled in Cannes, Nice, San Remo and Monaco. Juliet, who was uncharacteristically gambling at Monaco, went back on their 'agreed' plan to live together and made speeches about lovers becoming friends. He retorted with a sonnet: 'What is this prate of friendship?',[25] and wrote furiously in his diary, 'I shall leave Nice tomorrow'. Four days later he was asking Juliet, 'Do you care for me or do you not?' They parted inconclusively. He and Anne boarded the train two days later, 20 March, Wilfrid expecting up to the last some sign from Juliet. Sure enough, as the train was moving, a man rushed up the platform with a letter. It was from Madeline saying she was at Hyères, but he must not come. 'I felt the world slipping from my grasp, and I burst into tears.'

The tears poured down for more than an hour, Anne watching but not daring to sympathize. Once again he thought of suicide. But 'Anne, in her goodness, made me eat, and I became more sane'. They decided at Arles to return to the deserts of the Camargues, away from the civilized world. That night Anne came to him crying in her turn.

He said bitterly, 'Ah, the day will come when you too will abandon me.' 'How can I ever abandon you?' 'If *she* has abandoned me, why not you?' 'What has she to do with me?' 'Nothing except that she once loved me as you do.' And they shed their tears together.

The following morning Wilfrid went through one of his bizarre religious performances. He ordered a carriage and drove with Anne across the Camargues to the village of Saintes Maries, where he knelt at the triple shrine, promising the saints three golden images to the value of £100 apiece if they would give him back Juliet's love. He never had to pay up.

In any case, Anne would probably have paid, for she was the one who had ready cash; though she was beginning to worry about the mismanagement of their financial affairs. (Her capital of £12,000, Francis' of £4,000 and Wilfrid's of £2,000 had fallen to a total of £7,000 after six years of marriage.)

Anne's unselfishness during the Juliet crisis did not pass unnoticed by Blunt. 'What other woman would have this generosity', he wrote in his diary on 21 March, remembering her tears of sympathy the night before. Yet it is doubtful whether he really appreciated the half of his wife's nobility or the full agony behind her tears. Her diary recorded so much pain that she later cut out the account of these days in Nice – except for one fragment following the page dated 19 March. This fragment, however, tells us all we need to know: that Anne had hitherto suspected nothing of her husband's unfaithfulness and was prostrated by the cruel knowledge.

> I cannot write down any facts, but I am like one who has suddenly lost everything – or rather it is worse than that, I have discovered that I never had anything to lose – I who thought myself rich! Henceforth I will care for stones and sands – birds and beasts, the stars – anything in the universe but no human being except with a sorrowful pity – Why did I ever dream . . . [*sic*] But there are some sufferings I cannot bear to see and not help, only I cannot help.

She meant the sufferings of Blunt.

Minnie Pollen met them at the station when they arrived back in England, her image having replaced Juliet's even as Blunt crossed the Channel. It was she who was now to help him bear his sufferings – at greater future cost to herself. Blunt was soothed.

A visit to the studio of Sir Edward Burne-Jones set his heart again towards the ideal. (For the Juliet of Nice could no longer be described by that word.) After gazing at three pictures of beautiful women he wrote: 'I realized intensely that I had taken a wrong road in life, and the ideal, here sought and found so nobly, was worth all the reality of joy I have sold my soul to win.'

On arriving home he found a letter from Juliet lying on the table, 'like a serpent coiled to spring'. It proposed a new relationship between love and friendship but without passion – which indeed eventually developed. But at the time Blunt wrote angrily in his diary, 'I shall not answer this', and instead composed his 'Farewell to Juliet', a sequence of fifteen poems in the *Love Sonnets of Proteus*.

If only the literary vein could have continued until he and Anne were able to go abroad again. (She was still 'brooding over unaccomplished wishes' for a child, and prepared to 'keep quiet for a very long time', once another started.) John Murray the publisher accepted in principle Blunt's *Sonnets and Songs by Proteus* – 'A day of literary vain glory' – though when Anne showed Murray her sensitive African sketches he asked, 'Why no wild beasts?' A dinner party at the Lyttons brought Blunt face to face with George Eliot, whom he took in to dinner.

> She is a remarkable looking woman with a large rugged face, pale and calm, without pretension to good looks or other grace than that of manner – a pleasant soft voice, however, for the utterance of excellent English. She talks as she writes (a nominative case, a verb, a preposition, and all the other parts of speech in regular order), listens to what others have to say and thinks before she answers – a woman of mind with sense enough to sink her intellect. You might take her at first sight for a very superior governess, the type of decorum and respectable feminine virtues.

Her husband (as Blunt called him) George Lewes, with whom this type of decorum had already lived for over twenty years unmarried, Blunt found 'obtrusively ugly', but redeemed by piercing black eyes and dramatic conversation.

Murray sent Blunt's sonnets to Lewes, who described them flatteringly as 'a genuine source'. He had intended to dip into half a dozen but found himself reading every one, some twice, thereby showing that Blunt's vintage was 'truly that of the grape, not of the gooseberry'. Admittedly they were very unequal, some bottles being corked and others acid; but all were original, and all *'coulent de source'*, and carried the promise in the writer of a remarkable poet.

Blunt then sent them on to his cousin Godfrey Webb ('Webber') for a social vetting – 'I mustn't be blackballed next year at the "Travellers".'

One cannot quarrel with Lewes's verdict. Blunt's sonnets do indeed *'coulent de source'* – flow from a living spring of inspiration. That source was largely autobiographical; and there lay the danger. Though the sonnets were 'fierce', as Lytton noted, with the impetus of real emotion, they were rarely filtered (to return to the spring metaphor) or channelled deep underground. They always told a story that, in the nineteenth century, made them compulsive reading to all who knew Blunt, and to many who did not. When they were published anonymously in 1875, the *Graphic* reviewer found them too 'fastidious' and 'rebellious' to attract the general reader; but Edmund Gosse, the young literary critic, praised their 'passionate cry of revolt and insubmission' picking out the lines beginning 'Give me thy heart, Juliet' (written to Minnie Pollen) for their strength, and 'Esther' for its 'almost savage realism', born of 'love-resentment'.

Blunt had achieved realism in his sonnets at the cost of depth. But even if he had worked at them (as he frankly did not propose to do, having as yet no ambition for a poetic career), would he have climbed into the class of a Rossetti or even a Meredith? It may be that he was smothered by too great a fertility of gifts; that he attracted too many happenings; that he had too much external personality, so to speak, ever to reach beyond what Lewes had called the promise of becoming a remarkable poet.

While Blunt was waiting for the publication of his slim yellow volume early in June, Byron's letters to Lady Melbourne had come into the possession of Mrs Dudley Carleton, later Lady Dorchester; she was the eldest surviving daughter of John Cam Hobhouse, Lord Broughton, Byron's friend and executor who had died in 1869. Wilfrid and Anne, already aware that these letters dealt with Byron's alleged incest, were given them to read by Mrs Carleton on 14 May. Five days later Wilfrid had finished them. In his view, if published, they would 'convulse the universe.'*

In a long critique that followed, Wilfrid showed that the universe would be convulsed with merriment as well as outrage. He found the account of Byron's love affair with Lady Fanny Webster 'the most amusing part of the correspondence', and developed an interesting theory that it led on directly to August Leigh's downfall: 'He spared her [Fanny] and as a natural result had his heart hardened by it, a hardening which showed itself immediately after in the seduction of his sister, an amiable good woman who loved him and whom he loved and honoured all the more for it. . . .'

Two days later Blunt received a letter from Mrs Pollen, now back in Germany, and decided hers were quite the best letters he possessed.† Moreover, he could not help seeing that Mrs Pollen had much in common with Mrs Leigh, Augusta being 'a thoroughly good kind woman, devoted to her children and her husband, religious too and strangely entangled in a sin not natural to her. Minnie is far more my sister than ever Augusta was to Byron.'

* Published unexpurgated in *Famous In my Time* (1973) and *Alas! the Love of Women* (1974), being volumes II and III of Byron's Letters and Journals, edited by Leslie A. Marchand.

† Nevertheless he sent back all but one or two of Minnie's letters on 12 June 1875.

Blunt's self-identification with Byron, incipient ever since he was nineteen and even more tempting when he married Byron's granddaughter, was now carried a stage further. 'I find in [Byron's letters] views of love and women very like my own – how different from the conventional Byron.' To Blunt the 'conventional' Byron would have been a heartless seducer.

> They are the views of a man dependent on love for his very existence yet unsatisfied in what be clings to in obstinate despair; whose love is given in proportion as he is loved; to whom the soul is the real object of passion, the body the ostensible; a man devoured with the ambition of knowledge, the ambition of power, the ambition of happiness; in whom is a hope never wholly attained, a desire never wholly satisfied, a strength which turns like a sword upon itself.

If this moving passage tells us more about Blunt than about Byron, it must not be forgotten that only a fraction of what is now common knowledge about Byron had as yet been published.

Lord Lovelace did not share his son-in-law's enthusiasm for the Byron letters. He told Anne that Lady Byron had given him three different reasons for her separation from her husband, none of which was incest. However, Lord Lovelace had recently discovered for himself that Byron's marriage to Annabella was bigamous. He was married already. Thus Ada and all her descendants including Anne were illegitimate. 'This must be nonsense', wrote Blunt. 'Perhaps he meant to frighten Ralph by this into more submission.' Lovelace also told Anne – correctly this time – that her mother during her last illness had confessed to past infidelity, forgery and swindling.

Blunt's excursion into Byronic history seems to have made his reactions increasingly Byronic; he expressed, as Byron did, his aversion to female 'blues' and atheistic talk. He went to one of George Eliot's afternoons, and found it full of 'tiresome' literary people; while the dinner-table conversation at his cousin George Currie's had been ruined by general dogmatism. 'It is disagreeable to hear the existence of God denied over one's soup and tirades against priestcraft with the roast.' He felt a relief when dinner ended and conversation became frankly obscene. More relief still when he and Lytton escaped to Brook Street, where they entertained the writer Augustus Hare to supper. 'Hare is a young man of excellent manners, good taste, good sense, good looks.' Byron would have thought the same about the whole evening.

There seemed a chance now that the Blunts would begin a Vita Nova together at last. Wilfrid had shown Anne his farewell sonnets to Juliet, and Minnie was still in Germany. His house had been swept clean of the demon of lust.

Blunt, after his break with Juliet, wrote about being left 'in much nakedness of heart but cured of pain'. A heart stripped, light, and empty; but in Blunt's case that was an invitation to enter rather than a 'no entry' sign. And in fact seven demons worse than those that had been there before were soon to take possession of the house.

[5]
'Carnival of Folly' and Founding of the Stud 1875–1878

'The year 1875', wrote Blunt, 'saw the climax of my young man's follies and also their catastrophe.' The catastrophe began with a marriage and ended with a divorce suit – both in the same year. Among Anne's many aristocratic cousins was Robin Zouche,* the young Lord of Parham, a splendid Elizabethan manor in West Sussex. Robin had visited the Blunts at Crabbet, Anne finding him charming and humorous, Wilfrid less so. Now at twenty-six the only male representative of a historic family and estate, he had a duty to marry. Anne heard on 10 June that he was engaged to the Hon. Dorothea Fraser, daughter of Lord Saltoun. A few weeks later Lady Burrell, also a relative of the Curzons, gave a party at 44 Berkeley Square to celebrate. She asked Blunt privately to let her know afterwards how he, as a man of the world, assessed the young couple's chances of happiness; Robin being young and unsophisticated, and Doll barely eighteen with an impecunious father and a scheming mother.

Blunt had no thought to betray his trust. He approached the girl as Robin's friend, not hers. Doll, however, turned out to be of the gypsy type he always found it hardest to resist; a black-haired little beauty with the dark bright eyes of a bird such as he had once admired in Anne. Horses were at present her only loves. She talked vivaciously to Blunt, inviting him to come next day and see her riding in the Park. Whenever Zouche approached she dropped her eyes and fell silent.

Anne's comment was uncompromising: 'I do not think she is interesting, rather pretty, but like any and every girl – and her mother is very vulgar.'[1]

Blunt had no hesitation in advising Zouche to break off the engagement. Foolishly, Zouche wrote to Doll's mother, who promptly burnt his letter, requiring him to show up at St George's,

* Robert Nathaniel George Curzon, Lord Zouche, 1851–1914, died without issue. His only sister Darea succeeded him and died unmarried so that the family died out. His mother was a Wilmot-Horton, related to Anne through her grandfather Lord Byron.

Hanover Square, on the day arranged. The wedding took place on 17 July, the bride's going-away dress being a riding habit and her madcap whim, as it was then considered, to storm into Parham at a hand-gallop from Worthing.

Anne was not able to go to the wedding, for on the fifteenth she had had yet another miscarriage. A wail of anguish escaped into the diary:

> I am at my wit's end and see no hope or chance – I think Wilfrid is sorry and disappointed too. Oh why am I not someone else, why am I in the way of happiness – yet I have not the courage really to wish to die and be out of the way. Life in spite of everything is too sweet to me, but I think I ought to give it up. Oh if God would hear me. . . . *Can* God hear – or is there no God, it is too horrible.[2]

The wedding had depressed Blunt also. He wrote in his diary: 'My days of love are over. If I can succeed in wedding the Muse I may now settle down with her in life – a sad pis-aller.' Exactly a month later it was Doll, not the Muse, whom Blunt was wooing.

An archery contest and ball had been arranged by Lady Burrell at her Sussex home, West Grinstead Park. While dancing with her 'cousin' Wilfrid, Doll confessed that she loved no one in the world but her mare Bellona. She had the same strong, lithe body as the young equestrian Skittles. Her fringe of curls gave her a look of Queen Henrietta Maria. 'She shone like a star', wrote Blunt, 'among the dowdy country folk.'

But it was an angry star, shooting glances of resentment at the man she believed had trapped her, her husband. Blunt offered one way to freedom. While staying at Crabbet during the following week, she agreed to accompany Wilfrid and Anne on a projected ride through Abyssinia during the winter; and during a gallop with Wilfrid through the Forest she suddenly asked if he would run away with her. 'Whenever you like.'

She begged him to pay a return visit to Parham in September, bringing his own little horse Turkeycock but trying out her beautiful Bellona while there. He could also catalogue the books in the ghost room. With a sigh of anticipation she said at parting, 'I am afraid I shall love you'. In the meantime she wrote him the letters of an excited child:

> There is a nice large damp room ready for you with I should think *lots of rats* and *mice* and crammed with books, every day I carry some more there and I have mixed all the volumes, so I am afraid that you will be a long time over your catalogue.[3]

The longed-for week came, beginning on Saturday 11 September. Wilfrid and an old South American friend Alec Fraser, who was staying at Crabbet, rode over to Parham, while Anne, still hampered by the 'inner machinery', came by train. Next day Doll set the pace. She refused to go to church though her husband and all the men went – except Blunt. He and Doll sailed on the lake, sank their boat and, when the church-goers returned, made South American bolases under Alec's instruction out of egg-shells filled with lead, fired pistols from horseback, stalked about in suits of ancient armour, ransacked hidden corners and forgotten rooms for family treasures and played hide-and-seek by moonlight in the Long Gallery. Blunt wrote in his journal that night: 'To me it has been all the evening one of those delicious dreams in which one wanders in impossible places with the best beloved, and always the supreme pleasure is delayed – "not now, not yet".'

The delay was not to be long. A week of ever madder sport was planned, based on a supposed mixture of life in Abyssinia and Patagonia, and punctuated by Doll's particular outrages; as when she, Alec Fraser and her brother Pagan burst into the parish church, jangled the bells, preached mock sermons and played waltzes on the organ. The culmination came on 13 September, which Blunt described as 'a day of youth and glory'. All morning they hunted a deer in the park, Fraser trying to capture it with bolas and lasso, Blunt's Algerian greyhound coursing it and his little Turkeycock bounding over fern and under the low boughs. In the afternoon they raced their horses on the downs. Then someone suggested sleeping out.

They decided on the heronry in the North Park woods as their encampment. The family servants, faces strained and bewildered by this week of riot, loaded a dog-cart with blankets, mirrors, candlesticks, cooking-pots and food. Pompey was to be chief cook, and while he roasted partridges they lit a fire for themselves under the giant fir-trees. Blunt wrote:

> One huge bed was spread for all the party which we called the 'Bed of Ware', and we sat talking far into the night. Doll in her ulster coat a true gypsy, had hung a piece of looking-glass near her on a tree and was tired now after her long day of violent life, and sad and tender. She sat watching me with great black eyes in the firelight . . . we lay down, our pillows almost touching and our faces. It was long before we slept. The fire burned at first too brightly and the moon was nearly at its full. After the rest were silent we two were still awake and always when I looked at her, her eyes were wide and fixed on mine. There were rooks above us which fidgeted overhead, and once a heron coming back to roost settled a moment, then with a ghostly croak seeing there were strangers there flapped hurriedly away. . . . At last the fire burned down and the moon set. . . . That was our marriage night.

As to his other marriage, Anne lay in the Bed of Ware parallel to Doll, but her head to Doll's feet, a sadly symbolic position. Anne woke to find two affectionate dogs curled up on either side of her. An unwilling Robin was also present.

The rest of the week proceeded with unabated extravagance, Parham being an earthly paradise and 'in all Sussex the perfectest and best, and most ideal framework of romance'. The very danger of discovery spurred Blunt on to make ghostly journeys from his room in the east wing to Doll's in the west, up and down the long creaking staircases and across the great uncurtained hall, watched by the moon and Zouche effigies in armour.

It was time on the nineteenth to return to Crabbet, stopping on the way at Newbuildings to see Minnie. Doll and Blunt had agreed on their joint future. 'We are to love each other for ten years, since it is best to fix a limit to human happiness', meeting in London and visiting alternately Crabbet and Parham. She gave him her wedding ring in exchange for the little ring he gave her.

Minnie looked tired and ill. 'She told me what I had guessed, that our last meeting had borne fruit. Ten days ago this news would have given me a world of delight. Now I feel ashamed. She fainted in church on Sunday. . . . Thus it is we hunt after happiness, and cut a throat at the end of every pleasure. Woe is me!'

This was not Blunt's only expression of disgust. When making extracts from his diary for the year of folly, before editing and then burning it, he found traces of a guilty conscience at the very beginning of the Zouche tragedy. He himself had not even the excuse of youth; he was now thirty-five. Nor was his love for Doll what he had called in the cases of Juliet and Minnie a passion of the soul. Rather 'a buccaneering whim', embarked on because Robin had abdicated and Doll – 'Swingkettle', as he called her – was far too pretty to remain long without a lover.

The return visit to Crabbet began on 30 September. But now a new element of risk appeared. Blunt's young cousin Dermot Lord Mayo had succeeded to his assassinated father, the Viceroy; he came to stay at Crabbet and there met Doll. Her passion for horses was shared by Dermot, who was engaged in driving a coach twice a week from Brighton to Arundel. Robin had been cajoled into giving a house-warming party on 15 October consisting of a tournament organized by Dermot and Alec, followed by another ball at the Burrells'. Doll confessed to Blunt that both Mayo and Alec Fraser were in love with her, Mayo being eager to elope; but she would prefer to bolt with Blunt. As for Zouche, his jealousy was directed against Mayo not Blunt, and he loathed the idea of the tournament.

There was to be an order of chivalry to which the men could belong, wearing the ribbons of Doll its queen – Queen of Abyssinia, in anticipation of the projected tour. The house-party included the

Pollens, Edward Curzon (a cousin), Doll's brother Pagan Fraser, Harry Brand, son of the Speaker, and the Burrells. Henrietta Burrell arranged that Doll's bedroom should no longer be accessible to nocturnal visitors, by having it changed to one opening into Robin's. She scolded Blunt, as the oldest man present, for having encouraged so many 'improprieties'.

Blunt had no difficulty in promising Lady Burrell to preach decorum, for his one thought now was to prevent disaster. Meanwhile Doll had confided in Anne that her mother had forced the marriage on Robin, who did not love her. When she wound up with a burst of tears, Anne 'changed the subject'.

The day arrived, golden in the autumn sunshine. Blunt had told Doll he would raise an admonitory forefinger if she showed signs of naughtiness, to which she would respond with clasped hands, meaning 'I will be good'. After some dull sword exercises, tilting with billiard cues and firing at flower-pots from horseback, where Blunt excelled, the real excitement began with a sham fight: Doll and the girls to be Christian ladies attacked by Moorish brigands and rescued by knights in armour. The whole worked up to an Arab fantasia, much applauded; but not before Doll's jealous suitors had laid about them in earnest, Alec Fraser being cut over the head and arm and Mayo felled by Blunt. At the ball Blunt felt it prudent not to dance the cotillion with Doll, despite the clasped hands. Among other things, 'Minnie was watching and I know it gave her pain'.

Next day Doll rode alone with Mayo, returning to give Blunt the joyful news that 'Dermot had promised to elope with her, had made a declaration of love and tried to kiss her'.

Monday 18 October proved to be the fatal day. It had been arranged that Doll and Alec Fraser should ride part of the way with the Blunts to Newbuildings, Fraser then escorting her home. While the Blunts were packing, Mayo rushed in to say there had been a violent quarrel between Zouche and Doll, Zouche forbidding the ride and Doll crying that she would leave him. She had indeed vanished; but they found her in the stables, sobbing as she saddled Bellona. Blunt begged her to go to Zouche's house in Arlington Street and wait for him there, and she begged Anne to look after her dog Bess. Then away she went, alone, at a gallop; none knew exactly where or why. It was an elopement without a man. But because it led to Doll's divorce the scandal was always referred to in Sussex annals as 'the Parham elopement'.

The party broke up, Fraser vowing he would run away with Doll himself, 'if the lassie got into trouble', and the Blunts sombrely aware that they might never see this lovely place again – as indeed they did not, Parham being yet another paradise lost. Only Zouche remained cool.

Next morning Doll telegraphed for Blunt from Arlington Street. He met her this time flanked by his wife – 'there was need of circumspection' – to find all the tears dried and the incorrigible Swingkettle enchanted at her escapade. They made her promise to wait for Zouche there, and meanwhile telegraphed him. Too late. When they returned in the morning, Doll had left for a private hotel in Albemarle Street, having sent an urgent telegram: 'Dreadful things have happened come and see me here.'[4] Blunt guessed at once that Zouche must be retaliating. In this crisis he was forced to tell Anne something of his own involvement. (If he had seen her diary he would have realized that she already guessed a good deal. As the crisis deepened she seemed actually to enjoy the role of protective wife.)

Blunt decided that decorum now forbade him to take his wife to the scarlet woman's hotel. He found Doll in a state of high excitement, expecting Mayo any moment and asking Blunt's blessing on a proposed trip to Paris and Rome. He had just wished her God speed when a cab drove up with Mayo himself and his brother Maurice Bourke. Doll cleverly shuffled Blunt out of her bedroom door as the brothers entered her sitting-room – only to be persuaded by Maurice not to elope with Dermot, for the sake of his career. Alec Fraser also had been summoned by Doll and he showed willing. He too had been hidden for a time in her bedroom. But while she was hesitating, her brother Pagan arrived and carried her off to their father's London house. Lord Saltoun made her write a repentant letter to her husband. The affair, however, was already in the hands of the divorce lawyers.

All feelings of romance had died in Wilfrid. 'Me she still professed to love', he wrote, 'and perhaps she did, but she had made our scheme of life together impossible on any lines within my contrivance.' Blunt's friends soon left him in no doubt that he, as well as Mayo and Fraser, would be cited as co-respondent. Harry Brand, who had been Doll's 'fugitive lover' at Parham, was now drawn in as the Blunts' chief adviser. 'I told him all I thought I ought to seem to know',[5] wrote Anne, playing her new part of deceiver with unexpected pleasure; but she caught Percy Wyndham looking at her as if in pity, when he came to shoot at Crabbet in November. Distress and anxiety quite numbed Minnie Pollen, while John implored Wilfrid to keep out of London for the present.

Anne was deeply relieved when they decided to take refuge abroad for the rest of the winter. The Abyssinian trip, as planned, had of course foundered: not only were the Zouches unavailable, but an Egyptian–Abyssinian campaign was in progress. Alec Fraser, however, was still free to acompany them to the Delta villages of Egypt. Anne had consulted Minnie about the advisability of a journey, supposing – just supposing – there were the prospect of another child. The two women agreed that Anne must risk it; 'It would be very awkward and perhaps objectionable to give up going, as another person might go instead of me which would be a scandal and have a disastrous result. . . .'[6]

They left by P & O steamer on 23 December, Anne well pleased to have Wilfrid to herself, even if it meant crossing swords now and then with 'my master'. He expected her, for instance, to attend the New Year Anglican service in the ship's saloon, and when she explained that she had made a vow never to go to another Anglican service, he protested, partly in jest, 'But you have no right to make a vow without my leave.'

There was another curious interchange when she went on deck next day to 'look at the sky'. Wilfrid, suspecting 'the sky' to be a euphemism for some admirer, took to teasing her by repeating the question, 'Would you not like to go and look at the sky?' Anne found these signs of jealousy not unwelcome, but instead of replying with flirtatious tenderness, she came out with a brusque example of the angularity which he had noticed on their first meeting:

> I said I hated skies and I don't see why I should be bothered by being supposed to like any person's attentions, especially as I have a poor opinion of people in general and in particular, and don't believe in any one.[7]

On reaching Cairo from Suez, they read in the newspapers of 14 January 1876 that the Earl of Lytton had passed through Egypt to take up his glittering new post as Viceroy of India. Wilfrid telegraphed a request to accompany him as the Viceroy's secretary, confident that his request would be received by Robert as 'a cry for help', and encouraged to make the offer by Anne who hoped 'it would be something to interest Wilfrid and perhaps would cut out other interests'. The highlights of their tour, meanwhile, were camping by the Great Pyramid, which Anne sketched, and enjoying Bedouin hospitality in the Delta villages. Though Egyptian politics at present meant nothing to the Blunts, they instinctively chose to travel rough in the company of fellahin.

All had gone well on the return trek to Cairo in mid-February, apart from one small characteristic incident. Anne, having been invited by her master to shoot a teal, missed it and indulged in pathetic self-abasement: 'I had spoilt the pleasure of his walk, I was in despair.'[8] There were better reasons for despair in the news that awaited them at Cairo.

Wilfrid had left Anne and Alec Fraser on their camels outside the consulate door, while he collected their mail. First came Robert

Lytton's rejection of Wilfrid's proffered assistance. His obvious inability to take Wilfrid as his secretary (even Wilfrid later saw how absurd had been this escapist dream) was unfortunately couched in the form of a homily. Robert wrote:

> ... We have chosen different paths in life, you pleasure, I duty, which others will mistake for ambition of which I have not a grain. I know not which of us two is the wisest or the least foolish in his choice, but probably we have both made a mistake, for neither pleasure nor duty are any guarantee for happiness. Of this however I wish you a full store by the free gift of the Gods. Adieu.

Blunt felt that his 'cry for help' had been, however deservedly, forced back down his throat: 'It made the blood rush to my face as I read it.'

By the same mail, Blunt received a 'still more lugubrious document', namely, a legal summons in the case of Zouche *v.* Zouche. Putting the two letters together, the one from H.M.'s Viceroy and the other from H.M.'s law courts, Blunt saw a double blow to his pride, from which he was to date a change in his life. To be sure, folly was to dominate half of his middle life. But from now on, the other half began to be more serious.

Blunt's humiliation was temporarily forgotten in the rigours of travel. Their homeward journey to England – Cairo, Sinai Peninsula, Jerusalem, Malta – led them at first through tracts of wild country that struck terror into Anne's heart. But when they came to Mount Sinai she was able to express in paint her pleasure at the contrast between the living spirit of a Christian monastery and its frame of lifeless mountains and inner ring of savage ramparts. Years later Wilfrid was to express in poetry his feelings for the desert life of Israel's Mount Horeb:

> A living presence in the unliving waste,
> A couchant lion with a mane of stone.

On 9 March Anne had to reduce her activities to a minimum because of what seemed to be a threatened miscarriage. 'Travelling is not the time for having children....', she wrote. 'If I can only get safely to Jerusalem, I hope all will be easy to manage after that.'[9]

They did reach Jerusalem safely, but only after a hair-raising experience in the Wady Ghervor near Aqaba. The Blunts, in their dislike of interpreters, had decided to venture northwards with no guide but an Arab boy, Haïd, from Sinai and his friend. On the evening of the twenty-sixth an altercation, to them unintelligible, arose with a sheykh at their camp in a narrow ravine. 'Have your revolver ready', said Wilfrid to Anne, as they left next morning after a disturbed night, 'and mind, if there is any row, that they don't get your gun from you.' The sheykh and his followers were Tiahas, a tribe particularly frightening to Haïd, and there were only six of them – the Blunts, Fraser, the two Arabs and Pompey – against a threatening band that followed them all through the wady. Two nights later, at 3.30 a.m., the Tiahas crept up but retired when they saw the guns 'bristling in the starlight'. The Blunts' party abandoned sleep, dressed hurriedly and rode away, only to find themselves dogged by thirst instead of Tiahas. At their last gasp, they chanced upon the oasis of Sidi Khaled – 'Shades deep as midnight, greenness for tired eyes' – but again provoked a quarrel by rushing to drink without first asking leave of the local Bedouin.

These two disagreeable encounters had a stimulating rather than a depressive effect on the Blunts. They decided to learn Arabic. Two pleasant incidents spurred them on. Blunt was moved by a love-sick young Bedouin to write a letter for him to the father of his beloved; and the Arabs who were entrusted, after much haggling, with the sale of his camels at the end of their trek, carried out their bargain with complete honesty. Contrary to European opinion, Blunt found that Arabs existed with the same passions and probity as himself.

Leaving Anne at Jaffa to conserve her strength, he went on ahead to Jerusalem. It was 'the finest place he had yet seen', he told her. But the latest news from home, which he did not tell her, was not fine.

> At Jerusalem I found another letter which affected me with shame and a half resolve towards a once more orderly life. It was from Minnie announcing to me the untimely birth of a child, her child and mine.

Minnie's pathetic letter, dated 3 March, begged Wilfrid not to send her the desert wild flowers he had promised: 'The history of my life ended a few weeks ago . . .', she wrote. 'I have buried all my dear flowers that I loved. I cannot care for any others.' This was Minnie's last child, born at the end of 1875 and christened Benjamin.

The Blunts reached England at the end of April. More serious tribulations awaited them; for Anne the eternal disappointment over child-bearing, for Wilfrid the Zouche divorce case.

Anne had become so ill on the way home that they had to send for a doctor at Chichester, who charged £5 for saying there was no child, 'but there was something or other there . . .'. At Crabbet, Dr Cumberbatch still had hopes, but by June they seemed to have evaporated: 'Bad news', wrote Anne, 'no present prospects.' Further professional consultations in November produced one medical opinion of 'nothing wrong' and another of 'some flaw'. Taking Minnie's advice, Anne decided on an operation – 'Chloroform makes it all right' – followed by three months resting, to be fit for a desert journey in February 1877.[10] But now she had a new anxiety. Wilfrid had told her he thought of going abroad for a year – but not whether he intended to take her with him. If he did not, of what use was the operation?

Meanwhile, what Blunt called 'the trial' had been crawling forward through thickets of intrigue, invention and compromise. He saw Doll Zouche once more but decided not to repeat a legally dangerous assignment. After this he never saw Doll again; she fled from her father's house with Mayo that July. Her departure had made Zouche's divorce a simple matter. Not so simple was the question of co-respondents; there looked like being an *embarras de richesses*. Was it possible that Lord Zouche would still insist on identifying, in the words of W. B. Yeats about another situation, 'three notorious adulterers' – Dermot Mayo, Alec Fraser and Wilfrid Scawen Blunt?

Anne was beside herself with anxiety. She heard that Mr Ballantyne, Zouche's counsel, wanted to subpoena *her*. Nothing would induce her, she vowed, to set foot inside 'the walls of the abomination, the divorce court', especially since the Prince of Wales himself had said it would be a disgrace to draw in her name. Anne believed Doll was doing all she could to injure Wilfrid in the eyes of the world, in revenge for not running away with her. 'It is just he should suffer for doing wrong', she wrote in her diary, 'but the suffering was likely to be severe enough without this additional attack.'[11] Wilfrid was to see Lord Saltoun and make his daughter retract the 'lies' she was telling about him. Lord Zouche was asking for £7,000 damages! Both the Zouches were as bad as one another, raged Anne. She did not know exactly what Doll's 'lies' were, but was determined to find out. In this, the most serious public crisis of Blunt's life, Anne not only behaved as but was, to the depths of her being, the loyal wife.

It is clear that Wilfrid had told her quite early on about Doll's fantastic invitation to bolt with her and his reply, given in the same spirit, 'Whenever you like.' There is no record of this in Anne's diary; but then, numerous pages written during the Zouche crisis were later excised. Further proof that Wilfrid did tell her is found in his daughter's memoirs 'Myself and Others'. Judith there quotes her mother's 'piteous cry', expressed in her diary, allegedly at standing in her husband's way after he had told her that he was in honour bound to elope with Doll. 'And what is to become of me and our child', had been Anne's alleged response. This may be a basically correct account, for Judith had read her mother's diary, though not before it was cut.*

* According to Judith, Minnie Pollen had 'commandeered' Anne's diary and made the cuts, after Anne consulted her about Wilfrid's 'concubines', all unconscious that Minnie herself was one of them. ('Myself and Others.')

On the other hand, the 'piteous cry' at standing in Wilfrid's way, which Judith found in her mother's diary, was surely not over Wilfrid's proposed elopement with Doll, but over Anne's failure to give him more children. It was not beyond Judith to telescope her facts in order to strengthen her argument.

Wilfrid's lamentable temptation to tease the nervous and inarticulate Anne was growing. He had had no intention of eloping, desiring as usual to 'contrive' (his own word) another double marriage. But he could not resist trying out the effect of his fanciful dialogue with Doll on Anne. At the same time, Anne's own temptation to retire into her shell was also growing. For instance, in October he had gone to see his lawyer, without telling Anne whether or not she was involved. 'Why did he not say?' Why did she not ask?

In the same month, after a dispute over the disposal of the house sewage at Crabbet, she wrote: 'It is always best not to give an opinion. However I was foolish enough to say openly what I thought.' Both temptations had developed from their respective childhoods and youth; Wilfrid bullied and spoilt, Anne repressed.

Blunt summed up the results of the divorce case with economy:

> ... after much legal wrangling, some forswearing on our part ... and hers by affidavit, and a formal appearance of the parties concerned at Westminster law courts, it was arranged that if the names of the other co-respondents were withdrawn no defence should be made by those two [Dermot and Doll] to the petition – a decree nisi was therefore pronounced in Zouche's favour in December of that same year 1876.

Anne reported that the case had opened on the seventh, Wilfrid very harassed. Next day Wilfrid brought home the *Pall Mall Gazette* – accurate but 'slip slop' about the names, 'e.g. *de la* Zouche'. The case had come before Sir James Hannen and a special jury, the allegations against 'Mr Wilfred Blunt' were denied by him and by 'Lady de la Zouche' and were consequently withdrawn, and costs were given against Lord Mayo. That evening a telegram arrived for Wilfrid. He pocketed it without a word. Despite her anxiety, she kept her rule 'not to ask needless questions whatever it may cost me, and I waited the whole evening and heard nothing'.[12]

Was it Wilfrid's 'tease' not to tell, or necessary secretiveness? Probably the latter. For there had been more drama attached to the dropping of the case against Wilfrid on the last day, 9 December, than Anne suspected. On the eleventh, John Pollen wrote to her, 'I thank God that Wilfrid is free from a most odious implication.'[13] Inexpressibly relieved and delighted, Anne kept the letter.

Judith was to sum up more cynically. She belonged to a generation that had lost her mother's Victorian horror of the divorce court, indeed she was personally to experience a divorce. In the end, wrote Judith, her father found that Lady Zouche, like himself, was 'running a team', and so the divorce proceedings were compounded and Lord Mayo took Blunt's place as co-respondent.

This last sentence was inaccurate. Lord Mayo was always the senior co-respondent, so to speak, and after the divorce he and Doll left for Jersey, intending to marry when the decree was made absolute. But Dermot had reckoned without his family or the Channel Islands' laws, by which his brothers could treat him as insane. Maurice and Terence Bourke got him shut up for two years, at the end of which period Dermot emerged as a perfectly sane and indeed public-spirited citizen, while Doll showed an 'inexplicable' aversion to marriage, preferring a lover to a husband. She married Lord Trevor twenty years after the Parham scandal, only to die almost at once. 'Poor Swingkettle!' The last sentence of her last letter to Wilfrid, dated 17 November 1881, seemed to sum up the tragedy of her life: 'It is not a bad world with one thing and another – the people in it are rather trying – but one consolation it cannot last for ever – and goodbye and I wish you very good luck. Yours Doll.'[14]

For Blunt, the follies that began at Parham finally produced both debits and credits. High on the list of debits was a serious break with the whole Bourke and Wyndham cousinship, not to mention the Burrells and other Sussex neighbours.

Blunt felt that while the Burrells were justified, the Bourkes were wrong to blame him for Mayo's entanglement. After all, he had tried, with Anne's help, to return Lady Zouche to her rightful lord. His strongest argument, however, could not be made public; namely, that far from encouraging Dermot, he had at first regarded him as 'an unwelcome rival'. In his distress at the Bourkes' estrangement, Blunt wrote to Madeline Wyndham for sympathy and permission to visit her. For the first time he met with a repulse: 'Dear Wilfred [*sic*], I cannot well tell you when to come here because I think just now you had better not *come at all*. The Bourkes are constantly in and out. They feel very strongly against you.'[15]

'Damn the Bourkes', exploded Blunt to Anne, 'it is not *their* business to sit in judgment, and *they* are no patterns of virtue.' In his rage he was tempted to call out Mayo, until dissuaded by Brand.

On the credit side was the loyalty of Skittles. Blunt had found no censoriousness among the satins and perfumes of Park Street. Indeed it was to Skittles that he owed his eleventh-hour escape. After Wilfrid's visit she had spoken to her most illustrious patron, and through her 'intervention with the Prince of Wales', wrote Blunt, 'my name at the last moment was withdrawn by Serjeant Ballantyne, the opposing counsel and a friend of the Prince's, from the list of co-respondents, a timely succour'.

The conclusion is irresistible that the mysterious telegram which Wilfrid silently pocketed at dinner on 8 December 1875 brought the news of his reprieve.

Blunt also gave credit to the humiliations of 1875–6 for his return to religion. It began in June 1876 with Minnie's grief and remorse over the death of their infant.

> She begged me to let her make her peace with Heaven and that I should make mine. . . . Poor Minnie. She cannot be happy, and I am miserable; and it would be better in every way there should be an end of certain things between us . . . but I am powerless to resist. I promised I would attempt what she asked as regarded herself, but for me there is no hope.

Nevertheless he admitted to himself that, with the world slipping through his fingers, pleasure an illusion and pride overset, he was in 'a state of soul' he had not known for years. To Minnie he wrote the sonnet beginning 'I am tired of folly tired of my own ways'.[16]

During 1876 and 1877 a correspondence developed between Blunt and his old Oscott tutor, Father Charles Meynell, which was to result the next year, 1878, in a published book. Even Anne was interested. She still described herself as 'the least spiritual person', but she was now forced to admit that she did believe in God, whereas 'Wilfrid probably *not*'.[17] If not a believer, he could write at the end of 1876 about beginning a 'new life' – Vita Nova once again.

With Anne's operation safely behind her, she was enchanted to learn that Wilfrid did mean to take her abroad. And not only her but their horses; for they possessed three Barbs imported from Algeria. It was to be a riding holiday based on Gibraltar. Her mother Ada had written as a young girl that being on 'a leaping horse' was the greatest pleasure she knew. At thirty-eight Anne echoed: 'I do think there is nothing in the world like a good gallop.'[18] To her the long Gibraltar holiday (January–April 1877) was a splendid whirl of theatricals, hunting and steeplechases. She stuck the play-bills and race cards into her diary – 'Marabout. W.S. Blunt up', 'Yellowboy. Lady Anne Blunt up.'

Blunt managed to get through without any new adventures. On returning to England, his thoughts remained rather more interested in the possibilities of conversion than seduction. There were two supreme questions which he set Meynell to answer: did God exist, despite science's enthronement of evolution; and could there be an afterlife for the soul when the body had died? Blunt frankly admitted that he had only come to Meynell because he was in 'a sea of troubles'. As long as amusement, pleasure and joy beckoned him, he could not resist them. But in the dark night of unhappiness he had an intuition of things better than joy:

Night is wise
And joy's full sun-light never guessed the stars.[19]

It was not only joy, however, that blotted out the stars but Blunt's intellect also, and in course of arguments covering some 180 pages Meynell was never able to convince him. Today the battle of evolution has rolled away over distant hills, invisible alike to the scientists and to the religious believers of the twentieth century. This is no place to re-examine Meynell's ancient armoury. The chief interest of Blunt's arguments lies in his personal examples. At the death of Francis he *saw* the soul die with the body. His present predicament he illustrated by a story of Robert Lytton's about his uncle the ambassador, Sir Henry Bulwer. The ambassador had a paralysis which necessitated his being carried to his coach by his servant Forster. One day there was a disastrous fire on board the ambassador's river-steamer; the captain lowered a gangplank and behold, the paralytic Sir Henry was the first to walk nimbly off. Having reached the bank he shouted, 'Forster, carry me!' But Forster refused, and ever afterwards Sir Henry was able to walk unaided. Would some comparable disaster do the same for Blunt's paralysed faith?

As well as corresponding, Blunt conducted his dialogue with Meynell through personal visits. Anne kept him in touch with his home and child (whom they now called 'Beebee' or 'Bibi') by letter. The tone of her letters was often reproachful – as reproachful as Anne dared to be. On 4 June 1877 she wrote: 'My master ... Beebee suddenly said at dinner, "Papa's gone to London he isn't taking care of his little dogs"' – nor of his little child. Wilfrid replied airily to 'Dick': 'I hope my Bibi is well – the monkey.' A few days later (8 June) Anne wrote again: 'I hope, my master, that this anniversary finds you well and cheerful and that you have not forgotten what it is that happened this day 8 years ago.'[20] He had either forgotten or decided on a 'tease', for he wrote on the same day sending Bibi his blessing – but with no mention of their wedding day.

The 'Proteus controversy', as Blunt called his correspondence with Meynell, was sent off on 17 July to Cardinal Newman. So enthusiastic was 'the divine Noggs' – Cardinal Newman's affectionate nickname at his Birmingham Oratory – that he urged publication, offering to edit the book himself. On second thoughts, however, he delegated the task to Aubrey de Vere, the Irish poet and writer.* Newman did not quite like to stand over Meynell's semi-evolutionary views himself. In 1878

* Aubrey de Vere, 1814–1902. He was received into the Roman Catholic Church in 1851 despite the warning of Thomas Carlyle not to join: 'You were born free. Do not go into that hole.' *Recollections of Aubrey de Vere* (1897).

a small monkish-looking volume in brown and black hard covers duly appeared entitled *Proteus and Amadeus: A Correspondence*, Proteus being the mythical god of many shapes, and Amadeus meaning 'Lover of God'.*

The editor, de Vere, rightly praised the book's 'ability, freedom, and friendliness'; but today, as a polemic, it lacks bite. Blunt's contemporaries were more puzzled than pleased. Who was this Amadeus? Was it Cardinal Manning? And Proteus? 'Proteus is a creature of a gentle and somewhat feminine imagination', wrote the Catholic *Tablet*. 'There is a daintiness about his methods of treating subjects which is very peculiar' – and it would carry little weight among the 'coarser' spirits who frequented 'dissecting and lecture rooms'.

Meanwhile, Cardinal Newman had invited Wilfrid at the beginning of October 1877 to a three-day retreat at Birmingham. Wilfrid described it as 'an errand of despair', particularly as he arrived with raging toothache, contracted while fishing in the west of Ireland. As he pulled the Oratory doorbell he was in such pain that he said to himself, 'It is useless, I can neither talk nor think. I shall not be able to listen or to say an intelligible word.'

Father Ryder, Newman's second-in-command, opened the door, but the great man himself led in Wilfrid by the hand. Wilfrid never forgot that hand, indeed it was later to set up in him what can almost be called a cult of the hand:

> It is a hand of the finest possible texture, warm, nervous, sympathetic, so soft that it might have been a woman's had it been less strong, an electrical hand in which all life seemed centered, the seat of his consciousness, of his soul.

In a voice 'inexpressibly sweet and gentle', Newman explained that argument could not restore to the soul belief in God and immortality; only 'humilty and prayer' could do that. Wilfrid listened – and suddenly realized that his toothache had vanished. It had left him instantaneously at the touch of Newman's hand.

At the end of the retreat Wilfrid was overflowing with affection, reverence and emotional acquiescence. But his major hope, 'the coercion of my intellect', remained unfulfilled. On parting, Father Ryder, whom he greatly liked, instructed him to say nothing about the small miracle of the saint's hand. 'And so I went my way on the third day', wrote Wilfrid, 'once more into the world of sin. My quest, except for this small miracle, had failed.'

The Blunts' journey of 1876 had whetted their appetite for something more adventurous; a deeper penetration of the desert.

* Dr Meynell once suggested that Wilfrid should call one of his horses Proteus – 'Out of Matter by Evolution'

They both seem to have taken it for granted that they would go East again in the winter of 1877, though Anne sometimes felt her departure from home as a looming shadow. 'The place so beautiful with greenness and birds singing', she wrote of Crabbet in June 1877, 'that I can't think of leaving it again.'[21] Her diary included a photograph of this amply-staffed paradise – fifteen house-servants, eight women in the front row, six men, a boy and Pompey at the back.

According to Wilfrid, the journey had two major attractions for Anne; her delight in riding, whether on horse or camel; and her 'wonderful facility in acquiring languages'. He did not mention what was probably her strongest reason, that she could not trust him to go alone. That autumn a new siren had visited Crabbet, a Mrs Thurlow. Aged twenty-two, she and her military husband had met the Blunts in Gibraltar, where Blunt flirted with her for want of any other occupation. He had been caught in Seville Cathedral by the beadle with his arm around her waist, but explained she was his *novia* – fiancée. They later became lovers 'by accident rather than romance', as Blunt wrote, and his Arabian preoccupations were to end it 'without quarrel'. Anne wanted no more such accidents.

Blunt's own motives for making the great desert treks were more complex. After Cardinal Newman's failure to convert him he spoke of returning to 'the world of sin'. But he had burnt his fingers at Parham and his social ostracism was still in force. Beside Mrs Thurlow, there was a second lady potentially more dangerous, a Mrs Singleton, who wrote romantic novels under the pen-name of Violet Fane. She was to refer to herself and Blunt skittishly as 'we authors'. If the phrase were to become 'we lovers' there would be complications, since Blunt's cousin Philip Currie was already her lover. Yet she had confessed to 'a strange interest' in Blunt. At least the world of sin stopped short on the frontiers of Arabia.

Then there was the 'very competent travelling unit' (his words) that he and Anne made together – far more harmonious than as a stationary unit in Sussex. To her proficiency in languages which eliminated interpreters, he added a sharpness of vision and sense of direction that did away with guides. There is no need to believe, however, with his daughter that his powers of sight were almost if not quite supernatural. Judith was to state more than once that he could see the Moons of Jupiter with his naked eye (a possibility with a few individuals), and that his eyes glittered with 'double lights'.* His own diagnosis was more rational:

* The famous 'double lights' shown in an early photograph of Blunt cannot have come from within his eyes but can only have *reflected* 'double lights' in the room – perhaps touched up by Judith with white paint, for she was an expert photographer.

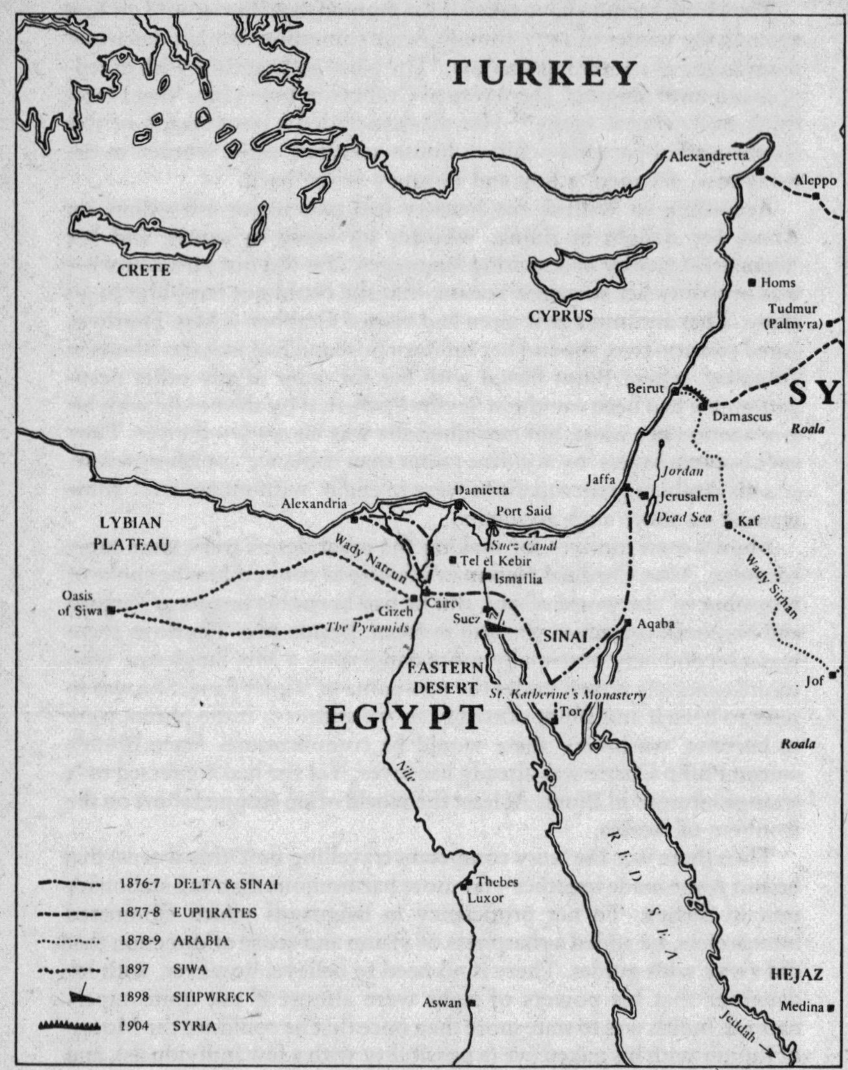
TURKEY
CRETE
CYPRUS
Alexandretta
Aleppo
Homs
Tudmur
(Palmyra)
Beirut
SY
Damascus
Roala
Jordan
Jaffa
Jerusalem
Dead Sea
Kaf
Wady Sirhan
Damietta
Alexandria
Port Said
LYBIAN
PLATEAU
Wady Natrun
Suez Canal
Tel el Kebir
Ismailia
Oasis
of Siwa
Cairo
Gizeh
The Pyramids
Suez
SINAI
Aqaba
EASTERN
DESERT
St. Katherine's Monastery
Jof
EGYPT
Tor
Roala
Nile
RED SEA
Thebes
Luxor
1876-7 DELTA & SINAI
1877-8 EUPHRATES
1878-9 ARABIA
1897 SIWA
1898 SHIPWRECK
1904 SYRIA
HEJAZ
Aswan
Medina
Jeddah

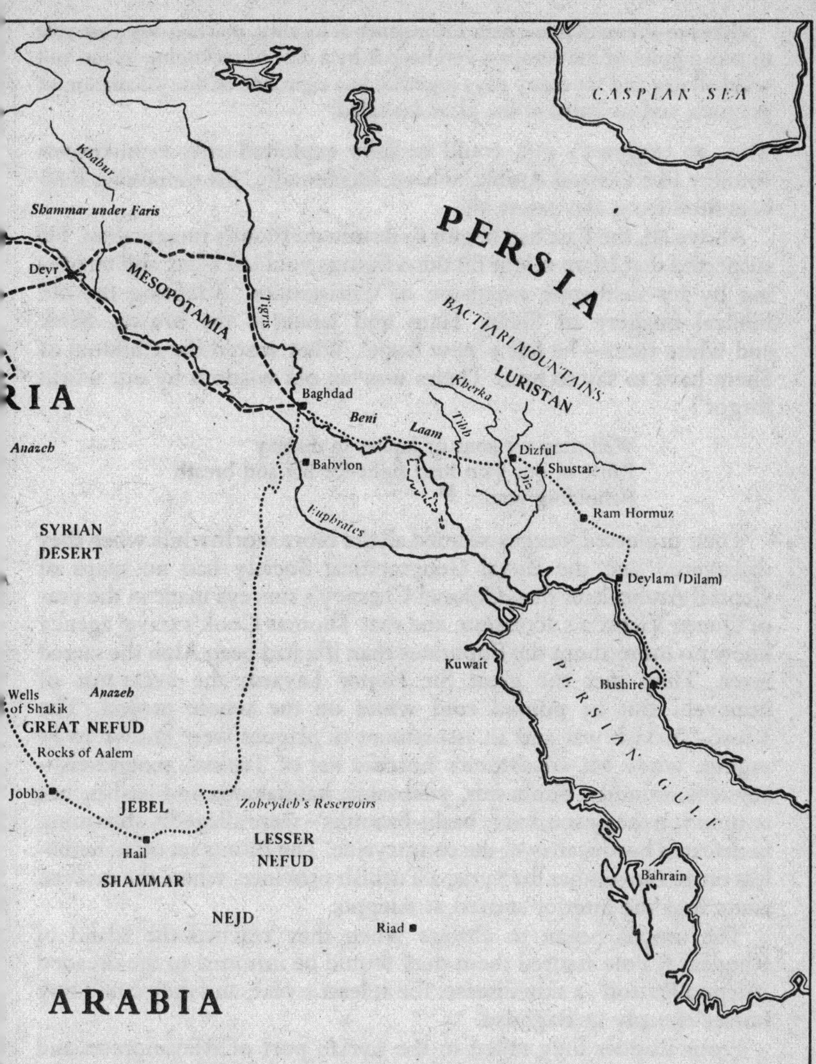
CASPIAN SEA
PERSIA
Khabur
Shammar under Faris
Deyr
MESOPOTAMIA
Tigris
BACTIARI MOUNTAINS
LURISTAN
RIA
Baghdad
Beni
Laam
Kberka
Tibb
Dizful
Shustar
Dis
Anazeh
Babylon
Ram Hormuz
SYRIAN
DESERT
Euphrates
Deylam (Dilam)
Kuwait
PERSIAN GULF
Bushire
Wells
of Shakik
Anazeh
GREAT NEFUD
Rocks of Aalem
Jobba
JEBEL
Zobeydeh's Reservoirs
Hail
LESSER
NEFUD
SHAMMAR
Bahrain
NEJD
Riad
ARABIA

I have to a remarkable extent the instinct of locality, that is to say I am able to take a point of the compass and keep it by a date of reckoning of sun and wind all day and for many days together in a right line of due calculation of the pace, and so arrive at the place intended.

This, an explorer's gift, could be fully exploited only in unknown country like Central Arabia, where, incidentally, his remaining lung benefited from the desert air.

Above all, the East had begun to dominate Blunt's imagination. He suspected that Islam might fill the religious void left bleak and terrifying by his deliberate expulsion of Christianity. Adopting the old biblical imagery of Shem, Ham and Japhet – the brown, black and white races – he felt a 'new hope'. What would the Children of Shem have to say to him? Theirs was 'an old wisdom by our world forgot':

Well may we sons of Japhet in dismay
Pause in our vain mad fight for life and breath
Beholding you....[22]

Their projected journey seemed all the more worthwhile when they discovered that the Royal Geographical Society had no maps of Central Arabia later than Colonel Chesney's surveys made in the year of Queen Victoria's accession, and that Thomas Cook's travel agency knew no more about the Euphrates than if it had been Alph the sacred river. They met the great Sir Henry Layard, the excavator of Nineveh. But he poured cold water on the whole project. The Russo-Turkish war and an assortment of plagues were known to be raging, while Mr Gladstone's horrific list of Turkish scoundrels – zaptiehs, mindirs, bimbashis, yuzbashis, kaimakams and pashas, not to mention the unspeakable bashi-bazouks – were allegedly swarming in defeated hordes all over the countryside. The Blunts set off nonetheless on 20 November for Syria, a Turkish province, where the caravan route into the interior started at Aleppo.

The omens began to change when they reached the island of Rhodes. A Pole assured them they would be immune to the dreaded 'Aleppo Button', a skin disease, for at least a year, and they could buy horses cheaply in Baghdad.

From Rhodes they sailed to the Syrian port of Alexandretta and thence rode on mules in four days to Aleppo, supplied with thirty flat Arab loaves, salt, pepper, oil, frying-pan and string of onions. 'With bread and onions one may travel far', wrote Anne. They arrived on 9 December exhausted, having stayed at small khans or inns on the way, sniffed at by cats, bitten by insects and stiff with sleeping on wooden platforms like the dogs in the Crabbet kennels. But at any rate, as they battled with icy winds and rain, wrapped in their Bedouin cloaks and yellow 'fellah' or peasant turbans – equally good as helmets, bandages, girdles or pillows – they no longer looked like the Children of Japhet.

The British consul at Aleppo with whom they stayed was to be a strong if short-term influence. James Henry Skene, an elderly charmer and fourteenth cousin of Anne through some Scottish princess, had seen the Crimean war as General Vivian's secretary, studied horse-racing and been consul at Aleppo for twenty years. He mapped an adventurous tour for the Blunts.[23]

Instead of going to Baghdad by Euphrates steamer, as Layard had cautiously advised, Skene said they should join one of the tribes of the Anazeh (Fedaan, Gomussa, Roala, Sebaa) and ride with them by camel towards their winter quarters, somewhere in the southern desert. Many of the best horse-breeding tribes were of the Anazeh. 'They know every detail of their own pedigrees and those of their horses', said Skene, 'and still remember the Darley Arabian' – that famous eighteenth-century stallion about whom Blunt had read in *Silk and Scarlet* as a boy.[24] Skene would give the Blunts an introduction to Jadaan, the Anazeh's wild warrior sheykh and Akid of the Sebaa Anazeh, and himself accompany them to the town of Deyr, west of the Euphrates, near which the Anazeh encampment was said to be.

While the December rains poured down, Anne stuffed saddles for their two riding mares, Hagar and Tamarisk, made a horse-rug and directed three Jewish tailors to stitch them a tent, sitting cross-legged each day in the consul's drawing-room. Blunt and Mrs Skene cast seventy-two extra revolver bullets, for the Anazeh had a running feud with the Shammar, another of the great desert tribes.

When all was ready, Anne found herself writing down three invaluable things they had learnt from Skene, beginning with 'Never take a gift'. The Blunts religiously observed this rule. But they could *give* presents, and indeed they were equipped with cloaks, boots, tobacco and sugar for that purpose. Next, Skene told them about the Arab oath of brotherhood, based on Abraham's oath to Abimalech at Beersheba. Most important of all, Skene taught them what points to look for in an Arab horse: the sloped shoulder; the tail carried horizontally like a streaming banner; the beautiful head with huge eyes, parallel ears and flaring nostrils, giving the effect of what might be called, in a woman, a tip-tilted nose; in all, an impression of 'great spirituality', of strength without a shred of coarseness. Lastly they must look at the knees – had they ever been broken? As they began buying, under Skene's direction, the picture filled out and they were able to assess the numerous mares and horses brought to them, each and every one pronounced by the Aleppan salesmen to be 'first class plenty werry good'. They made their most important purchase in Aleppo on 5 January, four days before departure. Kars, a pure-bred young Arab stallion but in desperate condition, cost them £69. He had been hit by a ball at the siege of Kars, and left for dead. It is clear that Skene and the Blunts had now matured between them the idea of a Crabbet Arabian stud.

Skene believed, like Napoleon I, that a pure Arab was the best horse in the world, and that to develop the Arabian's full glorious potential it must be bred from the best only, and bred in England, where it would grow large and beautiful on good conditions and food. In a letter to his brother-in-law Nep Wheatley, Wilfrid outlined their plans; for Nep might agree to receive the first batch of horses. Nep must keep the plans to himself, though Ralph Wentworth, a potential partner, would be informed of them by Anne. She and Wilfrid might even march with the Anazeh into the great unknown, the desert of Nejd. If it came off it would be the first thing of its kind ever done. Expect them home probably in April, certainly in time for the Derby. And look out for their gold medal from the Royal Geographical Society!

Their small caravan, accompanied by Skene and a few Turkish zaptiehs (police) in case of Shammar raids, left for Deyr on 9 January 1878. The zaptiehs were not the slightest use, wrote Blunt, 'for they sing one half of the night, and then sleep soundly the other half'. One dark night Anne was woken by a sound of lapping. She seized some four-footed beast by the hind legs and flung it out of the tent with a shout, waking Wilfrid. Probably a jackal or hyena, he wrote, though she had thought it a wolf. The omens were again not good – 'Grey crows sitting on dead trees'.

Sure enough, at Deyr they found themselves held captive by the Turkish pasha, an obstinate man who suffered from the 'button' and believed them to be British spies sent to reconnoitre the pickings from a rapidly collapsing Ottoman empire. The presence of the British consul with the Blunts deepened Turkish suspicions, though Skene returned to Aleppo on 27 January promising to meet them again at Deyr in March.

The small-town life of Deyr had begun to bore them stiff by the time they were allowed to depart – only to be bored even stiffer by the equally frustrating big-town life of Baghdad. For they had escaped from Deyr on condition that they gave up their quest for Jedaan, the Anazeh and the south. At Baghdad, though they were entertained in the picturesque residency, there was nothing to do but inspect some more 'werry good' animals in the horse-market.

Having cut out the Anazeh they decided to double back north-westwards from Baghdad through Mesopotamia, in the hope of an encounter with that receding desert mirage – a true Bedouin sheykh. By good luck they met a distinguished Indian exile, the ex-king of Oude, who loaded them with regal introductions to Shammar sheykhs. So they slipped off secretly once more into the desert, without the pasha's leave, Wilfrid pronouncing their perilous enterprise 'perfectly easy'.

This was the beginning of a memorable experience for Wilfrid. He led his private caravan across the wastes of ancient Babylon from minor sheykh to sheykh, eating with them but relying mainly for fresh food on his own superb marksmanship – as he would also rely on it in the extremity of a *ghazu* (raid). Wilfrid had a double-barrelled gun and Winchester rifle which fired fourteen shots without reloading. Always they slept outside the village in their own tent, surrounded by the four expensive young camels they had bought in Baghdad and a delul or she-dromedary, and attended by their two loyal servants, fat Hajji Mahmud who had followed them from Alexandretta, and Hanna, a Christian from Aleppo who spoke 'mincing town Arabic'.

Anne with her sensitivity to a side of Wilfrid's character that she admired, wrote in her diary that he was 'perfectly happy' to be without guards, police or guides but master '"in his own tent" and having besides his own camels and his own servants . . .'. Her reiteration of the word 'own' was to find a significant echo in one of Blunt's best-known poems:

Nor has the world a better thing,
Though one should search it round,
Than thus to live one's own sole king,
Upon one's own sole ground.[25]

In that case he was 'sole king' of broad-acred Crabbet in Sussex; in this case, of a few tents in the desert. No matter; among the Victorians to be sole owner anywhere was the very poetry of life.

At last their goal was achieved, in the discovery of Faris, one of the two rival leaders of the whole Shammar tribe. Anne immediately set about sketching his beautiful Arabian face, so truly *asil* (aristocratic) with its olive skin, fine curved nose, flashing eyes and smile, sweeping lashes and frame of plaited hair. Faris recognized in Blunt not only a tall handsome hunter from the West, who could hit a saucepan thrown up into the air (Faris took two minutes to fire a gun) but a man of breeding equal to his own. In Faris' tent they swore blood brotherhood according to the ritual Skene had already explained: 'Oh my God! By my God! By thy God! Brothers' – each meanwhile holding up the forefinger of the right hand, signifying 'one God', and grasping with the left hand the girdle of the other. At the end of the ceremony all three, wrote Anne, sat for a while in awed silence. 'I felt at that moment a real affection for him', recalled Blunt, 'and I dare say I shall feel it longer than he is likely to feel it for me.' Henceforth neither Faris nor any other Shammar could take Wilfrid's life or property, and vice versa.[26]

At Deyr there was a serious set-back. No Skene or message. It seemed that their last hope of meeting Jedaan, now said to be not far away, fighting the Roala (also of the Anazeh) to the south, had evaporated. Wilfrid rode off in search of news, leaving Anne to cope for five days with the townspeople, who at once tried to 'swarm like bees' into her tent. She put Hanna on guard and bravely endured.

Wilfrid returned with no news of Skene but bad news from the governor of Deyr. Still resolved to head them off from Jedaan, the pasha would send them under escort to Tudmur (Palmyra) whence they must proceed direct to Damascus and Beirut. 'Mind one thing', the pasha had said to the Blunts' guide, holding him by the ear, 'the English are to go straight to Damascus and above all must not be allowed to see anything on their way.' They spent a wretched night prepared alternately for execution as Russian spies or precipitate flight on their mares. Blunt's diplomacy triumphed, however, when it turned out that their escort, led by Mohammed-Ibn-Aruk, son of the sheykh of Tudmur, could be persuaded in the usual manner (bribery) to make a detour in the direction of Jedaan.

Blunt supported his bribe with an appeal to Arab honour: it would be *aib* (shame) for the English travellers to return home having seen nothing. At the word *aib* the Arabs burst into applause. What an invaluable public asset H.M. had lost, wrote Blunt, when he was allowed to leave the diplomatic service!

Skene eventually caught them up, bringing with him two mares for their stud, one a magnificent grey named Sherifa.

> Her hoofs fly forward faster even than flies the whirlwind.
> Her tail bone held aloft, yet the hairs sweep the gravel.[27]

Jeddaan, the folk-hero, proved to be a frost – at any rate, his brown eyes were cold and he plunged at once into questions about Sherifa's breeding. 'This struck us as rather rude', wrote Anne. Jedaan, unlike their charming Sherifa, was not well-bred. He was more interested in his fifteenth wife, recently acquired, than in potential blood-brotherhood. He redeemed himself to some extent by laying to heart Anne's beautifully spoken dissertation in Arabic on the madness of inter-tribal feuds. Would she try to induce his enemies the Roala 'to abstain from encroaching on pasturage' that belonged to another? On the way to the Roala, they joined up with a tribe of the Sebaa, the

Gomussa, and once more Wilfrid took an oath of brotherhood. This time his brother was Meshur-Ibn-Mershid, nephew of the Sheykh Suliman; they exchanged gifts, two silver-mounted Arab pistols for Wilfrid's revolver, a transaction which apparently did not breach Skene's rule. Anne's peace mission to the Roala was less successful, since their sheykh had grown too old to control his wild young men; but the first breathtaking vision of the Roala encampment made up for the failure of her mission. It was a sea of 20,000 black tents and 150,000 camels.

Anne's romantic feeling for what she called '*our own* desert' was matched by an aristocratic contempt for non-*asil* townees. She found their landlords in Deyr 'impertinent' for sitting down at table with them and even making conversation. 'We speedily set them in their proper place, which was on the floor....'

On their last night in the desert, 15 April, Wilfrid acquired in Mohammed-Ibn-Aruk his third Arab brother; for to Wilfrid's intense pleasure, their young guide chose the romance of brotherhood in lieu of the pecuniary reward he had been promised at Tudmur.

Next day the Blunts entered Damascus, to make two more highly romantic friends: Medjuel, sheykh of the Mesrab tribe, and his English wife Jane Digby el Mesrab, the former Lady Ellenborough. Both the Blunts were carried away by the seventy-year-old Mrs Digby and her unselfish devotion to her husband's tribe. It was only a pity, thought Anne, that she adopted the worst Arab fashions, such as daubing her eyelids with kohl and dying her hair black, while wearing an ugly European-style dress of beige silk with self-coloured bows and a dark plum underskirt. Her manner was quiet, dignified and unassuming. How utterly unlike the outrageous picture of her drawn by Mrs Richard Burton in the press.

Sadly the Blunts felt they were re-entering civilization, as they stepped into the diligence for Beirut at 3 a.m. On 26 April they reached the city, where they found an invitation to breakfast from Mr Eldridge the consul. Wilfrid bought a black straw hat 'to look European',[28] but Anne, with her usual insouciance about hats, found a battered old felt in her luggage, around which she draped a scarf. They were delighted to learn that Richard Burton's name stank in the consulate. 'Syria is not large enough to hold both you and me', Eldridge had informed Burton on his arrival, 'and one of us will have to go.' Burton agreed and said it would not be him. 'But it was!'

If only a party of wealthy English visitors, men and women, could have been dealt with in the same swift way. A dozen scantily-clad aristocrats arrived in their yacht from Malta, invaded the Blunts' hotel and took possession with loud, probably drunken laughter. One girl's golden hair, wrote Anne, hung 'quite loosely' down her back. It was not the only loose thing about a group which had its affinities with Parham. Who, after all, were truly *asil* – well-bred? The Children of Shem and their wonderful mares, whom the Blunts had just left behind, or these blue-blooded Yahoos, to whose world they were returning?

Wilfrid arrived home to find his religious dialogue, *Proteus and Amadeus*, about to be published. Meynell assured him that only a few corrections had been made since he delivered the manuscript. For instance, Aubrey de Vere, Father Ryder and even the publisher Kegan Paul, had objected to Wilfrid's question on the nature of a personal deity – 'Has God a smell?'. Meynell had changed it to 'scent'. After publication (May 1878) Meynell reported that the divine Noggs considered it wonderfully good.

As it happened, Blunt's travels among the Bedouin had made the whole Christian argument seem to him redundant. He wrote in his memoirs:

> I found among the bedouin with their 'bird-like minds' [a compliment from Blunt], their happy nonchalance, their plain materialism, their facile consciences, their lack of spiritual fancies, a freedom from all bondage religious or political, above all their practical unbelief in any but the corporal life... a solvent for the puzzles which had perplexed me.... I felt that these wild people were wiser than ourselves. They had solved the riddle of life by refusing to consider it, or even understand that there was a riddle at all. Thus I came back to Europe strengthened and consoled.

Moreover, a new book was superseding *Proteus and Amadeus* in Blunt's mind. His wife, urged by him to conquer her diffidence, was writing up her desert diary into a two-volume travelogue totalling between six and seven hundred pages. Blunt was to contribute the last seven chapters of Volume II, on the geography of Arabia, its tribes, especially the Anazeh, its villages inhabited and deserted, its caravan routes, safe and otherwise, and its horses.

The book was published in 1879 as '*The Bedouin Tribes of the Euphrates* by Lady Anne Blunt, edited with a Preface and some account of the Arabs and their Horses by W.S.B.'. His initials were the furthest Blunt would go as yet towards breaking his anonymity.

Giving full credit to earlier explorers of Arabia – Chesney, Kiepert, Burkhardt, Niebuhr, Layard, Ainsworth, Porter, Tristram, Cunninghame Graham, Palgrave – Blunt nonetheless claimed to have corrected some of his predecessors' mistakes (Chesney had put Tudmur fifty miles too far south and Kiepert placed the Jebel Gorab seventy miles too far south-west) and also marked a line of fresh-water pools near Damascus, with other springs and wells. 'I fear none of this', he added disarmingly, 'will allow us to claim a R.G.S.'s medal.'

The Bedouin's characteristic flaw he summed up as venality; their virtue, hospitality. They were hot-tempered, but not violent, because of the Prophet's veto on alcohol. Without being the least religious in a western sense, they constantly used the name of God: a sick mare had been known to recover when a verse of the Koran was whispered in her ear. Death they neither feared nor thought about. No one was left alone for one instant, so there was no time for brooding. A winding-sheet was a very acceptable present. He predicted a new Bedouin supremacy in the valleys, as the Ottoman empire declined into benevolent impotence and the tribes acquired firearms. 'My sympathy is with them', he concluded, 'and not with progress; and in their interests I cry "long live the sultan".' Then he began to wonder. 'But will no other power appear in the desert?' He envisaged the new power as European, perhaps Russian. Would he have cried, 'Long live oil'?

Towards the end of the Blunts' joint book, Wilfrid had raised the question of deterioration in Bedouin horses north of the Jebel Shammar. What was the cause? He found two answers; lack of stud horses and 'in-and-in-breeding'.

The foundation of the Crabbet Arabian Stud in 1878 was to remedy these defects, not only for Arabia but for the world.

If Skene was the father of the scheme and Blunt its inspiration, Lady Anne bore its labour pains. Without her to write the letters and raise the money, it might have remained for ever a hubble-bubble dream. Among her many achievements was getting her brother Ralph Wentworth involved as a partner in the Stud. A character capable of generous though sometimes evanescent enthusiasms, he promised to send Skene £500 purchase money early in May, raising his share to £750 by the end of June.

At this date the stud was intended to be a triple partnership, with the Blunts and Skenes as the other two. Skene, however, was in financial trouble and dropped out, having performed the essential service of choosing the first horses.

After entering in her diary Ralph's current contributions of £730 on 27 June, Anne went on to deal with their own. 'We (or rather I) £573, so that I must send £157 [to Skene at Aleppo] to be equal with Ralph.' Note the 'we (or rather I)'. It was Anne's money not Wilfrid's. In pointing this out years later, when fierce quarrels had arisen over the Stud, Judith was perfectly correct. On the other hand, her assertion that Ralph put up £10,000 was a piece of characteristic exaggeration. Ralph's share was to reach £1,000 and remain there.

Throughout June and July Anne busied herself with letters and telegrams to the Skenes, visits and letters to Drummonds her bankers, letters to agents and tripartite discussions with Wilfrid and Ralph.[29] She pored over the Stud accounts; these led her on to the more intractable finances of the Crabbet estate.

'I do not quite understand how Wilfrid manages his money matters', she wrote on 28 June. Neither did Wilfrid. Six years as 'Squire' had not served to neutralize his distaste for figures. It was the devoted Anne who discovered the inefficiency of the new Crabbet agent, and how Wilfrid's personal income had been dribbled away on the purchase of 'scraps of land'.

The clouds lifted spectacularly on 2 July when the first horses arrived. They were battered by the journey – bruises, bad eyes, colds, emaciation; but all were loved, and some seemed already to love their new owners. Anne tenderly snipped off a lock of Sherifa's hair and sealed it in an envelope. By September the Stud was improving rapidly, as Anne found when she made two lists of weights – the children's and the mares'. On the thirtieth Wilfrid entered their first horse for a public race – Kars, at Streatham. He did not win but ran well and was much admired in the paddock.

Nevertheless, Wilfrid was becoming restless. He had finished his part of the *Bedouin Tribes*, and announced to Anne that he needed a change from exercising mares. If only the change could be in his social life. But the doors of the Wyndhams and Burrells, and of all those he had scandalized or offended over Parham, were still not open to them. They could look back on only two rewarding visits during the year; Wilfrid to Lord Salisbury and Anne to Edward John Trelawny.

An invitation in April to call on Lord Salisbury, the Foreign Secretary, had come to Wilfrid through Philip Currie, his cousin. Philip had been struck by Wilfrid's clear cut and up-to-date accounts of the Middle East and his idea that Syria and Egypt should combine to loosen the Ottoman stranglehold. Salisbury and Blunt were impressed by one another's personalities but not by all one another's views. Though evidently a live wire, Blunt must not receive encouragement for his dream of a quasi-independent Near and Middle East. For Salisbury had already become secretly involved in the Cyprus agreement with Turkey. On the futility of a Euphrates valley railway, however, Blunt felt that Salisbury not only agreed with him but was strengthened by his eloquence.

Of the venerable Trelawny, Byron's friend, Anne wrote on 20 October:

> He described how Lord Byron would have liked to be a man of action but in the midst of talking about projects and plans, when excited he would rise

from his chair and at that moment suddenly feeling his infirmity would throw himself back with passionate violence.*

It was back to Arabia in November. 'Miseries, oh, Miseries!' Anne lamented. 'But for Wilfrid's sake we *must* go immediately. Good-bye my happy home – God grant *not* for ever.'[30]

* Trelawny told Anne that Byron's lameness was entirely due to his Achilles tendons being too short; very much too short in one foot and slightly in the other. It is generally accepted today that only Byron's right foot was affected, and that it was dysplasic. Trelawny, who described Shelley's wife, Mary, author of *Frankenstein*, as having an 'utterly commonplace mind', had shaken hands with Anne on parting – 'a rare compliment'.

[6]
The Children of Shem 1878–1880

The Blunts' first long journey through Arabia had been for pleasure. This was to be a pilgrimage of exploration – to the Nejd, meaning 'highlands'; the vast desert highlands of Central Arabia which must be approached by way of the Nefud, or 'sand passes', running like fingers into the ocean of sand beyond.[1] Of these sand passes, the explorer William Gifford Palgrave had written in no flattering terms; they were 'daughters of the Great Desert' and bore only too close a resemblance to their 'unamiable mother'.*

For his Arabian journey William Palgrave had disguised himself in 1862–3 as a native travelling doctor or quack, loaded with enough drugs 'to cure half the sick of Arabia'. He in turn had criticized a European explorer for entering Arabia disguised as 'a wandering darweesh' (dervish), since a religious disguise was both immoral and easily spotted. Richard Burton's disguise for his *Pilgrimage to Al Madinah and Meccah* had consisted of a false passport and the name of Dr Abdullah, aged thirty, a British subject. Away with all disguises, said the Blunts. They would be the first European Christians to penetrate the Nejd boldly and openly.

The initial voyage through the Mediterranean was less auspicious than the previous year's. They met a 'restless' Sir Garnet Wolseley in Cyprus – Cyprus, the ill-fated lynch-pin of Disraeli's secret treaty. After a talk with Sir Garnet, Cyprus' first British Governor, Anne wrote in her diary that the island was 'not a desirable place or worth any sacrifices'.[2] That the deal over Cyprus had been thoroughly undesirable was more than confirmed for the Blunts when they met their friends in Damascus. Cyprus, they were told, was 'bakshish' – the tip from Turkey to Britain for services rendered.

The odious word 'bakshish' stung Blunt's pride. Less than ten years

* William Gifford Palgrave, *A Year's Journey Through Central and Eastern Arabia 1862–1863*, Vol. I, p. 90 (1865). In today's maps Nefud is spelt Nafud, and Nejd has become Najd, according to the general change of 'e' into 'a'. Blunt and his contemporaries wrote sheikh, Feysul, Queyt and Meccah; we write Faisul, Kuwait and Makkah – at least on the maps.

had passed since he was a member of H.M.'s foreign service, and he still half believed that his country's diplomatic methods were uniquely pure. 'Bakshish' made him think again.

Because of the disenchantment with his own people and their means of procuring the 'Pax Britannica', Blunt at first felt a magical peace on entering Asia. Anne later agreed that the opening page of their joint book, *A Pilgrimage to Nejd*, should reflect this spell:

> It is strange how gloomy thoughts vanish as one sets foot in Asia. Only yesterday [5 December 1878] we were tossing on the sea of European thought, with its political anxieties, its social miseries and its restless aspirations.... The charm of the East is the absence of intellectual life.... Nobody here thinks of the past or the future, only of the present.

It was pure pleasure to see Medjuel el Mesrab riding to greet them on his white horse, and to spend from 6 to 7.30 p.m. with his wife Mrs Digby on their first day, hearing that their equestrian bargains of last year were the talk of the tribes – 'quite a sensation in the desert'. There were visits to two exiles, the Algerian Abd-el-Kader and the Turk Midhat Pasha; and to Sir Edward Malet on leave from Constantinople. Wilfrid and Mrs Digby agreed that the Blunts should buy a house in Damascus next to theirs ... maybe start up a branch stud ... perhaps get official employment. It was all a delicious part of the 'Pax Asiatica' which substituted harmonious dreams for restless aspirations.

Their preparations for the great journey took them a week. They engaged the emotional but loyal old Hanna to cook for them again, a relative of Hanna's and two camel drivers for their four deluls and four baggage animals. Through the presence of young Mohammed-Ibn-Aruk of Tudmur, they added a romantic quest to their serious explorations – his reunion with relatives living in the desert and the acquisition of a truly *asil* wife from among them, through whom he might uplift his own pedigree. And at the back of Blunt's mind was an even more romantic quest. In the Nejd he now thought to discover the original homeland of the Arabian horse.

The atmosphere of 'Pax Asiatica' was not to last for long. They found themselves marching out through the Damascus gate on Friday 13 December. They both felt 'dark forebodings', though Blunt reassured his wife with the thought that 'it would not be safe to begin a journey in a cheerful frame of mind'.

Their first target was the town of Jof (Al Jawf), 400 miles away, at the southern tip of the Wady Sirhan. After three days travelling along a stony road listening to Mohammed on Bedouin morals and oppressed by heat, flies and a head cold, Blunt regretfully revised his plans about a sequel. If they were to approach Central Arabia by the hazardous route they had chosen – straight across the Nefud and Jebel Shammar – they would arrive too late in the season to continue through Persia into Baluchistan, as he had hoped. Already even Mohammed was feeling the heat and one of the minor sheykhs they met along the route asked the Bey (Blunt) the favour of divining a well for him.

Things looked up for a bit as they entered the Druse territory, where the ruler was 'very ceremonious but not cold', and gave them the best dinner for days: chicken, horseradish vinaigrette, spiced tea, cream cheese and water melons. But soon they were in a 'diabolical' country of volcanic stones, made more horrible on Christmas Eve by a huge *khabra* or rink of cracked mud varnished so that it looked like water. Blunt shot a young camel for their Christmas dinner (it tasted fine, between beef and mutton), but during Christmas night an icy wind blew down their ill-secured tent. They crouched under the ruins till dawn, their eyes full of sand, and next day battled against a violent sandstorm. The camels, seen through a haze of sand and swept along in a huddle, with noses stretched out and ropes flying, looked 'gigantic and helpless', wrote Blunt in his diary, 'like antediluvian creatures in the flood'. Their ark turned out to be a high cliff at whose base reigned a strange and blessed calm. Here they camped, only to suffer a worse misfortune on the following morning.[3]

Anne was leaning over arranging something on the offside of her saddle when her delul sprang forward, pitching her over its head on to her left side and seriously injuring her left knee. She somehow managed to mount her mare and to continue the journey, writing in her diary: 'I think to have been awkward and a fool is worse than the pain though that is bad enough.'[4]

The evil results of Anne's sprain were quickly apparent. After resting on the twenty-eighth in a hospitable village with palm gardens and a black stone castle built by successors of the Prophet, they entered a depressing land of salt lakes and wretched communities (a consumptive child lay dying in a street) all paying tribute to Ibn Rashid at distant Hail. Even the locusts were torpid with cold – though easier therefore to fry – and the camels developed a raging thirst through eating salty vegetation. Blunt celebrated New Year's Day 1879 by losing his voice. But there was a burst of sunshine and high spirits on 3 January, which tempted him and Anne to gallop to the top of a hill, where they dismounted, tying their mares to some bushes, and began to unpack their 'mid-day mouthful' of bread and mishmash. Suddenly they heard the thud of hooves and saw twelve Bedouin horsemen coming for them at full tilt. Mohammed had taught Blunt to distinguish the Roala from other tribes by the thickness of their spears, and these twelve spears were extremely thick.

Blunt shouted to Anne, '*Ghazu!* Get on your mare!' They might have got away, but the tied horse and agonizing sprain prevented her from mounting in time. No questions were asked by the raiders or words spoken. Their motto was, 'Strike first, talk afterwards'. In the silent scuffle Anne was knocked down and Wilfrid, after being prodded by half a dozen lances, had his head and left arm belaboured by the butt of his own unloaded gun, until the stock broke. Then he heard Anne's wise words of surrender, '*Ana dahilak*', and repeated them himself. After which there were no more beatings, but enquiries at last from their captors as to who they were and where they were going.

Blunt, whose Arabic could be fluent in emergency, replied, 'To Jof; and be as good as to come to the caravan and you shall hear all.' Permission was granted and down the hill they both walked, Anne hobbling, for their mares had been seized. But once at the caravan, the Roala were in for a disagreeable surprise. It emerged that their prisoners had enjoyed the hospitality of one of their own sheykhs last year, and so their persons and property were sacrosanct. 'Ah, the beautiful mares, the beautiful gun', they lamented loudly as they handed their prizes back to the Blunts, and sat down to the consolations of the best dates in Nejd.

When the Blunts reached Jof two days later, Wilfrid had a sheep killed which he had vowed if they escaped. Anne had not yet forgotten her humiliation. Never again, she vowed, would she tie a horse to a bush. As for Wilfrid, bumps and bruises were the only concrete results of the *ghazu*, for his turban had saved his head and his layers of clothing had proved even thicker than the Roala spears. Anne reported that he now found it 'interesting' to have been '*taken*'.[5]

Was she frightened? they asked her. There had not been time. But the question gave an opportunity for the 'teasing creature' that always lurked inside Wilfrid to get a rise out of her. *He* was frightened, he said, and had almost left her in the lurch. For once she refused to believe him.

The first thing they had to do at Jof was to win permission from the governor to cross the Nefud with a guide provided by him. For this purpose they endured the terrible meal sent to their tent which only Wilfrid could eat. Anne described it as masses of soppy bread with lumps of floating pumpkin. Later they admired his two twelve-pound cannon called Nassr and Mansur, partook of wild cow and lemonade with him and watched a sword dance. Anne called him a tyrant. But he produced the necessary guide, after assuring them that the way to Hail and Riad (modern Ryadh, capital of Najd) was perfectly free from robbers – 'all persons found away from the high roads have their heads cut off'.

On the first day in Jof Wilfrid discovered a Painted Lady butterfly on a rock. His lifelong interest in butterflies told him that the nearest food for caterpillars of this species was at Hebron, 400 miles away across the Dead Sea. If a Painted Lady could cover that distance, an indomitable, unpainted lady could surely do half that amount – the two hundred miles across the Nefud – despite a lame leg.

Their second task was to arrange for the marriage of Mohammed, for some of the relatives he was seeking were at Jof. Anne selected a doe-eyed girl from the harem, while Blunt took the chair at the bargaining conference, persuading the girl's father that she could be married before her older sister and himself paying the bride price of £50. Mohammed had fallen passionately in love simply by talking about her. As Anne shrewdly observed, Arabs never saw young ladies, and so to talk about one was enough.[6]

At last, on 12 January, they were ready to start. Blunt kissed his male 'relations' all round, Anne doing her bare duty in the harem (which she thankfully found did not involve wholesale kissing) and, with dates, bread, a kid and eight water-skins, they set out for the first well of the Nefud. There would be only one other well, situated about two-thirds of the way across. The whole journey should take them ten days, instead of the thirteen required for the longer but safer route. They had chosen this road, 'if only to see the Nefud at its worst'. To them it had always been the *ne plus ultra* of deserts, the object of all their dreams.

In a state of something like exaltation, they stepped out on to the *hamad* or plain that represented 'the shore of the great Nefud'. It was absolutely level, absolutely bare of vegetation and black in colour. On and on they rode southwards towards a black horizon.[7]

A sudden shout on the thirteenth, 'The Nefud!' They could not believe it. The colour was so extraordinary, so unlike the sand colour they had expected. Wilfrid saw it as deep red gravel with a slight layer of white saltpetre. Anne saw it in terms of every Victorian's favourite aperient, rhubarb and magnesia.* 'Yet the Nefud it was', Anne wrote, 'the great red desert of Central Arabia. In a few minutes we cantered up to it, and our mares were standing with their feet in its first waves.'

Bright red in the morning dew, the sand was not watered by a single spring, yet it was far from barren even in January. Matted vines and bushes grew everywhere, and several kinds of grass would multiply in the spring rains. The Nefud was in fact the home of many Bedouin tribes during a great part of the year. Its waterless condition and the scarcity of wells did not worry them. Their female camels were in milk.

Spirits were still high at the first wells – the wells of Shakik, which

* Sir Henry Bulwer a hypochondriac, when minister at Washington, had welcomed his nephew Robert Lytton as attaché with the words: 'You look tired; would you like a drink?' He then sent for a rhubarb and magnesia. (Neville Lytton, *The English Country Gentleman*, p. 225.)

they reached on the fifteenth. Their heavily laden caravan, noisy with singing and story-telling, had been ploughing the desert waves in solitude. At the wells there was no other caravan, but the remains of a Roala *ghazu* that had got lost in the Nefud ten years ago while raiding the Shammar. There were also desert larks, linnets, a pair of kestrels, house-flies, huge black ants and purple flowers. As they filled their water-skins for the last time before reaching their second oasis at Jobba, Blunt had to issue warnings to his merry men; one drink a day, or they would all die of thirst. In front of them lay a hundred miles of fathomless sand.

On their first day out of Shakik a thunderstorm made the sand firm enough for galloping; an uncovenanted blessing which in fact was to save their lives. The camel-drivers sang, while Blunt made notes on two red and black sandstone *tels* they reached on the sixteenth. These *tels*, or Rocks of Aalem, were welcome landmarks, showing they had not lost their way. But the view from the top, though splendid, was intimidating: a blood-red desert landscape, the rounded crests and 'red-hot' waves of which Palgrave had written, rolling on to a fiery horizon. They seemed to be winding and tacking aimlessly through it, up on to hilltops, down into troughs, though always skirting the dreaded *fuljes* or bottomless pits. On the two following days there were black frosts. Carcases of camels lay around and they saw wolf tracks. During the second evening the hills of Jobba came into view, backed by the pale blue range of the Jebel Shammar. Would they ever reach Jobba, far less the hills of Nejd? Anne at least captured the hills in a careful drawing.

The crunch came on the nineteenth, though this utterly dry sand did not crunch but sucked in the camels' feet, so that one delul broke down completely and more and more of the baggage had to be off-loaded on to the towering Hatheran. Then the men had to walk, barefoot, all except Blunt, who cursed himself for being so manifestly less valiant than the Sons of Shem. And the singing had to stop, just as Palgrave described: 'The boisterous gaiety of the Bedouins soon died out.' When their water ran out a new sound arose: prayers to Allah. They were making only a little over one mile an hour. Everywhere there were clouds of locusts. 'A terrible day for camels and men', wrote Blunt in his diary. But Allah had heard their prayers – indeed, how should he not hear, having already sent the saving thunderstorm which had enabled them to make good time at the beginning? That very evening they saw the oasis of Jobba.

After the ocean of red sand, the green of Jobba's gardens seemed the brightest in the world and its purple and mauve sandstone cliffs veined with yellow sounded, as described by Anne, more like a giant bed of crocuses than rocks. Its sheykh, though only in his twenties, gracefully did the honours of an excellent mutton stew and wheat mishmash. After a day's rest they plunged back into the crimson rollers, but the evenings were now pleasant 'without onward feats of strength'. Wilfrid found orange caterpillars and coffee-coloured beetles, and drew the long-haired Nejd sheep which could go without water for thirty days; Anne wrote the musical notation of the desert lark's song, from G to D, and then six short and one long note on D; their Bedouin were singing again and turning somersaults down the sandhills. Before them, the blurred blue ridge of the Jebel Shammar, natural bastion of Nejd, had defined itself as fantastic gothic pinnacles and ramparts.

When they reached the first village in the plain of Hail, they sent ahead one of their servants with letters of introduction to the emir Mohammed Ibn Rashid. How would he receive them? Spine-chilling stories had been fed to them, of his usurping the throne after murdering all his brothers and nephews. Never mind, said Wilfrid, as they sat on a rock to write their diaries, they would die happy after seeing Jebel Shammar, 'even if we have our heads cut off in Hail'. Wilfrid's maxim had hitherto been, 'All places are alike.' Now he confessed to knowing of no beauty like this; Mount Sinai was *like*, but less lovely.

They entered the granite streets of Hail on 23 January, to find that a house had been prepared for them. A scarlet chamberlain received them in the palace courtyard, among crowds of soldiers, pilgrims and supplicants, and led them into a reception room seventy feet long by thirty wide, its ceiling supported on five huge pillars. After days of tents or huts, it seemed scarcely credible. Suddenly there was a buzz; the emir, strongly guarded by an immense throng of soldiers, entered; the two Blunts advanced with outstretched hands, then all sat, to hear Wilfrid's speech of pleasure. After a breakfast of dates rolled in bread and dipped in melted butter, the emir accepted the Blunts' gifts and took them on a tour of his estate.

Beginning with his gardens where he showed them his cheetahs, gazelles and antelopes, they passed on to the stables, filled with his treasured Nejd mares, all about fourteen hands, many greys, some from Feysul's great stud; and so through to the palace kitchens, in which were seven vast cauldrons each capable of boiling three whole camels. The sovereign of Hail did not forget to show them 'his latest toy', a telephone.

Next day they were given a glimpse of the great Persian pilgrimage, or Haj, camped outside the city walls. Anne noted in her diary, 'too *much rubbish* and too many *rags*' among the pilgrims, (though some were rich Persians) and was glad they could not accompany the Haj.[8]

Years later Wilfrid was to describe their visit to the emir in a throw-away manner, as if it had been 'from one country gentleman to another',[9] one of the gentlemen being accompanied by his wife. The other, however, had seemed at the time more like Richard III than a country gentleman. Anne remarked how thin, sallow and careworn the emir looked; Wilfrid noted the restless, claw-like hands for ever playing with the hem of his tunic, and deep-set eyes. 'It was the very type of a conscience-stricken face, or of one which fears an assassin.'[10]

A trivial incident reminded them that, country gentlemen apart, they were still Christians among Asiatics, indeed among Wahhabis, the most fanatical of Islamic sects.

Mohammed's marital success had gone to his head. He let it be known that *he* was the great man of the party, his the gifts; the Blunts were creatures of no account. Emir Ibn Rashid was too polite to ask questions, but quietly had the Blunts' rich food changed to camel meat and ceased to invite them to his audiences. No more delicious lamb joints on rice, no boiled ostrich egg for breakfast.

Wilfrid discovered the cause of the trouble, Mohammed was 'put in his place', and the emir quietly renewed his attentions.[11] But the Blunts had learnt their lesson. They decided to stay no longer provided they could make a decorous exit. Nor would the horses of Nejd detain them. The Hail stud had been something of a disappointment. In their shaggy winter coats the emir's mares could not compare with the Gomussa studs in Mesopotamia – always kept sleek and fit, ready for a *ghazu* – and the Blunts gathered that Ibn Saoud's stud in Riad was no more spectacular. Nejd was the land of the camel.

One other report may have caused a suspicion of disappointment. There was talk in Hail of a Christian gentleman who, *undisguised* and with little Arabic, had got there just before them. This was Charles Montagu Doughty, best-selling author of *Travels in Arabia Deserta*. But as Doughty did not publish his two immense volumes until 1888 – by then replete with Arabic words as well as English archaisms – the Blunts beat him to it, at least in print, by bringing out their own two volumes seven years before his. Nevertheless, Doughty too had seen the 'sand-pools' of the great Nefud; he too had sketched the weird sandstone hills looking like human heads and hands. So the Blunts' summary of this part of their journey was incorrect: 'No European nor Christian of any sort', they wrote, 'had penetrated *as such* before us to Jebel Shammar.'

A way of decorous retreat from Hail while the going remained good was opened up to the Blunts by Ibn Rashid himself. He took them into the plain where the Haj was waiting to depart, and gave them and the leader of the Haj a breathtaking display or 'fantasia' by his mares. The Blunts again had to revise their opinion of the little Nejd horse. For dash and agility it was incomparable.

They also made friends with the pilgrim's leader, one Ali Koli Khan, whose father turned out to be Khan of the great Bactiari tribe in the wild mountains north-east of the Persian Gulf. Here, they learnt, was a marvellous Arabian stud. Despite Anne's reservations, they decided to join the Haj (though camping apart), travel with the pilgrims to Baghdad and visit Ali Koli in Persia. Anything seemed possible in that desert air, 4,000 feet above sea level. They wanted to shout and sing, like the emir's curveting horsemen. They thought there could be no air so pure except perhaps on the moon.

They left with the Persian Haj on 1 February. The Blunts, especially Anne, got no thrills whatever from the proximity of 3,000 pilgrims with all their '*rags* and *rubbish*', and 5,000 camels. Nevertheless Anne meticulously described the three-mile-long procession, headed by dervishes and a green and red banner. Buzzards and ravens sat around looking out for locusts to eat or anything better. Many camels died including one of their own, and they continually passed animals' skeletons as well as the bones of 'plague pilgrims'. In a sandstorm near Mershid, Ali Koli was lost, reported dead; but they found Mohammed Ali's Aruk relatives and made a detour to visit them. The sheykh Mutlakh Ibn Aruk's excellent manners had a salutary effect upon Mohammed. In his thankfulness to the Blunts for finding his lost tribe he composed a ballad:

> Oh Lord keep safe my brother and the khatun [Anne] ...
> Guide them through Persia and far Hind [India] ...
> Let them once more behold their friends and London
> Let them relate the things that they have done.

This Aruk tribe also needed the Lord's help. They were almost starving owing to the failure of autumn rains. But for the locusts, they and their horses and camels would all have died. As Anne noted, 'Locusts eat everything green and everything that moves eats locusts'.

The prayer in Mohammed's ballad – 'Let them relate the things that they have done' – was generously answered. Ever since reaching Hail, Wilfrid had been drafting and adding to a long account of their travels for the Royal Geographical Society, with special reference to each *fulje* or deep pit in the Nefud, all the wells both on the outward and return journeys to Hail and the return to Baghdad, and such archeological touches as caught their fancy: Phoenician inscriptions and animal drawings on the Nefud rocks, the reservoirs of Queen Zobeydeh (only vaguely indicated on Chesney's map), Babylonian brick kilns, and the Tower of Babel just above the horizon. And from the residency at Baghdad, which they reached on 6 March, telegrams were sent out far and wide; among others to Mrs Pollen at Newbuildings, to Mrs Digby in Damascus and to Lady Lytton in Calcutta. For the desert had changed Blunt's mind for him on several points.

His 'thirst for exploration had not yet slaked', as Anne somewhat ruefully put it, and Minnie must be mother to Judith (as well as her own ten) for another half-year. Though it was pleasant for Anne to sleep in a bed again, Wilfrid could not forget the excitement of having hunted a hyena in the Nefud with his two greyhounds, shooting it and making a memorable meal off it in his 'house of hair'. He had turned against the idea of a house in town. Better the Bactiari than Baghdad or Britain; Ali Koli Khan was now reported alive and well. They resolved to visit him in his mountains. Who could tell what treasures they might find in a Bactiari stud? Anne telegraphed to the Vicereine of India, Lady Lytton, in Calcutta; 'En route from Central Arabia to Persia. Shall we pay you a visit April or May?'

They had become progressively more independent in their desert journeys. Now they were forced willy-nilly to stand on their own feet. All their old servants had been paid off. The Residency provided them with a trustworthy *kavass*, Hajji Mohammed, but within nine days of their start they were to have no other servants whatever. As a sign of Blunt's self-reliance, he had agreed to assist an African explorer, Captain Cameron, who was mapping a possible railway from Tripoli to Karachi. Both parties would start from Baghdad and join up at Bushire on the Gulf – the Blunts taking the dangerous route east of the Tigris and leaving the easier west bank to the experienced Cameron.

The Blunts left Baghdad on 20 March in a deluge. Almost at once, the local peasants brought Wilfrid piteous tales of devastation wrought by wild boars. Would not the great Bey rid the land of these pests? A boar-hunt was better than a hyena-hunt any day. Blunt rode forth on his mare Ariel like one of the seven champions of Christendom and slew five boars and a sow on the first day. On the second day, 23 March, he set out again, taking his lady and a crowd of attendants with him. A giant among boars was located, rust-red and villainous; Blunt wounded him twice, but as the men dashed in for the kill, he suddenly sprang up and charged. 'Turn him!' shouted Blunt to Anne, but instead, 'he turned me', wrote Anne, 'coming at me with a savage grunt and toss of his head'. In a moment he was among them all, Blunt whirled Ariel round and fired again, mortally wounding the boar, but not before he had tossed Ariel and her rider into the air, 'as in a bullring'. Blunt escaped all injury but Ariel's leg was caught by the tusks and terribly gashed. They staunched the wound with dung and bound it with their head handkerchiefs, but their beautiful Ariel had to be sent back to Baghdad.* For Anne, the journey was already 'ill-starred'.

* According to legend, desert sand rather than dung was the styptic which saved King Abdullah's life in 1818, fanned into the wound by the wings of loyal locusts.

Two more days, and they had lost a camel by death and their cook and a groom by desertion. Hailstones fell on the twenty-eighth as big as dates. They reached the turbid river Tibb the next day, servantless but for Hajji, and had to load and drive their camels across themselves.

They were actually worse than servantless, for they had come up with forty Arabs of the poverty-stricken, degraded Beni Laam tribe, travelling to Dizful to 'buy' corn. They refused to help the Blunts over the Tibb but asked 'impertinent questions' or galloped around, wrote Anne, 'shouting out their unasked for advice. It was very annoying'. She likened them to a gang of roughs on Epsom Downs. Nevertheless they had to use the Beni Laam as guides for lack of any others. Hajji muttered that they were not 'respectable Bedouins', but Khurdish robbers – in fact forty thieves. Their leader Ghafil, added Anne, had a squint, his second-in-command Saadun only one eye and all had 'a soft manner with great flabby faces, and a black look in their eyes, which, with their rows of glittering white teeth, give one a shudder'. But if these thieves made them shudder, it was only man who was vile in this lovely no-man's-land between Turkey and Persia. The sun shone and they rode through grass and flowers knee-deep in every hollow.

Next night Hajji, who was a Suni like their previous servants and therefore fair game for these Shias, crept to the Beni Laam camp-fire after dark and overheard a plot to murder and rob the 'kaffirs' (infidels). Indeed Anne was woken by one-eyed Ghafil lifting their tent-flap. 'Who goes there?' she cried, as if she were a stout British sentry at one of the thousands of outposts of empire. Wilfrid made her promise to gallop on her mare straight for the next river if they were separated, where she might find a friendly tribe. But Ghafil withdrew, though he remained prowling round 'like a hyena' all night.

Thanks to Wilfrid's expertise they got their camels safely across the next river, Dueri. Impressed, the forty thieves began to call Wilfrid 'Bey', instead of 'kaffir'. He assured Anne that Ghafil's Arabs would never assist him to murder them, since the Blunts were technically Ghafil's guests and might even be needed to fight off a Persian attack. The poor Beni Laam were great cowards.

They crossed the Kerkha, swollen with melted snow, on a raft, accompanied by the shouted comments of the forty thieves on their camels' chances of survival: 'Yetla!' 'Ma yetla' – 'he's over' 'He isn't'. But they all got over, and on the other side the Blunts presented letters of introduction to the local chieftain, one Kerim Khan, the most powerful chief of Luristan after Husseyn Koli Khan of the Bactiari, their friend's father. Having crossed two more streams and then the great River Diz, they found themselves in Dizful town, prepared for once to enjoy the 'blessings of civilization' in the shape of police and soldiers. The forty thieves were at last shaken off.

Anne found Dizful a 'tiresome city' despite its beautiful plain studded with shady canora trees and dells full of anemones and borage. The Persians were even more interfering than the Arabs, a hundred at a time standing around advising, or asking 'foolish questions', instead of helping them prepare for their next stage, from Dizful to Shustar, taking in Husseyn Koli Khan who was reported to be camped somewhere between the two. Horses had to be shod, mangy camels doctored.

Why were these Persians so impertinent? Hajji Mohammed, their servant, cleared up the mystery. The Blunts were not using the 'respectable road' or wearing respectable clothes or travelling with an escort of fifty men and a respectable number of servants, namely twenty-five.

Far from being mistaken for Queen Victoria's cousin, as Anne had once been in Spain, it was not quite certain that she was an honest woman, or that Blunt was not a Bedouin outcast. Indeed their ragged, commonplace clothes and laborious do-it-yourself mode of travel had brought the old argument about disguises full circle. Their determination to be themselves – white explorers with a practical preference for the clothes of the country – acted in the end as a most unwelcome disguise. And they were both, of course, sunburnt and naturally dark, Anne with black eyes and hair. When she once rolled back her Bedouin sleeve and showed a white wrist, there was utter amazement. If they had read Richard Burton more carefully they might have carried with them some better clothes. 'Throughout the East', he had written in his *Pilgrimage to Al-Madinah and Meccah*, 'a badly dressed man is a pauper, and, as in England, a pauper . . . is a scoundrel.'[12]

Their meeting with the great Husseyn Koli Khan kept up the 'ill-starred' record of their journey. He was on the way to Teheran and therefore could not invite them to his mountain fastnesses nor show them his mares. This was a crushing blow.* Nevertheless he was hospitable; he gave them excellent tea, poured *into* the hot water, which made it taste less bitter.

Nothing could have been more bitter than Shustar, and the fate that befell Wilfrid there. For Anne, it was to have dramatic consolations.

After they had turned their faces away from the lovely, snow-capped line of the Bactiari mountains, they realized that the heat was becoming insupportable. It was already April. They must make for

* The Blunts' views on the horses would have been invaluable. Nearly a hundred years later they have been saved from extinction and their Stud Book accepted by the World Arab Horse Organization. (Information from Peter Upton.)

Shustar and the Gulf at once. Had not Wilfrid cheerfully announced, while they were debating the journey in Baghdad, that if it became too hot they could always get down to the Gulf 'at any moment'?

Shustar was approached by a fifty-foot-high road-bridge over a deafening weir, which they could see through huge holes in the road, large enough for their camels to fall through. They were put in the absent governor's 'fairy pavilion', with a fountain, terrace and exquisite view of the river and natural parkland. 'Here at Shustar', wrote Anne under the date 7 April, 'our troubles were thought to end. So little can one foresee what is to come.'

On the night of the eighth Wilfrid went down with violent dysentery. Two days later, still very weak, he decided to leave this stifling inferno at all costs. But the governor's agent prevented their exit on the excuse that it was unsafe to travel without an escort of 2,000 horsemen. When Blunt tried to telegraph the legation at Teheran, his message was stopped. To the agent, however, it seemed that a man who tried to send a telegram must be respectable. He gave the Blunts an escort of seven. By now Anne's only aim was to get Wilfrid to Bushire alive.

They made an unlucky start on Friday the eleventh. After loading in the hot sun and riding all day Wilfrid was again desperately ill, and delirious all night. Anne treated him with homeopathic bryonia and laudanum. (For dysentery Richard Burton had recommended 'a purge and extract of opium'.)

Next morning Wilfrid, somewhat revived by Anne's cold tea, was lifted on to a delul, having decided that they should proceed but only by night (though the clouds of flies clung to their heads even in the dark), Anne taking the starry Scorpion as a guide. Their camp on the thirteenth was covered with spiked grass like fish-hooks that invaded their bedding.

At dawn on the fifteenth they saw the town of Ram Hormuz in the distance. Wilfrid suddenly felt an impulse to ride again on his mare. Before they knew quite what was happening, he and Anne had broken into a wild gallop, their two greyhounds Sheikha and Sayad bounding joyfully ahead. As Wilfrid drank orange-flavoured tea in Ram Hormuz with the ferraz-bashi (governor) and camped in a garden of pomegranates and nightingales, he realized that he was cured. To him it was a miracle – but a miracle wrought by human will-power, speed and the rush of healing air.

Anne's experience had been quite different but characteristic of her secretive and sensitive nature. She had finally become convinced of Christianity on the day after Wilfrid's delirium, when he rose from what had seemed his death-bed and was carried out to his camel under the stars. God – who else? – had answered her prayers.

Associated with this day was a vision; though it was a year before Anne disclosed the exact place on the road to Bushire (rather than Damascus, as it were) that the vision had been granted to her. It was in fact outside Shustar on the twelfth, when she first left their tent. She saw the heavens opening and a vision of her three dead children in glory.

Her mind was now made up to become a Catholic. But it was to be a year before she told Wilfrid of her intention, nearly forty before she disclosed to him its cause. The nature of her vision was never known to him.*

From pomegranates and nightingales to what Anne called 'a feverish dream of heat and flies' for the last lap. Through the dream they saw the shadowy crossings of three more rivers, sometimes deep, but the camels by now were used to swimming; a descent through a pass leading to a plain swarming with cuckoos, bee-birds, doves and francolins; constant alarms of robbers necessitating their sleeping under arms; a first sight of the Gulf, 'simmering like melted lead to the horizon'. They saw Bushire on 28 April. More startling, Bushire saw them. These ragged 'Bedouin' strangers, one of them gaunt and wasted to a skeleton – they had no business at the Residency. The smartly dressed sepoys barred the door with their muskets. 'Now we shall be sent away', said Wilfrid sardonically. But Mr Edwards the agent received them, introducing them to the 'small pleasures of washing and of eating and drinking like Christians'.

In their book they were to call the Arabian part of their journey a 'pilgrimage' and the Persian part a 'campaign'. Looking back, they were still amazed after a year by the distance they had covered – a 2,000-mile trek overland from the Mediterranean to the Persian Gulf, 500 miles of it driving their camels unaided through country said to be impossible.

Wilfrid commented that Anne had passed over the risks 'lightly' in their book, and he in his memoirs emphasized their months of hard manual work, with no one to help but Hajji the Turkish *kavass*, loading and unloading camels, swimming them and the horses across rivers, freighting goat-skin rafts, pitching tents; and all 'under arms', because of dangerous company. Wilfrid had nearly died of dysentery and Anne according to Judith (though this was an exaggeration) had dislocated both knees and her right shoulder and broken several ribs.†

If Anne had treated their hardships lightly in their book, she did not

* The full story was told by Anne only to her granddaughter and namesake, Anne Lytton.

† The injury to Anne's other knee took place in the following year, October 1880, when Judith herself accidentally trod on her mother's dress as she walked downstairs.

do so in letters to her brother Ralph. Their Persian 'campaign' she described to him on 30 April as fit only to be damned with six Ds – 'not only disagreeable, difficult, dangerous, and all but disastrous, but disappointing and disheartening.... Wilfrid will *never* want to go *any* hard journey again, I will swear to that!'[13] She was right.

The explorer David George Hogarth in his *Penetration of Arabia* (1905) considered that the risks taken on the Nejd 'pilgrimage' had been fully justified by what the Blunts had discovered about Arabia and its people, despite their being amateurs equipped only with compass, barometer, skilful pens and paint-brushes, sharp eyes, intense curiosity and guns. Hogarth particularly approved of their 'imaginative sympathy with Bedawin society... their actual narrative will bear comparison with any other....'[14]

In Wilfrid Blunt's opinion their Persian 'campaign' was equally valuable, for it pointed out the contrast between a free Arab society as in the Jebel Shammar and Nejd, and an oppressed national minority such as the Beni Laam, corrupted by an alien empire. At present the positive beauties of the Bedouin way of life were uppermost in Blunt's mind, rather than the burden of Turkish imperialism. He acknowledged later that perhaps he had idealized these primitive peoples, seeing no difference between nineteenth-century emirs – the Ibn Saouds and Ibn Rashids – and the kings of Arabia who had brought their gifts to Solomon. Nevertheless, writing as late as 1915 in his unfinished 'Religion of Happiness', he still remembered the Bedouin as

> a people... more moral than their neighbours and free from all contemptible crime, whose public life was based not in word only but in fact on those three principles so much abused in Europe, Liberty, Equality and Brotherhood.[15]

When Doughty's *Arabia Deserta* eventually came out in 1888 the world was to see the black spots that Blunt had omitted from his picture: the rampant diseases in Hail, headed by ophthalmia and dysentery; the exorcists and superstitions; the hypochondria raging among a third of all Arabians; the feuds and factions that rent the whole country. Looking solely, however, at the Bedouin villages, Doughty was to take the Blunt line: 'Under the mild and just judgment of their home-born sheykhs' they were in truth 'happy'.*

Wilfrid had only a few days in which to digest his thoughts before he and Anne were off again. For a letter had awaited them at Bushire

* Sir Henry Layard in his *Discoveries in the Ruins of Nineveh and Babylon* (1853), p. 291, wrote that the Bedouin villages were relatively free from disease compared with the towns, their chief enemies being ophthalmia and rheumatism. Cure for the latter: place the affected limb inside the reeking skin of a freshly slaughtered sheep. The Boers in South Africa were curing gangrene in the same way.

inviting them to visit the Viceroy and Vicereine of India at Simla. At the court of King Robert, Blunt was to leave the entirely male society of the desert and plunge back into a mixed white society – with the usual results. But for the first time he would also see the Sons of Japhet as a ruling caste, they and their works to be judged against life among the free Children of Shem.

'You tell me you are going to Simla', wrote his radical friend Harry Brand on 18 May 1879. 'You must take care of yourself there. For a man of your quick temperament, and lively sympathies Simla is a dangerous place. I fully expect to hear of you in some scrape before the winter.'[16]

Health, not morals or politics, was Anne's anxiety. After landing at Karachi from the Persian Gulf, she telegraphed Lady Lytton to send help if Wilfrid's health broke down again during the long rail journey up the Indus valley to Lahore. But nothing untoward occurred; indeed, there was a pleasurable moment when they saw their *Bedouin Tribes of the Euphrates* advertised in a Lahore newspaper by a Calcutta bookseller. At 3 p.m. on 16 May the 'sharp eyes' of Wilfrid were the first to detect the viceregal flag through the cedars and rhododendrons above them, as they were carried, first in tongas and finally in jampans, up the steep winding road to the high saddle on which Simla was built, over 7,000 feet above sea level. They were welcomed to Peterhof, the Viceroy's glorified country house, by Edith Lytton, 'more lovely than ever', according to Anne, and by Robert who seemed 'fatigued' though not actually ill. To the Viceroy and Vicereine, their visitors looked frankly extraordinary; both travel-worn to a degree, and Anne 'quite the wanderer' in a straight white woollen skirt (ladies' skirts were normally full) and wearing one of her more inventive hats made of a red silk handkerchief tied under her chin with a cap perched on top – and of course no ball dresses in her baggage. One of Lady Lytton's beautiful gowns sent out by Worth of Paris was adapted for Lady Anne to wear at dinner next day.[17]

Now began a whirl of parties, balls, 'rinking' (roller-skating), theatricals, a gymkhana and the Viceroy's Cup, for which Anne and Wilfrid entered the two mares they had brought with them. (Afterwards they sent home a horse from India, Hadban, which was to have a lasting influence on the Crabbet Stud.) Robert's conversation at dinner struck Anne as dazzling and daring. There seemed to be only one flaw in his character; he kept a medium, a boy of ten years old, whose frivolous information about the next world shocked her. The highlight of her diary was the grand ball on the Fourth of June. Supper was a triumph of the art of Bonsard, Lytton's French chef: soups, truffles, stuffed eggs, foie gras – 'unfortunately I did not get hold of the Pâté'.

Wilfrid's first impression was of mingled simplicity and grandeur in the British way of life, here in this remote hill station on the edge of the Empire. It was due, he realized, in no small part to a dichotomy in the Viceroy's own nature between imperial glory and bohemianism. One note of simplicity was struck by the small chalets in which guests stayed, so that they could eat magnificently at Peterhof but enjoy solitude when they wished. Edith Lytton had remarked that society at Simla was either 'dowdy' or 'fast'. Wilfrid was to analyse the fast set more closely, detecting certain conventionalities even in this 'very immoral' Anglo-Indian world. These his friend Robert flouted. He smoked cigarettes at all times and did not go to church on Sundays. If the spirit moved him, he would sit the whole evening talking to one pretty woman on a sofa, instead of doing the rounds of his guests. It was only the tact and charm of Edith that saved him from severe criticism. His attitude to men was equally remarked upon. 'My dearest fellow' was his regular way of addressing members of his council; and Wilfrid himself witnessed the Viceroy strolling up and down the lawn with his arm around the neck of his Finance Minister, Sir John Strachey. Wilfrid found the sight deliciously amusing, since the object of the Viceroy's embraces was a bilious, bespectacled and elderly official who walked with his head habitually on one side, 'like a sick raven'. Others found the display lacking in decorum.

One of the prettiest women with whom Lytton flirted was his private secretary's young wife, Mrs Batten. Lytton's dalliance, however, was strictly limited, owing to the security imposed on the Viceroy's court after Lord Mayo's assassination. Guards were on duty day and night. Mrs Batten divined in Blunt a better proposition. She made him her confidant from the very first evening, complaining of a husband much older than herself whom she did not love, and regaling him with her own love-affairs and those of all Simla. He summed her up as 'gay, fond of pleasure, quite depraved, but tinged too with romance'. For the present he went no further than to let Mrs Batten know that she attracted him.

At Simla it was politics that took hold of Blunt's imagination. Afterwards he was to feel that he and Lytton had awakened one another's latent desires: Lytton's for romance and irresponsible freedom, his own for 'achieving something in the great world of men'.

Blunt had reached Simla at a crucial moment for Lytton. The Viceroy had been conducting the Afghan War by telegraph from Simla, assisted by his abnormally self-confident military secretary, George Colley. Lytton's own self-confidence was based, it seemed, as much on superstition as on military expertise. One day he took Blunt with him to see some fire balloons, 'by whose directions of ascent he augured his military success or failure'. When the Afghan War was apparently brought to a triumphant end by the Treaty of Gandamak, Lytton duly noted that Blunt was with him at the signing. To him, Blunt had been born under a lucky star and was bringing his friends luck. But Blunt's magic did not work for the three men at Simla with whom he had been connected over the Afghan War. Major Cavagnari (soon to be Sir Louis), who had become friends with Blunt after negotiating the Treaty of Gandamak, was sent back to Afghanistan in July as British agent; he and his staff were assassinated less than two months later. Within two years, in February 1880, Sir George Colley met his death, Blunt thought by his own hand, at the battle of Majuba Hill.

As for Lord Lytton, General Roberts was temporarily to save him by reoccupying Kabul in October 1879. But a more subtle enemy than the khans of Kabul and Kandahar was on Lytton's trail. Though a Liberal in youth, Lytton had become publicly associated with Disraeli's glittering (and Tory) imperialism. When Disraeli's supremacy collapsed at the general election of 1880, Lytton resigned also. Liberal opinion already disliked him, and was to dislike him even more, as the alleged cause of the Second Afghan War.

Meanwhile during May and June of 1879 at Simla, Lytton's belief in Blunt's mystique led him to pour a stream of confidences, political and private, into his friend's attentive ear; Blunt kept a small red note-book entitled 'Notes of a Conversation with Lytton at Simla, May 20th, 1879.'[18] The main point made by Lytton was that the war in Afghanistan (the First Afghan War) was necessary in order to establish a 'scientific frontier' between India and Russia – 'not for the sake of extension of territory' but to prevent Russia from absorbing Afghanistan. The war, added Lytton, was demanded by Indian public opinion. Other notes followed on Indian finance, the salt tax, military establishment, public works and depreciation of silver, as well as draft letters from Blunt to various friends.

In view of the red note-book there is reason to believe the truth of Blunt's assertion in his 'Alms to Oblivion': 'Thus for these few weeks I may truly say that the whole machinery of the Indian government was laid bare to me with its hidden weaknesses as well as its strengths.'[19]

For the moment, Blunt's faith in the Empire's 'strengths' overrode the weaknesses. He accepted even the Afghan War. This is proved by the amazing secret imperial mission that he plotted with Lytton for himself and Anne, during the winter of 1879–80.

The idea was to extend British influence in Central Arabia. This would provide both a counterblast to Russian designs throughout the East and encouragement to the Arab peoples against their Ottoman masters. The Blunts would revisit the Emir of Hail in the Nejd, bringing the Viceroy of India's compliments and suitable gifts from the Indian government stores, including a small cannon. A third partner in the plan was Lytton's Foreign Secretary, Sir Alfred Lyall.

There is every reason to believe that a new diplomatic 'Pilgrimage to Nejd' was seriously planned. We know that during the first 'pilgrimage' Blunt had offered Ibn Rashid his services as unofficial liaison officer with Europe. The only exaggerated statement in this passage from Blunt's 'Alms to Oblivion', partly quoted above, refers to his own revulsion against the British Empire and all its 'weaknesses' even before he left Simla:

> I have described elsewhere* the effect of these revelations [by Lytton] on me, and of the study I made of Indian finance, at Lytton's recommendation, with his then Financial Secretary Sir John Strachey, and how I left Simla with my faith in the British Empire and its ways in the East shaken to its foundations.

It is clear that the diplomatic 'Pilgrimage to Nejd' would never have been planned if Blunt's belief in the British Empire were already 'shaken to its foundations'. As it turned out, the diplomatic pilgrim was forestalled by Cavagnari's murder and Lytton's fall.

By the time Blunt was ready to air his views on the East in book form, the 'weaknesses' of the British Empire were indeed uppermost in his mind. He was to envisage a future for the peoples of the East entirely independent of the British Empire and *a fortiori* of the Russian; ultimately of the Ottoman also. But at Simla, though the first jolt to his patriotic confidence in British imperialism was administered, he still hoped that radical opinion at home might reform the Empire, changing it into an instrument of pure benevolence. This is shown in the most important of the draft letters kept in his red note-book – that to his radical friend Harry Brand (reprinted in the preface to Blunt's *Ideas about India*, 1885):

> The 'natives', as they call them [wrote Blunt] are a race of slaves, frightened, unhappy, and terribly thin. Though a good conservative and a member of the Carlton Club, I own to be shocked ... and my faith in British institutions and the blessings of British rule have received a severe blow.

If the British went on 'developing' India at the present rate, 'the inhabitants will have sooner or later to resort to cannibalism for there will be nothing but each other left them to eat'. Why were starving Hindus given railroads, turnpikes, gaols, lunatic asylums, memorial

* In articles in the *Fortnightly Review*, 1884, republished in book form as *Ideas about India*, (1885).

buildings to Sir Bartle Frere, immense armies of police, magistrates and engineers?

> They want none of these things, and they want their rice very badly, as anybody can see by looking at their ribs.... All public debts, even in a self-governing country, are more or less dishonest, but in a despotism like India they are a mere swindle.

Nevertheless, continued Blunt, the intentions of the British Empire were good, while those of other empires were bad, and the Viceroy's own views were relatively enlightened. It was all the fault of officialdom. As Lytton put it: 'India is a despotism of office-boxes tempered by the occasional loss of keys.'*

This draft letter may be taken as Blunt's first sighting-shot in an anti-imperial crusade that was to become thunderous.

No small part of Blunt's later reputation for being unpatriotic and dishonourable stemmed from the uses he made of information gleaned at Simla. His daughter Lady Wentworth, in her *Authentic Arabian*, wrote of her father's 'dangerous' friendships with highly placed friends – dangerous to the friends, because his disarming charm and 'hypnotic eyes' would lure them into confidences which he did not intend to respect. Though Blunt's son-in-law, Neville Lytton, was dazzled by the man's personality and gifts, he drew the line at the Simla story as he knew it. In his *English Country Gentleman* (1925), Neville Lytton accused Blunt of starting an anti-British Empire campaign 'from the very steps of the Viceregal Palace. This was a typical instance of Blunt's political actions.' Blunt, he concluded, had behaved in an 'unnatural and 'unchivalrous' manner, contrary to the 'common code of honour'. Lastly, after Lord Lytton's death, Lady Lytton was to criticize Blunt bitterly for his breaches of trust.

On 3 July the Blunts said goodbye to the small, concentrated world of Simla; goodbye to the Lyttons' two clever girls, 'Bina' (afterwards Betty, wife of Gerald Balfour) and Conny (the suffragette Lady Constance Lytton); goodbye to the baby in arms Neville, Wilfrid's future son-in-law, and to Neville's elder brother Victor, whom Wilfrid's daughter Judith would have preferred to Neville; goodbye to Lady Lytton herself, for whom Wilfrid had learnt to feel at Simla a new kind of love, hitherto unfamiliar even to this growing specialist in the art of love.

It was Edith, Wilfrid decided, who had been responsible for his own renewed intimacy with Robert at Simla. From this fact he was to make a further deduction:

* Blunt here attributes this epigram to a Simla 'wag'; but in his later *India under Ripon*, to Lytton.

> There is no more certain rule in friendship . . . than that, unless one makes a little love to one's friend's wife, the love that was with him soon languishes. There is a point where it becomes a condition of its continuance, just as the continuance of one's love for a married woman depends so often on the pleasant relations one may establish with her husband. These are the secrets of the heart which are not known even to our best novelists.

In Blunt's system of ideal loves some kind of communal set-up was still haunting him, such as Shelley had enjoyed at Geneva, Pisa and Lerici. Better still, kinship or connections by marriage would facilitate the interchange that Wilfrid longed for. Even in the later Victorian age society was still small enough to allow of many such relationships within its close walls. The Parham disaster had temporarily destroyed them for Wilfrid in Sussex. At Simla he had found them happily at work. The Stracheys and Plowdens were interrelated, and Mr Batten was Lady Strachey's brother. Mrs Batten, daughter of General Hatch, Judge-Advocate General of India, had a sister Emma who was married to Wilfrid's cousin Edward Bourke, another son of Lord Mayo, the assassinated Viceroy. Like so many of Wilfrid's future loves, Mrs Batten got off to a flying start through being in some sense his 'cousin'.

A little tourism was indulged in on the way to Bombay, Wilfrid as usual appointing Anne as keeper of the diary. In her terse but effective way she recorded their first vision of the Taj Mahal at Agra, on the evening of 4 July: 'The Taj was to be seen like a ghostly balloon on the horizon.' On drawing nearer, Wilfrid called it 'a wedding-cake', but, wrote Anne, 'it had a sepulchral gleam with the stormy sky behind it'.

The glowing sandstone of the Red Fort, with its Elephant Gate and vast courtyards, they admired as much as the Taj, though they omitted to remark on the enormous British sarcophagus in the Great Court. It commemorated John Russell Colvin, Lieutenant-Governor of the North-West Provinces who had died inside the Red Fort during the Indian Mutiny. Colvin was a name that Blunt would soon know well and heartily dislike. Meanwhile it was back to England, where another 'Vita Nova' awaited Blunt. This time the expression had some justification.

A life of public endeavour had never hitherto been his. He had avoided having his name in print, never stood on a public platform or made a speech even at a tenants' dinner. The man whose handwriting was soon to become all too familiar to the editor of *The Times* had never yet signed a letter to a newspaper. He had remained in the background when Father Meynell published their joint correspondence and Anne their joint travelogue. Only intimate friends knew who was the 'Proteus' of the poems.

But the Viceroy's India had changed all that. It had convinced Blunt that the germs of a true doctrine were contained in his Eastern ideas and admiration for the Children of Shem. 'I screwed up my courage to come forward', he wrote, 'both in speech and print.'

Blunt's first appearance in print was thanks to an introduction from Lytton to the Liberal politician John Morley, editor of the *Fortnightly Review*. Blunt sent Morley a piece on the proposed Euphrates valley railway, arguing against it on the grounds that it would not pay the European investors. His real fear, however, was lest a railway should imperil the pastoral life of his Bedouin brothers.

His first talk had been given several months earlier to the British Association meeting at Sheffield. A few weeks later he followed it up with a lecture to the Royal Geographical Society, and then a meeting with the rationalist explorer Palgrave, who loved the Arabs but not their 'disgusting monotheism', and blithely described his own house in Constantinople as 'a *centre* of *sedition*'.

Blunt's lecture to the Geographical Society was 'a distinct success',[20] perhaps because he had tried it out during a visit to Madeline and Percy Wyndham at Wilbury in Wiltshire. It was here that Wilfrid first took notice of their daughter Mary 'and that, so she told me, she first fell in love with me'. Mary was still young enough to have a governess, but already lovely. When Blunt kissed her goodbye with all the rest of his cousins, Mary blushed, and was scolded afterwards by her mother. Her parents, however, had forgiven him for his Parham excesses. His growing repute as a traveller showed him in a different light, and the Crabbet Arabian Stud fired their imagination.

The Stud's fame was indeed beginning to spread. In August 1879, Blunt received a polite note from the explorer and horseman, Robert Cunninghame Graham, asking if he might visit Crabbet to congratulate Lady Anne on her *Bedouin Tribes*, to hear about Blunt's travels and 'to see his equine acquaintances'.[21] Joseph Edgar Boehm, an expert on horses, and sculptor of the Wellington equestrian statue at Hyde Park Corner, was shown over the Stud; so were Skittles and her 'husband', Alec Baillie. 'What an event this would have been for me once!' sighed Blunt. Now he was glad when they had gone and he could take Bibi out fishing, alone.

Blunt himself paid his first of many annual visits to Newmarket that year. As a result, the Crabbet Stud took a long step forward when the all-powerful James Weatherby agreed to include 'Arabians' in his stud lists of thoroughbreds. Blunt also persuaded the Newmarket pundits to schedule an Arab race for 1883. In this connection Blunt was to send an article to James Knowles, editor of the *Nineteenth Century* in 1880, advising the owners of Arabs to go for increased size. He afterwards renounced this ambition to develop Arabs above their natural height of about fifteen hands. For the ordinary purposes of the turf, the English thoroughbreds would remain supreme.

But that did not rule out the value of an Arab strain. 'The Arab cross', he was to write much later, 'gives courage, endurance, and especially jumping power, besides that soundness of wind and limb in which the English thoroughbred is so often defective', while pure-bred young Arab mares were 'a delight to ride', and could be driven in pairs, or better still in a team of four, 'by a child'.*

Blunt was probably thinking of his own offspring, Judith, whose accomplishments with horses were far beyond those of any ordinary child. And despite Judith's many criticisms of her father, she was to credit him with an eye for beauty and symmetry which drew him to the Arabian horse and made him an admirable judge of the stud horses he bought and bred.

Moreover, the *Nineteenth Century* article caught the eye of the new Prime Minister. Mr Gladstone found time, amid the excitements of his 1880 election victory, to wonder about the horses of ancient Greece. What was the origin of the flesh-and-blood Trojan horse? He asked the editor, Knowles, to put the question to Mr Blunt. Blunt had now no doubt that the first horse of all came from his beloved Arabia. By September 1880 he had written for Mr Gladstone an article entitled 'The Origins of the Kehilan'. 'It had cost me a deal of trouble.'

Wilfrid called on his mother's old friend, Cardinal Manning, a few weeks before Gladstone's election victory. Manning had been Gladstone's best friend at the time of Blunt's birth, but the statesman would hardly have appreciated the dialogue that took place in the Cardinal-Archbishop's house at Westminster on 16 March 1880:

MANNING: 'How are you going to vote at the election?'
BLUNT: 'I shall vote only on one consideration, a £5 note.'
MANNING: 'You mean you won't vote at all?'
BLUNT: 'I cannot get up an interest in these things. I look upon European civilization as doomed to perish and all politics as an expedient which cannot materially hasten or delay the end.'
MANNING: 'I take the same view though probably on different grounds. Europe is rejecting Christianity and with it the reign of moral law. The reign of force is now beginning again as in the early stages, and bloodshed and ruin must be the result.'

On that same day, at breakfast, Blunt had discussed the Sudan with Sir Rivers Wilson, one of his Foreign Office friends who had helped him ship his Arab horses home from Alexandria. The conversation revolved round the famous General Charles George Gordon, now aged forty-seven, who had turned his back on Europe to govern

* Pamphlet by W.S.B., no date. Printed at the Chiswick Press.

Zanzibar. Popularly known as 'Chinese Gordon' for his imperial victories in the Far East, he had successfully ruled the Sudan singlehanded for the last four years, suppressing the slave trade.

On his retirement, however, Gordon picked a quarrel with Blunt's friend Lord Lyons while passing through Paris, browbeating the ambassador about the urgency of a successor to himself at Khartoum. If the English would not appoint one, he, Gordon, would make the French do so. His last rude letter to Lyons had ended, said Wilson, with the words: 'I have one comfort in thinking that in ten or fifteen years' time it will matter little to either of us. A black box, six foot six by three foot, will then contain all that is left of Ambassador, Cabinet Minister or of your humble servant.' That sentence, noted Blunt, had stamped Gordon at the Foreign Office as a madman. Yet it contained a prophecy more accurate than Blunt's or Manning's. For the doom of Europe was not to come in their lifetime, whereas Gordon's calculation about his own black box was a mere half-dozen years out.

A third, seminal conversation on Eastern politics had taken place just a month earlier at Frant in Sussex between the Blunts and Lord Stratford de Redcliffe, the former Sir Stratford Canning. Though now ninety-four, he gave the Blunts a vivid account of the Lords cricket match in 1805 when he had played for Eton and Byron for Harrow; and of riding every day with Byron at Constantinople during his 'Childe Harold' pilgrimage. To Blunt the old man was a hero, because of the 'sublime' pro-Turkish part he had played as ambassador in Constantinople during the Crimean phase of English politics. England was now entering a new phase. 'I was beginning to imagine myself', wrote Blunt, 'the rising prophet of the new [phase] . . . which would see a regeneration of Islam with England's help in Arabia.'

It was too much to hope that Blunt's 'Vita Nova' in politics would extend to his inner life. Once in England he soon drifted back into the habits of romance which he was powerless to break. In his own words, 'a new passion took me as it were by the throat and compelled me to its service'.

The new passion was for 'Angelina', alias Mrs Minnie Singleton, alias Violet Fane the writer and poet. 'Angelina' was the name Mrs Singleton had given herself in a story called *Edwin and Angelina*, where her morose husband Henry Singleton appeared as Edwin, and Wilfrid's cousin Philip Currie as D'Arcy.

The affair was intrinsically of no great importance in Blunt's life. In seeking to explain it, he claimed to have been 'abandoned' both by Minnie Pollen and Anne his wife when he reached England, and so to have been driven to this new passion. He also believed that Christianity had come between him and his 'double marriage'. Minnie had had one of her many revulsions against his love, brought on by jealousy of Angelina, and had gone off on a pilgrimage hoping either to die in Rome or be 'born again'.

He answered one of her letters: 'I was looking at old journals yesterday and see what a wretch I was before you came to console me. I am a wretch still, but not *such* a wretch. This is your doing. If I could I would be happy and good like you, but you know what I am. There are days and weeks when I am helpless as a child against pleasure – and we cannot control our fate.' A week later came an ecstatic reply from Minnie: 'I feel as if I might begin a new life....' *Might* was the operative word.[22]

But Anne's 'Vita Nova' was to be permanent. While travelling in India she had deliberately refused to think about her vision outside Shustar; but in England she soon felt that she had been wrong to do so. 'Bibi' was being brought up a Catholic by the Pollens. Anne's poignant memories of Francis and Alice Blunt drove her in the same direction. And her beloved brother Ralph Wentworth showed signs in 1879 of wishing to marry Anne 'Pansy' Pollen. The Blunts felt a sharp disappointment when, after being rescued by them from the claws of an American novelist with a 'vulgar middle-class mind', he married the strongly Protestant Mary Wortley instead of the Catholic Pansy. Anne regretfully described him as 'unstable as water'.[23]

She herself took the plunge in 1880. Having put her in touch with Cardinal Newman at her request, Wilfrid received from her the following announcement on 5 March: '10 James Street [the Blunts' London flat near Buckingham Gate]. My master, I wish you were here because after thinking much I want to tell you the result. It is that I am convinced of the *reality* of the Church and that when I see the Cardinal I shall probably be able to ask him to receive me into it.'[24]

After telling Wilfrid that she would telegraph him, Anne then introduced the subject of Shustar:

> The conviction first came to me the day after we left Shustar, but it got clouded over again and I feared it might be only a baseless vision till I found it stand against everything that seemed certain to upset it. If Cardinal Newman could and would receive me without delay I should want you to be there. I could not be so happy without you.

Ralph had promised to travel with her to the Birmingham Oratory for her reception, but her brother and husband both failed her. 'Wilfrid was engaged seriously,' she wrote ironically in her diary, 'on his usual duty of amusing himself and was not yet returned from hunting with and visiting his cousin Mr George Currie at Brighton.' At the last moment Ralph did in fact turn up. But it was the faithful John Pollen who was with Anne all the way.

That same evening, 5 March, Wilfrid returned from Brighton, and after dining with Minnie at Pembridge Crescent noted in his diary that John was away in Birmingham, 'where he is seeing Anne through her conversion – a strange revenge'.

Why 'revenge'? Wilfrid was gradually to persuade himself that he had lost his wife to the Church, just as John Pollen had lost *his* wife to Wilfrid – 'a strange revenge' indeed, if it were true. That Wilfrid was thinking along these lines is suggested by an earlier entry in his diary, on 21 February: 'I think religion would make them both [Anne and Ralph] happier, though possibly I might be the loser.'

Cardinal Newman was too frail to perform the actual ceremony, but he was carried downstairs and spent twenty minutes with Anne. She was received into the Church next day, 6 March 1880, by Father Thomas Pope. A week later Wilfrid attended her Confirmation in Cardinal Manning's private chapel.

With both Anne and Minnie newly arrived in Rome – Anne in the Church, Minnie in the city – Wilfrid reacted to a feeling of rejection in the only way he knew. He gave full rein to the new passion.

'Wholly pagan' were the words with which Blunt described his love for Angelina. He had already said much the same thing about his liaisons with the dusky Anita in Rio and 'gypsy' Swingkettle at Parham. The dark-eyed Angelina had true gypsy blood through her mother, who had made a runaway match with Sir Charles Lamb of Beauport Park in Sussex. Another oft-repeated feature was the element of 'cousinship'. Though Blunt found his rivalry with Philip Currie in some sense distasteful ('I would really rather give Angelina up than him'), it also gave the affair a cachet.

The pages of his 1880 diary were largely destroyed by him, in shame at what he called his 'carnival of folly'. This included renting from the Duke of Bedford's French chef a love-nest opposite Victoria Station (recklessly close to the family flat at Buckingham Gate) under the alias of 'Mr. Walter Bingham an Irish gentleman residing at Streatham', and an agreement to live with Angelina in Italy. His peak of passion was reached in mid-April, after which Angelina began to wonder whether his 'papistical twist' might not make him 'suddenly repent of his sins and abandon her'. Angelina finally chose Philip – in fact she was to marry him in the 1890s after Singleton died, and become Lady Currie, a beautiful ambassadress in Constantinople. Blunt kept among his papers a bunch of everlasting flowers she had given him, tied with crimson ribbon. They are there still, having proved more durable than his six-months' 'pagan' romance.

Her combination of wit and emotion sparked off in Wilfrid a new electric storm of poetry. In a sonnet, written to her on St Valentine's Day after a hunt over the Sussex Downs, there was genuine feeling:

I knew the spring was come. I knew it even
Better than all by this, that through my chase
In bush and stone and hill and sea and heaven
I seemed to see and follow still your face.
Your face my quarry was. For it I rode
My horse a thing of wings, myself a god.[25]

His 'orgy of poetry', as he called it, overflowed into other literary activities: preparing the first edition of the *Proteus* poems under his own name; finishing the *Pilgrimage to Nejd* with a fresh onslaught on Eastern railways; shaping up a new book to be called *The Future of Islam*. Beyond that he explored new aspects of London literary society, often in the company of Angelina.

There was Tennyson, 'with no play of feature to relieve a rather heavy countenance'. And the historian Lecky with his 'philanthropic head and a benign expression of dullness'. And Browning's 'loud brass instrument of a voice' attacking the poet Rogers for stationing a servant behind his chair in old age to prompt his stories. And Dean Stanley defending Trelawny's prose in that 'quick eager way' that all Stanleys had.

Now that Robert Lytton was expected home for good from India Wilfrid was again interested in forming some kind of literary coterie. He and Robert would escort Angelina to Rome for the winter, and between the three of them would 'produce a poet'. The difficulty was not Anne, Edith or even Mr Singleton, but the 'oath of brotherhood' which Blunt had already taken with Angelina (sitting on the hearthrug of the love-nest each wearing a silk jibbah and girdle) and intended to take with Robert. Blunt therefore could not quarrel with Angelina, even if she insisted on bringing D'Arcy (Philip Currie) along; nor with Robert, over Mrs Batten. That was a thornier problem, since Robert had made Mrs Batten promise not to have an affair with Blunt when she returned from India. Perhaps the solution was another 'ménage à trois'? Anyway, here was Mrs Batten in July staying at Crabbet for Goodwood, and for much else. 'I found her door ajar about 12 o'clock', wrote Blunt, 'and stayed with her till daylight.' Next morning he drove a team of Arab mares from Arundel station to the racecourse – 'My horse a thing of wings, myself a god'.

And Minnie and Pansy were back from Rome, Minnie at first glowing with piety but soon with the old love. In May, Blunt took her and Pansy to the Royal Academy to see Val Prinsep's Indian pictures of Lytton's durbar. They decided that Lord Lytton looked rollicking, Lady Lytton lackadaisical and the herald reeling. Minnie's 'new life' was to be very different from the one she had dreamed of in Rome. 'It is certain now', wrote Blunt on 1 August 1880, 'that she is with child, and in spite of all former disappointments, this gives us a hope. It should be born, if all goes well, early in March.'*

17 August 1880 was Blunt's fortieth birthday. It was to be, he hoped, the hinge of the door which would open on a new life, a door separating the youthful ardours of 'Proteus' from his now serious political manifestations. Blunt was aware of a pleasing rhythm in the fact that his friend Lytton would see the revised edition of the *Proteus* poems through the press. For Lytton, he believed, was withdrawing from politics into the realms of poetry, while Blunt would resign his poetic dreams for the world of politics.

Plans for his political life had crystallized into a winter visit to Jeddah, the port for Mecca on the Red Sea. This would be the centre for his Arabian mission. In June he had met Malkum Khan the Persian ambassador, a little old man with a long nose and black eyes who had been brought to the house of Angelina by Philip Currie. Anne was learning classical Arabic from a teacher named Sabunji, editor of the Arab paper *The Bee*, and together they were translating Blunt's *Fortnightly* articles for distribution in the East. With quiet satisfaction Blunt reviewed 'the pretty good diplomacy' he now had at his private disposal: Plowden moved to Baghdad, Henderson at Aleppo, Jago at Damascus, Ross at Bushire – 'all my correspondents'. At home, there was his friend of many years, Eddy Hamilton, appointed since the election to be Mr Gladstone's private secretary. In the Foreign Office were Philip Currie, Rivers Wilson and Robert Lytton. Early in July Blunt dined at Limmers Hotel with another group of friends interested in the Middle East, among them Percy Wyndham, Harry Brand and Whittaker, editor of the *Levant Herald*. An informal committee was set up to receive news.

On the thirteenth he met the Grand Old Man himself, at a party of Mrs Gladstone's. Blunt arrived early and had twenty minutes alone with him. Though he found Gladstone 'totally ignorant of the ABC of the question' – the question being 'the regeneration of the East' – Blunt felt he had succeeded in 'grafting him with two ideas'; that the Sultan of Turkey was 'no Solomon', and that the Caliphate need not necessarily be vested in the Ottoman Turks, but might be Arabian.

At the end of the month, there was a set-back from the Foreign Secretary, Lord Granville, an ultra-cautious Whig of sixty-five known as Puss. Blunt had offered to go on the 'secret mission' to Arabia already discussed between himself and Lytton in India. Granville wrote stiffly that it was 'impossible under present circumstances to

* In his 'Alms to Oblivion', FM. 44, p. 67, Blunt wrote that in Spring 1881 Minnie bore and lost a son who was christened Benjamin, 'her latest and her last'. This last infant does not appear on the Pollen family tree under this date, but in 1875. See above, p. 116.

accept ...'. Gladstone, however, was genuinely interested and had circulated a memo to the Cabinet on Blunt's idea of the Arabian Caliphate. 'The government are no paladins', wrote Blunt in his diary. 'Some day they will come back to me, or I am much mistaken.' But two months later he was asking Sir Charles Dilke at the Foreign Office to appoint him consul of the Hadramaut or somewhere else on the Red Sea, for the sake of prestige. No response.

On 3 November the Blunts left for Arabia – 'perhaps for ever', wrote Wilfrid. 'I beg my wife to believe I love her truly, in spite of all, and my daughter with a pure and honest love.' His diary for 1880, he continued, contained 'the story of my sins'. He hoped that 1881 would have a different tale to tell. Had not Lord Byron's 'nobler vision' come to him 'in the midst of his debaucheries in Italy'? What Byron had done for Greece, 'and so retrieved his soul', Blunt would do for Arabia.

But he had made a mistake in the crystal. It was Egypt that he was to champion.

PART II

'Manhood in Battle'

[7]
Egypt, Arise!
1880–1882

Blunt's first action after 'closing for ever his account with youth'[1] was to open an account with Islam.

This meant educating himself in certain new liberal ideas which were fertilizing the Muslim world. Two names stood out. The mastermind of the whole reform movement was the Sayyid (descendant of the Prophet) Jamal al-Din al-Afghani, a wild spirit from the mountains of Afghanistan, who nevertheless preached the need for progress in religion. He had been banished from Cairo by the reactionaries, but not before his genius had left its mark on the Azhar, or religious university. Al-Afghani's chief disciple, Sheykh Mohammed Abdu, was destined to be Blunt's lifelong friend. His photograph forms the frontispiece to Blunt's *Secret History* of Egypt written during this period – a handsome, intelligent man with a broad forehead, level brows, serious dark eyes and a black crescent of a beard, dressed in the sombre kaftan and white turban of the Azhar sheykhs. Both al-Afghani and Abdu had become known to Blunt through the lucky chance of a distinguished teacher he had acquired at the Azhar, named Khalil. All three of them, al-Afghani, Abdu and Khalil believed passionately in one semi-political reform: an Arabian Caliphate at Mecca. Only if the tyrannical, materialistic Turkish Caliphate at Constantinople were brought to an end would a true spiritual revival be possible.

An Arabian Caliphate made no slight appeal to Blunt. Had he not cast himself as the apostle to the Arabs from the Giaours? 'The reshaping of the Islamic world' seemed about to begin, 'with the help as I then thought of England.' But Blunt's love-affair with Islam was not to work out as he expected.

He made for Jeddah, as being the Red Sea port for Mecca. His plan was to saturate himself in Islamic philosophy before offering himself to the Arabian tribes. At Jeddah even the shopkeepers spoke of 'things divine'; even the European vice-consuls 'prophesied'. This spiritual paradise, however, was infested by mosquitoes and Blunt went down with malaria. While Anne was questioning the sheykhs' wives about the desert tribes, Wilfrid was floating in and out of delirium. Every night the face of a sheykh with long teeth would haunt him. At last Anne decided he would never be fit until they went north.

From Jeddah he carried away with him a growing faith in Islam – and an 'ugly' story of Christendom. While he was in the port, he heard of a British captain having abandoned his storm-bound vessel when loaded with pilgrims. Their lives were saved, wrote Blunt, thanks only to the captain's nephew who volunteered to remain on board. Though Blunt did not mention it, this good young man was reluctantly assisted by the second engineer, whom the pilgrims prevented from leaving the ship. Together the two of them may have contributed to the portrait of Lord Jim in Joseph Conrad's novel of that name.*

Blunt's forced return to Cairo enabled him to continue his studies at the Azhar. Egypt he believed to be in a hopeful ferment. He began to wonder whether a reformed Islam did not hold the solution he had looked for but failed to find in Catholicism: a dogmatic creed to satisfy his heart, but one so simple as not to affront his intellect. 'There is no other god than God' was all he needed to believe, said Abdu and Khalil. 'To a mind like mine', wrote Blunt, 'this teaching is not convincing, but at least one possible of acceptance.' Perhaps the ninth-century Mosque of Ibn Tulun best symbolizes what Blunt found so congenial in Islamic teaching. Its four huge plain walls, and minaret with winding outside staircase that might have come from ancient Babylon, seem to call forth the utmost simplicity and dignity of which human nature is capable.

'If I can introduce a pure Arabian breed of horses into England and help to see Arabia free of the Turks, I shall not have quite lived in vain.' This had been his entry in a fragmentary diary of 1880, 26 June. Hence his visits to the *ulema* or divines of Cairo alternated with periods of camping outside the city, where Bedouin sheykhs would bring in their horses for sale. As the Blunts were setting out in February 1881 on a new drive for horses in the Hamad of Syria, a walled garden caught their eye. How exquisitely beautiful were its apricot trees all in full flower. Within a year this magical garden was to be their own.

The tribes of the Hamad, or great desert south of Palmyra, yielded Blunt no fresh political ideas but many fine horses, including the mare Rodania. Conditions were often dangerous. One night Blunt almost

* See Graham Greene's letter to *The Times Literary Supplement*, 6 December 1974. He makes the point that biographers of Conrad have missed Blunt's account, which occurs in his *Fortnightly* articles on which his *Future of Islam* was based.

lost his mare to two horse thieves, even though both the Blunts usually slept with their horses chained to their wrists. Wilfrid, who had evidently left his mare unchained, awoke to the sound of clanking, chased the thieves in the dark and recovered her, having been prodded with his own spear but fortunately with the blunt end. On another night a foal crept into Anne's bed and she awoke in the morning to find the little creature lying by her side.

In Damascus, where the Blunts camped for a week in what was still their own house next door to Jane Digby and her Medjuel, Wilfrid came to two important conclusions. The exiled Algerian patriot, Abd-el-Kader, whom he now got to know, seemed cut out to become the new Arabian Caliph, once Sultan Abdul Hamid had disappeared from Constantinople.

And did not the domestic bliss of the 'Digbys' contain a lesson for Anne and himself? Jane was held in high honour by Medjuel's tribe just because she was their 'benefactress'. The implication was surely, at least in Blunt's mind, that Anne's benefactions to the Stud, the Crabbet estate and now perhaps to her husband's new Arabian vocation, were entirely praiseworthy and in Anne's own best interests as a wife. It did not strike Blunt that a woman who had recently become an ardent Catholic convert might not wish to devote her benefactions to an Islamic Reformation.

The lessons Blunt drew from Medjuel's happy life were perhaps more obvious. Jane's attitude to her husband, wrote Blunt, was maternal and his to her one of filial affection. Medjuel would leave Jane occasionally for a spell in the desert 'to refresh his nomadic soul, but the rest of the time was devoted all to her'.[2] Blunt may have felt that Anne similarly should allow her younger husband his moments of romantic refreshment.

Oddly enough it was just at this moment that Anne's feminine charms received an outsider's tribute. The temporary military consul at Aleppo, Captain J. D. Hamill-Stewart, had had the Blunts to stay. 'Lady Anne is a clipper', he wrote to his sister in April, 'a jolly plucky woman with lots of brains, a good traveller and, withal, exceedingly ladylike. I assure you I am quite in love with her.' As for the 'clipper's' husband with his strange passion for interfering in the East and his unnecessarily good looks, he and the temporary military consul did not hit it off.[3]

England in May presented Blunt with few romantic temptations. He worked hard all the summer and autumn on his articles for the *Fortnightly*, which were to appear as a book during the following year entitled *The Future of Islam*. In the last chapter, written during the winter of 1881 when the Blunts had returned to Egypt, he wrote: 'The events of the last year in Egypt are significant. For the first time in its modern history a strong national party has arisen on the Nile. . . .'[4]

What were these events of 1881?

Egypt in 1879 was emerging from utter prostration. Ismail Pasha, the high-flying, extravagant Khedive or Sultan's viceroy, had attempted to carry Egypt fully into the nineteenth century. But Ismail's debts soared even higher than the telegraph poles and dock-cranes he introduced. In 1875, as a last resort, he sold nearly half the total of Suez Canal shares to Britain. From now on the European shareholders, or 'bondholders' as they were called, were to hold Egypt in bond. After a year Egypt was under the 'Dual Control' of Britain and France, with half of her revenue devoted to paying her public debt.

Captain Evelyn Baring was sent to Egypt as British Commissioner of the Debt. He set about clearing up the Egyptian shambles in his own way. Ismail was made to accept a civil list in place of his hereditary revenues, and a pro-European Prime Minister, Nubar Pasha, was installed. Ismail retorted by resurrecting the ancient Chamber of Notables, as it might be a native parliament to confront the foreign-sponsored ministry. A mutiny among half-pay officers gave him the chance to dismiss Nubar. Baring resigned, returning to India, and Ismail tried to govern through the army and Notables, headed by a constitutionalist named Sherif Pasha. Sherif, however, did the unforgivable thing: he suggested a reduction in the bondholders' interest.

Immediately there was an international outcry. The Sultan forced Ismail to abdicate in April 1879 in favour of his eldest son Tewfik. Tewfik's Prime Minister, Riaz Pasha, lightened the burdens of the fellahin, and pleased the Egyptians as a whole by emphasizing the country's Muslim character. When Blunt studied conditions in the countryside between Cairo and his camp during January 1881 he was amazed by the fellahins' prosperity, as compared with their wretchedness in Ismail's day. Tewfik he described as a promising though dull ruler.

Then, in the manner of all down-trodden nations who are at last on the upgrade, the Egyptians found that their whiff of success inspired them to demand fuller rights. The national uprising began in the army. While Blunt was planning his mission from Jeddah, Cairo had already become the scene of disturbances. Tewfik's War Minister was one Osman Rifky, a reactionary belonging to the ruling officer caste of Turkish-Circassians.* Rifky now attempted to deal a final blow at the

* The Turkish-Circassians had originally come from the Caucasus many centuries earlier, and the Mamelukes, whom Napoleon defeated in 1798 and Mohammed Ali exterminated in 1811, were of this race.

indigenous element by excluding all fellah officers from the Military Academy. Three fellah colonels vehemently protested, led by Ahmed Arabi. They were arrested by Rifky but released by their own soldiers. At once they became national heroes with the army as the centre of popular hopes. This, though not an ideal development, was no one's fault but the government's. For the civil and religious wings of the national movement, as represented by Sherif Pasha and Sheykh Jamal al-Din al-Afghani, had both been suppressed.

The army demanded reforms; and during the spring and summer of 1881 there was a prospect of peace or at any rate armistice – or so it seemed to the Khedive's two British advisers, Auckland Colvin and the Consul, who was none other than Blunt's old friend Sir Edward Malet, now grown into a reserved, self-doubting diplomat. Neither Colvin nor Malet would make excuses for the nationalists if things went wrong.

What went wrong was the character of the young Khedive Tewfik. An intriguer by temperament and a weakling who agreed with the last person to whom he spoke, Tewfik was soon surrounding the three colonels with a network of spies. There were rumours of a murder plot against the colonels, and on 8 September a well-founded report that Ahmed Arabi and a colleague were to be sent with their regiments out of Cairo, as a preliminary to picking off each separately. Arabi decided to pre-empt the Khedive's blow by the famous action of 9 September.

Colonel Arabi and 2,500 men with eighteen guns marched to the Abdin Palace, where they occupied the square. Meanwhile Tewfik had sent for Colvin his British Controller-General (Malet was on leave) to help him face the 'rebels'. This was the moment for which Auckland Colvin, stout limb that he was of the old imperialist tree, had been born. Years later Baring (then Lord Cromer) was to rhapsodize in his *Modern Egypt* over Colvin's response. 'The spirit of the Englishman rose high in the presence of danger', wrote Baring. 'It was not the first time [Colvin] had heard of mutiny. He knew how his own countrymen had met dangers of this sort.'[5]

'Shoot Arabi', Colvin urged the Khedive. The Khedive hesitated. Arabi, however, was not out to kill but to end Turkish arbitrary rule. Dismounting and putting up his sword at the Khedive's request, he made three demands: dismissal of all the ministers, a parliament sympathetic to the nationalists, an army of 18,000 men. Tewfik turned to Colvin:

'You heard what he said.'

'It is not fitting for the Viceroy to discuss questions of this kind with Colonels', replied the representative of the British Empire.[6] But Tewfik accepted Colonel Arabi's first point, agreeing to submit the other two points to the Sultan. With Sherif Pasha once more heading the ministry, for three months there was peace, even euphoria. Had not the Egyptian people achieved their bloodless revolution? They had made a nation, and only Colvin and Malet called it a mutiny.

It was during this happy period that Wilfrid Scawen Blunt turned up again in Cairo.

Anne's latest offering to Wilfrid had been a ten-foot-square equestrian portrait. She was painting her 'master' throughout the autumn, bushy-bearded and in Bedouin head-dress and robes, seated with casual grace upon the rearing stallion Pharaoh. They had bought Pharaoh through Skene in 1878 for £192.6s., a 14·3 dark bay with black points, celebrated among the tribes as 'the handsomest colt bred by the Sebaa for twenty years'. He had been foaled in 1876, a Seglawi Jedran of the Anazeh. The carriage of his tail was magnificent and he had 'eyes like the human eye, oval and showing the white'.[7] Judith, now aged eight, had sketched her mother painting Pharaoh, Anne on a ladder, Pharaoh with his forefeet on a box. Wilfrid's old friend the painter Molony began by calling the picture 'beastly'. But Anne plodded on. She finished just before leaving for the land of the Pharaohs on 21 November 1881, Wilfrid having gone on ahead. Anne's last view of Judith was of her face peering through the blinds of the drawing-room at Pembridge Crescent, the Pollens' London home.[8]

The Blunts had intended to make a second 'Pilgrimage to Nejd'. The situation in Cairo, however, and the opportunities for helping their friends persuaded them to stay there: 'When we can leave Cairo we don't, alas, know', wrote Anne in her diary on 10 January 1882. 'I long to go away to the desert and live with our camels. But we cannot leave this turmoil and confusion.' At least they were able to conduct the affairs of their stud throughout this period.

Prince Othman introduced them to Count Roman Potocki, owner of the famous Antonine Stud. On 3 February they went to see the walled garden of Sheykh Obeyd near Heliopolis, their apricot paradise of last year, with a view to purchase. They camped there for the first time on the seventeenth, having bought its thirty-seven acres, small steam engine, 'rubbishy' gardener's house and shrine of the Bedouin saint Obeyd, for a total of £1,500. It was, in part, a gesture of faith in nationalist Egypt.

But new trouble had begun in Europe. In May 1881 France had forcibly established a protectorate over Tunisia. Gambetta, the French Prime Minister, feared the repercussions of the Egyptian revolution on France's Tunisian conquest. Would the Sultan promote a 'Jehad' or holy war against all Christian aggressors? In Blunt's words, a wave of Muslim anger was rolling eastwards from Tunis towards Cairo. Gambetta's new policy could only be hostile to Egyptian nationalism.

Blunt saw the Tunis invasion as one of the two milestones on the road to revolution throughout the Near and Middle East; Britain's acquisition of Cyprus in 1878 was the first. Britain had been obliged to concede a free hand to France in Tunis as a *quid pro quo* for Cyprus. Nor would Britain dare diverge from France in the future; for only a solid Franco-British front would keep Bismarck's Germany within the bounds of the Congress of Berlin. Such was to be Blunt's (not altogether tenable) view of power politics.

When Blunt arrived in Cairo the autumn euphoria had not yet evaporated. Nevertheless he realized there was room for improvement in the relations between the Egyptian nationalists and his own official English friends. His first move was therefore to meet Arabi. He himself was still half inclined to take the line of the British press: namely, that the alleged national movement was a mere military coup. At the same time he was aware of hostile forces gathering against Egypt. On his way to Paris he had happened to travel with Sir Charles Dilke of the Foreign Office. After amiably recommending some pornographic literature, Dilke revealed his intent to bargain for a new trade deal with Gambetta. 'That man means to sell Egypt for his Commercial Treaty', said Blunt to himself. Moreover, his cousin Philip Currie had thrown out an imaginative hint before he left: 'Perhaps you might find in Arabi just the man you have been looking for.' With some such hope, Blunt had brought with him Lady Anne's teacher, the 'learned Arabic professor' Louis Sabunji.*

Pushing their way through a crowd of suppliants, Blunt and Sabunji were received by 'El Wahid' – the 'One' – as Arabi was now called among his doting followers. Blunt recognized in him a typical son of the fellahin, tall, heavily built and making up in eloquence for a lack of decisiveness. Someone had told him that this English well-wisher was married to Byron's granddaughter, and he praised Byron warmly as a freedom fighter.

After this interview, the practical Blunt at once began on what he saw as his mission – mediating between the two sides. Success seemed to attend him. Largely through his good offices, Arabi and Colvin were brought together, Arabi accepting Colvin's plans for the Chamber and an army of no more than 15,000 strong on financial grounds. However, in acting as liaison officer with British opinion at home, Blunt ran into trouble.

* Converted to Islam, Sabunji, a Syrian Christian, had once been in holy orders. When it suited him Blunt would still refer to him as 'the Rev. Louis Sabunji'.

He had cast the nationalists' programme into written form, sending a copy to Gladstone. He wondered whether to publish it also in *The Times*. Malet had advised against. But Blunt now had robuster friends at his elbow. Sir William Gregory, a retired governor of Ceylon and an Anglo-Irish landowner, who had once defended the Confederacy in Parliament, was living in Cairo with his young second wife. Both took a sanguine view of Arabi, and Blunt acted on their advice to publish. Unluckily the programme was to appear in *The Times* on 1 January 1882 as if from Arabi's own hand. This was to give Malet his chance to question the document's authenticity and by implication Blunt's good faith. Blunt's friends in England became alarmed. 'People will want to know who this Don Q. Wilfrid Scawen Blunt is', wrote Harry Brand on 10 January, 'whose reckless machinations are knocking down Egyptian stocks . . . ! But seriously speaking, Arabi Bey is doing no good. . . .'[9]

Meanwhile, Blunt as usual underestimated an opponent's annoyance: 'Except for this small difference of opinion', he wrote, 'my relations with Malet remained perfectly and intimately friendly.' Anne, however, referred in her diary to Malet's 'sudden bitter tone'. In any case, Malet's relations with Blunt were a storm in a teacup compared with the coming whirlwind.

On 6 January 1882 the British and French governments issued their disastrous 'Joint Note'. The Joint Note was ostensibly an assertion of support for the Khedive Tewfik. In fact it was an iron fist raised against the nationalists. 'They will take it as a declaration of war', said Blunt when Malet showed it to him. Neither Malet nor Colvin (nor Cromer in time to come) could regard the Note as anything but a gross blunder, a veiled challenge to Arabi to do his worst just as temperatures were falling. When Blunt visited Arabi (now Under-Secretary for War) on 9 January, he saw for the first time 'a peculiar gleam in his eye'.

In vain Blunt tried to make him accept Malet's pacific gloss on the Note. Did Malet think they were children? Arabi retorted. By mid-January the united nationalists – fellahin, soldiers, Notables, *ulema* – were already issuing their own joint demand. It was one to which Colvin, Malet and their French colleagues could never concede. For it touched on things sacred, finance.

The Chamber of Notables proposed a new right to vote on the revenues not assigned to the public debt. If half of Egypt's budget was sequestrated, at least Egypt should have a say in the allocation of the remainder. Beneath this demand lay a further proposal to cut the salaries and numbers of foreign officials. Even Malet privately admitted that four men were doing what could easily be done by two, and all four were being paid £3,000 where £2,000 was enough.*

The crisis arrived on 2 February when Sherif Pasha, who favoured a compromise with the foreign Controllers, was dismissed by Tewfik. Arabi became Minister of War. In the words of the wit, Lord Houghton, 'Sherif has resigned and a Gregory-Blunt Ministry is talked of!'[10] Again the fellahin rejoiced. Surely this meant that their triumphant army would at last regulate the water-rights, abolish the *corvée* and destroy that age-old instrument of torture, dried hippopotamus hide twisted into a *kurbaj* – the Egyptian cat.

Colvin admitted to Blunt on 31 January (their last meeting) that 'annexation' of Egypt was the probable end of his policy. 'England would never give up the footing she had got in Egypt....'[11] The use of words like 'annexation' and 'intervention' was a warning which Blunt passed on to the nationalists. Meanwhile his last words to Colvin were, 'I defy you' – 'I defy you to bring about English intervention or annexation'. Henceforth he and Colvin were on opposite sides. On 13 February Wilfrid was the only European at a Cairo meeting to celebrate the nationalists' parliamentary victory. Abdu spoke of liberty in ringing prose, others in verse. 'Was there ever any other nation', asked the gratified Blunt, 'which gained liberty by reason and not by the sword?'[12]

On 20 February Malet was writing to Granville:

> Wilfrid Blunt continues his optimism and declares that if Egypt is only left alone all will come right.... He has arrived at the conviction that the pure Egyptians are quite capable of governing and administering the country. I do not share this view....[13]

On 27 February, the Blunts and Lady Gregory paid a farewell call on Arabi and his household before returning home to continue their propaganda in England on Egypt's behalf. Just as Arabi had talked about Byron to Blunt on their first day together, so Blunt returned to Byron at their parting. He reminded Arabi of Byron's warning to the Greeks: 'Trust not for freedom to the Franks [Europeans].' Egyptians must be prepared to defend their new found freedom with their own arms. It was not the foreign politicians, added Blunt, but the financiers who threatened Egypt. A firm stand in Cairo would soon frighten off the City, for bondholders dreaded above all things 'a long and costly war'.

There can be no doubt that this advice to Arabi involved several

* General Sir Frederick Goldsmid went further than Malet. He described meeting three Chiefs of Caisse (Debt) at £3,600 each, in their office, one reading a newspaper, one sitting, one walking around; a single man at £1,000 could have done all their work. (Lady Gregory, *Autobiography*, p. 43.)

reckless misjudgments. The politicians were quite as hostile to Egyptian freedom as the bondholders. Blunt had forgotten Suez. Nor could 'a long and costly war' against British millions ever be sustained by 'El Wahid', the 'Only One'. The world would have to wait another twenty years before seeing a small people, the Boers, actually waging a long war that was more costly to the British than to themselves.

Arabi's mother and wife, meanwhile, explained to the two ladies his opposition to education for Arab women: it would fill them with frivolous European ideas and contaminate their religion. He had even threatened to put a match to his wife's trailing green dress, if she insisted on wearing French clothes. But what else could she wear, asked Arabi's wife, when visiting the Khedive's wife?[14]

To Anne, these things were no problem. As soon as she arrived in England on 5 March, with the prospect of many social and political calls, she simply bought a long black cloak 'to hide deficiencies'.

In England, the Blunts' chief aim was to establish an Egyptian lobby. This was no easy task, for all thoughts were at present on the coercion of Ireland rather than of Egypt. The parallel between Ireland and Egypt was brought home to Blunt by a chance conversation with Anne's Irish cousin, Lord Miltown: 'The trouble was got up by agitators', Miltown insisted; 'the Irish fellahin are not really with the National Party.... Armed intervention would set things right.'

The first person whom Blunt deliberately sought out was Eddy Hamilton, Gladstone's private secretary and Blunt's old friend. The P.M. was not at all angry at Blunt's 'interference' in Egyptian affairs, Eddy assured him; on the contrary, he appreciated Blunt's flow of information and promised, through Eddy, to see Blunt personally.

With a key man such as Hamilton at hand, Blunt's whip-round for other supporters was less vital. Nevertheless he called on Godfrey 'Webber' Webb and Algernon 'Button' Bourke for social and political news. Button, whom Blunt now described as a sort of 'sub-sub-sub-editor' of *The Times*, promised help with that journal. Unlike Gladstone, he would more than keep his promise.

Blunt's first ever visit to the House of Commons took place on 9 March. His escort was the Liberal M.P., George Howard, Rosalind's husband. 'He is a very sensible man', wrote Blunt; but it was on Rosalind that he chiefly relied, 'for she is a generous woman and is glad to find me doing good at last'.

At the Foreign Office on the tenth Dilke was volubly hostile, and so was Granville, though to do him justice he tried to discuss Blunt's horses rather than his politics. Would the Egyptians give up their claim to the domestic budget? No, replied Blunt. 'Then I look upon their case as hopeless', said the Foreign Minister. 'It must end by their being put down by force.' How could the Liberals 'put down' liberty? Thoroughly alarmed, Blunt wrote in his diary, 'I *must* see Gladstone.'

Meanwhile he filled in time with visits that somehow did not seem to further the cause as much as they should have. The likable president of the Asiatic Society, Sir Henry Rawlinson, far from supporting Egyptian freedom, called Blunt 'an enthusiast' who refused to accept the brutal truth: that 'Egyptians, like all Eastern races, were meant for despotic rule and always would be slaves'. The best thing for them was for England or Russia to absorb them. John Morley, editor of the Liberal *Pall Mall Gazette*, Blunt found deeply impregnated with Colvin–Malet propaganda; indeed Colvin was Morley's special correspondent in Egypt. Equally blinded by *his* correspondent, Moberly Bell, was John Walter, M.P., proprietor of *The Times*, whom Blunt dubbed 'the Banal Conversationalist or Every Man His Own Bore'. Walter, however, did promise to send a special correspondent to Cairo. More promises. 'Natty' Rothschild, who might have provided him with a more realistic picture of the bondholders' nerve, was summoned abroad to a relative's bedside on the very morning he had promised an interview.

The only person from whom Blunt gleaned anything important was Sir Garnet Wolseley, the good-humoured Anglo-Irish general whom he had met in Cyprus four years earlier. Wolseley questioned Blunt closely about Egypt's Eastern desert between the Delta and the Canal. 'I feel pretty sure', wrote Blunt soon afterwards in his diary, 'that if intervention takes place, troops will be landed from that side.' Blunt was to prove dead right. This information about the British landings was in fact the only absolutely accurate story that Blunt was able to pass on to Arabi, as a result of his March campaign in London. Unhappily for the Egyptians, Arabi was not equipped to take advantage of it when the landings occurred.

Blunt's passionately desired meeting with Gladstone took place at last on 22 March, but with disastrous consequences. The Grand but slippery Old Man convinced Blunt that he was on Arabi's side. Had he not won the election of 1880 against Disraeli on his championship of small nations and denunciation of imperialism? And had he not produced an article in the *Fortnightly*, forswearing any aggression towards Egypt? As late as 20 January this year, Gladstone had even written personally to Blunt, reaffirming these principles.

Now in the course of a remarkable forty minutes Gladstone twisted the impressionable Blunt around his finger. He had on his table in front of him a letter Blunt had written two days before to Lord Granville, arguing that Colvin should be withdrawn from Cairo and a Commission of Inquiry sent out. This seemed to Blunt a good start. Better still was the moment when Granville himself tried to interrupt the interview by sending up his name: 'The wily old man went out for an instant, and sent Lord Granville away, and then came back with a sort of skip across the room and rubbing his hands as one might do on having got rid of a bore.' Blunt took what he thought was his cue. He asked Gladstone for a message of goodwill to Arabi.

There was a pause. Then in a voice deliberately changed from the human to the official, the Prime Minister replied: 'I think not. But you are at liberty to state your own impressions of my sentiments. . . .'

Blunt took the Grand Old Man at what he thought was his word; and there was a parting squeeze for his hand that brought tears to Blunt's eyes. He posted a sheaf of good tidings to his friends in Cairo. 'With Gladstone on our side, what more was there to fear?'

There was everything to fear. It would need exceptional firmness on Gladstone's part to hold the ring for the nationalists against their many enemies. Neither the Khedive nor the Turkish-Circassian officers could be relied upon to make the new system work. And naturally the white settlers were in a fever of fear and animosity. News of an ugly racial incident at Shepheard's Hotel in Cairo, when the Khedive's cousin had breakfasted in the dining-room with a white woman and been handed, for a start, a tarbush full of salad, was only one of the symptoms. 'Altogether as pretty a business as one need hear of', wrote Blunt.

He was soon to hear of a 'prettier' business still. Meanwhile the First Act of his English campaign, as he put it, had ended on April Fool's Day. He met the Prince of Wales at supper, having sat by his sister Princess Louise at dinner and talked to her solidly on Egypt. But when he later tried to interest the Prince in Egypt, he was less than successful. H.R.H. steered off all subjects but Arab horses and an earlier scandal at Shepheard's Hotel also involving a lady. It was not long before the curtain had risen on Blunt's Second Act, and the Prince was asking why nothing could be done 'to stop this disloyal and eccentric Jesuit'.[15]

[8]
Wind and Whirlwind
1882

The Circassian Plot, as it was called, suddenly propelled Egypt into a new storm.

News reached England during the third week of April that the displaced Turkish-Circassian officers of the army had conspired to murder Arabi. To the establishment at home the news was not displeasing. It seemed but another proof of their belief that the Egyptian upheaval was due to a mere clash of 'opposing military coteries' within the army.[1]

To Blunt and his friends, it was exciting to learn that Arabi had been warned in time by his loyal soldiers, and had used this chance to arrest fifty plotters, including the reactionary Osman Rifky, and had sentenced them to exile on the White Nile. There was anxiety however in the report that the ex-Khedive Ismail was behind the Circassian Plot; for if true (as it probably was) it meant that his son Tewfik secretly opposed his own ministers.

Within a very few days came an appalling blow to nationalism in another part of the world. On 7 May in Phoenix Park, Dublin, Irish terrorists stabbed to death the new Irish secretary Lord Frederick Cavendish and his permanent under-secretary T. H. Burke. Next day Blunt was taken into the lobby of the House of Commons where Charles Stewart Parnell and John Dillon, two leading Irish M.P.s, were pointed out to him as 'the conspirators'. In fact they had nothing to do with the murders. Blunt commented characteristically in his diary: 'They looked very much like gentlemen among the cads of the lobby.'

Nevertheless the Phoenix Park Murders made a 'pretty' pair (to use Blunt's word) with the Circassian Plot. Nationalism the world over stank in British nostrils. Tewfik took the hint. On Malet's advice he had already refused to sign the order banishing the Turkish-Circassian officers. He had learnt from Malet that he would not be deserted if he reacted strongly against the nationalists: British and French naval squadrons were being despatched (the French very reluctantly) to Alexandria.

In great agitation at this build-up of explosive forces, Blunt telegraphed Arabi, 'Do nothing rashly.' At the same time he called at Downing Street offering to go out as mediator between the Khedive and his parliament. It may have been during this visit to Downing Street that Blunt ran into Lord Rosebery, the future Liberal Prime Minister. What did he think about Egypt, Blunt asked. Rosebery replied shortly, 'I have no views at all but those of a bondholder.'[2]

The British government's only reply to Blunt's offer was a tough speech in the House of Lords on 15 May promising support to Tewfik on the lines of the Joint Note, and announcing that Arabi's movement was split, the majority having gone over to the Khedive. This was not true, though the nationalist President, Sultan Pasha, had changed sides and the weakened nationalist government had resigned as a protest against Tewfik's intransigeance.

All that night Blunt tossed and turned, as he was often to do that summer. By the morning he had decided that only a 'bold step' would stop the present intrigues and perhaps halt the fleets. He himself launched a fleet of eight telegrams to the Egyptian ministers (at a cost of some £200 in today's money): to Arabi, 'United you have nothing to fear.... But stand firm'; to Sultan Pasha, 'Do not quarrel with Arabi. The danger is too great'; and remembering Colvin's threats of annexation, to six other deputies, 'If you let yourselves be separated from the army, Europe will annexe you.'

The first answer came that evening as Blunt sat down to dinner at peaceful Crabbet. 'The difference between the Khedive and his Ministers', telegraphed Sultan Pasha, 'has completely disappeared....' Other telegrams in like tone followed, including one from the Sheykh El Islam, head of the Azhar. Blunt's spirits rocketed, as they were apt to do given the slightest excuse. He rushed up to 10 Downing Street on the seventeenth and was delighted to find that Gladstone's two secretaries, Eddy Hamilton and the high-minded Arthur Godley, shared his joy. Did not the Egyptians' telegraphic replies prove that Colvin, Malet and Co. were feeding the Foreign Office with 'false information'?

Next morning came a cruel reverse. The Sheykh El Islam publicly recanted his telegram to Blunt. Swiftly his recantation was followed by that of the President.

Blunt saw no alternative but to publish a long open letter to Gladstone in *The Times*. Having dissuaded him once, Eddy Hamilton persuaded his friend to hold his fire yet again. 'Europe will annexe you' had been an unfortunate telegram, Eddy said; the fleet was being sent out simply to protect British lives; and Blunt's idea of a Commission of Inquiry was being acted upon. All this in good faith. But the result of Blunt's acquiescence in his friend's plea was to prove fatal.

The Foreign Office were to push on with their aggressive programme, undeterred. As for Blunt, the failure to explain his telegrams, or the recantations, left him wide open to attack. That evening the Liberal *St. James's Gazette* denounced him as an 'incendiary', the *Observer* followed suit and other papers were soon in full cry. As long ago as 14 April, Lord Granville had described Blunt to Malet as acting 'almost as an agent for Arabi'.[3] And this was the man whom the Egyptian nationalists had been led to believe was the friend of the Prince of Wales and Mr Gladstone's conscience.

Blunt was later to have many regrets, but his defiant advice to Arabi was not among them. He did greatly regret the retraction of his open letter to Gladstone. It had been such a near-run thing. Blunt had had to send his manservant David Roberts on the nineteenth to receive it back from the very hands of Thomas Chenery, the sympathetic editor of *The Times*. To the last, Blunt believed that if he had gone ahead and published his denunciatory letter he might have quenched the rising fires of British jingoism.

There were still a few days to go before the final crisis. Sixty people assembled on the evening of the nineteenth to hear Blunt address the Anti-Aggression League. Sir William Gregory was not among them. 'People don't mind being cowards and curs', wrote Anne in her diary.[4] Ignorance was perhaps a worse enemy than cowardice. One old gentleman at the meeting asked what 'a sheykh' was.

By the following day, 20 May, at least the naval ratings knew what 'a sheykh' was, for the British and French squadrons anchored off Alexandria. On the twenty-first Anne and Wilfrid unexpectedly met Lord Granville, still fuming over the fleet of telegrams, at a house-party given by yet another of her noble cousins, Lord Portsmouth. News arrived that Arabi had called up 4,000 reservists to face the foreign fleets. 'His Lordship looks worried', wrote Blunt hopefully, 'so I augur well for the Nationalists.' Two days later 'His Lordship's' brow cleared as he shifted responsibility on to Malet, giving him and his French colleague a free hand in Egypt.

It took Malet less than no time to decide on action. For at last he understood perfectly what his government wanted. On 25 May the Egyptian nationalists received an ultimatum, a second Joint Note more shattering even than the first: Arabi to go into voluntary exile under threat of force, and law and order to be preserved under Tewfik's restored authority.

Blunt was in agony. The ultimatum spelt ruin for Egypt or at least its reduction to a Tunis. 'Vicisti O Colvine!' were the last words in his diary of the twenty-eighth before trying, and failing, to sleep. At 3 a.m. he was up again and roaming about the silent corridors of Crabbet, only to learn from the morning newspapers that there had been another violent turn in the wheel. 'Cairo has risen', recorded Blunt in ecstasies on the twenty-ninth, 'and has demanded Arabi's recall as Minister of War, the Khedive acquiescing.' Hasty but happy preparations were begun. 'We are to go to Egypt', Anne wrote in her diary. Wilfrid dashed up to London leaving Eddy with a long memorandum for Gladstone describing his eccentric new plans. He would urge the nationalists to sink their petty differences, warn the Khedive not to listen to Malet and his French colleague, advise everybody to keep on good terms both with the Sultan and European powers; he would explain that the British government, while sympathetic, were bound by their predecessors' actions, the French by their financiers' ambitions, the Germans by their need to break the Anglo-French alliance and the Sultan by his Caliphal dreams, a matter, added Blunt, 'which they probably understand at least as well as I do'.

It was hardly surprising that Blunt was to hear the British naval commander would arrest him if he so much as tried to land at Alexandria.

There appeared to be only one setback, however, on that joyful 29 May. The Blunts showed their beautiful Pharaoh at Horsham but he was passed over, wrote Anne, in favour of 'a mongrel'. And she knew why. Either the 'mongrel's' owner was related to the judge, or it was because bondholders flocked to such shows, and they 'loathe the name of Blunt'.[5] It was not always easy to drive that lively pair in harness, Egyptian nationalism and the Crabbet Arabian Stud. Moreover, the Blunts, with their interest in auguries, should have attached due importance to the defeat of a Pharaoh.

It was part of Egypt's tragedy that the nationalist movement, when it was unaggressive and almost starry-eyed, had been misunderstood, suspected and thwarted. Now the arrival of the Anglo-French squadron was changing the people's mood into something more like the dangerous excitement that the Control had all along been depicting. Yet when Gladstone, on 1 June, turned against Arabi in Parliament, accusing him of having 'thrown off the mask', Gladstone had got it back to front. The dreamy, religious Arabi had put on the mask – the mask of a practical soldier.

In Blunt's eyes, Gladstone himself was the traitor who had 'thrown off the mask'. Never again would he trust Gladstone's protestations, or indeed those of any other 'mere Parliamentarian'. Nor would he underestimate the political animosity that might accrue to himself. There had been an angry question in Parliament about his proposal to go to Egypt. Was it true that Mr Wilfrid Blunt was about to put himself 'at the head of the insurrection?'[6] Dilke was able to soothe honourable members with the news that Mr Blunt had changed his mind – as indeed he had, thanks to Eddy Hamilton's third round of impassioned entreaties. Instead Blunt sent Sabunji at his own expense.

On the same day – 7 June – that Sabunji reached Egypt, a commissioner from Constantinople made his appearance. This was Dervish Pasha, an unscrupulous veteran whom the Sultan vainly hoped would subdue his Egyptian vassals before the Europeans intervened. On the day of Dervish's arrival Blunt happened to meet Dilke's secretary at his club. 'I hear you are sending a barrel of salt to put on Arabi's tail', said Blunt. 'No, the salt is to pickle him', was the reply. But Dervish was not to be the one to do the pickling. Four days later another of those catastrophes occurred which can only be compared to one of the seven plagues of Egypt, modern version, the Circassian Plot being the first.

On 11 June a riot broke out in Alexandria. Sixty people were killed and many hundreds wounded. Most people agreed that the riot had originated in a trivial dispute, but Arabi's enemies were quick to accuse him of fomenting the disturbance. To this Blunt replied cogently, why should Arabi promote a massacre that was to do him and his cause nothing but harm? Colvin had long been hopefully waiting for just this outburst of lawlessness and disorder, so that in the name of law and order Europe might intervene. Not only was Arabi guiltless of the riot, argued Blunt, but his enemies had conspired to begin it and to let it rip.

That is as may be. What is incontestable is that Arabi's former reputation for moderation, goodwill and above all effectiveness was destroyed on that single day, 11 June.

It took Blunt some time and many telegrams from Sabunji to reach these conclusions. His first move had been to apply for a ticket to the House of Commons through Speaker Brand who, in supplying it to the 'rebel Blunt', felt bound to add, 'he does not deserve one'.[7] After listening to a speech by Dilke about Dervish's success, Blunt returned to James Street, where he and Anne were visited by Lady Malet, mother of Edward. She strode up and down their drawing-room muttering 'traitors' under her breath. 'Poor Lady Malet!' Blunt wrote; '... she looks upon me as Edward's murderer'. (Malet was in fact to escape from Cairo within a few days, suffering from alleged *febris perniciosa*, induced as he thought by poisoning.)

If the nationalists were not above poison, the financiers could stoop to bribes. The first fat bribe to Arabi was said to be £4,000 a year from 'Natty' Rothschild, provided he left Egypt. Solution by bribery was to crop again later when the *New York Herald* correspondent in Cairo suggested that Arabi should be invited to the USA and given £1,000 a year, in return for writing a weekly column in the paper and appearing on the platform of Barnum's Circus.[8]

Blunt, however, took financial, as all other moves, in deadly earnest. By mid-June Sabunji's stream of telegrams was beginning to get him down.

> June 14 – I am quite worn out. Mrs. Howard, whom I met in the Park, said I looked altered. And in fact I have not had Egypt, sleeping or waking, out of my head since the crisis began....[9]

It was the wildly fluctuating rumours that were wearing Blunt out. To each new item, whether good or bad, he would react with the full force of his temperament. One day he would be 'very uneasy', the next sure that 'the game is won'. His diary for the 17 June reported, 'Very troubled night', due to reports of British troop movements. But had not France, Germany and Austria come to terms with Arabi? 'So England does not matter.'

England, however, did matter. 'We think they mean mischief', he wrote on the twenty-second. There was only one way to prevent it. Next day he published in *The Times* his long-deferred letter to Gladstone. If Gladstone had 'finally hardened his heart against the Egyptians', as Blunt rightly suspected, he himself would sharpen his steel against Gladstone.

His letter appeared on the same day that an international conference met in Constantinople (though boycotted by the Sultan) to decide Egypt's fate. 'It created a great sensation', wrote Blunt – of the letter not the conference. His letter contained a long historical analysis and ended with Blunt's habitual act of faith: that if once the British people understood the situation in Egypt, they would never perpetrate a great public wrong for the sake of a mistaken interest 'in Egyptian finance and in the Suez Canal'. He was appealing over the heads of the government to the British people. 'The Suez Canal', he concluded in his letter, 'cannot be better protected for England, as for the rest of the world, than by the admission of the Egyptian people into the comity of nations.'

The 'sensation' caused by his letter rapidly changed into a prolonged 'storm of abuse'. Edward Malet's brother Henry attacked him in *The Times*, and was supported by a 'nasty' leading article. There was anger in the *Sunday Observer* and the *Saturday Review*, while the *St James's Gazette* was to castigate this 'impulsive, credulous, and exceedingly vain man'. Again there were questions in Parliament, this time over Blunt's 'unofficial negotiations' with Arabi. One peer called him 'only another Arabi in a frock coat'. Lady Wynford considered him 'very wicked' for putting Egypt out of bounds to tourists.[10] Lord Houghton had decided weeks ago that both Blunt and Arabi ought to be shot.[11] Even his friend Mrs Singleton felt sure that Wilfrid would not have supported Arabi had he been an Irishman instead of an Arab. Time would show how wide of the mark she was. Colvin and Malet denied ever having used Blunt as 'mediator'.

All this local in-fighting suddenly gave way to stories from every quarter that Alexandria was to be bombarded. 'We have got the Grand Old Man into a corner now', said Joseph Chamberlain, Dilke's imperialistic accomplice in the Cabinet, 'and he *must* fight.'

Blunt felt that it was Arabi who now '*must* fight', when a new ultimatum was delivered to him in the second week of July. Either he must surrender the forts of Alexandria to England's naval commander Sir Beauchamp Seymour, or take the consequences. Arabi was given twenty-four hours in which to hand over.

Blunt's own attitude hardened, in line with the Egyptians'. When one of his pro-nationalist Liberal friends, Lord De La Warr, begged him on 10 July to make Arabi compromise, Blunt declined: 'The Egyptians could not give up their forts honourably.' He went home to Crabbet. The devoted Lady Gregory, who had helped to sustain his morale throughout his long days in London, now marvelled at his sudden blood-thirstiness. 'W.S.B. does not seem to mind', she wrote: 'says there must be bloodshed before things come right.'[12]

Arabi was still negotiating, or stalling, according to one's view of the situation, when the guns from H.M. ships opened fire at 7 a.m. on 11 July.* Old John Bright the Quaker pacifist resigned from the Cabinet. By sunset Arabi's forts were in ruins and all his gunners dead or wounded. His forces retreated under a white flag to Cairo, leaving Alexandria burning fiercely behind them and at the mercy of looters. They omitted to take the Khedive along with them, thus giving him the chance to desert his ministers yet again, and to put himself under the protection of the British.

A political tug-of-war raged in Egypt throughout the rest of July, Blunt doing his best to reflect it in England. He boldly accepted an invitation to Marlborough House on the thirteenth, where the Prince of Wales shook hands with him, but in silence. 'Her Majesty was looking beaming', recorded Blunt in his best vein of irony, ' – I suppose elated at her bombardment.' Next day Blunt passed on to Gladstone a letter dictated by Arabi to Sabunji stating the Egyptian position. *The Times* called it a 'blunt announcement', which *Punch* parodied as a 'Wilfrid Blunt pronouncement' to Gladstone Pasha. Not long afterwards the Prince of Wales was giving Granville the ludicrous information, 'on very good authority', that the 'disloyal and eccentric

* It later emerged that the Egyptian guns were not threatening the fleet but facing eastwards, away from it.

Jesuit', Mr Wilfrid Blunt, was about to join Arabi, having raised £20,000 by the sale of his family jewels and furniture.[13]

The bombardment, burning and looting of Alexandria may be taken as the third, fourth and fifth plagues of Egypt, 1882. While the diminishing band of Arabi's friends in England protested that the burning had either been caused accidentally by the British naval guns or deliberately by the Khedive, Blunt boldly attributed it to Arabi's military wisdom. 'I say he ordered it, and was right to do so. This is the policy of the Russians at Moscow.' Little Lady Gregory was once more wonderstruck by Blunt's audacity.

In mid-August General Wolseley, at the head of 30,000 trained and disciplined men, prepared to attack Arabi on his flank at Ismailia opposite the Suez Canal. Blunt had warned Arabi of the danger months ago; but only at this eleventh hour did Arabi's army begin to entrench.

And now the sixth plague was upon them, in the person of Ferdinand de Lesseps and his precious Canal. To block the Canal was vital. Indeed it was Arabi's only chance of holding out and prolonging the war until world opinion should intervene and bring British intervention to a halt. But 'Make no attempt to cut my Canal', de Lesseps telegraphed to him superbly; 'I am there. Fear nothing from that side. . . . I answer for everything.'[14]

History unjustly has made Arabi wholly responsible for the Egyptians' consequent military disaster, de Lesseps not at all.

Arabi was surprised and defeated by Wolseley on 13 September at Tel-el-Kebir, in forty minutes. The Egyptians suffered 10,000 casualties, the British 80. Blunt aptly described their forty minutes of glory as 'a mere butchery of peasants'.

Tel-el-Kebir, the seventh and last plague, wrecked Arabi's career for ever and postponed Egypt's independence for half a century. The Egyptian fellah leader surrendered his sword to General Drury Lowe at Cairo on 14 September. He thus became a prisoner of the British.

Before he knew Arabi's fate General Gordon had written from Cape Town to his friend Blunt: 'As for Arabi, whatever may become of him individually, he will live for centuries in the people; they will never be "your obedient servants" again.'[15] Whatever may become of Arabi. . . . That was to be Blunt's overwhelming concern for the rest of 1882.

Virtually at his own expense, he vowed to obtain for Arabi and his colleagues a legal trial and proper defence counsel. Otherwise they would surely be handed over to the Khedive and certain death. Only the British government could force the Khedive to agree to a public trial and only Blunt, it seemed, could make the British government force the Khedive. Time was short; Moberly Bell telegraphed from Alexandria that the white settlers demanded 'exemplary punishment'. General Sir Samuel Baker told *The Times'* readers that nothing short of execution would do: 'In the Oriental mind clemency is a token of weakness.'[16] Nubar Pasha suggested that Arabi should be beaten in front of Bedouin sheykhs. The *Egyptian Gazette* was for 'condign punishment' all round.

Thanks to that anonymous power in the corridors of *The Times*, Algernon 'Button' Bourke, Blunt brought off his first coup. Bourke persuaded the editor Chenery to announce in his paper as a government decision what was in fact only Blunt's 'unauthorized programme': namely, that Arabi would not be executed without the British government's consent, and that he would not be tried without legal aid. No such thing had been decided. Gladstone, however, could not go back on so obviously humane a 'decision', after it had been seen in print. Blunt's enemies, meanwhile, hoped that he would soon be requiring legal aid himself. 'The fellow knows he has a handsome head', said Lord Houghton, 'and he wants it to be seen on Temple Bar.'[17]

Queen's Counsel, in the shape of A. M. Broadley, was engaged by Blunt to defend Arabi and his friends. Broadley had been *The Times'* correspondent in Tunis and had defended the Bey against the French. With him went the Hon. Mark Napier as his junior, a delightful and original character who was to be Blunt's friend for life.

Then came a hitch. Blunt wrote a letter to Arabi, to be delivered through Malet, giving details of his plans: Blunt himself would arrive in Cairo with Broadley and Napier to help Arabi with his evidence. Not only was Blunt's letter never delivered to Arabi, but if Blunt had landed at Alexandria he himself would have been delivered into the hands of the police. This we know from Malet's book on Egypt published in 1909.

'Am I to have this letter delivered?' Malet had asked Lord Granville in a style that expected the answer 'no'. As regards Blunt's proposed public landing in Egypt, added Malet, the Egyptian government would have him taken into custody and Malet would *not* interfere unless instructed by Granville. But suppose Blunt arrived in disguise?

> If Mr Blunt comes here secretly, and is discovered, he will be arrested. In that case, unless instructed by your Lordship to the contrary, I should not exact his release, but should insist on his being sent out of the country. . . .[18]

Lord Granville agreed with Malet's plan of campaign. So on 4 October Blunt received back his letter to Arabi, with the coldest of covering notes from his erstwhile friend: 'Sir . . . herewith . . . 22nd ultimo . . . I am, etc., Edward B. Malet.'

Blunt was not so foolhardy as to risk Arabi's life and perhaps his own by getting nabbed, especially as Button's sleight-of-hand with *The Times* had made sure that Arabi's defence counsel would get through. Yet the weeks of discussion by letter with Broadley, and of money-raising in England, kept Blunt in a perpetual fever.

To begin with Broadley did not like Arabi. 'He can talk, and do little else', Broadley wrote. And Arabi would have much to explain away. The centre of Alexandria, according to Broadley, was a ruin occupied by shanties and grog-shops with names like 'The British Tar', 'The Tel-el-Kebir' and 'The Wolseley Arms'. Translation of Arabi's documents presented another difficulty. How about this for Arabi's (translated) letter appointing Broadley and Napier as his counsel: 'Mr Broadley, of Lincoln's Inn', had come out as 'Mr Broadley of Long Street', and 'the Hon. Mark Napier of the Inner Temple' as 'the Hon. Mark Napier son of Officer Campbell'.[19]

The trial at last began in mid-September. Three main accusations faced Arabi, as well as an overall charge of rebellion: abuse of the white flag in his retreat from Alexandria; the riots; and the fire after the bombardment. Arabi's counsel showed that the white flag episode was within Wolseley's own rules of war, and that none of the violence had been perpetrated with Arabi's consent. In regard to the general charge of 'rebellion' against the Sultan, Arabi had defended Egypt at the Sultan's own initial (though since cancelled) command, and if anyone was a rebel it was Tewfik when he betrayed the country to the British.

On 30 October, Mark Napier was able to inform Blunt that 'we are masters now'. By November the British government's case for a court martial rather than the civil trial was in such 'a hopeless muddle' that Granville had to send out their ace negotiator Lord Dufferin to cut the knot.[20]

Blunt, in a state of elation, had begun to bank on complete exculpation of the nationalist leaders; but the British government's resolve to save official faces, and Blunt's own inability to go on paying for an indefinite trial, suggested the need for a compromise. If Blunt accepted a compromise in principle, wrote Broadley urgently, would he telegraph in code the word 'Pax'; if he refused, the word 'Bellum'.

Pax it was. With much inward groaning Blunt consented that Arabi and his friends should plead guilty to 'rebellion'. They were formally sentenced to death but their sentences commuted forthwith to banishment.* 'Arabi delighted at result and sends thanks', wired Broadley, 'Dufferin brick Anglo-Egyptian Colony furious.'

Blunt continued to badger the British government until what he

* Malet was later to write that this was exactly the result he himself had hoped for – but as a result of a court martial not a public trial. *Shifting Scenes* (1901), p. 74.

considered a suitable location for the exiles was agreed. Not the Amdaman Islands, far less South Africa, but Ceylon: 'the traditional place of exile', wrote Blunt, 'of our father Adam when driven out of Paradise'.[21] As an expert on lost paradises, Blunt could conceive of no better retreat. Meanwhile the fellahin firmly believed their absent leader was merely making a thirty-day celestial trip through the heavens, and would shortly return as their Mahdi and saviour.[22]

Any claim by Blunt to fame as a political animal must rest largely on the 1882 balance-sheet. He himself was fully conscious of his heavy responsibility for making Arabi fight and for the grievous consequences in blood and suffering. Even so he did not ultimately regret his incitements. At least since 1882 Britain was no longer able to ignore Egyptian complaints of exploitation by foreigners in general and Turkish tyranny in particular. Lord Cromer's social and economic reforms which were to follow the war proved one side of the nationalists' case: reforms were long overdue.

On the political side, Blunt's antennae were miracles of sensitivity compared with the obtuseness of his opponents. He had an instinctive feeling for a nation's right to be free. A man like the statesman Lord Milner, though much younger than Blunt, could never get beyond the conventional view that 'Egypt for the Egyptians' was 'an ominous and misleading watchcry'.[23] Even Cromer called it 'impossible', at least in the foreseeable future. Blunt's cherished hope, however, that Egypt could be won for the Egyptians through a fellah prophet like Arabi was utopian, as he himself came to realize. It might have been said of Colonel Arabi as it was later to be said of Colonel Dreyfus: 'L'homme était bien inferieur à l'affaire.' Indeed, a sympathetic Scottish royal governess in Cairo was to use almost those words in saying to Blunt that Arabi was 'not quite à la hauteur de la situation'. That granted, both General Gordon and Blunt were right to see in Ahmed Arabi Pasha a national hero whose name would not soon be forgotten. Seventy-four years later, at the time of Suez, the name of 'Ourábi' was still a talisman.*

The Egyptian tragedy also brought out the weaknesses in Blunt's character. His influence with the British Cabinet was not so great as he led the Egyptians to suppose; just as his responsibility for events in Egypt was not as weighty as many people in Britain – including perhaps himself – imagined. In denouncing Gladstone in his diary for the bombardment of Alexandria – 'I believe him capable of any

* One of Blunt's mistakes was to 'correct' Colvin's spelling of the hero's name from Ourábi or Urabi to Arabi; thereby emphasizing, as he thought, the profound connection of the man Arabi with Arab nationalists. Unfortunately the English pronunciation (Araby) is totally unlike the Egyptian, which is nearer Colvin's spelling. Recently, when I tried to discuss 'Araby' with an Egyptian he did not at first know who I meant.

treachery and any crime'[24] – Blunt was carrying exaggeration to the point of mere rhetoric. Nevertheless, the sometimes wild and whirling words of his diary do convey, as nothing else does, the complete disillusionment of all generous spirits with Gladstone's behaviour in 1882. The Grand Old Man was not seen at his best.

Another of Blunt's errors was gradually to forget the 'route-to-India' argument in the British government's calculations. More and more he tended to see Gladstone and Granville as manipulated by the bondholders. In his defence it can be said that the financiers' pull was indeed powerful. Why did *The Times* accept loaded stories from Moberly Bell? asked Lady Gregory one day of Chenery, the editor. 'I will tell you', replied Chenery. 'It is because of the influence of the European bondholders. . . .' Her husband's comment was: 'Don't tell that to Wilfrid Blunt or he will have sandwich-men walking with it down Piccadilly tomorrow.'[25] On the Canal question, Blunt was told personally by John Bright in 1882 that Britain's communications with India depended on the Cape, not the Canal. Gladstone himself had proclaimed this 'truth' in 1880, during his violent election attacks upon Disraeli.

The theme of 'selfish financiers' led on inevitably to 'greedy Jews', since great names like Disraeli and Rothschild were prominent in the story of Egyptian economic development. It is no extenuation of Blunt's fault to say that many of his contemporaries argued likewise. Nevertheless he was not a racist. He knew well that both Arabs and Jews were of the same Semitic stock. As one literary lady had expostulated to him at the time of the Arabi crisis, he, Blunt, was an 'Aryan' and had no business with his poetic talents to involve himself with the 'Semites' – meaning Arabs.

Blunt's moral courage, loyalty and persistence were qualities that far outweighed his mistakes. He never ceased to work for a free pardon for Arabi, boring as the subject became to successive British governments and, ultimately, useless to Arabi himself. Nor did Blunt labour just for one man. He stood out against a whole policy; against the annexation of Egypt.

The band of trusted political friends with whom Blunt worked during that summer included a significant mixture of Tories and Radicals: Lord Randolph Churchill, Drummond Wolff and John Gorst of the Tory 'Fourth Party'; Blunt's Tory country neighbour W. J. Evelyn, M.P., whose ancestor had been responsible for the famous diary; and the Radicals Sir Wilfrid Lawson and Sir George Labouchere. Blunt's cousin Percy Wyndham, husband of the lovely Madeline and father of the lovelier Mary, was the only Tory to vote with the tiny minority of nineteen against the war.

Though Blunt paid ten times as much as anyone else towards the

Arabi Defence Fund (£3,000 against contributions amounting to some £300) the smaller sum he raised put him in touch with many interesting characters hitherto unknown to him. Frederic Harrison the left-wing pamphleteer and Comtist sent ten guineas, and Alexander William Kinglake, Oriental traveller, historian and author of *Eothen*, gave £5. 'There is a fire about Mr Blunt', he said, 'which must command a following.'

Being the man he was, Blunt could not conduct an arduous and prolonged campaign without the help of a romance, if such were available. In 1882 it was available with that queen of empathy Lady Gregory.

Augusta Gregory, born a Persse in County Galway, Ireland, had been married to Sir William Gregory for two years and now had a baby son. She and Wilfrid Blunt met in the winter of 1881, he a revelation to her of bold masculinity, she to him 'a quiet little woman of perhaps five and twenty, rather plain than pretty, but still attractive, with much good sense, and a fair share of Irish wit'. In fact she looked extremely like Queen Victoria, having smooth hair parted neatly in the centre, a clever unstylish face and diminutive figure.

Blunt added that Sir William kept her 'rather in the background'. Sir William's initial enthusiasm for the Egyptian nationalists had faded, Blunt said, because Sir William did not wish to risk his popularity as a clubman and diner-out. On the other hand, Sir William may have suspected the effect on his unobtrusive little wife of a romantic lost cause. Blunt was to describe its effect in his 'Secret Memoirs':[26]

> This naturally drew us more closely than ever together, and at the climax of the tragedy by a spontaneous impulse we found comfort in each other's arms. It was a consummation neither of us, I think, foresaw, and was a quite new experience in her quiet life. It harmonized not ill with mine in its new phase of political idealism and did not in any way disturb or displace it. On the contrary to both of us the passionate element in our intercourse at this time proved a source of inspiration and of strength. It was under its influence that I was able to carry on that hardest public battle of my life, the rescuing of Arabi from the vengeance of his enemies – she working with me and advising and encouraging.

The child of their passion was Blunt's long, moving poem, *The Wind and the Whirlwind.** The first draft was transcribed for him by

* Published in his Poetical Works (1914), Vol. II, pp. 221–35, and in *The Secret History of the Occupation of Egypt*, republished 1969. It is interesting that as late as 1970 Blunt's name was twice celebrated in Marxist literature. A Russian author Alla Mihailovna Lynbarskaya published in Leningrad her *Wilfrid Scawen Blunt: Life, Work & Struggle*. In a note on this book, the editor of a British Communist organ, *Marxism Today* (August 1970), pointed out that Karl Marx, a few months before his death, was reading and making marginal notes on Blunt's 'The Egyptian Revolution' in the journal *Nineteenth Century*.

Lady Gregory and filed with his private papers. There it remains today, all 103 verses of it, in her neat handwriting. It is vibrant with bitterness and indignation. To Blunt, the defeat, imprisonment and exile of Arabi had raised a wind of resentment against Europe in the East. Europe would surely reap the whirlwind. And in the centre of the whirlwind's path would lie a doomed British Empire:

> Thou hast deserved men's hatred. They shall hate thee.
> Thou hast deserved men's fear. Their fear shall kill.
> Thou hast thy foot upon the weak. The weakest
> With his bruised head shall strike thee on the heel.

[9]
A Passage through India 1883–1884

Egypt's defeat had reduced some of Blunt's friends to despair. Rosalind Howard, for instance, unable to endure the jollifications of the Liberal 'jingoists', had preferred 'to stay at home and gnash my teeth'. When her will for action drove her out again it was along new roads. By February 1883 she was 'wholly occupied in converting our local town to teetotalism – 1,400 converts in 3 months! Ceaseless work ... and now the difficult process of keeping the weak from relaxing.'[1]

Blunt also had problems of making and keeping converts. But his thwarted energies had turned from Egypt to India.

A first hint that India might be his new field had come from General Gordon, who had gone out as private secretary to Lord Ripon the new Viceroy and Lytton's successor, but resigned on reaching Bombay. He had called on the Blunts at James Street towards the end of 1882. This 'quiet little unmilitary man with grey eyes and hair turning grey' had some disquieting things to say. India was a hopeless proposition for reformers because of British vested interests, especially the Civil Service; nothing would ever be done for the people 'except through a revolution'.

Wilfrid's imagination was fired and Anne found Gordon not 'touched' in the head, as Eddy Hamilton had once suggested, but 'in perfect possession of perfect common sense'.[2]

The next person of note to bring forward India was Blunt's old friend Jamal al-Din al-Afghani. He suggested that Blunt should call on the Egyptian exiles in Ceylon and then explore 'native society' in India, with a view to their possible interest in 'home rule'. An important side issue would be the Indian Mohammedans. Were they 'a living force in Islam', equal to furthering the Islamic reformation of which al-Afghani and Blunt still dreamed?

A third person to encourage Blunt was Lord Randolph Churchill. On 'Button' Bourke's advice, Blunt wrote to Churchill asking him, as a leading member of the Tory Opposition in Parliament, to defend the

Egyptian nationalists against the charge of complicity in the Alexandria riot. Churchill made a rendezvous with Blunt at a chess tournament in the Strand, and here for the first time Blunt met this 'decidedly good-looking young man, smartly dressed and with a certain distinction of manner which marked him from the common herd'. There was nothing aggressive in his appearance, except for the 'strong moustache curling up above his cheeks'. Nevertheless he was soon flaying the Liberal government for allowing some Egyptian hangings; so effectively indeed, that twenty-five years later Lord Cromer still thought it necessary, in his *Modern Egypt*, to repudiate Lord Randolph's case and Blunt's theories.

Here was a man after Blunt's heart: ferocious in public attack but frank and natural, even boyish, in private. He seemed ready to learn from Blunt, deferring charmingly to him as writer and poet. (Blunt noticed that Churchill's eloquence did not prevent him from manhandling the English language, a characteristic phrase of his being, 'between you and I'.) All through that parliamentary session of 1883 Blunt was impregnating an instinctively sympathetic Churchill with his own ideas for justice and liberty in the East. 'Before the session was over', wrote Blunt, 'I counted him as, on those points, already my disciple. My success with him confirms me in my ambition to become a preacher of reform.' India should be his rostrum.

It was without any apparent wrench that Blunt prepared to part for another long period from his daughter Bibi and his friends. The parting from Lady Gregory was rather more serious; for theirs was one of the passions that had to stop, in deference to the new era of 'doing good'. Their separation, wrote Blunt, resulted in a beautiful sonnet-sequence by Augusta. Ten years later it was printed, with her consent, in the Kelmscott edition of Blunt's *Proteus*, under the title of 'A Woman's Sonnets'.

> She wrote them for me as a farewell to our passion and put them in my hand the morning that we parted after a last night spent together in the room over the bow-window at Crabbet ... and they tell all our love's history that needs the telling.

The twelve originals, still among Blunt's papers, were written out by Augusta Gregory herself though in a disguised handwriting. In the last sonnet Augusta sent Wilfrid away with a line typical of that period: 'Go forth dear! thou hast much to do on earth.'

By a strange coincidence, another document was being written by another victim of a dead passion just three days after Wilfrid received the package from Augusta Gregory. But in the second case there was no 'mutual pact'. Indeed, Wilfrid was thoroughly taken aback by the statement suddenly handed to him by his wife, without further explanation. The statement was long, covering over two pages of lined foolscap, and deeply moving. It began abruptly with no heading but the date:

> *August 10, 1883*. This paper is written to state a fact and explain its cause – as neither the one nor the other seem to be understood. The fact is that all keen interest I have in life is gone past recall – the cause the shock of discovering that I have spent many years under a false impression.

Anne then explained that 'an earthquake' had reduced the 'house' in which she had lived to a heap of ruins. Ivy might some day cover the ruin but it would never be a house again. She did not expect 'external assistance' in bearing the 'unceasing pain' though it would be a relief if care were taken not to stir it up. Give the grass time to grow over the grave.

> This is no question of 'Me and Thee' or 'Thee and Me'. Nor do I now complain that I once was rich – and now am poor. It is too late. I accept harsh truth preferring it to a false dream. . . . I have lived long years hoarding an unreal treasure and thinking 'while life lasts this will be there'.

She compared herself to a foolish traveller who failed to see that behind the desert mirage of a caravan and oasis lay nothing but 'a desolate waste'.

> I believed in what was not, nor ever had been. And the knowledge of the truth came suddenly like a bitter wind destroying all that had taken years to grow up, and killing all hope. Time is needed to recover – and some day perhaps – Alas! Time is short and that 'Some Day' may but be the Nothing of the phantom caravan.

Nevertheless there would be no outward change in her behaviour. Whatever work there was to do she would take her share of it. Willingly, even gladly (if she could still be glad), she would help where she was pledged by her marriage vows to give help.

> Have I not written this plain? Perhaps I have failed. Like the dumb creatures that have no voice to speak their suffering I have no words on my tongue. Then those who are poets . . . despise us and think in their hearts that we have nothing to say no sense of grief – no souls. How often have I tried to write this? . . . Shall I try once more?

Anne then tried to explain her tragedy with yet another metaphor. Two ships were steering a parallel course round the world when a sudden fog separated them. 'All night long my ship signalled. No answer came.' Instead her ship struck a rock and sank, destroying all her treasured possessions except her compass, a scroll of Arabic and herself. Alone she must sit in an open boat, learning to row against the long waves – waves that from her tall ship's deck had once looked so smooth.

Now from the sea level they seem like mountains. I strain my eyes for a sight of land. I care for nothing but to keep the straight path.

She signed it A.I.N.B. – Anne Isabella Noel Blunt – in Arabic letters.[3]

What exactly had gone wrong? Writing many years later, Blunt confessed that he still did not completely understand. Yet he was able to make a guess, part of which is convincing, part bogus. His explanation (which is also his 'Apologia pro Vita Sua') begins as follows:

In the long history of my vagrant heart I have said little of what was my conjugal life at home. This in spite of my many lapses had in reality been quite a happy one. Though I have loved other women, I have not for that reason been less kind to my wife, nor has she had cause to reproach me with the neglect of those duties for which matrimony. . . . was primarily ordained. No one in truth had ever a stronger desire for 'the procreation of children' . . . and as yet we had no heir.

Now, however, the day of such hopes was fairly at an end. I was forty-two, Anne forty-five; and, with the vanishing of what we have so long desired in common, a certain estrangement had begun between us, for which I do not in my conscience think I was seriously to blame. Nevertheless to Anne the gradual separation *a thoro* [from the marriage-bed] was a matter of grievous concern, and, though she said nothing and though I did not suspect it, it was in secret making her unhappy.[4]

Here at least Wilfrid was right. There are several references in Anne's 1883 diary to some such hidden grief: in June during a tennis weekend at Crabbet she goes to bed writing, 'I am tired – extinct[5] – Would that my thoughts could stop – it is unbearable'; in July she records, 'Conversation about the hearts of poets – who have no heart, by the way, as it all dissolves in vain words. A wound years ago remains a wound for ever to me, poor worm of the earth, as long as I live, but those who talk pass unscathed. I don't know which is more despicable.'[6]

Wilfrid's analysis took a more dubious turn when he considered Anne's reaction to the loss of his physical love:

She interpreted it, not for what it was, a physical effect of time's hand laid on us, but as revealing a lack of constancy in my affection which had sapped the foundations of her married life. My infidelities she had condoned as due to my poet's nature, but my inconstancy, for so she deemed it, filled her with despair. . . . If I did not continue thus to love her, it was a proof that I had never loved her truly.

None of this rings true. Did Anne ever really 'condone' his infidelities? Or did she not find them 'despicable' (to use her own word)? And if it was only a matter of *anno domini*, Anne may have asked herself why 'time' should lay his hand on her and Wilfrid but not on Wilfrid and Lady Gregory? For there is no reason to suppose that Anne did not know about that adulterous night at Crabbet on 7 August, as she had known of so many others.

Even less acceptable is Wilfrid's final suggestion that Anne's conversion to Catholicism had contributed to the 'ill result'. Priests in the confessional, he implied, may have urged her no longer to 'condone' her husband's sins. 'I had been, as it were, for all these years a god to her', he concluded, 'and now she had come to acknowledge another god and another service. . . . She had accepted a new standard and by it I stood condemned.'

When she heard this theory, often voiced by Wilfrid, Anne repudiated it utterly. Never, never had Wilfrid been her 'god'.

It was soon evident to Anne that her continuing pledge of help to her husband in his work might involve fresh strains. Wilfrid had approached Lord Randolph Churchill and Father Coffin, she noted in her diary on 27 August, with a view to standing for Parliament as a Home Ruler – but it would have to be in Ireland. Anne was lukewarm:

> I think English constituencies are bad, and probably Irish are worse. His whole life of political action has been transparently straight and I doubt the possibility of his getting into Parliament without sacrificing that. I consider that the pledges given by M.P.s are a sacrifice of their integrity.[7]

Others thought differently. Blunt's portrait was already commissioned for *Vanity Fair*, in whose pages he would shine like Gladstone and Disraeli, but as 'The Prophet'. And on the same day that Anne was hesitating, 27 August, the Catholic journalist Wilfrid Meynell was asking for biographical details to fill out an article on Blunt in his *Merry England*. Two days later came an even more intriguing proposition, from Gladstone, again using as his intermediary Thomas Knowles, editor of the *Nineteenth Century*. According to Knowles, Gladstone's idea was that Blunt should encourage the Egyptian Nationalists to elect Arabi to their new, allegedly democratic consultative assembly, thus giving the government an excuse to bring Arabi back. Blunt was later to call the consultative assembly 'that mockery of self-government . . . without legislative power, without control over Ministers'.[8] But now he felt it imperative to make the most of this initiative.

However, he had learnt his lesson this time; no soaring hopes were allowed to delude him. True, his position at Cairo would be much stronger than last year. Malet and Colvin had both been moved; and the new man was none other than Evelyn Baring, appointed with carte blanche to govern Egypt. Baring had just written an article for the *Nineteenth Century*, said Knowles, 'full of the most liberal ideas', and would receive Blunt 'with open arms'. On 8 September Blunt wrote to Rosalind Howard:

> If there is anything in Knowles' argument I shall find the field open for me with Baring. At the same time I confess I am far from sanguine. In the first place I do not trust Mr. Gladstone as you do, and then I *know* the difficulties. These will be immense, and without really cordial cooperation from Baring I could do nothing at all. . . .

He finally decided that half an hour's talk with Baring would be enough to settle the matter. Until then, his future was again in the melting-pot. Would it be worthwhile staying in Egypt instead of going on to India? He began once more to keep a regular diary.

The Blunts' first stop was in Paris where they met al-Afghani and other nationalist friends. Wilfrid drew up three points on Egypt to put to the government: the public debt to be reduced; the Canal to be internationalized; the Sudan, where an Arab rebellion had broken out soon after Tel-el-Kebir led by a fanatical 'Mahdi' or saviour, to be independent.

On the voyage to Suez Blunt addressed himself to the many money-lenders, Syrians and Greeks, on board. What did they predict? One and all favoured annexation by England. Baring was 'a master of finance, a man who knew his own mind and as firm as a rock'. A Greek who did not know who they were recommended them to visit Arabi in Ceylon as 'une bête curieuse'. Sherif Pasha, said the Greek, had advised the English government to show Arabi publicly at 1s. a head and use the money for the Egyptian debt; the waxwork of him at Madame Tussaud's was 'beaucoup trop beau'. He referred to the Indian peasants as 'les animaux'. At Port Said postcard-sellers came on board and the Blunts bought a ghastly photograph of the hangings.

From the train to Cairo they caught glimpses of the Tel-el-Kebir battlefield: a skull or two, many bones and hundreds of broken food cans. Arabi's celebrated 'lines' turned out to be nothing but a low bank and shallow dry ditch. 'They would hardly stop a hunting-field', wrote Blunt ruefully.

The breakfast with Evelyn Baring took place on 26 September at noon. As his power and success waxed, Baring was to rebuild the British Embassy in a style that still enunciates nineteenth-century views of imperial grandeur. (As if that were not enough, Lord Kitchener was to add a vast ballroom wing, now occupied by the visa department.) When Blunt arrived there in 1883 the charming garden ran right down to the Nile. Today a busy city street roars between the embassy and the east bank.

Baring had arrived in Cairo as Resident only a few days before

Blunt's call. This was Blunt's first sight of the man who was to be known as Lord Cromer, the architect of modern Egypt, or simply as 'the Great Builder' – everyone knew who that meant. His staff nicknamed him 'Over-Baring', overbearing to his superiors rather than to his inferiors. Blunt thought he looked about fifty; in fact Baring at forty-two was a year younger than Blunt.

The conversation began in a friendly manner. Blunt felt that he was dealing with 'a man of sense and integrity'; perhaps not exactly brilliant, but 'capable of original ideas'. This being so, Blunt decided to try out the original idea confided to him by Gladstone. What about restoring the nationalist exiles, beginning with civilians, and finally bringing back Arabi?

Quite out of the question, snapped Baring. Impossible without another revolution. In any case, had not the nationalists alternative leaders still in Egypt?

The Khedive's reign of terror, replied Blunt hotly, had crushed all courage out of the few who had not been hanged, exiled or imprisoned.

The amiable tone that had hitherto characterized the conversation now vanished. Blunt saw that in reality he and Baring had from the outset been in 'hopeless disaccord'. When Baring finally declared his intention to give the Khedive all-out backing, and Blunt retorted that then it was goodbye to Egyptian self-government and reform, the breakfast-party broke up. Blunt did mention a desire in Downing Street for 'something in the nature of a restoration of the National Party'. But he tactfully refrained from uttering the name of Gladstone. 'I saw that it was useless talking further....'

And useless to put off his journey to India beyond another week. In that short time, however, Blunt was able thoroughly to blot his copy-book with Baring.

He was asked by his Arab friends to visit some of the Nationalists now held in the Zaptieh prison. Having written to Baring for permission and received no answer, he decided to go anyway. A warder obliged with a key, and in the few minutes allowed him, Blunt was inundated with pleas to look after the prisoners' interests and remember them to Arabi.

Three days before his departure came a belated answer from Baring: the Khedive said no. 'Rot!' wrote Blunt in his diary; it was Baring's own doing. Blunt's last act was to inform the Resident that he had in fact seen the prisoners; and to recommend them to his mercy. As a result the prisoners were eventually released – but Blunt himself was punished by exile. It would be three long years before he was allowed to see Cairo and Sheykh Obeyd again.

Of Sheykh Obeyd, his beloved garden and orchard, he carried away with him a last, ironic memory. It had been ransacked by the Turkish authorities after he left in 1882 and a cache discovered of twelve Winchester rifles, four revolvers and one small brass cannon. Gun-running to the rebels, of course! The weapons were rushed to British military H.Q. (where Blunt claimed them many years later) and the Blunts marked down as terrorists.

In fact the guns had been acquired for their abortive desert journey in 1880, the cannon being intended as a present to Ibn Rashid.*

If the revolt of Islam was not to happen in Egypt, then surely India might awake and rise? Alas, the prophet of India's awakening – 'Blunti' as the Muslims now called him – was himself laid low almost at once with acute malaria during the voyage to Ceylon. It was left for Anne to report on the 'Anglo-Indian' planters who were their fellow passengers. She expressed her horror of the planters' ladies, for ever shouting 'Boy – Boy – Bo ... y', to give or countermand an order.

BOY: 'Mem no take tiffin?'
MEM: 'Oh no, Boy, I'm so ill today, Boy.'

Five minutes later the sick memsahib would be shouting at the top of her voice for chops, jam, rice, chicken.

In revenge for Anne's censorious expression, the passengers got the captain to send her a nasty note:

> Madam you are requested not to appear at your meals in your hat and ladies are not allowed on deck [where Wilfrid slept] before eight o'clock [Anne had joined him for early morning tea at 7 a.m.]. A compliance with above rules is desired.[9]

A tea-planter who consented to converse with Anne was hot against the Ilbert Bill, which Lord Ripon the Viceroy of India sponsored and Wilfrid intended above all to study. According to the new Bill, India would at last get a touch of self-government in the law-courts. For Englishmen accused of crime would in future be judged in the ordinary native courts instead of coming before white tribunals. Anne's planter friend explained: 'The sole idea of the natives is to sweep the English out of the country', and the Ilbert Bill would encourage them 'to begin using their brooms'.

A vast concourse of joyful Muslims watched the Blunts being brought ashore at Colombo on 19 October, Wilfrid only half-conscious in his beflagged steam-launch, with six other boats full of exiles, and sons of exiles, and supporters of exiles, in tow. In response to showers of rose-water, flower petals and addresses, Wilfrid could

* Judith Wentworth fell for the canard, writing in her autobiography that her father had 'imported arms' at Sheykh Obeyd and 'plotted' with nationalist conspirators against Cromer.

only say, very slowly, 'The Muslims have no better friend than I.' Indeed, he had renounced wine and was reading the Koran. If he had subsequently found himself at death's door, he wrote, 'I would have made my profession of Islam and attained perhaps to the honour of Mohammedan saintship, so great was the devotion of all the community to me.'

But he was dragged from death's door and potential sanctity thanks to a diet of goat's milk and expert nursing by Cowie, Anne's maid. 'Anne in a sick room with all her devotion was of little use.' Wilfrid was soon receiving a daily stream of visitors, Hindus as well as Muslims. Their numbers and enthusiasm at first amazed him. Then he learnt that his old enemy Sir Auckland Colvin, now back in India, had attacked him in the *Pioneer*, an important Anglo-Indian newspaper. In fact the *Pioneer* acted as a free advertisement for Blunt's travels; wherever he went he was met by those 'natives' who had the courage of their convictions, whether of reform or revolution. A grand banquet attended by 450 prominent Muslims of Ceylon was followed on 10 November by Blunt's farewell breakfast, at which Arabi toasted Queen Victoria for giving him such a pleasant place of exile. They kissed Blunt goodbye one after the other on the quay next day. It was the humane rule of Sir William Gregory, Blunt generously decided, that had made the people of Ceylon so friendly.

A series of train journeys through south-east India to Madras took it out of Blunt. He could walk only short distances and was trundled to the Hindu temples in carts. At Tanjore they were shown Sivaji's bull and Ganesh the elephant god. Perhaps it was too much to expect a Victorian guide to explain to Anne the 'mysterious black posts' which she took for some kind of altar. She drew one in her diary, not having heard of the sacred *lingam*.

They found politics again in Madras. Two clever young Hindu editors consulted Blunt at 1 a.m. about the salt tax, irrigation, the tax on forests, and the community relations of Hindus and Muslims. Should their paper back *one* party in England? No, replied Blunt, who had not yet made up his own mind. Tipu Sultan's grandson was disappointingly cautious, being a government official, and a Muslim judge was afraid to be seen talking to them in their hotel. But the wise old Brahmin Ragonath Rao, cousin of a raja, was good value as an exponent of old-fashioned Indian patriotism. He did not believe in full independence. 'We make very good seconds', he said; 'but the highest offices should always be filled by Englishmen – Englishmen of course of the best class.'[10]

On the way to Hyderabad they inspected villages, Anne meticulously noting the numbers of population, children, bullocks per family, secret salt meadows, debts to taxmen, new wells, famine sufferers and the type of village, whether 'caste' or 'pariah'. At Hyderabad they were guests at the magnificent Palladian-style Residency. Mr Cordery the Resident and his staff of civil servants at first regarded Wilfrid with suspicion. But after Wilfrid had boldly informed them that he favoured abolition of the entire Indian Civil Service, as at present constituted, they all relaxed. At least he was an open enemy.

The Blunts felt happier here, under the rule of a Nizam, than in the 'mournful towns under English rule', like Madras. The place was the busiest in the Mohammedan East after Cairo – 'a great flower-bed' of bright dresses, as seen from the backs of their elephants. Young Salar Jung, the liberal-minded son of the late Prime Minister, seemed to Blunt cut out for a great role in emancipating India. True to his own prophetic urges, Blunt had soon devised a mission for himself to Lord Ripon, the Viceroy, on behalf of the leading Muslims.

It was no less than an attempt to redirect the ruling forces in Hyderabad. The Nizam, hitherto a minor, was about to be installed on the *musnad* (throne) by Lord Ripon. Cordery's plan was to appoint the Peishkar, a docile veteran reactionary, as the Nizam's Prime Minister. This was the heaven-sent moment, decided Blunt, in which to get Salar Jung, aged twenty-two, appointed instead, so that the two youthful Muslim nobles, the Nizam and his Prime Minister, could light the torch of freedom for all India. Admittedly, for the Nizam's torch to produce a really spectacular blaze Cordery would have to be removed. How could Cordery, 'who drinks too much sherry every evening, be his proper mentor?' Salar Jung, on the other hand, would keep the Nizam straight with a 'time-table of daily work'.[11]

In Calcutta Blunt's hopes at first thrived. Lord Ripon, a Catholic convert, was piously dedicated to reform; one of his A.D.C.s happened to be Walter Pollen, Minnie's son, while his chaplain was Father Kerr, cousin of Blunt's old friend Schomberg. Though nervous, Blunt put Salar Jung's case to Ripon. The Viceroy's friendliness enchanted him; indeed nothing had impressed him so much since the first interview with Gladstone in 1882. *Absit omen!*

But even more absorbing than interviews and parties in Government House – that dazzling confection of pillars and steps high and wide enough to lead to an Anglo-Indian heaven – were Blunt's meetings with small groups of liberal Muslims. To be sure, not all the auguries were happy. Mrs Ilbert, in tears, gave them the shameful news that her husband's great Bill was to be emasculated as a result of Anglo-Indian pressure.

'I cannot understand anyone paying a moment's attention to the Anglo-Indians', said Blunt.

'If you had been Viceroy', sobbed Mrs Ilbert, 'I have no doubt it would have been so.'

For his part, Blunt felt bound to castigate those faint-hearted Muslims who were switching to the government's side on the Ilbert Bill. How suicidal to desert the Hindus on this pivotal battle – the Hindus who, in Blunt's candid opinion, were intellectually 'far our superiors'. Only the most drastic measures would win the people's rights. When an optimistic Indian editor suggested that the Civil Service would soon be opened to Indians, Blunt replied sternly: 'Nothing will be done without a Revolution.'

Perhaps the Indian National Conference would bring that revolution about? Blunt spent the last days of the year attending its meetings, in company with its dynamic secretary Mr Bose. On hearing that Mr Wilfrid Blunt was present the delegates burst into cheers. Rising to his feet Blunt said: '*All* nations are fit for self-government and few more so than the Indians.' He was again loudly applauded after begging the delegates to take up the cause of the poor, as Arabi had. Less acceptable was his suggestion that the problem of fund-raising should be solved by passing the hat round. Bose replied that if he did so the delegates would never show up again. Blunt's concluding words on what he called the first session of the Indian Parliament were: 'May it be memorable in history.' As precursor of the Indian National Congress, it was.

The magical sights Blunt was next to see in Benares, Delhi and Jaipur hardly found a place in his diary. It was left again for Anne to expatiate on the Monkey Temple of Benares, the magnificent view from the Mutiny Monument outside Delhi and the touching bunch of marigolds on Humayum's tomb, not to mention the studs they inspected and the races they attended. True, Blunt noted any little ironies: the last of the Moguls at Benares, for instance, taking his guests to a cock-skirmish rather than cock-fight, since he was too poor to replace a bird if it was killed.*

Blunt was more concerned with two political issues: the arrogance of Anglo-Indians towards 'natives'; and the foundation of a new liberal all-India Islamic university in the Deccan, preferably at Hyderabad.

The horror of Anglo-Indian arrogance was suddenly brought home to him after a scene on the platform at Patna station on 8 January 1884. About thirty Muslims had come to see him off, headed by the venerable Nawab Villayet Ali Khan. Suddenly a furious white man lent out of the next compartment window brandishing a cane and shouting to Blunt's Indian friends, 'Clear off! I shall strike you if you come in reach

* In regard to the Mutiny Monument, Blunt would have appreciated the new plaque put up by a twentieth-century Indian government, to supplement but not obliterate the British plaque which Blunt saw: 'The "Enemy" of the inscriptions on this monument were those who rose against Colonial rule and fought bravely for National Liberation in 1857. Unveiled 28 August 1976.'

of me.' Blunt, in his own words, 'jumped at him, of course', and Anne, who was sitting behind her husband, heard and jotted down the following exchanges:

'What is your official position, to give orders?'

'What the d – is that to *you*? These people must move off – they're in my way.'

'They're not in your way. They came to wish me goodbye – my friends – they don't interfere with you.'

'They are very much in my way, *very* much.'

'You're behaving like a blackguard.'

At that moment the train started. (The man turned out to be Brigadier-Surgeon B. C. Kerr, Chief Medical Officer of the Punjab.)

This was a situation demanding all Blunt's courage and pertinacity. He had recently told his Muslim friends to 'show a little teeth' over the Ilbert Bill. Now he sank his own teeth into the Patna case, and would not let go until an apology had been received many months later. Lord Ripon was treated to several sarcastic letters from Blunt himself ('Dr. Kerr . . . doubtless considers that I have unwarrantably interfered with his time-honoured privilege of ill-treating men of an inferior race to his own. . . .'); and also to extracts from the outraged letters of eight Indian eye-witnesses. The Anglo-Indian *Statesman* denounced Blunt for his part in the Patna incident and described him as 'a paid spy' – though who paid him was not revealed.

A second example of Blunt's practical imagination was his work for a new centre of Islamic reform in India, the al-Azhar having so far failed. The idea of Hyderabad as its site had come to him as he lay unable to sleep one night in Calcutta. Salar Jung and the Nizam had both reacted warmly. The whole project turned on a Salar-Nizam regime being installed at Hyderabad rather than a Cordery-Peishkar regime, and Blunt did not hesitate to bombard Ripon's staff with his views. A signal triumph followed when Salar Jung took the prime ministerial seat next to the Nizam's throne at the durbar of 5 February, the 'poor old Peishkar' having to be shunted aside, while 'poor Cordery' looked black as thunder. 'A day to be marked with white.'

A photograph of the event bears out Shane Leslie's words that it was 'worthy of the British Empire's oddest scrapbook'.[12] Lord Ripon sits in the centre with Anne two places away very upright and comely. Wilfrid with a bushy beard stands immediately behind the Viceroy's chair; further along, stout Cordery scowling.

Blunt wrote jubilantly in his diary, 'Our balloon has gone up at last.'[13] He only wished Cordery had known that his opponent was going about with his subversive poem *The Wind and the Whirlwind* in his baggage and 'a decree of exile from Egypt' in his pocket; that such a 'proclaimed rebel' as himself should defeat the Resident and advise the Viceroy added an exquisite touch of irony to Blunt's joy.

The speed with which his Hyderabad project had been accomplished took his breath away: 'I doubt if ever a university was imagined, planned, preached and accepted before in six weeks from its first conception.' When the Nizam invited him to return to Hyderabad next winter and complete the work, Blunt wrote, 'This "crowns the edifice".'[14]

All he now wanted was to go home. He had been away five months, four of them touring India. He sailed from Bombay on 1 March as confident as ever, despite the warning issued by the Vice-Chancellor of Bombay university, a Mr West. The Muslims' religious fanaticism, said West, would be a fatal impediment to their advancement in the world. 'You might as well run a race with a knapsack on your back.' Blunt replied angrily: 'Perhaps if the race was a long one, and the knapsack full of bread, you might not find it an encumbrance.'

He and Anne had decided not to risk arrest by trying to land at Suez. To get him behind Egyptian prison bars, wrote Blunt in his diary, would be a victory for '*them*'; to go straight home a victory for him. Sure enough, when they reached Suez on 12 March a voice hailed him over the blue waters from a government launch – 'Was a Mr. Blunt aboard?' – and then a lieutenant-colonel in Khedivial uniform told him that if he tried to land he would be arrested. He did not try.

They sailed blithely home with a valuable cargo of horses bought in India, occasionally inspecting the syces' quarters to make sure that they did not use the horse-rugs as extra blankets for themselves. They reached England on 28 March, Wilfrid well aware that he might not see Egypt again for years. What he did not guess was that he had seen India for the last time.

Why did he never return to the scene of so much action, so much more promise?

In a chapter of his *India Under Ripon* entitled 'An Apology for Failure', he was to find the main causes deeply embedded in his own character. Despite the influence he now wielded among many prominent Muslims and, to a lesser extent, Hindus, he could still be distracted by new interests, new countries. And the drama of the Sudan and later of Ireland would be irresistible to one of Blunt's temperament. Moreover, the essential religious basis of an Islamic university demanded of Blunt himself a degree of faith which he did not possess. While still on Indian soil he continued to assure his friends that he never drank wine and could say with them the traditional formula: 'La Allah ila wa Mohammed Rasul Allah.' But on arrival in England he realized how much more than that was required if he were to dedicate his life to Islam in India. Teetotalism was not enough.

Beyond this personal area there were other reasons why India was never to see Blunt again. Cordery and his sherry proved immovable; therefore there was no new 'great Resident' such as Blunt had envisaged to guide the youthful Nizam and his Prime Minister. These two young men slipped back from the foothills of reform into the traditional rut of pleasure. Lord Ripon himself resigned, frustrated in his ideals, and the new Viceroy, Lord Dufferin, urbanely steered the government machine back into its 'old grooves'. If Ripon could not achieve reform, who could?*

On the Blunts' voyage home one of the horses they had bought in India died. His name was Reformer.

* Perhaps it was due to a sense of contrition at 'wasting' the harvest he had sown in India that made Blunt unusually critical of men like Cordery and Dufferin. Having become a teetotaller himself in 1883, he became a keen spotter of excessive drinking in others. He regarded Dufferin as a 'farceur', though one who might prove a 'successful viceroy'. (FM 26/1975, 3 February 1884.)

[10]
'Am I a Tory Democrat?'
1884–1885

The idea of entering Parliament had been floating about in Blunt's head for over a year. Anne was not enthusiastic. Paradoxically, however, it was due to domestic quarrels over Judith, after they returned from India, that finally drove Wilfrid to London and the political arena.

For the first time in their married life a long journey through the East had not brought them together. Until 1884 it could be safely assumed that Wilfrid when abroad would draw nearer to Anne. Now the pattern changed. Wilfrid's turning to Cowie during his serious illness of October 1883 in Ceylon, rather than to Anne, was perhaps the first sign. A sudden despairing entry in Anne's diary for 1 February 1884 showed how far the estrangement had developed in three months:

> Wilfrid begins again to look much worn and tired and yet he is too independent of any sympathy from me to care about having it, so that I shall no longer venture to make even the smallest advance.[1]

Nothing of this appears in Wilfrid's own diary. It is possible that a certain querulousness in Anne, resulting from her innate self-depreciation had begun to get him down; as his unkindness was certainly crucifying her.

A comment in her diary on the death of her cousin Edward Noel in Greece, soon after their return from India, illustrates the bitterness that mingled with her sadness. Noel was a 'brute', Anne wrote, for burdening his widow with a last request to support 'another woman'. Wilfrid himself was engaged during these years in helping to support his son by 'another woman' out of the money that his wife and daughter were later to feel should have come to them. In 1882 Mrs Georgie Sumner had written to Blunt suggesting that from next year he should begin paying for their ten-year-old son Berkeley's boarding-school.[2] But when, after two years' payment of fees at £120 a year, Wilfrid had still not been allowed to set eyes on his son, he declined to go on 'making these payments blindly'. Either he must be given some real interest 'in the educational and practical control' of the boy or payments would cease. Wilfrid's well-meant blackmail did not work, for Georgie was now as deeply religious as Anne herself.

Anne's child Judith was also becoming a source of dispute rather than harmony between the parents. Neither was entirely to blame. The over-protectiveness that Anne showed towards her adored daughter is easily understood. 'Oh God give me patience', she wrote: 'and take not away this one, my only Child.'[3] While Wilfrid laughed at her 'fussing', she added, he behaved as if he himself possessed 'the concentrated wisdom of fathers and nurses – as if he had other children surviving'. Except for 'necessary information', he hardly spoke to Anne. 'I am to be in a less good position than a nurse.'

For Wilfrid's part, his wife's 'fussing' drove him to treat Judith with masculine toughness. After the first disappointment that she was not a boy, he had chosen to treat her as the son of his house. Beautiful, athletic, high-spirited, a good head taller than the average girl of her age, Judith revelled in the country sports her splendid father devised for her, and himself took part in. They would ride together through the Forest, go rabbiting together, fish for trout together on Crabbet lake. Once when Wilfrid commented on his friend Robert Lytton's being 'foolishly in love with his daughter Betty', Wilfrid added, 'It is like me and Judith.'

He delighted above all in Judith's conservative romanticism over Crabbet. She objected to 'trees being cut down or new cottages built or old ones repaired . . . this is as it should be. I remember how angry I was with my Uncle Chandler for thinning the trees at Witley when I was about her age.'[4]

It was only long afterwards that Judith began to remember his teasing and taunting and testing: his forcing her to jump gates almost too high for her pony and his derision at her tears when she fell off, since 'his son would never have cried'.[5]

In those early years Judith's natural wish for freedom made her take her father's rather than her mother's side. 'You can come riding with us if you like', she would say condescendingly to her mother, making it clear that two was company. Anne, deeply resentful at finding 'my own child put over my head to give orders and occupy *my* place', only tightened the domestic reins, extending her restrictions to Judith's moral as well as physical health. When Judith and her governess met and talked to two young farmers in the Forest one day, Anne was not at all pleased. Nor would she take Judith at Lady Gregory's invitation 'to meet the little Fergusons' (great-nieces of the editor of the Ceylon *Observer*) because Anne herself had not yet vetted them; nor even to see 'the little Brands', at Wilfrid's own wish.

Well before this Eastern journey, however, Wilfrid had begun making more and more frequent trips to London, as an express result of his paternal irritations at home. 'What, not eat an egg with me?' he exclaimed when Anne kept Judith in bed for breakfast because of a slight cold, on his very first day home from India. 'I shall go away and see some of my friends and when my Bibi can eat an egg with me you can send me a telegram.' A few weeks later Judith was not allowed to dash out riding with him ('she must prepare properly'), and Wilfrid again exploded: 'I HATE being at home.'

'My friends', to whose homes Wilfrid now retreated for periods of relaxation, led him deeper into politics. Most of them were politically minded: 'Button' Bourke, Eddy Hamilton, Rosalind and George Howard, M.P., Lord Randolph Churchill, and even Skittles with her informal circle of Establishment gentlemen. And events abroad had long seemed once more to be demanding Wilfrid's intervention. This time it was the Sudan and General Gordon; though whether Gordon remained, as hitherto, among 'my friends' had become doubtful. For Gordon had been sent out to Khartoum in January, after Hicks Pasha's force had been cut to pieces by the Mahdi during the previous November. Who but 'Chinese Gordon' could now halt Mohammed Ahmed ibn Abdullah, the 'Expected Mahdi of Islam'?

Blunt's first direct participation in the Sudan imbroglio had taken the form of a letter to Gordon. Dated Delhi, 24 January 1884, it was in effect a portentous warning against Gordon's mission. Blunt did not as yet know whether the Liberal government had sent Gordon out to evacuate Khartoum leaving the Mahdi in charge, or to impose the Khedive's (and therefore Britain's) authority. If it was evacuation (which by and large it was) Blunt wished Gordon God speed. If it meant the occupation of Khartoum, Blunt predicted death and destruction. Gordon's 'great name' with the native peoples would count for nothing, since Mohammedans the world over saw right and justice on the Mahdi's, not Tewfik's side. Blunt's final words were prophetic:

> Also consider what your death will mean; the certainty of a cry for vengeance in England and an excuse with those who seek no better than a war of conquest. I wish I could be sure that all those who are sending you on your mission do not foresee this end.

The last point was put more brutally in Blunt's diary for 30 January: 'I feel certain the Foreign Office has sent him out on purpose he should be killed, so as to excite public opinion. . . .'[6]

A week later the report that Gordon had been taken prisoner on his march to Khartoum sent Blunt hurrying to Lord Ripon with a first offer of mediation between Gordon and the Mahdi. Though sympathetic, the Viceroy told Blunt he was probably too unpopular with the government to be used.[7]

It was announced a few days later that Gordon had not been captured after all: 'so I hope he may yet get my letter in time', wrote Blunt, 'and take my advice'. The letter probably never reached Gordon, who in fact arrived at Khartoum on 18 February but was hemmed in by the Mahdi from mid-March onwards. Nor did Gordon mention Blunt's letter in his journal, though there were references to the prospect of 'Wilfrid Blunt making a nice row' about 'this and that', if he, Gordon, deviated from the strictest principles of justice.

Back in England from India towards the end of March, Blunt was to find Gordon the subject of universal discussion. His own sympathies were now flatly with the Mahdi, and he was to shock Anne after the news of a British defeat at Abu Klea by saying he hoped the whole expeditionary force had been wiped out. Blunt indeed had scarcely expected anything but British defeats, after meeting the Commander-in-Chief of India that February 1884: 'an inept old noodle, who fuddled himself into incoherency with champagne and curaçoa. I should like to be the Mahdi, with such a Commander-in-Chief opposite me, especially after luncheon'.[8] His only reservations about the Mahdi's fitness for command concerned the slave trade. As an orthodox Mohammedan the Mahdi was not against the trade and in fact had close relations with slavers. Wilfrid's friend al-Afghani, however, had an answer. Did not African slaves positively gain by the chance of exchanging their freedom – freedom to eat each other – for a better life among Mohammedans?

Having exchanged his lonely breakfast egg at Crabbet for a dizzy round of political luncheons, dinners and suppers, Blunt was soon composing a letter to *The Times*. Two of his eccentric aristocratic friends, Lyulph Stanley and Auberon Herbert, agreed that Gladstone ought to have taken his advice and made a deal with Arabi; but it was not too late to restore him. Both Rosalind Howard and Button Bourke advised him to enter Parliament as a moderate; Rosalind hated to hear her brilliant Wilfrid talking in support of a mere 'fanatic', the Mahdi.

'It is so stupid of you', she raged, entering one of her storm zones, 'because you have so much sense, and if you would be moderate you might have great influence.'[9]

'My influence will never be great in England', Blunt thundered back, 'because English people care nothing for principle, and everything for party, and I am not a party man.'

Blunt's great and immoderate letter to *The Times* was published on 10 April. Sweeping settlements in the Sudan and Egypt were proposed: British troops to be withdrawn from both countries, peace made with the Mahdi, a 'European Congress' to settle the Egyptian question on the basis of self-government under the protection of the Great Powers; the Khedive to abdicate and all Egyptian exiles to be repatriated (including of course Wilfrid Scawen Blunt).

The chances of this radical solution being adopted were nil; indeed George Buckle, *The Times*'s new editor, printed a disparaging leading article alongside Blunt's letter. The best that Blunt could get in the way of reaction from the Establishment was Eddy Hamilton's cry after reading his letter – 'sick of the whole thing and wished Egypt at the bottom of the sea'. His friend Blunt replied inflexibly: 'We will plague you in turn with all the plagues of Egypt until you let the people go.'

Blunt's less cautious friends were enthusiastic about his letter. Sir Wilfrid Lawson, the Radical M.P., agreed that the sooner Gordon was out the better. 'Why on earth should he spend his time "shelling the rebels"?[10] I should prefer to see the rebels shell him.' Skittles repeated that the Prince of Wales was 'really so pleased with it, and it is a real good letter'.

> Darling Winny Boy [she wrote on 21 April] . . . I have read all your letters to The Times with great interest. How right you were in saying what you did to me two years back about all the trouble we should have. . . . That vile man Gladstone will be the ruin of us all e'er long. . . . It is a pity some of the Irish don't blow him up to save the country, no man is hated is CURSED more by the English . . . than he. *Still* I fear he will live on, bad weeds grow apace and the wicked survive. . . .[11]

Skittles continued to press Blunt's views on the Prince of Wales:

> My dearest Winny – Last night [10 September] the Prince was here and we had a talk about you as I told him you had been so kind coming to see me etc. [Skittles had been ill.] He said of course he would be kind to you and *ought* to be for we were once something very dear to each other. I said yes but people are cruel and change so. He said I like Blunt although I may not agree with him on certain things.[12]

Meanwhile the *Pall Mall Gazette* argued, somewhat cynically indeed, that Mr Wilfrid Blunt should be sent out on a mission to the Mahdi. If Khartoum was to be evacuated and all its treasure handed over, Mr Blunt rather than General Gordon was 'our proper agent' in the Sudan. Gordon would fight to save the garrison; Blunt would not injure the hair of an Arab. That was precisely the Liberal government's policy. 'Mr. Blunt is not less brave than General Gordon', concluded the author (W. T. Stead), 'and he could be sacrificed at least as safely.'

In fact Blunt had already in February vainly proposed himself to Ripon as the government's envoy to the Sudan. Nevertheless the idea was now getting around. On 18 April, Mark Napier and his brother

Jack rushed into Blunt's room. Help us to save Gordon, they cried; it only needed a 1,000 sportsmen – the type who would 'go a 1,000 miles to shoot a lion'[13] – to force a passage up the Nile and rescue Gordon at the point of the skinning knife or the elephant gun. 'They thought,' wrote Blunt indulgently, 'that I might like to join them and show them the way.' A few days later it was Auberon Herbert writing to Blunt in the same romantic vein. 'I suppose you are not going to Khartoum?' he enquired. 'If you want a companion – and cannot get a better ... I will gladly come....'[14]

Blunt now wrote a sober letter to Gladstone, offering himself as mediator for the relief of Gordon. Gladstone found himself faced with a volunteer who promised to beard the Mahdi personally (or if preferred to send al-Afghani or Abdu) and demanded only three promises in return: no British military operations against the Mahdi during the Blunt mission; no revenge in the event of his death; no expeditionary force if he were captured. The return of Arabi from exile went almost without saying.

Blunt had to wait until the beginning of May to hear from Gladstone. The answer was a brief 'no'. Mr Blunt's journey would be superfluous, since H.M. Government and Mr Gladstone 'have no other desire than to promote the evacuation of the country'.[15]

Thwarted in his attempts to become a mediator, Blunt trained his guns on Gladstone personally. Why had the Prime Minister encouraged him, albeit indirectly through Knowles and Hamilton, to go to Egypt last autumn and then forbidden him to return to his estate of Sheykh Obeyd in the spring?

Blunt was no more successful as an aggrieved exile than he had been as a mediator. Having imagined he had got Gladstone and Co. 'in a wonderful fix', he received a bland reply from the P.M.'s secretary denying the whole Gladstone-Knowles-Hamilton affair and deploring Mr Blunt's 'proceedings in Egypt'. Blunt, however, got his cousin Percy Wyndham, M.P., to take up in Parliament the case of his exile. Though the order against his entering Egypt was not rescinded, he felt the debate had gone well.

As fast as one mission failed he thought of another. The *Fortnightly* was publishing his 'Ideas on India', and it might be that the reformation of Islam he there envisaged was more likely to spring from source – that is, from Constantinople – than in the outlying Mohammedan dominions. He would go on a mission to the Sultan.

There were other consolations, before he set out with Anne in September. The Crabbet calendar had never been merrier. On 30 May he had driven his oddly assorted friends Harry Brand and Frederic Harrison to Epsom for the Oaks. It was also an 'odd' turn-out – the phaeton and four Arabs. One of the Arabs, Bozra, had never been in the team before and they arrived late, too late, Blunt was told by officials, to reach his accustomed stand. Unabashed he drove full tilt up the course to his place, amid the cheers of the bystanders.

He considered the defeat of Halfa, the Arabian he entered for the Newmarket race, as another 'political' set-back. 'For success on the turf', reflected Blunt, 'seems always to have been held in England as in some measure connected with political capacity....'[16]

But he was pleased in spite of everything that he and Anne had been invited to Mrs Gladstone's evening party on 11 June. Wilfrid thought Mrs Gladstone 'looked rather askance' when their names were announced, and Anne decided that Gladstone's hand-shake 'seemed to pass me on or hand me on, as it were'.[17] Nevertheless Wilfrid's rapport with the Grand Old man was apparently re-established. His hand reminded Wilfrid of Newman's when the Cardinal cured his toothache – 'soft, warm and nervous'.

'How do you do, Mr. Blunt. I am very glad indeed to see you', Gladstone said, to Wilfrid's amazement. If it had been the Duke of Wellington, he said to himself, it would have been, 'Damn you, sir, get out of my way.'[18]

Hardly less gratifying was a letter from the famous socialist H. M. Hyndman, founder of the Social Democratic Federation, sending him some literature and an invitation to 'join our ranks'. He felt that Blunt must be aware that the poverty of India and Egypt was due to 'the infamous capitalist system', while the solution lay in Democratic Socialism. If men like Blunt 'should work side by side with the workers' the coming revolution would be peaceful. 'I hope you will join us', Hyndman ended. 'I am quite certain that if you do you will never regret it – if, as I judge, you are a man capable of making sacrifices for a great cause.'

Blunt could not accept; but it was heart-warming to be asked.[19]

The Blunts were abroad for two months. On the way to Constantinople they visited the magnificent Potocki stud at Antonin, in Russian Poland. Judith would be happy here, wrote Blunt to his daughter, as there were 180 splendid Arabian horses, rides every day and coursing with eight greyhounds. In Constantinople Judith heard that the sea-water came up to their windows, 'so one can bathe without getting out of bed'. But the Sultan remained enigmatically out of reach. After having seen the royal stud, the palaces, princes and bazaars, and waited interminably for an audience that was always promised but never granted, Wilfrid decided to go home. He was perhaps naïve ever to have imagined that Abdul Hamid II, otherwise Abdul the Damned, would inaugurate the Reformation of Islam. Fear of assassination made him 'un misérable et un fou', as the wise old ex-Grand Vizier

Achmet Vefyk warned the Blunts. 'Already he is probably asking himself why you have come, and when you mean to go.' They went on Guy Fawkes Day, Anne noting grimly that the palace coffee had not *yet* poisoned them.[20]

On Christmas Eve 1884, back in England, Blunt made one last bizarre attempt to get himself nominated as peace envoy to the Mahdi. He was persuaded by the Arbitration and Peace Society to join them on a pilgrimage to Hawarden, Gladstone's home near Chester. Their tactic was to send in a message that certain 'gentlemen' wished to wait upon Mr Gladstone, withholding the name of Blunt until they were safely inside. Gladstone, however, was about to go into dinner, and his butler smelt a rat. 'Deputation', he snorted, and shut them out. They arrived home by the Irish Mail train in the grey chill of Christmas morning suffering from political frost-bite.

The frost was soon to invade Crabbet. Two days after Christmas Wilfrid felt bored, complaining, 'This is the only house in England in which people *never* come to stay.' He asked Anne to invite Lady Gregory, his cousin Miss Chandler and C. Molony the Irish painter. Anne said Molony had 'better come *after* Lady Gregory, for if he were told not to flirt with her, he had "an example"'.

'If you mean *me*. . . .'

'I do mean you.'

'If you mean me, you will never find women will talk to *you* as they do to me.'

Anne retorted that his conduct had cut her off from her oldest friends – meaning the Zouches.

'I have now got to the age', Blunt insisted, 'when I like to be amused without giving myself much trouble, and there are several women who amuse me. I don't care which of them it is, but I must have someone.'[21]

Offered Lady Gregory, Mrs Batten, Mrs Thurlow or Mrs Singleton, Anne opted for the first. At least Lady Gregory would not have a bad effect on Judith. The religious views of Mrs Batten were suspect, and she had told Anne some 'queer things'.

The battle of Abu Klea in the New Year of 1885 overwhelmed Blunt with bitterness towards the Liberal leader and grief over the Arab casualties. What were British soldiers doing in the Sudan?

> What are they? a mongrel scum of thieves from Whitechapel and Seven Dials, commanded by young fellows whose idea is the green room of the Gaiety – without beliefs, without traditions, without other principle . . . than just to get their promotion and have a little fun. . . . On the other side men with the memory of a thousand years of freedom . . . worshipping God and serving him in arms like the heroes of the ancient world they are. It is over the death of these that we rejoice.

All Blunt desired was to see the butchers butchered and sent to hell.

> Gladstone! Great God, is there no vengeance for this pitiful man of blood, who has not even the courage to be at the same time a man of iron. What is he that he should have cost the world a single life? A pedant, a babbler, an impotent old fool.[22]

On 5 February he heard in London the news of Khartoum's fall – news as glorious as it was unexpected: 'I could not help singing all the way down in the train.'

The announcement on the tenth of Gordon's death drew forth no pity for the man who had once been his friend but whom he now believed – wrongly he later confessed – to have ratted on the native peoples. All Blunt now felt was relief that Gordon was dead, not captured. He rightly predicted that this would mean the ultimate evacuation by Britain of the Dervishes' country. On 20 June the Mahdi, whom Blunt had once said never made a mistake in his life, now made the mistake of dying. The rising collapsed for lack of a leader of the Mahdi's calibre. Blunt's only consolation was a 'beautiful' sonnet on his death by Lady Gregory.

Blunt and Lord Stanley of Alderley, meanwhile, were busying themselves with deputations to Lord Ripon, Hassan Fehmy the Sultan's envoy, and indeed anyone else who would listen to them about the problems of the East. They made a strange pair: Stanley an anarchist who believed in no taxes whatever and 'free trade' in everything including prostitution;* Blunt a politician manqué who needed to harness his restless political energies to the parliamentary chariot.

Advice was flowing in from all quarters that he should fight a seat. There were two small problems, however. Which seat would have him? And under what flag should he fight?

Sir Alfred Lyall like Harry Brand wanted him to stand in 'a good radical constituency'. The Howards were divided: Rosalind being violently against his entering the House of Commons at all but suggesting that he should get a peerage as peacemaker and operate from the House of Lords; her Liberal husband George Howard, M.P. favouring a Tory seat for Blunt so that he might 'ruin the Tory Party'.

Wilfrid himself found Randolph Churchill's Fourth Party – running under the colours of 'Tory Democracy' – a major attraction, but his friend Button Bourke was strongly opposed. Lord Randolph would not be able to get him a safe seat, protested Button; far better to try for an Irish constituency through Mr Parnell and go in as a Tory Home Ruler.

* He had persuaded some American anarchists to publish Blunt's *The Wind and the Whirlwind*. God was mentioned in the poem far too often, the editor being 'agin God first last and always'. Nevertheless Blunt's poem was 'very fine'.

Bearing this advice in mind, Blunt nevertheless saw Lord Randolph on 14 April, only to fall headlong for the Churchill charm: 'I really like him better than any of them personally.' They discussed India which Churchill had just visited partly on Blunt's advice, and then Blunt was assigned his first Tory task. Would he write a poem for the Party which Sir Arthur Sullivan might set to music?

'With something about a primrose in it?' asked Blunt, on his guard. It would be Primrose Day in memory of Disraeli on the nineteenth.

'Yes, if you like – but it does not matter so much what it is, so long as it is patriotic.' Blunt would try, but feared he couldn't manage the primrose. 'This worship of an old Hebrew gentleman', he wrote afterwards in his diary, 'under the form of a primrose is certainly one of the most ridiculous ever imagined.'[23]

Lord Randolph found some of Blunt's views equally ridiculous. Here was Blunt, a would-be Tory candidate, suddenly describing himself as a nationalist in Ireland. Lord Randolph 'made a face at the word "Nationalist"', advising Blunt merely to say he had 'wide opinions' on the Irish question. 'You could not come forward as an avowed Nationalist.' Once in Parliament he could take his own line.

'But what is Tory democracy?' rejoined Blunt, wondering why the Irish in a democracy could not govern themselves.

Lord Randolph confessed to dreading this question in public. Being now in private he replied with commendable honesty: 'To tell the truth I don't know myself what Tory democracy is. But I believe it is principally opportunism.' And in that context Blunt had better try defining it himself and send the written results to Churchill, who would then see if any constituency would have him. Far better than joining Parnell and the Irish obstructionists.

Blunt went off willingly to draft his memorandum, 'Am I a Tory democrat?', feeling that 'perhaps, after all, I shall be freest with Randolph...'. He was determined nonetheless to see the Irish Nationalists.

On the twenty-seventh he called on the McCarthys, father and son, at their humble lodgings in Ebury Street. Both Justin and Huntley pleased him by their openness. 'I feel more at home with these people', he wrote, 'than in the Carlton Club.' He had told Justin he was prepared to follow Parnell 'on all Irish questions short of dynamite'. Perhaps the deciding factor had been Justin's remark that both Arabi and the Mahdi were heroes in Ireland.

He met Charles Stewart Parnell on 6 May at the House of Commons. A cold douche awaited him from the leader, whom he nevertheless found frank, straightforward and charming. Parnell could not get an Englishman one of the much sought-after Irish constituencies; it would create too many jealousies. But if Lord Randolph would get Blunt an English seat, Parnell would deliver the solid Irish vote.

That settled it. 'Am I a Tory democrat?' had to be answered in the affirmative, and next day the hopeful author was showing his piece to Churchill. On home affairs he called himself a Conservative, on Indian affairs a protagonist of 'large reforms' leading to self-government, on Egypt and the Sudan a nationalist, and on Ireland a Home Ruler. Again Churchill winced. Why not use some vaguer expression than 'Home Rule'? Of course it must come to this in the end, 'but we haven't educated the party up to it yet ...'.

For the next month there was ceaseless activity on Blunt's part, a good deal of 'educating' people up to his ideas, but precious little 'conservatism', apart from his going to a levée in his old diplomatic uniform. A scrutiny of his diary, political and social, shows how far the conventional uniform belied Blunt's extremely unorthodox feelings.

8 May: Great meeting, predominantly Liberal, at the Birmingham Town Hall where Blunt inserted and carried with acclamation a Peace Association resolution, demanding the recall of General Wolseley from the Sudan.

9 May: Interview with the Conservative national agent, after which Blunt reflected, 'I don't know whether I shall gain most or lose most by being in Parliament. But I am determined, if I do get there, to lead the party in their foreign politics and about India.'

11 May: Dinner at South Street with 'Lady C' (Skittles) to hear an account of how she had 'captivated no less a personage than the G.O.M. himself!' Skittles had often heard of the Prime Minister's craving to know ladies of light character, but this Saturday was her own first meeting with him. 'Saturdays and Sundays are his evenings out.'

Nothing improper [wrote Blunt] seems to have happened, except that the old man kissed her hand saying in a rather formal manner 'If it is permitted for an old man'. On the contrary she seems to have forced the conversation into politics and attacked him on his wickedness in killing the Arabs.... But he took it all in good part.

What did he think of Mr Blunt? asked Skittles. 'A charming person', replied Gladstone, 'but on politics mad.' To which Blunt rejoined in his diary, 'The mad always think other people mad.' The interview ended somewhat abruptly when the Prince of Wales called and by his rudeness forced Mr Gladstone to take up his hat and leave.

Next morning, after revelling in Skittles' tale, Blunt sent the Prime Minister his *Proteus* sonnets in a new edition – to be thanked with the gracious remark that 'Mr. Gladstone would turn with pleasure from the Sudan to Proteus'.

'These little interchanges of courtesies in wartime', reflected Blunt complacently, 'are agreeable, and the old man appreciates them, looking on all politics, as he does, in the light of a debating Club.'

17 May: Dinner again with Miss Walters to hear of her second meeting with Gladstone. The Prime Minister had arrived alone, having sent in advance twelve pounds of Russian tea and bringing with him a bunch of narcissi. 'I have not come to talk politics', he said, remarking instead on the smallness of her waist and going on to test the size (she told Blunt) 'by manual measurement'. If she wrote to him, as Gladstone hoped she would, she should mark the envelope private, followed by a little cross thus, 'Private x'.

Skittles afterwards heard that Gladstone had been 'struck with all my go and charming ways ...'.[24] She looked forward to rather more politics '*next time*', for the Prince of Wales had warned her 'not to trouble him about *politics*' at first – 'but when he has got into the habit of coming', Skittles ended triumphantly to Blunt, 'then I mean to let him have it'.

21 May: Great Liberal wedding of Laura Tennant and Alfred Lyttelton at St George's, Hanover Square. Laura was the society beauty who most 'amused' Blunt at the moment. She gave him her hand as she swept down the aisle. 'Her hand thrilled me....' His reaction to Gladstone's speech proposing the couple's health – 'full of finest moral sentiments about virtues of wedded state' – was more cynical. 'I laughed in my sleeve as I thought of his visits to South Street.'[25]

4 June: Speech by Randolph, a 'capital one', which provoked Blunt's comment, 'He is educating the Tory Party and I am educating him.'

8 June: Manifesto from Blunt to Churchill, stating Blunt's opinions. But before this educational document could be sent, still less published in *The Times*, a political bombshell had fallen upon Gladstone.

Gladstone's government fell on 9 June. He was succeeded by Lord Salisbury and the Tories who were, however, dependent for their majority on Irish votes. Lord Randolph Churchill, Blunt's patron-protégé, took the powerful India Office; Drummond Wolff, another of the Fourth Party, was sent on a conciliatory mission to the Sultan; Baring might be recalled. It was now or never for Blunt.

At first things looked rosy. The London borough of Southwark would probably select him as their candidate despite the suspicions of a few 'fossilized Tories'. To his intense annoyance, however, 'Master Button' double-crossed him by putting his own brother Mayo up for Southwark, while he himself tried for Clapham. Blunt did not blame Mayo after the Zouche affair. 'But Button!' (Neither Mayo nor Button, however, was adopted.)

On the same day, 14 July, as Blunt received this bad news, he delivered his maiden speech as a Tory at East Grinstead in Sussex. 'This commits me to party politics', he noted without enthusiasm, 'a thing I have avoided all my life.' He observed again that 'the party will require educating'. Two days later a deputation waited on him from another South London constituency, Camberwell North. Blunt compulsively played his two lowest cards: he was a Catholic, he told them, and a Home Ruler. They were 'staggered', until he assured them it was 'best to call a spade a spade'. He would pay his own expenses and in return they would give him 'an easy time of it in the way of work'. He was adopted on 23 July, despite one of the venerable selectors voting against him as a Roman Catholic. There was to be no 'easy time' for him.[26]

His old friend Cardinal Manning, on whom he called, promised to recommend him to the local priest. His almost equally old friend Rosalind Howard made scenes about his Conservatism while he was her guest at Castle Howard. In retaliation he threatened to draft his electoral address on Castle Howard writing paper, and she to turn him out of her carriage and make him walk home.* The Camberwell constituency he loathed as 'a chaos', his chairman being 'a sweating tailor', his small election audiences 'very degraded', the best of the electors strongly radical (though this tended to make his 'Tory Democracy' acceptable), his organization nil and he himself required to 'educate the voters' on the ABC of politics. Added to all this was a repulsive conglomeration of pub parlours garnished with stuffed pike, tench and bream and dim with pipe and beer fumes; 'frowsy fellows' in stuffy schoolrooms 'talking nonsense to each other'; Tory churchmen alienated by his Irish views. What a terrible come down from 'the politics of the golden East'.[27]

For he had by no means dropped his Eastern mission, however incomprehensible it might seem to 'the miserable Camberwell rabble'. He had brought over the Sayyid Jamal al-Din al-Afghani and two Muslim friends as soon as Gladstone fell, in order that Lord Randolph and Salisbury might be in the closest possible touch with authentic Mohammedan opinion. As his honoured guests, these three were harboured at 10 James Street for three whole months. Unfortunately, however, Wolff told Blunt 'it would never do' to raise the question of Arabi with Salisbury just yet, on which Blunt remarked predictably, 'Lord Salisbury requires educating....'

At the end of the three months a dispute arose at 10 James Street between the learned trio about religion and politics. It resulted in two of them belabouring one another with umbrellas until the blood

* He drafted it on Carlton Club paper – he had been a member for ten years – calling himself the 'Constitutional' candidate.

flowed. Their exasperated host incontinently sent them packing and al-Afghani followed them in a huff. Blunt excused himself with the thought that three months was 'the full term of Arab hospitality'.

His adoption meeting in Camberwell was spoilt by Lord Folkestone's 'rhodomontade against the Irish' and Sir Henry Fletcher's 'prosing about the love of the agricultural labourer for the parson' – both speakers sent down by Head Office. A Primrose League meeting held at Worth School near Crabbet inspired Blunt to a speech on peasant proprietorship. 'It gave satisfaction', he wrote dryly, 'to the Radicals at the end of the room.' There is no record that a mass Tory rally at Crabbet gave satisfaction to the host. Another election crowd in Camberwell listened to the candidate expounding for two hours his doctrine of 'Tory Socialism'; the meeting ended in fisticuffs.

Nevertheless, his hopes were still high, perhaps inordinately so, on his forty-fifth birthday (17 August). What he afterwards described shamefacedly as 'vainglorious words' found their way into his diary:

> When I look at my life, I see that it is progressing, and while there is progress there is happiness. I look forward to parliament, as the beginning of a new phase. I shall be Cabinet Minister in five years' time; head of my party, perhaps in ten. But shall I get in? I think it is in my fate.[28]

Ten days later, after an open air meeting which sang 'Rule, Britannia' in honour of Blunt, Churchill and Tory Democracy, Blunt wrote: 'I have a conviction that I shall carry all before me, or why should this opportunity have been placed before me? If I fail I shall take it as a sign that my mission has failed.'

During the later weeks of canvassing Blunt allowed his euphoric mood to expand in the warmth of a shamelessly socialistic campaign. His inexperience as a candidate probably led him to adapt himself to the radical street crowds he was now addressing; not that he himself was without a layer of genuinely revolutionary emotion. At any rate, by November he had knocked up a record of preaching 'pure socialism' in the streets, attacking 'the capitalists and the party of money', and 'pleading the cause of Labour'. He had spoken in favour of open diplomacy; had persuaded al-Afghani and a Persian visitor to support him with orations delivered in Arabic and Persian respectively (the one meeting that the Camberwell electorate really enjoyed – no 'education'); had attacked the Burma war in *The Times*; had organized a Camberwell rally for the restoration of Arabi; had visited and rhapsodized over the Salvation Army H.Q.; and had subdued a hostile assembly by quoting four lines from James Russell Lowell's 'Stanzas on Freedom':

They are slaves who fear to speak
For the fallen and the weak.
They are slaves who dare not be
In the right with two or three.[29]

There was only a fortnight to go when he dropped a political bombshell that lost the support of the 'two or three' who really mattered to him. On 12 November he suddenly came out fair and square for Home Rule and Parnell. It was at a meeting specially convened for the Irish. Again Blunt was carried away by too much empathy; again inexperience and temperamental optimism had caused him to misinterpret the temporary parliamentary alliance between Salisbury and Parnell as a permanent Tory move towards Home Rule; and as in the Arabi affair, Blunt overrated his own influence over Cabinet ministers. Lord Salisbury of course could not countenance his impetuous move from 'Tory Democracy' to some inventive dream of Parnellite socialism. His friend Lord Randolph Churchill had hoped up to 11 November that Blunt would pull his election through, despite his attitude on Burma; but the declaration of the twelfth was too much. All along Churchill had been trying to tone down the Home Ruler in Blunt. From now on they were no longer to act on their 'familiar and intimate footing as political allies'.[30] As for Camberwell, where he made his declaration of the twelfth 'almost on the spur of the moment', Blunt admitted that some of his supporters 'looked rather aghast'.

Nomination day at Camberwell was on 24 November. The only moment of drama happily did not concern Blunt this time. Miss Helen Taylor, member of a school board and the step-daughter of John Stuart Mill, presented her nomination papers to the returning officer, 'a perky sandy-faced scrubby-looking youth', as Blunt described him, with the intention of standing for Parliament. She was quicky demolished by Sandy Face, who simply read out the Franchise Act, in which every pronoun was either 'he' or 'his'. One feels that Blunt was within an ace of adding to his other electoral burdens a declaration for Women's Suffrage.

His campaign ended with a torchlight procession preceded by a denunciation of Dilke who stood in nearby Chelsea and was said to have scraped in by taking the Sacrament at Chelsea Old Church on the Sunday before his election. 'There is no greater cad than this man.'

On election day Wilfrid and Anne drove round the polling stations in an open carriage, attended by children who climbed into the carriage, and faithful supporters like the Pollens, Wilfrid Meynell and the Duke of Norfolk. Blunt felt 'fairly confident' of the result. The count took place on the twenty-eighth at the Masonic Hall. It was neck and neck all the way. Blunt just led during the morning but was overtaken in the last hours, beaten by 2,975 votes to 3,137, a majority against him of 162 out of 6,112. Anne, who had regarded the campaign as 'a ceaseless grind', though she did not complain, attributed Wilfrid's defeat to party mismanagement and treachery – no checker at the count, no counting agents, no 'personation clerks' to prevent the dead from voting.* Wilfrid knew better. In every English constituency he reckoned that five per cent of the electorate would give an anti-papist vote if they could. In Camberwell North the five per cent had no need to sniff out papistry; the Tory candidate was a self-confessed, self-advertised Catholic and Home Ruler.

Blunt did not minimize his personal chagrin, nor the wider hopes which his defeat had frustrated. He wrote, 'I take defeat as final', and told Meynell it was a 'death blow' to their cause.[31]

Letters of condolence flowed in: Cardinal Manning congratulating him on his 'manly fight' fought 'with visor up as a Catholic – the first man who has faced an English constituency in the metropolitan elections'; Skittles applauding his 'real good fight', urging him not to cave in but to have another try if only because the Prince of Wales said he must 'stick to it as they really wanted someone like yourself in the House . . .'.[32] *The Times* took up the tale, calling the defeated candidate for Camberwell North 'a peculiar specimen of a Conservative': all the more peculiar, when on 17 December Gladstone made a volte-face and came out with the very Home Rule programme that Blunt had so long wished upon Salisbury. And this burning Liberal crusader for Ireland was the man whom Blunt had written off as 'an impotent old fool'!

Deeply troubled, Blunt wrote to Churchill on Christmas Day, wondering if he could still be of any use to the Tories. 'I fear I have not in me the spirit of a good party man, but I thought at one time I could help you individually in the pursuit of better things.' The answer came back short and sharp. 'There is no doubt about the matter. If you want Home Rule you must go to Gladstone for it. We cannot touch it.'[33]

So it seemed that Blunt must end the year 1885 in the same mood of despondency he had recorded immediately after the Camberwell count:

> It is seldom that great states depend upon a single Election. Had I succeeded I could not have failed to carry all before me on my own subject in the House of Commons and I might have founded a party which should have been the beginning of something great for England as well as Asia and Egypt.

* Anne could not bear the Tory Party officials, and when Wilfrid asked her to order a new stair carpet for Crabbet, she felt sure it was to keep up with the Party chairman. 'We shall have *velvet flock* papers next!' (BL. 53953, 25 August 1885.)

Instead of this, Camberwell had chosen 'a vestry man' who would never open his lips in Parliament but be content to put on airs as an M.P. before 'his fellow grocers'.

> So be it. . . . I do not complain, and the Eternal Government of the World is strange in its ways. Finis.[34]

But it was not the finish.

[11]
A New Pilgrimage
1886–1887

Wilfrid escaped to the Howards' castle of Naworth on New Year's Eve, confident of forgetting Camberwell in the rowdy 'communistic' atmosphere of children, governesses, tutors and guests that pleasantly reminded him of a Bedouin camp. 'The racket does one good', Blunt felt, 'for all our evils come from too much ease and selfishness.' And a fellow-guest at Naworth had shown him that a man could be hopeless and happy at the same time. James Anthony Froude the historian delighted Blunt by his 'lightness in hand. Though a pessimist in politics, he is one who smiles through it all. . . .' Froude was equally enthusiastic about Blunt, later telling Mrs Howard that Blunt's literary style in his letters to *The Times* was perfect.[1]

Hunting rabbits with Judith in the Icehouse wood at Crabbet also helped to console him. 'She is so absolutely without despondency.' But a visit to William and Janey Morris and their two daughters May and Jenny set him back: 'There is an indescribable gloom about them all' – apart from the artist himself. Morris was 'different from all this, a hard-working cheerful Welshman, full of his plans and projects. . . .'

This was exactly what Blunt desired for himself. Plans and projects. Perhaps a new pilgrimage. His friend Harry Brand had laughingly told him to found a 'Fourth Party' of his own, now that the Conservative government was unlikely to survive. 'I am in the mood', Blunt had conceded, 'to form a Fourth, Fifth or Sixth Party, being for the moment in a cave all by myself.'

The moment, however, had prolonged itself into two months, the Conservatives been defeated in Parliament and Gladstone declared Prime Minister, before Blunt emerged from his cave – into the glare of Ireland. He had meanwhile tried all the usual remedies for despair with no effect: re-reading his memoirs and poetry – 'sad work' or even 'rubbish'; visiting the old Crabbet servants – Mrs Selwood at nearly ninety seemed younger than he; calling on pretty married women like Blanche Hozier and Laura Lyttelton – but Laura was waiting for her first baby (and by April she was dead in childbirth); dining with

1 Self-portrait of Wilfrid, aged fourteen.

2 Wilfrid in diplomatic uniform.

3 Alice Blunt, Wilfrid's sister.

4 Newbuildings Place.

5 Crabbet Park.

Poetical Vision of yr. reception in London

Goodbye

Prosaick reality for me.

[Please I wish you w. write

6 Letter from Lady Anne Blunt to W.S.B. probably 1874.

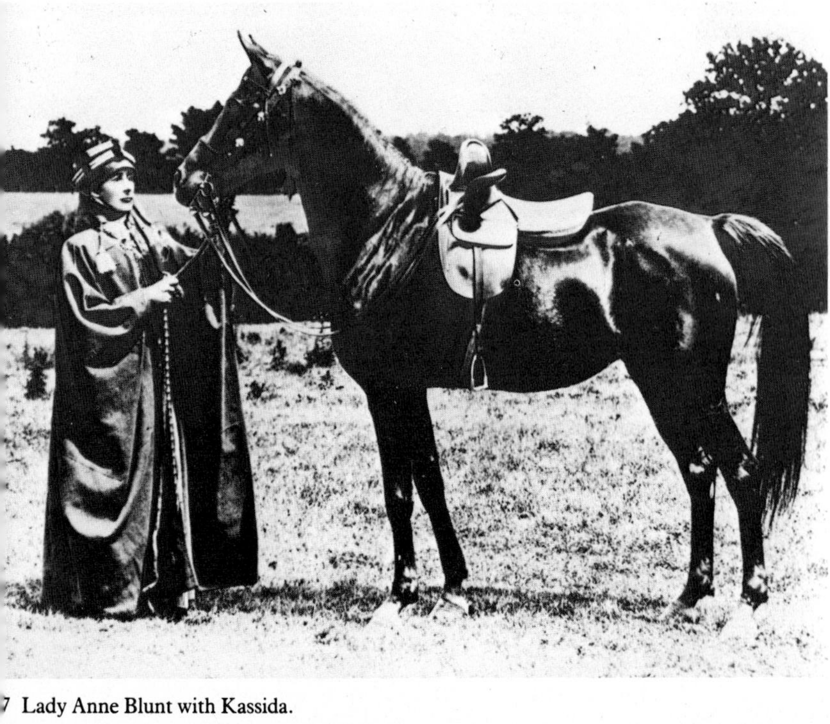

7 Lady Anne Blunt with Kassida.

8 Catherine Walters ('Skittles').

9 Lady Anne Isabella (King-) Noel.

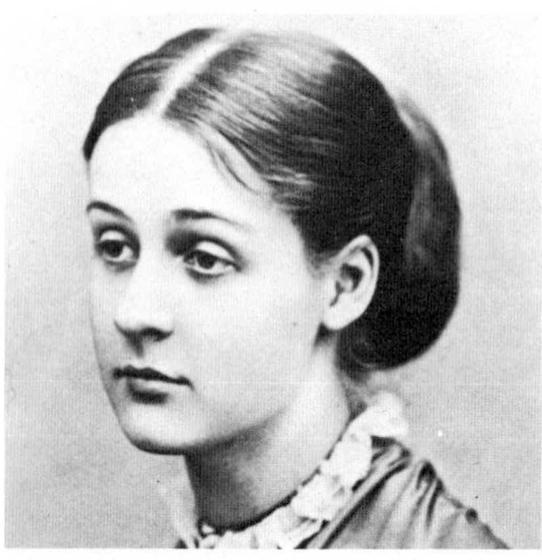

10 Margaret Maria Laprimaudaye, afterwards Mrs 'Minnie' Pollen.

11 'Georgie' Sumner.

12 Mrs Ella Baird.

13 Madeline Wyndham, 1873.

14 Mrs William Morris (Janey) at Kelmscott House, Hammersmith.

15 Lady Elcho (Countess of Wemyss).

16 Margaret Talbot.

17 Lady Mary Charteris about 1904.

18 Dorothy Carleton.

20 *Right:* Ahmed Arabi, 1882, drawn from a photograph in Cairo prison.

19 *Below:* W.S.B. on Pharaoh, by Lady Anne Blunt, 1881.

22 *Above:* W.S.B. in prison clothes, 1888.

21 *Left:* Lady Anne in Dublin, 1888. W.S.B. regarded this as her best photograph.

23 Lady Emily Lytton, 1892, wearing W.S.B.'s overcoat.

25 Anne, Winnie and Anthony Lytton.

24 Judith and Neville Lytton and their spaniels at Crabbet.

26 After the 'Peacock Dinner', January 1914. W.B. Yeats stands on the right of W.S.B., Ezra Pound on his left.

27 W.S.B. in old age by Neville Lytton.

Angelina to meet Oscar Wilde; attending demonstrations for Ireland in Shoreditch and for the unemployed in Trafalgar Square. But Ireland was faced by 'the same unscrupulous gang of financiers, property holders, mortgage companies, and speculators as Egypt', while the Trafalgar Square riot took place after Blunt had left for tea with William Morris, so that he missed the 'destructive part of socialism', the part he liked. ('It is only the constructive part I cannot stomach.')[2]

Gradually, however, as February passed into March, Blunt concentrated his activities on Ireland. He declined to address the Cambridge University Carlton Club on Egypt or Tory Democracy; Home Rule was the raging topic of the day and on Home Rule he would speak. Was he not co-founder of the Home Rule Union in Britain and the first Englishman to be elected to the Irish National League? Gladstone was busy shaping a Home Rule Bill for Parliament; Blunt was re-shaping his own career.

He had been thinking of making a political tour of Ireland since January. On 23 March he wrote in his diary, 'I am leaving for Ireland tonight', and then added the words, 'alone and in very low spirits'.

Those last six words were seemingly inexplicable, coming from a man who had left his cave and was going on a journey he had long desired and planned. They can be understood only after a digression into his private memoirs.

Blunt believed himself to possess fatally sharp vision. In situations where other men might be duped into feeling happy, he, the poet, would perceive his true state of suffering. The afternoon before he left for Ireland seemed to him just such a moment. But the picture of his sufferings could be described as mostly fantasy, a case of poetic licence. He wrote an extraordinary threnody for love and litany of self-pity in quasi-biblical language, like a distraught psalmist:

> I am leaving for Ireland tonight, *alone, alone.* I never thought that it would come to this. But the sorrows of the grave are closing in upon me and the loneliness of old age. [He was forty-five.] Of all things this is the most terrible. There is not in the world a soul of all who have loved me who loves me still enough to go with me on this short venture.

He then specified that Anne had refused to go with him, while Minnie, having promised to see him off, had not turned up.

> I am going without a benediction or a cheer; and so it will be to the end. Oh truly the pleasure of life is dust and ashes. The love of women and the love of children and the love of friends – which is the most empty? I know not. In public life I have striven to do justly and the world is full of my enemies. In the world of my own life I have striven to be loved, and none loves me – no not one.

Queen Victoria was holding a Drawing-Room that afternoon and Blunt went on to extract an added pang from the stream of carriages passing under his windows. He imagined each one was about to stop to bring him a message:

> But they pass on. . . . What profit to have eloquence, to write in verse, to say in the language of the gods the misery of men? To be a poet is only to suffer more. . . . Why was I not dull to all this as the mass of the world is dull? Then I might delude myself with dreams. I might think that Judith loved me, that the world remembered me; and that there were souls who still clung to mine. But I am wise, and I see all things like an eagle, and I know that there is none to love me, no not one.

What might be called the Cardinal Wolsey note ('If I had loved my God as I have loved my King he would not have deserted me in my old age') now combined with the psalmist's plaint:

> Oh, if I could have loved God in other days instead of women, he might comfort me now. . . . I have loved woman and woman loves me no more. And I have not loved God. How should he love me more than these? No. There is none to love me either on the Earth or in the Heaven, or in my own home. I have loved myself and even myself loves me no more. There is none anywhere to love me. No, not one.

It was true that Anne had refused to go with him to Ireland. But she had been kicked out hunting in February. And she told John Pollen that Wilfrid had not asked her. Minnie had been unable to see him off for the simple reason that her son Arthur was ill. While Wilfrid was away, she wrote to him almost daily.[3]

The love of Judith was unquestionable. She adored her father, though at thirteen may have been still also subject to her mother's rule. She slept in Anne's room when only slightly unwell, and had not yet been allowed to visit the Howards or ride with the Wyndhams; indeed no other children but the Pollen boys and Lytton girls seem to have been her close friends. Anne recounts how one day the door-bell rang and Wilfrid said to his daughter, 'There's Mrs. Meynell, Bibi; wouldn't you like to come and see her?'

'Certainly not', replied Judith haughtily, then only twelve and a half. 'I would not stir a foot to see a person I don't know.' Many years later Judith was to write that Alice Meynell resembled 'a ghostly bundle of dusty cobwebs tied to a stick' and 'spoke in a wailing cry baby voice'.*

Anne's reaction to Judith's 'impertinence' was pleasure that her

* But compare the poet Coventry Patmore's lines on Alice Meynell: 'Straight as a stalk of lavender/Soft as a rope of silk.'

daughter could 'hold her own' – against her overwhelming father, perhaps?[4]

Blunt arrived in Ireland to find the 'Land War' being waged with the utmost ferocity. The great landlords, mostly men of alien race, alien religion and an alien way of life, rack-rented their tenants until mounting arrears ended in eviction. Then the cabins were burnt to the ground and the land that the peasants had reclaimed from the bogs for potatoes was turned over to grass. The evicted peasants and their friends retaliated by 'moonlighting': organizing night raids and maiming cattle. The policy of the government and landlords was law and order; of the National League peasant proprietorship, protection for all tenants and a parliament in Dublin to make and enforce just laws. The problem was far from new.

In the course of one month Blunt collected many samples of the problem. To begin with he found Home Rule agitation rampant among the Catholic clergy. Dr Walsh, Archbishop of Dublin, jumped up and down with excitement as he told Blunt that 'landlordism' was doomed; the outrages in Kerry and Galway, however, he deplored. Old Dr Duggan, Bishop of Clonfert in Galway, was even more to Blunt's taste: a white-haired, snuff-taking patriarch of saintly violence, he lived in extreme poverty in a wretched little house known as the 'palace'. He took Blunt to see the site of the last battle that the Irish had fought against William of Orange, the Battle of Aughrim. 'They call it the last battle but the battle is still going on.' Then, raising his arm, he pointed to the miles of empty grass where he himself could remember cottages and families.

> Where are they now? O England, England! They are engulfed in your great cities, Liverpool, London.... They would have lived here happy, and died, and saved their Christian souls; and they have been driven out to live like devils and die like dogs, and be damned to eternity, and all for the sake of making a few English landlords rich.[5]

As soon as Blunt returned to England, he was to weave a poem of seventy-seven verses around that scene with Dr Duggan. Entitled 'The Canon of Aughrim', its first verse had been drafted several years ago and was originally destined for a poem on Egypt. But now Blunt felt it fitted Ireland as well or better:

> You ask me of English honour, whether your Nation is just?
> Justice for us is a word divine, a name we revere –
> Alas, no more than a name, a thing laid by in the dust.
> The world shall know it again, but not in this month or year.[6]

The way that Ireland had slipped into Egypt's place in Blunt's mind became more obvious as his tour progressed. 'They adore Davitt here', he wrote in Donegal on 4 April, 'as Arabi used to be adored in Egypt.' Michael Davitt was the most radical of the Irish leaders, founder of the Land League and in favour of land nationalization. Though gaunt, one-armed and altogether 'odd looking', he deeply impressed Blunt, being less 'communistic' than Blunt had expected and glad to see plenty of clergy in the movement as a steadying influence. (In somewhat the same way, Blunt himself had always welcomed the effect of their religion on the Egyptian Nationalists.)

Another great Irish name that Blunt conjured with during his tour was that of John Dillon, M.P. Dillon was absent from Ireland in April. Indeed all the Nationalist M.P.s were on duty in Westminster for the introduction of Gladstone's Home Rule Bill. But Blunt had met Dillon previously in the House of Commons and now he spent a day and a night with Dillon's devoted cousin Mrs Deane, at Barraghderin in Sligo.

'A great day at Barraghderin', wrote Blunt, for it was 8 April, the very day of Gladstone's speech. In between speculating how the G.O.M. would get on, Blunt and Mrs Deane had a question-and-answer session which was to stand Blunt in good stead later. Dillon, she told him, had been in Kilmainham gaol with Parnell in 1881; he intended to retire from politics 'as soon as he had freed his country'. Of Parnell she said that he was 'an aristocrat at heart' but a true patriot. It was Davitt whom the poor Irish loved most. What 'excellent well-bred people these Nationalists are', reflected Blunt.

So much for Blunt's new Nationalist friends, his Irish substitutes, as it were, for Arabi, al-Afghani and Abdu. What of the opposite, the landlords?

These were often his friends also. Lady Gregory was the closest; and there were older friends dating from his first days in London society, or even further back, to his youth in the diplomatic service: the Earl of Pembroke, for instance, an Irish landowner but also the genial host of the 'Wagger' Club at Wilton, shortly to be reborn as the Crabbet Club; the Earl of Arran, with whom as Lord Sudley Blunt had served in the Paris embassy; the Marquess of Clanricarde who, as Hubert de Burgh, had also been a diplomat with Blunt but had failed, unlike Blunt, to win Skittles's favours. Now Blunt found that Arran was a by-word in Donegal for serving seventy-five evictions on the tenants of his family estate, having visited it for the first time that spring and stayed only for forty-eight hours. In Galway, Lord Clanricarde was the most loathed of many hated landlords, because he 'will not give another lease or renew it when one falls in' on his vast estates.

Fortunately the unpopular families of Roscommon were not bound to Blunt by ties of early friendship. So he felt no compunction about hitting them hard. On the estates of Lord Kingston and of Colonel King Harman, M.P., Blunt saw the results of recent evictions – 'emergency men' living in the empty cottages, with constables to guard them against the homeless tenants who still wandered around. King Harman's rent-roll, Blunt was told, stood at £45,000 a year of which £40,000 went to 'the Jews in London "clean away"'. Blunt promptly exposed the evictions in Stead's *Pall Mall*, and a wordy war broke out between him and Kingston and King Harman. He returned in April to Roscommon in the hope of stopping or mitigating the next round of evictions. They went on for three days amid ritual barbarity: hundreds of armed men throwing out half-starved women and boys, their bits of furniture and even a book or two; one man's father had been a scholar, and as the son left, a volume of Horace's *Satires* was thrown out after him.

The details of each eviction were taken down by Blunt. 'The sight made me so angry that I was positively ill, my heart hurting me.' Even the constables were disgusted, subscribing £5 among themselves for the outcast families. He sent the strongest letter of his life to the *Pall Mall*: 'What absurd laws! What a ludicrous scheme of government!' Perhaps £20 was collected for the landlord at a cost of £1,000 to the government – not to mention the price paid in brutality and suffering.

Eviction proceedings on the fourth day were a mere 'sham'. Only one eviction; but an indignation meeting at the roadside called by Blunt and Father Reddy, the local priest. Blunt spoke for half an hour. Better still, he was sent for by Lord Kingston personally (it was Blunt's policy always to meet the landlords if possible). This also turned out to be an indignation meeting. Kingston swore that Father Reddy was a liar and all the tenants quite rich enough to pay higher rents. Blunt answered,

'Come with me to their houses and hear what they have to say....'

'If I went into a single cottage', retorted Kingston, 'it would encourage them so much they would never pay rent again.'

Blunt then asked Kingston for a fifty per cent reduction of rent all round. That, said Kingston, would reduce him to beggary and after all, 'we all must live'. Blunt felt like replying in the words of Napoleon III, 'I do not see the necessity'. Instead he said,

'Then it means war?'

'Yes, it must be war.'

'I shall fight you with every weapon in my power, in the press, by questions in Parliament, by helping your tenants against you.'

He rather liked young Kingston personally – 'but he is helpless, with the prejudices of his class....'[7]

Blunt reached England four days later (21 April) to find that 'the prejudices of class' had made him a host of enemies. Sidney Herbert said King Harman was thirsting for his blood (Blunt took this to mean a duel and was quite ready to fight until Button headed him off); Lady Gregory was 'up in arms' and only silenced by Blunt's saying that 'property blinds all eyes';[8] Skittles reported the Prince of Wales as 'very angry' at his doings in Ireland; and Button told him that Lord Pembroke and indeed 'everybody' was 'very angry' at his attacks on Lord Kingston's evictions. 'Everybody' knew about evictions. Why tell the story again? 'Their anger, however', noted Blunt, 'means that I have hit them hard, so I don't mind.'

Before he went back to Ireland, he had to deal with two awkward personal matters. His Crabbet agent Charlie Laprimaudaye was instructed to lower one or two of the rents: 'It will not do to neglect the mote in my own eye while plucking the beam out of Lord Kingston's.' At much the same time a letter reached him which made him a benefactor of the Sussex 'peasants' to the tune of £3.3s.od.:

> Box Hill, Dorking. 27 April. Sir, You are in communication with Mr. Wilfrid Blunt, and may not be unwilling to send him the enclosed cheque for three guineas in aid of the peasantry round about, as he may choose to dispense the small sum.[9]

The writer was George Meredith, poet and novelist. There is no clue to the intermediary's name.

The other awkward matter was 'the division', as Minnie called it, between Wilfrid and Anne. Minnie had begged him on 17 April to come home at once rather than stay longer in Ireland, as he proposed. 'You know dearest Wilfrid that I really do only want your happiness, and IN THE END you know quite well it is only in your home that you will be happy.' But though Wilfrid did break his Irish tour, the breach between him and Anne was not healed. Anne twisted her knee this time while hunting at Easter and again could not go with him when he returned to Ireland on 15 May. She wrote in her diary that he was 'offended'.[10] He wrote in his: 'I left London by mail for Dublin in low spirits as I always am when leaving home, nervous and anxious without cause.'

There was enough travelling during Blunt's second Irish tour (15 to 31 May) to disperse his melancholy at least for that fortnight; though when he saw Crabbet again on an unseasonable June day, the fog returned. 'One certainly leads a solitary life in England as country squire', he complained, 'and I am not sure that the Irish peasants with all their troubles are not happier.'

Blunt had met everyone this time from bishops to moonlighters, from informers to schoolboys. For his previous brush with King

Harman he was praised again and again; in one of Lord Listowel's strongholds the people presented him with an address and made him deliver a speech on the Town Council premises. In Waterford his fighting spirit was roused when he heard that his cousin Lord Leconfield of Petworth in Sussex owned property near Limerick – 'Fr. Ambrose has promised me to find out how it is managed.' (The management was good.)

On his return to London he found politics at fever-heat; it was the run-up to the crucial second reading of Gladstone's Home Rule Bill on 7 and 8 June. Blunt felt bound in honour to put the case of the wretched families he had so recently visited, refusing to admit that it was not the moment to plead the cause of Land Reform. When he offered to explain the whole eviction question in detail to John Morley, the Irish Secretary, he received the cold reply: 'Why cannot you write me a short memo about Kerry? It is in a profoundly demoralized state.'[11] Blunt felt that he himself would soon be as demoralized as Kerry unless he could break through. Only one way remained: to enter Parliament at the forthcoming election and fight the cause of the Irish tenants from inside.

'I have been tormenting myself all night', he wrote on 4 June, 'about what to do in regard to the Election when a letter comes from Wyllie the Liberal Agent ... inviting me to stand as a supporter of Mr. Gladstone's Irish policy.' A year ago Blunt had questioned himself, 'Am I a Tory Democrat?' Now he did not need to ask, 'Am I a Liberal?' The Liberal agent's invitation bound him to nothing, he decided, beyond his own opinions. 'I shall accept.' Two days later one of the Liberal Whips repeated the invitation, and even got Blunt into the lobby of the House on the evening of the great debate. He heard the hectic betting on the Bill, watched members milling around and was sad to catch sight of the once radical Harry Brand now whipping for Hartington's Liberal Unionists. Then he walked home to his new flat in Buckingham Palace Road. But not to sleep. 'I could not sleep all night', he wrote on 8 June, 'thinking of the probable fate of Ireland being decided, and at seven I went out to buy a paper.'

In his own words, the result of the voting had been not far from 'irretrievable disaster'. Gladstone, in the greatest speech of his old age, had besought the House to 'think, not for the moment, but for the years that are to come'. The House did so; but not in the sense the old prophet hoped. By a majority of thirty they decided that Home Rule for Ireland should again be withheld, thus ensuring that the bloodshed of the moment should be carried forward into the years to come. It was Chamberlain and his Liberal waverers who had voted the wrong way, going into the lobby with Hartington's Unionists and the Tories.

Blunt comforted himself by a visit to Skittles, who had some agreeably nasty things to say about the two villains, Hartington and Chamberlain. Of Hartington she remarked that she couldn't understand how 'so stupid a fellow as Cav had ever got anywhere in politics'. As for Chamberlain, 'he had come to her house and given himself airs of gallantry which didn't suit him'; his new aristocratic friends, Hartington, the Prince of Wales and the rest, 'all hate and despise him in their hearts for the cad he is'. Blunt commented: 'If the Birmingham working men could see their tribune in South Street, I fancy they would be astonished.'[12]

To be a tribune of the people: that was Blunt's aching ambition. As before, however, only a rabble of Londoners were ready to have him as their candidate; this time St George's in the East and Rotherhithe – 'but I loathe these London constituencies'. After kicking his heels in the lobby for over a week, there seemed a chance at last of the Exchange division of Liverpool (full of Irish) or Galway. But both seats were dependent upon Parnell's approval, and Parnell would not answer Blunt's letters. (Blunt could not know that Parnell was contemplating the greatest mistake of his life – giving Galway to his mistress' husband, William O'Shea.) 'One needs to have a hard skin to lead this life', wrote Blunt forlornly on 17 June.

By the twentieth he had all but given up hope: 'I will fight a good place or none this time', he resolved. 'Still, I feel depressed at my being "out of it".' On the very next day he was offered a real opportunity of getting in.

The Birmingham Liberals, disgusted by their great Joe's defection to Unionism, wanted a Gladstonian Home Ruler. Would Blunt consider it? Blunt's faithful young secretary Edward Hope was sent to Birmingham to investigate. Hope, as the nephew by marriage of Skittles, had already reported that his aunt and her Prince were as keen as ever to have Blunt in Parliament; the Prince because 'there is a want of gentlemen in the House'. This time she promised to fix Birmingham for him through Cyril Flower, the Liberal Whip whose brother had once been her lover.

Within two days Hope had sized up the situation, sensibly but pessimistically. The Liberals of the Edgbaston division of Birmingham had no organization whatever, had done no canvassing and were split in two between Gladstonians and Chamberlainites. Of those who ostensibly wanted Blunt, half distrusted his past record of Conservatism, while the other half were motivated by private resentments. Father Pollen at Birmingham Oratory (one of Minnie's sons) told Hope (also a Catholic) that the Catholic vote in Edgbaston, such as it was, would go Unionist. Young Hope then summed up: the fight might be worth it – 'I should like a dozen such for the sake of a hard blow and excitement' – but it could not lead to victory.[13]

Meanwhile Blunt in London had met a dizzying mixture of encouragement and caution. Rosalind Howard, like some Boadicea urging a trainee on to the Roman swords, wrote to him:

> Once you have fought this fight your future career will be simplified even if you lose. Your present record is not wholly satisfactory and the Churchill taint must be effaced. A fight in the sacred vicinity of Birmingham will give you the requisite radical cachet. There is no more time for vacillation. . . .[14]

Vacillation, however, was the only response that Blunt could get out of Francis Schnadhorst, the organizer of the Birmingham Liberal caucus. Schnadhorst's own position with Chamberlain was so 'very delicate' that he really did not know how to advise Blunt. Labouchere on the contrary was emphatic. Blunt must not fight Edgbaston but West Birmingham, 'Radical Joe's' own seat.

After a midnight journey to Birmingham on the twenty-fourth Blunt found that Hope's worst fears were justified. Edgbaston was no-go. As for West Birmingham, could he make even a propaganda fight here against Chamberlain? (There was no question of getting in.) Not one of Joe's critics on the divisional council would publicly support Blunt. 'Who, then, has invited Mr. Blunt?' asked the *Birmingham Post* scornfully. 'The answer is – himself.' But before Blunt could relapse once more into despair, a deputation of five honest, energetic men from Kidderminster suddenly begged him to stand for them. The seat was winnable. 'The tide of misfortune has turned. *Inshallah*.'

Blunt promptly withdrew from Birmingham. He could not, however, back out of an open-air meeting already advertised for West Birmingham in Icknield Street on 27 June. Amid uproar and laughter he mounted a chair on the platform guarded by the police and had the satisfaction of shouting, 'Joe Chamberlain will end as a Tory peer.'

Immediately afterwards he caught the last train to Kidderminster, falling deeply asleep from exhaustion. He was woken by an unaccountable mob seething around his compartment in the small hours – Kidderminster out *en masse* to welcome their new hero.* There followed a triumphal torchlight procession through the town, with many spontaneous harangues by Blunt. For upwards of a week the fight continued, Blunt enjoying it as much as he had hated Camberwell. Anne was there, noting in her diary that the 'Primroses' of 1885 had ripened into the 'Oranges' of 1886. Young Hope was to write that Blunt had 'conquered a very strong position in the place'. Yet in the end he did not conquer Kidderminster. With Home Rulers falling, as

* One of the Quaker Peases had won Kidderminster for the Liberals with a majority of 150, but had seceded to Chamberlain on Home Rule.

he said, like ninepins round him and a total majority of 118 about to be declared against Home Rule in Parliament, Blunt was exhilarated to lose Kidderminster on 4 July to the Conservative A. F. Godson by no more than 285 votes. He loved the people of Kidderminster, especially after the weavers presented him with thirty square feet of carpet for the hall at Crabbet, featuring his coat-of-arms.*

For some months Blunt was to keep up his Liberal connection with Kidderminster, delighting the carpet-weavers with a discourse in the Town Hall on 'Arabia and the Arabian Horse'. Bedouin feuds were no more bloody than Birmingham elections, 'more like a game', he said (laughter), and the Bedouins paid no taxes (loud cheers). Edward Hope had discovered that entertainments in Kidderminster were 'rare', so Blunt might with advantage lecture there, 'possibly even joining the Liberal Club'.[15] During the Kidderminster election Blunt had announced his resignation from the Tory party 'publicly and absolutely and for ever' in *The Times* and other papers, because of 'their selfish class politics'. On 9 July he had taken the chair at Heathfield, Sussex, for the Liberal candidate, 'a fraudulent grocer'. Ten days later he faced the fact that his left-wing politics had driven away most of the old set from the Crabbet lawn tennis weekend. The meeting was 'very thinly attended'.

By the autumn he found that the continual disappointments (during the election he had been in touch with twenty constituencies) had sapped his interest in politics. He wrote in his diary on 8 September:

> I find myself falling into the same ways in politics that I did in love. The Arabs were my first love and I loved them passionately, but it was of no avail.... Since then I have wandered from love to love. Ardent for a while and then weary and always failing a little of my happiness.

In this self-critical and again self-pitying mood, Wilfrid allowed the rift between himself and Anne to widen. They were quarrelling over Judith. Anne had left her daughter at Crabbet while she herself visited the Wentworths in Porlock for several weeks. Judith, however, was forbidden to join her father at Castle Howard. That Rosalind Howard was 'aggressively unorthodox', Wilfrid freely admitted; nevertheless he positively disliked the Wentworths' influence – Mary 'a silly pretentious woman' and Ralph 'a mere chameleon' – and forbade them his house or Judith theirs. 'Anne seems to have gone mad over the

* His daughter Judith was to say that he lost Kidderminster by replying, when asked if he supported women's suffrage, 'I am a strong supporter of Godhood, womanhood, doghood and cathood', with the result, wrote Judith, that 'men were thrown to the dogs and women classed with cats'. ('Myself and Others.') Four years later Blunt's young protégé Herbert Vivian was bringing out a new magazine, *The Whirlwind*, which stood for the monarchy and the people against Whig oligarchy, vaccination, vivisection and 'female, childhood or Doghood Suffrage'. (Lytton Letters. FM. 1890, File 57.)

Wentworths', he wrote in his diary on 2 October, 'and I shall have to assert my right to Judith.' For the time being, however, they agreed to leave Judith once more in the care of the Pollen family, while they set out on what Wilfrid called 'A New Pilgrimage'.

His recent adventures in Ireland had turned his thoughts back to an old love, the Catholic Church. It was not for nothing that he had declared himself a Catholic to the English electors as well as the Irish peasants and had travelled around Ireland in the company of Catholic priests, many of them old men (Wilfrid always had a special feeling for the old). His mind was finally made up for him by reading during one sleepless night a volume of Rossetti's poems. 'I have resolved to end, before it is too late, my phase of active life and betake myself to that third and concluding phase of all rational existence, the life contemplative.'

He therefore decided to spend the winter in Rome with Anne, or at least, to start out with Anne.

They left Paris together on 28 October; but Wilfrid was already in half a mind to leave her for a life of 'contemplation'. The trouble was that at present he did not know whether to be a Christian hermit or a Mohammedan dervish, particularly as in some respects he was neither; just a materialist.

Happily oblivious of Wilfrid's concealed motives in visiting Rome, Anne shared his joy at this 'new pilgrimage' to the papal city of his youth. For his part he encouraged her and her maid Cowie to go sightseeing on their own. 'Anne rouses in me, I know not why, all my worst passions; and in her company I should be only an atheist.' But without her he felt himself approaching that state of religious rebirth which Cardinal Manning had wished him in a farewell interview just before he left for Rome. 'You will get back there', said Blunt's old friend, 'into the rut of the centuries, and it will do you good.'

The rut of the centuries.... What a seductive phrase! What a life it evoked of peace with holy men following a tradition as straight as the road to Rome itself, along which the wheels of time had rolled biting deep into the soil. And the alternative? As Blunt saw it, his fall from grace at the first assault of the world, 'to say nothing of the flesh and the devil'. It was only among holy men that his frail faith could grow. 'I do not really believe in anything', he had written after staying with Bitters in Paris on the way, 'except vaguely in God's providence and my own entire helplessness in His hands.' The week he had just spent in Paris 'proves how chameleon-like I am, taking the colour of the mud I sit on'.

Immediately they reached Rome Anne, with her impeccable Italian, set about wooing the Vatican officials into arranging a private audience for her husband. With the assistance of Blunt's friend Monsignor Stonor she was successful. And on 11 November Blunt approached what he felt might prove a turning-point in his life.

As he waited patiently two hours for the audience – 'What are a few hours in this Eternal City and in the anteroom of the Vicar of Christ?' – he remembered that he had been sick in mind and body when last in Rome twenty years ago. He was sick now, from a vicious boil and slight heart attack on 1 November. But he was glad of it. He felt more able to approach the penitent stool.

Pope Leo XIII sat on his throne, a little old man, thin and white, with a benign half-smile and very bright eyes – 'piercingly bright'. For a moment he reminded Wilfrid of Voltaire sitting in his chair in the foyer of the Français, but this was no 'mocking spirit'; it was 'an unearthly being, full of knowledge and wisdom, and with the heart of a child'.

Wilfrid approached, kneeling three times; kissed the slipper and then the hand which held his throughout the audience, reminding him of Newman's. Their conversation proceeded in French.

'You have something to tell me, what is it?'

'Holy Father, I have two things to say ... the first for others, the second for myself. About the others it is this. I have been of late in Ireland, where I have seen much of the clergy and the people, and I wish to tell your Holiness how good they are, and how unfortunate and how devoted.'

'Devoted? To what ... ?'

'To religion and the Holy See' – and Wilfrid begged Pope Leo to protect them.

'You are an Englishman and you love the Irish? Is there not generally antipathy?'

'Not with me.'

'And if I understand you rightly, you love the Irish?'

'I do, Holy Father.'

'That is well, *very* well.'*

Wilfrid now turned to his personal case.

'I am very unhappy. I have committed great sins; and I wish to lead a new life. But the habit of the world and the contradictions of my own mind stand always in my way. I cannot break through these; and my prayer to you, Holy Father, is that you will give me a blessing, with the object that perhaps some day I may retire from the world to make my salvation before I die.'

* There are slight variations in dialogue between Blunt's contemporary diary FM. 29/1975, pp. 65–67, quoted here, and his published version in *The Land War in Ireland*, p. 182. In the latter version also his private affairs are omitted.

The Pope broke in: 'What, are you married, and you wish to leave your wife?'

Though he prevaricated, that was indeed Wilfrid's thought. But Pope Leo would have none of it. He insisted that Wilfrid perform his married and religious duties, avoid occasions of sin and the company of unbelievers, so that his dual unfaithfulness might be a thing of the past.

Anne was then summoned and husband and wife were blessed together, with an injunction to make their daughter a bond between them. 'I could not say a word for my tears', wrote Wilfrid, 'and I have felt happy ever since, and with peace of heart such as I have not had for years.'

It did not last. In spite of ecstatic letters from Minnie about the Holy Father's curing Wilfrid body and soul; in spite of the word 'happiness' suddenly blossoming in Anne's diary like an autumn crocus, and of Wilfrid's going the round of 'superstitious devotion', as he called it, and kissing the toe again; in spite of all this, his new-born piety was dwindling within days and by the New Year his 'little burst of fervour' was expended.

The trouble was partly a return to full health. While ill he had not been able to go about, take exercise or even write: neither his memoirs nor the long poem *Griselda* he had started in England, sub-titled 'A Society Novel in Rhymed Verse',[16] had made any progress. Only Judith benefited from more letters than usual, one telling her to her delight how Cowie had wanted to sit in the Pope's chair but Pappa stopped her, remembering the story of 'The Three Bears'. And of course Anne benefited, for Wilfrid went to Confession before the Pope's Mass on 2 January 1887 and Anne had the inexpressible joy of receiving Communion at his side.

A week later they attended a party at the embassy and Wilfrid spent the evening talking to Mrs Waldo Storey, the wife of a sculptor, 'not in a way profitable to my soul'. His Egyptian memoirs, moreover, had been resumed. 'This leads my mind away.' His new heroine Griselda, with her 'noble carriage of the hips' and 'proportionate waist', had met Prince Belgirate on the Appian Way; and Wilfrid was working on an autobiographical sonnet sequence called *A New Pilgrimage*.

> O Rome, thy ways are narrow and aspire
> Too straitly for the knees of this halt age.[17]

Wilfrid was already half up from his knees, when news reached him that Ireland was again in eruption. His friend John Dillon had been arrested for his part in a new agrarian movement called the Plan of Campaign. Salisbury's Cabinet seemed to be crumbling: the Chancellor of the Exchequer, Lord Randolph, resigned and the former Foreign

Secretary, Lord Iddesleigh, dropped dead at the Prime Minister's feet. From Blunt's rejuvenated pen came a fresh flow of political letters: congratulations to Randolph on his 'breaking loose', protests to *The Times* on Ireland, requests to Salisbury for permission to visit his neglected estate of Sheykh Obeyd. As he grew more lusty, Blunt leapt into the saddle again and galloped madly over the Campagna, studied the crossing of Roman mares with Arab stallions, or hunted with the Duke and Duchess of Sermoneta at Folignano, yelling the tally-ho of an Arab in pursuit of gazelle.

On 17 January 1887 came at last the telegram from Lord Salisbury that Blunt had awaited for a year: 'Your letter received. Baring says no objection.' It was off and away to Sheykh Obeyd next day. '*Here therefore ends my sad soul's pilgrimage. . . .*'[18] And here begins a renewed bout with the world.

[12]
'Balfour's Criminal'
1887

'I expect they think I shall be less in their way in Cairo than in Ireland', wrote Blunt in his diary on 24 January 1887, as an Italian ship carried him and Anne back to Egypt after nearly four years' banishment. Even now Blunt had had to give Salisbury assurances that he would not dabble in Egyptian politics; but to be honest, the political ban was not a major deprivation. 'The East has become an irritant', he had written not so long before.[1] Ireland occupied his thoughts, especially since his Irish friends were temporarily under arrest for their part in the famous Plan of Campaign. This was a recent militant development in Ireland's land war. Rack-rented tenants had been advised by the Plan's organizers, John Dillon, William O'Brien and Tim Harrington, to offer their landlords a fair rent, and if that was refused to pay the money into a national fund.

In contrast with the Irish struggle, Blunt found his return to Egypt a frustrating anti-climax. No doubt his Sheykh Obeyed garden was still charming, despite the ruin of orange and lemon trees through lack of watering. 'At least, it *would* be charming', he wrote, 'if there were any regime at Cairo which would give me an interest in being there. As it is I find nothing but regrets and sad recollections.' In 1887 the occupying British, as represented by Baring, countenanced a government composed entirely of foreigners – Armenian, Greek, Syrian, Turkish. Blunt rightly pointed out that such an alien government could not last an instant without the support of British bayonets. Looked at the other way round, the British occupation of Egypt was indispensable until Egyptian self-government was restored.

But when Blunt put this view to Lord Salisbury in April, and the Prime Minister passed it on to Baring for comment, the comment was devastating: 'Make Blunt English consul-general', wrote Baring, and the whole modern Egyptian economy dependent on trade, capitulations (foreign privileges) and the external debt would disappear; 'make one of Blunt's friends ruler or prime minister of Egypt', and he would regard such a regime 'as little less absurd than the nomination of some savage Red Indian chief to be Governor-General of Canada'.[2] This view would have seemed sheer common sense to Salisbury, who considered offering Home Rule to the Irish as little less absurd than nominating the Hottentots. At the Cairo races, Blunt found himself standing beside Baring. He described the scene to Lady Gregory:

> Sir Evelyn Baring was there, with footmen running before him, in a white hat, and he came up to me, nose to nose . . . but I had the presence of mind not to see him, and as he will probably read this letter I shall not say how much like a grocer he looked. I hope and trust his reign here is nearly over, as Randolph will be Foreign Secretary before we are many weeks older and he will sweep the place out of the old gang.[3]

But there was still more disillusionment in store for Blunt. Baring was to survive as uncrowned king of Cairo for another twenty-two years, whereas Lord Randolph never returned to office after his petulant resignation, either as Foreign Secretary or anything else.

Bad as all this was, it paled beside the 'evil-looking' explorer Henry Stanley, whom Blunt had seen on Cairo station enjoying an official send-off on his expedition to relieve Emin Pasha at Zanzibar. 'I hope to Heaven he may leave his bones half-way', was Blunt's wish for the hard, squat-faced Stanley. 'All that Europe has done by its interference of the last thirty years in Africa has been to introduce fire-arms, drink, and syphilis.'

It was only the necessity of finding a new head gardener for Sheykh Obeyd that kept the Blunts in Egypt until 20 March. 'I feel restless and anxious to be away', Wilfrid was writing as early as 1 February, 'for I am convinced that Baring will play me some trick.'[4] Though Wilfrid had given his parole to Salisbury, he was nonetheless watched by the police and warned on 4 March by Valentine Baker Pasha, their chief ('for all the world like a fat Circassian'), against visiting a horse-breeding tribe in the Eastern Desert near Suez. Blunt was furious. 'For the future I shall give no pledges and take my chance of arrest.'

The Blunts' last adventure was indeed enjoyed without government permission – a visit to the religious pilgrimage (Mowled) of 12,000 Arabs far away in the desert south-east of Cairo. 'Baker would have gone into fits', wrote Wilfrid happily, 'if he could have seen us riding round the tomb with them. . . . But I was cautious and did not talk a word of politics. It is satisfactory however to see how well I am received by these masses, Englishman though I am.'

At last the rehabilitation of Sheykh Obeyd was complete, at a cost of £200 for pruning, irrigation and replanting. (The Blunts had lost some £150 a year during their exile, through the 'rogueries' of agents and gardeners.) The estate was now let to an old Muslim friend of Arabi's. Wilfrid planned to keep it as 'a place of retreat from the troubles of Europe, which one day must come'. But it was Anne who would eventually use it as a 'retreat' from the troubles of life with Wilfrid.

Wilfrid was enchanted to be home at Crabbet once more. 'Judith grown tall and good; and the horses likewise. I am delighted after being at Cairo to see with a fresh eye how much better our mares are than anyone else's.' The only blot was the Crabbet estate's indebtedness. He regretted having 'muddled away' several thousand pounds through carelessness. However, there were consolations: all landlords had 'fallen upon evil days'; his marriage had brought in far more property than he had squandered; he had no debts (only mortgages of £3,000); he gave away a tenth of his income every year, drove 'no hard bargains and exacted no unmerciful rents', and the £8,000 he had laid out on politics during the last five years had been well spent. Anne's comment on the situation was not so carefree. Her only privilege in their household, she wrote, was 'the right to pay'.[5]

It was pleasant for Wilfrid to be dallying in London again after an absence of five months: to be flattered by Sir John Millais for his tan ('Ah, I should like to paint you, your face is such a capital brown'); to hobnob with his cousin Madeline Wyndham in Val Prinsep's studio, and to learn that her son George's marriage to Sibell Grosvenor, widow of the Duke of Westminster's heir, now had the approval of both families; to call on W. T. Stead of the *Pall Mall* and hear about his attractive proposal for a 'League of all the Fanaticisms', and on Lord Randolph Churchill, who looked desperately ill but was as friendly as in the old days before the Camberwell election; and on the painter Burne-Jones – 'at least *he* has not wasted his life'. If Blunt were not to waste his, he must focus his talents as Burne-Jones had and keep in front of him some ideal. The ideal of the times was Home Rule for Ireland.

Lord Randolph had told Blunt that a last effort to rule Ireland by force was soon to be made. Parliament would almost certainly pass a Crimes Bill. Unlike previous Coercion Bills – of which in fact it was a particularly virulent species – the intended legislation was to continue indefinitely. If this long-term repression failed to pacify Ireland, admitted Churchill, Home Rule it would be.

Blunt saw at once that it was up to all Nationalists to oppose the Bill's passage and make it unworkable if passed. He therefore joined a massive anti-Coercion demonstration on Easter Monday, 11 April, in Hyde Park, taking with him in his brake a dozen members of the Home Rule Union which he had helped to found. Along Pall Mall they rattled, stopping to hoot outside the Carlton Club, up St James's Street where the Liberal Unionists in Brooks's earned another hoot, and into Piccadilly where they cheered Mrs Gladstone and her daughter Mary at a window. Guiding his Arabians deftly through the huge press in the Park, Blunt came to a dashing halt at platform 13, where he took the chair for the Nationalist M.P., T. P. O'Connor. Next door was the Socialist platform manned by Michael Davitt and William Morris's daughter May, looking like a French revolutionist going to an execution. The Irish agitation, noted Blunt, had given a great fillip to socialism. Blunt's and Davitt's platforms attracted a crowd of 10,000 each, all sober enthusiasts. There was only one drunk visible the whole afternoon, but several Liberal Unionists 'sneaking about'. Blunt's voice, said Frederic Harrison afterwards, carried better than anyone's.

Keeping up the pace, Blunt used an invitation by the Kidderminster Liberals to take the chair at a Women's Suffrage meeting ('my attitude on this occasion was one of friendly neutrality')[6] and to organize a Home Rule meeting next day at the Town Hall. He spoke to such effect that the people persuaded him to stand again if there were an unexpected election. 'I had not intended this, as I am sick of English politics. . . .' At the invitation of Arthur Pollen, Minnie's undergraduate son, he visited the Oxford Union on 12 May to debate against the Crimes Bill. A 'capital' evening, the opposing speaker from Ulster being 'dull'. After a tour of the colleges and a speech to the Palmerston Club next day on Egypt, Blunt decided 'I adore the young'.

When the Crimes Bill was debated in the Commons on the tenth, Blunt was able to hear Parnell speak for the first time. He feared it would be the last, so thin and ill did the Irish leader look. Another speaker new to Blunt was the Tory W. H. Smith, 'who looks like a grocer and is one'.[7] Blunt's mind seems to have run on grocers as a symbol of the bourgeoisie; in fact of course Smith was a stationer.

By July Blunt had actually been urged to undertake a mission to Dublin by Cardinal Manning himself. The Plan of Campaign was apparently causing Pope Leo some anxiety; enough to make him send Monsignor Persico from Rome to look into it. Who better than Wilfrid, suggested Manning, to explain the agrarian war to the papal envoy?

Meanwhile there were developments on the Egyptian and also on Blunt's domestic front.

After many ups and downs the terms of Drummond Wolff's Convention on Egypt had been agreed between Britain and the Sultan. Blunt heard the news on 23 May. 'Hurrah!' he wrote in his diary. This burst of joy was supplemented by a letter from him to *The Times* 'burying the hatchet formally with Lord Salisbury', whom Blunt now believed must be irrevocably pledged to the evacuation of Egypt. Alas for buried hatchets. The Convention itself was soon buried in the dust of diplomatic might-have-beens. For among the Convention's articles appeared the stipulation that Britain should have the right to re-enter Egypt in case of emergency. France and Russia immediately issued a massive protest. By 18 July it was clear even to Blunt that the Convention would never be ratified by the Sultan.

Amid all this political exertion he reacted rather tepidly to Queen Victoria's Golden Jubilee. The celebrations had a bad beginning for Wilfrid when he and Anne quarrelled over a visit to Witley, the old home of Wilfrid's mother in Surrey. He had looked forward to showing all the landmarks to Judith: the names cut on trees, the lanes he loved, 'the sacred places of my youth'. Unfortunately, however, he had got 'entangled' in the lanes on the way there, and they arrived at Witley after a long detour on a piping hot day, to find Jubilee junketings in full swing: roundabouts, Punch and Judy, fireworks – 'a strange unholy spectacle'. Anne insisted on going straight home again. Judith saw nothing. This was a bitter disappointment to Wilfrid who was finding his daughter an ideal companion:

> I dawdle with her talking nonsense and quarrelling exactly as I used to do thirty years ago with my sister Alice. This is very nice, as the time seems to have rolled back. Judith is really an extraordinarily good tempered child, far more so than we ever were.[8]

On Jubilee Day itself he took her to watch the procession with the Pollens in London, Anne declining on principle – she loathed junketings. Next day he lent Crabbet Park for sack races and running through casks. But he himself preferred to take tea with old Mrs 'Woodie'. She told him about Queen Victoria's coronation, and how pleased the young Queen had seemed 'to bow to the gentlemen'. Wilfrid's warmest feelings for Victoria were to be aroused when he chanced to see her driving through Hyde Park in July. 'She has much improved in appearance in the last years, in the way women do when they become old instead of middle-aged.'

Jubilee month also saw the transformation of the annual Crabbet lawn tennis weekend into the Crabbet Club.

The foundation of the Crabbet Club represented a renewed flirtation on Wilfrid's part with youth. There were other signs of a slide towards what he sometimes called frivolity. He discovered, for instance, a bundle of letters from his father to his mother and aunt (Lady Leconfield). Unlike the Lady Byron letters which Wilfrid was reading also and described as 'a putrescent mass', he found his father's 'light and amusing', full of pleasures, little peccadillos, sport, Derby Days, 'little political ambitions'; and, a little while from the end, religion. 'Perhaps I too may succeed in this.' Wilfrid now felt for the first time that though his father had been a better husband, better brother, better friend than himself, 'much of my own triviality was inborn'.

Another sign was a sudden friendship with pretty Dora Swinburne, a wild girl of twenty-one whose father, Sir John Swinburne, took the chair for Wilfrid at a Home Rule meeting. To his distress Wilfrid found that she was engaged to Richard Chamberlain, brother of Joseph ('delighted with the great diamond ring'), but could still be an amusing gossip about her prospective relatives. Lord Rosebery had said to her: 'One must draw the line somewhere with one's political friends, and I draw mine at the screw-making fraternity, the brothers Chamberlain.'

In planning the Club, Blunt drew the line at women and old age. His successful visit to the Oxford undergraduates had prompted him to remodel the Crabbet tennis weekend on a younger basis, inviting Arthur Pollen to bring a dozen friends from Oxford and Herbert Vivian to come from Cambridge. Moreover the new Club was to run on bachelor principles, since Lord Pembroke's marriage and consequent introduction of ladies into the Wagger Club had ruined it. As president, Blunt addressed the members to this effect after dinner – Anne listening unseen from the gallery and deciding that Wilfrid had been 'on the edge of rudeness' to the ladies. She rejoiced, however, that her young guests did not go in for 'noisy conviviality' like the older ones.

A week later Wilfrid had drafted the Club's aims and constitution:[9]

1 The Crabbet Club is a convivial association which has for its object to discourage serious views of life by holding up a constant standard of its amusements.

2 It consists of a President, four public officers and forty ordinary members, who engage to meet annually at Crabbet Park on the invitation of the President, there to promote the purposes of the Club.

Blunt was entranced with his new creation. 'It is curious', he reflected, 'how much closer I am in sympathy with the pleasure of youth than I was ten or twelve years ago when we began our annual tournaments. Then they only half amused me. Now I am wild with delight.'

Nevertheless, even if the Crabbet Club existed to ignore 'the serious side of life', that side of life would not ignore Blunt. On the day that the Wolff Convention collapsed, Blunt went straight round to Cardinal Manning. From Manning he learnt of the papal mission to Dublin. Taking with him young Arthur Pollen, his favourite among the Pollen sons, he set off on 18 July on his third political visit to Ireland; it was to last only a week.

He met Monsignor Persico the papal envoy at the Archbishop of

Dublin's palace on 19 July: 'old Persico', as Blunt called him, 'a diplomatist of the silent, sleepy school, with an enormous nose'. But not too sleepy to formulate for Blunt the problem set by the Irish Land War, with which Pope Leo was wrestling. 'How should people behave when the law was bad', asked Persico, 'until it was repealed?' Blunt bowed out of this one – 'I said I was not casuist enough to answer that' – but instead gave the envoy a factual account of the peasants' plight in Ireland. 'There was no means of forcing attention except by breaking the law.'[10]

A visit to fiery Dr Croke, Archbishop of Cashel, partially opened Blunt's eyes to what might be expected from Rome, and the Pope's true attitude. Dr Croke had once argued the Irish case with the Holy Father himself, as he gleefully told Blunt:

POPE: '... Revolution in France, and revolution in Germany, and revolution here, and revolution there, and now there's to be revolution in Ireland too. I won't have it, and you're the man that's doing it.'
CROKE: '... There's revolution *and* revolution, revolution with guns against law and order, and a moral revolution against injustice. It's the latter we're having in Ireland.'
POPE: 'Oh, no, it's a disturbance you're making, and I have given my orders to stop it.... I can't sacrifice the Church to Ireland.'
CROKE: 'No, nor Ireland either to the Church.'[11]

If Monsignor Persico came to Wexford, Croke told Blunt, he would 'open his eyes for him, or shut them, too, if he liked it better'.

The day before this interview, Blunt had called on two other Catholic patriots – Mr and Mrs Michael Davitt of Land League Cottage, Ballybrack. Davitt was out to stop evictions at all costs. He had himself been arrested so often that to risk it again did not worry him. 'Why, it will only call more attention to the facts.' There followed two days' attendance at a court trial in Gorey, Co. Wexford, where everyone convicted under the Plan shooks hands all round, especially with the local priest – 'Only six weeks, Father. That's a small thing for the Plan.' The tour was concluded by Blunt with a meeting near Athy, where William O'Brien spoke to test the Crimes Act. O'Brien knew when to be moderate, and Blunt in turn resisted pleas to go on the platform himself or allow Arthur Pollen to orate: 'There was really no call for English intervention.'

Two things that particularly struck him during the tour were both the work of women. He was shown over George IV's dazzling ballroom in the Mansion House by a little, middle-aged Irish Catholic woman, Mrs T. D. Sullivan, now the Lady Mayoress of Dublin: 'These are the little revenges of history', wrote Blunt, 'which console us for much injustice in the modern world.' The other was the flag which Mrs Davitt, a gay Irish American, had flown over Land League Cottage on Queen Victoria's Jubilee day. She showed it to Blunt – a strip of black material worked with the white letters EVICTORIA.[12]

It was at Crabbet on 31 July that Blunt gave his pledge of help to Dillon. He and his friend were sitting on a bench in the Icehouse wood. Dillon declared that the Plan of Campaign had won the people's confidence and all but stamped out agrarian crime. However, the government might still 'mean mischief' and Dillon and O'Brien find themselves arrested in the autumn. If not, Dillon would accept the Blunts' invitation to winter with them at Sheykh Obeyd for his health's sake. There was a threat of tuberculosis. 'He has promised me', wrote Blunt at the end of an hour's conversation, 'to let me know if I can help him in any way.' Blunt in his turn promised to respond.[13]

Some three weeks later came the first sign that Dillon was right and the government did 'mean mischief'. A chance encounter with his cousin George Wyndham in the lobby of the House brought Blunt the startling news that the Irish Land League had been banned.

Young George Wyndham, after leaving the army and winning Sibell Grosvenor from an alleged list of eighty besotted rivals, had gone into the Irish Office, where he was private secretary to Arthur James Balfour. A nephew of the Prime Minister Lord Salisbury through his mother, Balfour had been given the key position of Irish Secretary in Salisbury's government. Now, on 19 August 1887, Balfour was 'showing fight' as a novice in the Irish arena. Blunt and George Wyndham met again in September at Clouds, the imposing new country house in Wiltshire of Percy and Madeline Wyndham. The Blunt family, including Judith this time, arrived at Clouds on 31 August. Nothing could have exceeded Wilfrid's elation. The peerless Madeline was unchanged, Percy 'larger-minded and kinder', their daughter Mary, Lady Elcho (expecting her third child), 'the cleverest best and most beautiful woman in the world, with just that touch of human sympathy which brings her to the level of our sins'. Then there was Sybil Marchioness of Queensberry, a cousin whom Wilfrid had loved as a small boy forty years ago; and her schoolboy son Lord Alfred Douglas (Bosie) playing a noisy rhyming game throughout dinner with another child, Pamela Wyndham, Mary's young sister. 'Among these Judith sits like a mouse', Wilfrid noticed, 'too shy to talk.'

It was not till the Saturday afternoon, 1 September, however, that the fun really began – with the arrival of the Irish Secretary A. J. Balfour himself. He brought with him Henry James the novelist, on whom Blunt commented: 'For a man who writes so lightly and well it is amazing how dull-witted he is', trying hard to keep up with the talk but 'always a little behindhand'. Blunt had met Balfour before. The best he could say of him now was that 'as a young man he must have been charming, and still has some of the ways of a tame cat'.

'Lackadaisical' was what a Liberal M.P., Philip Stanhope, had just dubbed Balfour in Parliament; but Blunt found him curiously hard and cynical. On reflection he attributed these qualities to Balfour's pseudo-scientific philosophy: an unwarranted deduction from Darwinism, as Blunt saw it, justifying the Tories' aggressive racialism, whether against the Arabs or Celts, because it promoted 'the survival of the fittest'. After Mary Elcho had scored off him that evening at a game of reversi, Balfour took the opportunity to enunciate his creed: 'There is no more vain and foolish feeling than remorse.' This dictum seemed to explain some remarks made by Balfour at dinner about John Dillon which Blunt found 'not altogether pleasant'.

'I am sorry for Dillon', Balfour began, 'as if he gets into prison it is likely to kill him. He will have hard labour, and it will be quite different from Forster's ridiculous imprisonments at Kilmainham.'* 'There is something almost interesting about Dillon', Balfour added patronizingly; 'but it is a pity he lies so.' Then he repeated the threat: 'He is afraid of prison, and he is right, as it will probably kill him.'[14]

Next day, Sunday, after beating Balfour in a foursome at tennis, Blunt felt able to tackle him on Ireland. Everyone knew that during the afternoon the full fury of the Crimes Act was to be tried out against a meeting at Ballycoreen. 'I suppose it's all over now', Balfour had remarked to George Wyndham as they strolled in for tea. The Irish Office had strict orders that telegrams were not to disturb Balfour's Sunday. So it would not be till the Monday that Balfour heard there had been no disturbance in Ireland either. Meanwhile Balfour and Blunt had had their second ding-dong match of the weekend – over Ireland.

Blunt argued that Home Rule was a certainty. 'The Nationalists needed only to sit still and win.' Balfour disagreed. 'He seems to imagine', wrote Blunt afterwards, 'that by locking up and getting rid of Dillon, O'Brien, and half a dozen others he can take the life out of the National movement, and he wants an excuse for doing so.' Blunt left Clouds convinced that the Irish Secretary intended to 'take the life out of' Dillon personally, as well as the National movement.

No doubt Blunt's impressions owed something to Balfour's relations with Mary Elcho. Like the rest of the house-party, Blunt knew

* The Liberal Irish Secretary, William Edward Forster, 1818–86, sent Parnell, Dillon and others to Kilmainham jail in 1881. They were liberated after Parnell negotiated the 'Kilmainham Treaty' with Joseph Chamberlain through the mediation of Mrs O'Shea.

that Balfour had a *grande passion* for Mary – 'that is quite clear' – and she obviously had a 'tendresse' for him.

> But what their exact relations may be [Blunt continued in his diary] I cannot determine. Perhaps it is better not to be too wise, and as all the house accepts the position as the most natural in the world, there let us leave it.

He left it – for seven years at any rate – and left Clouds full of distrust for Balfour, but no longer regarding him as a weakling. Mary Elcho's 'tame cat' had claws for Ireland.

Hardly had Blunt settled down to a non-political holiday at Naworth Castle reading his poetry to the Howard ladies, before he was jerked back by his conscience to Ireland. He had just come in from shooting partridges when he heard news of very different shootings. Under the Crimes Act, the police had fired on a crowd at Mitchelstown in Co. Cork on 9 September, killing two people. Blunt left for Ireland with some of his Home Rule Union colleagues, much as he hated being part of deputations. But he must not shirk 'committing' himself. 'I have so often resolved to wait for the first blood and now it has been shed.'[15]

His spirits rose after a packed meeting at the Rotunda in Dublin on the fourteenth, where he spoke; after which he sent Judith a merry sketch of two burly men with shillalaghs, one labelled 'Rotund', the other 'Rotunder'. By the next day, however, he felt less buoyant. John Dillon told him during a walk along Killiney Strand about the razor edge on which he himself operated. If he and all the leaders were locked up (O'Brien was already awaiting trial in Cork gaol), the 'violent men' would take over. On the other hand, Dillon and his friends must not 'turn tail'. Blunt's revelations about Balfour's ruthless character and cruel intentions only sharpened the razor's edge for Dillon.

A week later Blunt spent two memorable days with Dillon and Davitt at Mitchelstown, where the Court House was chock-full both for the inquest on the riot and O'Brien's trial. Dillon, striding up and down outside, dark and tense 'like a black panther', narrowly averted another clash between the police and crowd, but O'Brien, the enthusiast, was cheerful inside. As for Blunt, 'I cursed my country with its red coats and black coats and its absurd truculent ministers of an infamous law.' He was to curse it still more next month. Irish throats might chant 'Remember Mitchelstown!' till they were hoarse. Nothing made any visible difference to Balfour's drive against Home Rule. For the murdered – no remorse; for the agitators – no mercy.

Blunt had just squeezed in a poetry-orientated visit to Knebworth when, with a suddenness that boded no good, Dillon summoned him on 14 October by telegram to Dublin.

His excitement rising, Wilfrid telegraphed for Anne and Cowie. They all met at Crewe, Wilfrid after a twelve-mile gallop from Kidderminster where he cut short a speech, and just caught the night mail. Arriving at dawn on the fifteenth, Wilfrid rushed off with O'Brien to Limerick without waiting either for breakfast or Anne. There were to be anti-eviction meetings in the 'proclaimed' (banned) areas. Did this mean, Blunt asked himself, 'something in the way of a fight with the Government'?

The night of the sixteenth was pitch dark. O'Brien and his small party had spent the day in Limerick attending various evictions there in order to put the police off the scent. Their true destination was Woodford in Galway, a proclaimed area and already well known to Blunt. The party, consisting of O'Brien, Blunt, a visiting English M.P. named James Rowlands and two press men, slipped off unseen to Woodford in a brake. As they approached the small town the surrounding countryside burst into welcoming flame – gorse commons set on fire and turf torches dipped in paraffin flaring along the road. There were no police or reporters waiting, for the telegraph wires Woodford had been cut. From a window in the main street, O'Brien leant out and symbolically burnt the government proclamation against all meetings in the area; the two Englishmen following with suitably eloquent harangues. In the theatrical atmosphere Blunt forgot his whirling words almost as soon as they were spoken. But his presence at the burning of the proclamation was to be remembered against him for many a month.

For the next three days they attended, with John Redmond, M.P., the first trial under Balfour's new Act, at Wexford. Anne, who had joined them, jotted down some highlights: the brilliant but venomous Crown Counsel, Edward Carson, turning round and putting out his tongue at his opposite number for the defence, after the latter had made an effective speech; the Resident Magistrate saying ingenuously to Tim Healy, M.P., Counsel for the defence, 'Well, Mr. Healy, I think you will *very likely* get fair play in this court.'

Back in Dublin on the twenty-first, Wilfrid heard that there were to be more evictions in Woodford. This seemed the moment for a definitive English gesture – not secretly at midnight this time but in public, in broad daylight; to be exact, an anti-eviction meeting in Woodford at two on Sunday afternoon 23 October. Blunt spent the twenty-second arranging for Woodford and Loughrea to be plastered with notices of the meeting, and in showing a French artist – a kind of minor Gustave Doré working for the *Graphic* – the horrors of eviction.

Last thing that night came a thrilling telegram from O'Brien to say that Dublin Castle had banned Blunt's meeting by name.

Wilfrid and Anne slept the night at Woodford in the house of a militant miller named Roche whose children, sent out to scout at daybreak, reported the presence of 150 police and a company of Scots Guards. Wilfrid dashed out, found a copy of the proclamation on the bridge, its paste still wet, and tore it down. Signed by the Lord-Lieutenant and Arthur James Balfour, it accused him of aiming at 'intimidation' and 'a breach of the peace'. Then Blunt drafted his own individual proclamation and despatched it to the O.C. Police and Scots Guards: 'I do not recognize the right of the Lord Lieutenant causelessly to interfere with a meeting convened by orderly Englishmen', not to cause alarm and terror, as the proclamation said, but to 'encourage the victims of Lord Clanricarde's rapacity to a steadfast patience and endurance of their wrongs, which cannot now be of long duration. . . . Signed. Chairman of the Meeting. Wilfrid Scawen Blunt.'[16]

Punctually at two (so that the notoriously unpunctual Irish should not collect in too large numbers for their own safety) the platform party of perhaps fifteen people marched quietly to 'Keary's Meadow', a field in the centre of the town at the foot of sloping plough land and surrounded by small hills dotted with trees. As Wilfrid and his friends trooped in and mounted the platform, they were aware of the police advancing step by step from the back of the field behind them.

'Are you the Mr. Blunt whose name is on the handbills?' demanded Major Byrne, the Magistrate. 'Then it is my duty to prevent this meeting.'

'It is my duty to hold it', replied Wilfrid, rising as chairman.

'Men of Galway!' he began. Next moment Byrne gave a signal from the rear – 'Clear the platform!' The platform was rushed by the police and the whole group including Lady Anne and Mrs Rowlands were swept from the commanding heights on to the ground three or four feet below.

Immediately Wilfrid, followed by Anne, clambered back and again the same opening words, 'Men of Galway!' echoed across the field, by now a buffeting mass of police and villagers, only to be silenced once more by a new wave of Byrne's men. 'Clear the platform! Put this man down!' This time, however, Wilfrid was prepared for the assault. He pulled the police down with him and they all toppled over the edge of the platform together. There was a fine scrimmage, the police pulling and tearing at Wilfrid's overcoat until Anne thought, 'What an astonishingly strong coat that is.' (It was to become a famous coat in a few months' time.)

Meanwhile Byrne seized Anne by the throat, dug in his fingers and nearly throttled her as he tried in vain to drag her off Wilfrid. 'Take her off! Take her off!' Byrne yelled; 'but, thanks be to God', wrote Anne in her diary, 'I was able to hold firm.' They began twisting Wilfrid's arm until he roared out 'Torture is abolished so leave it alone'. By now he was lying passive, determined not to 'offer resistance'.

'Let go or you will kill him', Anne screamed, thinking he had lost consciousness. The police stood back and might have let him go had not Wilfrid suddenly determined to force the issue, making the meeting a test case. He sprang up.

'Are you all such damned cowards', he shouted, 'that not one of you dares arrest me?' Sergeant Wade then stepped forward, took him by the coat-collar and shoulder and arrested him.

'It's all right now', Wilfrid whispered to Anne. 'Come along.' And they were marched off.[17]

Blunt and Roche were locked in for the evening at Woodford police station but, having refused bail, were conveyed to Loughrea gaol, some miles away, for the night. Bonfires in their honour illuminated the road, and rocks to impede their police van were rolled across it. A shadowy throng of well-wishers surged round them outside Loughrea prison, and Blunt fell happily asleep in his eight-feet-by-six cell conscious that he had already become 'we' against 'them'. For a moonlighter had tried to stab their police driver outside the gates, but when questioned about the incident Blunt stoutly denied ever having seen anything.

Two magistrates considered Blunt's case next day, 24 October, one a Limerick grocer, the other a racing tout about to be arrested himself for debt. Again Anne noted some features of the occasion: Crown Counsel Ronan always 'puffing with anger' and his junior, Carson, 'panting with rage'; Ronan declaring, 'English politicians coming over here must be taught that they will be treated as if they were the *ordinary* inhabitants of the country.' At the end of the day Blunt was sentenced to two months' imprisonment. He lodged an appeal to Quarter Sessions, having been refused leave to cross-summons Byrne and Balfour.

Released on bail, he and Anne returned to London. For Wilfrid the experience was not unenjoyable in retrospect, as an illustrated letter he sent to Judith from Loughrea gaol showed: first, a sketch of the affray, Anne clinging to the prostrate Wilfrid and 'Bibi a sad helpless orphan'; then these 'merciless cannibals' waiting to try Pappa – 'But it is better to be good than happy and I have often been far more mauled on the lawn at Crabbet by a sacrilegious child.'[18] In later years he was to regard it as a memorable landmark:

> It had a large political importance in its day, and ... deserves to be remembered in Irish history as being the first recorded instance, in all the four

hundred years of English oppression, of an Englishman having taken the Celtic Irish side in any conflict, or suffered even the shortest imprisonment for Ireland's sake.[19]

For Anne the experience had been harrowing, though she was as always intrepid. Her throat ached and her wrist had been struck by a stone. In those days, as Wilfrid pointed out, it was most rare for a woman to take part in 'political scrambles'. The suffragettes of the future were still only children. Nor was Anne at all happy about Wilfrid's new decision to fight Deptford as an anti-Coercion candidate. As early as July she had suspected that 'political mania' once again threatened to afflict her husband, despite his renunciation. 'One can never count on anything with Wilfrid.'[20] Nevertheless, as soon as canvassing for the Deptford by-election began, Anne was at her post, diligently marking down 'outs', 'very cordial' and 'doubtful' – far too many of the last, since Conservatives were angry at having the notorious Mr Blunt 'foisted' upon them. 'I wish Deptford was given up', Anne wrote in December.[21]

Woodford had indeed brought Wilfrid both notoriety and fame. Lord Randolph Churchill wrote expressing 'profound regret' at his goings-on in Ireland. But the Crabbet Club, through Arthur Pollen, telegraphed congratulations, and Herbert Vivian was converted to Home Rule. Even Rosalind Howard, who hitherto had regarded Wilfrid as above all a poet, now changed her mind. 'You are through and through a man of action – a man one can utterly trust. . . . You will have Ireland's love as well as Egypt's.'[22]

Heartening letters about British public opinion came from other women friends. Minnie Pollen rejoiced with him, particularly at 'Randy' (Lord Randolph) criticizing the Blunts by name at a meeting in Nottingham, and causing them both to be cheered – 'though it was a ticket Tory meeting'. What the people liked, said Minnie, was the story of Wilfrid climbing back on the platform after being thrown off: 'That is enough for an Englishman, and has done you more good than every word you *ever* wrote or spoke.'[23]

Skittles, though most unhappy 'to see how those *horrible* brutes and blackguards behaved towards you poor boy', had a fighting message to wind up with: 'Shame, shame on them! You are so brave and good. Without exception Clanricarde is one of the villains on earth. I know the man *too* well. . . .'[24] 'What a splendid commotion you have made!' Janey Morris wrote to Wilfrid. 'People are wildly enthusiastic about it, I dined at the Burne-Joneses last night, and all were loud in your praise.'[25]

'Remember Woodford – and Wilfrid', was the headline in the *Pall Mall Gazette*. Two distinguished Liberal statesmen, Sir William

Harcourt and Sir Wilfrid Lawson, were soon bear-leading their prize around the north of England. Blunt had never met the burly, jovial Harcourt before, but found him greatly to his taste. He could hardly believe it when Harcourt told him his popularity with the Liberals was 'second only to Gladstone's'.

[13]
In Chains for Ireland
1888

'A bright and lovable New Year', was Skittles' wish to her 'dearest Winny' for 1888. Lovable was perhaps not quite the word. For Wilfrid was to open the New Year by surrendering to his bail. He appeared at Portumna County Court, between Loughrea and Galway Town, for his appeal. Anne was present and his new youthful secretary Herbert Vivian,* as well as other loyal friends, including old John Evelyn and young John Pollen, who headed all his letters from court 'In the den of thieves'.

Intense party political interest had been aroused by Blunt's appeal. The press was there in force. It was felt that if Blunt first won his appeal and then won Deptford, 'Bloody Balfour's' Coercion policy and his uncle Lord Salisbury's 'twenty years of resolute government' might end ignominiously in twenty days.[1]

The trial began on 3 January and lasted five days. Blunt's defence was conducted free by The MacDermot and Tim Harrington, in front of Mr Justice Henn. There was no jury. Prosecuting counsel were Atkinson and Edward Carson again as junior, 'two of the Castle bloodhounds'. Anne kept records, sometimes adding portraits with colour-notes: an Irish R.M. ('Face and pocket-handkerchief – crimson. Hair – red'); Carson, dark and angular; the defendants, whoever they were, always Christ-like.[2]

Atkinson for the Crown opened with a package denunciation of Woodford and its champions: 'This Woodford is in a district remarkable for crime and *murder* [Lord Clanricarde's agent had been shot the year before] – a most turbulent district addressed by these gentlemen who know how to appeal to the passions of these people.'

The first task for Carson was to convince Judge Henn that passions had indeed been roused by these 'gentlemen' and not by the police. He got from one police witness the statement that in seizing Blunt by the coat collar he had exclaimed solicitously, 'Take care of the lady'; and

* Edward Hope had resigned his post at the end of 1887 and planned to emigrate to South America, thanks to a loan from Blunt.

from another, that no assaults had been committed on anyone, 'except by Mr. Blunt' (laughter); and from a third, that when Mr Blunt climbed back on the platform 'the crowd groaned fiercely'.

The MacDermot's speech for the defence began on a strong emotional note. 'Mr. Blunt comes here – an English gentleman – comes on a noble mission as I shall show and is met by accusations.' He then dealt with the accusation of violence. Supporters of Home Rule, he insisted, were *against* violence, and he quoted Parnell's saying, 'He who commits a crime gives strength to the enemy.' At the Woodford meeting, what violence had there been? Only *one* policeman injured. The prosecution would argue that Blunt's meeting was illegal and the police, therefore, doing their duty in dispersing it. He denied both claims. There was laughter when he dealt with one police witness's account of the struggle on the platform. 'Mr. Blunt is driven off, again attempts like a true Englishman to ascend – again he is on the ground. And a policeman says, *while falling* his wife was "Whispering to him conspiracy" – on the way to the ground!' Mr Blunt's behaviour was lawful, yet he had been sentenced to two months' imprisonment. 'I believe, Sir, firmly', he ended addressing the judge, 'that you will find it impossible to convict Mr. Blunt.'

Judge Henn did not find it impossible to convict Blunt. He sentenced him to two months' hard labour, though not without a tribute of crocodile tears: 'With deepest pain I must confirm the sentence of the court below', he pronounced. Mr Blunt's conduct was 'courageous if not wise', though Henn wondered about 'his good feeling as to the risks to life and limb – of the danger to the *lady*'. (*Damn* Hunn, wrote Anne in her notebook.) So it was to be Galway gaol.

Wilfrid now had an hour or so, wrote Anne dramatically, 'to prepare for death' – death for two months anyway 'and maybe for altogether'. She was thinking of the Balfour threat to kill off the Nationalist ringleaders in prison.

They were taken that afternoon by train to Galway Town, Anne quietly talking Arabic with Wilfrid, to the confusion of their guards. (Wilfrid reckoned that Arabic had not been heard in the extreme west of Europe since the Moors occupied Baltimore, Co. Cork, in 1637.) At the station an enthusiastic crowd surrounded their carriage, one girl seizing Wilfrid's hand and blessing him. An omnibus took them on to the gaol, while the crowd followed them with deafening cheers for 'Mr. Blunt' and groans for 'Mr. Balfour'. Before and behind rode mounted police, their swords drawn. A police officer also occupied the driver's seat on the omnibus, since the usual coachman refused 'to drive Mr. Blunt to gaol'.

Anne had slipped into the omnibus beside Wilfrid before they could stop her. Inside the gates Captain Mason the prison governor, a short purple-faced man in a top hat, with walrus moustache and whiskers, allowed them time to say goodbye 'properly'. Then suddenly Anne found herself alone outside under the gas flares, unable to see John Evelyn's carriage which was waiting for her, because of the darkness and thronging people. She got a lift to her hotel. All night she dreamt of police charges, waking up Cowie next door with her moans.[3]

Galway gaol was an old-fashioned, rambling place with many pleasant irregularities both in design and discipline. Blunt could see a good patch of sky from his window and, if he stood on his cell stool, jackdaws, sparrows, a tom-tit and an occasional sea-gull; best of all, he could see a warder's house opposite with his daughter's shadow sometimes moving on the blind. The roar of the Shannon weir at night he mistook for the open sea.

Most of the warders, being Nationalists themselves, allowed him small privileges: an obliging fellow-prisoner to sweep out his cell; permission to sit cross-legged on the floor Arab-fashion, with his Bedouin rug under him as if in the real desert, instead of perched upright on his stool according to the regulations; an occasional copy of the *Freeman's Journal* dropped by the head warder; surreptitious gifts of food which he fed to his birds and the prison mouse. A young spider was coaxed into spinning its web across the Prison Regulations on his cell wall, so that flies might know about the rules governing Sentence of Death. Another whimsical pleasure was picking oakum. Wilfrid enjoyed the 'good healthy smell' as he deftly unravelled an end of old tarred rope. The warders would come in to admire the fine texture of his growing pile, 'hardly less attractive than that of a woman's golden hair'. After he had got wise to the boredom of workless Sundays he would secret a rope's end on Saturday nights.

Beside becoming an oakum addict, Wilfrid enjoyed the daily visits of Captain Mason the governor to give him the news; of Dr McCormack the bishop, the provider of pinches of snuff as well as spiritual stimulus; and of the prison doctor, the kindly recipient of a note from Sir Andrew Clarke, M.D., who had 'thumped and sounded' Wilfrid before he left England for Galway in December. To think that Clarke pummelled Gladstone also, and better still, Skittles, alleviated his sufferings.

For suffer he did. He, a writer, had no writing materials, a fact that his political friends could scarcely credit. They fondly imagined him to be a 'political prisoner', whereas he was a 'common criminal'. Nor was he entitled to any reading material other than the prison Bible, whose cramped print was illegible except during the moments when a ray of sunlight slanted into his cell.

Nevertheless a memorandum on prisons that he wrote for the

Home Secretary Winston Churchill in 1910 dwelt kindly on his first fortnight in the lax old institution:

> Thus Galway was for me a house of penance rather than of punishment, and my time in it, for the first fortnight, a kind of spiritual retreat. I still look back on it with affection as a softening influence in my life.[4]

This affection, however, was to freeze up in a burst of January weather, made darker by the growing monotony of his detention and a tightening of discipline.

Wilfrid had always suffered from the cold. For this reason he insisted on wearing his own socks under the prison ones and his own top coat of thick woollen frieze over the prison uniform, day and night. The wearing of the overcoat prevented him from taking any exercise, since only regulation clothing was allowed in the yard. That in turn meant that he was never healthily warm, never physically tired. Lying on his plank bed in a totally unheated cell through the long, long January nights, he would drop off for an hour or two, wake up expecting it to be morning and hear the prison clock strike nine. Ten more hours of blackness with nothing to do but think bitter thoughts – and gather his precious overcoat more closely around him.

Sleeplessness affected his imagination. Small things began to irritate, like the catching of his mouse by a well-meaning warder. Then came a bigger thing. News of his overcoat had percolated to the Prison Board at Dublin, of which the chairman was the Hon. Charles Bourke, formerly land agent to the Burrells' Sussex estate, but unlike Button Bourke his nephew, a violent Unionist. On 11 January Wilfrid secretly wrote to Anne on a single sheet of tissue paper that though he was otherwise well his coat might cause trouble. 'But I *will not* give up my coat.'

That very evening the governor came into his cell with some strange warders and tried to make him surrender it. (His own warders had been permanently removed on orders from Dublin.) A substitute prison coat was left in his cell. But the new prison coat from Dublin was hopelessly inadequate for the tall Blunt. 'So I cling to my coat as I do to my life.' He began to imagine that 'bloody Balfour', in wishing to deprive him of his overcoat, was really after his life. Already slightly unbalanced by the nightly 'torment' of thirteen hours' darkness, Wilfrid's mind kept running on the Balfour threats uttered after that dinner at Clouds. 'Sorry for Dillon . . . prison . . . likely to kill him . . . hard labour . . . something interesting about Dillon. . . .' Change the name Dillon to Blunt, and Balfour's own Plan of Campaign seemed to be revealed. In Blunt's exaggerated state of suspicion it was easy to put two and two together and make five.

The crisis came on 13 January. Under Bourke's instructions,

Captain Mason seized Blunt's overcoat by a token show of force, Blunt formally resisting. He was furiously angry; and he knew from a warder that on this very day two of his Irish friends had been thrown again into gaol, one of them William O'Brien who, 'half comically, half tragically', had already made a stand against prison clothing. The overcoat question being now indissolubly linked in Blunt's mind with the honour of political prisoners if not their life or death, he demanded to see the Visiting Justices forthwith.

Six local magistrates accordingly met Blunt on the morning of the fourteenth in his cell. Wrapped only in a blanket, he was resolved to deploy his full case from the pulpit of his plank bed and in the strength of his John-the-Baptist raiment. His powerful harangue included the disclosure of Balfour's threats made privately at Clouds.[5]

In a sense he was preaching to the converted, for the local magistrates all disliked Clanricarde and respected Blunt both for the Crabbet Stud and his friendship with the important Gregorys of nearby Coole. One of the J.P.s was the distiller Persse, a kinsman of Lady Gregory's who talked horse-flesh with Wilfrid. They ordered him a made-to-measure overcoat (though the sleeve measurements were too short and the body too long), pen and paper, books and a larger lighter cell. Bishop McCormack was allowed to procure him a quarto Douai bible with big print and illustrations. Wilfrid scribbled verses in the fly-leaves:

> Long have I searched the earth for liberty,
> In desert places and lands far abroad,
> Where neither kings nor constables should be . . .[6]

and read all the historical books of the Old Testament, rejoicing in the names of places he knew and loved, like Horeb and Sinai, and much gratified to find that the Lord would undoubtedly 'bring my soul out of trouble' and 'destroy mine enemies'. When he came to assemble a sonnet sequence on his imprisonment entitled *In Vinculis* – 'In Chains' – he found that it was not the forgiveness of the New Testament but its story of betrayal and suffering with which he could identify:

> From Caiphas to Pilate I was sent. . . .
> The garment of my life is rent in twain.[7]

His new cell unfortunately was damp and even colder than the last, so that he was tortured by rheumatism. Even worse than the cold were the consequences of his disclosures about his private conversation with Balfour at Clouds. Garbled and exaggerated as it probably was by a clerk's transcription of Blunt's oral testimony, it immediately appeared in the press, bringing down a torrent of invective on Blunt's head. Balfour denied Blunt's account totally.

Even though some of his friends accused him of 'hitting below the belt', he did not afterwards regret his disclosures politically. (Similarly, he had never regretted the use he made of Lord Lytton's conversations in India.) For it was his considered opinion that by the end of 1888 some of the things he had been fighting for were won through his intervention. Their own clothes were no longer removed from the backs of political prisoners nor menial tasks forced upon them; nor was Dillon killed by cruelty when he fell once more into Balfour's hands. On the contrary, Dillon was to leave the prison hospital, after six months' confinement, a healthier man than he had entered.

Meanwhile new anxieties came crowding in: an ill-omened visit from Charlie Bourke and the Prison Board; the Deptford by-election; people who had promised but unaccountably failed to visit him, like Morley, Ripon, Manning; above all, a new civil action for damages that Blunt himself was about to bring against Major Byrne in Dublin.

The Dublin Four Courts were the scene of Blunt's last battle in Ireland's Land War. He was moved from Galway to Kilmainham gaol in Dublin at five in the morning of 8 February. Galway was paradise compared with Kilmainham. Blunt was to describe it, with effect, to Winston Churchill as the epitome of an up-to-date inhuman prison. The Kilmainham system – invented to deal with urban criminals – was known as 'silent and separate'. Blunt was to find it entirely odious. Through this system the prisoner's sense of proportion was destroyed 'and the mind revolves upon the axis of its own imaginings, to its spiritual hurt'. Blunt found himself siding with the worst Dublin criminals, his fellow-sufferers, and revolting with them against 'the barbarities of civilization'. Better a thousand times the dirty prison yard of Aleppo where he had seen murderers and honest men marshalled cheek by jowl 'on a common basis of humanity', than this 'convent without God', this 'school without a teacher'. In Kilmainham there was no humanity, only hygiene. Under the blanket of 'stupefying silence' and 'encircled by a hell of repellent regularity', 'absolute uniformity', 'abominable exactitude', Blunt made no friends.

And last the gaol – What stillness in these doors!
  The silent turnkey their last bolts have shot;
And their steps die in the long corridors.
  I am alone. My tears run fast and hot.[8]

He fell rapidly into a black melancholy, from which his civil action barely aroused him.

The case against Byrne for assault at Woodford had been brought in Blunt's name by the Irish National League. Wide political interest was therefore again focused upon Blunt, both Irish Nationalists and English Liberals believing that a victory in the Four Courts would bring Balfour's policy into total disrepute. Before leaving England, Blunt had obtained the best legal advice on his chances, with the result that on 28 November 1887, H. H. Asquith, Sir Charles Russell, Robert Reid and W. S. Robson had given their joint opinion: 'Mr. Blunt has a good cause of action for assault' against Byrne and Balfour. All four were M.P.s and Q.C.s, and all were to be even more distinguished in the future, the first as Prime Minister, the second as Lord Chief Justice (he was already Attorney-General), the third as Lord Chancellor and the fourth as a later Attorney-General.

Nevertheless there were strong forces arrayed against Blunt. The judge in the case was Christopher Palles, Chief Baron of the Exchequer in Ireland and famous for his condemnation of the Plan of Campaign. The Crown lawyers were Peter O'Brien the Irish Attorney-General, known as 'Peter the Packer' for his skill in packing juries, with two other Q.C.s, Atkinson and Lynch, as his juniors. 'Pether', as the Nationalist press derisively called O'Brien because of his extravagant brogue, only had to make sure that *one* out of the twelve jurors was against Blunt, to win. The plaintiff required a unanimous verdict. The jury was in fact swiftly challenged and weeded out by Peter the Packer until it contained the one strong Unionist he needed: Mr Pease, a Quaker. Blunt's counsel were The MacDermot, Q.C. and Tim Healy, M.P.

When Anne saw Wilfrid in court the first day, 11 February, he looked to her ill, 'as if the life had gone out of him'. Anne added percipiently: 'In some degree he seemed *to be someone else*.'[9]

The court was perishingly cold, and Wilfrid wore his uncouth prison overcoat. Anne felt that he had nonetheless made a great impression on the judge in his first speech. Wilfrid himself, however, realized it was simply that Palles behaved with politeness towards him, unlike 'Old Henn' at Portumna. A 'great sensation' was caused when the judge ordered two of Wilfrid's anti-Coercion speeches to be read aloud in court and Wilfrid endorsed their sentiments with a bold 'Hear, hear!' But during lunch he dared not eat the mutton cutlets offered to him, contenting himself with jelly, since the prison porridge and cocoa had given him chronic indigestion. He was driven back to Kilmainham wearing his own greatcoat over the prison one, with four officers riding in front and one behind.[10]

On Monday 13 February, when the hearing was resumed, there was a pleasant diversion in the witnesses' waiting-room. Their friends arranged for Anne and Wilfrid to be photographed separately and together.* The portrait of Anne in a neat jacket and bonnet was afterwards described by Wilfrid as the best likeness ever taken of her.

* Judith's account of the incident was inaccurate, for she wrote that Blunt put on his prison uniform again *after* he had been released, *in order* to be 'photographed for the Press'.

Wilfrid wore his short prison jacket and round felt cap in one photograph, the prison overcoat in another. Etchings made from the photographs were sent to his friends. One of the friends may have been Skittles, for it was said that King Edward VII later saw a copy. 'What uniform is he wearing?' asked the King. 'Your Majesty's.'

On the same day, 13 February, Mr Gladstone was penning a letter to Mr Blunt full of 'warm and cordial sympathy' for the indignities he had suffered and stating his belief that Mr Blunt had acted in the Woodford affair 'as a loyal and law abiding citizen in defence of the most cherished rights of our countrymen....'[11]

Mr Pease, as Pether's twelfth man, did his duty; and in voting for the Crown on the seventeenth made sure that Blunt's suit was rejected. All the other eleven gave their votes for Blunt.

Sick at heart and with a severe chest cold, not to mention grey hairs discovered in his beard, Blunt was reincarcerated to work out the rest of his sentence. 'One especial drop of bitterness was mingled with my cup', he confessed in his memoirs. On the very day he returned to Kilmainham gaol, Balfour, George Wyndham and George's family, including his sister Mary Elcho, had arrived at the Chief Secretary's Lodge in Phoenix Park to hold what Blunt called 'high revel '. Their rejoicing was in no way lowered by the thought of Balfour's criminal doing the 'silent and separate' nearby. During his now utterly sleepless nights, Blunt passed the time making anagrams of his enemy's names on a slate. 'The Right Honourable Arthur James Balfour of Whittinghame' yielded 'How! Am I not Arthur B., a huge thief, the brutal gaoler of Irishmen?'[12] The prison doctor, alarmed at Blunt's melancholy, ordered a book to calm his nerves. Under the impression that it was a book of devotions, the chaplain supplied Victor Hugo's *Notre Dame de Paris*. Blunt's neurosis, as a result, was deepened by nightmares of medieval as well as modern dungeons.[13]

Another bitter drop was the thought of Deptford. At a critical stage in the campaign the news reached Deptford that their anti-Coercion Radical candidate had been 'non-suited' in the Dublin court.

No one could have worked harder for him in Deptford than Anne, though the canvassing, crowds and speeches she described in her diary as a 'troubled dream'; it needed Wilfrid's presence to give them reality. Scarcely less devoted than Anne were the massed ranks of the Pollens. John and Minnie had organized an army of 'lady scribes' at Pembridge Crescent to despatch 10,000 potted biographies of Wilfrid Scawen Blunt in 10,000 envelopes, while Minnie gave him news from the constituency and messages from her own fiery heart. The Pollen family had no friends left, added Minnie, because in London society Home Rulers were boycotted. Four days before polling she went to bed at three and was up again at seven. Having only just discovered that Wilfrid could receive letters, she took the precaution of addressing him as 'My dear dear nephew ... from your very affectionate aunt.' Margaret Pollen, Minnie's spinster daughter, added her quota of comfort: 'Dear Cousin O'Blunt. ... You will be delighted to hear that you are in the pantomime and every other illustrated paper has pictures of you picking oakum in a classical costume consisting of blankets mostly.'

As the campaign neared its close, Minnie assured her 'nephew' that the poor of Deptford were being 'wonderfully nice' about him. It was not surprising, since at Mass that morning (26 February) the priest had told the whole congregation to pray for Mr Blunt's success. Mrs Gladstone's canvassing visit to the Deptford constituency 'did much good', and they expected Lady Ripon to drive round tomorrow. Everything was in fact 'going beautifully'.[14]

Wilfrid's opponents however had three or four quite dangerous weapons. To begin with, Deptford was a Conservative seat, from which John Evelyn had resigned in his favour. Wilfrid had a formidable Conservative opponent in Charles Darling (later Mr Justice Darling, then Lord Darling). As early as 1886 Darling had put it about that the Catholic idol of the London poor, Cardinal Manning, was against Home Rule. It was Wilfrid who obtained a message from Manning denying 'this mischievous statement'.*

Later, Wilfrid's friends had more difficulty in rebutting the charge that his repetition of Balfour's after-dinner conversation at Clouds was 'treason to the privacy of the mahogany'. John Pollen might write stoutly, 'Great bosh that.' But the Conservatives who had had their knees under the mahogany regarded the election cry of social treason not as bosh but a bull point.

Yet another matter was being used against him. Darling read aloud an 'improper' sonnet from *Proteus* at a Nonconformist meeting with the comment, 'That was written by the man who wants you to elect him. And who did he marry? The granddaughter of Lord Byron, the man who wrote *Don Juan*.' Darling also accused Blunt of being 'in intimate alliance with the Socialists', since the Socialist candidate had withdrawn.[15] Worst of all of course was Wilfrid's legal failure in Dublin. Why should Deptford accept what Dublin had rejected?

On the night that the poll was declared, 29 February, Wilfrid awoke in his cell, and the prison was suddenly shaken by a great gust of wind like the roaring of a crowd. 'It is the Conservatives cheering our

* Message from Manning's assistant secretary the Rev. W. Fleming: 'I am desired by the Cardinal to inform you that the use of his name in Mr. Darling's handbill, classing his Eminence with the opponents of Home Rule is contrary to the truth. ... He has always been in favour of giving to Ireland the power of administering its own local affairs.' (Lytton Letters, FM. 25 June 1886.)

defeat', he exclaimed. The Conservatives of Deptford were indeed cheering at that very hour outside the Carlton Club in Pall Mall, twenty minutes before midnight, in a whirlwind of joy.

The result of the by-election was as follows:

Charles John Darling, Unionist,	4,345
Wilfrid Scawen Blunt, Anti-Coercion	4,070
Unionist majority,	275

The Times announced that Darling had won through 'sheer pluck and cleverness'. His opponent (whose name it did not deign to mention) had lost because Englishmen were repelled by 'martyrdom'.

Release from prison came on 6 March. Taken before the governor, Blunt was given 8½d., his wages for picking oakum, and spared the usual words of advice to a freed prisoner. Instead Governor Beer told him that his own new-born son was to be called, after the prison's late distinguished inmate, Wilfrid Blunt Beer. Wilfrid was too despondent to raise a smile of gratitude.

> No, I will smile no more. Love's touch of pleasure
> Shall be as tears to me, fair words as gall,
> The sun as blackness, friends as a false measure,
> And Spring's blithe pageant on this earthly ball,
> If it should brag, shall earn from me no praise,
> But silence only to my end of days.[16]

Anne, however, was inclined to brag about the 8½d. wages, which she wore on a silver chain round her neck.

The psychological aftermath of prison – in Wilfrid's case deep gloom and withdrawal – was to last for many months, indeed after five years he was telling Lady Gregory that he still shuddered at sight of a policeman. In his conclusion to the Prison Memorandum drawn up much later for Winston Churchill, he wrote: 'I left Kilmainham at the end of my two months in a spirit of revolt against all society, a feeling which I am sure is the predominant one in every released prisoner at its gates.'

Anne took him for calming drives round Dublin on the first days of release, and in the evenings to receptions given in his honour. 'Here all are kind', he wrote in his diary, 'and I sometimes think it would be better to remain. I dread the cold douche of English society more than I can say.' Then he introduced a significant note on his marriage. 'Anne has behaved admirably all these past months. She worked night and day at Deptford and all for nothing. Yet she is perfectly content and happy.'

It is possible that if Wilfrid had really settled in Ireland instead of

Egypt for the winters, his married life would have settled down too. The religious forces playing upon it from Catholic Ireland would have been very different from those of the Muslim world or English society. Yet one must doubt whether his intention was ever more than another of those yearnings for 'a better life' that had often overtaken him in the past and vanished as often under contrary influences.

True, in May 1888 he was asking the M.P. for Cork to look out for a farm near Queenstown where he could found a branch of the Crabbet Stud and hunt in the winter. And a month earlier he had chanced to run into an old priest who had known his father and mother, Father Lockhart, with cathartic results:

> I am here [he wrote from St Etheldreda's in Ely Place] once more desperately resolved to lead a better life. My meeting Father Lockhart at Epsom was a Providence, as I have confessed my sins. I suppose there never was a worse record than mine has been in certain ways.[17]

But this time the obstacle to his 'better life' was to be the 'cold douche' awaiting him in England. So much colder was it even than he had expected, that in the end only fresh loves seemed to offer life-giving warmth.

The 'Welcome Home' planned for him at Crabbet on 10 March was the first wet blanket. Instead of the glittering gathering of Liberal M.P.s and perhaps a Tory magnate or two, there was a popular demonstration led by three Irish M.P.s and a Radical village shoemaker. Wilfrid, exhausted by his journey from Ireland, might have backed out of receiving them, but for Anne. 'It is a pity', she urged, 'to speak discouragingly and even slightingly of the first attempts of the timorous population of Sussex to make head against the domination of class.'[18]

However, there was a letter lying on the hall table from Mark Napier which showed that at least one friend realized Wilfrid's emotional predicament. Having congratulated and condoled, Mark concluded:

> But now it is done, I wish you a season of rest and peace. Blake says somewhere 'damn braces. Bless relaxes'. You have had enough of braces for a time – let me commend you to take a few of the relaxes.[19]

Cardinal Manning, too, advised him to stay quiet and await events. 'I had done enough, he thought, for Ireland.' Blunt had not yet read (if he ever read) Oscar Wilde's judgement of the effect of Ireland on his poetry:

> Prison has had an admirable effect on Mr. Wilfred [sic] Blunt as a poet. . . . Literature is not much indebted to Mr Balfour for his sophistical *Defence of Philosophic Doubt* which is one of the dullest books we know, but it must be

admitted that by sending Mr Blunt to gaol he has converted a clever rhymer into an earnest and deep-thinking poet.[20]

One of the finest sonnets of the *In Vinculis* series still exists on its original sheet of prison paper, written in his indelible pencil with a note attached, 'To be framed – glass both sides':

> To take my place in the world's brotherhood
> As one prepared to suffer all its fate;
> To do and be undone for sake of good,
> And conquer rage by giving love for hate;
> That were a noble dream, and so to cease,
> Scorned by the proud but with the poor at peace.

A noble dream. . . . Could this ideal really be for Blunt more than a noble dream? To live with the poor at peace was not beyond him. But to scorn the proud? Two equally strong instincts urged him to cope with the proud rather than ignore them – the proud being symbolized by Balfour and his circle. One instinct was to re-enter the magic circle and, to adapt Blunt's sonnet, to live 'with the proud at peace'. The other, to have one more fling at them.

An interchange of letters with George Wyndham soon after Wilfrid's release from gaol illustrates this conflict. George, though still profoundly shocked by his cousin's revelations about Balfour, hoped they might yet be friends on the basis of sport and poetry. 'This has done me good', wrote Wilfrid in his diary. His reply was dated 19 March:

> Dear George, I accept your letter in the spirit in which it is written. In cases of this sort it is better not to argue, and I say nothing except that the whole matter has given me more pain than any incident connected with my public life. I am trying to go back to my resolution of last summer and be quit of politics, but one is not always one's own master and I may not succeed. But when the present political bitterness is over I hope we may see each other again.

A letter from George at the end of the year, thanking Wilfrid for a copy of *In Vinculis*, showed how similar the cousins were in their ambivalence over politics. 'I hope', wrote George, 'for a pure break of poetry to clear my lungs of the poisonous dust of political controversy.'[21]

Gladstone and the Irish between them soon had Blunt back in the arena, poisonous dust or no. Gladstone now wanted to use the English hero of the Plan of Campaign in the Liberal cause. It was a game of skill at which Gladstone was a master and Blunt remained an unwary innocent.

Gladstone's opening move was a letter in March suggesting Blunt should repeat his allegations against Balfour in print under his own name. 'Perhaps you may be contemplating (and I hope you are) a full and detailed account of your prison and court experiences.'[22] An interview between Blunt and Gladstone followed. It began with the G.O.M. affecting deep embarrassment at the thought of Blunt's perhaps expecting a Liberal seat. After Blunt had been manoeuvred into disclaiming any such desire, the air artificially cleared and Gladstone gave Blunt the heartiest encouragement to make a full disclosure of Balfour's table-talk at Clouds. Again poor Blunt took the bait, and agreed to publish, while knowing that there was nothing further to disclose.

It was indeed the dampest of squibs. Nevertheless it rekindled the fires of animosity against himself, without in the least pleasing the Liberals. The Hon. Reginald Brett, a Liberal (later Lord Esher), revived the cry of post-prandial betrayal on *The Times* correspondence page; a *Times* article trumped up an accusation against Lady Anne Blunt regarding evicted tenants on one of the Lovelace properties, which required a legal threat by Blunt to quell it; Balfour in a triumphant speech on 24 March issued a general denial that he had ever wished the death of any human being.

Blunt battled on. He was persuaded by two of his Irish M.P. friends, T. P. O'Connor and John Dillon, to speak at a banquet in the Free Trade Hall, Manchester, given in honour of 'Balfour's Criminals' – the released Coercion prisoners including O'Brien, T. D. Sullivan and Blunt himself. But a week or so later Balfour more than got his own back at a banquet given in *his* honour at the St James's Hall, London. He '*danced* on me to his heart's content', wrote Blunt bitterly. Not a word in his defence from the Liberal *Daily News*. *The Times* and *Pall Mall* had both gone over to the enemy.

Gladstone in fact had lost interest in this political guerrilla who fell flat on his face. He had expected Blunt at least to do the dancing. Philip Stanhope, the Liberal Whip, had earlier warned Blunt that the Liberal front bench was 'very weak-kneed and tired'. That was to put it mildly. In his mortification, Blunt was tempted to exaggerate the effect on events of his own personal discomfiture: 'The result has been O'Brien's new arrest on Saturday, and the issue of a warrant against Dillon.'

Even before Balfour's banquet and O'Brien's arrest, Blunt had decided to have nothing more to do with English public life:

> The Liberal leaders look upon me with suspicion; Society is in arms against me for Balfour's sake; and the Irish for whom I risked everything will not take me into their party. I am like a man who has swum out to help a wreck and whom the sailors on it refuse to take on board. I now have to swim back to shore as I can.[23]

Mingled with self-pity was a dawning realization that he had got Arthur Balfour all wrong. He was beginning to understand Balfour's curiously frivolous idiom, according to which even the gravest subjects had to be rinsed in a colouring of wit. This trait was characteristic of the house of Cecil, from which Balfour was descended through his mother. Shortly before Wilfrid's Portumna appeal, his friend Lady Alice Gaisford had asked Lord Salisbury if a prison sentence was likely. Salisbury thought not. But what about the proclamation from Dublin Castle? pursued Lady Alice. 'Oh, that was to amuse Arthur.'[24]

Salisbury's reply was also to amuse Lady Alice. And Arthur's original threat at Clouds had been to amuse Wilfrid – or so Gerald Balfour suggested to Blanche Hozier during that autumn of 1888. 'Arthur must have said more or less what Mr. Blunt repeated', admitted Gerald, 'but he said it in fun.'[25]

If Wilfrid could not yet fully accept this, he did appreciate Arthur Balfour's formidable apparatus as an opponent. He might be called 'lackadaisical' and nicknamed 'The Ineptitude'; his philosophy might be one of doubt and his feelings grey; Minnie might say that she had seen him in the House looking like 'a sick vampire bat';[26] but his debating was steely and his ruthlessness black as the pit. Wilfrid had completely revised his opinion of the 'tame cat', and he seldom bore a personal grudge where he could understand and even eventually admire.

Not everyone was as open-minded as Blunt. The Conservative circle of his own relatives (apart from George Wyndham) could not forgive his 'treason' to family, friends, party, class and code. And what had the inner circle of Liberals to offer him in place of his kith and kin? He had no contacts with the great Whig houses, such as the Argylls or Lansdownes. A friend like Sir Wilfrid Lawson had a dissenting lifestyle that was not Blunt's: copious meals, luscious greenhouse fruit, but a passionate belief in temperance and also daily family prayers and church twice on Sundays, with no tennis. Only on Sir William Harcourt's Hampshire estate of Malwood did Wilfrid feel really at home with a Liberal.

The attentions of Sir William Harcourt, however, could not straighten out Blunt's ambivalent feelings for Balfour. His nerves were in a bad state, and he was waking at night with an overpowering sense of disaster. 'This is ageing me.'

Moreover he was bound by ties of loyalty and affection to make two last visits to Ireland. There was O'Brien's trial to be attended; friends who had aided him in his own extremity to be looked up and thanked; Dillon to be supported before a prison ordeal that might prove fatal to one already ill.

The first of these visits took place from 24 April till 10 May. His spirits rose as he landed at Kingstown and was warmly greeted by a news-vendor: 'Here's the *Freeman* for your honour and a welcome back to Ireland. We'll run you in presently for the St. Stephen Division and good luck to you.'* His spirits rose higher as the train carried him with O'Brien and other friends to Loughrea. 'A merry party we were – you would think going to a wedding rather than a trial', wrote Blunt. 'But the Irish have the blessing of high spirits. ...'

They needed it. For at the height of the court proceedings Pope Leo XIII dropped his bombshell. Known as the Papal Rescript, it gave an account of the Plan of Campaign which none of Blunt's friends could accept as a true one, and then proceeded to condemn them and the Plan. For one day they were dashed. 'The news lies like an incubus on us all.' Next day, however, Dr Duggan exorcized the incubus by laboriously translating aloud the Rescript from its solemn Latin into pithy English – with plenty of asides. Each paragraph was received with a clinking of glasses and 'roars of laughter'. In England, the Papal Rescript might make Blunt and the dangerous people he was associating with seem even more undesirable. But in Ireland he was to witness the sleight of hand by which 'Balfour's Criminals' avoided becoming 'Pope Leo's Criminals' as well. They neither admitted culpability nor dropped the Plan; but as loyal sons of the Church they discovered that the Pope had been 'bamboozled' by a group of English and Irish peers.

There were some personal moments of pleasure. Blunt picked up his large-print Bible – the one that Charlie Bourke had confiscated – in a Galway bookshop for ten shillings. It was labelled proudly 'Blunt's Bible'. The name of Blunt was one to conjure with in Ireland, though he had not a drop of Irish blood. (He was to bequeath it to Lady Gregory.) When he called on old Mrs Pope-Hennessy at Youghal, mother of the anti-Colonial governor Sir John Pope-Hennessy, she welcomed Blunt as the reincarnation of Daniel O'Connell – 'a new Liberator'. All the cottagers around recognized him from the pictures in *United Ireland*. But the old scar was not allowed to heal; when one member of the Irish hierarchy asked him to stand for the Longford seat, he had to reply, 'I cannot even discuss it until the proposal comes from Parnell.'

His next and last visit to Ireland was over in a week. That too was to have its unexpected pleasures. He had reluctantly left Crabbet on a June day because Dillon's trial loomed ahead. 'To London [on the eleventh] in an unhappy mood. I am determined to clear my soul of its political baggage; but I cannot leave the Irish battle just where it is, with Dillon under sentence of death.' Arriving in Dublin alone with Anne on the fifteenth, his depression worsened. Would he ever be 'disentangled'?[27] In his neurotic state he wondered if perhaps Dillon

* The St Stephen's Green seat in Dublin for which a Nationalist candidate was required.

did not want him. He could do him no good now. Had he ever really been of use?

He felt better after Dillon was civilly treated by the judge in court, though sentenced to six months in gaol. And better still when Dillon's confidante, Mrs Deane, assured him Dillon and O'Brien believed that his exposure of Balfour's savage intentions had nipped them in the bud and 'saved their lives'. He left on the twenty-second, never to visit Ireland again.

Why in the end had Blunt never got either a Liberal or an Irish seat? An admirer of a younger generation, Sir Shane Leslie, put it down to jealousy: Gladstone did not want 'a real champion of the downtrodden' in the House to show him up, nor Parnell 'another aristocrat, especially one who resembled him in looks and was often mistaken for him in the lobbies of the House'.[28] There were, however, genuine political reasons for the failure to use Blunt. His support had become a liability to Gladstone in the parliamentary game since the 'Balfour–Clouds' fiasco. And Parnell could never put an Englishman into an Irish seat. As for Blunt's likeness to Parnell, it was a question of opinion. Minnie Pollen was as good a judge as any, and she considered that it existed only in certain tones of Blunt's voice. On the other hand, Wilfrid Meynell had sent Blunt on 3 October 1887 a copy of the *Weekly Register* that referred to the likeness. 'Many thanks for the W.R.', replied Blunt. 'I have constantly been taken for Parnell both in Ireland and in the lobby of the House of Commons, so I suppose we must be alike.'[29]

Perhaps the best comment on Blunt's situation comes from his own pen, when advising young Herbert Vivian about joining a political party. Vivian should remain neutral until the future of parties became clearer:

> I being older am obliged to join either party as I can, where they go with my ideas, only reserving to myself the right to drop them where we differ.
>
> The Irish struggle is the noblest our age has seen and you ought to be in it on the right side.[30]

Blunt always believed there was only one side – Ireland's.

Meanwhile he echoed Cardinal Manning's advice as to his own future. 'I shall stand aside and wait', he wrote in his diary. 'The world has other things for me to do, and time is short.' On returning to Crabbet he wrote again on 26 June: 'Here ends the History of my political life.' It ended with him still 'in the depths of gloom'. But there were indeed other things to do. 'Had the young mares out to look at.' The young. The beautiful. The loving.

[14]
Disentanglement 1888–1890

Two more years and Blunt would be fifty. They were transitional years, during which he detected a gradual but irrevocable change in the whole pattern of his life. To begin with, there were no more active politics after 1888. When someone suggested his standing for Parliament – as a Mohammedan – he was not even tempted.

The end of Blunt's militant Irish connection set in motion other changes, away from the Liberal Party, Catholicism, and the recent spell of austere married life. He himself would always point to the wedding of William O'Brien in London on 11 June 1890, two months before his own fiftieth birthday, as the flourish with which his Irish connection ended. 'This was a really wonderful event. . . . It is all very well to scoff at the wickedness of the age in which we live, but the Catholic Irish are a standing miracle of God's grace.'

He envied these Irish for living at a time in their country's history when noble sacrifices were possible.

> In England I find nothing noble. We are too rich and strong and prosperous to have any cause left us worth dying for. What a miserable mountebank old Gladstone is, compared with the least of these poor Irish Members![1]

Nevertheless his connection with the Grand Old Mountebank and Liberal Party had also ended with a flourish, if a reception given by the Attorney-General Sir Charles Russell in 1889 is taken as the last Liberal event the Blunts attended. The press called it 'the political party of the year'. Predominantly a great Liberal occasion to meet the Gladstones, the guests included the Campbell-Bannermans, Lefevres and Pollens; but Parnell, Oscar Wilde and Lord Randolph Churchill were also present, Churchill preferring even the most Radical of his fellow-guests to 'the old *frumps* of the Tory party'. Another face seemed 'politically rather incongruous', commented the press, 'the sharp, small features of Mr. Darling. Hard by was the prisoner whom Mr. Darling defeated at Deptford, Mr. Wilfrid Blunt with Lady Blunt.' Anne noted that Gladstone had shaken her hand at the door with 'a sort of repellent *shove*'.[2]

Paradoxically it was Rosalind Howard, the dedicated Liberal, who now put Blunt in touch with a frivolous life she herself so much despised. The connection was made accidentally, though Blunt 'hungered for a new romance which should have nothing at all to do with politics and which should give me back that taste of happiness which I knew so well and had been so long without'.

Rosalind invited him to stay for a tennis holiday with her children in July 1888, adding, 'Blanche Hozier comes about the 15th and when you want frivolity you will find abundance of it in its pleasantest form in her.'[3] Blunt seized on the last phrase. What could it portend but 'a new passion complete in its surroundings'? He felt a romance at Castle Howard would recompense him for the 'squalor of prison life'. And he already knew something of Lady Blanche's own romantic past, having first met her briefly at Rosalind's in July 1880, dined with Blanche and her husband that October ('a strange couple') and called on Blanche once in 1886.

She was the clever daughter of Lord and Lady Airlie, and had married Henry Hozier, a member of Lloyds and centre of a divorce case that had attracted maximum publicity. Instead of marrying the 'other woman' when free to do so, Hozier had unexpectedly won the 'bonny' Lady Blanche Ogilvie. She was now the mother of two small daughters, Kitty and Clementine, and twins, Bill and Nellie, born that April, 1888.*

Lady Blanche Hozier's marriage was already on the rocks. She was to confide in Wilfrid in 1892 that the gallant 'Bay' Middleton, superb horseman and escort to the Empress Elizabeth of Austria in the shires, was, unknown to Hozier, Kitty's and Clemmie's father; while Hozier refused to acknowledge the twins as his.[4] Blanche invited Wilfrid to stay in her little house in Forfarshire, where she took him on a round of visits including Glamis and Airlie (he was forbidden to enter the latter castle, not because of anything in his relations with Blanche, but with Ireland) and he went on to Auberon Herbert at Loch Awe and the Wagrams at their (rented) Castle Menzies. The latter, Wilfrid described with satisfaction, as 'the most frivolous section of the world's frivolity'.

If not a grand passion, his friendship with Blanche Hozier was far from superficial. Beginning with a week in which they rode together through Scottish glens, it was to last throughout Blanche's lifetime, based upon her gift for writing sharp, gossipy letters, such as the one sent to Crabbet on 1 February 1889:

> I always feel ashamed of sending London gossip, which is as unfresh and unclean almost as the London air, into the fresh sweet English country – and I

* Kitty and Bill died unmarried, Kitty as a girl of seventeen; Clementine became Mrs Winston Churchill, and Nellie Mrs Romilly.

feel the same about doing so to you now. . . . Oscar Wilde came into Bruton Street while I was there – an affected unpleasant creature – but he says amusing things in an amusing way – complained that 'Macbeth' at the Lyceum was too dull for anything – 'a series of Scotch dissolving views'.[5]

Despite her many misfortunes, involving battles against Hozier that ended in her separation, poverty and the threat of losing her children, she avoided self-pity. Where others of Blunt's women friends affected a coy or sentimental prose style, Blanche wrote as she talked. A note she scribbled on Sunday 18 September after the first enchanted week was over, shows her as a lover:

> Dear Mr Blunt. . . . I don't think church has done me much good, at least I could not keep my thoughts of you out of my mind. I want you – so much, so much, your pleasant talk – your kindness – your dear and beautiful face to look at – I can't write more luckily – perhaps – for my guests will talk – goodbye – my dear friend – Blanche H.H.[6]

By the following month 'Mr. Blunt' (Blanche was never to use his Christian name during all their years of friendship) had become anxious. The lady was urged to send back his love letters (which he destroyed, while keeping many of hers) and to restrict her language in future to 'the proper limit in letters'. Perhaps thinking of old Gladstone's instructions to Skittles, he suggested that 'a cross' would express all that was necessary.

Yet it was not fear of scandal that brought the passionate side of their friendship to an end. Having returned to England in spring 1889 after a long absence, Blunt took a house near hers in Mayfair and found her 'just as passionately inclined as ever' but screwing up her courage to tell him something she called 'the truth'. All too soon the mystery was cleared up and with it their love affair.

There was another man. 'I feel bound', she wrote cryptically, 'to a man I once liked.' The man was Ellis Ashmead Bartlett (soon to be knighted), successful Conservative politician and pleasure-loving brother of Lady Burdett Coutts' husband; according to Blunt: a 'ridiculous personage . . . a rather absurd middle-aged Member of Parliament, married with many children, of no personal attraction but with much underbred pretension . . . at whom the world generally laughs'. Blunt tried to laugh too, especially after the jealous M.P. sent Lady Blanche a telegram from the Carlton Club on April Fool's Day, signed 'Wilfrid'.

The laughter faltered, however, when Bartlett threatened to have Lady Blanche's Mayfair house watched and to blackmail her or shoot himself, having involved Blunt in a public quarrel. The laughter stopped altogether when Bartlett forced his way into her bedroom one night, after Blunt had dined with her in the company of Henry James,

Lord Carlisle, Lady Arabella Romilly, and then gone home. There was a scene in front of her maid in which Blunt's exposure was again threatened, unless Blanche took back Bartlett. This she proposed to do, in an unhappy note to Blunt.

It was too much, transgressing as it did against the code of love, by which a husband had rights but not a previous lover. It also offended Blunt's vanity. 'Fond as I was of her [he wrote years later] I could not accept the position it seemed to propose, that of a furtive lover playing at hide and seek with a personage who had not even the right of being her husband.' He declined by letter, 'in all kindness'. Their friendship, though no longer 'on the same unreserved footing', was not impaired. 'But the romance of our intimacy had died out and never was renewed.'[7]

Blunt liked the danger of 'forbidden fruit', as he called it, but not humiliation. Now something worse was in store. His profound affection for the whole Pollen family, with all its Catholic, artistic and Liberal associations, came to a devastating end.

The drama opened in 1888 with Judith Blunt and Arthur Pollen on the stage: Judith a tall, beautiful girl of fifteen and Arthur, the cleverest of the Pollen brothers, with whom Judith had been brought up as a younger sister.*

After the quarrel, Judith invested her childhood with the Pollens at Newbuildings Place with the blackest of memories. Spoilt during the summer months at Crabbet, she found the Newbuildings winters spartan. Snow whirled through every crack in the casement windows, owls hooted and hissed, rats squeaked and ghosts haunted the priests' holes, thanks to Minnie's interminable tales of hell fire. According to Judith, Minnie never went to Mass herself, got up late and slumped about the house in an old dressing-gown; but when Pappa called she could look gloriously beautiful in pre-Raphaelite velvets. The Pollens were too poor to afford enough fuel or blankets, so Judith would perforce pile mats and rugs topped by the fire-irons on to her flinty bed – or better still, smuggle her dog Butterfly into it, where the two would shiver together. Her dislike of Minnie, she recorded, was equalled only by her distaste for Minnie's son Arthur – the brother most frequently at home – whom she found 'vulgar'.[8]

This picture is hardly borne out by contemporary letters. At eleven Judith was thanking Arthur for a letter because it was so 'beautiful', and at fourteen for another because 'it is so nice to know exactly what you are doing in the day . . .'. She sent him a photograph and sketches

* Arthur Hungerford Pollen, 1866–1937. Revolutionized 'fire-control gunnery' for which he was awarded £30,000 after controversy and delay. His intellectual Catholicism helped to inspire the 'Second Spring'.

of herself playing tennis in a long skirt and hat. From Minnie's and Wilfrid's letters about her, she appeared to be going through 'tomboyhood' (Wilfrid's word) rather than girlhood, Minnie remarking that at lesson time (with a governess) 'she bangs down the pen and rushes up ladders and sits in the hayrick'; Wilfrid writing to her even at eighteen, 'I am glad my dear child that you are amusing yourself. At your age it is natural and graceful if not done headforemost downstairs.'[9]

To Arthur Pollen she appeared more than graceful. Some time after her fifteenth birthday he told her 'I love you', held her hand, kissed her when she was unhappy and said 'he wished *there was no one* else in the world but himself and her'. This was his crime; no more, no less. In September 1888 Judith complained to her mother of his attentions.

Anne was at once thrown into a state of agitation. She decided to institute a scrupulous investigation. Did she not recollect Arthur carrying up the tray when Judith had chicken-pox at Pembridge Crescent, and she, Anne, trying to stop him because of the infection, but really because it was 'improper'? She thought of the many times that Minnie had sent Arthur unnecessarily down to Crabbet to recuperate from alleged overwork – especially the week when Judith was convalescing at the seaside and Arthur arrived uninvited.[10] Putting two and two together Anne convinced herself of a Pollen conspiracy to carry off the Blunt heiress. She consulted Wilfrid.

This 'tuppenny ha'penny' dispute, this 'childish business' – that was to be Wilfrid's first reaction to his wife's story. He felt sure that Judith, after all still only a child, was exaggerating. He swore he would not get involved in a 'nursery squabble'.

Nevertheless Anne's anxious voice had struck one answering chord in himself. He was passionately devoted to his family inheritance; he was the 'Squire'; and hardly had the Squire's daughter reached her teens before Blunt was dreaming of the marriage that should carry on his line. In a burst of confidence, he had told Minnie about a 'little scheme' that came to him in Kidderminster of marrying Judith to a remote kinsman and local squire named Edward Blount of Imberhorne – 'an arrangement which appealed to my imagination as consonant with Arabian ideas where a return to some faraway strain of kindred blood is so much in fashion'.

From Anne's diary, it appears that Wilfrid at first hoped to end the Pollen association on other than sexual grounds, by the tactful deployment of his own financial embarrassments. He needed to sell or let the Newbuildings land for shooting, but could not do so with the Pollen family entrenched in the house.

The Pollen exodus duly took place, Arthur referring with some justice to 'the great eviction'.* Not all evictions were in Ireland. Anne, however, was far from pleased by such a circuitous way out. On 23 October she decided the moment had come for Wilfrid to confront Minnie with the truth. Minnie 'blazed into fury', demanding to know when Anne had first heard about Judith's charges. Anne had not kept her journal ... could not say exactly. ...

But Anne was keeping her diary now, and she describes how the 'scene' escalated, 'floods of Billingsgate' pouring from Minnie. Anne's greatest crime, according to Minnie, was 'to speak to Wilfrid or anything else without *leave*. So long', concluded Anne with extraordinary vehemence, 'has an influence come between us, but no longer shall it!' Her diary was finally reduced to floods of Arabic.

For the next week or so there were attempts by the two families to back-pedal on the accusation. A second 'stormy scene', however, was enacted in the Crabbet library when Minnie demanded that Wilfrid write Arthur an apology: 'the honour of her son and her own were at stake'. Wilfrid's own anger thereupon erupted for the first time. 'He went black from anger and rage', wrote Anne in Arabic. Finally he restored peace by saying he would tell Arthur he had misinterpreted his behaviour. Minnie then insisted that Anne also withdraw her charges. This Anne declined to do, since it would be a betrayal of Judith; though she agreed with John Pollen, who alone maintained 'his dignity', that Arthur's attentions could have been misunderstood. Nevertheless, said Anne to Wilfrid, 'I must listen to my own child, when distressed.'[11]

Wilfrid cut the knot by sweeping both Judith and Anne off to Paris on 9 November, then to Sheykh Obeyd. 'This always gives me a new start in life. ...' But not before he had sent a farewell letter to Minnie:

> Crabbet 7 November 1888. If you hear of my having spoken unkindly of you in any way, do not believe it. Neither will I believe it if I hear the like of you. ... Our friendship has been a blessing to me in many ways and for many years. It is not a case of 'tout lasse' but of 'tout casse'. Yr. aff. W.S.B.[12]

Yet a feeling persists that Wilfrid was tired of Minnie ('tout lasse'), quite apart from the rupture ('tout casse'). Minnie forgave Wilfrid, but not Anne. How far was the secret love affair between Minnie and Wilfrid involved in this quarrel? The behaviour of both suggests at the very least that they were assuaging their guilt by each rushing with unnecessary fervour to the defence of their respective offspring. To what extent was their liaison actually responsible for the violence of the quarrel?

No one mentioned the liaison as a specific cause except Judith – very

* No sale of Newbuildings land followed. But the fact that Blunt ever contemplated a sale casts a curious light on his later fury with Judith for selling part of the Crabbet estate. See below, pp. 406 and 431.

many years later – in a section of 'Myself and Others' entitled 'Growing up at Newbuildings'. Judith wrote that four out of the seven Pollen boys fell in love with her at thirteen:

> A terrific parental explosion followed the discovery of the rival lovers in which high words of blame revealed the possibility that one young Apollo was my half-brother – an extraordinary resemblance to my Father's outstanding good looks seemed to confirm this. In a storm of vituperation the families parted and I was summarily removed to Egypt. ...[13]

This passage bristles with inaccuracies. If there was a youthful rivalry among the Pollen boys, it had little to do with the quarrel. At most, Judith may have magnified Arthur's crimes because she preferred his brother Stephen; indeed she was to fall in love with Stephen a few years later. The 'half-brother' theme was sheer invention. As we have seen, Minnie's children by Wilfrid died before or at birth; her affair with him did not begin until 1872; the youngest Pollen boy, Arthur, was born in 1866.

The 'high words of blame' during the explosion may none the less have 'revealed' something. Was it the love-affair itself?

The adult Judith undoubtedly knew of the affair, referring to Minnie as her father's 'concubine' in her autobiography. How did she discover? Not from the younger generation of Pollens, to whom the secret was never disclosed. Then from Anne? We have hints, if not evidence, that the quarrel was the occasion of Anne's learning the truth. Did Minnie in her anger give some accidental clue to her own position with Wilfrid?

For the next few months Anne's relations with Wilfrid were unusually affectionate; the inference perhaps being that she had guessed, he had confessed, she had forgiven.

There was a short spell of politics for Wilfrid as he passed through Paris. But it served only to puzzle his political friends still further. Skittles gave him an introduction to General Boulanger, and he wrote a sympathetic letter to the press about that right-wing demogogue. In the same week he met 'la Citoyenne' Louise Michel, a French Passionaria, who presented him with a black and red poster advertising the coming social revolution. She had added some verses signed 'Souvenir à M. Wilfred [sic] Blunt'.

Which side was the man on?

Before settling at Sheykh Obeyd for the winter he decided to show Greece to Byron's granddaughter and great-granddaughter for the first time. At Piraeus he read Byron's *Childe Harold* to Judith, and Miss Tricoupi, daughter of the Greek leader who had pronounced Byron's funeral oration, showed Anne a precious miniature of the hero given to Tricoupi by the Duke of Sussex. It was the one that Anne's mother

Ada had asked to see before she died, but the message was passed on too late. When Miss Tricoupi criticized Lady Byron, Anne defended both her grandmother and her grandfather, saying she 'loved him better than almost anyone'; but one could be fair to both.[14] Wilfrid and Judith raced from top to bottom of Mount Lycabettus as Byron might have done had he not been cursed with a lame foot, and made the acquaintance of the Noels at Achmetaga on Euboea, where the pretty blue-eyed child Irene was Anne's distant cousin.*

Sheykh Obeyd seemed to Judith no less enchanting, with brigands constantly sighted on the desert edge (she said her father paid one brigand 'protection money'), and the garden taken over by strange animals that found asylum inside its long, high, mud-brick walls: wolf, jackal, fox, ichneumon, hedgehog, hyena, rat. Beyond the huge wooden double-doors with their classical pediment were rippling water-channels and a fountain by the shrine of Sheykh Obeyd, descendant of the Prophet; bees humming in the orange blossom and acacias, camels munching the green barley and Arab horses tethered in the court-yard, some of them always saddled up ready for a dash into the desert hills. Judith's only complaints were that no proper furniture stood upon the white sanded floors, only two wooden chicken coops for a table and divan, and Wilfrid's precious oriental mat on which he sat happily cross-legged, while Judith got backache as they played endless chess together; and no doors to the house, so that a wolf might get in. Often she beat Pappa at chess. If she did not, well, he had drawn a sketch in her scrapbook of what happened then. 'Stalemate' – Judith kicking over the chess-board.

Wilfrid gave her a colt for her sixteenth birthday in an Aleppo headstall, for both of which Anne paid. But, 'I don't mind so as he is pleased', Anne wrote in her diary. Even at night they all slept in Arab clothes, including head-dress. 'I am sure I never spent such happy days as now.'[15]

Wilfrid returned to England on 5 April 1889 in advance of his wife and daughter, propelled by what he called 'the rage of migration which seizes me in the springtime'. His idle life at Sheykh Obeyd – 'not even written to the Times' – had made him restless. In London he became deeply depressed. 'The secret of happiness is to move onwards and to feel that it is from good to better, and the whole of my life, as I plainly see, is in decline.' Galway gaol he now saw as his peak; the decline being symbolized by a renewal of his quarrel with the Pollens. Arthur resigned from the secretaryship of the Crabbet Club, and when Anne ran into him accidentally at 'the stores' (Army and Navy)

* Irene Noel's grandfather had bought Euboea after the War of Independence. He was the natural son of Thomas Wentworth, Lady Byron's uncle. Irene Noel married Philip Baker, now Lord Noel-Baker.

accused her of maligning the Pollens to common friends, a fact that Anne indignantly denied.

By June Wilfrid was grasping at a new solution: the appointment of a third party, Father William Kerr, as umpire. No move could have been more disastrous; it simply reopened the case on more extensive lines. Everybody repeated with emphasis their original charges. Anne considered Father William to be biased in favour of the pious Pollens ('four religious' in *their* family to set against Wilfrid's 'supposed shortcomings'), while Wilfrid argued that Father William ought to hear Judith's full story from her own lips – a step which the priest refused to take in Judith's own interest. Stalemate; but, alas, no chance for Judith to solve it by kicking over the board.

During August and September Lord Carlisle (as George Howard had become) tried in vain to break the deadlock and get the quarrel decently interred: 'I advocate white sepulchres', he wrote, and was supported by Blanche Hozier. To this Wilfrid replied, 'I agree with you entirely about whited sepulchres, but the first thing is to get your dead man buried.' That autumn, it was the family friendship, not the family feud, which they buried. Minnie's last two letters to Wilfrid were not even opened by him.[16]

A wearisome tale of Victorian prejudice on both sides? Yet one aspect of it was to figure strongly in Wilfrid Blunt's future. His taste for what George Carlisle called 'semi-judicial enquiry' was to develop not only in himself but in his daughter Judith Lady Wentworth, until it became extreme litigiousness.

Now there was no Minnie, Wilfrid had to turn somewhere else. He turned more and more to Janey and the William Morris household. Wilfrid liked the two Morris girls, despite what he considered May's fanatical socialism and Jenny's epileptic fits; his admiration for the lovely Janey might well replace his old love for Minnie. The one difference was in the influence of William Morris. Here the ambience was materialistic rather than Catholic.

During long conversations, Blunt discovered that Morris had once possessed intense faith both in religion and in political action. But there had been changes: 'He, like myself, was going through a period of disenchantment with regard to public affairs and was beginning to turn away from futile attempts to improve mankind and return to his older love of poetry and art.' Also like Blunt he had been unable to recapture his belief in the supernatural, 'contenting himself with material beauty and work of a material kind'. Morris's powerful influence was thus another nail in the coffin of Blunt's religion. The irresistible temptation presented by Janey Morris was to be yet one more.

Blunt called his *In Vinculis*, in which his own prison sufferings were described in the language of Christ's passion, his 'final farewell to Catholicity'; he corrected the proofs at Kelmscott Manor, the Morris' country home near Lechlade in Oxfordshire.* 'Mrs Morris, who loves me, has designed the cover of it with shamrock leaves....' They had loved one another 'on and off', he added later, for about nine years. But it was in writing of 1889 that he first depicted the scene and circumstances of their love's climax.

The marriage of Janey and Top or Topsy (Morris' nicknames) was loveless as far as Janey was concerned – or so Wilfrid believed. 'She was a loveable and noble woman but he had never touched her heart.' Dante Gabriel Rossetti, however, had done so:

> What had taken place between her and Rossetti he [Morris] knew and had forgiven. But he had not forgotten it. I used to think too that he suspected me at times, for her intimacy with me was not very explicable otherwise.[17]

Blunt noticed that Morris would sometimes leave the two of them alone together. Then he would suddenly re-enter the room on some pretext, but treading heavily, as if he were ashamed of his suspicions. Finding nothing, he was 'far too generous' not to put the base thought aside. 'And yet', wrote Blunt, 'there was reason.'

Kelmscott Manor, explained Blunt, was a romantic but extraordinarily uncomfortable house, where almost all the rooms were passage-rooms, both below and above stairs. To reach the upstairs tapestried chamber, where they all sat in the evening, they had to pass through Morris' bedroom where he later lay alone at night in a great square Elizabethan four-poster. 'Mrs Morris slept alone at the end of a short passage at the head of the staircase to the right. The hall was uncarpeted with floors that creaked.... To me such midnight perils have always been attractive.' It was not of his own younger self, however, that he thought now, but of Gabriel Rossetti, dead since 1882:

> Rossetti seemed a constant presence there, for it was there that he and Janey had had their time of love some fourteen years before and I came to identify myself with him as his admirer and successor.

As the years passed, Blunt realized how 'very curious' this friendship of himself and Janey was. They had little in common. Janey was such a silent woman that they could not have become intimate 'except through the physical senses'. They never even used one another's Christian names. 'I wonder whether it was so with Rossetti?'[18]†

* Not to be confused with their town house, Kelmscott House, in Hammersmith Mall.

† It was not so. See *Dante Gabriel Rossetti and Jane Morris: Their Correspondence*, edited by Bryson and Troxell. 'My dearest Janey', 'My dear Gabriel.' Janey at least once addressed Blunt as '*Caro Mio*' in a letter. (FM 252/1975. 8 November 1888.)

But if Janey was silent, she was not inarticulate on paper, as her letters to Blunt of 1889 show. *21 August* (on the effect of Blunt's first visit to Kelmscott): 'I move about in a sort of dream as if a spell had been cast over me and the whole place. Are you sure you have brought no magic arts from Egypt and have employed them against a poor defenceless woman?'

As time went on, Wilfrid's 'Secret Memoirs' also became more articulate about his relations with Janey than they had been in 1889. Three years later he was writing quite openly of his doings at Kelmscott Manor:

> We slept together, Mrs Morris and I, and she told things about the past which explained much in regard to Rossetti. 'I never quite gave myself', she said, 'as I do now.' Perhaps, if she had, he might not have perished in the way he did.[19]

Janey explained a few months afterwards that it was the sight of Rossetti's 'great rows' of empty chloral bottles in his lodgings at Bognor, and his possible effect on her children, that had brought their love to an end seven years before he died.

On his way through Rome for his usual family winter at Sheykh Obeyd, Wilfrid again underlined his rejection of religion. The spell of the mystical hand – Pope Leo's and before that Newman's – could no longer work. He kissed St Peter's toe and still felt 'a presence' in the basilica, but that was all.

> All one can do is to kneel and kneel on, waiting for a sign and the touch of a hand. These came to me before, why not again? I think if I could bring myself to burn my poetry and these journals, and cast off my intellectual as I have my political life, I might in abject nakedness creep up to heaven. But I have not the courage to part with the few rags left me. Instead I cling the closer to my past life.[20]

But if some new passion should arise? Then indeed it might sweep away what Blunt called 'the ignoble phantom' of the present together with his clinging nostalgia. 'I am convinced that a religious life is best', he concluded, 'and equally that I am made for pleasure. Love is to me what a dram is to a drinker.'

He had just downed a dram in the form of Mrs Marie Stillman, née Spartali. But the 'splendidly beautiful' and once bejewelled model of Rossetti and Burne-Jones was not for Blunt. Mrs Stillman lived with her husband William and children in Rome. Though nearly fifty, she still possessed 'star-like beauty'. Blunt called on her one afternoon and questioned her for an hour about Rossetti, with whose poetry, personality and women he was fast becoming obsessed. 'Going away I kissed her hand.... Rossetti *must* have loved her.' His own love-making, in her case confined to the hand alone, was continued during a visit to the Sistine Chapel; the touch of her hand was again 'an electric current'.

Next year, 1890, he was to meet Marie for a few lyrical September days in Cambridge. But when Wilfrid came to say goodbye Marie scolded him for his love-letters.

'I suppose you thought I liked them.'

'I suppose I thought you liked me.'

'Yes, I do like you, but you must not talk to me of such things and you must not look at me, as you do.'

Wilfrid obediently lowered his eyes and covered her hand with kisses. 'So we sat for half-an-hour with the life pulsing through our fingers.' He would never forget it while he lived. 'There is no woman in the world who has such hands, such eyes and such a voice – oh, her voice! Look at Burne-Jones's pencil drawings and you guess something of her face. But her voice is sweeter a thousand times, each syllable a note like pearls dropped into a stream.'

Six months later still his love for Marie blossomed for the last time during a spring afternoon under the trees at Frascati. In a mist of blue anemones, dog-tooth violets, periwinkles and forget-me-nots he deflowered – her hand. 'I undid the button of her glove and held her wonderful hand naked in mine, and so all the way home to Rome.'

But she would not go again with him into the country and he realized that for her to begin 'the ways of love' at fifty was too late. 'There is nothing about her of this modern age, and I feel that just this one day I have lived the life of the *Divina Comedia* with Beatrice's self.'*

Meanwhile he himself had entered his fiftieth year, and the century its ninth decade, the Naughty Nineties as they were to be called. His winter in Egypt had been 'unemotional', he wrote in February 1890, and the return through Paris seemed to offer compensation in the spirit of the new decade. He had already noted the change in English women's behaviour, compared with those far-off days when he had initiated his cousin Madeline Wyndham. Today a young lady and her chaperone would visit even the *danse à ventre*. 'English women are astonishing at Paris . . . they seem to have seen and done everything it is possible to see and do and some things which are impossible.' His brief but concentrated affair with the Hon. Mrs Reggie Talbot, wife of the Military Secretary at the embassy, was one of these 'impossible' things.

* Rossetti wrote to Jane Morris on 30 July 1869, 'Mary Spartali has given me one sitting to paint the hands of the Beatrice I did from you, and she is to give me another.' (Bryson and Troxell, p. 12.)

Margaret Jane Talbot was thirty-five – she had a white lock in her beautiful hair – and had been married eleven years to a husband with whom she was profoundly happy, except that they had no child. A photograph of her shows a pointed face, classical features and huge blue eyes. As the elder sister of Wilfrid's sister-in-law Mary Wentworth, Margaret could offer Wilfrid his favourite kind of love – love 'within the tribe'.

Their passion suddenly expanded and flowered in a single week of April 1890. They met on the twenty-fifth in the Lyttons' ambassadorial circle, and had a discussion about love and marriage – 'I have been in a state ever since like a young man of thirty'; next evening at the theatre Wilfrid pressed her arm – 'what is more delicious than these first little tendernesses, let what will come after'. He kissed the 'little left hand' she held out to him on parting.* On the third day she confessed that she had made 'the leap' so rare in a woman of her background; she had decided to take afternoon tea alone with him at Bitters' apartment in the rue Mazarine. On the twenty-seventh Wilfrid spent with her at the rue Mazarine 'two of the most passionate hours of my life', though her terror of having a child that resembled him came to some extent between them. Next day, 1 May, she looked pale and ill, asking him to leave her. Her 'farouche' look of virtue sent him home to England with a special pang. 'What a delicious life we might have had together, brother and sister, friends and lovers, all in one.'[21]

A few days at Castle Howard with Rosalind Carlisle and her daughter Mary, now the wedded wife of Gilbert Murray, further convinced Blunt that his own romance with Margaret was potentially perfection, theirs a travesty. Mary argued that married happiness was founded on 'uniformity of opinion', not passion, and that her husband, the brilliant young professor of Greek at Glasgow, having been a virgin when she married him, had set a standard for all marriages. 'Greek or no Greek', commented Blunt, 'I am almost glad that I have not led the ideal life if these are its apostles.' He and Margaret had certainly not been bound together by 'a unity of belief in the progress of humanity', as Rosalind Carlisle declared all love and friendship should be. If this was 'the new philosophy of the twentieth century', retorted Blunt, he would prefer the affection of Rosalind's dog Wolf.

What he was to call 'the dear July days' in Paris lasted from the ninth to the fourteenth, when he and Margaret, after walking in the Champs Elysées, giving a franc to a beggar ('good omen'), sitting in the embassy garden, climbing the Arc de Triomphe and watching a

* '*The Little Left Hand*: A mid-Victorian verse drama in three acts' by W. S. Blunt, written in 1897. One line reads: 'A hand is a soul'.

procession in the Place de la Concorde, sealed their love in the rue Mazarine on the thirteenth. Margaret arrived late, having gone back home after the procession to give her husband his tea:

> The delay however was all to our greater delight, and there our marriage rite, which is to be eternal, was fully consummated. There are to be no more flights or hesitations, and we are to enjoy our love as nature wills it to our lives' end. She is a delicious woman, of that divine chaste type we only find among our own people and the noblest of them. Our love desecrates this a little but leaves something more touching and more dear. When it was over she rushed to the looking-glass and surveyed herself. 'What a bacchanalian figure!' she said. 'And to think that it is me!'[22]

But next morning the penitent wife sent Wilfrid a frantic note: 'Go from me, go – go.... Give any excuse, letters, telegrams from home, anything, but only go please.... He will ask me questions. I shall not be able to lie.'

Wilfred, not really surprised, set off at once to nurse the dying Bitters Currie in Switzerland. He consoled himself by flirting mechanically with an importunate fellow-guest at his hotel and making sure that Bitters received the last rites of the Church (he had become a Catholic). At midnight on Wilfrid's fiftieth birthday Bitters died. Wilfrid was bequeathed £1,000, which he earmarked for two tapestries designed by Burne-Jones and woven in Morris' workshop, the 'Visit of the Magi' and 'Primavera'.*

Meanwhile his own Primavera of that lost Parisian April, Margaret, was now moving into a tempestuous autumn. Lytton had warned Blunt that this would happen. By disposition and habit a flirt, he wrote, Margaret had played long and confidently with edged but harmless tools, 'the very blunt edges furnished by the prurient platonism of the little sentimental clique [the Souls] she has lived in'; now she had cut herself deeply 'with an instrument of a different temper' – Wilfrid being 'the kind of man to fascinate and stimulate her imagination, thus keeping physical feeling alive in separation'. At the same time she worshipped her husband. In a crisis she would sacrifice both Wilfrid and herself to him, thereby sacrificing all three.

To which Wilfrid replied, first, that danger was an attraction: 'Danger in love always acts with me as a physical stimulus, and passion is never so strong as when I am conscious of a tragedy approaching and hear its footsteps already in the next room.' And second, that a liaison conducted in the teeth of society had no attractions for him whatever. He loved Margaret for her 'very troubles of conscience', would not for worlds have her without them 'or loving her husband less'. If she left her husband it would end Blunt's romance with her. In concluding this

* The 'Visit of the Magi' hangs in the hall at Newbuildings, the 'Primavera' (in which Judith's lovely head is represented) in the drawing-room.

letter to the oldest, most intimate, wisest of his friends Blunt expressed more lucidly than ever before his philosophy of illicit love:

> A liaison, if it is not part and parcel of our lives in the world, not only becomes wearisome but *is* also from the very beginning – and even on a first night is I think indistinguishable from a demi-monde connection.

What attracted him to Margaret was the possibility of an attachment to a really good woman, under ideal circumstances of kinship. And if anyone objected that this ideal was itself immoral, Blunt had his answer:

> The little sins of the flesh do not in themselves degrade where there is love, any more out of marriage than in it. But it does degrade both men and women to be moral outlaws in the world.[23]

In other words, his ideal was a liaison discreetly encapsulated within marriage and society.

But Margaret was 'not the sort of woman to manage a harem discreetly or quietly', wrote Lytton. In November she confessed her sins to her husband, which convinced Blunt that his spring goddess had vanished for ever. So, making an autumnal anagram of her name – 'Margaret Jane Talbot: better again a mortal' – he retreated to 'unemotional' Sheykh Obeyd.

'I was by this time fifty years old and all that seemed to lie before was a sad acquiescence in the emptiness of things', he was to write in his 'Religion of Happiness' many years later. Such a mood, however, was deceptive or else inaccurately remembered. An account of his situation written actually on his fiftieth birthday, 17 August 1890, gave a fairer picture of his prospects. This birthday ought to be a turning-point, he wrote, but he found it hard to realize he no longer had his full youth before him: 'Physically and mentally I have never been much better equipped than now, and my capacity for enjoyment is certainly greater than it ever was. Life smiles on me in many ways.'

His domestic life was happier and more prosperous than most men's, Judith an ideal daughter, the son that Anne never gave him no longer a grief, Anne herself safely through the first matrimonial storms: 'Anne and I are like two ships in the regular trade winds, going pleasantly on together without trouble and without anxiety.'[24]

Anne's diary fully confirms the improved relationship. She gave him for his birthday a red-lined cloak and a red silk down pillow; when her dog Bangle strayed, it was he who sympathized most kindly, presenting her with his own Bulbul tied with blue ribbon, 'the apple of his eye'. A few weeks later she turned up a photograph of Butterfly that Judith had given her three years ago, and wrote: 'How many memories it brings back and how happy we are *now* – What a blaze of sunshine *now*, and what darkness *then*!!!'[25]

'What more do I need to make me happy?' asked Wilfrid. Perhaps ten more years to finish his poetry and diaries – and a constant 'element of romance'. Life without a tangle would be savourless.

[15]
The Amorist
1891–1894

At least one of Blunt's wishes for the nineties was to be abundantly granted. To say that he enjoyed an 'element of passion' would be an understatement. Passion was the element in which he lived, as a bird in the air or a worm in the earth, according to his mood.

Sometimes he despised himself; at other times 1891 was 'this happy year'. Past sins often seemed beautiful to him. Present ones always. On this principle he continued meticulously to record every detail of his sins in the nineties. In the same spirit, he persuaded Janey Morris to lodge with him her remaining packet of 'beautiful' love letters from Rossetti. She had burnt the majority ('foolish woman') and thought of building the survivors into the wall at Kelmscott, to be found or not as fate should decide, years hence.*

That present passions were always beautiful did not seem sufficient explanation to Blunt for the accessibility of women in the nineties. Was it due to a discovery that the old-established social *mores* no longer worked? Was it, as a Frenchman told Blunt, that English women were devoured by unsatisfied passion because their men had latterly become so chaste? Or was it a lethargic *fin de siècle* lowering of all standards? Or the foreshadowing of a dynamic twentieth-century world? Or simply the seductiveness of women's clothes? The first pretty style Wilfrid could remember was the Marie Antoinette fichu worn by Ella Baird; before that the monstrous crinoline 'made love-making ridiculous, almost impossible'. In the nineties Sibell Grosvenor shopped with him for bewitching chintzes, while Margaret Talbot wore 'a dear provocative little dress' with a low neck filled in by successive veils of chiffon and lace.[1]

In a conversation with Father Lockhart, Blunt appears to have settled for an end-of-century weakening in religious faith. English upper-middle-class Protestants, said Father Lockhart, had greatly

* Blunt noted in his journal the reception of Mrs Morris' packet of Rossetti letters on 12 November 1892. Later she asked for them back, and May Morris' executor gave them to the British Museum in 1939. They were opened in January 1964, fifty years after Janey's death.

changed as regards faith and morals. Fifty years ago 'the women were all pure and the men all impure'. Now public opinion no longer demanded that a young man should 'sow his wild oats with harlots. But, on the other hand, the women are less severely chaste.' Blunt and his friend reached the conclusion that, 'while public opinion was capable of doing much in restraining conduct, virtue would not stand any really strong test unaided by religious belief'.[2]

To Blunt, religion was still occasionally a worry, never a restraint. Indeed, he was working out a 'Religion of Happiness' (to be first expressed in literary form in 1895 but never finished) by which men would regard curiosity and courage in sexual adventures on the part of women as belonging to a better century. 'Duty is pleasure, pleasure duty, that is all we know on earth and all we need to know.'[3]

He felt hungry for the romance of Europe, he wrote in April 1891 on leaving Sheykh Obeyd and its 'child's life' – chess, dawdling, donkey-rides, talking nonsense; all with Judith.

The first lady to stay Blunt's hunger was Lady Edmund Talbot, Margaret Talbot's bosom friend. Mary Caroline Talbot had been recommended by George Wyndham as 'one who was artistic, literary and beginning to speculate about life'. She had attended Blunt's trial in Dublin and read his poetry. She was 'just the sort of good romantic woman' Blunt liked best, with 'a nervous sensitive hand worth much beauty'. He took her to see Ibsen's *Hedda Gabler* to encourage the new woman in her. Six weeks later she stayed at Crabbet. 'I told her I should come to her room at night, and she did not much protest', except to ask Blunt if he believed in a hereafter. He replied, 'I say my prayers, and hope for the best.' Acting on that principle he crept up to her room at midnight. 'I quite expected after this to attain the end of love'; but the door was bolted. Though the romance continued, 'the end' was never achieved, Lady Edmund being one who went to Paris for her bonnets, but on to Lourdes for her soul.[4]

Blunt was hardly to suffer; for meanwhile George's wife Sibell Grosvenor was in his sights – not to mention Dora Chamberlain – 'So here is another woman in my life!' – and Margaret Talbot's sister Caroline Grosvenor – 'She is one I could be in love with if I had time' – and Lady Helena Carnegie – 'an unmarried girl . . . interesting according to the fashion in this *fin de siècle*, inquisitive, unbelieving, sad, but with a wild love of life and of love' – and Margaret Talbot herself, who would seek his arms now and then, each time rendered a little more haggard by what she called her 'remorseful demons'. Margaret, incidentally, shared the *fin de siècle* obsession with sin. A gigantic python watched by her and Wilfrid at the Paris zoo seemed 'a vision of sin' and as such fascinated her. Wilfrid, himself the least *fin de siècle* of creatures, was wholly repelled by its flat glassy eyes and gloomy leer.[5]

It was during this visit to Paris that Skittles, suddenly sending for him, had to be put off. 'Truly time brings its revenges.' (She wanted money, which he posted.)

Sibell's love for Blunt varied inversely with her husband George's love for her; when George was neglecting her she would turn to the cousin. It began on 24 June, after Blunt had breakfasted with them and for the first time kissed Sibell goodbye.

'I wish it were possible I could love you', he said.

'You have so many others that love you.' So she knew about Margaret, and Lady Edmund Talbot? He invited her to Crabbet next day, but with the mental reservation, 'This must go no further. I cannot run risks with George. Heaven knows I have not sought it . . . and yet it tempts me, like looking down a precipice.'

At Crabbet he took her to the lake isle.

'How can I love two people? – and you know I love my George.'

'Of course it must not be – and yet –'

After 'a merry dinner' the Wyndhams returned to London by the last train.

Staying in September at Saighton Grange, the Wyndhams' country house, would be like 'the problem of the fox the goose and the cabbage'; except that the expected fox and goose (the two Talbot ladies) did not turn up, while the cabbage, Sibell, had returned to George. 'Fortunately, I am the least jealous of men', wrote Wilfrid, 'and the easiest consoled.' Nevertheless, a grouse drive was made melancholy by Sibell's refusal to say yes or no to his request for 'a fulfilment of our love'. He lay crouched in his butt all day thinking in despair of Sibell's green stockings.

A fortnight later he failed to console himself at Castle Menzies with Mrs Algernon ('Queenie') Grosvenor:

Other days shall forgotten be,
But not the journey you made with me,
The Tweed* in flood, and the angry sky
And the love we talked of, which could not be
With Eternity standing by.[6]

Eternity was standing guard also over the young Princess Hélène of Orleans. She had hoped to marry Prince Eddy of Wales, nicknamed 'Collars and Cuffs'; but Eternity, in the form of her Catholic religion, saved her from that fate. Wilfrid was never to venture on more than an intense romantic friendship. Yet she too demonstrated to him the change in women, by walking alone over the Scottish hills with no company but her dogs.

* 'The Severn's flood' in *Poetical Works* Vol. I.

'Have you no governess with you?'

'I should like to see the governess who would undertake to look after me.'[7]

As the Crabbet Club's president in Arab robes, Wilfrid sometimes felt it had developed too licentiously during the nineties. Perhaps he had encouraged the younger generation by allowing a nineties subject like 'Sin' to be chosen for the poetry contest. In 1888, when Arthur Pollen was still the Club secretary, the tone, if deliberately frivolous, was what the Victorians would have called wholesome.*

The change came in 1891. There were to be four 'brand new' visitors staying at Crabbet for the appointed day, 4 July, wrote Anne anxiously in her diary, wondering how to allot the bedrooms: H. C. Cust, 'the great Harry', who would expect a room to himself; Lord Houghton, poet, 'not suited to roughing it in dormitories'; the Hon. George Curzon, 'used to discomforts [on his Persian travels] but would not like them here'; Dick Grosvenor. All four ought to have a room each. (One of the single rooms was called Kilmainham – 'separate and solitary'.) And Anne suddenly remembered, 'Oh there is a fifth person I forgot! *Oscar Wilde*. Certainly he would expect a separate room.'[8]

It was a great coup to get Oscar Wilde. His friend Frank Harris has described him as over six feet with greasy bilious skin, flabby hands and heavy colourless lips. (To Rudyard Kipling's sister Trix his lips resembled 'big brown slugs' and he seemed to be 'roughly modelled in suet-pudding'.) While talking he pulled at his already pouchy jowl. Nevetheless, there was an incomparable charm in his talk, his voice being a 'musical tenor' and his eyes 'soulful'.[9] In 1890, after being driven over to Airlie Castle by Blanche Hozier in the same dogcart as Blunt in 1888, Wilde urged Blunt 'you must write a definitely Oriental volume. "Love and the Sphinx."'

The first new member to be elected that year was George Curzon, and after him, Wilde. When Wilde's name came up, a devil's advocate was appointed to oppose him, according to Club practice, in this case Curzon.

> He had been at Oxford with Wilde [wrote Blunt] and knew all his little weaknesses and did not spare him, playing with astonishing audacity and skill upon his reputation for sodomy and his treatment of the subject in Dorian Gray. Poor Oscar sat helplessly smiling, a fat mass, in his chair.... (He was sitting on my left and when he rose to reply I felt sorry for him – it seemed hardly fair.) But he pulled himself together as he went on and

* Extensive quotations from the Crabbet Club verse are given in the Earl of Lytton's *Wilfrid Scawen Blunt* (1961), pp. 219–38, 'The Crabbet Club'. There is also a volume of Crabbet verse in the Fitzwilliam Museum Library.

gradually warmed into an amusing and excellent speech. It was full of admirable epigrams and of those ingenious paradoxes which are his manner in writing. The discussion went on a long time between them, and I doubt if anything better of its kind was ever heard, even from Disraeli in his best days.[10]

Years afterwards Blunt noted that his own contemporary diary, quoted above, did less than justice to the brilliance and ferocity of the Curzon–Wilde duel.[11] More than once he thought that as chairman he ought to intervene, for Wilde was handicapped by deafness. The Club members present reacted with alternating hilarity and disquiet; fortunately the antagonists kept their temper. 'All the same [continued Blunt] the indictment was too home a thrust for Oscar not to feel it, and I think that it was for this reason that he did not come to our Club parties again.' When in 1893 Blunt reproached Wilde for non-attendance he replied blandly: 'I am very happy leading a country life.'

What is really memorable about it all is that, when two years later he was arraigned in a real Court of Justice, Oscar's line of defence was precisely the same as that made in his impromptu speech that evening at Crabbet.

Next day, Sunday, Wilde read out the competing poems on a subject of his own choosing, 'In Praise of Myself'. George Curzon was complimentary to Wilfrid as well as to himself:

Charms and a man I sing, to wit – a most superior person,
Myself, who bears the fitting name of George Nathaniel Curzon....
In tents of wandering Bedouin I have harkened more than once
To tales of prodigies performed by the great race of Blunts.

But it was George Peel, grandson of the former Prime Minister, whose 'Walt-Whitmanian Ballad' best exemplified the new nineties' spirit.

I am myself: I am not anybody else:
I am not Loulou Harcourt or Wilfrid Blunt....
The perfume of my body is delicious
I desire to prove this by taking off my clothes....
My hair is in a most curious state;
There are buzzings and whirrings in my top-knot:
Whom am I? I rather think I am Wilfrid Blunt....
I have read and thought enormously: Hume, Mill,
Herbert Spencer, Curzon's Russia in Central Asia, first chapter and a half....

An article by George Wyndham in the *New Review*,
Carlyle, Emerson, a rather stupid attack on Wilfrid Blunt in *Modern Society*,
My own Poem and the *Morning Papers*....
I am somewhat irregular in the morning after breakfast:
In this respect I am an artist.

On the Monday Wilfrid felt somewhat of a Frankenstein. 'The whole thing was rather ribald', he wrote, 'more perhaps than it should have been, but most certainly entertaining, though I feel this morning rather ashamed of myself.'

Wilde's own account was given to Frank Harris. After 'a delightful dinner, quite perfect', with Blunt 'a most admirable and perfect host', Curzon had got up and delivered a speech 'bristling with innuendoes, sneering side-hits at strange sins'. The audience thought it 'the height of bad taste ... and cheered and cheered' Wilde's reply. This was an indictment of Curzon's mediocrity – toiling and moiling for a second-class degree and destined for a second-rate career – no defence of the 'strange sins'. The Club roared with laughter, Curzon apologized and was 'charming', and 'a great night' of solo talk by Wilde followed. He continued:

In the morning we all trooped out to see the dawn, and some of the young ones, wild with youth and high spirits ... stripped off their clothes and rushed down to the lake and began swimming and diving about like a lot of schoolboys. There is a great deal of the schoolboy in all Englishmen, that is what makes them so lovable. When they came out they ... began playing lawn tennis, just as they were, stark naked, the future rulers of England. I shall never forget the scene. Wilfred [sic] Blunt had gone up to his wife's apartments and had changed into some fantastic pyjamas; suddenly he opened an upper window and came out and perched himself, cross-legged, on the balcony, looking down at the mad game of lawn tennis, for all the world like a sort of pink and green Buddha....[12]

The 1892 weekend, wrote Blunt, was almost as brilliant. 'These occasions are the salt of the earth.' The subject chosen being 'Marriage', it earned first prize for a bachelor, the future legal luminary Theobald Mathew; the runner-up was another bachelor, Harry Cust, 'of great abilities but given up, so his friends say, to vice, the vice of women'. Cust wrote:

Yet even cursed Cust, who may not nibble
  Those darling dainties made for married man,
May envy still the spouse of Lady Sibell,
  And bow before the lord of Lady Anne.*

* Cust was shortly to 'nibble those darling dainties' in the case of a woman he did not love but was forced to marry, thereby forfeiting a woman he did love, Pamela Wyndham.

Two of Wilfrid's verses give his views on the contemporary marriage lottery:

Marriage! Graduate of Girton.
Wedding gown an old chintz curtain.
Went to bed with flannel shirt on.
  O the fair fortune of marriage!

Marriage! Heiress. Best of marriages.
Noble father. Forty carriages.
Church St George's. Breakfast Claridges.
  O the fair fortune of marriage!

In 1893 George Curzon became the Crabbet laureate with his poem 'In Praise of Sin' – 'frank and systematic and premeditated Sin!'

The Club's peak was reached a year later. Its subject was 'Civilization' and the weekend frolic well illustrated the meaning of civilization, 1894. All the poets treated the subject with irony, except Lord Alfred Douglas (Wilde's friend 'Bosie'), who sent in a love-lyric that had nothing whatever to do with civilization: 'Because my love is fair and white and kind.'* Bosie won the annual tennis cup. The laureateship went to Godfrey Webb, a 'Soul' and popular man-about-town. One of his verses gives a sympathetic picture of Wilfrid as president in his Arab dress.

Fresh from the desert Wilfrid quite believes
He finds it [Civilization] when his Arab tents he
        leaves,
And gathers round him at those annual dinners
Some score of civilized and modern sinners;
Though still his savage nature we can guess
From the barbaric splendour of his dress.

Wilfrid's own poem sarcastically urged the Crabbet Club, especially the 'three Georges', Curzon, Wyndham and Leveson-Gower, to fulfil their imperial destiny by bringing 'civilization' to the savages:

Teach them your virtues, your plain ways, law
        courts and parliaments.
Build them South Kensington Art schools, sky signs,
        gasometers. . . .
Take control of their home life. Show them how
        royalty
Does it at Osborne and Windsor, you of the Bedchamber!
Go to them, Lords of the Household! Teach them
        your thirstiness,
How to behave on occasion, drunk but decorously. . . .
Go – only leave me protesting, pleased and polygamous.

* Bosie explained that the 'love' of his poem was a beautiful youth. It can hardly have been Oscar, whose skin and hair (dyed), wrote Wilfrid, were by now of a coarse 'Milesian' brown. In 1891, however, Blunt had written of Wilde's 'sort of fat good looks'.

By now Blunt was no longer critical of his young guests' high spirits. As his diary shows, they had learnt how to behave 'drunk but *in*decorously', to adapt his poem:

We sat on in joy at the dinner table till 3 o'clock and then went out to see the sunrise, Cairns playing the bagpipes on the lawn and Mark Napier dancing bare legged. Then George [Wyndham] and a number more went down into the pond and sang operatic choruses, after which they danced naked on the lawn in full daylight till ½ past 4.[13]

This was the last meeting of the Crabbet Club. It was not to survive when, next year, the rising tide of Wilfrid's 'polygamy' was to cause serious difficulties. Nor had the members appeared to the cold young gaze of Judith as the gods that her father remembered. Oscar Wilde was 'a great wobbly blancmange trying to serve underhand'; Bosie had hair 'like damp seaweed'; Harry Cust, reputed irresistible, was 'fat, podgy and coarse', his hair and eyes too light for his red complexion; George Wyndham, the undisputed Adonis and lord of the universe, had been spoilt by a mother (Madeline) who would say at table, ever since he was fifteen, 'Hush! George is going to speak!'[14]

Nevertheless, for an all-male mutual admiration society, the Crabbet Club had wit, intellect and astringency enough.

Blunt's 'polygamy' was beginning to oppress him. In 1891 he found himself handing to three different women – the two Talbots and Sibell Grosvenor – copies of precisely the same verses on the same day. 'All this I am afraid is very *fin de siècle*, and very immoral. But what can one do? Love is no respecter of time and place.' Happily no clash between the women was to be feared as long as the i's were not dotted. 'Women are not jealous in this way as men are', he told himself, 'for it is in the order of nature that a man's love should be divided.'

At times he found himself being used by hostesses like one of his own stallions, but for the extra-matrimonial consolation of unhappy pedigree ladies, rather than for breeding. It had begun with Princess Wagram insisting on his flirting with her sorrowful friend Lady Wenlock, who unaccountably was not satisfied with her 'excellent' husband. 'She is a type of our modern age', wrote Blunt, 'a highly cultured flower of feeling, in love with beauty and virtue, but curious about love and frightened at the thought of growing old.' (She was about thirty.) He dutifully kissed her glove, but unfortunately she was deaf and he soon tired of sitting over-close to read his poetry into her disabled ear.

Meanwhile, with the approach of Sheykh Obeyd, his eroticism slid into lassitude. 'I have written to Sibell and Mrs. Grosvenor', he recorded in his diary on 18 November, 'feeling rather guilty towards both. I wish I could simplify my life, and am determined in any case to begin nothing new.'

Simplification of course ruled out politics. He found nothing but confusion there. His two most congenial political friends, Sir Wilfrid Lawson and William Morris, each seemed increasingly disillusioned, Lawson seeing no hope in anything but 'a really democratic parliament' (an idea less than alluring to Blunt), and Morris offering his communistic utopia, *News from Nowhere*, to the world, but not believing in its possibility. 'I fancy', wrote Blunt, 'I may have influenced him in this.' Dropping in on another utopian experiment in Rome – the Peace Congress – Blunt could detect in it nothing but 'an amusing show where the eccentrics from every parliament in Europe were trotting their hobbies'. There were two debates; the first on arbitration, the second on Christianity, each violent.[15]

The Blunt family were to spend a tranquillizing four months planting the Sheykh Obeyd garden with palms and pink-washing El Keysheh, the small new house in the garden. The purchase of the white horse Dahman Shahwan was the main event of winter 1891–2. Wilfrid wrote on 7 December 1891:

> It is wonderful how the hopes and fears and loves and plans that busied me so a fortnight since have vanished under the influence of this clean atmosphere, I care nothing now for any European thing. Even my love for Margaret is laid by and put to sleep. It is a holy change.

He liked looking at Malruka, a pretty girl with smooth brown skin and white teeth, picking the maize – looking at her; that was all. He had never tried to make love to an Oriental woman, and never would. There was virtue and continence in the East, as in Ireland. Enough to share home pleasures with Anne, Judith and Cowie. Women occupied his thoughts, if at all, at certain periods of the moon, namely its second quarter, when the Bedouin had their mares covered.

The visit of a brilliant young social star and her family for tea at Sheykh Obeyd on 31 December, followed by a return visit by the Blunts to lunch with them in Cairo, apparently caused not a tremor in Wilfrid's heart. He simply found the girl 'very charming and very amusing'.[16] A rather more complicated impact, however, had been made by him on her. Her diary recorded:

> *31 December*. Papa, Mamma, Godfrey [Webb] . . . and myself visited Wilfred [sic] Blunt, an enthusiastic Radical poet, vain as a peacock, with an elaborate plan of living like a Bedouin, under the impression that people in the world are saying, 'Strange man that! one never sees him; buried as he is in his wild desert life, writing, reading, etc.'; whereas the world has not yet missed him, I

think. He is very handsome and cultivated, and, I am told, extremely susceptible. I saw nothing of this.[17]

The diarist was Margot Tennant, and her father Sir Charles Tennant, the wealthy Scottish manufacturer. Her vision of the poet – Margot was to nominate Blunt one of the four most beautiful men she had ever seen,[18] the other three being Lord Pembroke of the 'Wagger' Club, Lord Wemyss (father of Hugo Elcho) and Lord D'Abernon – may have sharpened her growing resolve to escape from Papa's factory chimney, known as the Tennant Stalk, into matrimony.

Infinitely refreshed, Wilfrid returned to Crabbet at the beginning of April 1892. Judith was to have a 'season'. In his own way he expected to have one too. He took a flat in Mount Street. After a slow start, all went superlatively well, though Margaret was aged and thin and their romance reduced to 'quiet affection'. For a few weeks the beautiful black-eyed Julia Peel, with 'white nervous hands' (sister of George and Willy, the Crabbet Club members) seemed about to take Margaret's place. Julia asked the Blunts to lunch at the House of Commons with her father the Speaker, and on the way to the terrace for coffee, in a little dark passage, Blunt felt that a caress had been invited. 'She is an odd girl, and I hardly know what she wants with me – probably nothing.'[19] It turned out that she wanted two things: Judith in marriage for her brother Willy and a talk – only a talk – with the much-talked-of Mr Blunt about the love she had never yet experienced. Nothing came of either project.

There was also Mary Elcho, to confide in him her wish to play a walk-on part in Wilde's new play, *Lady Windermere's Fan*, from which Wilfrid dissuaded her; Berthe Wagram, to take him to see the play; Sir Philip Currie, with Mrs Singleton as his hostess, to entertain him at a large dinner-party where he, Wilde, T. P. O'Connor and Philip sat up talking until the small hours; and Blanche Hozier to assure him that his name had never been mentioned in her divorce proceedings – no second Parham scandal.*

At Newbuildings he got nostalgic pleasure from walking round the plantations and discovering again the bench between two oaks where he and Minnie had sat, and the overgrown nook where Minnie had hung up a piece of looking-glass to warn them of chance comers – 'now like a hare's form when the hare is dead'. But love – 'a little love' – was alive in Crabbet; he read his poems to Caroline Grosvenor in the

* Sir Henry Hozier later agreed to a separation. Blunt recorded: 'Lord Napier tells me that the scandal . . . was very public. Hozier found Ashmead Bartlett in her bedroom and turned her out at once into the street. Lady Gregory . . . adds that there were nine others. (FM 31/1975, 29 May 1891.)

woods there. Being Margaret's sister, Caroline gave him a feeling of Eastern symmetry, as in the 'Arabic Ballads' he had just finished writing.

Poetry, craftsmanship and joy bubbled out of his friend William Morris at Hammersmith, where he took Judith to lunch. Morris showed the Blunts all over his Kelmscott printing press, the sheets of his own *Golden Legend* hanging out to dry. He had already honoured Wilfrid by printing his *Proteus* lyrics.

It was at another luncheon to which Wilfrid took Judith, towards the end of July, that his 'little loves' of the early summer suddenly showed signs of being supplanted by a new romance. The Tennants had invited them to Grosvenor Square. To his surprise, Margot took him up to her room at the top of the house.

'Why don't I know you better?' she asked, coming close to him. So he kissed her, and they made a love-pact. But she still hesitated.

'If I saw you oftener you would probably not like me', she wrote to him on 29 July. She preferred to remain 'a stranger, a mystery, an effort to you, and *quand même* yours – *quelquefois*'.[20] He decided their love was not serious, although she sat by him at the Gerald Balfours' gay evening, fanning herself with an eagle's wing. There was something of the eagle in her: a beaky nose, brilliant eyes, mordant wit, strong short hair; though her hair was wiry rather than feather-smooth.

On 2 August he gave a dinner-party for her at Mount Street and rode with her next day in the Park. Coming back, she told him her life-story: she had loved Peter Flower for eight years, and was now awaiting someone who combined Peter's charm with the intellect of a Haldane or Balfour – 'the intellectual ones are rather dry and awkward'. As they passed through the stables to her home she pointed to a table. 'There on that table Peter used to kiss me.' In return for kissing her likewise, Blunt made her promise never to quarrel, 'whatever happens'. She promised. He followed it up with a serious letter, for he did not want a flirtation. 'It would be too noisy a pleasure. But love, *yes*.' 'I am grateful for your interest and affection', she replied, 'especially as I feel I am not a very satisfactory person to love, although I am charming to *like*. Does this amuse you? You must come to Glen, and I will show you my home and the country that is *me*. . . .'[21]

The Glen – the Tennants' Scottish paradise – had to wait, however, for one of Blunt's August tours through the English countryside. After making love to Janey Morris in Oxfordshire, this time in a gig with a half-breed; usually it was a splendid Arabian four-in-hand,[22] and writing off Mr Henderson in Berkshire for being 'a nouveau riche' (he had bought Burne-Jones's 'Briar Rose' series for his home, Buscot Park), Blunt presented himself to the Elchos at Stanway in Gloucestershire. The party consisted only of Arthur Balfour, Hugo and Mary, 'certainly the strangest ménage', Hugo Elcho cynically going his own way, refusing to make up a four at tennis; Arthur the friendliest of companions because Mary so openly loved him. Blunt felt impelled to draw a line under the Irish chapter by lending Balfour his coat after tennis: 'When one taketh thy coat give him thy cloak also.'[23] From his next country house, Saighton, on 17 August Blunt wrote: 'My birthday of fifty-two and I never felt younger or more pleased with life.' He arrived at the Glen on the following day.

In going to the Glen, Wilfrid was putting himself more firmly than ever under the social jurisdiction of the Souls. Though Arthur Balfour at Stanway was their high priest, Blunt regarded the Glen as their temple. He had analysed the nature of the Souls at some length in his 'Secret Memoirs' the year before.[24] They aimed first, he noted, at aesthetic and cultural pleasures: dumbo crambo and witty evening conversation. Notwithstanding high intelligence, however, they were essentially shallow, and in this sense had a 'demoralizing' or even 'debasing' influence on Blunt. 'They read the Bible and they read the Morte d'Arthur in the same spirit.'

Their second aim was liberated morals; but Blunt believed they always stopped short of what he called 'the conjugal act', their motto being: 'Every woman shall have her man but no man shall have his woman.' Blunt had long been associated through kinship and sentiment with many of the leading Souls – Mary Elcho, Laura Tennant, Margaret and Mary Caroline Talbot, Violet Granby, Ettie Grenfell – indeed in describing them he was to use the pronoun 'we'. Nevertheless he could not accept the dictum, 'No man shall have his woman'.

What they put out of bounds as the conjugal act, he demanded as the essence of love, without which all friendships between men and women were incomplete. When the Tennants let him into their shrine it was as a temple-robber. 'The temptation to me was to break down this restriction', he had written the year before, 'and to treat seriously the less than serious game of passion I found being played and prove to these fair Souls that Love could be master.' Now came the golden opportunity. Margot had invited him to the Glen, having twice made him kiss her in London. He came down like a wolf on the Souls.

Not that Margot was afraid. She herself had burst into the circle of broken lilies that was the Souls, wrote Judith, like a bomb in a lily pond. Despite her long nose, jutting chin, eyes too close together, no make-up, fuzzy negro hair and stumpy figure, she could dance like a professional.* She had once toasted Queen Victoria standing on the table: 'Here's to Tum-Tum's dam!'

* Judith added that Margot's mother may have danced at the Moulin Rouge!

Nevertheless it was as 'a very sweet friend' that she took Blunt up to her bedroom at the Glen. She showed him her shrine to her dead sister and many of Laura's treasures, among them a skull. 'Her bed is a little iron one', he noted, 'plainly virginal.'

It was arranged that he should come to her room on the night of the twenty-fourth:

> At about midnight I found her there, very sweet and gentle in her little virginal bed, and stayed with her a great part of the night, she talking of a hundred delicious things in her wonderful way hour after hour which hardly even love could stop. Of all the nights of my life I remember not one more perfect, soul and body. Not that Margot is a great beauty, but she has a sweet little body, and I found her a virgin still, in spite of her great love for Peter and her little loves for the rest. Of her soul who can tell what it is except that it is unique in all the world.[25]

Blunt was ready to find in Margot the 'ideal love' he had lost when first Ella Baird, then Minnie, then Margaret failed him. 'People may say what they will, but a night like this is the purest and most exquisite delight our lives can give.'

In the early morning they agreed to take the Arab oath together one day. Then he left her. 'What a treasure to have won from Time!'

But time was to have its revenges. Though they did indeed swear the oath of brotherhood, Margot never invited him again to her room or visited Mount Street for tea. She made promises (which she broke), occasionally sat on his knee after a party. That was all. Blunt's language of excessive tenderness – the recurrent 'sweets' and 'littles' – was his response, however unconscious, to Margot's need for a heroic father as much or more than for a lover. When her father Sir Charles Tennant had arrived home on the twenty-seventh, Blunt had noticed that he 'grated' on his brilliant daughter, as 'a jarring element in the house though kindly in his way – the way of the nouveau riche'. Blunt did not see, however, that Margot had found in himself the romance of fatherhood Sir Charles lacked. He could not understand why their love had ended so abruptly. It depressed him:

> I think she never really loved me at all – spent that night with me perhaps through weariness of her virginity – and is now ashamed at what she has done.... I am sorry too, for I have begun really to love her.... There seems a curse on all my loves, that the moment my heart is moved to its inmost core, then fate ends it.[26]

Yet when Margot turned to him, as she would to a father, and asked whom she should marry, Evan Charteris or Henry Asquith, Blunt readily gave what he thought was the best advice. Marry Evan Charteris. He was in her own circle. And like a daughter, Margot did not take it. She married into a more magical circle, that of Prime Ministers: H. H. Asquith.*

Blunt prepared for another winter at Sheykh Obeyd in unusual gloom. 'I leave hardly a loving heart behind me.'

Contrary to expectations, 1893 was to be a memorable year for the amorist, not only for summer love adventures, but for an earlier burst of spring politics at Cairo. The Khedive Tewfik had died in January of the year before and his successor, Abbas II, was a sensitive youth of only seventeen. Blunt, after calling on him in February, described him to Judith as 'a short fat boy in the tightest of Hussar uniforms'. Lord Cromer (Sir Evelyn Baring now exalted to the peerage) gave the impression of patronizing him; and the Liberal victory of 1892 did not help Abbas, according to Blunt, since Lord Rosebery became Foreign Secretary. 'He will continue to represent the bondholders.'

Blunt steamed into Alexandria on 1 December 1892, noting in his diary, 'There is always something exciting in coming into port in rough weather.'

A flash of lightning came on the last day of the old year, 31 December 1892, with the publication of Alfred Milner's book, *Britain and Egypt.*† One of Milner's chapters, entitled 'The Veiled Protectorate', was to tear the veil that since 1883 had been drawn over the Egyptians' eyes. For it demonstrated beyond doubt that the British occupation of Egypt was to be permanent.[27] Milner gave two reasons why this should be so: Britain's commercial interests and Egypt's geographical position. So powerful, indeed, was the imperial drive, that Blunt himself for a few days, deeply impressed by Milner's apologia, believed Cromer a better bet than Riaz, the wizened conservative Turkish pasha who was soon to support Abbas.

On 15 January 1893 Abbas II, assisted by the resurgent Egyptian Nationalists, brought off his coup. Abbas, exercising his supposed legal right as the Sultan's viceroy, appointed Fakhri Pasha to lead the first Egyptian Nationalist government since the fall of Arabi.‡

Blunt would have done battle gladly for the new regime. However, his own residence at Sheykh Obeyd represented in itself a kind of veiled protectorate. Ever since returning to Egypt in 1887 he had been under an obligation not to take part in active politics. Nevertheless

* It was said that another future Prime Minister, A. J. Balfour, when asked if he intended to marry Margot, replied that he rather thought of having a career of his own.

† First published 1892, fourth edition 1907, in answer to Blunt's *Secret History of the English Occupation of Egypt,* 1907.

‡ But the legal rights of Abbas II had in fact been abrogated by Lord Granville's despatch of 4 January 1884, laying down the Khedive's obligation to accept British advice as long as the British occupation lasted. (Afaf Lutfi Al-Sayyid, *Egypt and Cromer,* p. 107 and *passim.*)

there were ways in which he could show solidarity. Having kept in close touch with prominent Nationalists like Sheykh Mohammed Abdu, he planned to pay a solemn call on young Abbas II at the end of February. Even his dress should mark the importance of the occasion. He would array himself (to use Anne's words), in his 'peacockest garments'. This meant acquiring from Cairo a superlatively conventional black morning suit. Fortunately a tailor had one in stock: black striped trousers and tail coat ordered by the lately deceased Hon. Oliver Montagu, and never worn.

His ceremonial support of the Khedive had been supplemented by a spate of his favourite press activity. Within a week of the January coup he was drafting a long memorandum on the situation (still among his papers) in which he outlined a ten-point programme for the evacuation of Egypt, the only alternative being 'to declare an open protectorate'. The nub of his criticism was in paragraph 8:

> Lord Cromer, in my opinion, while a great and successful Administrator had failed politically in Egypt. He has introduced valuable reforms for the material benefit of the tax-paying fellahin, but has done nothing for them morally or intellectually. He has left the governing power in the hands of the old privileged class, the Turkish Pashas. Latterly he has attempted to transfer the power to Englishmen. He has not in the remotest degree attempted the better half of Lord Dufferin's programme, namely the education of the fellahin in self-government.[28]

On this memorandum was based a letter, article and interview with the British press. But despite his bold language, Blunt was ready to compromise on a temporary solution of the crisis. Asked by a high official, Sir George Bowen, what was his own policy, Blunt replied with moderation: 'The English garrison might be withdrawn to Suez, as a compromise. That would satisfy the cry about England's route to India.'[29]

Blunt was once more in the news as 'at once the laughing-stock and the tool of the natives'; a 'poetic politician'; author of 'wild and whirling charges against Mr. Balfour' which he had failed as miserably to substantiate as those against Lord Cromer now. Even his devoted Lady Lytton trounced him for giving an interview to the *Pall Mall Gazette*: it might result in his again being exiled from Sheykh Obeyd – and anyway, she could not now come and stay with him.[30]

In high spirits, however, Blunt left Egypt on 18 April for Constantinople, where his Muslim friends again led him to hope for an interview with the Sultan, to discuss the evacuation of Egypt on a basis of 'neutralization', with the possible acquisition of Suez by Britain. The earlier, disappointing pattern, however, was repeated: no Sultan, but Arab stallions galore. Moreover, Blunt's ally al-Afghani, now living at the Turkish court, was no longer an intimate as in the days before the umbrella fight at James Street. Nevertheless, al-Afghani did promise 'to manage matters with the Sultan', and perhaps send for Blunt in the course of the summer. So Blunt returned to England in the hope of re-entering the only kind of diplomatic service he really enjoyed – an *un*accredited position. 'I am to write letters on political affairs in England to Jemal which he can show the Sultan. Thus I shall be his unaccredited ambassador.'[31]

In fact Blunt's services were not to be required as unaccredited ambassador to Constantinople, since the Nationalist ship broke up a year later between the rock of Cromer's solid material success and the whirlpool of the Khedive's youthful vacillations. There was no strong Nationalist leader in Cairo; nor had Cromer yet made a mistake grave enough to imperil his position. Moreover the 'Armenian massacres' of 1894 prejudiced people against Islam and Egyptian nationalism. By April the Egyptian whirlpool had subsided and the Khedive – still only nineteen – had made his reluctant peace.

Meanwhile, Blunt arrived back at Crabbet in high feather. In parting from George Wyndham the autumn before, he had agreed with his cousin that they both needed another 'grande passion'. For Blunt at least an emotional feast was prepared in this summer of 1893, though the first bite at the cherry was apparently a failure. He wrote to the poet Alice Meynell on 14 June inviting her to 'a poetical dinner' – never more than six, in Mount Street, 'and I try to make them amusing & we sometimes read out after them. Only it is a rule of the house that ladies do not bring their husbands or husbands their wives. But perhaps this would be too "fin de siècle" for you.' Perhaps it was. Or perhaps the adoration of three poets, Patmore, Meredith and Thompson was enough for Alice. There is no record of her acceptance.[32]

To call his romance with Lady Galloway a 'grande passion' was perhaps a little theatrical. For one thing, it began almost accidentally. At a luncheon-party given by Mary Galloway, Blunt was wondering whether to make a 'declaration' to his hostess or to Lady Helena Carnegie, also present; it was only when Lady Helena retired into the back drawing-room to write a letter and Lady Galloway began to talk romantically about an occasion when they had met in Paris two years earlier, that Blunt decided it should be Mary's hand he kissed. In these moods all he needed was *a* hand.

For another thing, it was Lady Galloway herself who introduced the words 'grande passion'. Clever, cultured (she was to write a monograph on Wagner highly approved by the musician's widow) the former Lady Mary Cecil had married the first comer in a desperate bid to escape desolation caused by leaving Hatfield on her father Lord Salisbury's death; this being followed by her widowed mother's second marriage to the fifteenth Lord Derby. Here was a potent source of 'grandes passions' among middle-aged Victorians (Mary Arthur Arabella Galloway had turned forty, being the god-daughter of Arthur Duke of Wellington and born in 1852, the year of his death) – the loveless marriage as an escape from home.*

Writing from Hatfield House on 12 June 1893, Lady Galloway began:

> How did you divine, dear Bard, all that this place is to me and has been all my life. I never told you anything about my feeling for it – and yet you knew. I suppose it is because you are a poet, and you know all that is in my heart.... Shall I walk round the garden at 5 o'clock? as we must be home soon after 6. How could you think you read too long on the river? The kingfisher, the trees and sunlight, and river charmed me. Even more than the little dark college room. Write and tell me if 5 o'clock will do.... I am here like an escaped bird.[33]

Wilfrid had not the slightest intention of helping the bird to escape altogether. He might call her 'the little savage' and allow her to address him as 'My dear Don Juan'; but when in August he received a wild letter from her threatening to break with her husband, he wrote sharply in his 'Secret Memoirs', 'I trust she will do nothing of the kind.'

In September he stayed with Lady Galloway in her Scottish home of Cumloden, where his fellow guests were the clever Margaret Jersey and Lord Sackville's daughter, Amalia West. He wrote in his diary on the twentieth:

> I have a very comfortable room arranged for me by Mary conveniently near her own. It is the anniversary night of my first love adventure thirty years ago [with Skittles] and how different at Cumloden from the squalid surroundings of the London streets! Here she is queen as well as woman, and our romance has taken new royal wings.

But still the 'royal wings' did not mean flight or escape for her. She wrote him a frustrated letter from the Alpes Maritimes next March, 1894, complaining of 'domestic suppression' and boredom: '*You* can never realize what it is to live *alone* and yet dragging a chain as I do. I am like one of your arab horses shut up in a tiny paddock alone – and unable to find full bent for its capacities.'[34]

Like so many of Wilfrid's loves, she had too long a pedigree and too small a paddock.

· · · · ·

* Judith was to describe Lord Galloway as 'weird', bent double, and always wearing cotton gloves. He also had 'a predilection for girls below the age of consent'. (Violet Powell, *Margaret Countess of Jersey*, p. 73. London, 1978.)

Meanwhile, what Blunt consistently called 'a little love', never a grand passion, had emerged to entrance him in 1893. Emily, daughter of his best friend Lord Lytton, had become Judith's best friend – yet another instance of the Blunt family's lifelong intertwining with the Lyttons.

Three years earlier Blunt had dedicated his *New Pilgrimage* to the sick Lytton, promising him, if he would come to convalesce in Egypt, camels' milk to drink – 'the real fontaine de Jouvence'. But there was to be no fount of youth for Robert Lytton, either in camels' milk or poetry. He died as ambassador in Paris on 24 November 1891, a fortnight after Blunt's visit ended. On Blunt's final evening with the Lyttons he had put a dog-rose brooch beside Emily Lytton's plate, in gratitude for her 'unostentatious kindness' throughout his visit. The wording was ironic.

Emily, youngest Lytton daughter, pretty but teased for her plumpness by her brothers Victor and Neville, got her own back on the world by an adolescent talent for repartee. Teasing between her and Blunt was rampant.

Next year, 1892, the bereaved Lyttons were housed in Elm Park Gardens, Chelsea. Emily, becoming slimmer and prettier every day, but still very shy, now dissociated herself both from fashionable and cultural society. She was a rebel against authority, especially her mother's and sisters'. When the eldest sister, Lady Betty Balfour, whose husband Gerald and brother-in-law Arthur were both Souls, produced an eligible young man for her and asked what she thought of him, Emmie would reply, 'I think he's a beast.' As for the Souls, 'If Souls could but have their thin coat of paint scraped off', she wrote on 27 June 1892 to the Rev. Whitwell Elwin, the seventy-six-year-old parson who was her beloved father confessor, 'what poor wooden blocks they would be. Don't tell Betty.'

Such an attitude did not displease Blunt. Two days later she was photographed after fishing with him at Crabbet – a smiling figure in an enormous hat and Blunt's overcoat holding a long pole. Another ten days and he was 'very nearly saying and doing something foolish' after the Eton and Harrow match. 'This must not be.'[35]

That autumn and winter the Souls and Emily were going strong on their opposed courses. Margot Tennant and her friends planned a Souls' bi-monthly magazine to be called *To-morrow: A Woman's Journal for Men*. Its motto, suggested Blunt, should be '*Solus cum Sola*, with an armorial coat bearing two flat fish osculant all *proper*'. The project was too proper, however, for old Sir William Harcourt. 'Ah, it is their bodies that I like', he joked over the port, 'and now that they are going to show us their souls all naked in print, I shall not care for them.'

Emily was another who did not care for Souls, but only for Wilfrid's soul. 'My dear Enemy', she wrote on 5 November, 'Though I have many and more important calls upon my time, my desire for your welfare compels me to write to you these few lines' – followed by two pages of flirtatious scolding. On the twenty-third, 'My dear disciple ... from the only person who tries to improve your mind. ...' As a Victorian girl of seventeen, Emily did not realize what she was up to. But her brother-in-law Gerald Balfour did: 'I call that flirtation.' And so of course did her 'dear Enemy'.

When the Blunts returned from Egypt in May 1893, Lady Lytton and Emily were on Victoria Station to meet them – 'Emily grown very pretty and nicely dressed in the new fashion with a cape of white lace and a pretty hat.'[36] Judith and Emily were to combine against the whole ambience of the Souls, founding their own 'Pawsoff and Rude Club'. But did Emily include Judith's father in this ban? It was in fact the beginning of a three-year 'spell' that she said he put upon her. As an older man, he did not make her feel shy. And he was the handsomest, most physically attractive man she had ever met, especially his beautiful hands – long, sensitive. ...

At Elm Park Gardens on 11 May she began teasing him 'in her pert way'. Suddenly he kissed her hands. On this first occasion it was indeed 'Pawsoff': she turned pale, snatched her hands away and ran upstairs. 'She is a pretty, provoking child. I hope I have not frightened her', he wrote. That evening she looked as if she had been crying, 'but I hope I am mistaken as I must not make her or any of them unhappy. It was a foolish thing to do.'

Foolish or not, he followed it up by laying light-hearted siege to Emily during a week at Crabbet, when she and Conny came to act in Blunt's *Bride of the Nile*.[37] This specially written closet-drama he admitted was 'not very good', but it had interesting features. The play was set in Egypt under the Roman occupation, thus enabling Blunt to parody Lord Cromer's 'high mission'. Blunt also solved the problem of two heroines' love for the same man (one heroine being played by Emily) by making the hero marry them both. The later triangles of Emily, Judith, Wilfrid, and of Judith, Wilfrid, Mary Elcho, were thus handled in advance at least to the poet's satisfaction. Blunt felt in himself an infinite capacity for loving.

One morning he took Emily to the woodlands hitherto sacred to Minnie:

> Today after two years of silent sympathy I have had a talk with Emily. It was a lovely morning ... the heath is splendidly in flower. We stopped and sat on the bank. She told me of a novel she is writing of which I am one of the characters [the villain] and she another, and I asked if she loved me, and she said very simply 'Yes'... It was all very sweet and delightful, but it must not go much further.

But it did go further. A few days later, he proposed, 'not quite in earnest', to 'bid her goodnight' in her room. She refused and he saw that he had frightened her. Next day she was 'a little cross' and there were explanations, again in the woods.

'I have been rather curiously brought up', Emily began. 'I have been told it is not wrong for friends to kiss and that friends may be trusted, but you must not misunderstand me or think ...'

'I think nothing, only that you have the prettiest blue eyes in the world.'

They agreed to correspond, meet when possible at his flat in Mount Street, spend a week together in Paris 'some day'. Before dinner, they sat opposite one another on the drawing-room floor, he in his Arab dress, she in her blue fellahin acting-clothes, 'making a little covenant' of Mohammedan marriage with 'a little ring' of coloured stones which he put on the 'little finger' of her left hand.

'With this ring I thee wed, with my body I thee worship.' It was all said, she admitted, 'half-playfully'.

After dinner she danced for them in her swirling robes (within a week Margot was doing the same at the Glen); then left next day, but taking with her an acrostic sonnet written by Blunt. Her favourite couplet dwelt on 'ideal love':

> Ideal love is sealed in her blue eyes,
> Love without words, the deepest, holiest, best.

Blunt's real message, however, lay in the last two lines:

> O sun, shine bright to-day on hill and dale.
> Nurse O soft wind, to-night my happiness.[38]

Moreover, for Emily and Blunt the word 'holiest' had very different meanings. According to his new religion of pleasure, holiness and happiness were interchangeable. Emily, on the contrary, persuaded herself that she was disciplining his soul to a higher love – despite the evidence of a 'very hot embrace' the evening before.

There was to be only one more day of unclouded happiness for Blunt and holiness for Emily. On 29 August she wrote him 'her first love letter':

> My dear Thing. ... I wear your ring and it is lovely. Whenever I see or feel it I think of you, and as there are little sharp points on it which stick into my fingers when I press them together, I have to think of you very often. ... Your affectionate adviser, Emily Lytton.

He thought the letter 'very pretty'.

She did not tell him that she had sent a copy to her darling 'Rev'.

At once the venerable Jupiter of Booton Rectory hurled a sizzling thunderbolt. Blunt was a villain, Emmie blind. She must never see him again. (What would Booton have thought had it been known that Blunt was at that very moment writing an ardent acrostic sonnet to Margot Tennant? For the E and N in Tennant he chose the lines, 'Each passionate fibre of your being pressed/Nearer to mine'. Margot asked him to change the 'passionate' into 'delicate', so that the acrostic could go into her album.)[39] For a moment Emily was stunned by Booton into revulsion, agreeing that she had been 'a blind fool' and delivering to Blunt a minor thunderbolt of her own, based on the parent missile: 'I now realize that the love you said you felt for me was a love which you should have been ashamed to offer, and which I would rather die than accept or return – all friendship is impossible between us.'

Blunt had no alternative but to resign. 'The thing I loved in you', he wrote, 'was that you loved me, and since that is gone I shall not seek you out.' He admitted to having said 'many foolish things', but 'perhaps not all of them quite meant'.

Yet when Emily visited Crabbet again that October she suffered from 'a kind of perpetual internal tremble'; and by November, after Blunt had departed to the East, she was again confessing to Booton her 'infatuation'. She had long been unable to think of him as a villain.[40]

The villain was indeed harmlessly engaged on visiting the four Coptic monasteries of Wady Natrun. In this strange hide-out in the Western Desert, half fortress, half hermitage, Blunt showed unusual interest in sight-seeing. He was amply rewarded. In one of the monasteries sixteen packing-cases contained the remains of holy persons wrapped in linen; the monks uncovered St Basil's toes for him to see.

'Are you still afraid of attacks by the Arabs?' asked Blunt, impressed by the huge keeps and drawbridges.

'There are always dangers.'

'But not of recent years?'

'Well, there were the Beni Hellal.' That attack, Blunt recalled, had been made in the tenth century.*[41]

In June 1894 Booton again ordered a total 'break' with Crabbet, despite Emily's friendship for Judith. Booton was inexorable: 'His whole design towards you is that of a demon ... infamy ... ruin ... Satan in person.'

So in July Emily brought herself to write a letter to Satan threatening to tell her mother all unless he avoided her. 'Not very graciously worded', noted Wilfrid in his diary, 'and in the gracious way of youth.' However, he promised Emily to avoid her. 'Take care of your

* Today there seems to be no fear of the outside world at Wady Natrun. Conference buildings are being erected and unscreened visitors are welcomed with coffee in plastic cups. The beautiful murals can be photographed by flashlight. But I saw no saintly toes.

precious life and make those who love you happy. Your affectionate W.S.B.'[42]

The day before, at Margot's, he had attended the most brilliant luncheon-party he could remember. Everyone sparkled – Mrs Ettie Grenfell, Lord Ribblesdale, Oscar Wilde – everyone, that is to say, except the new husband, Henry Asquith. Blunt sat next to him, feeling sorry for this timid talker who was afraid of saying the wrong thing: 'a good preacher but distinctly bourgeois'.[43]

His August visits included one to Shakespeare's shrine at Stratford, accompanied by his cousin Lord Alfred Douglas. They sat on the tomb and read Shakespeare's sonnets 'as an appropriate form of prayer'. Wilfrid found Bosie, who had never in his life seen the sun rise, 'a soft traveller'. Though Bosie could not wait to join Oscar Wilde in Worthing, Wilfrid felt the trip might have done the boy good. He had had many opportunities of talking to Bosie 'in the way of precept', he wrote to Anne, 'in which as you know I excel.'*[44]

After Stratford, Wilfrid went on alone to Stanway to join the Elchos' house-party, which included as usual Arthur Balfour. 'By a sudden inspiration in the evening', wrote Wilfrid, 'when we were once more alone I kissed Mary's hand. She turned pale, said nothing and went away to Arthur.'[45]

That was the last recorded kiss of the season. Who now could he depend on for love? Margaret said she wanted to be a nun, Emily said goodbye. Perhaps Lady Galloway? 'But my mind is already on the wing and free of entanglement', he wrote on 5 October. 'I shall if possible keep it so and am making arrangements to stay abroad over next summer. But I promise nothing to myself. I go to Tunis to pay Terence a visit.'

The visit to his twenty-four-year-old cousin Terence Bourke, Button's younger brother, only strengthened Wilfrid's desire never to return home. Terence had gone native in Tunis with a thoroughness that Wilfrid could not match. An Arabic speaker, he was 'duckless' in a silk shirt, slippers and tarbush; watchless, never in a hurry or a temper; 'the mosquitoes do not bite him nor the flies annoy ... he knows everything, and has a wisdom about the things of life – the really essential things which is altogether wonderful'. The little house smelt deliciously of cinnamon and oil; they ate saffron, capsicum, pounded wheat, gourd, fish, sweet rice, pistachios and plums. There were cobwebs hanging from all the ceilings and piles of clean dust in all the

* Blunt later added a note on the love-sick Douglas. 'I did not quite understand the full character of his relations with Oscar though they were plain enough. It was difficult to realize that there could be *passion* felt for one so physically repulsive as Wilde was. Yet the fat sensual man had already thoroughly debauched the boy, as a girl is debauched, mind and body.' (FM 3/1975 9 August 1894.)

corners. So captivated was Wilfrid by Terence's 'hermitage' that he vowed to establish one of his own on Mount Sinai. Or perhaps with Terence at Cyrene, where they might both become Muslims.

Fortunately or unfortunately, the idea appealed also to his women friends. Janey Morris had always longed to share the desert with him, though 'we are more likely to retire to Kelmscott', she had written in 1889, 'and live on vegetables'. Mary Galloway had 'longed for your hermitage on Mount Sinai'. Amalia West wrote, 'I shall have to come and join you!' Helena Carnegie also felt 'the hermit spirit strong upon me . . . I suppose we must not join forces in our solitudes.' Even Emily, next year. Above all, Lady Elcho. In 1893 she had told him how much she envied his Egyptian life: 'Some day I must take my children there!'

Now she was committed to come in the New Year, 1895.

[16]
Grande Passion
1895–1896

The amassing of cottages by Wilfrid Blunt was to become a favourite legend among his friends. Not exactly *cottages ornées* since they were most plainly furnished, they nevertheless served the same purpose as in the eighteenth century – to make secluded love.

El Kheysheh, the new Pink House built by him at Sheykh Obeyd, had been meant all along for Mary Elcho. Looking forward to her visit early in 1895, Wilfrid wrote: 'Once her mind is made up, obstacles only strengthen her purpose. So I hope at last to enjoy the delights of her being in the house I first designed for her.'[1] A sketch of El Kheysheh by Wilfrid shows a two-storey building with many windows, many servants; its walls pink, its garden walls white. Through a gate in its white wall was the garden of Sheykh Obeyd. In this pink paradise, this garden, this shrine of Sheykh Obeyd and desert beyond, Wilfrid was to know 'the greatest happiness' of his later years – followed by his greatest sorrow. 'I touched for a moment the ideal I had through life pursued and held it, like a captured bird in my hand, and then it slipped through my fingers and was gone.'[2]

Lady Elcho brought with her the three children, Ego, Guy and Cynthia and their governess Miss Jourdain, Ego returning in due course with Lord Cromer's boys to Cheam School. Lord Elcho was an obstacle; his mistress of many years, Hermione Duchess of Leinster, by whom Wilfrid understood he had a 'Fitzgerald' son, was dying in Mentone. His thoughts were returning to his wife. But Mary genuinely felt it was his duty to sit by his mistress' bedside to the last.

At the magical age of thirty-two (sixteen, when girls were fighting off childhood, and the thirties, when women were fighting off age, were both magical in Wilfrid's eyes), Mary was in the full beauty of her half-Irish inheritance – raven hair, pale skin; but she had extreme slenderness rather than her mother Madeline's pagan power, and dark eyes instead of the Campbell grey-blue inherited from Pamela Fitzgerald.

It was past midnight on 5 January, with a harder frost than Wilfrid could ever remember at Sheykh Obeyd, when the Elcho party arrived. Scarcely three days later, on 'a sparkling morning', the lines were drawn for the siege of El Kheysheh, as Wilfrid's Peninsular father would have said. 'I have spoken to Mary', Wilfrid wrote in his diary.* She had come to the Blunts' house dressed in her Bedouin clothes, the gift of Wilfrid. On the way back to her garden gate she asked to see Sheykh Obeyd's tomb, whose small dome shone white through the trees. Wilfrid took her down the low step and into the shrine, where the gaunt stone sarcophagus filled almost the entire space, a blue-green turban placed over the saint's head. 'I made a prayer to Sheykh Obeyd', wrote Wilfrid, 'for good fortune with her.' That done, he kissed her. Under the gemeyseh trees outside they sat down on the sand, talking of past times. Mary recalled that she had first been kissed by him as a child of six at Wilbury, 'in a cousinly way'. Now he must still think of her as a child, or as an old woman; 'in either case too young or too old'. But she agreed to go with him in February up the Nile.'

Next day Wilfrid took her to the little jessamine garden and there presented her with an acrostic love-sonnet. This broke down her reserve, to the extent of her admitting that he had long ago won her childish love. 'She is the most reserved of women, and, if I had not first written it in verse, the word [love] I think would never have been spoken.' But she was 'not free'.

What did this mean? Arthur Balfour? After she had said 'the little things of life would not prevent me', Wilfrid decided the big thing must be a vow to Arthur. Mary's unfathomable reserve about herself was among her attractions: 'a mystery not one of her woman friends pretends to have solved'. (This was inaccurate, for Margot Tennant had assured Wilfrid categorically that, as Souls, Mary Elcho and Arthur Balfour never slept together.) Wilfrid continued:

> Her secrets are close shut, impenetrably guarded with a little laugh of unconcern, baffling the curious. She reminds me so much of her mother, whom I also loved thirty years ago. She has the same large-minded view of things and, when at last reserve is broken, the same sincerity. But her nature is a finer one, being without the worldly touch. She is an ideal woman for a lifelong passion, and has the subtle charm for me, besides, of blood relationship. I was happy here before she came, but this is more than heaven.

* This diary caused Blunt many changes of mind. At first he thought an expurgated transcript would do; then he preferred the original diary; in 1921 he was still wondering whether or not to destroy it; finally the original, after being cut out of the 'Secret Memoirs', was sewn together again and laid loose in a 1895 volume.

The day before, half in jest and half in earnest, his daughter Judith had said to him, 'I warn you that if you leave me for Mary I shall do harm to both of you.' It was a voice he did not heed.[3]

On the fourteenth, El Kheysheh surrendered. 'This afternoon my extremest hopes were fulfilled.' Mary was alone in the house, her maid in Cairo, the children and governess out donkey-riding. When Wilfrid called with his poetry book she was resting in bed, the shutters drawn, a large envelope on her table addressed to Arthur Balfour. There was no pretence this time of Wilfrid reading to her, the room was too dark; but he did not think 'she intended quite all that happened'. Afterwards she reproached herself gently, but not him, 'Then the others came in, and I went away and have gone about since like one distracted with my happiness.'[4]

A pencil note appeared in Judith's diary: 'Found H.F. [for 'Head of the Family', as he liked to be called] sitting on Mary's bed to-night when I went over unexpectedly. They looked horribly confused, but I suppose it means nothing.'

During the next few days Mary, his 'fairy queen', wandered through the gardens with him, talking of the possibilities and the impossibilities of the future, or listening to his poetry, or to the Arab boy playing for them on his *rebab*. When she appeared all in white with a red scarf round her waist, wearing the *kefiyeh* and *aghal* on her head like an Arab woman, but with vine leaves in her hair, he burst into his song of Solomon:

> She is the ideal for which I have all my life been waiting.
> She cares for nothing really but for love, an oriental woman whose life it is to be kissed and kiss.

It was the influence of Arthur Balfour's philosophy, Wilfrid later decided, that had turned Mary into a pagan.

Soon they were off on an expedition to the sandhills, the children on donkeys, Miss Jourdain and the *rebab* player on camels, Wilfrid and Mary on Arab mares, a foal following Mary's. The two romances of his life had met – the desert and love. At the sandhills they sheltered from the sun under Wilfrid's blue and white striped travelling carpet. They scooped up sand for pillows and Wilfrid read her his translation of the Arabian poem *Ántara*.[5]

The mysterious Mary explained something of her situation to him:

> Though she and Hugo live affectionately together, it is not conjugally, this for the last six years. He goes his way; she had her 'friend'. To him, her friend, Arthur Balfour, she is pledged far more than to Hugo. She loves and honours and respects him, and he is constant to her, and she has been always constant to him, and she is bound to him by a thousand promises never to give herself

to another. On this understanding he has been content that their love should be within certain limits – a little more than friendship a little less than love. She cannot desert him – and yet – and yet? I must be content with this.[6]

They agreed that in the summer she would return to her old life, saying goodbye to this as to a dream.

Next day, the twenty-fifth, came a sheaf of letters for Mary – from Lady de Vesci, Godfrey Webb, Hugo, Arthur Balfour – all warning her not to fall in love with Wilfrid.

Early in February they made a more audacious expedition, called by Wilfrid their 'desert honeymoon'. It was quite a party, Anne and Judith riding with them on the first day, but then turning back. However, Miss Jourdain brought the children all the way, since it would be 'less than proper' they should go alone. There were many servants. Each night they camped in a different wady, the first overlooking Cairo and the pyramids, black against a yellow sky. The ladies had tents and Wilfrid his striped carpet-shelter a little apart, where Mary came to him. 'I think the Arabs with us knew that we were lovers – indeed they must have known it, for there were Mary's naked tell-tale footsteps each morning in the sand. . . . Mary is now my true Bedouin wife.'[7]

What if there had been one wakeful child? But it was Arthur Balfour who was to cast the first shadow. The fat letter Wilfrid had seen addressed to Arthur at El Kheysheh contained a confession that her cousin and host had 'made a little love'. By return, Arthur protested. Mary felt desperately guilty. Arthur had been such an unselfish lover . . .

Other ill news was that poor Randolph Churchill had died. And that Stephen Pollen, whom Judith had not seen for seven years, was coming home. Many suitors had been turned down by her, including that most devoted and eligible Everard Fielding, son of a Catholic peer. Now, to Anne's intense alarm, Judith professed to be in love with a Pollen.[8]

There was a bitter blow on 15 February. Hugo had got a 'reprieve' from the Duchess' bedside and was coming to stay. And on St Valentine's Day, Wilfrid's Bedouin wife had told him that 'it being the thirty-sixth day . . . she is certainly with child'.

Mary had all along spoken with natural concern of the possible 'consequences'. 'A little troubled and anxious' (the adverb 'little' no doubt contributed by Wilfrid) she had decided even before Hugo's visit to return home in March.

'For me it is a pure gift from heaven', wrote Wilfrid of the coming child. The arrival of Lord Elcho, however, in a billycock hat with a chow chow dog on a chain, brought a touch of hell.

When I came out this morning before sunrise to the tent I found his Christian hat in it where he had left it yesterday, and it moved me to anger. I feel that she has brought a stranger into my tent, she who was my Bedouin wife, and that when I get her once more into the desert I shall cut off her head.[9]

When Hugo went out on the lake, 'after the fashion of Englishmen', to shoot something, and only succeeded in upsetting his boat, the Bedouin husband wrote, 'served him right'. But worse was in store. It emerged to Wilfrid's consternation that Mary and Hugo had long ago planned a complete reconciliation once the Duchess was dead, with another baby to clinch it. Could the reconciliation be pre-dated? Otherwise she would have to tell Hugo and he might make a scandal. Above all she feared Arthur getting to know. 'She will not, if she can help it', wrote Wilfrid, 'give up her husband or her children or her friend.'

Yet such was Wilfrid's power over her that during a second camping excursion into the sandhills, comprising Hugo, the governess in a Margate Sands straw boater, the children, Frederic Harrison, a host of Arab servants and Mary herself (in an English riding-coat and top boots, white blanket over her head and white umbrella, green-lined), Wilfrid made her sleep with him until the Scorpion had risen on the horizon.

I would not allow Mary to share her tent with Hugo, as that would not have been proper, Suleyman and all the Arabs know that she is my Bedouin wife, and I would not hear of it. So Mary and Judith had one tent to themselves, and Hugo and Harrison the other, while I slept under a bush a little apart, where Mary could come to me as in the night of our honeymoon.[10]

Frederic Harrison, a stocky figure with a loud voice who enjoyed sliding down sandhills because they reminded him of the Alps, gives an idyllic picture of Sheykh Obeyd.[11] The tomb in the garden, the ruined well; the rustling pods of acacia, the olives, apricots, roses; the first meal of dates and hot fresh camel's milk taken lounging in cane divans on the flat roof, shaded by the giant lebbek tree;* the surrounding Bible lands – Matarieh where the fleeing Virgin Mary washed Jesus' napkins, Goshen, where they camped on the site of Potiphar's house and Harrison asked, 'Blunt, are you Joseph?'; Lady Elcho and Lady Anne dressed like Roxana and Fatima, Judith like the Queen of Sheba; above all, the Sultan of Morocco as impersonated by Blunt – 'Allah! Biswallah! Sheykh!' saluted Harrison – and the fierce, lacerated sunrise behind Sinai.

* Blunt's great tree, around which he had built his house, was probably *Albizia Lebbek*, as described by Mary Stout, *Gardening in Egypt* (Egyptian Horticultural Society, 1935): 'the best known shade tree in Egypt . . . large, ornamental . . . deciduous for only a few weeks in spring . . . flowers occur with new foliage and are deliciously fragrant'.

But for Wilfrid the end was in sight. Whereas his first acrostic poem to Mary had brimmed with love – 'Mary sweetest name of any' – he now wrote gloomily, 'Make my grave here, Emira, when I die.' A visit to the Cairo Museum underlined his fate, the whole party, even himself and Mary, being dressed in smart European clothes. 'With the change of raiment, the beauty of our life here passed away like a dream and we both felt degraded, as angels must.' Next day they all sat under the lebbek tree while Judith and Mary mended Wilfrid's blue and white carpet, Mary embroidering it with a red scorpion. But the scorpion now had a sting.*[12]

Nevertheless there was to be one more 'honeymoon' for Wilfrid after Hugo returned to his Duchess, and before the end came. On 26 February they plunged into the virtually uninhabited Eastern Desert between the rugged Kalala range and the Gulf of Suez, their target the historic monastery of St Anthony. It was ironic that, of the first European women to visit the saint's retreat in fifteen hundred years, one should know so much about temptation, the other so little. For Anne had come too.

This in itself was tempting providence. Despite Anne's presence, Wilfrid tapped on Mary's tent the second night. 'It is the voice of my beloved that knocketh saying open to me, my sister, my love, my dove, my undefiled, for my head is filled with dew and my locks with the drops of the night.'

Towards morning a tremendous hot wind blew down their tents, Wilfrid discovering Mary under the debris, her mass of black hair tangled with the canvas – fortunately the canvas of her own tent not his. The tell-tale footsteps in the sand never ceased, whatever their adventures: losing their way; running out of water and food, except for a few biscuits and the apples Mary always carried in her pocket 'like a schoolboy'; freezing at night; trying not to notice the ring of black and white Egyptian vultures sitting in a circle around their camp till dark; Mary sick and perhaps in danger; wading and creeping round the narrow boulder-strewn Red Sea shore, with Wilfrid acting Perseus to Mary's Andromeda; finding 'secret nests' in the deep sand for himself and Mary, by moonlight. Before returning to Sheykh Obeyd Wilfrid lit three candles in a stony wady for Mary's safety, much as he had lit candles during Anne's pregnancies a quarter of a century ago. They arrived back exhausted after sixteen unforgettable nights and days.[13]

There was a telegram from Hugo, 'I am unhappy shall await you at home', which Mary took to mean the Duchess was dead and Hugo would reassert his marital rights. 'I dare not advise', recorded Wilfrid's diary, 'for women in such cases are wiser than men.' Mary departed on

* Blunt later added a note about his carpet: 'I have directed that I am to be buried in it.'

26 March. 'I have been sad, sad, sad, these last four days past', Wilfrid wrote on the thirtieth, 'sick and sorry of my life.'

Mary confessed to Hugo, and they both wrote to Wilfrid. He had rushed round to Mount Street on his return expecting a love-letter. Instead, Mary announced that the end had come. 'You did try and wreck my life', she wrote, 'and the only thing that prevents my being utterly angry with you is that I believe you *did care* for me in a way.' Utterly angry, however, was a fair description of Hugo's mood, and his letter Wilfrid described as 'a ferocious insult':

> You have wrecked the life and destroyed the happiness of a woman whom a spark of chivalry would have made you protect. She was thirty years younger than yourself [actually twenty-two]. You had known her from childhood. She was your cousin and your guest. She was a happy woman when she went to Egypt, and her misery now would touch a heart of stone.[14]

Both the Elchos insisted on Blunt's absolute silence henceforth; Hugo threatening to tell all if Wilfrid so much as tried to get in touch through Madeline or George Wyndham.

It would have been well for Wilfrid had he kept silence, at least throughout the first three agonized months of his return to Crabbet. but a serious illness attacked him while still in Egypt, probably the beginning of a tubercular condition that was to afflict him on and off for several years; this further lowered his morale. At the same time his daughter showed herself charmingly affectionate to her ailing father. Fatally, he succumbed to the temptation to make Judith his confidante; fatally, because she was to write afterwards in her diary of 26 December 1897 about 'the happy days before Mary Elcho and that child came to ruin my life'. Did he even tell her about the baby?

Judith told her children that he did: though he tried at first to disguise from her the full truth, dwelling only on his love for Mary, Hugo's jealousy, his own need for a go-between. When Judith burst into sympathetic tears as they walked under the spring trees of Crabbet, Wilfrid persuaded himself that she was his sister Alice over again, consoling him in these same woods for his loss of Skittles.

He got through the summer in a state of hysterical despair. It was torture when people were nice to him. 'Yes, I heard *entrancing* accounts,' said Pamela, Mary's sister (about to marry Eddy Tennant, Margot's brother), 'from Mary and the children about Egypt! She *did* enjoy it all so much'; conversely, it was unendurable when people were nasty, like Hugo cutting Judith in the street. Wilfrid had lost two stone since last year.

He tried to write a long 'romance of the 19th century', parodying the Souls, called *The Court of Love*. But he could not finish it. The final passage of its first draft, however, was to be quoted by Blunt at a symposium about Heaven, conducted verbally under the auspices of Alfred Austin, the new Poet Laureate, on his lawn at Swinford two years later. When asked for his idea of Heaven, Blunt replied:

> ... to be laid out to sleep in a garden, with running water near, and so to sleep for a hundred thousand years, then to be woke by a bird singing, and to call out to the person one loved best, 'Are you there?' and for her to answer, 'Yes, are you' and so turn round and go to sleep again for another hundred thousand years.[15]

In an otherwise generous review of Blunt's *My Diaries*, Volume I, where this passage first appeared in print, E. M. Forster used Blunt's picture of Heaven as a rod to beat him with. The quotation, argued Forster, proved that Blunt was fundamentally a lover of earthly grace, lacking that 'fiery whirlwind' which sweeps a man into eternal regions. 'The hope that the Creation may be a garden', continued Forster, 'wherein the nations and the worlds blossom sweetly each after its kind is the deepest he knows'; he cannot be classed with those who have seen 'Creation's flaming ramparts or have heard its inexpressive nuptial song'.[16]

Apart from the inevitable question – what sort of nuptial song did E. M. Forster himself hear? – it is worth pointing out that Blunt's heavenly vision was not of a gentle Sussex garden but of a wild paradise whose backcloth was indeed the 'flaming ramparts' of Mount Sinai. And when, in 1895, Blunt first described this garden of Heaven, it was not in 'exquisite hope' but in numb despair. His 'inexpressive nuptial song' – 'open to me, my sister, my dove, my undefiled' – had fallen for ever silent.

Crabbet became so distasteful to him that he let it, moving with Anne and Judith into Newbuildings, to begin yet again a 'hermit's life'. Judith's romance for Stephen Pollen came to nothing – 'Stephen cares more about his parents than about Judith' – and though Blunt had not wanted the marriage, Judith's depression added yet another black cloud to his own.*

His horses were the first of his interests to return. That autumn he was to buy a colt and filly from Poland, and more importantly, in 1896 to buy up the whole remainder of Abbas I's famous stud – six mares and four stallions. Ali Pasha Sherif had inherited the stud on Abbas' death in 1855; part he sold to King Victor Emmanuel of Italy. When on Ali Pasha Sherif's death in 1896 the Blunts acquired what was left, their Crabbet stud leapt into a class of its own. No stud in Egypt, Syria or Turkey could touch it.

* In 'Myself and Others', Judith gave a different twist to the story, as sketched above by Blunt and incidentally corroborated by letters from Emily Lytton and Stephen himself: 'My childhood's fancy' for Stephen, she wrote, 'no longer held its glamour.'

Punctuating the despair were moments of unwarranted hope. Mary's love had never quite been written off by Blunt. They met secretly on 16 August 1895 on the train from London to Brighton. Mary told Wilfrid that Hugo had been thunderstruck for three days. 'If it had been Arthur', he said, 'I could have understood it, but I cannot understand it now. I forgive you but I shall be nasty to you.' Yet he was very kind. Would he be kind to the baby? asked Wilfrid. He would not be unkind – 'would not hurt a fly' – but would take no notice of it, and nobody would remark that. Wilfrid's idea that George should be a godfather – George guessed their secret – delighted Mary. She hoped for a girl, so as not to complicate the Wemyss inheritance, 'for I know', she added, 'my own children will die as a punishment to me'.

Did Arthur know? 'He was a little jealous about me at first but he does not suspect.' Nor would anyone else trouble to compare the dates about the child's birth. Hugo had begun by fearing the Duchess' relatives would consider him heartless for returning to his wife while his mistress still lived. On the contrary, said Mary, the Fitzgeralds were grateful to Mary for her long forbearance. So Hugo had come round too. 'Now we can never either of us say anything to the other', he said. She would see Wilfrid casually, and let him see the baby when he came back from Egypt, next year.

'This has put me once again', wrote Blunt, 'into the highest of high spirits.' He made a new will, settling his property after Anne, Judith and Judith's children if any, on George and Mary, 'hoping in this way best to secure the interests of the baby that is to be. The child would be my natural heir both as my own child and as a descendant through Mary of my father's sister.'*

There was one other agreeable interlude on which, however, Blunt did not lay great stress. The child Emily was still faithful to her 'little love'. Hardly more than a week after his happy au revoir to Lady Elcho, he accepted Emily's invitation to join them at the Lockers' in Cromer. There was a visit to the sea with Emily before breakfast, followed by 'a quiet day of almost innocent love. It is pleasant to be loved like this and I do not feel it an infidelity to Mary.'[17]

And an almost quiet night? There was indeed a quiet evening when they all played the letter-game, Emily holding Blunt's hand under the table. That night, however, she heard someone trying her bedroom door. As usual when Blunt was around, it was locked. She said nothing about it next morning; instead, kissed his hand when they said goodbye, 'which I always think a true sign of love', remarked Blunt complacently. A shower of what he called 'real love-letters' from

* This was to be the first of many wills that aroused Judith's ire. As a result, she produced a story in 'Myself and Others' of Hugo's threatening to divorce Mary but being bought off by Wilfrid.

Emily quickly followed, the first dated 23 August, beginning 'Dear Thing ... I think I had better come and be a hermitess with you on Mount Sinai.' In another (3 September) of nine pages she wrote, 'Dear Thing ... You don't know how miserable I was last year when you went away. The night before you left I cried myself to sleep.' Blunt was enchanted – 'for it is sweeter to be loved even than to love'.[18] They had exchanged rings, hers to him of twisted wire, his to her a garnet from Vienna.

For he was off on his travels again. Paris. Poland. The Ukraine. Armenia. Therapia. Egypt. He had left England this year as early as 5 September, perhaps to be abroad when Mary's confinement approached. Anne saw him off. 'Goodbye my beloved', she said, a word he had never heard before from her.

Sweeter to be loved. ...

It was the Eastern studs rather than Eastern politics that carried Wilfrid through the autumn, though his cousin Sir Philip Currie, now ambassador to the Porte, had a good deal to say about Egypt, Armenia and the Russian nihilists. His view on Egypt was, no evacuation – '*never*' – though Britain might one day be driven out. The cousins talked at dinner happily with Angelina, now Lady Currie, between them. 'I have always maintained', wrote Wilfrid, 'that it is a great bond between men to have loved the same woman – have loved, in the past tense.'

He was away again in October to see the Upper Nile after a fortnight in his Sheykh Obeyd hermitage. 'Dearest Anne', he had written, 'Here I am, a real hermit at last, sitting alone in my Shish [upper room] like a white blackbird in its cage.'[19]

On the return journey, at Aswan, there was a message from Judith. Mary had a splendid girl with thick black hair. 'For a moment I had an Arab pang of disappointment', confessed Blunt, 'that it was not a boy.' He had dreamt on 30 October (it was born on the twenty-fourth) of a wonderful black-eyed son. Wilfrid hoped the baby would be called Zobeydeh. But she was to be little Mary; 'the family baby', wrote George tactfully, since the godparents were nearly all Wyndham relations. Her mother wrote on 9 December that she was 'very knowing very temperful and quite fascinating ... highly stringed', according to the nurse. Her huge glittering black eyes looked one through and through, as if she were 'gazing fearlessly across the desert'.

The child was ten months old before Wilfrid set eyes on her. It was carefully planned that while Hugo was away ('a meeting might be very terrible', wrote Mary) she and Wilfrid should drive to the Rising Sun at Cleeve Hill, near Cheltenham, where the nurse and baby would be awaiting them. All Wilfrid carried away from this emotive meeting was the memory of two black eyes in a sunburnt little face following him with a friendly stare round the inn parlour – and a bill of three shillings and ninepence for a baby's hair-brush. Nevertheless – 'I kissed its little face ... and told it how beautiful it was. ... It is something to have lived for such a moment as this.' On leaving the Rising Sun he was asked by the proprietress to sign her visitors' book. He scribbled his name he hoped illegibly in pencil, giving his address as Bath.

Mary Elcho was already pregnant again. Unless the new baby was Arthur's (which Wilfrid thought improbable) 'he' – Arthur – 'must be something more or less than a man'. A few days later Mary gave her own explanation: 'Arthur is not jealous', she said, 'you know he is not like other men.'[20]

Scarcely a year after little Mary's birth, the blonde Ivo was born, Hugo's youngest son. 'The new baby is the most hideous little monster imaginable, ignoble, pale, with wandering weak blue eyes and an idiotic stare, palpably legitimate', wrote Wilfrid. But as the two children grew up together, one dark, the other fair, Wilfrid had to admit that they made a dazzling pair.

Not a single hour of his daughter's childhood was to be spent in any of her natural father's homes, despite his pleadings. A notification of a children's tea-party at which she would be present occasionally came his way; or he could watch her shooting toy arrows with her half-brother in Belgrave Square. If he wrote to her mother – which he often did, in protest – the letters must never go to the Elchos' town or country addresses, in case Hugo saw the handwriting. 'There's a letter to you from Wilfrid, Mary, extraordinary fellow that he is!' said Percy Wyndham one day to his daughter; 'why doesn't he write to you at your own house?'[21]

And so the secret was kept. Wilfrid drew what comfort he could from Mary's rare concessions to affection in her letters. She was still his 'Bedouin wife', she would sometimes write, putting kindness before truth.

If the child's birth in the autumn of 1895 brought no immediate happiness to Blunt, it helped indirectly to break up his own family life.

Judith was bitterly jealous of Mary; what more natural than that she should turn from the father who had thrown her over to her now 'best friend', Emily Lytton? Indeed there is reason to believe that Judith's love for Emily equalled or excelled anything that she was to feel for a man. Suddenly a horrific idea dawned on her. The adored father, whose love for herself Judith had had to relinquish to another, was reappearing on the scene as her own rival. Blunt noted sadly on returning to England in the spring of 1896 that Emily's 'little love' seemed to have exhausted itself, since she had not answered his last two letters. What had happened?[22]

We know that Judith was sent by her father to look at baby Mary and report. Judith's feelings as go-between must have been painful enough, especially if we accept the accuracy of her diary entry some two years later, when she referred to her early discovery of her father's adultery: 'After I found him on her bed at El Keyshi's, H.F.'s new pretence was threadbare.' The same diary entry of Judith's, however, goes on to recall an even more poignant element in the situation. For she linked up the blow of her father's adultery with a new development on the Emily front. 'Even his confession', wrote Judith, 'might have failed to alienate us but for Emily's amazing confession that she was going to elope with him to Paris at the same time', that is, in the same year 1895. 'My frustration of this plan is a crime for which I have forfeited my birthright and my blessing.'

There is nothing improbable in Judith's story. That Emily, like so many other ladies, wanted to join Blunt 'on Mount Sinai' was well known to all, including Lady Lytton, who finally put her foot down, saying Emily must stay with the Gerald Balfours in Ireland and 'find herself a husband'.

But the elopement to Paris? Blunt had indeed suggested to Emily a week in Paris 'some day'. What more natural than that he should travel to Paris in 1895 to meet this twenty-year-old girl, Judith's friend, and bring her on to Egypt?

But here Judith's friend had reckoned without Judith. The instant Emily confided in her, Judith acted. Did Emily really believe she was Wilfrid's one true love? Out came the story of his love-affair at El Kheysheh, with no doubt a mention of the baby. 'This naturally made Emily extremely angry', wrote Judith in 'Myself and Others', 'and crashed the whole scheme.'

The end of the story is told partly by Emily herself with the charm of transparent honesty, in her remarkable book, *A Blessed Girl* (1953). When Wilfrid returned to England, still sore at Judith's suspected 'treachery' of the previous autumn, Emily again found herself in his toils. Judith therefore confronted him in May 1896, 'out of pure love and friendship' for Emily, not only with the Paris plan but also with the episode of the bedroom door at Cromer. Some sixty years later, Emily was to remember that he had been 'staggered' by this latter revelation, never guessing that she had seen the door-handle move. His magic for her finally departed when he exculpated himself by letter, blaming her for their three years' entanglement.

Judith, in her diary for 1897, was to describe her actual confrontation:

H.F. told me I was a fool to interfere and I am not sure he wasn't right. He boasted that it would have done Emily all the good in the world – she wasn't pretty enough to get much of a husband and wasn't likely to get such a chance again.

Judith, whose passion for her father was never entirely to cool, thought that his 'monstrous conceit' as exemplified here, did contain 'a substratum of truth'.

How wrong they both were. Emily found herself a brilliant husband that very summer. The future architectural genius and creator of imperial New Delhi, Sir Edwin Lutyens (Ned), fell in love with her at a party because she looked 'so cross and unhappy'.[23] They were married at Knebworth on 4 August 1897, Wilfrid giving her a necklace of moonstones, for which she thanked 'Dear Mr. Blunt' politely. There was no one to console Judith for looking just as 'cross and unhappy'.

H.F. could not forgive her, she wrote in 'Myself and Others', for thwarting his plans with Emily, 'and from that day he and I could never trust one another again'. He put her under a ban not to approach him. When Anne accused her of coldness, Judith dared not tell her mother the true reason, 'for fear of breaking her heart'.

Partly to get this unhappy daughter out of the way, partly to get an heir to his Sussex squiredom, H.F. renewed his campaign for Judith's marriage. Anyone would do, provided they had some breeding: Lord Alfred Douglas, the immediate cause of 'poor Oscar's' spell in Reading gaol; an ancient bewhiskered French marquis, cast-off lover of Princess Wagram; even the eccentric Maurice Baring seemed to catch her father's eye as a possible son-in-law. Lady Lytton contributed the suggestion of young Lord Beauchamp: 'I wish I could be a fairy', she wrote, 'and arrange for him to marry Judith.' 'Fairy' was at least the right word.* There was nothing wrong with marrying 'a respectable dummy', her father had told Judith, 'and waiting for happiness till the other man appears'.

Blunt's diary confirms Judith's account of their estrangement. He concluded bitterly:

> What I resent in the matter is not so much the treachery, as the proof it gives of Judith's lack of affection for me, for the jealousy is not about me but about Emily. This quarrel is a most unfortunate thing; it breaks up my whole life. Emily was like a second daughter to me and here they are both gone. I am left like Adam when Cain had killed Abel, alone at my fireside.[24]

Blunt's fireside, in fact, was rarely happy from start to finish of 1896, though a guilty conscience does not seem to have been among the

* Lord Beauchamp later had to flee the country.

disturbing influences. Fireside peace was not enhanced by Anne's growing impatience with Wilfrid's vocal anti-imperialism. She had a daughter to marry off. Wilfrid, on the contrary, was becoming more extreme. On his next desert exploration he withheld his maps from the Royal Geographical Society, on the ground that it was 'the instrument of Europe's penetrations and conquests against the wild races of mankind'.[25] What had happened, he demanded, after King Menelik and his wild Abyssinians defeated the Italians at Adowa that spring? Why, Kitchener penetrated to Dongola, as a white man's diversion to help the aggressor.

'Misfortunes never rain but they pour', he wrote in June of the domestic front. His son Berkeley Sumner – by now a handsome blond sailor – came to see him for the first time; but only because his illegitimacy, discovered that spring, was in danger of causing a family scandal. Thanks mainly to George Wyndham's advice, a satisfactory solution was reached. Berkeley renounced the Sumner money in exchange for £250 allowance from Blunt and payment of his debts. Wyndham had also persuaded Blunt not to admit paternity publicly but to let Berkeley follow the precedent of their cousin Alfred Montgomery. Though known to be the Marquis Wellesley's son, Alfred had never taken his father's name.

Blunt was now prepared to enjoy a son at last. 'I have lost confidence in Judith as an "eldest son"', and Berkeley came 'like a chance plank in a shipwreck'. He even told Anne about him. She kissed him, 'an unusual thing', saying she had 'long done fretting about such matters'. All she wanted was to know all.

'I hope you have no more skeletons in your cupboard', she added.

'I have many skeletons.'[26]

Alas, Berkeley Sumner was not to become the consoling 'skeleton' Blunt had hoped. Whenever the young man tried to communicate with his natural father by letter he floundered in confusion, unable to marshal his thoughts. At twenty-four he ought to be able to express himself. At least Judith's faults were not intellectual. 'He is a good fellow but I am afraid a fool.'

A final blow of that year was the death of William Morris on 3 October. Blunt composed one of his perfect appreciations – honest, feeling, original – later picked out by E. M. Forster for special praise:

> He is the most wonderful man I have known [wrote Blunt], unique in this, that he had no thought for any thing or person, including himself, but only for the work he had in hand. . . . He liked to talk to me because I knew how to talk to him, and our fence of words furbished his wit, but I doubt if he would have crossed the street to speak to me. . . . I should say half-a-dozen were all the friends he had. I do not count myself among the number, intimate as I was with him and much as I loved him. . . .[27]

With Morris, and perhaps only Morris, Blunt found it 'sweetest to love'.*

He called at once on Janey, lying as usual on her sofa in her blue shawl, her hair pure white. He kissed her; the first time for several years. (Her last invitation to love had been in 1894 when she left a pansy in his bedroom at Kelmscott Manor, but he ignored its message.) She said now: 'I am not unhappy, though it is a terrible thing, for I have been with him since I first knew anything. I was eighteen when I married but' – and she repeated her earlier confession to Blunt – 'I never loved him.'†

Blunt lent her his Mount Street flat and had her and May Morris to stay at El Kheysheh. It was not a success. Neither of the ladies rode, though Janey tried, and the sand was too deep for walking. Twice a day Blunt would visit them indoors, finding the socialist May 'a most obstinately silent woman'.

Judith found her worse. She wore a transparent yellow chintz dress and lorgnettes; but at any rate not knickerbockers, as in London, where Judith heard she tricycled about the streets despite the catcalls of urchins – 'I suppose *he's* in bed, ma'm, while you've got 'em on.' The Morris ladies bored the Blunts and, wrote Blunt, 'I fear they are likely to be a little bored by us. . . . I cannot make love to either of them, and what else is there to be done?'

What else indeed? One November morning Blunt saw a mottled body with flat head lying inert in the sand under his window. A venomous snake! He rushed down to kill it. It was a cactus. 'Such are the hallucinations which come of complete idleness', said Judith. But the malaise went deeper than that. Paradise had eluded him again. He was left as a mere character in romantic poetry. William Morris had given him his Kelmscott *Morte d'Arthur*, and he saw himself as an echo of Sir Lancelot:

> His search for 'worshippe' in the world; his secret backslidings on the one count of love; his quest of the Sangreal made abortive through his sin; his repentance; his return to love; the woes it wrought; the destruction of his 'fellowship'; his separation, in spite of their love, from his Queen; and after the great tragedy, his retirement to an 'ermytage', where his life ends. I am more than ever determined that the last act of his drama shall also be mine.[28]

* (FM 354/1975, 5 October 1896.) 'Reading this over while transcribing my journal', Blunt noted in 1911, 'I feel that the judgment given in it of Morris's lack of tenderness is too hard a one. Nevertheless I leave it as I wrote it, for it was my thought at the time.'

† Janey seems to have changed her mind. Blunt wrote in his diary of 10 August 1903: 'Of Morris she said that, though selfish in little things, in great ones he was most magnanimous, the least selfish of men. After all, she said, I suppose if I was young again I should do the same again.'

Soon afterwards Ralph Lovelace, Anne's brother, lent him the Byron letters. So he became a shadow of Lord Byron, the lover who wrote, 'I never could love but that which loves' – Judith his 'moral Clytemnestra', Mary his incestuously beloved Augusta, Emily his Clare Clairmont before her fall.

And now here he was beating a plant to death, tilting at windmills. This must stop.

PART III

'Old Age in Meditation'

[17]
'Poor Wicked Century, Farewell!' *1897–1900*

No diarist was ever more aware of changing times than Wilfrid Blunt. Indeed, as the run-up to the twentieth century began, he accelerated the rate of change, like a child playing a pianola-roll at double speed. He half-envisaged his own end as part of the *fin de siècle*. He almost welcomed it. The setting was to be the Western Desert, somewhere in the Senussi kingdom, around Siwa. Or perhaps as far afield as Tripoli or Benghazi. It was to take 'forty days at least', forty days in the wilderness, 'and there is just a little risk in it, especially as I am far from well'.[1]

But what was there to make life precious? He and his friend Mohammed Abdu had a disillusioned talk. Life in Cairo was worse than it had ever been. Even in the bad old days of Ismail, 'there was a good deal of liberty of thought and speech'. As for Constantinople, things had never been so shocking. 'But all the old-fashioned ideas of liberty and humanity are fast disappearing from the world. Abdu and I find ourselves almost alone in our views.'[2]

If Blunt did not actually expire in the desert, he might rediscover the Islam that civilization had tainted. Better still, he might establish there that permanent desert hermitage of which he and Terence Bourke had dreamed.

The dangers were to be such as he had never conceived of, quite apart from his own ill health, depression and reckless mood. It was the season of Ramadan, not a propitious moment for a white man to penetrate the wilder Muslim tribes. Nor did Blunt have adequate guides. Setting off on 5 February 1897 with personal equipment of under £55, three guns, his mare Yemama and the Scorpion carpet-shelter, he camped the first night in the sand between the Pyramids and the fashionable Mena Hotel, 'nobody recognizing me'; for he was in Arab dress. Next day he rode up the green Nile valley to the right of the Step Pyramid at Saccara. The first desert sheykh whom Blunt met, Abdallah Minjowar, a dear old friend, furnished him with two Harabi guides, Beseys and Minshawi, strict Muslims of the *Tarik* order, and also with letters of introduction to the same religious brotherhood at Jarabub; so impressed was Abdallah with Blunt's religious vocation.

In the letters of credence Abdallah described Blunt as an Arab, one Naif, a son of Hajji Mahmud of Aleppo. 'I do not like this', wrote Blunt of the deception.[3] But he was assured it was necessary, since the Muslim brotherhood hated all Europeans, and to appear undisguised would be courting 'real danger'. As it happened, Blunt had once met the real Hajji Mahmud's father, Hajji Batran, in Aleppo. He must try to impersonate the latter's grandson.

All seemed to go well. They reached a miraculous spring on the thirteenth whose stream, said his guides, would water any number of camels if you just called out to it, 'Ha, ha, ha, ha, ha!' That sounded cheerful. Three days later they lost their road, so absorbed was old Beseys in advising Blunt about his Muslim 'vocation'. Beseys in fact was useless as a guide; he had not been on this road for over forty years. Blunt got his guides back on to the road by following a hyena track.

At this point Beseys devised a more complicated disguise for Blunt. He should be a kinsman both to Sidi el Kader of Damascus and Hajji Batran of Aleppo, travelling to see his relatives in Benghazi. Another two days, and Beseys's assistant Arab guide decamped, Minshawi replacing him by a black Sudanese slave named Osman. Unfortunately Osman had only once travelled this road before, twenty-five years ago, and that at night, in the opposite direction, when escaping from Asia. He did not tell Blunt this.

On the twenty-first they were hopelessly astray again and in a bad way. Once more it was Blunt himself who saved the party, but through a fortunate accident. He mistook some distant black stones on the barren shining plain for *tarfa* bushes in the Sittarah oasis. By sheer luck, however, the black stones were not far from the great caravan route to Siwa.

They arrived at the Senussi monastery of Zeytoun in the Siwa oasis on the twenty-sixth, after yet another agonizing spell of helpless thirsty wandering, Blunt calling on all his saints from St Winifred to Sheykh Obeyd. The Senussi monks were friendly. Should he settle for their Muslim order? But he went on to camp just outside the town of Siwa on the twenty-seventh – the preliminary to 'a day of disasters'.

Ominous signs had in fact appeared that night, though Blunt did not fully recognize them. Two factions from Siwa came to call on him under cover of darkness, the first from the eastern, the second from the western town. Beseys rashly invented yet another identity for Blunt, telling the Westerners – already suspicious – that he was a certain Sakr, from Nejd. The Siwans went on questioning, Blunt stalling. In the night his precious Scorpion carpet was stolen.

At dawn Blunt's personal servant Suleyman excitedly announced an iminent *ghazu*. Immediately Beseys and his friends vanished, leaving Blunt alone with the faithful Suleyman and Osman to face 200 armed men from the western town. The three travellers were knocked about, Blunt's tent being pulled down over his head, his weapons seized, his clothes torn off in a search for money – "the drachmas, the money! you have a thousand? you have two thousand?' – all amid the hubbub of shouting men, roaring camels, neighing horses, the clash of antique swords, clatter of old-fashioned blunderbusses and every other kind of 'impossible weapon'. Blunt was beaten over the head and his cheek gashed by some of the very men who had visited him the night before and drunk of his coffee.

As luck would have it, he had just been reading Charles Doughty's Arabian travels. His advice for an emergency was to 'remain passive'. Blunt therefore kept his temper, simply clutching one of the sheykh's cloaks as an act of surrender; '*ana dahilak*' – 'I am your prisoner'. He was borne captive into Siwa, his head wrapped in other cloaks to save him from further battering. A chorus of triumphant women greeted him from every housetop: 'Ulu – lu – lu – lu!'

After appearing first before the governor in the council chamber and then in the police office, Blunt gradually, with many furtive and humiliating whispers that he was an Englishman, succeeded in making his position clear. His servants and property trickled back, including Beseys, but not his money or the Persian sword presented to him by Mohammed Ibn Aruk at Tudmur; and only one of his guns. But Ramadan was ending; and so were his troubles. He afterwards blamed the Senussi fanaticism on their internal factions (in which they suspected Blunt of being involved because of his disguise) and on Ramadan, which drove them 'mad'. At last on 3 March he was allowed to leave Siwa, and after many forced marches, doggedly relying on his own compass and sense of direction, his guides in open dissent, he saw the welcome dome and huge keep of the westernmost Coptic monastery at Wady Natrun, 'a good bit of navigation'. He was home in Sheykh Obeyd on St Patrick's Day, 17 March, after exactly forty days in the wilderness.

These auspicious Christian landmarks should have headed off Blunt from Islam and redirected him to his old faith. They were not enough, however, to offset the general anti-religious effect of his rough 'Ride to Siwa'. He laughingly referred to his disaster of 28 February as the Battle of Jupiter Ammon, in memory of Siwa's nearby Roman temple. But what was the good of an Islam reformed along the Mahdi's lines, if it produced the 'mere madness' of Siwa? 'I had made myself a romance about these reformers', he wrote in retrospect on 24 March, 'but it has no substantial basis . . . The less religion in the world perhaps, after all, the better.'[4]

That last sentence has often been quoted by Blunt's humanist admirers, such as E. M. Forster and Edith Finch his biographer, the future wife of Bertrand Russell. They take it to be Blunt's final verdict on the subject of religion. On the contrary, religion was to pursue him like the 'Hound of Heaven' in the poem written by one he was later to know, Francis Thompson: 'I fled him down the nights and down the days . . .' Blunt's apparent conclusion – 'the less religion in the world the better' – must not be wrenched from context, but seen as an angry reaction to the Battle of Jupiter Ammon.

A further reaction on Blunt's part to the Siwa débâcle was an aggressive call on Lord Cromer. How dared the Egyptian Government claim suzerainty over the Senussia? They should either keep order or clear out.

Cromer returned as good as he got. It was all Blunt's own fault: he ought never to have gone to Siwa. He ought not to have consulted Abdallah. He ought to have gone in English dress. It was all 'most inopportune', since the Senussi chiefs were traditionally friendly to Britain.[5]

At any rate, Blunt got back his Scorpion carpet.

It looked at last as if Blunt were going to make his exit from the nineteenth century in a low key. Women seemed not to excite him.

> Here I feel an absolute calm as one no longer interested . . . even about Mary I have somehow grown indifferent, she has not written and I do not care. The smaller pleasures of living interest me more than the greater ones and I am content to abdicate.[6]

Chronic indigestion assisted Blunt towards abdication, the first attacks having been brought on by the thirst, starvation and general hardships of Siwa. His weight had fallen from fourteen stone six pounds in 1895 to ten stone ten now, exactly the same as when he had first come to London as a boy of eighteen. 'The thought of dying does not trouble me', he wrote on 1 May 1897, 'but the pain of it is wearisome and I am glad of any relief.'

His condition justified Dr Philpot in providing relief through morphia. Other sources of content were Anne's quiet company, and a new pied-à-terre at Caxtons, a pretty, half-timbered sixteenth-century cottage in a lane near Crabbet. 'I have long wished to occupy a real labourer's cottage and this is precisely one.' Its last labouring occupant, Bates the estate forester, had hanged himself in the cart shed. The dead never haunted Wilfrid; indeed 'poor old Bates' death-shed was later re-erected at Fernycroft in Hampshire, another new pied-à-terre of Blunt's.

The Stud itself was the supreme source of comfort, 'which never diminishes and keeps us young'. There were months of special satisfaction when Wilfrid succeeded in saving the life of one of the Ali Sherif brood mares, after three of them stampeded and Bint Helwa broke her leg. 'She was the most beautiful of all', wrote Wilfrid, 'and I would infinitely sooner my own leg had been broken.' Sam Webb the stud groom was for shooting her. But Wilfrid sent for the vet and insisted on his setting the leg, using the bark of a young elm as a splint, and 'hanging her' from a stable beam for over nine months. As it happened, she had been served by Mesaoud ten days before the accident. In due course she produced a fine filly foal, and later seven other foals during the remaining ten years of her crippled but valuable life.[7]

A final cause for quiet content was financial. Wilfrid's own income was £3,300 a year net, and Anne's £3,500. 'We therefore live now well within our income, a happy state of things which never used to be the case.' He was encouraged to apply to the Somerset Herald for permission to represent the Scawen family, and to quarter the Scawen arms with his own. 'George thinks it should be done.'

There is some evidence that George Wyndham was responsible for Wilfrid's re-occupation of his throne in the Court of Love. King Arthur and his Round Table were much in vogue among the Souls; George had written lyrically to his cousin about 'an enchanted land of Arthurian romance', called St Fagan's Castle, near Cardiff, the home of Lord and Lady Windsor. 'The house is Elizabethan with gables', continued George, 'built within the enceinte of a Norman fortress, there is a pleasance and terraces and fishponds, and mazes of cut yews.' Next year, 1896, without actually saying he was in love, George told Wilfrid he had never been so happy in his life – 'which', noted Wilfrid, 'generally means the same thing.'[8]

By 1897 Wilfrid was securely re-established in the bosom of the cousinship. He was a guest, for instance, at Madeline Wyndham's birthday party on 20 June, where he formed a 'ring' with Mary Elcho, Sir Edward Burne-Jones and Arthur Balfour – the last 'thickened and reddened till he looks quite the country squire'. Two days later Lady Windsor invited him to stay at St Fagan's for a week. 'In the wilderness where my heart now is', wrote Blunt, 'this seems a pleasant oasis if not the goal I sought.'

He arrived resplendent in white, drawn by four Arabians, on 10 August. Present at St Fagan's were Walburga ('Wally') Lady Paget, Gay Windsor's German mother married to the diplomat Sir Augustus Paget, and three bare-footed Windsor children. The whole family were vegetarians, kept early hours (breakfast at seven-thirty, bed at ten) and were addicted to 'air baths'. Dressed all in white, Gay Windsor took Wilfrid for an evening walk. She confessed to having read his *Proteus* sonnets as a girl, until they were removed from her, and cross-questioned him about Mary Elcho's visit to Sheykh Obeyd, half promising to come herself. Wilfrid hardly knew where this new friendship would lead, 'but it must surely lead to something'. It might have led to rivalry with George Wyndham.

Meanwhile Wilfrid spent a happy week debating with Gay the merits of love as against friendship between the sexes. She was thirty-two or three – 'the exact age of romance' – having been married off by her mother at eighteen; tall, still slight, fair with wide pathetic eyes. Wilfrid understood that George had been an unsuccessful wooer. 'I must ask her however about this before we go further, for I am determined to establish this love, if love it is to be, upon a sure footing.' But when he enquired she became negative: 'I will be a true and faithful friend to you', she said, 'but you must not expect more than this, perhaps it is a defect in me that I cannot feel in any other way.' Nonplussed, Blunt wrote in his diary:

> Friendship plain and simple with a woman is to me an impossibility. It is not that in theory I should not delight in such a friendship, I have often wished for one but in practice and in spite of all goodwill I find it freezes me. If I do not make love, I don't know what to do or say and she is bored and I am bored and insensibly the friendship and all else withers away.[9]

Next day Gay was dressed in white again (she had worn black the day before, to reject him) and they agreed to visit Jerusalem and Damascus together. 'She loves me' – because he reminded her of her adored father.

Wilfrid wrote for Gay Windsor what he considered to be his best poem, an Arabic form of prose with rhymed endings:

> Ghost of the beautiful past, of the days long gone,
> of a queen, of a fair sweet woman.
> Ghost with the passionate eyes, how proud, yet not too
> proud to have wept, to have loved, since to love
> is human.[10]

That autumn he prepared a vegetarian dinner for Gay in Mount Street – spinach, cauliflower and sago pudding – but he had to eat it alone. She did not come. Nor did she visit Sheykh Obeyd that winter. Her letters petered out. 'Something has gone wrong, I know not what ...' The something was George. In July of the following year, George and Gay stayed together at Newbuildings. Wilfrid sent them into the woods alone to read Swinburne, while he took old Weatherby of

Tattersalls to see the mares. 'I promised George long ago that I would do my best to further his designs.'

The politics of 1897 demanded of Blunt patience and self-control rather than self-sacrifice. There was no sparkle for him in the Queen's Diamond Jubilee. Mary Elcho had arranged to meet him at the Achilles Statue in Hyde Park, but the crowds of 'ridiculous sightseers' were so dense that he caught a glimpse only of Mary's parents, her sons and cousin Dorothy Carleton. Blunt 'shed tears of rage'. He celebrated Jubilee Day itself, 22 June, by retiring in one of his Egyptian tents on Chanctonbury Ring, with his servants David and Sam. At least the ninety-seven surrounding bonfires, one at Newbuildings, were 'inspiriting'.

Blunt detected the hand of Queen Victoria in the Report on the Jameson Raid, 'the most scandalous ever jobbed'. It was she no doubt who had managed the whitewashing of Cecil Rhodes. 'She is pleased with her title of Empress, and likes to enlarge her Imperial borders. I should not indeed be at all surprised if she was really in the Jameson affair with her ministers. How else explain the connivance of the Liberal opposition?'

However, George Wyndham was able to convince his cousin that it was not the Queen but he himself who had been so clever; forcing Chamberlain's hand into the support of Rhodes, capturing old Harcourt, bamboozling the 'stupid M.P.s'. So Blunt turned his invective against a political era that could seduce a young man like George, 'the heir of all the ages', into joining such a 'scoundrel crew'.

He saw no good in the Queen's Speech of 1898. 'There were the usual lies.' In his published *My Diaries* he was persuaded to change 'lies' into 'insincerities'. But subsequent events were to show that the word 'lies' had been nearer the truth. For what else were all those protestations of peace and goodwill but 'lies', in a year that was to see Omdurman and Fashoda?

The news of Omdurman, fought on 2 September, reached Blunt on the sixth. His 'bile rose', and he dashed off a furious letter to *The Times* which was printed, to his astonishment, on the tenth. Denouncing the unspeakable slaughter of dervishes,* he exposed the pretext of avenging General Gordon, that true Christian who loved above all the coloured races. Saddest of ironies was the death of *The Times'* own correspondent, Hubert Howard, adventurous young son of Rosalind Carlisle, the only man for whom Blunt cared in Kitchener's ferocious army. (Button had told Blunt that 'a heavy butcher's bill' had been ordered.)

* The final figures were some 20,000 dervish casualties to 482 British and allied – 40 to 1. (P. Ziegler, *Omdurman*, p. 216.)

Among the courageous sympathizers with Blunt's letter – for the whole country had 'gone mad with lust of fighting' – was old Percy Wyndham, George's father. But Percy had to cut the letter from his copy of *The Times* at Clouds, lest his house-guest Princess Christian, daughter of Queen Victoria, should see it, 'so bloodthirsty are the Royal Family'.

Next month came the showdown with France over Fashoda, the disputed military post on the White Nile. Again Blunt's bile rose as Tories, Liberals, Radicals, Churchmen, Nonconformists all combined to extol English virtue and denounce French greed. But what could you expect when 'Imperial plunder' was in question? There was no more difference between England and France, in Blunt's opinion, than between two highwaymen or two cardsharpers. He had it out with George Wyndham on 17 October. With 'brutal frankness', George told Wilfrid that the purpose of all African operations, whether French or English, was to 'civilize' Africa in the interests of Europe, the only argument being about who should 'civilize' where. Britain intended, come what might, to possess the Nile. 'It is not worth while drawing distinctions of right or wrong', added George; 'it is a matter entirely of interest.' Africa's interest would be best served, thought Blunt, if the two civilizing powers should 'bash each other's heads'.[11]

One unexpected result of Blunt's letter to *The Times* about Omdurman was a flattering approach from Herbert Spencer. So much moved had the humanist philosopher been that he invited Blunt to write a diatribe in verse against Church and State, making Satan the hero. During the course of literary negotiations, Blunt visited Spencer at Brighton, having been warned by letter that the philosopher had taken to his bed many years ago, worn out by brain-work; Blunt must dine alone, since his host dared not add the burden of 'table conversation' to their other talks. Blunt found the old hypochondriac unimpressive. Nevertheless Spencer's suggestion did bring forth Blunt's dramatic poem, 'Satan Absolved: a Victorian Mystery'.

In the poem Satan calls the attention of the Lord God (represented by Blunt as an ignorant fuddy-duddy) to the appalling crimes committed in his name by the white man: animals slaughtered for pleasure, birds for their plumage, the earth scorched and wasted, primitive peoples maimed and enslaved. Today the poem reads as an early, spirited plea for conservation:

> The wise amorous seal
> He flayeth big with young: the walrus cubs that kneel
> But cannot turn his rage, alive he mangleth them,
> Leaveth in breathing heaps; outrooted branch and stem.

Impressive also was his lampooning of the Anglo-Saxon achievement:

> ... His Mansion House funds floated, alms economised,
> His hospitals, museums, baths, parks, workhouses,
> And that last glorious marvel, his free Daily Press.
> A wonderful Saxon truly, each day interviewed
> By his own wondering self and found exceeding good.

Most successful of all was his attack on the British Empire, with its allegedly God-given mission

> To bear the 'White Man's Burden', which he yearns to take
> On his white Saxon back for his white conscience sake.

Satan promptly exposes the whole solemn imposture:

> Their poets who write big of the 'White Burden'. Trash!
> The White Man's Burden, Lord, is the burden of his cash.*

Blunt never wrote lines more genuinely impassioned or effective. They got under the skin of his contemporaries, particularly as the poem was published during the Boer War. As a result it was savagely mauled in the press. One reviewer was amazed that gentlemen like Mr Spencer and Mr Watts had allowed their names to be associated with such 'puerile logic and indifferent literary workmanship'. (The poem was dedicated to Spencer, and G. F. Watts had designed the frontispiece.) The *Athenaeum* pronounced it queer, offensive, flatly blasphemous and stinking. The *Hastings Western Mail* was saddened that a Sussex squire with a charming wife and famous stud could write anything so 'cumbrous, incongruous and unconvincing'. Mr Blunt's rhymes appalled the *Pall Mall Gazette*: 'God' rhymed with 'wood', 'stop' with 'hope'. Only *The Times* and *Glasgow Herald* were reasonably friendly, the former seeing in it 'a great deal of terrible truth'. An obvious criticism was made by Wilfrid Lawson:

> Your work on the Devil, dear Blunt, I have read,
> What a curious fancy to enter your head.
> The world, I admit, is as bad as can be,
> But how *he'll* make it better I scarcely can see.[12]

And what of Blunt's own record on those blood-sports for which Satan so violently condemned Man – Blunt, the crack shot of Crabbet?

* *Poetical Works* vol II, 'Satan Absolved'. Kipling had published his 'Take up the White Man's Burden' in 1898, as an antidote to his Jubilee poem 'Recessional', which might be misunderstood.

His sensibilities were too fine not to be aware of this dilemma. He solved it, but only to his moderate satisfaction:

> While birds and beasts who do not harm man have a right to be left in absolute peace, those we help to breed by giving them protection may fairly pay a certain tribute, just as tame beasts are made to do – though the higher law would be to let *all* live.[13]

Since Siwa, he had remained obstinately irreligious; so much so, that when he met W. B. Yeats for the first time on 1 April 1898 he reacted to Yeats's spiritual experiments with extreme scepticism.

Yet the moment a painful illness struck him, on the sixth, Blunt made a bee-line for St Winifred's miraculous well, Holywell in Cheshire, admitting to himself that his feelings about religion, though illogical, were not extinct. The deeply religious Sibell Grosvenor, George's wife, took him to the fifteenth-century shrine, since it happened to be situated on the Westminster estate. Here Wilfrid waded three times up to his chest through the chilly water (52 degrees). He slept well that night, and was still without pain next day. No pilgrim, he remarked, had probably ever washed in Holywell with less Christian faith but also with 'so little of the mocking spirit'. Hardly had he included St Winifred in his canon of prayers, however, before the saint abandoned him. From that date, 13 April, until 8 May, he was racked by such violent agony that he made another will and then 'definitely took to my death-bed'.

More important, he took a brilliant young secretary named Sydney Cockerell, a disciple of Morris, on 1 May, and a professional nurse, Elizabeth Lawrence. With the combined help of his two new attendants, of 'my dear good Cowie', David his valet and perhaps even St Winifred, he just pulled through, after breaking a blood vessel on 8 May and hovering on the brink of death for a week. By the end of the month he had graduated from a diet of iced water to 'meat of an ethereal kind' and diluted wine, 'the first that I have tasted for fifteen years'.

> I mean to live a quite different life now [he wrote], to anything I have lately lived. Eating and drinking seem to me the only true pleasures and to read and toddle about in the sun. My life is purged and clear, and here I will remain.[14]

Recognizing that St Winifred had chosen to cure him by natural rather than supernatural means, he sent her a thanksgiving note, his crutches and a cheque for £20.

Cockerell's usefulness surpassed all expectations. In return, with characteristic generosity, Blunt was to lend him £500 and give him such 'overwhelming largesse' on marriage that Cockerell thought instead of 'making the Grand Tour!'[15] Meanwhile he sorted Blunt's papers, making possible the publication of *My Diaries*, and gave him 'really new interests in life'. One was the pleasure of buying antiquarian books, among them *Gerarde's Herbal*. This in turn inspired Miss Lawrence to collect wild flowers for Blunt, which he would paint. Soon Blunt was writing verse again, notably an inscription for the scrubbed oak refectory table made by Philip Webb the architect for William Morris' former home, the Red House. Janey had presented it to Wilfrid after her husband's death.

> At this fair oak table sat...
> William Morris, whose art's plan
> Laid its lines in ample span...

Today Morris' table is still in the hall at Newbuildings, beneath Burne-Jones' tapestry, with Blunt's verses engraved on a brass plate at one end.

Perhaps it was as a result of Blunt's own illness that he felt sympathetic towards the Meynells' shy young Catholic protégé, the consumptive poet Francis Thompson. The two poets, Alice Meynell and Thompson, made 'a lugubrious pair' when Wilfrid Meynell brought them over to Newbuildings in October: she 'with her tearful voice', he 'weak-eyed red-nosed'.[16]

A point about Thompson's health that interested Blunt was the connection between inspiration and morphia. 'He has written no poetry now Meynell tells me for some years, being cured of his morphia, but he [Meynell] thinks the fountain may some day break forth again.' Did this influence Blunt in maintaining his own 'fountain' by means of the usual 'doses'? Blunt does not say. But certainly the morphia continued, Dr Philpot telling Anne to let him have 'as much as necessary'.

Another book that Cockerell bought for Blunt from William Morris' sale was a sixteenth-century edition of Malory's *Morte d'Arthur*. This treasure – he paid £35 for it – was to rekindle the flame of love.

At the end of 1898 Blunt was still too weak to travel abroad. He rented a cottage called Gorsey End near the Harcourts in Hampshire, and from Lord Montagu of Beaulieu bought another cottage called Fernycroft, deep in the New Forest. Not far away from Fernycroft lived Lady De La Warr and her highly poetical daughter Lady Margaret Sackville. Though only sixteen, Margaret had already written love-sonnets which she wanted to publish, but which her mother feared might be 'misunderstood'. Would Mr Blunt dissuade her on one of their walks by the Beaulieu river? Thus thrown together, Margaret and Wilfrid discovered their shared love for Arthurian legend – and for one another. Margaret showed him a sonnet of hers beginning, 'Arthur still lives for those who love him well.' To which Blunt replied, 'Why wait for Arthur, he too long has slept.' Here was King Wilfrid, unmistakably alive and awake, ready to satisfy her.[17]

Poems passed between the girl of sixteen and man of nearly sixty, Wilfrid considering himself passionately in love for about two months. Then the romance faltered, as far as Blunt was concerned. Like Emily, Margaret tended to mix up 'passion' in her sonnets with 'souls' and 'holiness' and a 'sanctified' future. 'Literature without love', wrote Wilfrid, 'is tiresome in a woman. . . .'

However, another Arthurian maiden was available. Madeline Wyndham had an orphaned unmarried niece on the Campbell side of her family, named Dorothy Carleton, whose home was with her and Percy at Clouds or 44 Berkeley Square. Blunt had once or twice noticed how attractive she was, 'very rosy and pretty, a true gypsy's face'. At first Dorothy was no more to Blunt than one of a pair of lively girls staying at Clouds in 1900 (the other being Dolly Paget) who were prepared to listen to his poetry-readings, ride over the Downs with him, tell ghost stories in a cave by starlight, dress up in Arab clothes for dinner and arrange sixty wax tapers round his birthday cake on 17 August. But on that birthday morning it was Dorothy to whom Blunt made a 'declaration' in a church on the Downs; it was Dorothy who made the speech in his honour; Dorothy who followed up with yearning letters; Dorothy who saw in him not Arthur nor Lancelot but Merlin the magic-maker.

Magic was precisely what Dorothy needed. She had no money or position of her own, and lived as unpaid companion to her aunt and uncle. After the Clouds visit she wrote to Blunt:

> *31 August 1900*. 'Dear Mr. Blunt, All your wonderful, lovely gifts arrived this morning – oh! they do give me such pleasure – the silky scarf and the glistening beads with their strange scent . . . you really *are* the Necromancer Merlin and much too good for me.'

Then came a visit from Dorothy and her Aunt Madeline to Fernycroft.

> *1 October 1900*. Clouds. 'Well, I shall not try to thank you, but indeed your sympathy and interest in my rather aimless existence have touched me very deeply. . . .'
>
> *5 October*. Clouds. 'Nearly midnight. Dear Merlin. . . . I have pulled down my hair, and slipped into the Arab kaftan . . . partly to get into the right spirit for writing to you. . . . I find I am more and more conscious, particularly the last year or so, of a kind of second existence, a feeling as if the outside "cloud castle" life were calling, *shouting* to me. . . ."[18]
>
> On the twenty-fourth she elaborated her dream of 'the *larger* life – as if there were something wide and splendid *outside* oneself, not the orthodox religion but an almost unimaginable beauty and nobleness and strength which *might* be lived somewhere'.

Meanwhile a tragically unromantic wedding had taken place in Cairo the winter before. Judith Blunt was now a tall, striking woman of nearly twenty-five. Her face had her father's beauty, her mother's softness. She pined for an 'ideal love'. When the Crabbet Stud swept the board with prizes at the Crystal Palace Show in 1897, Judith wrote in her diary: 'I seem to be lucky with horses whatever I may be in love!' She had in fact fallen poignantly in love with Victor Lytton.

Emily had done her best to bring her brother up to scratch. He and Judith had spent one glorious May Week at Cambridge in 1897, not at the balls, but walking, talking and reading in blissful solitude together. Why did he not propose? Anne became desperately worried at rumours of their engagement. Judith must no longer go about with him. Wilfrid felt humiliated and wrote, 'Judith is in the wrong.' In August humorous ways of committing suicide occurred to Judith; perhaps a leap off Battersea Bridge with a tombstone tied round her neck: 'Hic Jacet Amor Eternus.'

Eventually it emerged that Victor, Earl of Lytton since his father's death, would be damaged in his career if he married a Roman Catholic – at least, this was what Judith gathered from his family. Victor's widowed mother had become lady-in-waiting to Queen Victoria, so was in a position to know H.M.'s mind. And Judith, in her diary, wrote that the Queen had forbidden the banns. In 'Myself and Others' she explained that Queen Victoria did not want the daughter of a 'red hot revolutionary and ex-political prisoner' at Court.

After this catastrophe, Judith was in no mood to consider marriage. She turned down various young men, including Hubert Howard, killed subsequently at Omdurman, George Duckworth, and Stephen Pollen, who had changed his mind while in India and now proposed to her – too late.

Yet she was bored at home, and Wilfrid bored with her. Since their estrangement over Emily, they could not talk together. All he wanted of her was an heir. Unhappily for both of them, there was a delightful boy of nineteen ready and aching to make Judith happy. Neville Lytton, still an art student in Paris studying under Bonnat, fell madly in love with the girl who loved his brother and was six years his senior. For many months Neville pleaded, Judith resisted, as in this letter of 1 April 1898: 'See here my young friend! . . . I've got a code of honour in spite of my parentage! . . . So – DANGER KEEP OFF THE GRASS.'

But the dice were loaded against her. One day in July 1898 her aunt Mary Wentworth gave an At Home for her at Wentworth House in Swan Walk, Chelsea. First George Duckworth proposed to her (second time round); then George Cole; then one 'Ernest' with no surname given – the unimportance of being Ernest. At last Neville

Lytton burst into the room, proposed for the hundredth time, put his dark curly head on Judith's shoulder and dissolved into tears.

'I will think about it', she said weakly. More weakly, she told her mother in strict confidence. Beside herself with joy, Anne told Wilfrid. Before Judith realized what was happening, Pappa had put the announcement of their engagement in the paper. He had forced her hand. 'H.F. has put a match to gunpowder with a vengeance', wrote Judith.

She knew she was not in love with Neville, indeed 'there is something about his face that repels me'. His eyes were too close together, neck too short, smile too constant and light. She felt a fraud accepting photographs from Lady Lytton of Neville as a baby. 'It maddens me that nobody sees how false the whole thing is.' When Neville visited Newbuildings she told him 'he must *make* me love him'.

Added to all this, having been brought up a prude by Anne, Judith was alarmed by warnings from her friends in the Paris embassy about 'the depraved atmosphere of Parisian perverted vice in all its ingenuity'. Her main anxiety, however, was children. Having seen a cow's insides hanging out at Sheykh Obeyd, she felt sure that childbirth would mean death for her. Neville assured her they needn't have children. But how prevent them? Anne, when asked, became confused and startled ... didn't know ... better ask the doctor.

Neville approached both a Cairo doctor and French priest. The latter said there was *no* prevention; the former gave Neville things which he said were called 'French Letters' (they were to prove an abysmal failure) and consoled Judith somewhat by predicting that physically she was incapable of conception.

Twice Judith broke off the engagement. She wrote to him on 10 November of her 'dream lover' to whom 'the *Prig*' (Victor) more nearly approached than Neville, whom she loved only as a beloved friend, 'like Emmie'. But the arrival of Neville at Sheykh Obeyd, all charm and affection, temporarily shook Judith's resolve. She tried again to release herself a few days before the wedding, having written to Mrs Amy Elwin, wife of 'his Rev.' and now Judith's chief adviser, 'Amy I can't do it.' Amy, however, entreated her to go forward, as all engaged girls felt that way. On the eve of her wedding she wrote in her diary: 'If only Cowie were here she would tell me I was buying the wrong hat again and galvanize me into resistance.... Goodnight to my Dreams.' The date of the wedding was fixed for 2 February 1899, four days before Neville was twenty and Judith twenty-six. They shared a birthday.

Blunt was too ill to go abroad that winter, and had asked Lord Cromer to give his daughter away in his place. This choice seemed to Anne 'astounding'; indeed she began opposing it, since Lord Cromer had in the past 'been treated as a personal enemy'.[19] Anne never quite grasped Wilfrid's worldly side; nor the nineteenth-century separation between private and political life.

Roland Baring, Cromer's son, was best man at the ceremony at the Roman Catholic church of Zeytoun; the reception was at the British embassy. Anne slaughtered a flock of sheep to feast five villages. 'Judith looked most beautiful', she reported to her husband, adding in her diary, 'They looked the picture of happiness.' She was not to know that Judith would write during her honeymoon at El Keysheh, the Pink House: 'Who will ever give me back my dreams . . . the poetry of Love?' No Arthurian romance, no romance at all for her.

Queen Victoria at least tried to inject a little romance into the event she had helped indirectly to bring about. 'I hope the marriage of young Mr. Lytton and Miss Blunt has gone off well today. V.R.I.', she telegraphed to Cromer, expecting, said Lady Lytton, something 'gushing' in reply. Lord Cromer wired back succinctly: 'Marriage duly performed.'

Wilfrid had wished Judith and Neville 'all the happiness that *he* deserves', saying he would be present in spirit at the cutting of the cake. Judith he advised to enter matrimony 'in a spirit of enjoyment, remembering that it is for this life only, and that in Heaven there will be neither marriage nor giving in marriage'. Cowie, looking after Blunt at Newbuildings, saw only a rather bad photograph of Judith's wedding with her 'dear little face' leaving the church; it made her look black – 'not that you will be sorry', she wrote to Blunt, 'as you think all black people more beautiful than white'.[20]

The Eighteen Hundreds, as Blunt preferred to call the nineteenth century, came to an end in a series of storms. There was the final disgrace attached to Omdurman: the Mahdi's head severed from his entombed body at Kitchener's command by young Major William 'Monkey' Gordon, nephew of the avenged General, the body thrown into the Nile, the skull intended by Kitchener for an inkwell or drinking-cup, and several finger-nails reserved for White's Club. The ensuing row caused Kitchener virtually to put the blame on young Gordon. Blunt let off steam by writing the truth in defence of Bill Gordon to the *Daily News*. His letter was published, but with Kitchener's version entitled 'The True Story' printed opposite. An agitation in February 1899 to oppose Kitchener's grant of £30,000 was joined by Blunt. The agitators failed and Blunt wrote: 'An abominable world it is, an abominable century, an abominable race.'

When the Boer War broke out later in 1899, Blunt's only interest was in the fate of the blacks. They might even gain from a Dutch–English fight. 'Anything is better than the general handshaking of the great white thieves and their amicable division of the spoils.' He assured Harry Cust that Chamberlain had put Milner on to 'work the press' over the Transvaal quarrel, just as he had worked it over the 'Veiled Protectorate' in Egypt. Only a brilliant operator like Milner would capture the Liberals by selecting the franchise as the cause of war, rather than Rhodes' money-bags. Cust was shocked at Blunt's cynicism. 'A poet', he said, 'should not be so unbelieving in honesty.'

Blunt contributed £50 to a 'Stop the War' committee, though with some 'qualm of conscience'; for if the war went on for another six months it really might smash up the British Empire.[21]

On first seeing Kitchener in the House of Lords in June 1900, he hailed him as 'a big brutal fellow fitly representing modern British soldierdom'.

Kaiser William's announcement that the twentieth century would begin in the German Empire on 1 January 1900 was enough to make Blunt decide otherwise. He was also aware that 'the Moslem centuries go down to the end of the hundreds, and begin again with the year one'. So, in his diary, he treated 1900 as the last year of the nineteenth century. It was within an ace of being his own last year also.[22]

He and Anne had successfully completed a short January expedition into what he called the 'Home Desert', equipped with tents and other comforts in deference to their age – he fifty-nine, she sixty-two. This journey accomplished, Blunt prepared immediately for yet another trek, though with Cockerell and Nurse Lawrence this time, Anne having returned to London for Judith's expected baby. (The priest had scored off the doctor.)

His goal was again Mount Sinai, after twenty-five years. Together with a throng of pilgrims for the Muslim holy places, Blunt and his party boarded the Khedivial steamer *Chibine* at Suez for Tor (El Tur) down the Gulf on 8 March. The *Chibine* was predictably jampacked and stifling. At one in the morning of the ninth Blunt awoke, opened his window. He lay thinking of Sinai twenty-five years ago and 'the poor issue of our short lives'. Suddenly there were two heavy blows. An earthquake shock? No. The *Chibine* had struck a reef. Despite the intense darkness Blunt could see the foaming breakers through his window.

In the course of four days and nights shipwrecked in the Gulf of Suez, Blunt heard that a seaman had been drowned trying to launch one of the four small lifeboats and a woman and child had succumbed to thirst. On the second day Blunt finished reading Tolstoy's *Resurrection* ('most depressing'); on the third, water came into his cabin turning the indelible pencil of his diary bright purple (as it still is), so he decamped to the pilgrims' deck – no sleep at night for the eternal hammering on the reef, pilgrims praying incessantly, Blunt addressing St Winifred, 'a superstition which quiets the mind', angry pilgrims forcing the incompetent captain to send out his last boat for help with Blunt's efficient servant Suleyman in it, Blunt seeing the Scorpion towards morning ('it reminded me of many things'); on the fourth day, higher winds, whiter foam, Blunt living on morphia and distributing his oranges to the parched pilgrims while the stewards sold soda-water at exorbitant prices to the rich; until at four in the afternoon a naval gunboat, HMS *Hebe*, unexpectedly rescued them.

For once, Blunt was to spend several weeks working hand in glove with authority. He was publicly thanked for his testimony to the naval court set up to enquire into the pilgrims' case, while the Khedivial steamship company's conduct was censured. 'I am so unused to being praised for "public spirited conduct"', he wrote to Anne, 'that I feel I must have done something very wrong.' There was only one blot. It turned out that his old enemy Sir Auckland Colvin was a director of the company and would 'do his best to bolster up the rotten system'. 'This is a good instance', Blunt decided, 'of the way public interests always give way to private ones.' But he had got out of Lord Cromer by 2 April a promise to appoint a director at Suez next week, with power to refuse passports to pilgrims sailing on uncertified vessels.[23]

On the way home Blunt's party visited the novelist 'Ouida'* and her dogs near Pisa, a little old lady who, like Byron and Blunt himself, preferred animals to the present breed of men. Blunt had left England in November 1899 with the words, 'The only thing I love now is my cat, and I am obliged, alas! to leave it behind.'

A pandemonium of poodles greeted the party on arrival at Ouida's villa. The largest jumped on Blunt's lap and another took his hat in its teeth. 'They do not often bite', said Ouida, 'except beggars.' Her acid pen, Blunt assumed, had condemned her to exile. She welcomed him as a fellow outsider. 'The world', she said to him, 'takes its revenge on us for having despised it.'[24]

At home, he found the 'Yellow Peril' scare mounting, as news of the Boxer Rebellion in China came through. Blunt's reaction was predictable. 'The Chinese, after a long course of bullying by the Powers, worrying by missionaries, and robbing by merchants and speculators, have risen, and are, very properly, knocking the foreign vermin on the head.'†

The air was full of change. Blunt had his first ride in a motor car, and his Arabian team had been frightened by electric trams in Southampton. Old Evelyn, who visited Sheykh Obeyd that winter, was the last of the Tory anti-Imperialists, and young Wyndham the worst of the Tory Jingoes – 'George represents all that is most brutal in modern

* Marie Louise (de la) Ramée.

† In *My Diaries* the original words 'foreign vermin' were softened to 'foreign invasion'.

English politics and it marks the decline of the higher traditions to find one like him proclaiming and defending it.*

The new woman had already reached the ranks of the aristocracy. Lady Cowper, Mrs Ettie Grenfell, Mrs Horner and Lady Emily Lytton were staying at Ampthill. All went out bicycling. When they got stuck in the verges of a ploughed field, Lady Cowper let out a stream of 'damns' and pulled out her cigarettes, while the other two married ladies pulled their skirts off over their heads. Emily commented to Blunt on the 'elegance' of their silhouettes.[25]

Blunt's first grandchild was born on 7 April. Christened Noel Anthony Scawen, later called Anthony, Blunt named the enormous baby (thirteen pounds at birth) with artistic hands and an expression as venerable as the century itself, 'Old Father Christmas'.

By 22 December 1900 he was seeing out the old century with ever more bitter adieus. That the new century might see out the British Empire was at least one possibility to be thankful for. He had written to Cockerell on 23 September: 'I am delighted to see the Boers in Cape Colony and hope that they may yet win their independence of our precious Empire, which may God confound with the Queen-Empress and all the Royal Family, including the Emperor William. This is my last wish in the rotten old nineteenth century.'[26] Indeed all the white races were anathema: the Americans 'spending fifty million a year on slaughtering the Filipinos'; King Leopold of the Belgians brutalizing the Congo for gain; the French and Italians grieved by their temporary inactivity. 'God's equal curse be on them all! So ends the famous nineteenth century into which we were so proud to be born.' On Christmas Eve he sent *The Times* an unseasonable gift in the shape of an article called 'The Shame of the Nineteenth Century'. It was rejected.

As the century expired he convinced himself that the British Empire was definitely doomed.

> *31st Dec.* I bid goodbye to the old century, may it rest in peace as it has lived in war. Of the new century I prophesy nothing except that it will see the decline of the British Empire. Other worse Empires will rise perhaps in its place.

He was at Sheykh Obeyd, and thoughts of the pharaohs came into his mind – 'but I shall not live to see the day'.

Joseph the son of Jacob may have looked up at the Pyramids, he speculated, perhaps from this very garden of Sheykh Obeyd, wondering about the future, just as he himself did now. Yet what a little matter the future seemed compared with that four thousand years of the past.

'And so, poor wicked Nineteenth Century, farewell!'[27]

* In *My Diaries* Blunt changed the word 'brutal' into 'extreme'.

[18]
The Shame of the Twentieth Century 1901–1906

Hardly had Blunt dealt with 'The Shame of the Nineteenth Century' before the shame of the twentieth was upon him, in the shape of the so-called Military Fox-hunting Case. This time Blunt could lay none of the blame at the feet of the Queen, for she had died six months before, on 22 January 1901.

The obituary of Queen Victoria that Blunt published in *My Diaries* was written with his usual frankness, modified somewhat by discretion;

> ... As to Her Majesty personally, one does not like to say all one thinks even in one's journal. By all I have heard of her she was in her old age a dignified but rather commonplace good soul, like many of our dowagers....[1]

In his original diary there had been no 'rather' in front of 'commonplace'; 'good soul' had been 'old soul'; the words 'and bourgeois' had occurred before 'like how many of our dowagers.' And the last sentence of all (deleted on publication) had run: 'Privately all lovers of liberty will rejoice at the end of a bloody and abominable reign.' The novelist Ouida wrote to him:

> I am entirely with you about the late Queen. She was a most mischievous fetish for a most hypocritical nation. Her influence on society was *nil*; she did not even know what society had become. She never entered it.... She liked dogs, but she sent her own when aged to the kennels, and she did nothing for the race.[2]

A few days after his diary entry, Blunt's feelings mellowed towards the Queen on hearing that she had 'expressed a strong wish for peace on her deathbed'. This seemed to be later confirmed when he met Princess Louise of Schleswig-Holstein, Queen Victoria's granddaughter. 'Yes', she said, 'Grandmama has several times told me long before it happened, that she only hoped to be spared living to see another war in South Africa.'[3] Peace was signed with the Boer Republics in 1902. And Arabi was pardoned by King Edward VII and permitted at last to return in peace to Egypt. Blunt celebrated with a letter to *The Times* advocating Egypt for the Egyptians.

Meanwhile Blunt had declared war against the British Foreign Office. At five in the morning of 21 July 1901, a party of eight British officers decided to risk trespassing in Blunt's garden of Sheykh Obeyd for the sake of some sport with his plentiful foxes.[4] Ignoring the notice of 'Sport Forbidden', they put up a fox with a great view halloo, Captain Harman of the 11th Hussars acting as 'Master' and winding his horn.

The horn awoke Blunt's overseer Mutlak, who collected two of his men. Then the Egyptians, all three on foot, assailed the eight mounted trespassers with sticks and belaboured their backs as they turned to flee. The police were called and the Egyptians arrested. They had 'assaulted' white men. There was a headline in the press, 'Natives beat Officers'. Within a few days they were brought to trial and sentenced to six, four and three months' imprisonment.

As soon as he received the news, Blunt rushed round to the Foreign Office, where he fell upon the Permanent Secretary 'Old Giglamps' (Sir Thomas Sanderson), who advised him to write a formal letter of protest to the Foreign Secretary in person, Lord Lansdowne. But Blunt was not well – 'I am getting old for these mental gymnastics and cannot sleep.'[5]

One of the disturbing factors was a confession extorted from his servants in prison that they had twice seen *him* belabouring trespassers with his own hands until the blood ran. The Foreign Office were chortling over the despotism of 'this bird of freedom'.[6] Blunt needed all the help he could get from young Sydney Cockerell (back as his secretary), Cunninghame Graham the buccaneering 'Don Roberto' of the Pampas, and the Irish M.P.s, whose leader John Redmond raised the matter in Parliament. Blunt and Cockerell planned a letter to the press in which Blunt should seem to pity the poor officers for their beating. 'This will make them very angry.'

It did. Margaret Talbot, whose husband was now the General in Cairo, wrote to her sister Lady Lovelace that the soldiers would never forgive Blunt for accusing them of cowardice. And all for a 'storm in *such* a teacup'; the 'large and valuable stud' that was disturbed turning out to be '*six*' – but 'veracity with a mixture of Wilfrid and Arabs doesn't exist'.[7]

Wilfrid, however, had the satisfaction of seeing the sentence on his Egyptian servants cut by two-thirds; of receiving a promise that sporting 'trespass' would in future be disallowed; and of extracting a complete Blue Book from the British Government on the incident.

To this his indefatigable pen added 'A Supplement to Blue Book Egypt 3, 1901. Printed for presentation to both Houses of Parliament, March 1902.' Blunt was particularly pleased with the two main reasons he adduced for objecting to the military fox-hunters at Sheykh Obeyd: the disturbance to his valuable brood mares and the desecration of his wildlife sanctuary – both of them objections he knew would touch the British heart. In a letter to Lord Salisbury Blunt pointed out the multitude of discrepancies between the Blue Book's account of the incident and that given in the court proceedings in Cairo – the one in English, the other in Arabic. Blunt had a secret weapon in Lady Anne, who laboured at the translations for him, laying bare the 'astonishing lies' of officialdom.

It was the fox-hunting incident that wrung from Anne the only poem of her life:

Oh for Kipling to sing of that glorious hunt
Of July 21st in the garden of Blunt!
Ryecroft, Rowe, Hartwell, Bradley, Buchan and Greer,
'Master' Harman and Keyser – a name slightly queer....

'We can put the hounds in where the wall is just low
In a trice they will find and our horn we will blow.
Never mind if the people in charge run and shout
We are eight British Soldiers, we can't be turned out.'

Anne presented her verses to Wilfrid on his sixty-first birthday. He congratulated her on having exercised at last her 'hereditary talent' (as Byron's granddaughter), and she wrote characteristically in her diary, 'Thirty-two years have I been waiting – I may say – for a compliment!'[8]

If Blunt had made his first complimentary bow to his wife, he had made his last to Lord Cromer. On 19 November he called at the Cairo agency, congratulating Cromer on his second marriage (as a widower he had married Lady Katharine Thynne) and on the new stricter regulations for pilgrim ships. But there the civilities stopped. Blunt's social call deteriorated into a series of skirmishes on the fox-hunting case. 'Did you read the dossier?' demanded Blunt. 'Yes.' 'All?' 'Yes. All in the Blue Book.' 'That', said Blunt, 'is a very small part.' Blunt wrote afterwards, 'Our attitude towards each other from this point has been one of hostility. I do not regret it.' Indeed, he was soon to attack Cromer personally in the London press (May 1902) for whitewashing the army of occupation and tampering with the Law Courts. Four years later, he was to congratulate himself on having done so. It was his 'attack', launched first in the *Daily News* and widely copied except by *The Times* and *Telegraph*, that enabled him to go for Cromer with redoubled effect, when the notorious Denshawai case arose in 1906.*

Blunt's blood was up, but during the rest of 1902 there was nothing and no one to spill it for.

His beautiful Mary Elcho and meek Dorothy Carleton were both keeping out of his way; possibly an interconnected decision. True, a threesome between himself, Wilfrid Meynell and Charlie Russell's wife Adeline was proceeding on its curious way, based upon a common Catholic circle, love of poetry and love of one another. Blunt found Adeline 'a dear good woman high-hearted and sincere'; she called him 'you dear person', a wonderful being who had given her happiness such as she had not known for years. Sometimes they would spend together an 'afternoon of love'; or they would walk home in the dark through the Park where almost every space was occupied by lovers reposing on the benches, 'according to the naïve English custom' in each other's arms. 'We took our places among them', wrote Blunt, 'when we found a vacant seat, and spent a half hour in imitation of their ways.... Altogether a sweet evening, profitable more than many devoted to good works.' But on 12 November, after one of these 'delicious' experiences, he seemed to hear, for the first time, the bell toll for him:

> I feel ten years older [he wrote soon afterwards] having made up my mind to the final renunciation. I suppose everyone comes to this at last, and my youth has been prolonged beyond its natural date. On Tuesday ... a sweet evening it was, moving me with the consciousness that there was at least this little element of happiness left in life, that I could make her happy.... I have had a warning since that my sixty-two years cannot be trifled with, symptoms of what I am certain is paralysis or would be paralysis if I took a step further in the road of pleasure. I have felt these slightly once or twice before, but yesterday I seemed to feel the hands of the angel of destruction on my cheek. Now, death I do not fear. But to be stricken helpless would be an evil fate and it has scared me.[9]

Adeline, meanwhile, had returned to her brilliant husband, a leading divorce lawyer, with whom she had not lived for seven years. Taking credit to himself for her renewed interest in sex, Blunt marvelled at the mysterious ways of Providence: 'My love, offered with no motive at all of piety or other than the end desired by lovers, has achieved the miracle and her domestic peace is signed and sealed. What wonder men are cynics who have made a study of the human heart.' Here spoke Blunt the student and practitioner of *Les Liaisons Dangereuses*; a role for which his time was running out.

Poetry-reading, to more and more unusual audiences, was to be an

* Today spelt Denshwai.

expanding industry for Blunt at this otherwise static period. He, Meynell and Adeline would read aloud Blake and Patmore, Mrs Browning and Crashaw, Meredith's *Modern Love** and Yeats's *Cathleen ni Houlihan*. Yeats tried to win over Blunt to his own 'chaunting' method of recitation; in vain. But Blunt admired him: 'He is of that most interesting dark Irish type with pale face and lank hair.' And Yeats did succeed in involving Blunt in the poetry and drama of the 'Celtic Twilight', then rendering Dublin a good deal more luminous than the London of Alfred Austin's noonday. *Fand of the Fair Cheek* was to be Blunt's contribution to the Cuchulain cycle of Irish plays put on by Yeats and Lady Gregory at the Abbey Theatre, Dublin. Blunt helped to obtain a patent for the Abbey through George Wyndham, the Irish Secretary, but he was humble about his literary offering, *Fand*. 'It is a wretched thing. I was ashamed to read it out.'[10] Certainly it was poor compared with the 'Celtic' poetry of W. B. Yeats, J. M. Synge or A. E. (George Russell). Nevertheless Blunt's verses are rarely without the interest of human relationships. Here is Queen Emer offering reconciliation to her rival the fairy Fand:

> And women need forgiveness. We are all weak. We stand,
> We two like children lost in a bewitched strange land,
> The land of one man's heart, where we alone are kin.

The public image of another poet greatly exercised Blunt during this period. His brother-in-law Lord Lovelace was about to publish *Astarte*, the clever but perverse attempt to vindicate his grandmother Lady Byron by exposing the incest of his grandfather Lord Byron with 'Astarte', Byron's half-sister Augusta Leigh. Blunt had been shocked by the violence of Lovelace's first draft. That the published version was more moderate Blunt put down to his own good offices in begging his brother-in-law 'to avoid bitterness or disparagement when speaking of Byron who was certainly a man of commanding genius, and also to spare him even morally as far as the facts would allow'.[11]

Success in one field always whetted Blunt's appetite for renewed activities in another. After the Fox-hunting Case, his intervention to improve *Astarte*. After *Astarte*, a long summer's work as intermediary on the great Irish Land Bill.

Blunt's cousin George Wyndham was approaching his political

* Blunt visited Meredith and found him 'boxed in' with box hedges at Box Hill. *Modern Love* (1897) is his masterpiece, though one wonders which of the trio had to read aloud its famous awful line, 'My feet were nourished on her breasts all night.' Meynell read it again at Newbuilding's – 'rather an ordeal' – in 1911. (V. Meynell, *Francis Thompson and Wilfrid Meynell*, p. 80.)

zenith. Here he was, Irish Chief Secretary, a Cabinet Minister in his thirties, with Arthur Balfour, his colleague of many years, intimate friend and honorary brother-in-law, now Prime Minister. (Lord Salisbury had resigned in 1902 and died this year, 1903.) If any moment was ever to be George's, this was it. True, his manly beauty was beginning to show signs of wear and tear. Though always a dandy he was soon to be described by Judith – that merciless diminisher of male idols – as having once been handsome but now 'repulsive', since his features were thickened by drink 'and shiny to the point of combustion'; his eyes tiny and voice mincing. Nevertheless George still felt the divine afflatus of poetry, writing love lyrics that his acolytes (including Wilfrid), considered masterly.* Far from being irritated by George's arrogance, as Judith was, Wilfrid thoroughly enjoyed him:

> He is certainly strangely egotistical, though not I think selfish, monopolising attention to his own talk and his own ideas. Some people resent this, but on me it has a stimulating effect and rouses me to repartee. Thus I am always happy in his company, almost as his mother is, who adores his self glorifications, which are a schoolboy's in simplicity.[12]

No one could have been more anxious to serve than Blunt, when Wyndham proposed him as go-between in the Irish agrarian problem. The post of 'unaccredited ambassador' still appealed to him. To act as unofficial intermediary between two politicians he admired as much as George Wyndham and John Redmond, the Irish parliamentary leader, was Blunt's idea of self-fulfilment. Redmond had succeeded Parnell as leader, after the party had been battered, first by the Parnell–O'Shea divorce case, then by Parnell's death in 1890.

The Wyndham plan was to buy out the Irish landlords through state loans to their tenants. In Blunt's eyes, this was no more or less than a step towards Home Rule, always his main object. Now in 1903 the Conservative government of Arthur Balfour – 'Bloody Balfour', no less – had been persuaded by George Wyndham to employ £150 million of public money on a vast, voluntary scheme of peasant proprietorship – the biggest thing, in Blunt's ecstatic opinion, since Catholic Emancipation.

But was the price right? This was where Blunt came in. A sum of £12 million had been set aside by the Treasury to subsidize the tenants.

* Judith again mocked him, writing a skit on his lines:

> Oh Phyllis in her kirtle, for so I choose to call
> The prettiest and the shortest petticoat of all. . . .
>
> Oh Wyndham in his tubulars, for so I choose to call
> The newest and the smartest trousers of them all.

Wilfrid unwisely showed George the parody, so that George never liked Judith again.

Acting as the tenants' representatives, John Redmond and William O'Brien insisted on a better deal. At the same time a group of reactionaries were threatening to withdraw their support altogether unless the Irish agreed that the scheme as it stood was 'final'. Parnell had once said, 'No man shall set a limit to the march of a nation.' Already Blunt's friend Michael Davitt, and to a lesser extent John Dillon, saw Ireland marching towards wholesale land nationalization rather than smallholdings.

George put Wilfrid in the picture on 31 March, explaining how the convention of Irish landlords had proposed the Bill, how a conference of landlords and tenants had followed, and how the convention of Irish Nationalists would discuss it on 16 April. This last convention was the crux. He would immediately see Redmond about it, Wilfrid promised George.

Next day Blunt lunched with the Irish leader, who was greatly relieved to negotiate privately through a friend rather than 'go openly' to the House of Commons and knock at Wyndham's door, without knowing who might observe him. On the day after, Wilfrid reported these arrangements to George over breakfast, mentioning some of the amendments to the Bill that Redmond would require. Two days later he brought a written statement from Redmond, and on the sixth the cousins agreed to send Wyndham's answer in his, Wilfrid's handwriting, changing George's 'I's' into 'We's'. By the twenty-third Redmond was back from his convention, demanding concessions at the second reading of the Bill, including the release of an Irish political prisoner named Kilbride before the debate. Why were the government, asked Redmond, 'deliberately placing his continuing imprisonment in their path?' On the twenty-fourth George agreed, through Wilfrid, that Kilbride's health was a sound ground for release.

During May and June, Blunt was seeing William O'Brien and John Dillon as well as Redmond and Wyndham, urging moderation on all parties, since the new Land Bill would be 'the first piece of quite honest legislation on Ireland' and the 'certain prelude' to Home Rule. To show his faith in Redmond, Blunt contributed £50 to the Irish Parliamentary Fund.

The second reading passed with a huge majority of 391 votes. Wyndham then agreed to consider amendments in the committee stage provided he could discuss them personally with Redmond at Blunt's house. This crucial meeting between the Irish Chief Secretary and the Nationalist leader took place on 23 June after elaborate preparations by Blunt. The letters exchanged between Redmond and Blunt show something of the latter's influence.

Four days before the meeting, for instance, on 19 June,[13] Redmond still considered the situation very serious, 'unless the Government can meet the Irish Party by accepting Mr. Duke's amendment, which is the very least they could do to soften Irish feelings and prevent fatal bitterness'. (Henry Duke M.P. was responsible for an amendment at the committee stage to the £12 million limit in the Land Bill.) Redmond continued to Blunt:

> Mr. Wyndham will make a fatal mistake if he thinks that the Irish hostility to Clause 1 is a game of bluff. The opposition to the Bill is intense and is rapidly growing uncontrollable. Some of us have had to strain our influence to prevent it showing itself in a much more dangerous form than anything that has occurred yet.

The unofficial ambassador, having passed on this sharp warning to Wyndham on the twentieth, replied to Redmond by return that he would arrange for 'G' to meet him at 'this house' next Tuesday to talk things over, 'this house' being Blunt's, in Chapel Street:

> Personally, it seems to me, [added Blunt to Redmond] that however imperfect the bill, it will be an immense step towards Home Rule, and if it is found not to work satisfactorily, nothing I should think would be easier in a year or two's time when the Liberals have come into power to get certain sections amended. However we will talk of this on Tuesday.

Tuesday arrived and all went well. In one of his best diary passages Blunt described the contrast between these two Irish types – 'for George is far more Irish than English' – as negotiators: George the descendant of the Fitzgeralds 'gesticulating a good deal with his hands and very eager'; Redmond born of solid Wexford farming-stock 'sitting with his hand nursing his great double chin seriously, but expanding from time to time in genial smiles when points of agreement were reached... This I felt was an historic event, as I saw George into his hansom at the door with his red box – a great day for Chapel Street!'[14]

Wyndham had agreed to adopt Henry Duke's amendment to 'the limit' in Clause 1 and promised to release a second political prisoner named McHugh, while Redmond graciously admitted that incarceration had saved Kilbride's life, since he had been drinking himself to death. As for the landlords' acceptance of the new clause, Blunt put it down not to graciousness but entirely to ignorance – 'most of them too stupid to understand the bill'.

Redmond continued to use Blunt during July, and on 14 August 1903 King Edward VII gave his royal assent to the Bill. By 1908, little short of a quarter of a million tenants had bought their farms under the Land Act.

Wyndham suffered recurrent nervous breakdowns from exhaustion aggravated by drink and political pressures. He resigned from the government on 6 March 1905, after the Prime Minister had written to Sibell, 'He is really hardly sane....'[15] Six months later, when the general election was in sight, Wyndham had moved away from the progressive ideals that had temporarily united him politically as well as personally with Blunt. 'I mean to win my own election here [Dover]', he wrote to Blunt on 30 September 1905, 'in the hopes of returning to the House as one of a small and chastened band of Medieval Reactionaries.'

Wilfrid, however, was more resilient. Moreover, instead of worrying about George's split with Redmond (over Catholic education) Wilfrid considered it 'a factor for the good', writing in his diary, 'As far as my policies are concerned I should be sorry to see entire harmony between Ireland and England for then we should have the Irish as imperialistic as the worst of us.'[16]

Before leaving England that autumn he summed up his state with distinct cheerfulness, despite three deaths that had caused him great pain: Mary Galloway's, Berthe Wagram's and 'the dear Cowie's'. (Berthe Wagram had been his lover briefly in the early 1880s – he remembered the first day she showed him Wagram's Napoleonic treasures in the Long Gallery at Gros Bois and her golden hair fell down 'by accident or design' and he kissed her – but he had 'imperceptibly transferred' his affection to her husband and children, 'as is so often the case in love affairs'.)[17] His romance with Gay Windsor was also at an end.

> Nevertheless I have been happier this year than in most years, partly I think through better health, partly through being more busily occupied, while there has been the undercurrent of Dorothy's affection and Mrs. Russell's love. The latter has counted for much with me, though I feel it cannot last. Dorothy, I hope, will not fail.

Mary Elcho, on the other hand, hoped that Dorothy would fail; for the best possible reason. 'I fear you make love to her!' she had written a month before.

> Judith's children too [Blunt went on] have grown to an age when they add a pleasure to the house and they have been much at Newbuildings.[18]

Anthony was now three and a half, and Anne a year old; Winifrid, to her grandfather's delight, was to arrive in 1904. 'I don't know why you should suppose me dissatisfied with your female baby', he wrote to Judith, 'which no doubt will be an interesting addition to the family, especially if it has black hair and eyes.'[19] Judith was to feel that her father had never forgiven her for her own hazel eyes and hair with golden lights. She replied to him on this occasion that Winnie might be followed by 'more grandsons'. This must have been written purely to please her father, for she was telling her sister-in-law, Lady Constance Lytton, this same year that she had never had any maternal feeling before marriage, so why after? Winnie, blue-eyed like all the Lytton children, was to be the last of the family.

Apart from the grandchildren, Wilfrid was glad to have made a settlement of Crabbet Park on Judith and to have persuaded her to take his name as an additional surname – 'Blunt-Lytton'. Blunt's sense of 'squiredom' was growing on him. Judith must inherit Crabbet at once, he explained to her in a long letter, since the estate plus timber was worth £240,000, and death duties later at 6½ per cent would ruin her. 'The Crabbet Estate is to me what a kingdom is to a king, a matter of duty more than any sentiment....'[20]

He had already crossed swords with rival potentates. He was ordered by the East Grinstead Rural District Council to pull down an experimental modern chalet built for his labourers, on the ground that only a brick-built cottage would be warm (David Roberts his servant spoke up for Blunt's cottage in court, after living there cosily for two years) and it contravened the bye-laws; and he put up a notice signed 'Wilfrid Scawen Blunt Lord of the Manor' to say that the fountain he had presented to the public in Crawley Lane had been certified by Allen & Hanbury the chemists as pure drinking-water, hoping thus to prevent invasion of the parish by a local water company – 'There is nothing more corrupt than English local bodies.'[21]

There have been no domestic or public worries [he concluded his summary of 1903] and the part I was able to play in Irish affairs has given me confidence that even in politics my life has not been quite wasted.

It was Blunt's own psychological clumsiness that produced five days later a near-break with Dorothy Carleton. Excited by some new photographs of his little Mary, he decided on impulse to tell Dorothy the romantic story. Hardly had he said the first words before it was plain he had dealt her a shattering blow. 'The light faded wholly from her face and the colour of her cheeks resolved itself into livid patches, as it might with one wounded and suddenly in agony.'[22] After he had written to her, 'You must forgive me as you can. I shall not forgive myself', there was no more correspondence between them throughout his usual winter stay in Egypt. It was then that he made his last desert journey; to Damascus in March 1904.

The following summer Dorothy finally got over the shock of Blunt's revelation. They met happily at Belgrave Square, where the child Mary devoted herself to a lanky doll she called her husband, caressing and beating it by turns; and also at Clouds in the autumn, where Dorothy and Wilfrid whimsically agreed that 'when she is tired of a celibate life – which she already is – we are to be married by Mohammedan law'.[23]

At Sheykh Obeyd on 10 December 1904 Blunt was struck down with a violent attack of (malarial) 'Mediterranean fever', that was to afflict him for two consecutive years, affecting his spine. This marked the beginning of tragic changes; for though he was soon to record 'the happiest year of my life' (1906), the overall effect can only be described as tragic. It was the indirect cause of his separation from Anne. Without the illness, there might have been no separation. And if Cowie had been alive the illness would scarcely have mattered. Cowie would have nursed him emotionally while Miss Lawrence nursed him physically, as they had done since 1898, leaving Anne to welcome him back to normal when the crisis was over. As it was, Cowie's last letter had begun pathetically in January 1903, 'I believe I am *wore* out', and she died next month. 'I feel that my home life is broken up in a way which cannot be mended', wrote Wilfrid to Judith.[24]

With no Cowie, he found the first three months of his illness at Sheykh Obeyd intolerably boring. It was a joy when Judith and Neville came out to visit him:

> Their arrival has ended my long silence, for up to now I have had no one but my nurse to talk to and it had been a great cause of depression. Anne with her many virtues is useless in a sick room, and whether from fear of infection or jealousy of Miss Lawrence . . . has left me entirely to myself, paying me a visit of two minutes in the morning and a minute and a half in the evening.

Anne was certainly not unenvious of Miss Lawrence's ascendancy, believing the nurse to have 'supplanted' her as mistress in her own home. Nor did she put it past the nurse to exaggerate Blunt's ill-health in order to increase her own power. In this suspicion Anne was encouraged by Judith. A note in the latter's handwriting, written during the height of her father's illness, bears the inscription, 'A good smacking was what he wanted!'

Anne may have hesitated at first to encourage his 'malingering' by too much solicitude; nevertheless, her main reason for absenting herself was not jealousy but fear of intruding. She felt Wilfrid had no wish for her company, while Wilfrid, resentful at her apparent neglect, began to react against her brief visits; a vicious circle. 'It seems as if he may be vexed sometimes if I am *not* with him', Anne wrote in her diary on 13 March, 'but that when I *am* there he does not want me!'

Scarcely well enough to travel, he set off for Cairo and the journey home four days later, on 17 March. Anne offered to accompany the invalid and his nurse as far as Ramleh station, to which Miss Lawrence assented: 'Her ladyship can look after the luggage. I cannot leave *him*.' Judith called this 'cheek'. To Anne it was a mortal, unforgivable affront. It did irreparable damage.[25]

When Anne returned to England a month later, she found the situation if anything worse. Unknown to Wilfrid (who was happy in the attentions of his 'Wyndham connections'), Sydney Cockerell had summoned Anne and Judith with 'an alarmist telegram'. Anne found herself 'less than welcome' (Wilfrid's words). Thinking the telegram had been Wilfrid's, she could not understand his coldness. 'It was one of the many small causes of our growing estrangement', wrote Wilfrid afterwards.

He had nearly died in Venice on the way home and had been saved, as he saw it, solely by the devotion of his nurse and secretary. He blamed his wife bitterly for having deserted Miss Lawrence '*in her trouble*' (Anne's sarcastic underlining) at Sheykh Obeyd. Still in great pain, especially in his arms, he was living on hashish. His fingers trembled so much that the handwriting of his diary, when he attempted to continue it, could not be recognized as his usual elegant but free script.

Secretly blaming herself for not having gone home with him, Anne did in the end offer an apology and he held out his hand to her – 'a thing that has not happened' wrote poor Anne 'for at least 20 years....'

Wilfrid and Miss Lawrence between them soon changed Anne's self-reproach into self-pity. There was a scene on Wilfrid's departure to Chapel Street early in June, of which he gave an honest but not very endearing account:

> I wanted to be independent while in London and was obliged to tell Anne so, so I have not seen her since I came up, though I believe she has been in London most of the time and is hurt at my prohibition. But last time she was constantly wandering about the house and this drives other women away.[26]

On 3 July the crisis arrived, with another of those hurtful phrases that cannot be forgotten. Dr Philpot had told Blunt that his lung – the one his doctors suspected of being tubercular – was healthy after all. At Cockerell's wish Blunt had consulted his secretary's uncle, old Sir Douglas Powell, the distinguished surgeon. Powell arrived, recalled Blunt, looking like an executioner and said in a sepulchral voice: 'I urge you, as I would urge my own son, to submit to a slight operation on the left lung, the merest touch with an instrument....' Blunt refused 'an operation which I afterwards learnt would have been almost certainly in my weak state fatal, while the lung was sound'. It became a family joke that neither he nor Anne trusted doctors; they preferred to call in a vet.* Philpot had Blunt's lung X-rayed at the

* The Powell story, losing nothing in the telling, was relayed by Blunt to Bernard Shaw in 1905, thus being 'among the contributary causes', as Blunt thought, of Shaw's *The Doctor's Dilemma*. In the Preface, Shaw described contemporary medicine as 'a murderous absurdity'. The play was first produced in autumn 1906. 'The first act', wrote Blunt, 'is quite the most witty thing that has ever been put on the stage.'

Brompton Chest Hospital. Once assured it was sound, Blunt decided to leave Newbuildings and seek another period of emotional refreshment with his women friends in Chapel Street. Anne asked, 'Can I go to London by the same train with you or not?' Wilfrid, feverish and full of drugs, replied,

'I will not have this sort of thing. I shall have to go away somewhere under a feigned name to escape.'

'What sort of thing?'

'I will not be followed about. If I had to choose one of you, I should certainly choose Miss Lawrence.' It was another unforgivable remark.[27]

Wilfrid tried afterwards to explain that he would have 'chosen' his nurse rather than his wife only in the sense that his very life depended at that moment on intensive nursing; nor was he quite sane, he added, what with the pain and the drugs. Anne, however, after giving the nurse a piece of her mind ('she looked scared'), called a family conclave consisting of Judith, Neville and her cousin Irene Noel, communicating also by letter with her brother Ralph Lovelace. Ralph's conclusion was that his sister must keep away from Newbuildings while the nurse's 'incongruous and dangerous' reign lasted – a reign that in Ralph's imagination involved a sexual connection of 'ludicrous bathos'. After Neville had consulted a solicitor, Francis Smith of Lincoln's Inn, to make sure that Anne did not prejudice her 'home rights' or rights in the Stud, by not returning to Newbuildings when Wilfrid did so, an ultimatum was drawn up for presentation to Wilfrid.

1 Anne was willing to enter Newbuildings only provided Wilfrid 'put the nurses on a proper footing', i.e. arranged for them to take their meals alone. (No more of Nurse Williams ordering the wine or of Miss Lawrence seizing the teapot and actually pouring out the tea at Lady Anne's own tea-table. If an Englishman's home was his castle, an Edwardian lady's tea-table was her keep.)

2 Unless Wilfrid agreed, Anne would resort to her only weapon, money. She would at once stop paying the nurses' wages; but not cut off other supplies while Wilfrid was so ill.[28]

Wilfrid caved in. 'Dearest Anne . . . I wish I could do without them [his nurses]', he wrote on the twenty-seventh, 'but for the present this is impossible. I am very little better and do not expect to do more than remain an invalid for the rest of my days, the fewer the better.' But the nurses should – as Anne wished – eat in Wilfrid's writing-room while he and Anne occupied the dining-room. He had the tact not to point out that Cowie had taken all her meals with them for the last ten years. He also dropped the hashish, though still requiring one-twelfth of a grain of morphia every night. By September, after a visit to Brighton, he looked 'wonderfully better', wrote Anne, and in October there was even a noticeable improvement in his manner to his wife. She asked him if he had any objection to her calling him 'Wilfrid' (presumably instead of 'H.F.' – Head of the Family) and he said none whatever; never had had. 'I don't know that he ever *said* he had', noted Anne, 'but it *felt* as if he had.' He went off to London with his nurse in the phaeton, 'and actually spoke several words to *me*, asked if I wanted him to do anything for *me* in town, and said "goodbye". What an astonishing change.'[29]

Dr Philpot had his patient X-rayed again in November, with the result that two of his vertebrae were shown to be too close together. Wilfrid must lie flat on his back for three months in an invalid carriage, while Anne set off alone for Egypt with instructions to sell off the 'outlying lands' of Sheykh Obeyd. Wilfrid would never return.

She said goodnight as usual on 27 November, her last evening at Newbuildings before the journey. 'He stretched out his hand to me, and, as I took it, pulled, and I leant down and touched his forehead with my lips as he wanted. What a change!'

Next morning at nine she innocently asked Wilfrid if his 'extraordinary behaviour yesterday was a new leaf?' Wilfrid pretended not to understand; then referred to the drugs; then was interrupted by Dr Philpot with the 'infernal machine' for his spine. But before Anne finally left at ten, there was another 'demonstration of kindness';

> For holding out his hand again as yesterday he drew me towards me [*sic*] – I was sitting on a chair beside the couch – and kissed me. Perhaps *really* there is a leaf on the tree that was dead.[30]

It was mid-June 1906 before Anne saw him again. The unusual length of her Egyptian visit (she generally returned in March or April) had been due to the rigours of her operations in the land market. Her success was phenomenal – too complete, as it turned out, for her own future happiness. She exactly hit off the Egyptian land boom. The price of land had slumped during the 1880s, when Wilfrid bought the Sheykh Obeyd garden as a mark of faith in Egyptian Nationalism. Now it was soaring, after twenty years of Cromerian rule, and thanks also to Sir Ernest Cassel's investment in the Aswan Dam. Anne presented Wilfrid with the amazing sum of £35,000 for his 'desert land', a profit of 4,000 per cent.

The rise in land values was not the only spectacular change in Egypt. As Blunt guessed, the Entente Cordiale with France in 1904 would have far-reaching repercussions. He rightly saw that an Anglo-French alliance boded no good for Egypt. After all, it had been at France's insistence that the British occupation had hitherto been 'temporary'.

Now, in the words of Sir Eldon Gorst, financial adviser to Cromer, 'the difficulty with France' had been swept away.*

On the other hand, the victories of the Orient over the West in the Russo-Japanese war encouraged Eastern Nationalism: 'great news', wrote Blunt on 11 February 1904. 'The Russo–Japanese war has begun, and some ironclads have been sunk at Port Arthur. This is to the good.'

At the same time the Egyptian Nationalists had got their own new head of steam, independently of the Khedive Abbas II, who by 1904 had finally accepted the occupation. Among the young Nationalists were Lufti-al-Sayyid, a moderate, through whom the emancipation of women was first heard of in Egypt; the brothers Zaghloul; above all Mustafa Kamel Pasha the mesmeric orator and leader, known in Paris as 'Caramel Pacha' and called by Blunt, who entertained him in the Jubilee Room at Newbuildings, 'a very wonderful young man'.

There were signs by 1905 of an even greater change in Blunt in regard to Egypt. Was he beginning to come round to Cromer, despite the fox-hunting incident of five years before? If so, it was due partly to the influence of Mohammed Abdu who respected Cromer, partly to 'the protection and encouragement given to the natives', but mostly to Cromer's strong line against financial corruption. Blunt recorded a conversation on 17 March 1905 with an Englishman (Hewat) who had lived in Egypt for forty years:

> We talked much about Cromer and his failure to re-establish any form of self-government in the country, but he agreed with me that, despot for despot, Egypt might be in much worse hands. He is the only guarantee we have at present against a new era of speculation and financial jobbery.[31]

The first critical incident of 1906 concerned a Turkish landing at Taba on the Gulf of Aqaba in January. Cromer advised Sir Edward Grey, Foreign Secretary in the new Liberal government, to order the Sultan off, fearing a pan-Islamic drive supported by Germany. Grey commanded the Turks to evacuate within ten days and they did so – but not before Blunt had criticized this rough diplomacy in a letter to Grey, and the Egyptian Nationalists had come out on the side of Turkey. Next month the whole Law School of Cairo went on strike, an unheard of act for those days. And two months later, in May, came the horrible Denshawai affair.

The story, as reported by Blunt, was that a fracas between Egyptian villagers and British army officers had taken place at Denshawai in the Delta near Tanta; the very place where Blunt believed one of Arabi's

* Sir Eldon Gorst, 'Egypt in 1904', Appendix III to Milner's *England in Egypt*, 4th edition.

followers, Abdu Dia, had been unjustly hanged in 1882. This time, invited by a village notable, seven officers had gone out to shoot the fellahin's tame pigeons; as it might be, an Englishman's poultry. But no notable received them; instead, a swarm of furious villagers rushed forward to save their valuable birds, and incidentally to punish these military vandals whom they believed had also set fire to their threshing-floor. A mêlée followed; one fellah woman and four men were peppered with shot and all the officers belaboured with *nabuts* (wooden staves). In an attempt to bring help, Captain Bull made a dash for his camp, collapsed on the way from heat stroke after concussion, was succoured by a villager, but died. Thinking the villager had killed him, Bull's comrades beat the man to death. No one was tried for this man's murder, but a court sentenced four peasants to public hanging, two to imprisonment for life, six to seven years, eight to fifty lashes plus one year for three of the eight.*

'This is exactly like all these cases', wrote Blunt; justice between Egyptian peasants and the army of occupation, when in conflict, did not exist. 'Yet we talk of civilizing Egypt.' He at once joined the stream of protests from British journalists and M.P.s, himself writing to the *Manchester Guardian* and the French *Figaro*. John Dillon was urged by Blunt to raise the matter in Parliament – he must go on 'torturing' the government, said Blunt's journalist friend William J. Moloney – and a long letter was despatched by Blunt to Keir Hardie the Labour leader, in answer to his enquiry whether Sir Edward Grey was justified in citing 'fanatical unrest' in Egypt as an excuse for the Denshawai brutalities. Blunt replied that there was no religious 'fanaticism' in the Delta, but much '*political* resentment' in Cairo, after Taba. 'Lord Cromer is a man of very high qualities, financial and administrative', he added, 'but he has had things too long his own way in Egypt to be always just.'[32]

Privately shattered, as Blunt later heard, by the Denshawai horror, Cromer was given the O.M. and allowed to resign next year on health grounds. 'Already the Denshawai pigeons were coming home to roost.'†

Meanwhile Blunt in July 1906 was working on a powerful pamphlet entitled *Atrocities of Justice Under British Rule in Egypt* (first edition

* Blunt differed from most Radicals in arguing that a *public* hanging was more dignified for a peasant, who would be supported by his friends, than a private hanging where he would be tortured. A folk-ballad on Denshawai suggests that Blunt may have been right: 'His brother, O you People, stood by him/And gazed till his eyes grew dim.' (Translated from the Arabic by Afaf Lutfi al-Sayyid, *Egypt and Cromer*, p. 173.)

† Peter Mansfield, *The British in Egypt*, p. 170. Mr Mansfield writes that 'every Egyptian schoolboy' knows the story of Denshawai, as every Indian knows that of Amritsar. Denshawai explained the 'anti-British outpourings of Radio Cairo', he was told, even before the Suez crisis of 1956.

1906, second 1907), assembling all the miscarriages of justice he could remember since 1882.* The pamphlet ended with the words:

> Let us remember the Dreyfus case. Is there no Member of Parliament, no body of members, with sufficient courage to rise in their places, and say publicly of Lord Cromer, and of no other, 'J'accuse'?

Deeply impressed by the pamphlet, George Bernard Shaw enquired of Neville Lytton, who was painting him, ironically, in papal attire, whether Blunt would give him further details of the Denshawai affair, so that he could use them in the Preface to his *John Bull's Other Island*. Blunt complied, and Shaw devoted fifteen pages of his Preface to 'The Denshawai Horror'. Others took a different view of Blunt's denunciation of Denshawai. The anonymous writer of a postcard threatened to murder him if he dared to show his face again in Egypt.

Anne had worked early and late for days to get the Denshawai documents translated from the Arabic. Then, on 11 July, she gallantly took down the whole long article at Wilfrid's dictation. Wilfrid's attack on Cromer she considered 'well merited'. But what of H.F. himself? She wrote in her diary: 'It is amusing his making use of me while longing to be rid of me!'[33]

Three weeks later she was out.

‡ Blunt felt particularly bad about the case of Professor Palmer, a British spy who had been murdered by Bedouin known to him through Blunt. They were indiscriminately and savagely punished.

[19]
The Parting
1906–1909

Among Blunt's papers is a card advertising bed and board in a Sussex farmhouse at the foot of Chanctonbury Ring: The Mill House, Ashington, near Pulborough; 12 acres of grounds, own dairy, paddock, orchard, garden, 4s. a day, 'Lights out at 11 p.m.'.

The 'lights out' rule did not worry Blunt and Dorothy Carleton, whose rooms were next to one another. On a sudden inspiration Blunt had decided to make a weekend excursion with Dorothy, taking Miss Lawrence as chaperone. A small cavalcade set out on the Saturday from this farmhouse, the 'ideal honeymoon cottage', Dorothy and Miss Lawrence driving the 'Texas waggon', Blunt in his donkey-drawn 'perambulator', a farm-cart bringing the picnic and Blunt's bed, which they set up under the beech trees of the famous clump. Sunday was spent reading poetry in the shade of a pear tree at the Mill House; on Monday morning they drove home. That night Blunt wrote in his diary:

> It is thus that one can be happy, if one has the courage to seize one's hour – even at the age of sixty-five. Dorothy is thirty-one and has known no real happiness till now. We have made a plan of life together which we are both determined to carry out whatever may be the difficulties, though indeed there should be none, for she is free and I am free, and the world troubles neither of us much. Who would have thought a year ago that such fortune was possibly in store when I was lying helpless and in pain?'[1]

The date of these raptures was 11 June 1906. Exactly a week later Anne returned to Newbuildings. She had not seen her husband for eight months, having been detained in Egypt by her exhausting duties as his land agent. Her first thought on return was not to visit him but to inspect the Crabbet Arabian Stud. The inspection was an unrewarding one. She knew that ten days before her arrival two important buyers had visited the Stud on behalf of the Indian government and given 1,180 guineas for four animals, including 530 guineas for Rijm; they had also made an offer for the colt Rifaat. Blunt had refused that offer against his wife's postal advice. On top of this, the general state of the Stud and fields may have irritated Anne. Land drainage had been stopped by Blunt to some extent in order to restore to his 'kingdom' its pristine wealth of heath and marsh.

At four on 19 June Lady Anne was hardly inside the 'little gate' of Newbuildings before she had begun a heated argument about the sale of Rifaat. An answer had to be given at once to the Indian buyers, and in the urgency of the moment it did not strike her that this was a brusque way of celebrating her homecoming. For her part, she found H.F. 'repellant and domineering'. Her later comment was: 'This began it all.' His comment: 'This was the beginning of the trouble between Anne and me which led first to a partition of the stud and then to a personal separation. At the outset it seemed a thing of no consequence and certainly was wholly remote from my thoughts and wishes.'

Still at the gate, Anne argued that he had given over to her the complete Stud management (during his illness of 1895). Did he now wish to take it back or what? He did. Then Anne would not give a *farthing* towards its management. He didn't care. She summed up that evening in her diary: 'I *see* no solution but to divide, as not having insisted on a signed document I have no legal status and cannot prove that he gave his share to me though he did so and that most emphatically.... It shows how unreliable he is.'

Blunt meanwhile hoped that Guy Carleton, Dorothy's brother and their Stud manager, would calm Anne down. 'But it has been a douche of cold water and a disappointment', he wrote in his diary, 'for I had been looking forward to Anne's return, as an element of pleasure.' Only '*an* element of pleasure'; nevertheless he had written to her affectionately throughout her long absence, and she to him. 'The violet you sent me', he wrote in March, 'smelt quite sweet on arrival.' And he was eagerly awaiting her help in finishing his diary-histories, *The Land War in Ireland* and *Gordon at Khartoum.*[2]

Next day Blunt and Guy Carleton drew up a memorandum for Anne's consideration, by which Blunt would cede to her the whole management and cost of the Stud, leaving him merely a right to veto sales on breeding stock (his forte being the judgment of individual animals). They would own the livestock jointly. 'Carleton however', noted Blunt, 'thinks Anne may insist on a division of the Stud. This I should refuse.'

A sale of their Arabians at Tattersalls on 2 July brought on the crisis again, for the experiment was a dismal failure. This confirmed Anne in her criticisms: 'I will have *no more partnership*,' she had written at the outset; 'What I have must be mine and mine alone.' As a first step, Anne consulted Judith and Neville, with the result that she sent Blunt an ultimatum via Carleton on 3 July. Since Blunt would not divide, she would throw up the whole management and withdraw all her subsidies – including the latest bill of nearly £70 for his nurses, payments she made as part of the total sharing of their responsibilities. For a moment H.F. was staggered: 'This is war', he said to Guy. He foresaw very serious domestic consequences. Could he afford to carry on the Stud alone? Could he keep up Newbuildings without Anne's help? He and Anne might even 'drift into a practical separation'. But after a talk with Guy Carleton he decided that the cost of the Stud would not exceed £1,000 a year 'at worst' (a 100 per cent under-estimate) 'and, now that the land in Egypt is sold, that will be nothing'. No more striking example could be found of Blunt's abrupt swings from despair to euphoria. Nor was this to be his last change of mind.

Suddenly it seems to have struck him that he had been fighting to avoid something which might prove the ideal solution for all concerned. Anne wanted to divide the Stud. He had opposed her wish because it might lead to their 'drift into a practical separation'. But that meant also the possibility of practical union with Dorothy. 'Perhaps it is better thus', he wrote in his 'Secret Memoirs', 'and if I could only be sure of retaining Dorothy as the companion of my widowhood I should hail it as a blessing. I have talked it over with her and though there are of course great difficulties I think I can rely on her.' He took her from Chapel Street to the garden of Belgrave Square where he read her Tennyson's 'Come not when I am dead'. It made her cry.

By 8 July Anne had consulted her solicitor and her brother Ralph, the latter regarding H.F. as a 'demonic influence';[3] Carleton had agreed to work solely for Blunt; the two Blunts were to meet at Newbuildings to conclude the division.

On the ninth the meeting – fatal for Anne – took place. Wilfrid was laid out under the oak trees. He suggested a 'stud talk', adding that he did not wish to be hostile. (Nor was he, said Anne.) But it gradually dawned on her that she was, to use her own vivid phrase, 'receiving her congé'. After reading aloud his memorandum to her, he said, according to her diary,

> that of course I ought to be *domiciled with* my half of the Stud (to which I have no objection only I must have time to find a place to inhabit). He was so evidently pleased at this prospect that I am really sure that it weighs much with him on coming to an agreement.[4]

After her acquiescence, Wilfrid at once suggested buying out one of his tenants' leases on the estate for Anne; alternatively, setting her up in a room with Judith and Neville at Forest Cottage.

'I will decide my *own* "domicile"', interrupted Anne.

That evening she wrote to her brother Ralph: 'You will have your wish that I shall cease to be a member, at least a resident member of this household, and I think that this prospect is what has put Wilfrid into such good humour.'[5] It was two days after this that Anne was finding it 'amusing' that H.F. should employ her on transcribing her Denshawai pamphlet, while longing to be rid of her.

On the sixteenth there were more 'hot exchanges' over the final destiny of the Stud, both eventually agreeing to bequeath their half to Judith and her children. (H.F. had begun by objecting to Judith's 'commercialism'.) Anne was collecting her belongings from Newbuildings during the next weeks – her family portraits and engravings; two chairs of Lord Byron's and one of Aunt Louisa's 'which the Nurse claimed!!' Two hired wagons carried the bulk of her furniture and her weeping servants to an ugly little villa in Three Bridges, towards the end of July.

Blunt went to London on the thirtieth, expecting to be back in time to say goodbye. But he was delayed and so 'This day, Monday, the 30th of July 1906, proved to be the last of my married life with Anne.' On 1 August Anne moved into Judith's bedroom at Forest Cottage. 'Farewell to Newbuildings after 37 years!'[6]

There were some things in Wilfrid's account of the separation which Anne could not know of. The day after Anne's written ultimatum of 3 July, another important meeting took place between Wilfrid and Dorothy. He found her torn. She was unhappy in her 'unmeaning life at home' but had not quite the courage to throw in her lot with him. A visit to Lady Gregory at Coole in Ireland was arranged for her by the Wyndhams, to see if she and young Robert, Lady Gregory's son, might fall in love. In that 'improbable' event, Wilfrid would have no choice but to make his peace with Anne. If however the Dorothy–Robert affair 'ended in nothing' as Wilfrid confidently believed it would, poor Dorothy would be considered more of a failure at home than ever. That would be the moment to interest her Aunt Madeline and Uncle Percy in the prospect of Dorothy's adoption as Wilfrid's niece.

From Coole Dorothy reported that the poet Yeats had delivered to the assembled guests a fine eulogy of Blunt: 'He is very handsome – and has written a volume of most magnificent Sonnets'; and then Lady Gregory chimed in with Blunt's bullfighting and Egyptian struggle, 'and now as the Crown and blossom of his life he has written a play [*Fand*] for our Irish theatre'. Yeats' praises recommenced with 'He is the only man I know who *constructs* like a poet, so many can write verse plays, but he is the only one who has the poetical construction.' Dorothy enjoyed mild flirtations both with 'Mr R.' (Robert Gregory) and Yeats, the latter proposing to mesmerize her and draw her horoscope. 'This is amusing', commented Blunt. 'There is much of the charlatan in Yeats.' Fortunately neither of Dorothy's wooers proposed.[7]

Wilfrid's story of the crucial 'domicile' discussion with Anne does not differ radically from hers. They went through his draft together, he recorded, Anne agreeing to remove her half of the Stud to Crabbet. Wilfrid continued:

> I asked her what she proposed to do and said that if she took away her half she would I suppose remain with them, and she said that was her idea. I said I think, 'certainly a separate domicile would be better seeing the friction there has been of late between us on many points besides the Stud, only let the separation be a friendly one and not a quarrel, I can still go to stay with you as a guest and you with me. Only we shall have our separate establishments....' To this she entirely agreed and so ... the whole of this thorny question has settled itself in half an hour....[8]

Blunt's spirits rocketed. He had got what he wanted, had he not, without so much as a frown.

Yet if he had 'conned' Anne, he had also deceived himself. Despite his vivid interest in his wife's grandfather Lord Byron, he did not see that the drama of Byron's turning out Lady Byron – and yet not turning her out – was in some sense being re-enacted; Dorothy Carleton playing Augusta Leigh's submissive role. It was only after Anne's friends and relatives accused him of using compulsion against her, that Blunt sensed the Byron *motif* at work – but used by the opposition. He wrote in his diary on 17 November: 'Certainly, when we parted, there was no quarrel.... I don't know quite what the influence was that changed [Anne's] friendly attitude into a hostile one, but I imagine it was first her brother's with his perpetual memories of the old Byron separation, and secondly a religious influence, the necessity of finding for herself a reason of conscience for leaving the conjugal home.'[9]

Neville later denied that religion had anything to do with Anne's attitude. The truth was that Anne felt too much unnerved in Blunt's presence (reduced to a 'nerveless pulp' according to Judith) to say what she really felt. It was only in her letters to Judith that Anne showed the pain.

As early as 1 May 1905 Anne was writing about Dorothy to Judith in a significant way. Dorothy and Guy had visited Newbuildings – Dorothy 'of course' taken into H.F.'s tent, while Anne showed Guy round. By November of that year Judith was writing of Dorothy: 'She is in love with H.F. I think.' On 18 May of the critical year 1906 Anne confided to Judith her fear of the 'Wyndham set' (which of course included Dorothy). After the break, Anne became more explicit.

There would be some hope of reconciliation, she wrote to Judith on 28 July, if only 'that fiendish influence' could be removed.

Four days earlier Judith had written in her diary: 'My Father has turned Mother out of the house and she has taken lodgings at Three Bridges. She cannot put up with Dorothy and H.F. won't give D. up.'

From Forest Cottage during August Anne worked hard with her solicitor, Francis Smith, to prevent Wilfrid's solicitor, Edward Chandler, from getting her Milbanke fortune (inherited from Lady Byron) settled on Wilfrid after Anne's death instead of on Judith. 'Of course the expectation of such an income', Anne reflected bitterly, 'has much increased the wish for my decease on Wilfrid's part and the looking forward to a new and young wife!'

When Wilfrid, in keeping with his own theory that he and Anne had parted in all affection, invited her to meet him, she did not answer. And when he expressed surprise (through Cockerell) she retorted in red ink:

> But I had received my 'congé' from you and had accepted it; as a natural consequence the habits and customs of life in common have come to an end.... My life has passed out of your life and the past precludes relations such as those of mere acquaintances; it is indeed surprising that you should imagine these to be possible.

Wilfrid's reply demonstrated that the reasons for Anne's departure were to be no less arguable than those of her grandmother Lady Byron's before her.* Wilfrid professed not to understand Anne's using the phrase 'my having given you your "congé"'. He wrote to her, 'It was of the two rather your proposal than mine, for, until you pressed the division of the stud and of all common financial arrangements, I was adverse to any change.' Alongide this letter Anne wrote, 'Humbug'. 'I am in a fight against the Powers of Evil', she told Ralph Lovelace, 'and am striking out as it were in the dark, against one who is more than a match for almost any lawyer.'[10]

Ralph's sudden and unexpected death on 29 August changed the situation totally, to Blunt's advantage. Financially he was henceforth to flourish like the green bay tree. Anne's salesmanship in Egypt had already gained him a small fortune; now his whole financial responsibilities for the young Lyttons' future and that of the Crabbet estate was suddenly lifted from his shoulders, and by none other than Lord Lovelace. Ralph had left the entire fortune of his mother Ada Byron to

* Anne was to tell her grandson Anthony at the age of about nine: 'Your grandfather and I separated when he put Miss Lawrence at the head of the table to pour out tea for guests in our house.' The tea-table controversy was certainly part of the general marriage breakdown and Anne would naturally not mention adultery to a child. But Judith always insisted it was Dorothy.

his wife Mary, but after her to his sister Anne, niece Judith and her children. Crabbet was therefore provided for.

Besides causing this financial windfall, Ralph's death had also removed at a stroke Blunt's only dangerous opponent. According to Judith, her uncle had been about to challenge the Stud settlement in the courts and get Anne a divorce. His death from heart failure in the heat of battle liberated Blunt for his own affair of the heart.

Forthwith Blunt went ahead with the 'adoption' of Dorothy Carleton as his niece. He could now afford to exert pressure on her guardians, Percy and Madeline Wyndham, by offering to settle on her, either as *dot* or legacy, the sum of £10,000. In 'Myself and Others', Judith was to attribute the Wyndhams' acquiescence purely to this bribe. Percy had found the £200 per year he allowed Dorothy 'inconvenient', and therefore agreed to 'hand over' to Blunt, provided the latter took on the finance.

The real consideration that weighed with the Wyndhams, however, as with all Blunt's friends (and even to some extent with Anne) was his precarious health. Confined to his couch or perambulator, he seemed to be still at death's door. Cockerell was only a part-time secretary and might leave him for other work.* If Dorothy acted as Wilfrid's secretary during the last few months of his brilliant but misguided life, what harm? On 24 September Madeline congratulated her 'most darling Dorothy' on Wilfrid's 'wonderful and generous offer and plan for you', entailing as it did an opportunity to do valuable work. And on 10 November 1906 a legal settlement was duly signed in favour of 'Miss Margaret Theodora [Dorothy] Carleton', the trustees being George Wyndham and Guy Carleton. Like Proserpine, Dorothy was to divide herself between the upper world of Clouds and the nether world of Newbuildings.

But Blunt did not die. Indeed by next spring, 1907, he was to mount his mare for the first time in two years. Nor was he unable to make Dorothy happy. Their relations he described as 'in everything but name a marriage'. Not surprisingly, the world began to talk. Had not his wife left him because of this 'other woman'? His old flame Mme Arcos came to tea and questioned him closely. 'I explained to her however', he recorded, 'that there was no woman in the case as she seemed to suspect.'[11]

If Mme Arcos considered this a bare-faced lie, she was wrong. Except for the Stud quarrel, Blunt would merely have entertained Dorothy at Newbuildings while Anne was in Egypt, quite contented, like the Pasha he was, to make two wives happy – or even three; for Mary, his 'Bedouin wife', was occasionally to fall into his arms again after the separation from Anne. This made Blunt feel guilty, for

* Cockerell was to become Director of the Fitzwilliam Museum, Cambridge, in 1908.

Dorothy's sake. And though he had rarely before felt guilt over Anne, he did now find room for remorse. After enumerating the joys of this his 'happiest year', 1906, he was forced to add:

> Now my losses must be counted. The greatest of them has of course been my quarrel with Anne, or rather I should say her quarrel with me. This is indeed lamentable and fills me at times with self-reproach . . . retrospectively I know the fault of our gradual disunion has been mainly mine. I have run after my own happiness at the expense of hers. . . .

And again two months later: 'I have been a prodigal and spendthrift in the ways of love and am ashamed now that I should still have love poured out on me.'[12]

At the end of his first year's 'marriage' to Dorothy, Blunt celebrated at Clouds. 'August 17, 1907 . . . she slept with me till morning in the winter bedroom, as sweet a birthday as one could wish to have.' But by now the suspicions of Dorothy's Carleton and Campbell relatives had become clamorous. Guy Carleton demanded that his sister's trust money of £10,000 – 'the bride price' – should be handed back to Blunt; while the Stud was partly reallocated in Anne's favour to increase her share, so that Guy could act as joint manager to Crabbet and Newbuildings, thus giving an appearance of family unity. Blunt was to keep only twelve brood mares and six horses, 'which will be quite enough to amuse me, and save me much expense and anxiety'. Through the alarmist letters of Madeline Wyndham, Dorothy was persuaded to quit Newbuildings until the hubbub had died down.

Dorothy herself had written to Blunt in deep distress. For besides being his beneficiary in her own right, she had also agreed to hand over certain other of his bequests to 'the child Mary' in due course; just as George Wyndham was to inherit Blunt's Fernycroft estate and leave it in turn to Berkeley Sumner who already lived there.* But Dorothy now felt that the burden of executrix might be more than she could bear. At least if the £10,000 trust was broken, she would not benefit personally. In March 1908 a 'deed of release' was signed by Dorothy's trustees returning the £10,000 to Blunt.

The last straw came when Miss Lawrence complained of Dorothy's impropriety in taking in her master's early morning tea. The nurse had to be upgraded as 'housekeeper' to keep her sweet. Blunt derided her petty jealousy, without apparently noticing the irony of the situation. Here was the woman who had helped to drive Anne from her tea-table, herself deprived of the morning tea-tray by a supplanter.

* Berkeley, now married, gave his father little trouble, except for an occasional letter of the 'if I could have a lump sum down to square off what we owe' kind. But, alas, he was good only at physical labour: grubbing out the roots of trees or working his wife's mangle. During the Great War he gained the MBE, OBE and Légion d'Honneur, but afterwards became a dock labourer.

Among all these troubles, Blunt was determined that his 'marriage' should not break up. He and Dorothy would 'live together – according to God's holy ordinance or otherwise – as long as we both shall live'. But if his mind was made up, he could not understand why Madeline had changed hers so strangely about the adoption. Madeline explained to him: 'You know things have altered', she said, 'since we agreed to it a year ago. You were then very ill ... now you are well and still comparatively young, and people know what you have been....'[13]

On 24 August Wilfrid Meynell and his son Everard brought the 'poor poet' Francis Thompson, now in the last stages of consumption, to stay at Gosbrook, one of Blunt's cottages, for a week. Never had Blunt seen so tiny a face on a man; Thompson looked like a dying child or a sixteenth-century Spanish saint. After resting at Gosbrook, he was driven by Blunt in the phaeton to Newbuildings for tea, where he revived a little. 'I took him a toddle round the garden', wrote Blunt – toddlers both. He was interested that Thompson still could not tell one flower or tree from another. (This was his second visit.) Except a poppy. 'Ah that's a poppy', he said, as if greeting a friend. He had not written anything for ten years and knew he would never write again.

Each day they lunched outdoors in the Jubilee garden and Francis Thompson would rest on Francis Blunt's old wicker couch in the Jubilee 'Speckled Room' on the ground floor, having tipped a little powder into his wine. On the third day he seemed much better.

What was the secret, Blunt asked himself afterwards, of this 'man of genius'? He believed it was the tragic experiences underlying Thompson's poetry, his very fine ear, wealth of imagery; above all, the shining goodness of his character. 'There is so little of material selfishness, so great a sympathy with all forms of suffering, such thankfulness for the small change of beauty in the world, scattered as alms to the poorest.'

Blunt commissioned Neville Lytton to make a drawing of the poet; and Lytton executed on 27 August a superb profile in coloured chalks, which hung first in the Speckled Room, then in Newbuildings hall after Blunt's death.*

When the elder Meynell came down for the day, Blunt took the opportunity to get from him all he knew of Francis Thompson's earlier days. It is set out fully in *My Diaries*. Especially moving to Blunt was the account of Thompson's vagrant life around Covent Garden, sweetened by the unselfish sympathy of a prostitute. Blunt's own vein of mysticism responded to the story of Thompson's visitation by the dead poet Chatterton, who warned him not to take a lethal dose of laudanum. The money Chatterton needed would have arrived next

* It is now on permanent loan to the National Portrait Gallery.

day and saved him, had he not committed suicide; and the money from Meynell did arrive next day and save Thompson.[14]

At the end of a week, the Meynells, whose goodness to Thompson was unbounded, had to leave; but Blunt suggested that the poet should stay on, being looked after by his own most trusted servant David Roberts, who lived with his wife and family in a cottage called Rascall's Corner at Southwater. Meynell agreed with enthusiasm.

For a day or so Thompson seemed pretty well; able to walk the mile between Rascall's Corner and Newbuildings for lunch and tea with Blunt, though mostly carried to and fro in the phaeton. On 5 September he had violent diarrhoea. The Horsham doctor said 'no anxiety', but Blunt and Miss Lawrence who both visited him were worried by his extreme emaciation. Blunt sent a report to Meynell on the fifth and Miss Lawrence on the seventh. 'I told him', she added to Meynell, 'it was very good for Mr. Blunt to have him here as he interests Mr. Blunt very much – & is not shy with him now.'*[15]

As autumn advanced, however, Thompson's strength failed completely, and he could no longer be driven to and fro in the phaeton, apart from the difficulty of getting it through the mud in the lane. He seemed happiest sitting in the cottage kitchen listening to Mrs Roberts's simple talk – when he was not sleeping off the opium sent to him by post from London, in a room with a fire and all the windows shut. On 7 October Blunt told Meynell that Thompson had only once had lunch at Newbuildings that week, and might be better back in London, since the weather had broken. Meynell replied by return:

> I was greatly interested in your letter. The elusive Thompson is a being I well recognize. His nerves forsake him. Everard will come down to conduct him to town some day next week. I think he should be attended. I have laid down my car, and am too rheumatic to get into a train.[16]

Blunt's health was no better than Meynell's, a fact that the American priest Father Connolly was probably unaware of, when he criticized Blunt's attitude to Thompson.† Convinced that a man whom he considered to be more of a 'Mohammedan' than a Christian could not appreciate Thompson, Father Connolly also questioned by implication the walks from Southwater and the 'thatched cottage built of corrugated iron – an extraordinary combination!' at 'Rascals' [*sic*] Corner'. The cottage was probably a relic of Blunt's building experiment which David Roberts had warmly supported. Beyond that, it is evident from Meynell's letters both that Blunt appreciated Thompson

* 'It is strange to see him twisting his moustache and pulling down his cuffs when Mr Blunt approaches', wrote Everard. (Viola Meynell, *Francis Thompson and Wilfrid Meynell*, p. 179.)

† Terence L. Connolly, *Francis Thompson – In his Path* (Milwaukee, 1946), pp. 50–7. There is a valuable description of Newbuildings and Dorothy Carleton in the 1940s. Fr Connolly founded the Francis Thompson Room at Boston College.

and the Meynells appreciated Blunt. Viola Meynell was later to describe Blunt as her father's best friend, which would hardly have been the case had Blunt treated the beloved poet less than generously.

Blunt indeed came to endow Thompson almost with the powers of a saint. Being terrified of wasps and once stung in the Jubilee garden, Thompson cursed them; after which there were no more wasps at Newbuildings for three years. Or so Blunt claimed.

On 13 November came a letter from Meynell to Blunt:

> Francis Thomspon died at dawn today. I was with him till late last night, and he made a pleased response when I told him you had made solicitous enquiries after him. He was so thin at last that I marvelled he could live.... Please send me two or three of your everlasting flowers to put into his grave.

Next day, 14 November, Blunt wrote a moving obituary of Thompson which was published in the *Academy* on the twenty-third. 'As I think of him', Blunt concluded, 'sitting with us under the trees I seem to hear him reciting his own verses:

> Suffer me at your leafy feast
> To sit apart, a somewhat alien guest ...
> Frail, strengthless as a noon-belated moon.
> Or as the glazing eyes of watery heaven,
> When the sick night sinks in a deathly swoon.'

On 31 July 1908 Blunt was thanking Meynell warmly for giving him the manuscript of Thompson's famous essay on Shelley. He would value it as an essay, 'and perhaps even still more as a palimpsest, and certainly shall not rub out a word of the pencil writing which may be full of good things yet to be discovered.'*[17]

There are signs, quite apart from Thompson's visit, that Blunt sometimes contemplated founding a literary 'coterie': perhaps the building of summer dwellings for artists and writers on his Gosbrook estate, perhaps the families to live rent free and all meet at Newbuildings for the main meal of the day, but otherwise keeping themselves.

The Meynells by now had their own house under the downs at Greatham, but Blunt had lent them Fernycroft several summers ago. He would arrive like a whirlwind to visit them with his Arabians and pitch his tent in the Forest. 'If life contained many such moments', said Alice Meynell after the Arabians bolted one day and crashed the carriage, 'it would indeed be a gift beyond price.'[18]

Another family who were to become only less intimate with Blunt than the Meynells were the Bellocs – Hilaire Belloc, the half-French Catholic writer, his wife Elodie and their splendidly untidy children. They had recently come to live under the famous windmill at nearby

* Today the MS is in Boston College.

Shipley. Belloc had first got into touch with Blunt when seeking an introduction to William Morris, 'whose work', wrote Belloc to Blunt, 'once all but converted me to approach the Great Beast of Socialism'. The consumption of claret by Hilaire and Elodie at Newbuildings – three and a half bottles in an evening – amused Blunt though he did not imitate it.

Yet other poets marked out for Blunt's circle were his cousin Lord Alfred Douglas and Alfred's wife Olive. Young Bosie's future had been of constant concern to Blunt. While badgering Meynell to give him literary work, Blunt believed that Bosie's real hope lay in marriage. He gave Bosie money the year after Oscar Wilde's death and again in 1902 to enable him to elope with Olive Custance, hitherto the fiancée of George Montagu. The Wyndhams were delighted. 'Anything short of murder in the Douglas family', said Percy to Wilfrid, 'is a source of congratulation.'[19]

Two more candidates for Blunt's literary and Catholic circle, introduced to him by Meynell, were the modernist priest Father Tyrrell and Miss Maude Petre in whose house at Storrington he lived. Maud Petre, about thirty-five, struck Blunt as being without much humour but essentially honest and good:

> I fancy all the same [he wrote on 15 August 1907] that both she and Fr. Tyrrell are conscious of the anomaly of their position, both religious and social, but this only makes them the more interesting to me. I hope to see more of them. . . .[20]

Ill-health had further circumscribed Blunt's political work. Journalism and exhortation were about all he could henceforth manage. In 1907 he encouraged a young Irishman named Frederick Ryan to edit a new left-wing organ, to be called *Egypt*, and wrote most of the first number himself. The Denshawai case continued to excite him. He proposed to establish a secondary school at Denshawai as a memorial to the victims. But only old John Evelyn among politicians joined him in contributing, and the government vetoed the project.

Bernard Shaw was to advise him about finding a publisher for Theodore Rothstein's pamphlet, *Egypt's Ruin*. Arthur Fifield knew 'the revolutionary market', suggested Shaw; better still Heinemann, who was already in the thick of conflict between Hall-Caine and Cromer over the White Prophet. 'It is possible that he may imagine himself enlisted under your banner ... being a Jew is naturally an enemy to Caesar, he might take on the job.'[21] Rothstein was a Jewish Marxist.

Blunt himself advised Dillon and the Irish party in February to boycott Parliament's vote of £50,000 for Lord Cromer on his resignation as Consul General in Egypt. Blunt had received the news of Cromer's resignation the April before somewhat melodramatically.

He had fallen asleep before dinner, exhausted by writing an article for the Liberal *Daily News* in answer to Cromer's annual report on Egypt. A telegram from Meynell announced the resignation. In a second Blunt was fully awake, shaking his four-poster with gargantuan laughter. 'Whoo-whoop!' he wired back to Meynell, feeling like a huntsman with Cromer's brush in his pocket 'and the mask of that ancient red fox dangling from my saddle'.

Later that same year on a sudden impulse Blunt shot a fine dog fox, 'fat sleek and beautiful', in the Newbuildings wood. 'If the officers of the 11th Hussars but knew! I feel now that I have passed the Rubicon of crime and am bound no longer to my fellow men by any moral restraint or fear of their disapproval.' From now on his social defiance over Dorothy and his political challenge to the British Empire were united, both symbolized by shooting that sleek red fox.[22]

Next year, 1908, when the Egyptian Nationalists' leader Kamel Pasha died suddenly, Blunt responded to his successor Farid Bey's request for advice with a long trenchant letter, of which the final paragraph ran: 'Have courage and always courage. Never miss an occasion to act strongly and to strike the enemy. Tapez et tapagez toujours. Voilà mon ordre. A vous de coeur. W.S.B.'

The Turkish revolution of 1908 filled Blunt with hope for Egypt also. His friend Professor Browne of Cambridge, the great Persian expert, visited him at Newbuildings. Surely if Sir Edward Grey the Liberal Foreign Secretary supported Turkish freedom, as he did, his government *must* give a constitution to Egypt? But no. Dillon told Blunt that Egypt as a subject was absolutely boycotted in Parliament. So Blunt could only write and write. C. P. Scott, the editor of the *Manchester Guardian*, felt 'great difficulty in troubling' Blunt for articles, as he would not accept payment; nevertheless he begged for pieces on Kamel and Farid, and later on Gorst. 'You seem to be the only man who takes a sympathetic interest and really knows about the people.'[23]

The Labour party propagandist H. N. Brailsford was one of those who congratulated Blunt on his *Manchester Guardian* article. 'The attitude of calm certainty' with which Blunt regarded Egypt's future liberation both impressed and cheered him. His wife Jane, a militant suffragette to whom Blunt had given a copy of *Satan Absolved*, found herself 'in such complete sympathy with Satan's view of humanity that there seemed nothing left to say'. When a butterfly sailed across her backyard at 32 Well Walk, Hampstead, she hoped it might be Antichrist.

With his romantic attitude to women, Blunt did not espouse the suffragettes' cause. But he advised Margot Asquith to cease ranting against them. Woman-rule in England was no more a peril than the

Yellow Peril in Europe or the Negro Peril in America. 'Women have never ruled men anywhere, and never will except indirectly by being better and kinder and less selfish than we are.' If only Margot would realize 'the folly of treating political enthusiasts as common criminals'.[24]

Blunt's social defiance was also strengthened by the flood of amusing or malicious gossip he received from visiting friends as he lay on his couch. It gave him a satisfactorily cynical view of that society before which he stood arraigned. Why should he respect a system, for instance, that had driven Mrs Crawford, Dilke's mistress, and Dilke himself to such extremities? It was Wilfrid Meynell who told Blunt that Mrs Crawford, desiring a divorce from her M.P. husband, had trapped Dilke into being her co-respondent:

'She made advances to Dilke and used to meet him at a house Dilke had for such purposes, writing at the same time anonymous letters to her husband warning him against Dilke. Dilke was thus entrapped. Fanny, the maid, who shared their amusements, was got out of the way by Dilke, who still pays her a pension at Buenos Aires where she lives.' In the end both were punished; Dilke was made to play 'a fool's part without profit of guilt or innocence', while Mrs Crawford, instead of being made an honest woman of by her lover after the divorce, became a Catholic, devoting herself to good works. Cardinal Manning, whose penitent she was, asked Meynell to introduce her around – he knew what the old Catholics were like – and she told Meynell the whole story.

On the ever-fascinating subject of Balfour, Blanche Hozier told Blunt that Arthur had proposed to her 'when she was very young, but she did not fancy him – he was very badly dressed in those days and not at all attractive'. Margot added that Balfour now looked upon all politics as a game – 'the world to come being infinitely more interesting and important'. He was entirely without passion, said Margot, though he may have kissed Mary Elcho.[25]

It was Skittles, however, who fed Blunt most of his gossip, especially that from the Palace. He and Skittles had been out of touch for ten years but in 1905 she was desperate for his help, being wretchedly ill (an operation and later radium treatment for cancer) and penurious: 'God bless you a 1000 times dear dear old friend Winny, for your noble generosity to me with regard to the lease of South Street.' For many years afterwards she rewarded him with stories about the Royal Family, often culled from the royal doctors who attended her at the King's expense. Her little jokes had always been adapted to the King's sense of humour. There was the time when she had produced a rather shabby umbrella and he said, 'It needs recovering.' 'Yes', she said, 'I have had it covered twice, but there has been no produce.'[26]

Skittles had not seen the King since 1904 and was never to see him again. Yet the flow of her information, whether true or false, was ceaseless. Sometimes it was His Majesty's health, even worse than her own, with cancer of the throat (not true), varicose veins and his bones turning to chalk. At other times it was his family and friends. 'He is terribly bored with the Queen, who is very dear and very stupid.' Jewish businessmen, she continued, such as Hirsch and Cassel were his particular friends, partly because they were financially generous, partly because of a blood relationship with Sir Ernest Cassel, who was the illegitimate grandson of Prince Ernest of Saxe-Coburg, King Edward's uncle. (Prince Ernest, said Skittles, had had an illegitimate daughter by an actress who married a Jew of Frankfurt named Cassel.)[27]

A year or two later Skittles was to excel herself, repeating a doctor's highly coloured gossip about the death of the sculptor Edgar Boehm. Despite all Queen Victoria could do, he had managed to die of a haemorrhage in Princess Louise's arms, leaving the courageous Princess to snatch the studio key from his pocket, call a cab and, covered with blood as she was, dash for a doctor on her own – she had no lady-in-waiting with her. She and the doctor afterwards 'concocted a story' that Boehm had died moving a heavy statue. Knowing nothing of this drama, the old Queen had the errant lover laid in Westminster Abbey. Skittles and Blunt were much amused. Blunt also considered the story to be of historical value:

> This is all very interesting and suggests to me that the scandalous paragraphs in papers etc. about Queen Victoria and John Brown were the work of Boehm, who with no real evidence spread the stories about Queen Victoria in order to cover up any revelations about his own relations with Princess Louise. It all fits in and there is a great deal of truth mixed up with the invention.[28]

Another day it would be Skittles and the poet Swinburne – 'Pussy' and 'Swinny' – trying to make love, but he was always too drunk. 'So very kind he was too, instructing her about birds and flowers, as one might a child, and especially the grasses on Wimbledon Common. How many sorts were there? "Never mind about that", she would say. "Give them all to the cow."' Swinburne loved Blunt's *Proteus* poems, she added, but would not meet him because of his Irish opinions – 'damned Jesuit', Swinburne called him.[29]

Then there were Skittles's reminiscences of politicians. When Blunt sent her a present of rabbits for the pot, she thanked him with a story of Disraeli and Gladstone: how Dizzy was 'a kind old fellow but very dull. . . . I loved old bully Gladstone far more than "Dizzy", old G. had a lot of fun in him and was a more powerful man to me than old

Dizzy.'* Or there was Blunt's old Irish opponent Lord Clanricarde. He had once lent her £500 on the security of her jewels, 'but he always refused to let her have them back except on a certain condition and that it should be in her riding hat'. He used to come 'sneaking outside the house at night', so that the then Prince of Wales and Lord Hartington were forced to empty a *pot de chambre* on his head.[30]

If this was society, and always had been, why should Blunt mind if it criticized him? But the reaction of his own family was another matter. A misconceived attempt on his part to get Dorothy accepted by Crabbet was to provoke a new and deep domestic rupture.

The quarrel began in spring 1908 when Judith and her family were moving permanently into Crabbet from Forest Cottage, and she invited her father for a few days' visit on 1 April to discuss their plans. Her invitation, sent on 15 March, was affectionate: addressed to 'Dearest H.F.' and signed 'Bibi', it was brought by two little messengers, Anthony the grandson and Nell the water spaniel. Judith did not want to make any changes at Crabbet without consulting him, she said, and offered him a permanent room in his old home, 'a refuge from the world – the long sought Hermitage!'

Wilfrid was pleased. But he saw the difficulty. Judith spoke of a hermitage. That assumed no Dorothy.

His first solution was a sensible one: 'My only difficulty', he replied to Judith on the thirty-first, 'is that Dorothy is with me just now and I cannot well leave her alone here, so we are writing to Guy to propose she should go to him for those two nights....' If Guy could not have her, 'I must put off my visit to you till a more convenient season'.[31]

Had Wilfrid stuck to that plan all might have been well. Guy's response, however, put his back up. It was not that Guy *could* not have Dorothy; he would not. 'Dear Squire', he explained after telegraphing his refusal, 'it won't do. She would not be received at Crabbet with favour', and her coming to Guy would emphasize the fact and start 'talk', which of all things he wanted to avoid. Wilfrid promptly sent for Guy, declared that if Judith was 'less than polite to Dorothy' she must not expect him, Wilfrid, at Crabbet, and asked Guy to tell Judith so. He wrote in his diary that day, 3 April, 'Judith has no real right to set up as my censor of morals, nor will I accept her as such.'

Next day Guy backed out of his mission. Instead, Neville sent a long conciliatory letter explaining, as he thought, the situation. Judith would refuse to have Dorothy 'not on moral grounds, but simply out of loyalty to her mother'. She wanted to remain neutral between her

* Button Bourke was to tell Blunt about the good advice old 'bully Gladstone' had once given to a prostitute Button knew. 'He told me', said the girl, 'to be honest in all my dealings and always to give full value for the money I received.'

parents. Why could not H.F. keep his affair with Dorothy separate from his daughter and grandchildren?

This was calling Wilfrid's bluff over the adoption formula, and Wilfrid did not deign to reply to 'this letter of a young man', except to send for Neville and Guy again on the tenth. By now Wilfrid felt sure that Anne's alleged disapproval was merely 'an excuse' to conceal Judith's own jealousy of Dorothy, expecially of her probable benefit from H.F.'s will.* Wilfrid therefore made Neville take a note to Judith, proposing to bring Dorothy over, 'to show her the house on her way to Clouds. . . . Can you give us luncheon?' Any further rudeness from Judith would mean no H.F. at Crabbet or Lyttons at Newbuildings. 'It is a matter of honour with me', concluded Wilfrid, 'which leaves me no middle course.' Judith laughed at the word 'honour' but felt obliged to reply: 'If you really wish it I shall expect you to lunch at one o'clock on Monday according to your letter. There will be a bed for Miss Lawrence. Yours. J.'[32]

Judith's diary celebrated 13 April with expressive bleakness: 'H.F. and D.C. came to lunch D.C. left 3 train. Miss Lawrence came. Tennis bad.'

Her father on the contrary was delighted.

> I slept in the big bedroom in the east front [he wrote] where I have spent many a happy night in the former times with loves that are gone to their graves. Now I am installed there in an old man's way with my nurse next door to me. I find Judith most anxious to make things agreeable to me; and I am sure I was right in showing my teeth about Dorothy.

But while Wilfrid was revelling in gentle nostalgia at Crabbet, Judith on 14 April eased her conscience by sending her 'darling Mother' an account of Dorothy's visit, and of how' 'uncomfortable' it had made her, Judith.

> But H.F. [she explained] said in a letter to Neville that he would take all responsibility and told him you knew all about her and approved of the arrangement and that there was no quarrel between you as you often wrote to him. You will be sure to hear of the visit from Guy so I had better just tell you. . . . I do think it hard that he should make his coming conditional on her coming too, but of course if you approve it is all right.

If Anne registered shock in her reply to her daughter, in her letter to Wilfrid her 'surprise and indignation' were nothing less than volcanic. Dated 22 April from Sheykh Obeyd, her letter accused him of immor-

* Blunt did threaten to change his will unless Judith received Dorothy, or so Guy told Judith on 7 April. However, Judith merely wrote in her diary: 'As he makes his Will afresh every six weeks and I have no reason to believe it is now in my favour and the said WILL has been used as a family Blackmailer for the last ten years this leaves me comparatively calm.'

ality, false pretences (over their correspondence), premeditated insult and revolting conduct in dragging Judith into it. She ended 'in great sorrow and anger'.[33]

Wilfrid assailed Judith on 5 May with a fierce indictment, penned as if by a double reincarnation of Jeremiah the prophet and King Lear. The ingratitude! – after inheriting Crabbet from *him* not from her mother. The lies! – about Dorothy's position (the personal aspect of it being none of their business). The treachery! – in writing to her mother secretly while her father was under her roof. The malice! – in causing fresh strife between her parents. After some two thousand scorching words, he finished up: 'I had intended in beginning this letter to make a last appeal to you to repair the wrong you have done.' But he now saw that it was useless.

> You are too hard, too self-interested, too double-tongued, to be trusted again.... It is better therefore you and I should remain apart.... Enjoy Crabbet for the future in you own filial way. I will never set foot inside its doors again. Wilfrid Scawen Blunt.[34]

This volley of wrath, misery and delusion was the grand climax of the quarrel. After that it began to subside. Judith sent her father's tirade to her mother who, having let off steam by contradicting it paragraph by paragraph in alternate red and green ink, afterwards in her goodness prayed for Christian charity. Then Blunt bethought him, not for the first time, of the risk he ran of losing his adored grandchildren. Anthony was 'the dearest boy in the world', Anne the prettiest and most unselfish girl, Winnie the cleverest. Soon subsidiary villains began to appear, who deflected his willing attention from his wife and daughter. It turned out that Miss Lawrence had made mischief while at Crabbet; and Guy Carleton composed a letter on 16 May that enabled Blunt to dub him the ultimate 'enemy'. After announcing that his work as Her Ladyship's stud manager would henceforth preclude him from coming to Newbuildings, Guy wrote:

> I don't think you and Dorothy know what a scandal you have caused. You and she only see a very small set of people and do not know what is being said. You may explain till you are black in the face but the world at large will not take your view of the matter.[35]

Accompanying these family eruptions, like the shriek of split rocks heard above the hissing of molten lava, were excruciating attacks of illness that hit Blunt in May and June. They may indeed have played their part in his violence. First an incipient hernia racked him, necessitating his wearing a truss. There was talk of cancer. Then a tubercular abscess blocked his throat. Luckily it burst before 'they' could operate.

But before all had subsided, he had been threatened with blood poisoning and a bone-splinter from his diseased spine piercing his gullet.

As a result, Dorothy was to go through many black depressions, though her personal relations with Blunt were not among the causes. Their love, as he was never tired of writing, remained 'unclouded'.

It was his constant nearness to death that kept her in a state of gnawing anxiety. And family quarrels were a scourge to her gentle nature. (Blunt was to call her 'the least self-assertive person in the world'.) On Christmas Day 1908, she woke up crying after a dream that Crabbet loved her (Judith and Neville had indeed paid a polite visit to Newbuildings in September); 'all the complications of Crabbet being smoothed away and reconciliation and kind words all round'. Then the Christmas post brought her Wilfrid's poem 'Sea Lavender', in which the 'Flower of passions unrevealed' reminded him of his and Dorothy's own nuptial dawn.

> Under the sky's multitude,
> Till the pulsings of their blood
> Led them into ways unknown,
> Flesh of flesh and bone of bone
> Clasped in one, till doubt was over,
> And they went forth loved and lover....[36]

Dorothy went to bed that night 'hugging the poem' in her arms.

In October 1909 Anne had not yet left for Egypt, being laid up with erysipelas. The doctor advised her to keep her head swathed even in bed – a habit which, like subsequent attacks of dermatitis – 'my hideous ailment' – became chronic and caused some mockery and misunderstanding. Hearing of her afflictions, Wilfrid once again suggested a meeting. Her response, or lack of it, chilled him. 'I should not mind meeting the H.F. in the open air', she told Neville, 'not in a house.' They might inspect the Crabbet Stud but only discuss Stud affairs; nor would she wish her seeing H.F. to be construed into any change of view. Her attitude was understandable, but not to Blunt.

'This is precisely the kind of letter Lady Byron might have written in answer to a message from her husband', Wilfrid commented unfairly. He replied, also through Neville, that 'it is not sufficiently encouraging to me to make any further move in the matter'. To go round the Stud with Anne and old Holman the groom under umbrellas (for a south-westerly gale was blowing) was less than tempting. 'I closed the door on that portion of my life once again, not to knock more at it.'[37]

Those words were to hold good for the next six years.

[20]
'Pilgrim of Distress'
1910–1913

On 28 November 1910 Wilfrid Blunt was pierced by an agonizing pain in his bladder, accompanied by a stricture that lasted all the morning. The doctor, while able temporarily to relieve him, explained that he would be an invalid for life. What Blunt philosophically called an infirmity of age was in fact prostate trouble – possibly operable but for Blunt's abhorrence of the surgeon's knife. He was to give up his Chapel Street house for good in 1912, never again travelling to London. His deepest grief was all along for Dorothy. 'Up to this moment I have not really felt my years', he had written after receiving the bad news, 'having it still in my power to make a woman who should love me happy. I can hardly hope any more for this, and the thought is depressing.' He need not have worried. He was her god and it was bliss to be with him in heaven, even if in heaven there was no marriage or giving in marriage.[1]

In the same year that his terminal illness began – though it took an unconscionable time to terminate – the Edwardian age passed away. Skittles was soon able to regale him with a blow-by-blow account of the scene involving two weeping women at the bedside of King Edward VII. 'You must kiss her', the King ordered Queen Alexandra. 'You must kiss Alice', pointing to the anguished Mrs Keppel. The Queen obeyed him; but the moment he had drawn his last breath she said to the courtiers, 'Get that woman out', cocking a snook as the door shut for ever on her rival. All 'very interesting', wrote Blunt.[2]

But his own long and brilliant summary of the King's qualities showed a real sense of loss. How far was King Edward truly a 'peacemaker'? He always patched up the quarrels of his courtiers and Blunt believed he was useful to the Foreign Office, 'especially under such insular Secretaries of State as Arthur Balfour and Edward Grey'. The King it was who had stopped the unpopular Boer War. He had been shocked by the brutalities in Egypt as well as by Cromer's 'unnecessary quarrel with the Khedive and Sultan. 'It was entirely due to him that Cromer was recalled.' He might even be called, like Solomon, the Wise.

They each had several hundred concubines and as we know 'The knowledge of women is the beginning of wisdom.' At least it teaches tolerance for the unwisdom of others. Of all this the newspaper writers say no word, being virtuous men and fools.*

A week after the King's death, Blunt had seen a great beech lying in his park uprooted by a storm the night before. 'It was a symbol of the dead King', he wrote, 'quite rotten at the root, but one half of it clothed in its spring green.' The parallel with his own case may have added sharpness to his experience.

The young eagles of the new reign did not please Blunt. In July 1911 he was invited to a party at Stafford House with Wilfrid Meynell, where 'literary gentlemen' were supposed to meet 'comical ladies'. At one stage in the evening, after loud and tiresome singing, the ladies sat in a ring on the floor while a group of Parisian can-can dancers showed their knees and knickers. Such displays, reflected Blunt, would have been impossible in the dance-halls, let alone drawing-rooms of his youth; yet now all present, ranging from 'ex-beauties' like Lady Desborough and Lady Randolph Churchill to 'young men and maidens', applauded wildly, without a suspicion of indecorum – 'for such are the manners of the day. It is not for me to find fault', admitted Blunt, 'and I suppose we enjoy our lives more. Still there was a certain brutality about it all which "gave one to think".'[3]

He championed the old-fashioned 'poor', whose children were mowed down on the Sussex highways by young motorists from London, while their gardens were trampled by a callous race of fox-hunters. 'It is near lunacy in this democratic age', reflected Blunt, 'for our gentry to go on with their amusements in the way they do, caring not a damn for their poorer neighbours.'[4]

Among his clashes with individuals, his worst was with the incorrigible Bosie (Lord Alfred Douglas). In 1909 Blunt had received a telegram from Bosie asking for £500 'by Wednesday' to keep his by now disreputable magazine the *Academy* afloat. Blunt telegraphed back: 'Just leaving for Clouds. You must not count on me in this matter.' To which Bosie replied: 'Many thanks for your kind and considerate telegram just received. Did not count on you. I never count on anyone who can't write sonnets.' Two years later Bosie, having become a Catholic, suddenly apologized to Blunt for his past rudeness. 'Dear Alfred, Your trespass against me was a small matter', replied Blunt, but his 'sins against others of your friends' could not be 'countenanced' – a reference to Bosie's mania for litigation. Bosie hit back: 'Of what value has your countenance ever been to any man? To

* Blunt himself 'virtuously' omitted from his *My Diaries* Vol. II, p. 321, the phrase italicized above, replacing it with 'that knowledge of women which as we know is the beginning of wisdom . . .'. (FM 10/1975, 20 May 1910.)

be known as your friend or associate has always been something in the nature of a social handicap.' What was Blunt but 'a contemptible cad', whom most people considered 'a half crazy old gentleman, with a bee in his bonnet'. It was only the intervention of George Wyndham and Mark Napier which prevented the row from developing into one of Bosie's court actions.[5]

In politics Blunt saw nothing but doom; the rush of the oncoming whirlwind, expected but none the less horrific. For the past forty years he had been mapping its path: Congress of Vienna, Canal Convention, Tangier, Egypt, Entente Cordiale, Morocco. And now 'the abominable Concert of Europe presided over by that pompous ineptitude Grey'. Twice in 1910 Blunt wrote extremist pamphlets on Egyptian anniversaries to rouse the Nationalists. But it all seemed hopeless. The milestones of doom followed one another so thick and fast that exhortations and warnings became meaningless. First the Italian seizure of Tripoli, then the Balkan wars. All in two years, 1912–13; the Ottoman Empire dismembered. Yet Blunt had spent thirty years of his life preaching the regeneration of Islam.

Some day Egypt might win her freedom, but not along the lines he had so passionately advocated: 'Egyptian patriotism must take a new direction and I am too old to begin with a fresh policy. Others may do so without inconsistency. I cannot.'[6]

In explaining this disaster to his Indian friends, Blunt deeply touched their tender hearts. 'I actually wept myself', wrote Syed Mahmud, a barrister from Bankipur. But Mahmud saw a ray of hope for the Muslims:

> They have now begun to realize [Mahmud wrote] the true meanings of what you told them years ago.... Your articles in 'Egypt' are widely read here. They are translated and reproduced in vernacular papers and let me tell you that they carry a lot of weight.[7]

There were other subsidiary misfortunes within the grand tragedy, which also caused Blunt pain and despair. The attempt of Sir Eldon Gorst (Cromer's successor) to establish a more liberal regime in Egypt had not been supported. Arabi, who had died in 1911, was described by Moberly Bell in *The Times* as 'an exploded windbag'. That was to be expected; but Arabi's memory was also being denigrated by the Egyptian leaders.* 'The Egyptians deserve their fate', wrote Blunt,

* Blunt had privately criticized Ahmed Arabi for making friends with the mammon of unrighteousness on his return from exile. He claimed a bigger allowance from government, since his family had grown enormously in Ceylon and his grandsons desired education to enable them to enter the government service, instead of remaining part of the fellahin, and proud of it, like their famous grandsire. On the whole, Blunt felt in his heart that in the changed circumstances of the twentieth century, Arabi had better have remained in Ceylon.

'when they treat with neglect the only man who showed any courage among them when it came to the pinch in 1882.' But the fathers of the present leaders had already deserted to Britain. The magazine *Egypt* was failing, as Frederick Ryan had lamented to Blunt, because Nationalist support was concentrated entirely in Cairo, whereas in Ireland 'every village had its National League branch'.[8]

The magazine was to collapse in 1913, Blunt having resigned his chairmanship the year before, after his violent attack of illness. Worse still, Ryan died of peritonitis in Blunt's house. He was only thirty-eight. Blunt mourned him in one of his most poignant sonnets, 'To a Dead Journalist':

> O soul of man, thou pilgrim of distress
> Lost in time's void! Thou wind of nothingness![9]

And what of the Irish Nationalists? Here too Blunt felt that most of his former comrades-in-arms had gone over to the enemy, leaving him more in sympathy with the revolutionary Fenians. The Irish parliamentary party were supporting Sir Edward Grey and his pernicious European policy, as a return for getting Home Rule. It would serve them right if they never got Home Rule after all. Blunt's aristocratic prejudices prevented him from welcoming Asquith's threat to create 500 new peers, if the House of Lords refused to pass Home Rule – even though Winston Churchill said Blunt himself should be one of the new peers!

That faithful Irishman John Dillon tried to comfort Blunt for the Balkan débâcle along the lines that appealed to more and more of their friends: 'I knew you would feel very much depressed.... It is extremely mixed up with the complete triumph, so far as European politics are concerned, of international finance.'[10] This theory was where the extremes of left and right met; Marxists like Blunt's friend Hyndman and Catholics like Belloc both believing in the conspiracy of 'international finance capital'.

Hilaire Belloc and the two Chestertons, Cecil and Gilbert Keith, whom Blunt occasionally met at Shipley, won his warm sympathy for their boldness in attacking the Marconi scandal; though at first when Belloc's paper *Eye Witness* became Cecil Chesterton's *New Witness*, Blunt remarked that it might be more aptly named *False Witness*. A few months later, however, Blunt was contributing his views to *New Witness* rather than to any capitalist newspaper, 'since experience has long taught me that the Press in the hands of Capitalism is the most dangerous of all forms of popular education in untruth, and that Democracy, guided by it, has become the engine of its own destruction'.[11] He had written a satirical ballad for Belloc at the beginning of 1912 entitled 'My Duty Right or Wrong':

I went today to talk to Israel
Who does my business in the 'Deodar'.
I had some preference stock I wished to sell,
A Chinese Labour thing in Zanzibar,
Which had grown shaky but still stood at par.
He praised my moral instinct, wired Hongkong
'We make the sacrifice.' I took my car
Repeating 'Yes. My duty right or wrong.'*

Over the Marconi scandal itself Blunt was predictably cynical. He did not particularly blame Sir Herbert Samuel, who was a Jew and related to financiers. Samuel had simply pursued his profession by other means. But Lloyd George!

And this is our Chancellor of the Exchequer! If he had had the manhood of a mouse he would have resigned, and if Asquith had had the honesty of a bookmaker he would have chucked him. We shall see him whitewashed and forgiven.[12]

Blunt felt no confidence in Asquith's ability to keep the peace at home, any more than abroad, after the disastrous coal strike of 1912. The country might even be in for a civil war. On 28 March he ordered £250 in gold and £50 in silver from Glyn's Bank 'as an insurance against political accidents in these days of stress'. In July of the year before he had obtained two other 'caches' of gold from Glyn's, because of the 'warlike' atmosphere, one of which he and Dorothy secreted above the kitchen ceiling, the other in the Forest beside a sycamore.

There were some consolations, even in the political field. Philip Napier, Mark's son, wrote to Blunt from Cairo that Lord Kitchener, Gorst's successor as Consul General in 1911, was now known locally as 'Kitchener of Chaos'. Blunt had tried to encourage the chaos by helping the May 1912 number of *Egypt* to be delivered to subscribers in Cairo, notwithstanding Kitchener's prohibition. 'The June number', he noted, 'will exhort Mohammedans in London to boycott him [Kitchener] when he comes here on the 20th.'

The politician who contributed most, after George Wyndham, to Blunt's happiness was the young Winston Churchill, still in his thirties, Home Secretary and the husband of Lady Blanche Hozier's daughter Clementine. On first hearing of Clementine's engagement from Blanche, Blunt wrote, 'Clementine and Kitty, who died, are both Blanche told me long ago her daughters by Bay Middleton, who I believe was a charming man but I never saw him. It is much wiser for a woman who has an inferior husband, to choose a suitable sire for her

* This is the second of three stanzas with an envoi. (FM. 410/1975, 16 January 1912.)

children, and both these girls were delightful, refined and superior in every way.'*

Blunt composed for Clementine a poem entitled 'Love's Novitiate', urging her to enter Love's courts, where she would find 'Realms wide of peace, joys won without amaze'. He attended their wedding in September 1908, several people asking Lady Blanche afterwards: 'Who was that beautiful, tall man sitting in the front pew?' Blunt himself wrote: 'I arrived at the church when all the seats were taken, but Blanche Hozier gave me a place in the family pew between her sister Maud White and Hugo Wemyss who is I think like me a former lover. Redesdale a third was with her in the front.'

On their honeymoon Winston wrote to his mother-in-law: 'I find love-making a serious and delightful occupation.' Two years later Clementine was writing to Blunt of her dazzling husband: 'I was very proud when I heard him from the gallery. I hope he will never catch the usual Official Mood.' He never did.[13]

Of Clementine, Blunt wrote in 1912: 'She is certainly the most beautiful woman now in society and one of the nicest.'[14] Her younger sister Nellie was one of those lively girls with whom Blunt was automatically tempted to have 'a little love'. But, as he remarked, 'in love one must either go forwards or go backwards', and from 1910 onwards he and Nellie fortunately went back.†

As for Churchill himself, Blunt soon believed he could influence the son even more creatively than he had influenced the father some twenty-five years before. He wrote to Judith on 16 March 1910, 'You may not know that Churchill has adopted nearly all the ideas of my memorandum on prison reform (Let Neville know this).'[15] Blunt rightly felt that he had not been a political prisoner in vain. While continuing to press on Churchill his full proposals that non-violent political prisoners should be placed 'in the first class of misdemeanours', Blunt asked the Home Secretary to a discussion at Newbuildings with himself and the socialist Hyndman. Churchill wired back: 'Shall be happy to meet any of your friends who will not blow me up.' Next day, however, the Home Secretary revoked his telegram and suggested meeting 'one of your Irish friends' instead –

* FM. 395/1975, 15 August 1908. In 1916 when Blunt lent Lady Blanche a cottage called Carpenters on the Crabbet estate, Margot Asquith told him that Blanche's brother-in-law Lord Redesdale was Clementine's father. After a gossip with the ailing but 'valiant' Blanche, Blunt wrote: 'Bertie [Lord Redesdale] in later years was one of Blanche's lovers but it was not true... that Clementine was his daughter. I doubt if anyone but myself knows who Clementine's father was.' (FM. 16/1975, 23 August 1916.)

† That Blunt took Nellie to his secret spot in Newbuildings wood, read her poetry, held her hand and generally flirted with her is further proof, if that were needed, that she was not his daughter. The legend that she *was* is based mainly on her dark eyes and features which certainly resembled Blunt's in a portrait painted of her at this date by Neville Lytton's friend Charlot Geoffroy Dechaume. Nellie was born five months before Blunt's affair with Blanche began.

who might have been thought handier with bombs than the Sussex county cricketer Hyndman. Blunt invited John Redmond.[16]

Just over a week later Winston came again, this time with Clemmie. Present also was Harley Granville Barker the playwright and Fabian socialist, 'a man of much political intelligence', wrote Blunt, 'besides being an excellent fellow and man of the world'. Blunt got Churchill to accept all their points except the abandonment of forcible feeding. This reform was to remain one of Blunt's chief concerns, for the health of the suffragette Lady Constance Lytton had been ruined by it, as he knew from the 'goal-bird confabulations' (her expression) they had together.

Blunt's fascination with Churchill continued to grow.

> Churchill has a wonderful memory [he had written earlier] which extends to scraps of poetry and fragments of speeches of a hundred years ago. He is also a great and very rapid reader of books. He told us he wrote his life of his father mostly while in the House of Commons and busy with all sorts of other work.[17]

Churchill had three outstanding qualities according to Blunt: 'great ability, honesty in politics, and a good heart'. The three things that he most resembled, said Meynell, were 'a seraph, a rat and ... a rat-catcher'. Dorothy Carleton said he was the image of Puck. No one as yet saw in him the British bulldog.

Memories of brilliant and bibulous evenings at Newbuildings with Winston and other choice friends abound in the Blunt diaries from 1909 onwards. There was the dinner for Winston with Harry Cust that October, 1909, when argument was borne forward on a river of champagne and Blunt's old Madeira 'of which Winston managed to account for seven glasses, not however being less clear in his arguments for it. Harry was more affected and when we were on our way to bed talked rather incoherently about the moon and forgot which floor of the house we were on.'[18]

Next night Clementine stole the show 'in a kind of Mermaid's dress which looked as if she had no clothes at all underneath her outer sheath of crimped silk. She whispered to me that it was almost so, when I remarked about it. She is certainly a lovely woman with no small share of knowledge of the fact, and still in love with Winston, as he with her.'

The crowning occasion was in 1912, when Blunt assembled his closest friends for dinner in the Jubilee room: Clementine in an embroidered dress brought from Smyrna, Winston in borrowed plumes (one of Blunt's Baghdad robes), George Wyndham in a blue dressing-gown, Blunt in his Bedouin clothes; only Mark Napier not dressed up. The 'feast of reason and flow of bowl' reminded Blunt of superlative nights at the old Crabbet Club. In his published account he left out all reference to the 'bowl's' contents of champagne, oldest Madeira and home-made sloe gin, which eventually rendered George 'too drunk to be any longer quite articulate'. And while admitting in print that the secrets of the Cabinet and Opposition front benches had all been 'gloriously divulged', he wisely kept dark that this was after 'George Curzon's arse had been kicked and Lansdowne been emasculated' by common accord.[19]

Churchill's political differences from Blunt never impeded their intimacy. 'I was glad to find from your letter of last month', Churchill had written from the Home Office on 17 October 1911, that 'my belonging to a government wicked enough to send Lord Kitchener to Egypt has not altered our relations!'[20]

This period of male conviviality, when Newbuildings was the Mecca of politicians with a good cause and good appetites, saw also Blunt's serene acceptance of a physical second childhood. He depended entirely on his nurse every hour of his day, being washed, dressed and undressed like a baby. 'There is something pleasant in this helplessness.' At Christmas 1911 Miss Lawrence asked for a little nursemaid to assist her. Blunt was pleased. 'I like this idea of being back in a real nursery as suited to my second childhood. The little girl Annie is terribly afraid of me but seems intelligent and good.' April Fool's Day he sometimes thought the best day of the year, when he would set elaborate traps for his household. Dorothy took him to see J. M. Barrie's play *Peter Pan* in 1912. Finding it bored him he wrote, 'I suppose I am not old enough for it....'[21]

Those 'merry souls', his grandchildren, entertained him with the standing joke that if Grandpa had a nurse he must be a child. A Japanese doll slept beside him on his pillow, presented by Winnie. This doll, wrote Winnie aged nine, held the unshakeable belief that 'two plus two makes five ... and six plus six makes thirteen'.

Anne was discovering a new youth behind the door Wilfrid had closed in 1909. Once the door was shut she found if 'a relief'. Judith was told of her exhilaration at riding and hitting a polo ball about in the desert; why did not the woeful Edith Lytton take up cycling? At the beginning of 1912 Anne wrote movingly to her daughter: her career, so long 'failing in everything I tried for (of course especially H.F.)' was now a success, through 'having *you* and through you everything else'. Her two granddaughters, at present visiting Sheykh Obeyd, made 'this home a Paradise'.

It is somewhat surprising to find Father Lawrence of the Crawley friary trying that same year to heal the breach on the grounds of Her Ladyship's failing health; though no doubt he was right in emphasizing Anne's unalterable devotion, despite everything, to her husband. Wilfrid rebuffed the friar – 'a dear good man' – with more honesty than grace: 'Anne and I are really happier apart.'[22]

Only in Judith was there no sense of recaptured youth, although her own successes as a poet had drawn her closer to her father. He had persuaded her not to publish hastily – 'If I had to begin life again', he wrote to her, 'I should *publish no* verse between eighteen and eighty.' Her first volume of sonnets, *Love in a Mist*, was to be acclaimed, but Blunt found it unaccountably sad. What had one so superbly endowed as Judith to be sad about? This was the measure of his insensitivity to Judith's sorrows.

The girlhood of his child Mary never ceased to stir Blunt. Dorothy kept him informed of her 'moonlight' beauty – pale skin and shadowy eyes – and ravishing clothes: 'a little rose pink crêpe-de-chine frock all embroidered with silken flowers' and a moonstone crescent in her hair; or 'white *charmeuse* draped on classical lines' for her Court Presentation dress; or dark velvet and champagne-coloured satin and black hat wreathed with a large creamy feather to match, for her cousin Percy Wyndham's wedding. But their meetings were still almost always accidental. When they met in Rotten Row he asked her if she had seen many people she knew. She gave her unknown father one of those devastating looks that so much disturbed him. 'I do not come to see people. I only look at the dogs and horses.'[23]

Then the glorious day arrived on 26 September 1912 when her mother brought the child, 'a miracle of beauty', to Newbuildings for the day. Blunt showed her the carved four-poster where that other love-child Berkeley had been conceived, with the shell of the ostrich egg on which he and Anne had breakfasted in the desert over thirty years ago, hanging from the top. Beside it was the bunch of everlasting flowers he had picked when he knew this love-child was to be born. She was enchanted by the Arab weapons, peacock's train and great Moorish straw hats in the hall, and by the Morris tapestry. Blunt was wild with joy at her loveliness, charm and above all her presence in his home.

Quite carried away by her 'noble countenance so unspoiled by the vanity of the world in which she lives', he gave her the most valued of all his treasures: a barbaric ornament set with a lock of William Morris' hair. Later the child's mother expostulated to him: 'Any little thing of beads' would have done just as well, and now what would people think – or Hugo say?' (Hugo, as everyone knew, had a mistress, Lady Angela Forbes. But even the introduction of the can-can into the drawing-room had not banished the double standard from the bedroom.)[24]

Blunt had feared lest his fashionable young lady should find the peace of Newbuildings dull. Her evident pleasure in it set him off on renewed sessions of will-making, with the concomitant match-making. These pursuits gave the 'old Squire' a relatively innocent, even childlike sense of power over his 'kingdom'. In order that Blunts and Wyndhams should marry well, or better still, should be inter-mingled with one another in the new generation, he promoted many bizarre romances, all of which came to nought.

As Blunt's matrimonial inspirations ebbed and flowed, so his wills were signed and superseded – 'fifteen hundred every six months', Judith once sarcastically observed. His cottage-hermitages were now coming into their own as prospective legacies: some for the grandchildren, others for George or Dorothy or the child Mary, depending on who was to have Newbuildings at any given moment. Even the recently formed National Trust received a tentative offer of Worth Forest. But a visit of inspection on the Trust's behalf by 'three old women like the witches in Macbeth', headed by Miss Octavia Hill, temporarily quenched Blunt's public-spirited plan for his beloved kingdom. 'If such are to be its guardians', he wrote, 'it would be a desecration.'

Blunt himself saw that the final travesty of his match-making had occurred in 1913, when Skittles formally offered him her niece Daisy, if ever he were matrimonially free. 'I laughed and said it was too late and I was no longer capable.'[25]

He was sitting under the apple trees on 9 June 1913, waiting for the carriage to take him to the Forest, when a telegram arrived. 'George Wyndham is dead. Meynell.'

Both he and Dorothy were distraught at the news. They had each lost a brother rather than a cousin, and Dorothy would now have to bear the full burden of trusteeship for the child Mary's legacy from Blunt, which George had hitherto shared. She hurried to Clouds to comfort Madeline, George's mother (old Percy had died of a stroke the year before), while Blunt learnt from a Horsham paper that George's sudden death had been in Paris from heart failure (afterwards corrected to a blood-clot). Next day Hilaire Belloc called in a distressed state. He had seen George in Paris, and spoke of his death as 'the end of honesty in English public life'. This was an exaggeration in Wilfrid's opinion; 'for George's politics were the least creditable part of him., . . . It was George's other side that I loved and admired.'[26]

This 'other side' was the poetry and romance, the medieval dreams and secret loves. When George's only son Percy had married Diana Lister that spring, George wrote to Wilfrid without fear of being misunderstood: 'It is extravagant to suppose that Percy and Diana are going to be lovers and, also, husband and wife. But it is pleasant to contemplate the hypothesis.' Could true love ever be respectable? George like Wilfrid was in every sense irrevocably a Lancelot. 'I know of a certain cure for the "mal du siècle"', he had once informed Wilfrid, 'and shall go, like Lancelot, into the wilderness whenever the world wearies me.'[27]

Now that the world would weary George no more, nor George sustain Wilfrid, it was fortunate that Wilfrid's settled love for Dorothy had at long last broken the cycle of his own Arthurian dreams, and lifted happiness on to a smoother if quieter plane. As a memorial to their common past, as well as to his dear friend, Wilfrid dedicated the second volume of his *Poetical Works* 'To a Happy Warrior'. George Wyndham he saw as the 'ultimate man', heir to all the earth's delights.

> For what is wisdom more than this one thought,
> To harvest happiness?

From this harvest George had

> Fashioned a new chivalry
> For days to be . . .
> Till in his hands
> It seemed the actual lance
> Of Lancelot trembled and took edge and shook
> Defiance at his foes in Lyonnesse. . . .

Ill-health prevented Wilfrid from attending George's funeral. He took his usual drive through the Forest that day. 'On our way back to Newbuildings', he wrote, 'we stopped at Crawley and I said an unbeliever's prayer for him at Francis's tomb, it being the exact hour of the funeral at Clouds.' Ten days later Gay Plymouth (Windsor) came to Wilfrid for comfort, in floods of tears, telling him that she had been with George virtually up to his death. George had died for love, interpreted Wilfrid, as he would have wished.[28]

In making up his accounts for 1913, Blunt could still find something on the credit side. There was his printing press in the Jubilee room – the Jubilee Press – where he and Dorothy worked together. It may have been partly due to his Jubilee Press that Blunt wrote so much verse this year; more in 1913 than in the previous ten. Then George's death, catastrophic though it was, had resulted in Blunt's more intimate relations with 'all the Wyndham clan'. Yet he continued his 'personal lament' at his failures. No converts to his anti-imperialism in Europe; no school of his disciples in the East, 'though my ideas are bearing fruit [in India] and will one day be justified in act . . .'. Even his Arabian horses seemed to be failing him. There had been only two genuine buyers during 1913. The motor-car had ousted the carriage horse, and only the hunter, he believed, was still in demand.

The sense of failure wounded him; and he despised himself the more for feeling it so keenly. 'Why should I mind? I ask myself, and I find no answer.' Now that 1913 was over Blunt felt relieved, as from an incubus.

Sitting up till midnight on 31 December in the gloom of a desolating frost, he wrote, 'We let in the New Year I hope of better omen.' He had misread the omens for 1914. There was another incubus ready to descend on the world; but also the unlooked-for honour of disciples on his doorstep.

[21]
Peacocks and Prophets
1914–1917

It all began, as far as Blunt was concerned, with a visit from Lady Gregory. Three days after Christmas 1913 she arrived at Newbuildings with a verbal invitation for Blunt to attend a complimentary dinner given in his honour by a group of young poets. 'I am of course much flattered by this', he recorded, 'and still more surprised for I have been quite unaware of having any following among the young in poetry....'[1]

His heart went out yet again to the heroine of what he called his longest-lived friendship. If anyone was to write his life, it must be Lady Gregory, for 'this is the sort of thing a woman can do better than a man'. Blunt may even have thought the idea of the 'Peacock Dinner' – as the complimentary luncheon was to be called – was originally hers. In a sense it was; though the poet Ezra Pound initiated the project.

Still in his twenties, young Pound was staying at Stone Cottage, Colman's Hatch, with Yeats, acting as the poet's secretary. He persuaded Yeats to approach Blunt through Lady Gregory. It was she who made the change from the proposed London dinner to a Newbuildings luncheon, after Blunt had pointed out that he could not go to London 'for any possible consideration'. Remembering that Yeats had once been disappointed of a peacock feast, it was she who suggested to Pound and Blunt the possibility of culling a bird from the Newbuilding's flock.

The date of the Peacock Dinner was fixed for 18 January 1914, Blunt warning Lady Gregory that he wanted no present – 'should not know what to do with one'[2] – just the poets' names and good wishes on paper, 'as simple as possible'. There was a letter in *The Times* on the eleventh announcing the occasion. 'They must all be curiously unbusinesslike', commented Blunt when he read it, 'for the Times letter explains nothing of the reason for their admiration.' Nor had there so far been any formal invitation. It arrived undated on the twelfth in

Pound's handwriting, making the poets sound even more unbusinesslike.

> Wishing in some way to show our admiration of Wilfred [*sic*] Scawen Blunt, a committee consisting of William Butler Yeats, T. Sturge Moore, John Masefield, Victor Plarr, Frederic Manning, F. S. Flint, Richard Aldington and myself made out an invitation to him inviting him to dine at the Hotel Dieu Donné at some convenient time in January. The original invitation bearing our signature has been lost or destroyed by Mr. Yeats's housekeeper, and as there is scarcely time to circulate another copy for signature by the whole committee, the three of us who are now together send this invitation. Signed Ezra Pound Secretary, W. B. Yeats, Frederic Manning.

Thoughtfully Yeats hired a car (£5) to carry Blunt's disciples to and from the *ashram* in good time. A last minute note from Pound said the committee of seven with himself would arrive at Newbuildings for lunch by motor, 'unless we break down en route'. Two poets were absent on the day; Manning unaccountably, Masefield because 'he is under the thumb of a wife who will not let him go anywhere'. Or so Lady Gregory told Dorothy. Two other young men, however, were asked by Blunt in their places and to give him moral support (he had 'only met Yeats and *heard* of Yeats and Masefield'): Lord Osborne Beauclerk; and Belloc for the afternoon only, otherwise Belloc would turn all the talk to 'Marconis and Jews'. Blunt's own account of the proceedings has never yet been published. Here it is:

> The Poets' Sunday. They arrived quite punctually by motor at 12.30, six of them under Yeats' escort bringing with them a small marble coffer with an inscription 'Homage to W. S. Blunt', and an absurd futurist bas-relief of a naked Egyptian woman the work of a Franco-Pole sculptor [Gaudier Brzeska] coming into fashion.* Inside there was an address signed by the poets in a kind of futurist verse without rhyme or metre or much reason with bits of verse in the handwriting of each ... queer looking young men with shock heads of hair but capital fellows as it turned out, intelligent, and with a great knowledge of literature ancient and modern also some wit and as far as I could judge good hearts. There was a peacock served up in full plumage on the table for them and they had excellent appetites [two helpings each 'and roast beef besides'] and some good conversation and all enjoyed themselves. The address was intoned by Pound and I responded with a brief speech and Yeats made another and Belloc looked in and they stayed talking till tea time after which all went back to London.[3]

Blunt's overall gratitude evidently struggled with small embarrassments. As a poet and prophet of seventy-four whose deeds were in the past, he could not be expected to appreciate 'futuristic' art. But *they*

* As secretary of the committee, Pound had written to Lady Gregory on 4 January, 'Gaudier Brzeska is making a marble pen-box or reliquary or whatever it may be. I hope his decoration won't be too ultra-modern.'

could be expected to get the facts of the past right. In the address that Pound intoned so fashionably, he confused the Egyptian Arabi with the Italian patriot Mazzini:

> Because you have gone your individual gait,
> Written verses, made mock of the world
> Swung the grand style, not made a trade of art
> Upheld Mazzini and detested institutions
> We, who are little given to respect,
> Respect you, and having no better way to show it,
> Bring you this poem to be some record of it.[4]

The 'bits of verse' by each poet are given in extract below. The general theme tended to gloom. Plarr's poem was to a burial urn:

> Who in this small urn reposes,
> Celt or Roman, man or woman
> Steel of steel, or rose of roses?

From Sturge Moore came 'The Dying Swan':

> O silver throated Swan
> Struck, struck! a golden dart
> Clean through thy breast has gone
> Home to the heart.

From Pound came 'The Return':

> Hail! Hail!
> these were the swift to harry
> these the keen-scented
> these were the souls of blood slow on the leash
> Pallid the leashmen.

From Flint 'The Swan':

> Into the dark of the arch the swan floats,
>   and the black depth of my sorrow
>   bears a white rose of fame.

From Yeats 'When Helen Lived':

> We have cried in our despair
> That men desert
> For some trivial affair
> Or noisy, insolent sport,
> Beauty that we have won
> From bitterest hours. . . .

From Masefield 'Truth':

Man with his burning soul
Has but an hour of breath
To build a ship of truth
In which his soul may sail
Sail on the sea of death....

From Aldington 'In the Via Sistina':

O daughter of Isis,
  Thou standest beside the wet highway
Of this decayed Rome,
  A manifest harlot
Straight and slim art thou
  As a marble phallus....

If Aldington thought Blunt would like what was strong, sexy stuff for those pre-war days he was almost certainly mistaken. Nor did Blunt like the marble box that contained all this Pandora treasure. 'I have been obliged,' he wrote to Cockerell, 'to turn [it] with its face to the wall.'[5]

A letter from Beauclerk to Cockerell fills in some gaps. (Lord Osborne was a great success, being mistaken for R. L. Stevenson's step-son, Lloyd Osbourne.) 'It took some time to break the ice, – (as you know W.B. is very shy) ... it was all quite interesting, though Yeats would interview W.B. for the benefit of the company.' After luncheon and a discussion of versification, Blunt read a 'clever little translation' of Gobineau's piece about Don Juan – 'prefacing it with the remark that he hoped they wouldn't be too shocked. When we read Ezra Pound's and Aldington's compositions next day, we realized how unnecessary W.B.'s fear had been.'[6]

In retrospect, Blunt found that his encounter with the six poets in search of a prophet had left him strangely disheartened. The prophet had of course been dressed in full Arabian fig. This, together with his Jacobean house and Morris' table off which they lunched, should have rendered him timeless. Instead, as he wrote next day, 'The modern poetry represented by these young men is too entirely unlike anything I can recognize as good verse that I feel there is something absurd in their expressing admiration of mine. They explain it by saying that I was the first writer of verse to rebel against the romantic convention of early and mid-Victorian poetry and to write about things as they are, but ... they do not follow at all in my footsteps'; their verse seemed to him nothing but 'word puzzles'.[7]

This mood melted in a pleasant aftermath of thank-you letters, generous publicity and further, individual visits. On 20 January Blunt opened *The Times* to find 'a very prominent account' which made the presentation look like 'a really important event'. Blunt himself was reported as saying modestly in his speech that he wrote verses rather than poetry, and wrote only when down on his luck in love or politics. However, having washed his hands of politics, it was now very pleasant 'to be considered a poet'.

A photographer arrived to take his portrait on behalf of several newspapers; and the group photograph, posed on the eighteenth, turned out to be 'a very good one of everybody except Yeats'. (Pound said Yeats looked like 'a very moulting eagle indeed'.) Aldington sent in a report to *The Egoist* on 2 February, and there had been a flattering letter from the absentee Masefield saying how much pleasure and help he had derived from Blunt's work. He recognized Blunt's 'special honour and power, in having kept poetry close to life in a generation that strove to part them'. Masefield rubbed in that he admired Blunt for his poetry, not for his politics or his horses. Mrs Masefield brought her husband for a weekend in April, making sure there was a return train early on the Sunday afternoon. Blunt had learnt from Pound of Masefield's rough youth as a farm-hand and then before the mast; and how he had been married by 'a strong-minded Fabian lady' who held him in subjection. 'I like them extremely', wrote Blunt after the visit.[8]

Ezra Pound also was to bring his wife to stay in July, having written to Blunt on 23 March:

> As it happens I am about to commit matrimony so . . . when we get back in June it would have to be 'the pair of us'. Of course the other section of the pair is much more charming and decorative than I am – and almost as intelligent. . . .! In any case I dare say we will have a high old row when you first behold with horror the depth and extent of my poetic heresies. Aldington wants me to forward his regards – but then he is a safe conservative person.[9]

Blunt politely invited Pound and Aldington to come at once, before matrimony was committed. They arrived together on 25 March. Blunt found Aldington a likable young fellow who copied Pound but was basically 'healthy'; bred in Kent. But Pound –

> Pound it turns out is an American born in Idaho and Europeanized at Paris, where he has contracted all the absurdities of the day, and is now a cubist. Here he makes himself a sort of understudy of Yeats, repeating Yeats' voice with Yeats' brogue, an odd nervous little man with a mop of reddish hair looking as if dyed and a jerky manner as if afflicted with St. Vitus' dance.

As much a human puzzle as his poetry was a 'word puzzle', Pound intrigued Blunt. Soon afterwards he sent Blunt a book of D. H. Lawrence's poetry (recommending the 'dialect poems' at the end), a 'sheaf' of Ford Maddox Hueffer, and a copy of Max Beerbohm's famous satirical verses, 'The King is duller than the Queen'.

Pound came to Newbuildings again in July with his bride, improbably the daughter of a white Anglo-Indian official. Blunt found her refined and sensible; she had already humanized and deodorized her husband – 'and he needed deodorizing'. Mrs Pound's thank-you letter included a tribute to Blunt's house and herbals, and news of Mr Yeats: 'He says that by writing his autobiography he has learnt a great deal about himself.'[10]

Finally came Yeats and Lady Gregory together in May of the following year, 1915. Yeats, after his lecturing tour in America, looked 'sleek and fat and well-dressed', wrote Blunt, 'as becomes a prosperous man and one taking himself very seriously'. A letter arrived from him in June:

> Dear Mr. Blunt, My housekeeper tells me that I carried off from you a towel. I suppose it got mixed up with my bath gown. She has now washed it and sent it back to you.
>
> The pleasant memory of sunlight and peacock comes back to me again and again amid the London noise and I thank you for that memory.[11]

Nevertheless Yeats in his heart associated Blunt's peacock with pride rather than peace. Before leaving for America he had written a poem, 'The Peacock', at Stone Cottage:

> What's riches to him
> That has made a great peacock
> With the pride of his eye?*

Pound had heard Yeats, in the throes of composition, chanting the verses aloud in the brogue that he himself so skilfully imitated. He was later to mock both Yeats' voice and Yeats' mockery of Blunt in his own *Pisan Cantos*:

> that had made a great Peeeeacock
> in the proide ov his oiye
> had made a great peeeeeeecock in the . . .
> made a great peacock
> in the proide of his oyyee
> proide ov his oy – ee.

In Blunt's eye Pound had seen the flash of pride that means liberty and an indomitable spirit rather than vanity. And so Pound also wrote:

> To have, with decency, knocked
> That a Blunt should open
> To have gathered from the air a live tradition
> or from a fine old eye the unconquered flame
> This is not vanity.[12]

* Published in *Responsibilities* (1914). 'The Peacock' and 'When Helen Lived' were among the first poems of Yeats' second flowering.

In early 1914 Blunt's attention was taken up by the crisis in Ireland and the suffragettes. Skittles wrote that during the presentations at Buckingham Palace in June 'one of the Miss B's' – pearls and satins and feathers and all – shouted 'We have no King but thank God we have a Mrs. Pankhurst' and then had tried to spit at King George 'but could not reach him'. Even Queen Mary had turned deadly pale, clutching the King's arm. Margot Asquith, that inveterate enemy of the suffragettes, had herself been knocked out by 'an anaemia of the brain'. Now she was well again, and wanted dearest Wilfrid to give her a bit of 'coozling'. He was not averse; but his eyes were fixed on Ireland.

Not that he had backed either side during the Curragh 'Mutiny' of March. He had never wavered on Home Rule, now at last made law by Parliament. It was inconceivable that he should sympathize with British officers at the Curragh camp who might or might not obey orders to use force against a rebellious Ulster. No more could he sympathize with the Irish Parliamentary Party in Dublin, whom he still regarded as renegades for voting in favour of Grey's foreign policy. Blunt's old friend John Dillon tried in vain over many months to bring him round to the moderate Irish point of view. But others had got in first, putting the militant case.

Temperamentally Blunt was always inclined that way. And he had Mrs Padraic Colum, wife of the Irish poet and Sinn Feiner, to write him spirited letters, and Casement himself to keep in even closer touch. Early in May, Mrs Colum asked for a message from Blunt to be read out at a women's meeting of the Irish National Volunteers, appealing for arms and funds. Roger Casement, she informed him, was one of their leaders. Let Blunt send a subscription if the spirit moved him. 'But above all things send us *your blessing*, in memory of your own fighting days, when you were in Galway gaol, for Kathleen ni Houlihan.'

Blunt's rousing message, advocating 'the stick behind', was a triumph. 'The young men stood up and waved their hats', wrote Mary Colum. As a result of the message and the stir it created, Casement sent three enthusiastic letters to Blunt from his lodgings in London: 'We *shall* have the Harp without the Crown' – 'We stand in the forefront of human freedom, fighting a battle that is world wide' – 'The Irish Volunteers are swelling daily!... If we had rifles we could get 100,000 men inside a month.' Casement himself paid a visit to Newbuildings between the second and third letters (13 May), agreeing with Blunt that Parnell's 'silly' love letters to Mrs O'Shea had been published purposely at this moment to belittle Ireland.[13] But Ireland would triumph.*

* Lady Gregory was mistaken in her belief that Blunt never met Casement. 'He had not known him,' she wrote, 'but had been tremendously struck with his speech after trial "envies him his death."' (Lady Gregory, *The Journals*, p. 13, 25 November 1916.)

As for Europe, Blunt was in no mood to believe the news from abroad put out by press or Parliament. His friend Theodore Rothstein, a refugee from Tsarist Russia and expert on Eastern Europe, told him that most of the foreign correspondents were fakes. The *Standard* had hired him to send bogus telegrams signed 'Our Special Correspondent' from all over the world, except Paris and Berlin where they had real correspondents. The other papers did the same, bar the *Manchester Guardian* and *Daily News* who had their own correspondents.

But despite his scepticism, the news of Sarajevo on 28 June made Blunt pause and think. Did it mean war? If so, he was anti-war. His next important visitor happened to be a noted pacifist, Ramsay MacDonald the Labour leader, brought to Newbuildings on 22 July at Lady Margaret Sackville's request.

When King George's conference, held at Buckingham Palace to find a compromise solution to the Irish problem, failed, Blunt rejoiced. He was not so happy at Austria declaring war on Servia and London going wild with excitement. On 1 August he started up his gold-store again (to be replenished in 1915). Mark Napier had told him the only safe investments were land and foreign securities. 'But gold in a stocking is better still', wrote Blunt. (When the sovereigns were returned to the bank in 1921, Blunt's solicitor counted some 500 in a trunk, 148 in a black silk stocking and 29 and 100 divided between two red stockings.) But for all his precautions Blunt believed obstinately that Britain would remain neutral. The alternative would be 'too stupid even for Grey'. After all, the treaty guaranteeing 'little Belgium' had been made eighty-four years ago, and Britain had broken many promises to small nations since then. In any case, all the ministers – Asquith, Grey and the rest, except perhaps Winston – were 'old men, quite unable to deal with a situation demanding virility'.[14]

The actual declaration of war staggered Blunt. He launched next day, 5 August, into a torrent of invective against the government's hypocritical stand on 'treaties':

> And now at last we are to fight for what? For Servia, a nest of murderous swine which has never listened to a word of English remonstrance, for Russia, the tyrant of Poland, Finland and all northern Asia, for France, our fellow brigand in North Africa and lastly for Belgium with its Congo record. And we call this England's honour![15]

Blunt was one of the earliest to denounce the 'little Belgium' ploy and the element of power politics which Grey introduced into other considerations. He developed an attitude to the war which satisfied his own conscience and did not outrage his country neighbours. He called it 'unarmed neutrality'. Ezra Pound heard that 'the fine old eye' had spotted the chance for yet another defiant jape – a notice on his front door saying, 'Belligerents will please go round to the kitchen.' The sick humour of war suited his mood: the local scouts' need for oceans of tea 'to keep up their courage'; Kitchener's pronouncing the east coast defences 'capable of repelling the Salvation but no other army'; Neville Lytton's 'Southdown Regiment', a replica of Falstaff's volunteers. 'I advised them all to surrender on the earliest occasion.'

Somehow he managed to avoid offending even his aristocratic friends. Lord Ribblesdale, though mourning for fallen sons, was to become one of his best friends in 1916; to Blunt, the finest type of Conservative county magnate.* There was no break with Lady Desborough when her two sons Julian and Billy Grenfell were killed, both 'glorious schoolboys' in Blunt's opinion. Though Ivo fell, the youngest son of Mary Elcho (now Wemyss), Mary still visited Wilfrid, referring to Newbuildings, that hot-bed of pacificism, as Blunt's 'dear Palace of the Winds'.

His dear 'Kitty', as Skittles now always signed herself, had become ultra-patriotic. Her tender recollections of the young Kaiser's 'very handsome face for a Germyn' and his infatuation for her – Edward would never leave her alone with his nephew – did not prevent her from selling the jewelled parasol he had once given her, to help the poor wounded victims of those cruel 'Germyns'.

Despite the rising war fever, Blunt's *Poetical Works*, published in August 1914, met with some praise, especially from fellow-poets, which was all Blunt cared about. Katharine Tynan – 'the best woman poet of our day' – paid him a tribute in *New Witness*, and Edward Thomas in the *Daily Herald* saw Blunt as the successor to 'the Byron inheritance'; one who could write of sport like a sportsman and love like 'no other lover in Victorian prose or verse'; very English, though more European than most, with 'a perfume of the East'. The *Glasgow Herald* bravely lauded him as 'A Militant Poet' concerned with the wrongs both of Ireland and the East. 'He is essentially a fighter and all fight braces.'

A fight put up by others in a noble cause would be bracing to Blunt himself. He saw such a cause in the Easter Rising of 1916, especially in his friend Roger Casement's heroic but disastrous attempt at gun-running – German guns – on behalf of the Irish Volunteers. 'The man in the jaws of the lion', quoted Blunt, 'will call to the tiger for help.' The

* To some extent Blunt identified with Ribblesdale: he was 'a poet without having written poetry', a man of the world without being the slave of pleasure, 'essentially an aristocrat and as essentially a lover of his own people, the country people among whom he lives in Yorkshire as I live in Sussex'. (Finch, *Wilfrid Scawen Blunt*, p. 368–9.)

failure of the Easter Rising and the death by shooting of the leading rebels reawakened in Blunt all the emotions of 1887.

Casement's part in the Rising has been justly described as 'melodramatic and pitiful'. He was captured at dawn on Good Friday, 21 April, having crawled up the beach in Tralee Bay. The separate ship carrying his arms had already been sent to the bottom. Unlike Blunt, Casement realized that a rising in the circumstances of 1916 could not but fail. Yet if it was going to happen, *he* could not fail it. 'Roger Casement and his twenty Germans', wrote Margot to Wilfrid, 'was a kind of Comedy Tragedy and the Countess dressed in green poplin etc.'[17]. The union of Ireland's green flag with the Prophet's green flag in a joint bid for Irish and Egyptian freedom had indeed been one of Casement's wilder hopes – one calculated to appeal to Blunt; and he may well have confided it to Blunt during his visit two years earlier.

Individual radicals gave sums of several hundred pounds for Casement's defence. According to the irate Judith, her father donated £10,000 (of *her* money); but as Judith was always free with the noughts, it is improbable that Blunt gave more than £1,000. The prisoner made a moving and powerful speech from the dock on 29 June: 'Since in the acts which have led to the trial it was the people of Ireland I sought to serve – and them alone – I leave my judgment and my sentence in their hands.' But it was Lord Reading (the former Rufus Isaacs, now Lord Chief Justice), who actually passed judgment, putting on the black cap and condemning the prisoner to death. He added the customary words, 'Lord have mercy on your soul.' Casement's devoted cousin Gertrude Bannister, who was present, added *sotto voce*, 'And may he have mercy on yours.'

Wilfrid Blunt's gloss on the tremendous scene was less charitable towards Lord Reading. He admired Casement for his ideals, his great height and handsome face reminding him of Michael Davitt. When the evening papers of 29 June brought him the news of Casement's condemnation, his own sense of drama and poetic justice turned in his diary to concentrated venom. He re-wrote the trial in his own words:

> 'Prisoner at the Bar have you any word to say why I should not hang you by the neck until you are dead?'
>
> 'Only one word my Lord, Marconi.'[18].

Meynell brought comfort early next morning with one of his telegrams: 'Blunt. Southwater. 9.15 a.m. 30 June 1916. Casement laughed at the death sentence.'

When Blunt read the speech from the dock he was lifted into a state of prolonged exaltation. 'A magnificent pronouncement, the noblest apologia ever made by a political prisoner before his judges in the whole history of Irish or any other national war for freedom. It moved me to a stream of tears....'

Petitions for the commuting of Casement's sentence were immediately launched by some of his English friends. His health had been affected, it was urged, by his arduous labours for Britain in Putumayo and the Congo. Behind this well-meant plea was a more sinister suggestion put about by his enemies. The man was insane; his pornographic 'Black Diaries' proved it. Copies were circulated underground by the government to alienate sympathy from Casement, particularly in America and Ireland.

While not accepting that the 'Black Diaries' were genuine, Blunt would have nothing whatsoever to do with petitions. He had already sent some reading matter for Miss Bannister to give her cousin. 'Since his condemnation', Blunt heard, 'the prisoner's chief reading had been of my Egyptian books, The Secret History and the others of the series.' Now, with Meynell and H. W. Nevinson pressing him to sign a petition and Miss Bannister asking him to write personally to Asquith, he sent Dorothy to London on 10 July with a prophetic letter for Miss Bannister: 'The government would be glad to boast that [Sir Roger] had weakened, that he had authorized our plea "ad miserecordiam", and so rob him of his dignity of sacrifice and the glory of martyrdom so nearly won.' Casement was no more a traitor in Berlin than Theobald Wolfe Tone and Lord Edward Fitzgerald had been in Paris in 1798: 'I know that every Irishman worth his salt will hold your kinsman morally excused, and if he seals his treason with his blood or on the gallows will revere him for all time to come.'

Gertrude Bannister took Blunt's advice; and at a crucial interview with Asquith she said, 'He is as sane as you are.' On 3 August Father Carey, Casement's confessor wrote: 'He marched to the scaffold with the dignity of a prince and towered straight over all of us.' Casement's last words had been, 'I die for my country.' What a glorious ending: 'Casement has accomplished everything I should have like to do.' But, Blunt continued, 'I was unworthy, and had the curse on me of my imperial English origin.'[19]

Six days after the hanging he sent Dorothy again to London to condole with Gertrude Bannister. At the end of their conversation Dorothy asked about the Putumayo diaries.

'Faked ...', Miss Bannister replied, 'and sent round to the press in the unscrupulous way we heard of by F. E. Smith [the Attorney-General]. Roger in his generosity thought Smith honest and told me to feel no bitterness against him, that it had been a fair fight. But I knew what was being said and I couldn't tell him.'

'Did he ever know it?'

'Yes, before the end he did know something of it.'[20]

Towards the end of the year Gertrude, now married to Sydney Parry, Casement's boyhood friend, visited Newbuildings. Blunt saw in her an 'exceedingly' attractive replica of Charlotte Brontë. Parry brought with him Casement's last letter, smuggled out by a warder's wife. Among the messages it contained was 'Give my love to Wilfrid Blunt.'

Judith's New Year resolution for 1915 seems to have been to bring about a general family reconciliation. She had already made successful approaches to her father towards the end of 1914, having apologized for her past attitude towards Dorothy and blaming it on Dorothy's brother, with which Blunt was glad to agree. Blunt had finished the year in a melancholy and therefore softened mood. The war had wrecked his calm.

> I have been too old to adapt myself to the new conditions [he wrote]. It is not merely another year that has passed away but a whole cycle of years, a period in the history of the world, and the history of the human intellect. The people who are growing up now will have different brains from ours, with different ideals of beauty and romance. They will not care for our art or literature, they will not understand our thoughts or read our poetry. This I think is the chief cause of my depression.[21]

After much negotiation between Judith, Anne and Wilfrid, the great day was fixed. Wilfrid was to give lunch to his estranged wife on 12 May at Worth Manor House, formerly known as Old House Warren, the last, most remote and romantic of the 'hermitages' he had built or rebuilt in the Forest. Wilfrid went to the Forest the night before, feeling 'some apprehension' about this first meeting for over eight years. His apprehension was banished by Judith's faultless stage-management. She drove Anne up in the carriage without any servants, so that no one witnessed their kiss of greeting or overheard the ninety minutes of absolutely natural conversation about the Stud, the grandchildren, Egypt, and the war (it had been agreed, 'no talk of the past'). Judith herself had tactfully disappeared. When she rejoined them for lunch it was a 'really gay' party. Judith, now forty-two, looked splendid, strong and healthy as a girl; Anne 'hardly at all altered' in her usual 'mouse coloured brown'. Wilfrid wrote: 'I have never been more impressed with her intellectual superiority and the pleasantness of her conversation ... the threads of life seem drawn together again, to the extent that it seems strange there ever should have been any quarrel.'[22]

As a result of many more meetings during the summer, it was decided between Anne and Wilfrid to reorganize the Stud on a basis summarized by Wilfrid in a letter of 22 September:

1 Revoking the deed of 1906.
2 My assigning the whole ownership and management of the stud for you as long as you live.
3 Its reversion to me, should I survive you.

Wilfrid gave her Caxtons (old Philip Webb his former tenant had died) as well as paddocks and stabling for her stock. Before Anne returned to Egypt in October, she had even stepped inside Newbuildings once more, accompanied for lunch by her widowed sister-in-law Mary Lovelace. (Dorothy, staying with her brother at Windsor, was carefully not mentioned.) On 15 October Wilfrid scribbled her a farewell letter: 'Dearest Anne. . . . It has been a very great pleasure seeing you . . . and it seems a pity it should end so soon. You have made Caxtons a very perfect little hermitage. . . . I wish I was going with you. . . . I shall expect you back about Christmastime, perhaps before. And so goodbye and God bless you. Your affectionate W.S.B.'

They were never to set eyes on one another again.

The one family storm at this time did not divide Wilfrid and Anne, but rather Judith from her parents. The expenses of Crabbet Park suddenly seemed more than Judith could bear, even with generous allowances from her mother and a contribution of £4,000 towards building the new real tennis court. She sacked Caffin, the trusted family estate agent and stud manager, accusing him of embezzling £14,000. Wilfrid was outraged. His old servant might perhaps be a muddler, but Caffin was perfectly honest. It was agreed that he should work for Anne at Caxtons as well as for Wilfrid at Newbuildings. As for Judith's financial difficulties, both her parents put them down to the 'extravagant' life she and Neville led.

Admittedly the real tennis court was grandiose; but the Lyttons' main expenses were due to the permanent employment of two professional coaches – one the delightful international champion G. F. Covey – and the 'country club' style in which the place was run. There was a squash court, later a swimming pool, and other facilities. Neville would bring down large parties of clever artistic friends from London studios and theatres. In an effort to retain the devotion of her much younger husband, Judith paid for the weekend whirligigs. When she called at Newbuildings in August driving her Baby Austin motor ('bought out of her poverty', wrote Blunt) she lost yet more of his sympathies.

About the time that Anne was leaving for Egypt, the row between Wilfrid and Judith began to escalate. Wilfrid unwisely allowed his grandson Anthony to become involved. Now fifteen, Anthony was encouraged to confide in his grandfather at Newbuildings about Crabbet's 'uncomfortable' state of affairs. 'He comes here as a refuge', wrote Blunt and succumbed to the temptation of enlightening

Anthony about his own future inheritance including Worth Forest, so that the boy might have a secret weapon against his mother. (Blunt could never resist the chance of expounding the duties and pleasures of 'squiredom' to a new generation.)

Anthony and his sisters had been taught by Judith to call her 'Jack'. While worshipping 'Jack', they feared her vein of masculine violence. In 'Myself and Others', Judith wildly accused Caffin of being her father's 'blackguardly secret service agent' (she sometimes half-imagined a nest of German spies at Newbuildings), and even more wildly, envisaged Anthony as the potential victim of morphia addiction, deliberately introduced by his grandfather. After a flaming row in the Forest, when Blunt shouted that Judith's head ought to hang with Cromer's on Traitors Gate, and Miss Lawrence screamed at Judith, 'Oh, what have you done to upset him so?' – after this drama, followed by a letter in which Judith was called 'a cockatrice's egg', and many virulent entries in their respective diaries, Anthony and his sisters were forbidden Newbuildings. A truce, however, was called at Christmas, partly because the unmaternal 'Jack' liked to send her children away as much as possible.

During the Christmas holidays, Anne and Winnie Lytton needed to visit the dentist at Brighton. Miss Lawrence was ill, so Blunt sent Dorothy with them. Vibrations from the grapevine at once convinced Judith that her children were being employed to whitewash the adulterous union. Newbuildings was again banned. ('When we were forbidden by Jack to go there', recalled Winnie many years later, 'it was as if the sun had gone out.')[23] Worse still, Judith seized the opportunity to do what she had long contemplated but had hitherto avoided for fear of parental wrath – sell part of the sacred 'kingdom' that was the Crabbet estate.

The effect on Blunt was catastrophic, as Judith had pleasantly foreseen: 'This bombshell', she wrote, would cause a flutter at Newbuildings in the ... 'I can't call it the dove cote ... shall we say the Hornets Headquarters. It will make "some" buzz I guess.' Though Wilfrid and Anne managed to buy back several farms at the auction, he could not forgive this betrayal of all he believed in as 'Squire', and all he had taught Judith. While mourning the loss of his grandchildren, he decided to cut himself off entirely from Crabbet, a drastic solution that Anne agreed with 'desperate grief' was the only possible one, at least for the time being.

A pair of terrible letters and one shocking interview in 1916 set their seal on the state of war between Crabbet and Newbuildings. First, Judith had defended her own alleged extravagance by citing with coarse vituperation the money spent by Blunt on avoiding divorce suits and providing for illegitimate children. 'What has been your example as a Father?' Then, half-repentant, she sent Father Lawrence to rescue Blunt from the latest immoral 'entanglement', Dorothy. Blunt retaliated by telling Father Lawrence that he was an atheist and loved Dorothy more than wife, child or grandchildren – a random thrust which the poor old priest saw fit to repeat to Judith, adding for good measure his own indictment of her father:

> He is a *most* dangerous and a most wicked man. He is determined to get hold of Anthony, and he will stop at nothing, mind you, *nothing*, in order to do so. He would get you certified as a lunatic to get the boy.

This last was the interpretation put by Father Lawrence on Blunt's view that Judith's hysteria was a function of the change of life. She did in fact believe Blunt to have set a detective on her, in the hope of discovering a liaison with Covey the tennis coach. In August she boasted of catching one 'spy' red-handed: Susie the maid, who had stolen her clothes, rings, and a bottle of dog medicine labelled Sexual Pills. 'I only hope she took them that's all!!'

Unfortunately Father Lawrence warned Anne also against Wilfrid, thereby taking some of the pleasure out of their reconciliation. Saying nothing to Wilfrid, Anne prayed for him harder than ever; nevertheless, a remark about Dorothy's 'wire entanglements' in which she held Wilfrid, showed a reawakened bitterness.

Finally, Judith in a furious letter to Dorothy threatened a physical attack. The following is an example of the many gratuitous insults her letter contained: 'Some years ago your possible condition was common talk, now my Father's age has turned the gossip into ridicule. All this is gall and misery and horror to my Mother and me.'[24]

Actually Judith's mother herself was by no means exempt from the lash. Anne was denounced for temporarily cutting off Judith's allowance, not out of spite inspired by Wilfrid, as Judith imagined, but because of Anne's confused belief that the war had reduced her to penury. With her fear of water (Anne's sole phobia) combined with her sorrows over Crabbet, she decided not to leave her beloved Egypt until the German U-boat menace was conquered. It never was, in the months that remained to her.

Anne spent the first six months of 1917 leading a spartan existence. To save money she even gave up riding and took to 'route marching' and 'pedestrian training' as she called it, instead. She was racing against time to finish both her fragmentary writings on the Arabian horse and her last will and testament. (Her fragments were to inspire Judith's book, *The Authentic Arabian*; her will to provoke, alas, a public feud.) As her strength failed, her whole love for Wilfrid strengthened. Nurse Lawrence, reporting on Wilfrid's physical sufferings, wrote that he wished for Anne's presence. Though the nurse's motives were not of the highest (she intended to suggest that he longed in vain to escape from Dorothy), her words comforted Anne. She took to re-reading his old letters. Then the two of them began recalling to one another nostalgic events from their past: he, Anne's very first letter to him of 1867; she, her vision of 1884 in Persia, the vision that up till now had only once been mentioned between them, though Wilfrid knew more of it from Neville. 'I have often wondered', she now wrote to Wilfrid, 'why what was given to me [faith] was not given to you.'[25]

She may also have been preparing to explain her sad diary entry of 10 August 1883, when she had seen herself and him as 'two ships' separated by a blinding fog. A typewritten copy of her account was apparently found among her last packet of letters.[26] If she did indeed intend Wilfrid to re-read it, she no doubt meant to annotate it, as in the case of her Persian vision, with her present less bleak thoughts.* In August a serious illness intervened. Dysentery was later diagnosed.

Her two last diary entries ran, '7 November Wednesday.... Quite flattened out.' 'Saturday Am a shade better, but no Mass for me on Sunday.' On 6 December Wilfrid received a cable from Philip Napier that Anne was ill – the first time she had allowed it to be mentioned. A telegram arrived for him in her name on 10 December: 'Thanks cable progress maintained love Blunt.' She died on the fifteenth in the American hospital in Cairo, where she had been constantly visited by Philip Napier and his wife Gabrielle. 'Love', wrote her maid Jeannie to Judith, was the last word she whispered. Philip told Wilfrid that her last wish had been for the end of the family estrangement.

She was buried in the small nuns' cemetery at Jebel al Ahmar, then a peaceful oasis looking out across the sands to Heliopolis with a desert ridge behind – a scene wholly Egyptian, wholly beautiful and within sight of Sheykh Obeyd. Two months later, Wilfrid found a 1770 headstone at Shipley from which he designed a granite sarcophagus. The inscription began, 'Here lies in the Egyptian desert which she loved LADY ANNE BLUNT.' She was a great lady.

After the Second World War Anne's grave was removed to the 'Roman' burial ground, a Catholic enclave within the vast spreading Abbasieh Cemetery of Cairo. There are no golden sands, but the sun shines on Anne's tomb; and palms, yuccas and eucalyptus saplings throw a lacework of shadow over the still sharp lettering.

The tumults in Blunt's domestic life were matched by the crises in his friends' war-time careers. After shooting three cock pheasants in

* Her grandson Anthony advised his mother not to show it to his ailing grandfather, advice which Judith did not take. Neither realized that Wilfrid had seen it already. See above, p. 195.

Marlpost Wood, he had written in his diary, 'It did me good but I could wish them to have been Asquith and Grey and George.' Sure enough less than nine months later, Asquith's Liberal Cabinet had been shot to pieces, a casualty of the Dardanelles fiasco. Asquith himself, having been first forced into a coalition, was himself out by the end of 1916. So was Grey. But instead of 'George' making up the trio of extinct cock pheasants, it was Blunt's friend Churchill who was to complete the bag. Worse still, Lloyd George, that 'contemptible little dog', came out on top.

Winston Churchill had in fact been the first to be shunted; from the Admiralty to the Duchy of Lancaster in May 1915. Blunt spent a memorable four hours with Winston and his family at Hoe Farm (converted by Lutyens) in Surrey, on 14 August. The fallen minister was deeply embittered, and but for the devotion of Clementine and the rest, 'he might', thought Blunt, 'have gone mad'. Nellie Hozier, patient beyond belief, had sat for hours allowing him to paint her portrait, which the family 'with splendid courage' were admiring. 'I too tried my best to praise the portrait', wrote Blunt, 'saying it belonged to the futurist school.' But soon he and Winston were on to politics and the war, Winston haunted by his responsibility, as First Lord of the Admiralty, for the loss of life at Gallipoli.

'There is more blood than paint upon these hands', he said to Blunt, showing his paint-smeared fingers with a queer little tragic gesture. 'All those thousands of men killed. We thought it would be a little job, and so it might have been if it had been begun in the right way. . . .' Grown stout and thick-set, Churchill reminded Blunt of Napoleon on St Helena.[27]

A fortnight later Churchill dined in Arab robes at Newbuildings, holding forth to an audience composed of Blunt, Belloc, an Oratorian priest and young Anthony, on the stupidity of the War Office, 'and how the war was likely to drift because all those who had the power of continuing it were profiting by it'. By November 1915 the virile strain that Blunt admired in Churchill had revolted against his humiliation and he resolved to go out and fight in Flanders. The news reached Blunt on the fifteenth, while he was entertaining Mark Napier and Hilaire Belloc to a roistering dinner. Blunt at once drafted a splendid letter to Winston:

> I am commissioned on our joint behalf and on that of the parish of Shipley to congratulate you on your courage in breaking loose from your official bondage to that gang of incapables which has been making a fool of the British Empire. We look to you now to take the supreme command of our gallant armies abroad and to revive the glories achieved by them in the past under your great ancestor.[28]

Next day Churchill made 'a great speech in the House of Commons', noted Blunt, '... and he leaves England for Flanders in an oriole of glory'. Then Blunt ventured a prophecy: 'He ... will come back some day and take the running for the premiership with a pretty good certainty of winning.'

In 1917 Blunt congratulated him on his return to office, despite his colleagues being 'a set of sweeps'. He crowned that autumn with a visit to Clementine at Lullenden, the Churchills' new farmhouse in Sussex. (Winston was away.) Like all very beautiful women, she was affectionate and kind 'to very old men'. When another Churchill baby arrived next year, Blunt wrote, 'I shall consider it in some sort mine, for ... did I not kiss her in that pleasant barn before we parted?'[29]

There is no doubt that Churchill looked forward to his sessions with Blunt. 'It would be so nice to have a talk', ran a typical note of 1917. 'Ireland. Russia. Turkey. Arabia. What a welter!' But it all depended on his 'scraping together enough petrol', as he blithely put it, from the Ministry of Munitions, where he was now in charge. Sometimes it was not the petrol but the car that let him down. 'My dear Mr. Blunt', wrote Clementine on Easter Monday 1918, 'We intended coming today to see you, but alas! the old motor broke some important part of its insides.'[30]

In some moods, Blunt thoroughly enjoyed his celebrity as a detached philosopher:

> I notice that people writing to me now seem to address me as a sage because of my having escaped the universal war fever and Newbuildings as a kind of Noah's Ark riding calmly on the waters of the Flood. This is amusing.... There is an advantage in being old, if I was twenty-five I should be called a slacker.

Not everyone, however, approved of his detachment. Minnie Pollen was to write when victory had been won,

> I am surprised and disappointed at the aloofness of your attitude to present events. It is a change to think of *you* as insular. It may amuse you to know that in the German plans of Sussex, for use of the invading army, Newbuildings is marked as suitable for an observation post!

With this parting shot, Minnie set off for the nearest church 'to say the Te Deum'. Some two months later she died in the odour of sanctity, according to her Jesuit son John, with 'nothing on her mind'.[31]

In other moods Blunt himself found his position a strain. At the end of 1916 – 'a very wicked year' – he had written: 'I feel my refusal to see the war a fine thing oppressive in its isolation, the extreme of selfishness. Yet I cannot for my life see it otherwise than a blundering and obstinate stupidity.' His feeling of selfishness may have been caused by the thought of two young men at the front, the husbands of his daughters. Neville Lytton had already received a flesh wound; and a soldier serving in Egypt had married his Mary on 20 November 1915 at Cairo. To Blunt's satisfaction, the young man was reported by Mary's mother to be well-bred and well-off, not exactly intellectual but tolerant of intellect in others. 'It's dreadful that Mary should be all alone in Egypt', wrote Lady Wemyss to Blunt on 18 November, ' – but isn't it strange that she should be married there. . . .'[32]

[22]
The Unconquered Flame
1918–1922

Beneath Anne's name on her monument appeared her second title, Baroness Wentworth 'in her own right'. It came through Lady Byron and the Noels to Anne on the death of her niece Ada Mary Wentworth, fourteenth holder of the peerage, on 18 June 1917. Anne was to hold it for only six months, but she and Wilfrid both felt proud of her transient honour. When Judith inherited it on her mother's death, Wilfrid wrote apprehensively that it would 'make her more arrogant than ever'. He added that there might be trouble over Anne's property. 'Fortunately the executorship of Anne's Will is in safe hands, Philip Napier's and Edward Chandler's [Blunt's cousin and family solicitor].'[1]

The first shock came on 7 January 1918. Philip Napier telegraphed that Anne had left her horses and land at Sheykh Obeyd, plus Woolborough in Sussex and 'the residue of her personalty', to her two granddaughters Anne and Winnie Lytton under trust; the trustees being Philip himself and the Public Trustee. This meant, as Blunt realized at once, that there would be no surplus money for running the Crabbet Arabian Stud. However, he himself had first suggested to his wife the idea of a trust. And without Anne's management, he could not cope with the combined eighty head of horses at Crabbet and Newbuildings. Now it was just a matter of still further reduction – perhaps to a dozen mares and fillies and three stallions all told. Never once did he doubt his own legal status as the Stud's 'reversionary owner' – a phrase continually used in the years of stud talk and correspondence between himself and Anne.

Anne's will, dated 14 June 1917, proved a bombshell; chiefly because of what it left out. There was no mention of the future of the Stud itself. Whether the Stud was to go with the property now became an issue of acute controversy.

While bequeathing to Judith all her plate, jewellery and private papers, including her poignant diaries, in a 'stand of four tin boxes painted white presently at Caxtons', and above all her precious MS of 'The Arabian Horse' with which Wilfrid had frequently helped her (every word written out in her own hand, wrote Everard Fielding, with the neatness and perfection of a medieval manuscript), she left Wilfrid nothing but her business papers on the Stud. No message. No kindly mention whatever. The stud groom Holman received a legacy of £100. But there was nothing for Caffin or Chandler, both of whom had been promised gifts by Anne verbally to make up for Judith's unfair prejudice against them.

Wilfrid jumped to the conclusion that Anne had been got at by his enemies. These he listed as anonymous letter-writers, hostile legal influences, and Judith. Anne's was a 'wicked will', he lamented, a bitter blow to his memories of their 'affectionate' last two years; just as her death had been a blow to his plans for spending the sunset of his life with her. (The particular part of the sunset, that is, when Dorothy was with her brother or Aunt Madeline.) Anne's horses at Sheykh Obeyd were already being sold up, 'and she seems in the few words alluding to the Stud in England to have forgotten that it would be mine'.

For all his fears, Wilfrid had not yet caught an inkling of the full horror, though there were mutterings in February, when Judith claimed part of the Stud for her daughters' trustees. H.F. paid no attention, beyond looking up the 1906 'Deed of Partition', according to which he was undoubtedly now sole owner. He had forgotten the interminable new drafts since then, by which the 1906 Partition was revoked in 1915, and by 1916 his whole share made over to Anne.[2]

Next month the Public Trustee, while apparently admitting Blunt's legal right to the whole Stud, advised him to allow Judith certain horses she claimed her mother had given her, including one special mare, Riyala. (These were the so-called 'free horses', bred by Anne apart from the Stud. Wilfrid knew nothing of them.) Blunt declined; indeed, he began compiling with Dorothy's help a memorandum of the Stud for Counsel to present to the trustees. Haig's great offensive was on the way on the Western Front and Blunt felt anxious on this count also, though the matter of the Stud was 'a more important issue perhaps than that of the British Empire for which Haig is fighting, in as much as the horse is more worthy than the man'.

By the end of March he believed that Judith was after the whole Stud – Riyala and every other brood mare and stallion. 'I intend to take my stand even at the risk of litigation,' he wrote. 'Fortunately we have I think every point of the law on our side, including the point of possession.' He had by now assembled the whole Stud at Newbuildings.[3]

On 4 April Blunt heard the astounding news that Judith had raided the Caxtons loose-boxes at the head of her three children, her coachman and her gardener. Finding Riyala's shut fast, she ordered Anthony to break the lock. At this point old Holman the Newbuildings groom, supported by Dulcie his daughter, ran out from their cottage to intervene, but were kept back by Anthony and the girls. Anthony was 'an athlete standing six feet one', wrote Blunt, and an expert at 'garrotting'; the girls were trained in 'gymnastic exercises'; Judith was 'possessed of immense strength' as a result of 'practising all athletic tricks'. The reports caused Blunt to believe, wrongly, that these gifts were abused. The mare's halter was wrenched from Holman's hand and in the scrimmage his nail torn off. Triumphantly, covered in blood, Judith led the mare away, to an accompaniment of screams and curses from the whole Holman family. Mrs Holman had joined the fray just too late to pull out the young ladies' hair. Some witnesses said she had been drinking; others that it was Judith who smelt of whisky. The young Lyttons came back for Riyala's foal and only just failed to get Rim also, who was in the paddock but refused to be caught.

Judith's story of the *ghazu* in 'Myself and Others' was not a whit less melodramatic than the above version which had reached Blunt. According to her, Holman sprang at Judith 'like a whirlwind' (a very venerable whirlwind), seizing her by the neck. 'I grappled with him and forced him away from the door and yelled to Anthony to hold him while I wrenched myself free from his frenzied clutches and got the door open. Nurse flung me a headstall which I whipped on to the mare [Riyala] and before reinforcements could arrive rushed her out and down the Park leaving the foal to its fate and pursued by frantic shouts and yells and oaths' – and by Winnie's conciliatory voice crying to friend and foe alike, 'Have a peppermint, have a peppermint.'

After locking up the mare at Crabbet, they returned to a tug-of-war for the foal, Anthony grasping its tail and Holman its head, while Winnie shrieked, 'Oh, don't pull its tail off, it's cruel!' Holman, worsted in the battle, flung himself upon Judith 'like a mad bull', but with Anthony's help she penned him against the railings. Bleeding and with bruised ribs, she called her 'platoon' and marched them and the foal home in triumph. 'You're a pack o' savages,' shouted Holman to Anne and Judith; and 'that boy of yours stole Riyala'. 'Possession is nine-tenths of the law', was Judith's reply, 'and we mean to keep them both.' Later, she and the Holmans were to become reconciled.

The persuasions of his friends prevailed over Blunt's furious desire to haul Judith before a magistrate's court. Lady Lovelace pointed out how damaging it would be to the children, while Mark Napier suggested that if Blunt could forgive the Germans he could surely forgive his own family. One of the best chances for a compromise was lost when he refused the suggestion of Sir Charles Stewart (the Public Trustee) for a settlement out of court, the idea being that he should leave the whole Stud to Judith after his death. Stewart was 'a dear old fossil', wrote Judith, 'not used to dealing with explosives'.

While the Germans were retreating Blunt was advancing new proposals for *his* stud: the trustees of course intended to disperse it piecemeal; *he* would make it over intact to a 'Colonial government' – or possibly to the King himself (Lord Ribblesdale's brainwave). In September he was lamenting to Meynell that he could not keep warm and his blood 'refused to circulate even at the news of the British Army marching into Nazareth' – but it raced fast enough at the thought of re-entering Crabbet to bring back his horses. 'Peace is really here,' he wrote of Europe in October, meanwhile coaching his own new trustee Charlie Adeane (a Wyndham) on the coming struggle. On Armistice Day Judith put ribbons in her own and her ponies' hair, but heard that Newbuildings had celebrated by shooting Regiz, lest she should get him, and serving up two steaks for dinner. As the Peace Conference dragged on through much of 1919, so did Blunt's negotiations. 'The case is entering now on its second year', he wrote on 27 February, 'and is no further advanced than at the beginning.' He and Ribblesdale decided definitely to approach the King at Michaelmas. But that monarch's advisers decided to keep out of a hornets' nest.

At last, in December 1919, the patriarchal warrior and his allies were ordered to take up action stations. Blunt sent to London for his old barber Mr Middleton to cut his hair. Already Judith had dealt with Philip Napier in court – 'I gave it him hot and strong in the neck' – and had submitted to and triumphed over a 'savage cross-examination'. She had also handled a press agog over the Crabbet *cause célèbre*, and a horde of agents from foreign studs eager to pick up cheap bargains. Prince Kemal el Din, she wrote, instructed his servant: 'Buy the whole Stud at all costs do not leave a single horse behind.' At one moment an ambassador from Egypt rushed hither and thither flourishing an open cheque; at another he was escaping from an American commission agent on a motor cycle armed with a knuckle-duster. Four days passed, but 'the Blunt faction made no progress at all'. Then Blunt himself went into court.

The court was his bedroom. Opposing counsel and a High Court judge repaired in a body to Newbuildings with Cockerell representing the public. But it was the defendant who wore the scarlet robes embroidered with gold thread; he lay supine on his magnificent Spanish bed with brocaded curtains, from whose canopy hung everlasting flowers and the ostrich egg. Blunt felt that he occupied the best position in the room, and with a small extra dose of morphia he was in high spirits, prepared to enjoy himself. Nevertheless he was a tragic figure. Like the bull in his ballad of Sancho Sanchez, he was baited with a stream of darts. Why had his wife left him? Was there another woman? Was her name Miss Carleton?

Blunt felt that the raising of these 'violent hares' in his bedroom, and afterwards in court by Judith, did the trustees' cause no good with the kindly referee – 'an old man', reflected Blunt, 'and I have no doubt has had domestic troubles at home'. But despite the referee's putative domestic troubles, Blunt's bellicosity probably injured his case. 'Under torture', wrote Judith's counsel to her, '(for he had his past put to him pretty mercilessly)', her father 'showed his fangs in a way which did him no good.' For her part, Judith admired him for being so 'diabolically cute ... with a concentrated cunning'; though at the end of his cross-examination she hoped he felt like 'a bit of mildewed boiled tapioca' whose friends would advise him to 'chuck it'. This time it was she who rejected a compromise.

Up to the last moment, the 'unconquered flame' in him expected victory. Again, on 11 February, he refused a compromise by which he would have had half the Stud, leaving it to his granddaughter Anne on his death. It was all or nothing. On 5 March 1920 his counsel wired him, 'Decision against you with all costs but you allowed cost of keeping all horses that you had from January 1918.'

Judith's lawyers sent her on the same day two sprightly messages. 'Congratulations. Enemy routed. Horse and Foot especially Horse.' 'Game set and match.'

Blunt was not as downcast as his friends expected. He regarded the result as 'a legal quibble'. Mrs Gabrielle Napier, who had been with Anne in Cairo right up to her last days, wrote: 'I could not help thinking how contrary the development was from dear Lady Anne's real wishes and intentions,' and Cockerell thought the same. Blunt's own comment was, 'Apart from the sense of a sharp blow which any unexpected news of defeat gives at the moment, it has not troubled me much.... The duty of preserving the Stud now goes to my grandchildren and they may or may not be found worthy of it. The burden is off my shoulders.' By November he had made himself forget it.[4]

Of his grandchildren, it is the delightful Lady Anne Lytton who still breeds and judges Arabian horses with incomparable skill and felicity. She has said of her grandmother's legacy: 'She meant my Grandfather to have the Stud, but did not separate the Stud from the rest of her property, which went to us.' At a centenary celebration of the Crabbet Arabian Stud, held at Newbuildings on 9 June 1978, everyone present who knew the story felt that this must be so. Who could leave creatures of such poetic beauty as were paraded there, the sunshine running in golden rivers along their coats, away from a man who was a poet?*

. . . . .

* See *The Crabbet Arabian Stud: Its History and Influence*, by R. Archer, C. Pearson and C. Covey, 1978. In this admirable account full justice is done to all, including Judith Lady Wentworth as a great breeder of Arabians.

Blunt's stoicism over this failure was partly due to his reviving interest in the post-war world; partly to his worsening health.

There was no end to the pilgrimages to Newbuildings, or to the pictures of the future painted for him by his friends. Ramsay MacDonald thought a Bolshevik revolution 'quite possible' when the soldiers came home from the war. A weekend of conversation with the Churchills convinced Blunt that Winston had caused the war even more than Grey. However, 'There is much of the schoolboy in Winston notwithstanding his crimes.... I am personally very fond of Winston and forgive him as one forgives a boy who has raided one's orchard.' He too thought a Bolshevik break-up in England quite possible. Old Brailsford, on the contrary, intended to work as a Labour candidate for a brave new world. 'Elections are much more elaborate than they were when you made your dashing intervention,' he wrote to Blunt. 'I am trying to learn this repugnant business.'[5]

The Peace Conference had stirred the hopes of subject peoples. Syed Ross Masood, a young Indian with whom E. M. Forster was in love, visited the prophet Blunt on Forster's recommendation. 'I come to you in search of wisdom and inspiration,' wrote Ross to Blunt. Aly Kamel, Vice-President of the Egyptian National Party and an exile in Paris, sent Blunt his 'filial homage' and longed to 'chake your kind and loyal hand'. A. M. Mischad and M. A. Zahra, both at English medical schools, were helped by Blunt to get their political propaganda published. At precisely the same time as the High Court took away his stud (March 1920) he was sponsoring an Independence Committee to give back their country to the Egyptians. Saad Zaghloul asked him to be president of the English branch, since all Egyptians looked upon him as 'their father'.

Blunt could not accept the invitation to attend the meeting for Imperial Justice to All Peoples organized by Lord Parmoor, the Labour peer and father of Sir Stafford Cripps, but he did urge Lord Parmoor to get in touch with 'that excellent man Saad Zaghloul.... I need not say that I sympathize with all the weak nationalities your meeting would protect'. Of course he ought to be among the fighters. But he no longer had the strength; not even for a newspaper war. 'So soon passeth it away', he quoted, 'and we are gone.'[6]

But his memory was not to pass away from India. Years after his death, Syed Mahmud was appealing to Lord Wavell from prison for reconciliation, and testifying to Blunt's influence as the first 'honest and frank' politician at whose feet he had sat, even before 'Gandhiji's'. Through Blunt and other friends he had come to admire English people. Blunt's name would long be cherished in the East 'and may even survive the Empire'.

Ten months before Blunt's death, he was being asked by Andrew

Rothstein, son of his old friend Theodore, to become a contributor to the *Labour Monthly*, amid a galaxy of young Communists, Socialists and 'bourgeois pacifists'.

That 'good fellow' St John Philby, an Arabian scholar and anti-imperialist like Blunt himself, the father of Kim Philby, had stayed at Newbuildings, and now sent Blunt his warm wishes for his eightieth birthday. He was off to Mesopotamia as a chief government adviser, and hoped to enjoy a 'sustained technical correspondence' with Blunt. A few days later a charming young man whom Blunt had been asked to address as Mr Lawrence ('Please not "Colonel" nowadays') visited him and told him about his extraordinary adventures in the Hejaz and Syria, one of his sayings being, 'The Syrians are monkeys and the Arabs lions'. Afterwards T. E. Lawrence told Cunninghame Graham that Blunt was 'a Prophet'. Next year Samuel C. Chew, an American professor at Bryn Mawr University, made a pilgrimage to offer Blunt, as poet and statesman, his homage of 'reverence and affection'. And Winston Churchill, now at the Colonial Office, wrote: 'I by no means exclude the possibility of what you suggest' – that Ireland should be evacuated and given complete self-government. '*Please*', Churchill added, '*keep this letter to yourself*.'[7]

That last sentence was probably written with Blunt's *My Diaries* in mind.* Their publication was a strong reason for Blunt's reawakened interest in world affairs; he hoped they might be in time to influence the Peace Conference and its aftermath. His friend Churchill was one of those who winced at Blunt's frank reports of private conversations; but he forgave him. Wilfrid Meynell was another. 'I am not a gossip,' he protested to Cockerell on reading Blunt's lively list of his stories. 'You are the prince of gossips!' retorted Cockerell.[8] Lest Hilaire Belloc also should be upset, Blunt wrote some verses in his friend's presentation copy beginning:

> Ho! to Hilarious, prince of good neighbours!
> Here take my last leaf of impotent labours.

The most violent of reactions came from Bosie, who found the *Diaries* 'odious' and 'truly revolting', showing as they did that Blunt had spent all his life on the side of 'rottenness and rotten people' – like Oscar Wilde and Abbas's ex-dancing boy, the Khedive Riaz.

By and large, however, *My Diaries* were received with acclamation. E. M. Forster, reviewing them on 19 July in the *Nation*, praised 'the wealth of Blunt's mind', his sincere feeling balanced by detachment, his valuable portrait gallery. If not 'great', his life was that of 'an English gentleman of genius' who was also the *enfant*

* *My Diaries* Volume I, 1888–1900, published 1919; *My Diaries* Volume II, 1901–1914, published 1920.

terrible of politics. 'Never was such a delightful book.' The young Shane Leslie wrote from New York that everyone wanted to see two things: De Valera (there on a visit) and Leslie's review of *My Diaries*.

Blunt himself was both amused and dazzled by the chorus of praise. 'I have never before had even a tolerably good press till today, when I have called all the political world knaves and all the journalists fools, and at last they are delighted!'

All the praise in the world, however, could not keep the infirmities of old age at bay. In the words of his 'Proteus', long ago, 'The Gaul is at the gate.'[9]

From 1917 onwards Blunt was trying desperately to cut down on the morphia which affected his nerves, though it kept the pain sufficiently subdued to allow of conversation and writing. 'I am my own doctor,' he wrote ill-advisedly. A subsequent twitching in his feet 'worse than any pain' at last persuaded him that the doctor's prescription of 'morphia-and-patience' was necessary. A prolonged choking fit in September 1920 convinced him that the end had come; he was cured none the less by Dorothy's reading aloud to him the Penitential Psalms, and by St Winifred.

There was no escape from that other bane of the old: the spectacle of social ties either weakening or vanishing altogether. On his seventy-eighth birthday Mary Wemyss sent him 'the thinnest of thin' notes, since visitors were waiting for her to pour out tea.

> Such is the grave of our *grande passion*! The pretence of a wriggle under a dust heap of domestic duty! but why complain? Are we not worms, all of us, however much we may have begun as Souls?

This was unfair to Mary, who was writing to him eighteen months later, 'The stars of Egypt are an undying memory – and footprints in the sand!'[10]

So many of his loves had gone: Georgie Sumner, Ella Baird, Madeline Wyndham, Janey Morris, Minnie Pollen. 'Kitty' Walters – Skittles – died of a stroke in 1920 attended to the last by her adoring Gerald de Saumarez. Blunt had already arranged for Kitty's burial in the Capuchins' churchyard at Crawley, but it remained for Gerald to help the good friars to skate over the difficulty that she was not in fact Mrs Baillie (as she had told them) but Catherine Walters, spinster, to her dying day. Nevertheless the initials C.W.B. appeared on her headstone.

Towards the end of 1920 the pilgrim theme returned sadly to Blunt's mind. He saw himself as the last survivor of a gay band who had crossed the desert together, each one falling off until suddenly there was no one at all to answer him when he called out in the dark 'Are you there?'

Those friends who had any influence with him cherished one overriding hope: that he would not end his own pilgrimage without becoming reconciled to his family. Through an accidental meeting with Lady ('Cosie') Burrell, he was persuaded to see his grandchildren again. Anthony, a soldier stationed in Ireland where the Black and Tans were raging – Blunt called them the Bashi Bazouks of fifty years ago – was still the flawless grandson he had so much loved and missed: 'a very beautiful young man', cycling over from Crabbet and ready to come at call. When Anne and Winnie visited Newbuildings – the first time for six years – Blunt was amazed and moved by their 'overpowering' affection. But it was no joy to him that Winnie was virtually pushed by her mother into marriage at seventeen with Claude Tryon, a man over twice her age. A month after Winnie's wedding (which Judith referred to as the 'Funeral day' in her diary, despite her own involvement), Neville Lytton wrote to Blunt from Paris that he and Judith were to be divorced.*

Blunt, never too old to plan dynastic marriages, entertained the final fantasy of again intermingling the blood of Wyndhams and Blunts in a union between Anthony and Daphne Currie, daughter of Lawrence Currie (a cousin on Blunt's maternal side) and of Sibell Adeane (a Wyndham).†

Judith alone, it seemed, was never to be forgiven. After her stud victory she offered to let byegones be byegones. An emotional letter arrived from her signed 'Always your Bibi' – but enclosing with exquisite cruelty Anne's tragic document of 1883, typed out and entitled by Judith, 'My Mother's Last Message'.‡ Blunt described Judith's letter as 'impertinence'. The truth was that in his failing state he dared not risk the excitement – and resulting physical agony – of further confrontation with his daughter.

Nevertheless, Blunt's last two years were not without poignancy. He had long been aware that his friends Meynell and Belloc were working to restore his lost faith. One of their instruments was the Dominican prior Father Vincent MacNab, first brought to Newbuildings in 1916. The friendship with Father MacNab was a growing source of light in Blunt's darkness.

There was another light. In his child Mary, now married with a

* Neville married a French woman *en secondes noces*, and his daughter Madeleine received a friendly welcome from her half-brothers and sisters.

† Anthony was to marry Clarissa Palmer in 1946, and their five children, Caroline, John, Roland, Lucy and Sarah are the great-great-great-grandchildren of Lord Byron the poet. After the deaths of Victor Lytton and his two sons, Neville became 3rd Earl of Lytton, to be succeeded by his son Anthony as 4th Earl in 1951.

‡ (FM. Letters, 1033/1975, 25 May 1920.) See p. 195 above.

handsome son, he saw all that was best and most beautiful: 'so perfect a creative being to continue what was best in me'. After a long argument with Mary Wemyss, who feared fresh scandal, he had been allowed to bequeath to his child Worth Forest estate, including that small house he had designed and built deep in its bracken. He called it rather ostentatiously Worth Manor House.

The pleasures of will-making being finally exhausted, Blunt laid his diary aside on 22 October 1921, as he thought for ever. His state was so piteous that in August Mary Wemyss had besought him to let a brilliant specialist operate on his prostrate in a London nursing home. 'I am determined to die here in my hermitage,' replied Blunt in a pathetically infirm hand.

The habit of his diary was too strong to be dropped. He began again less than a week later, sometimes dictating to Dorothy. He even contrived to compose long diatribes against the oppressors of Egypt. But the passage in his diary that had been intended as his last entry (22 October 1921) was a cry for spiritual help:

> I should like to die worthily but I feel it is beyond my power. I go out into the darkness where no wisdom can avail. I would wish to believe in another life beyond, for my life here has been a happy one. I would wish to believe a good God loves us all. I feel that [I] cannot be God's enemy but my foolish reason tells me I shall never know.

In fact Blunt's 'foolish reason' had been submitted by him to rigorous and fruitful religious discipline. Since 1916 he and Dorothy had been re-reading among other works the Gospels, Old Testament and writings of the Desert Fathers. These last he would constantly come back to, because of their account of man's eternal fight against the flesh and the devil. Towards the end of 1921 he was writing:

> The impossible severities endured by the hermits in search of a new life after death . . . have revived my hope of perhaps a pitiful God – and [I] wonder whether the visions seen by Anne might not perhaps yet be shown to me also *in articulo mortis*. It helps me to bear my pain.

At times he felt that his religious reading had made him more of an unbeliever than ever; and he admitted to the 'modernist' Miss Petre (Father Tyrrell's friend) that his prayers to St Winifred and even Cardinal Manning were 'superstitious practices'. Miss Petre smiled to find a portrait of Manning, the 'persecutor of modernism', perched opposite Blunt on the chair his mother had died in. Whatever happened, he would be buried in his 'dear wood', rather than at the Crawley monastery, and thus be prepared for utter oblivion – 'if so it needs must be'.[11]

When Meynell called at the beginning of March 1922, Blunt could not see him, it being one of his worst days, 'when I can only exist by having the most violent passages of the Old Testament read out to me'.[12]

After what had been another gap in his diary, he took it up again on St Patrick's Day, to record that Belloc had gone on holiday to Rome, bringing Blunt's homage to Pope Pius XI. 'How willingly would I believe if only I could but, woe is me, I cannot.'

A week later Belloc himself arrived with a crucifix blessed for Blunt by the Pope.

> It found me in a mood for conversion and an insistence on the necessity for me of a return to the Sacraments before I die. He urged that being already a Catholic and with no quarrel with the Church I needed nothing to entitle me to ask for these.

Blunt was finally convinced by a personal admission by Belloc: he himself often went to the Sacraments 'feeling little'. Blunt believed in the Church; he need not 'feel' its truths before making his confession.

Confession was no difficulty for him, replied Blunt, only all the priests who had been his friends were dead. Belloc suggested Father John Pollen, Minnie's son. 'I could not explain', noted Blunt, 'why he was the most impossible.'*[13]

It was then agreed that Father MacNab should be sent for, 'a man whom I like, a Sinn Feiner and an enlightened thinker with whom I have had talks already on early Christian theology'. Shane Leslie vividly imagines the 'great moment' when the Sussex sheykh and the Irish Dominican met, 'both wearing white robes'.

Having taken his decision, Blunt began at once a brief daily service of prayer, with a small altar on his bed formed by the Pope's crucifix, an Irish silver snuff-box and St Winifred's well-water. He felt himself again 'a pilgrim to her shrine'. It allayed his pain, enabling him to talk again, 'and what is more has added a sense of happiness and trust in some good thing after this poor miserable life. What matter if it is not true!' – this last out of respect for the agnostic Dorothy to whom he was dictating.†

But with a return of what Blunt called 'the pieties of my youth', came the punishing experience of repentance. He noted 'a terrible and

* Shane Leslie gives a striking but incorrect version of this incident. 'The Meynells', wrote Leslie, 'found a discreet priest, gentleman-born, to bring to his bedside, but Blunt motioned him away and fell back in unexpected silence. When Wilfrid sadly enquired the why of this relapse – "Could you not have guessed he was my own son?" groaned the sick man.' (*Long Shadows*, p. 254.) It was Belloc not Meynell who suggested Father Pollen, and as we have seen, neither John nor any of the other surviving Pollens could have been Blunt's children.

† (FM. 472/1975, 27 March 1922.) Dorothy afterwards told Lady Gregory that Blunt had summoned Father MacNab, 'I am broken with pain, you may send for that priest . . .' Sir William Gregory, however, had predicted even in Blunt's 'Mohammedan' days, 'You will see Wilfrid will die with the wafer in his mouth.' (Lady Gregory, *The Journals*, Vol. I, 6 May 1923.)

tragic incident' on 5 August when Margaret Pollen sat by his bedside, narrating the story of her mother's perfect life 'to its evil angel . . . in the very room which had been the scene of so many of our secret wickednesses including the first; things repented now but unforgotten'. He must have consulted Father MacNab in a panic, for a letter arrived from him dated 14 August: 'Do not be anxious. You have received all the Sacraments of the Church. . . . God keep you in his love. Pray for me.'[14]

And so the diary ended. But there were a few more letters to be dictated. On his eighty-second birthday, Sydney Cockerell wrote down for him a farewell message to Judith. He wished, he said, to forgive and be forgiven, however impossible it might once have seemed.[15] A letter he had written in 1917 to Lady Lovelace would explain why he had not answered Judith's messages. 'This is all I need to say as a dying man.' The last seven words were in his own hand: 'Once more your father Wilfrid Scawen Blunt.'[16]

Judith responded with a sonnet on the seventeenth ('Remembering all – Remember to forget'), among the best she wrote; a forgiving letter on the eighteenth to her 'most beloved Pappa'; a visit with Cockerell on the nineteenth; a letter of reconciliation to Dorothy on the twenty-first; and a passionately loving last letter to her father on the twenty-seventh: 'Now more than ever and in life and in death I shall always be your devoted B.B.'

On 5 September Blunt roused himself from the effects of a severe haemorrhage to address his friend Winston. Let him send the exiled Zaghloul back to Cairo: 'You will all be fools in Downing Street if you do not. . . . I tell you this practically on my deathbed. . . . With it I say a last farewell to this world's politics.'[17] It was indeed the last letter in this great collection. Winston sent a solicitous telegram in reply.

A letter of gratitude arrived for Blunt from India dated 12 September, announcing the release of a prisoner he had helped. Blunt never saw it. For he himself had been released two days before.

He died on the morning of 10 September 1922. His grandson has told the story most movingly. Though very weak, a sudden crisis of restlessness came over him, and he tried to get to the window to look out. The nurse who was with him held him down. When the sounds of the struggle brought Miss Lawrence into the room, she saw him gazing intently at the fire, through the holes bored at the bottom of his bed for that purpose. 'Into his eyes came a look of very great joy, so said Miss Lawrence. He threw his head back on to the pillow. He was dead.'

By order of Blunt himself, Judith was not to be notified of his death until Cockerell had arrived at Newbuildings; no doubt to safeguard the 'Secret Memoirs'. Thus Cockerell, not Judith, received the news by telegraph on 11 September: '8.15 A.M. Southwater. Mr. Blunt Passed Away Yesterday Sunday Please Come At Once ... Carleton And Lawrence.' Judith first saw the news in 'huge headlines' in the evening papers: *Death of Mr. Blunt.* She put the delay down to Dorothy's machinations.

Young Anne Lytton was brought by her mother to look upon the shrunken remains that once had been her glorious grandfather. To Anthony, who had recently visited him, he still looked beautiful. Two days after his death he was wrapped in his oriental carpet – the one that had seen so many adventures – and carried on a stretcher by six men from his estate, including Alfred Kensett, Felix and Jack Rapley and William Knight, to the appointed glade in Newbuildings wood. They were each bequeathed £10. It was all as quick and simple as possible, 'without religious or other ceremony, or intervention of strangers', according to a long-standing clause in the will. But his family and friends gathered round, as Anne Lytton and Nurse Lawrence cast handfuls of potpourri and everlasting flowers into the enormously deep 'pit', Dorothy meanwhile standing 'moaning' on the brink.[18]

Father MacNab, who had been away in Ireland at the time of Blunt's death, came back to bless the grave. Blunt had every right to be buried in his own ground, said the priest, and the land had already been blessed many times. Later he was to declare to Anthony, a devout Catholic, 'Your grandfather is all right – you have no cause to worry!'

A replica of Lady Anne Blunt's monument was erected over the grave, with six lines chosen by the inspired Cockerell from Blunt's sonnet 'Chanclebury Ring':*

Dear checker-work of woods, the Sussex Weald!
If a name thrills me yet of things of earth,
That name is thine. How often I have fled
To thy deep hedgerows and embraced each field,
Each lag, each pasture, – fields which gave me birth
And saw my youth, and which must hold me dead.

Today an avenue of yews that Blunt himself planted has grown up to shelter the grave in winter. In summer the butterflies that he loved, Fritillaries, Ringlets and Speckled Woods, add their flickering lights to the pattern of sunshine and shadow through oak leaves. Beyond, the daughters of his first Arabian mares stand under the trees of an open field with their foals.

'I shall probably be reckoned some day as a poet,' wrote Blunt at the age of seventy-one, 'but not till after I am dead. My politics are too damnable for that.'[19] But it is his 'damnable' politics even more than

* Blunt always insisted this was the correct spelling of Chanctonbury. (*Love Sonnets of Proteus*, XCVII.)

his poetry that have brought him immortality. Blunt was the first of the great anti-imperialists; the first to make the heavens ring with his indignation at a time when the British Empire seemed all but divine: 'God who made thee mighty, make thee mightier yet.'

No one has seriously chronicled the Empire's rise and fall without quoting from Blunt's published diaries. In his unpublished diaries from 1914 onwards, he hailed the First World War and its aftermath as 'The White Man's Suicide'. In old age, an unexpected note of sadness invaded his writings, even as he pronounced the Empire's doom. Was not the white race his own, and the British Empire no worse than others; better indeed than most? Nevertheless he saw that the coloured races could not come to full stature until the white incubus had been exorcized. How would the peoples of India, Arabia, Persia, Egypt or the Sudan fare in any given event? This was his touchstone. As he wrote to Meynell about the Boer War, 'it is of course abominable, but I do not wholly regret it. It is far better our military swaggerers should break their teeth over these tough old Boers than go on slaughtering helpless black brown or yellow people with impunity and calling it glory.'[20]

Sometimes the *enfant terrible* of politics slipped up. One of his last accusations was against Cecil Rhodes, for importing slave labour from the Sudan. *The Times* corrected Mr Blunt. Those dark-skinned 'labourers' reported to be entering Rhodesia were not men but donkeys. No wonder Blunt's friend Harry Brand had years ago implored him to desist. 'You are not fit for practical politics, you have a soul above them. Stick to poetry and religion. You will be happier for it, and the world quieter.' But the dark-skinned peoples did not want a quiet world if it meant their suppression. They listened for Blunt's voice. 'If the English nation possesses something really admirable and superior, it is that she has produced some great characters like you,' wrote Riza Bey Tewfik.[21]

Blunt recognized three main reasons for opposing imperialism: no nation was morally fit to rule another; no race should 'usurp' another's space in the world; and the characteristics of the coloured peoples were of such intrinsic value that they must never be absorbed into alien races or diluted by Anglo-Saxon rule, with 'its debased industrialism, its crude cookery and its flavourless religious creed'. Speaking of Blunt's *Golden Odes* of Arab poetry, Frederic Harrison praised him for retaining 'the whole of the fierce, wild, heroic fire of the bedouin, without European manners and Christian mawkishness'. Blunt's personal manners towards Egyptians and Indians were flawless. Those who were able to observe him, like Professor Browne and E. M. Forster, remarked on his rare chivalry, friendliness and 'kingliness' – the last in the sense of bounty.

It was to preserving the 'heroic fire' that Blunt dedicated his finest qualities as man of action – courage, love of justice and freedom, passionate feeling. He was too much of an intellectual not to be occasionally cast down by doubt. He had noted the same in old Gladstone; but how on reaching a decision the Prime Minister's spirits rose. 'Once one has chosen one's course, courage comes back.'[22] Like Gladstone's Midlothian campaign, Blunt's life was a 'pilgrimage of passion'. When T. E. Lawrence called on him there was 'a fire yet flickering over the ashes of old fury'. On justice, Blunt was fond of quoting an Arab saying: 'An hour of justice is worth seventy years of prayer.' Father Vincent MacNab recognized in him 'a justice-thirsting' soul, and it was his passion for justice that made him fight for freedom; that freedom through which alone justice is won.

He had numerous friends on the left. The Labour M.P. Keir Hardie opened a correspondence with 'a man for whom I have for years retained the very highest regard'. Blunt was nonetheless in many respects a country Tory. Though he did not actually join forces with his friend Belloc to attack the 'Servile State', the whirlwind of his fury was often raised against the small servilities demanded by local bye-laws. Yet he could preach Socialism in the back streets of Camberwell, and reprimand Lady Gregory for letting her ownership of Coole Park stand between her and Irish Nationalism. This made for contradictions. Notable ones were his wrath over Winston Churchill's and George Wyndham's politics, alongside his devotion to Winston and George as men.[23]

He once wrote to John Dillon: 'Without occasional incidents of physical revolt a national cause stagnates and gets lost in the slough of material apathy and increased well-being.' A clever suffragette tried to get his subscription for *Votes for Women* by saying that she knew he disliked the cause – but 'approved the militant methods'. His swash-buckling was a side of Blunt that contributed to the picture of him as an 'Elizabethan' or 'Renaissance man'. Like the aggressive goldsmith Benvenuto Cellini who wrote in his diary: 'Taking my corners widely as is my fashion', Blunt would invite retaliation by driving hated motor-cars off the road with his foaming Arabian steeds. His all-round proficiency as explorer, horseman, horse-breeder, shot, sculptor, painter, prose-writer, poet, caused Lady Gregory to search even further back for his like. She wrote: 'The many gifts, the mastery of living, seem to belong to the heroic ages of the world and show him as one of Plutarch's men.'[24]

But it is to an imaginary age compounded of the Renaissance, the medieval Courts of Love and the Land of Heart's Desire that we must go for Blunt the great lover. Raymond Mortimer has judged him 'the most picturesque Englishman of his time – poet, sportsman, amorist and rebel'. Blunt's amours were surely responsible for more than a quarter of the picturesqueness.

Ethics apart, there is no doubt that his love brought with it a quality of life-enhancement which was unique in that age. The drooping Janey Morris discovered an unsuspected 'capacity for enjoyment' in herself after visiting Newbuildings. Mabel Batten, a typically frustrated Victorian,* found none to satisfy her 'nameless cravings' until she met Wilfrid Blunt. He loved women in a way far remote from a Laclos or Casanova, appreciating their individualities without presuming to have understood them down to the last sigh. 'Women very seldom tell all about themselves', he wrote.[25]

His extraordinary virile beauty often did his work for him without the necessity for any seduction scene. He was well aware of this. But this was not all. His portrait of the poet Hoël in the unfinished 'Court of Love' was one version of himself. People would sometimes call Hoël a 'heartless' hedonist in his dealings with women; but Hoël could never have maintained his position in the Ghosts' Fellowship (the Souls) had he been other than 'affectionate, considerate and kind.... He had never needed to be a runner after women.'

How should we rate Blunt's lifelong championship of passion over friendship? At its lowest level it prevented him from seeing the point of the so-called New Woman. He wrote disparagingly of one of them: 'She has ceased altogether to be a pretty woman, and has become instead a "woman's delegate".' In extenuation it may be said that, with Blunt, friendship nearly always followed passion.[26]

His contemporaries believed that Eastern influences were responsible for his many loves. His interest in the East may indeed have accentuated his tendency to behave like a pasha. He may also have learnt from Islam that it is possible to make more than one woman happy. With his remarkable endowments it seemed almost a duty, a mission, to make as many happy as possible. At times, however, he was a medieval romantic, looking for the ideal woman on the road to the Holy Grail. He once described the devotion to the Virgin Mary as medieval Christianity at its highest. It is easy to be cynical about the process whereby one woman after another was hailed as his 'last', his 'perfect' love. External events, particularly husbands, were usually the cause of breakdown, not his infidelity. His relationship with Anne was the exception. Here the fidelity was all hers.

Again and again in this marriage fate seemed to have got its lines crossed. Surely it was Wilfrid, not Anne, whose grandfather had been

* 'Butterflies', his lyric written to Mrs Batten, shows this. (*Poetical Works*, vol. I, 'Love Lyrics of Proteus – Song–Butterflies'.)

Lord Byron? Blunt was conscious of a Byronic vein in himself. The unforgiving spirit of her grandmother Annabella had by no means entered into Anne; no more was her great charm of a Byronic kind. According to her contemporaries she was 'quaint', 'original', 'a trump', 'a brick', 'a good sort'. Her devoted grandson has written of her, 'Anne had very little insight into the character of others . . . was tight-lipped about little things with hardly any sense of humour – at least on Sunday mornings.'[27] Certainly it required a very good sort indeed to put up with the conditions of her marriage for thirty-six years. It is in the Blunts' joint Arabian adventures, visually recalled through Anne's entrancing water-colours and sustained by her scholarship, that the marriage achieves a reality never found in Byron's. In every sense her endurance was heroic.

Judith was the true casualty of her father's spendthrift love. In her way she longed for reconciliation, until at the reading of his will her love turned finally to gall. He had left Newbuildings and Worth Forest to 'strangers' – the former to Dorothy; the latter, including Worth Manor House, to his child Mary.*

This blow accounts for Judith's twisted mind in all her later recollections. She convinced herself that after Blunt's last letter, signed 'your father', he had changed his will in her favour, but too late to have it signed; too late, because Dorothy had poisoned him with an overdose of opium rather than lose Newbuildings. When Judith tried to get an exhumation order she found the body had been buried under tons of concrete. (Dorothy was to bequeath Newbuildings to Wilfrid's granddaughter, Lady Anne Lytton.)

In poor Judith's inflamed imagination her father's peaceful funeral became a scene from *opéra bouffe*. Here was little Cockerell leading the way in frock coat and grey trilby, for all the world like a tourist's guide. 'This carpet Mr. Blunt had travelled with . . . these rose leaves he had plucked . . . this dog – now where on earth is that dog? . . . Dot, Dot, come here! – Dot was his favourite dog. This grassy slope. . . . Steady please Kensett. . . .' Here then, intrusively, was Cockerell; there several ex-lady-loves, and Dorothy in trailing black looking 'hunted' (Judith indulged the fantasy that Dorothy too was an opium-eater);† Miss Lawrence prostrate and Jumbo (Anthony) arguing with Cock-

* The Worth estate and house were bought back by the Lyttons; but the isolated house was vandalized during the Second World War. Today only the foundations are visible, behind the huge yew tree where Anne and Wilfrid had tea together after their reconciliation in 1915. The present owner, with a sense of poetic justice, has preserved the foundation stone, on which Blunt's name and those of his carpenter and masons are graved. Like the Lady of Shallot's mirror, the stone is cracked from side to side, and a mouse's nest lies at the centre.

† According to 'Myself and Others', Judith got a Scotland Yard woman detective named 'M' to track down Dorothy to Savory & Moore's, the London chemist. (11 January 1919.)

erell about the depth of the hole. Cockerell, added Judith, wanted a 'domed mosque' over the grave. (She was always unjust to him.)

No name in Judith's vocabulary could eventually be too bad for Blunt, despite the 'magnetism' that remained 'hypnotic'. When thwarted, he became an 'Eastern potentate' or 'ex-Sultan' whose only desire was to cry 'Off with his head!' Or he was 'Kaiser Bill' or Hitler; not forgetting Byron, whom Judith vilified for his 'theatrical' womanizing. Even Blunt's poetry, in Judith's jaundiced eyes, was now and forever a function of his vanity.

Though Judith called her father a 'Quarrel Factory', her own record was decidely more pugnacious than his. She died without having seen her son Anthony for thirty years. 'Don't let the enemy come near me,' she said to a friend on her deathbed. 'The enemy?' 'My children....'

Blunt's vanity was widely accepted as a weakness. Cunninghame Graham, himself something of a peacock, was prepared to excuse: 'Without weaknesses no man can be strong.' An old friend like Lulu Harcourt would tease Blunt gently: Lulu was starting a garden with plants donated by famous people; would Wilfrid send some bulbs of *Narcissus Poeticus*? Lord Newton, however, regarded Blunt's vanity as that of a cad. At a party in 1891 there had been a discussion of male good looks. Newton put forward Parnell as an example. 'Ah,' said Blunt, 'I do not suppose that any two men have been mistaken for each other so frequently as I and Parnell.' On the other hand, Desmond MacCarthy, a most sensitive writer and welcome visitor at Newbuildings, wrote: 'He was vain but what is rare in the vain, extremely dignified.' E. M. Forster found the vanity in *My Diaries* 'not intrusive', though it spoilt the cumulative effect. There was too much of, 'they neglected my advice with the result that ...'.[28]

Blunt's own attitude to his diaries, both published and secret, must be properly understood. Truth and sincerity were his aims. When he was morally wrong – and he often admitted to being wrong in affairs of the heart – he must say so. If he was right and the establishment was wrong, he must say so too. Thus he hoped to present posterity with the most complete, candid and uncompromising personal record ever kept over so long a period in the England of his day. By that test he expected to be judged.

Both his political and his love poetry expressed what he had really felt or done. When W. E. Henley and George Wyndham edited a selection of Blunt's poems in 1898, Blunt was mortified that the political poems – *The Wind and the Whirlwind* and *Satan Absolved* – were excluded, as too 'damnable'. He felt vindicated when Macmillan in England (1919) and Knopf in America published the unexpurgated *Poetical Works*.

Yet it is by the lyrics and sonnets that Blunt's poetry will be remembered. W. B. Yeats believed that Blunt's best poems – few, but extremely fine – had an Elizabethan ring. His experiments in assonance, and in sonnets that had more than the statutory fourteen lines, foreshadow our freer future. The smack of finality at the end of his sonnets rarely misfires. We can agree with Sir Edward Marsh in picking out 'The Two Highwaymen', 'Chanclebury Ring' and 'Sidi Kaled' as favourites. The word favourite was too cold, said the rapturous Lady Desborough, when she chose Blunt's sole imperial sonnet, 'Gibraltar', as her 'most beloved'. The sonnet sequences played their part in subjecting willing victims to the spell of Merlin, when read aloud on winter nights.

Newbuildings itself was a potent source of magic. It had always radiated happiness. The three grandchildren felt 'wanted and cherished' there, as by God the Father. They remembered three special Newbuildings scents: jasmine at the front door; Persian roses at the back door and in potpourri all over the house; wood smoke. And three sounds: the cries of forty peacocks, a cuckoo clock, and a rebellious chiming clock that sang out midnight during dinner. Admittedly the unkempt beauty of woods and pastures was not always good husbandry. Blunt's solicitor wrote with alarm during the war that a landowner might be given hard labour if he failed in cultivation. 'If . . . the non-cultivation is with the intention of assisting the enemy, the punishment is Death. Please be careful.'[29]

It was to this paradise – or 'hermitage' as the old prophet preferred to call it – that the disciples came, to sit at the feet of their *guru*. His grandson was to call him the 'Sussex Tolstoy'. Even after the divorce, Neville Lytton professed himself H.F.'s disciple. Winston Churchill was not in the habit of geriatric visiting, and can only have stayed so often at Newbuildings for the sake of the stimulus he gained. 'It did me good also,' wrote Lady Gregory after a sick-visit to Newbuildings in 1919. Perhaps the most touching disciple was an obscure young soldier named Maitland Hardyman, who stayed with Blunt while on leave. 'As I tried to tell you, Sir', he wrote on 15 January 1917, 'both you yourself and the House, materialized to me what has always been a part of me. Very many thanks indeed to you, Sir, from a young and often very lonely "rebel".' In March he was trying to convert his mess to 'peace politics' – just before he was killed.[30]

If Blunt himself was anyone's disciple, he was William Morris'. There was a vast difference, however, between them. Morris' social conscience darkened his horizons. He wished he had not been born with a sense of beauty in this 'accursed age'. Blunt felt no incompatibility between his political conscience and his love of beauty. He gave full rein to all his impulses. He could equally well be elected President of the prestigious Arab Horse Society in 1917 and of the suspect Egyptian Independence Committee three years later. (There was one hitch in the former arrangement, as Judith gleefully pointed out. Owing to the High Court decision of 1920, the Arab Horse Society found themselves with 'a horseless President'.)

His feelings for Sussex were obsessional, at times irrational. Almost anything could make him indignant. 'I resent these Roman remains in Sussex,' he wrote after hearing of a dig, 'they have no business here, outlandish, imperialistic....' Judith had committed an unpardonable sin in selling some of the ancestral acres. When the *Petworth Posie*, a local publication, cited Kipling and Belloc along with himself as Sussex poets, he was affronted. They were not Sussex-born. Nor were the ex-soldiers whom it was proposed in 1916 to settle on Sussex soil. 'We don't want a lot of foreigners from the North of England', wrote Blunt, 'upsetting our native ways and introducing intensive cultivation.'[31] His servants learnt to treat their Squire as a deity. It was nothing but 'Yes, Squire. Quite so, Squire' from Caffin, scoffed Judith. Sometimes Caffin would say, by accident, 'Sir Wilfrid'.

Nevertheless, this late Victorian and Edwardian squire had no more in common with his Sussex predecessors than one of his fiery Arab stallions with a fat pony. As he discovered from an old Sussex diary, the Horsham people in the 1770s did little but eat, drink, pay calls and play cards. A little watching cricket, but no hunting or shooting. (This went for the mid-eighteenth-century Mr Blunts, Mr Scawens, Mr Burrells and Mr Evelyns.) But the world itself had been too tame for Wilfrid Blunt in the days of his manhood. It was the same with his religion. 'Religion is a wall to hold up the weak', said a sceptical friend. Blunt wanted no walls, but the possibility of a wider world with a new dimension.

In the end it was the strength of his personality that left the greatest impression. In *Heartbreak House*, Bernard Shaw was able to spread Blunt's personality over *two* characters, Captain Shotover and Hector Hushabye. Ezra Pound wanted some of Blunt's 'stuff' for the American magazine *Poetry* because of 'the glory of his name' – a phrase that Pound cannot have meant literally (Blunt's name was never strictly 'glorious' either in America or Britain) but which testified eloquently to his unforgettable personal impact. 'A thoroughbred human being' was Siegfried Sassoon's view of him in old age. While Blunt's genius cannot be pinned down either to his poetry or his politics, genius he had nonetheless. It was the light that hung outside his door, bringing men and women of genius to his home; the magnetism exerted by the warmth and brilliance of his inner world. It was there for others to enjoy even in his old age and illness. Working within him, it melted the last trace of his own human doubts.

Blunt was once much taken with an eighteenth-century tombstone in a Sussex churchyard. All told, it provides a fitting postscript on this restless giant of man:

Vast strong was I, and yet did die,
And in my grave asleep I lie.
My grave is stoned all round about
Yet I hope the Lord will find me out.

Bibliography

Bibliography

Unpublished Sources

Fitzwilliam Museum. The Blunt Papers.

Lytton Letters, at the Fitzwilliam Museum.

Lytton Papers, in the possession of the Earl of Lytton.

British Library, Additional Manuscripts. The Wentworth Bequest.

Tennant Papers. Mainly for material formerly in the possession of Dorothy Carleton.

Correspondence of Sir Sydney Cockerell and W. S. Blunt, in the possession of Mr Christopher Blunt.

Lovelace correspondence, in the possession of Lady Fairfax-Lucy.

Correspondence of Judith Blunt and Arthur Pollen, in the possession of the Hon. Mrs Pollen.

The Papers of Wilfrid Meynell, in the possession of Mrs Elizabeth Hawkins.

Letters of Professor E. G. Browne to W. S. Blunt, in the possession of the Rt Hon. Sir Patrick Browne.

Published Sources

ADAMS, W. S.: *Edwardian Portraits* (London, 1957).

ARCHER, ROSEMARY; PEARSON, COLIN; AND COVEY, CECIL: *The Crabbet Arabian Stud* (A. Heriot, Gloucestershire, 1978).

ASQUITH, MARGOT: *Autobiography* (2 vols, London, 1920).

BAKER, JOHN: *Horsham Diary*, edited by W. S. Blunt (Sussex Archeological Society, vol. LII).

BLUNT, LADY ANNE: *Bedouin Tribes of the Euphrates*, edited by Wilfrid Scawen Blunt (2 vols, London, 1879).

A Pilgrimage to Nejd (2 vols, London, 1881).

BLUNT, WILFRID SCAWEN: *Sonnets and Songs by Proteus* (London, 1875).

Proteus and Amadeus, A Correspondence, edited by Aubrey de Vere (London, 1878).
Love Sonnets of Proteus (London, 1881).
The Future of Islam (London, 1882).
The Wind and the Whirlwind (London, 1883).
Ideas about India (London, 1885).
In Vinculis (London, 1889).
A New Pilgrimage and other Poems (London, 1889).
The Love Lyrics and Songs of Proteus (Kelmscott Press, 1892).
Esther and Love Lyrics (London, 1892).
The Stealing of the Mare (London, 1892).
Griselda (London, 1893).
The Poetry of Wilfrid Blunt, selected by W. E. Henley and George Wyndham (London, 1898).
Satan Absolved (London and New York, 1899).
The Shame of the Nineteenth Century (Pamphlet, 1900).
The Military Fox-Hunting Case at Cairo (Pamphlet, 1902).
The Golden Odes of Arabia (Chiswick Press, 1903).
Atrocities of Justice under British Rule in Egypt (Pamphlet, 1906).
Mr Blunt and The Times (Pamphlet, 1907).
Secret History of the English Occupation of Egypt (London, 1907, reprinted 1969).
The New Situation in Egypt (Pamphlet, 1908).
India under Ripon (London, 1909).
Letter to the National Egyptian Congress (Pamphlet, 1910).
The Italian Horror (Pamphlet, 1911).
Gordon at Khartoum (London, 1912).
The Land War in Ireland (London, 1912).
Poetical Works of Wilfrid Scawen Blunt, complete edition (London, 1914, New York, 1923).
My Diaries, Part One 1888–1900, Part Two, 1900–1914 (London, 1919 and 1920).

BLUNT, WILFRID: *Cockerell* (London, 1964, New York, 1965).
Desert Hawk – Abd el Kader and the French Conquest of Algeria (London, 1947).
England's Michelangelo – A Biography of G. F. Watts (London, 1975).

BLYTH, HENRY: *Skittles – The Last Victorian Courtesan* (London, 1970).

BROADLEY, A. M.: *How We Defended Arabi* (London, 1886).

BROWNE, EDWARD G.: *The Persian Revolution 1905–1909* (Cambridge, 1910).

BURTON, CAPTAIN SIR RICHARD F.: *Pilgrimage to Al-Madinah and Meccah* (2 vols, London, 3rd edition, 1879).

COLVIN, SIR AUCKLAND: *The Making of Modern Egypt* (London, 1906).

CONOLLY, TERENCE L.: *Francis Thompson – In His Paths* (Milwaukee, 1946).
CRATHORNE, NANCY: *Tennants Stalk – The Story of the Tennants of the Glen* (London, 1973).
CROFT-COOKE, RUPERT: *'Bosie' – The Story of Lord Alfred Douglas* (London, 1963).
CROMER, EARL OF: *Modern Egypt* (2 vols, London, 1907).
DOUGHTY, CHARLES M.: *Travels in Arabia Deserta* (London, 1921).
EGREMONT, MAX: *The Cousins* (London, 1977).
FINCH, EDITH: *Wilfrid Scawen Blunt* (London, 1938).
FORSTER, E. M.: *Abinger Harvest* (London, 1936).
FURBANK, P. N.: *E. M. Forster – A Life* (London, 1977).
GLADWYN, CYNTHIA: *The Paris Embassy* (London, 1976).
GOING, WILLIAM T.: *A Peacock Dinner* (*Journal of Modern Literature*, Temple University, Pennsylvania, 1971).
GREGORY, LADY: *Seventy Years – The Autobiography of Lady Gregory* (C. Smythe, Gerrards Cross, 1974).
The Journals – Books 1–29, edited by Daniel J. Murphy (Vol. I, London, 1978).
GRYLLS, ROSALIE GLYNN: *Portrait of Rossetti* (London, 1964, Illinois, 1970).
HARRIS, FRANK: *Oscar Wilde, His Life and Confessions* (2 vols, New York City, 1918).
Contemporary Portraits (New York, 1920).
HARRISON, FREDERIC: *Autobiographic Memoirs* (2 vols, London, 1911).
HOGARTH, DAVID GEORGE: *The Penetration of Arabia* (London, 1904).
LAYARD, AUSTEN H., M.P.: *Discoveries in the Ruins of Nineveh and Babylon* (London, 1853).
LESLIE, ANITA: *Edwardians in Love* (London, 1972).
LESLIE, SIR SHANE: *Men Were Different* (London, 1937).
Long Shadows (London, 1966).
LUTFI AL-SAYYID, AFAF: *Egypt and Cromer* (London, 1968).
LUTYENS, LADY EMILY: *A Blessed Girl* (London, 1953).
The Birth of Rowland (London, 1956).
LYON, F. S. L.: *John Dillon* (London, 1968).
LYTTON, EARL OF: *The Desert and the Green* (London, 1957).
Wilfrid Scawen Blunt – A Memoir (London, 1961).
Mickla Bendore (London, 1962).
LYTTON, NEVILLE: *The English Country Gentleman* (London, 1925).
MACCARTHY, DESMOND: *Portraits I* (London, 1931).
MALET, SIR EDWARD: *Shifting Scenes* (London, 1901).
Egypt 1879–1883 (London, 1909).
MANSFIELD, PETER: *The British in Egypt* (London, 1971).

MEYERS, JEFFREY: *On the Warpath Against Tyranny* (*London Magazine*, August–September 1976).

MEYNELL, VIOLA: *Alice Meynell – A Memoir* (London, 1929).
Francis Thompson and Wilfrid Meynell – A Memoir (London, 1952).

MILES, ALFRED A.: *The Poets and the Poetry of the Century* (Vol. 6, London).

MILNER, ALFRED: *England in Egypt* (London, 1892).

PALGRAVE, WILLIAM GIFFORD: *A Year's Journey through Central and Eastern Arabia 1862–1863* (2 vols, London, 1865).

POLLEN, ANNE: *John Hungerford Pollen* (London, 1920).

PHILBY, H. ST. JOHN B.: *Arabia* (London, 1930).

REID, B. L.: *The Lives of Roger Casement* (Yale, 1976).

RUMBOLD, SIR HORACE: *Further Recollections of a Diplomat* (London, 1903).

SCHMIDT, MARGARET FOX: *Passion's Child – The Extraordinary Life of Jane Digby* (New York and London, 1976).

SHAW, G. B.: *John Bull's Other Island* (Preface, 'The Denshawai Horror', London, 1908).
The Doctor's Dilemma (Preface, London, 1911).
Heartbreak House (London, 1919).

STEEVENS, G. W.: *Egypt in 1898* (London, 1898).

TSCHIFFELY, A. F.: *Don Roberto – The Life and Works of R. B. Cunninghame Graham 1852–1936* (London, 1937).

TURNER, STEPHEN: *William Earl of Lovelace 1805–1893* (Surrey Archeological Collections, 1974).

UPTON, PETER: *Desert Heritage – an Artist's Impression of the Original Arabs Imported by the Blunts* (London, 1979).

WENTWORTH, JUDITH LADY: *Flame of Life* (London, 1930).
The Authentic Arabian Horse and His Descendants (London, 1945).

References

References

The following abbreviations are used:

FM. Fitzwilliam Museum, Wilfrid Scawen Blunt Collection

BL. British Library Additional Manuscripts Wentworth Bequest

Lytton FM. Lytton Letters loaned to the Fitzwilliam Museum

Lytton Papers. Lytton Papers in the possession of the Earl of Lytton

MD. My Diaries by Wilfrid Scawen Blunt

PW. Poetical Works of Wilfrid Scawen Blunt

The following names are abbreviated:

WSB Wilfrid Scawen Blunt

AINB Lady Anne Isabella Noel Blunt

J Judith Lady Wentworth *née* Blunt

Note. In order to keep the pages reasonably uncluttered, references have not been given for every one of the quotations from Blunt's diaries.

Part I

1 A Blessed Boy

1 *MD.* II., p. 475, 16 May 1914.
2 *PW.* II., 'Sussex Pastorals – "Sed Nos Qui Vivimus"'.
3 FM. 1400/1977. Various drafts of 'The Religion of Happiness'.
4 Lytton Papers; J, *Authentic Arabian*, p. 78.
5 Lytton Papers.
6 *Ibid.*, 29 November 1850, Mrs Blunt to the Rev. John Chandler.
7 BL. 54069, August 1873, WSB's 'Autobiographical Notes' dictated to AINB.
8 *PW.* I., 'Love Lyrics of Proteus – A Summer in Tuscany'.
9 *Ibid.*, 'Esther – A Sonnet Sequence', XXIX.
10 BL. 54069; Lytton Papers.
11 FM. 9/1975, 9 January 1909.
12 Tennant Papers, Lady Leconfield to WSB, 19 February 1860.
13 *Ibid.*, 28 March 1861.
14 *Ibid.*, 27 May 1861.
15 Lytton FM., 6 and 30 August 1861, Sir A. Malet to WSB.

2 Venus Discovered

1 Lytton Papers.
2 Finch, p. 41.
3 Lytton Papers, 22 and 28 August 1864.
4 FM. 729/1976, 732/1976.
5 *PW.* I., 'Esther – Sonnet LVII'.
6 Finch, p. 44.
7 Blyth, p. 150.
8 WSB, *Love Sonnets of Proteus* – 'To Manon, XXI'.
9 J, *Authentic Arabian*, p. 79.
10 *PW.* I., 'Esther – Sonnet LVIII'.
11 Lytton FM., 6 December 1863, Lady Malet to WSB.
12 FM. 633/1976, C. Walters ('Skittles') to WSB, May 1865.
13 *PW.* II., 'Sussex Pastorals – "Sed Nos Qui Vivimus", X'.
14 Lutyens, *Birth of Rowland*, p. 41.

15 *Ibid.*, p. 67.
16 *Ibid.*, p. 78, 27 July 1865.
17 *Ibid.*, p. 81.
18 *Ibid.*, p. 144.
19 *PW.* I., 'Love Lyrics of Proteus – Dead Joys'.
20 Lutyens, *Birth of Rowland*, p. 122, 14 August 1865.
21 *Ibid.*, pp. 164–5.
22 *Ibid.*, p. 217, 28 October 1865.
23 *PW.* I., 'Love Lyrics and Songs – The Broken Pitcher'.
24 *PW.* II., 'Worth Forest'.
25 FM. 41/1975, 'Alms to Oblivion', Chapter 4, p. 98.
26 Lytton FM., 1 September 1866, Lady Malet to WSB.

3 *Vita Nova*

1 WSB, *Love Sonnets of Proteus*, 'Juliet, XLVII'.
2 Lytton FM., 22 March 1863 and 5 September 1965, Lady Malet to WSB.
3 FM. 997/1976, 27 July 1865.
4 FM. 635/1977.
5 FM. 1000/1976.
6 WSB, *Love Sonnets of Proteus*, 'Juliet, XXII'.
7 BL. 54100.
8 *Ibid.*
9 FM. 1005/1976, 6 March 1869.
10 BL. 54100, 30 September 1868.
11 FM. 42/1975, 'Alms to Oblivion', Part IV, p. 7.
12 FM. 662/1977, 21 March 1869.
13 FM. 661/1977, 6 March 1869.
14 BL. 54100, 14 March 1869.
15 *Ibid.*
16 *Ibid.*
17 Lytton Papers.
18 FM. 25/1975, 1883.
19 FM. 378/1975, 1903.
20 BL. 53831, 6 August 1869.
21 Lytton FM, 24 October 1869, Godfrey Lushington to WSB.
22 BL. 54100.
23 FM. 42/1975, 11 January 1870.

4 *'What have we done to Death?'*

1 BL. 54100.
2 Tennant Papers.
3 *Ibid.*
4 BL. 53831.
5 *Ibid.*
6 FM. 666/1977.
7 FM. 1355/1976.
8 BL. 54100.
9 BL. 53835.
10 BL. 54100.
11 WSB, *Love Sonnets of Proteus*, 'Gods and False Gods – The Two Highwaymen, LXXI'.
12 *Ibid.*, 'To One to Whom He had been Unjust, LXXIII'.
13 FM. 1372/1976.
14 BL. 53835.
15 WSB, *Love Sonnets of Proteus*, 'Vita Nova – He is not a Poet, XCV'.
16 *Ibid.*, 'The Sublime, CVI'.
17 *Ibid.*, 'Roumeli Hissar, CIX'; BL. 54073, 23 April–13 May 1873.
18 BL. 53835–7, 8 July 1873.
19 WSB, *Love Sonnets of Proteus*, 'Juliet – On the Nature of Love, XXII'.
20 BL. 53835; see also WSB's brief travel diary, BL. 54075.
21 WSB, *Love Sonnets of Proteus*, 'Gods and False Gods – Cold Comfort, LXXVIII'.
22 *Ibid.*, 'He Desires the Impossible, LIV'.
23 BL. 53857, 18 April 1874.
24 WSB, *Love Sonnets of Proteus*, 'Vita Nova – On the Shortness of Time, XCVI'.
25 *Ibid.*, 'Juliet – To One who would "Remain Friends", XXXVII'.

5 *'Carnival of Folly' and Founding of the Stud*

1 BL. 53863, 10 June 1875.
2 *Ibid.*
3 FM. 1235/1976, 6 September 1875.
4 FM. 1230/1976, Wednesday [October] 1875.
5 BL. 53865, 7 November 1875.
6 *Ibid.*, 6 December 1875.
7 *Ibid.*, 2 and 3 January 1876.
8 *Ibid.*, 14 January and 1 February 1876.
9 BL. 53876, 9 March 1876.
10 *Ibid.*, 4 May 1876; BL. 53879, 3 November 1876.

11 BL. 53879, 30 May 1876.
12 *Ibid.*, 22 October 1876 and 8 December 1876.
13 BL. 53880, 11 December 1876.
14 FM. 1225/1976.
15 FM. 1208/1976, 29 May 1876.
16 WSB, *Love Sonnets of Proteus*, 'Gods and Gods – He would lead a better Life, LXXXII'.
17 BL. 53876, 6 October 1876.
18 BL. 53863, 13 June 1876.
19 WSB, *Love Sonnets of Proteus*, 'Vita Nova – Written in Distress, XCII'.
20 BL. 54100.
21 BL. 53887, 8 June 1876.
22 WSB, *Love Sonnets of Proteus*, 'Vita Nova – To the Bedouin Arabs, CXI'.
23 For this journey, see WSB's travel diary, BL.D.; AINB's diary, BL. 53889–901; their joint book, *Bedouin Tribes of the Euphrates*. For the Stud, see BL. 54130–33.
24 BL. 53889, 14 December 1877.
25 *PW*. II., 'The Old Squire'.
26 BL. 53889, 22 December 1877 (AINB's diary); BL. 54075, 15 March 1878 (WSB's diary).
27 *PW*. II., 'The Stealing of the Mare'.
28 BL. 53894, 26 April 1878.
29 *Ibid.*, *passim*.
30 BL. 53895, 20 October and 15 November 1878.

6 *The Children of Shem*

1 For this journey, see WSB's travel diary, BL.D; his FM. memoirs; AINB's diary, BL. 53902–3; and their book, *Pilgrimage to Nejd*.
2 BL. 53896, 1 December 1878.
3 BL. 54076, 20 and 26 December 1878.
4 BL. 53897, 27 December 1878.
5 *Ibid.*, 31 December 1878; BL. 54076, 3 January 1879.
6 BL. 54076, 5–12 January 1879; *Pilgrimage to Nejd*, I., p. 133.
7 BL. 54076, 13–23 January 1879; BL. 53899, 16 January–7 February 1879, 'In the Nefud' (AINB's diary).
8 BL. 53899, 25 January 1879.
9 Neville Lytton, p. 226.
10 *Pilgrimage to Nejd*, I., p. 216.
11 BL. 54076 and *Pilgrimage to Nejd*, II., p. 19.
12 Burton, I., p. 24.
13 BL. 54095 and J., 'Myself and Others'.
14 Hogarth, pp. 253–4.
15 WSB, 'A Religion of Happiness', FM. 1405/1977, and draft 'Preface'.
16 Lytton FM., 18 May 1879.
17 Extract from Lady Lytton's Simla Diary, by courtesy of Mary Lutyens.
18 Lytton Papers.
19 FM. 1190/1977.
20 BL. 58906, 15 December 1879.
21 Lytton FM., 21 August 1879.
22 FM. 1606/1976, 27 March 1880, Mrs M. Pollen to WSB; FM 43/1975, WSB to Mrs M. Pollen, 30 March 1880 and Mrs Pollen to WSB, 6 April 1880.
23 BL. 53905, 20 September 1879.
24 BL. 54100.
25 WSB, *Love Sonnets of Proteus*, 'Gods and False Gods – St. Valentine's Day, LV'.

Part II

7 *Egypt, Arise!*

1 FM. 44/1975, p. 62.
2 *Ibid.*, p. 66.
3 Letter in possession of C. Chevenix Trench, 20 April 1881.
4 WSB, *Future of Islam*, p. 205.
5 Cromer, *Modern Egypt*, II., p. 183.
6 WSB, *Secret History of the English Occupation of Egypt*, p. 151; Cromer, II., p. 185.
7 BL. 54131, old Crabbet Arabian Stud list, 1878–88.
8 BL. 53913, 17 October and 21 November 1881.
9 Lytton FM., H. Brand to WSB, 10 January 1882.
10 Lady Gregory, *Autobiography*, p. 36.
11 WSB, *Secret History . . . of Egypt*, pp. 200–1.
12 BL. 53915, 13 February 1882.
13 Malet, p. 265.
14 BL. 53916, 27 February 1882; Lady Gregory, *Autobiography*, p. 39.

15 Sir Sidney Lee, *King Edward VII* (London, 1925), I. p. 458.

8 Wind and Whirlwind

1 Milner, p. 15.
2 WSB, *Secret History of . . . Egypt*, p. 294.
3 Malet, p. 281.
4 BL. 53917, 19 May 1882.
5 *Ibid.*, 29 May 1882.
6 WSB, *Secret History of . . . Egypt*, p. 297.
7 Lytton FM., 19 June 1882, H. Brand to WSB.
8 Broadley, p. 161.
9 WSB, *Secret History of . . . Egypt*, p. 335.
10 BL. 53917, 23 June 1882.
11 Lady Gregory, *Autobiography*, p. 47.
12 *Ibid.*, p. 44.
13 See Chapter 7, note 15.
14 WSB, *Secret History of . . . Egypt*, p. 398.
15 *Ibid.*, pp. 427–8, 3 August 1882, General Gordon to WSB, from Cape Town.
16 Broadley, p. 2.
17 Lady Gregory, *Autobiography*, p. 35.
18 Malet, pp. 460–1.
19 Broadley, p. 65.
20 WSB, *Secret History of . . . Egypt*, pp. 453–4.
21 *Ibid.*, p. 475.
22 Broadley, p. 353.
23 Milner, p. 16.
24 WSB., *Secret History of . . . Egypt*, p. 369.
25 Lady Gregory, *Autobiography*, p. 44.
26 FM. 324/1975, pp. 55–9.

9 A Passage through India

1 Lytton FM., 13 and 15 September 1882, 12 February 1883, Rosalind Howard to WSB.
2 FM. 25/1975; BL. 53918.
3 FM. 44/1975.
4 FM, 25/1975, pp. 289 i–289 iii, 1883. Three loose sheets have been inserted into WSB's 'Indian Memoirs I', following extracts from AINB's diary for 1883 including her 'paper' of 10 August. WSB has also inserted a somewhat similar 'Note' into his diary of 1886 (FM. 335/1975, pp. 194–221) again including AINB's 'paper'. Both passages were probably written after the Blunts' separation; perhaps after AINB's death. See chapter 21, reference note 26.
5 BL. 53921, 2 June 1883.
6 FM. 25/1975, 6 July 1883.
7 BL. 53922, 23 July 1883.
8 FM. 25/1975, pp. 9–10.
9 BL. 53926, 8 October 1883.
10 BL. 53930, 22 November 1883.
11 FM. 26/1975, 6 February 1884.
12 Leslie, *Men were Different*, p. 252.
13 WSB, *India under Ripon*, pp. 184–5 and 190, 4 and 5 February 1884.
14 *Ibid.*, pp. 198 and 212, 9 February 1884.
14 *Ibid.*, pp. 198 and 212, 9 February 1884.

10 'Am I a Tory Democrat?'

1 BL. 53937.
2 FM. 1401/1976, 25 March 1882.
3 BL. 53950, 14 December 1884.
4 FM. 27/1975, 6 June 1884.
5 J, 'Myself and Others'.
6 FM. 26/1975, p. 155.
7 WSB, *India under Ripon*, p. 194.
8 FM. 26/1975, 25 February 1884.
9 Lytton FM., 26 April 1884, Rosalind Howard to WSB.
10 *Ibid.*, 10 April 1884, Sir W. Lawson to WSB.
11 FM. 635/1976, 21 April 1884, C. Walters ('Skittles') to WSB.
12 FM. 636/1976, 12 September 1884, same to same.
13 WSB, *Gordon at Khartoum*, p. 221.
14 Lytton FM., 7 May 1884, A. Herbert to WSB.
15 WSB., *Gordon at Khartoum*, p. 234.
16 *Ibid.*, p. 265.
17 BL. 53944.
18 FM. 330/1975.
19 FM. 249/1975, 9 July 1884.
20 WSB, *Gordon at Khartoum*, p. 309.
21 BL. 53950, 27 December 1884.
22 WSB, *Gordon at Khartoum*, pp. 362–3, 22 January 1885.

23 *Ibid.*, p. 418, 14 April 1885.
24 FM. 1018/1975, 14 May 1885, C. Walters ('Skittles') to WSB; FM. 333/1975.
25 WSB, *Gordon at Khartoum*, p. 432–3; FM. 330–3/1975.
26 WSB, *Gordon at Khartoum*, pp. 458–60.
27 *Ibid.*, p. 472.
28 *Ibid.*, p. 482.
29 *Ibid.*, p. 499; FM. 333/1975.
30 WSB, *Gordon at Khartoum*, pp. 503–4.
31 Meynell Papers, WSB to W. Meynell, December 1885; FM. 333/1975.
32 Lytton FM., 1 December 1885, Cardinal Manning to WSB: FM. 251/1975, 8 December 1885, C. Walters ('Skittles') to WSB; FM. 637/1976, 25 November 1885.
33 WSB, *Gordon at Khartoum*, Appendix D, pp. 615–16.
34 FM. 333/1975, 28 November and 31 December 1885.

11 *A New Pilgrimage*

1 WSB, *Land War in Ireland*, p. 12. Main sources for this chapter are WSB's diaries, FM. 334/1975–FM. 336/1975; FM. 29/1975; extracts from these diaries published in his *Land War*.
2 WSB, *Land War*, pp. 10 and 27.
3 FM. 24/1977, 27/1977, 35/1977.
4 BL. 53954, 22 September 1885.
5 WSB, *Land War*, pp. 65–6.
6 WSB, *PW*. II. 'The Canon of Aughrim', (Political Poems); also published in *Land War*, Appendix A.
7 WSB, *Land War*, pp. 73–6.
8 Lady Gregory, *Autobiography*, p. 203.
9 Lytton FM., 27 April 1886, G. Meredith to WSB.
10 FM. 36 and 38/1977, Mrs M. Pollen to WSB; BL. 53955, 19 February and June 1886.
11 Lytton FM., 5 June 1886, J. Morley to WSB.
12 FM. 335/1975, 15 June 1886.
13 Lytton FM., 23 June 1886, E. Hope to WSB.
14 *Ibid.*, 24 June 1886, R. Howard to WSB.
15 BL. 53955, June 1886; Lytton FM., 29 July 1886, E. Hope to WSB.
16 PW. I., pp. 205–78.
17 *Ibid.*, 'A New Pilgrimage – A Sonnet Sequence, 1887, XL'.
18 *Ibid.*

12 *Balfour's Criminal*

1 FM. 337/1975, 24 January 1887; FM. 29/1975, October 1886, p. 33.
2 Mansfield, p. 91, quoting Lord Zetland, *Lord Cromer* (London, 1932) p. 164.
3 Lady Gregory, *Autobiography*, 30 January 1887.
4 WSB., *Land War*, p. 218.
5 BL 53958, 30 March 1887.
6 WSB, *Land War*, p. 253, 4 May 1887.
7 *Ibid.*, p. 259; FM. 337/1975, p. 126.
8 FM. 337/1975, 1 June 1887.
9 BL. 53958, 25 June 1887.
10 WSB, *Land War*, p. 272.
11 *Ibid.*, p. 280.
12 *Ibid.*, p. 273.
13 *Ibid.*, p. 290.
14 FM. 338/1975, p. 77; *Land War*, p. 303.
15 WSB, *Land War*, p. 307.
16 *Ibid.*, p. 350.
17 BL. 53959; two notebooks of AINB's, (i) 6–20 October 1887, (ii) 21–6 October 1887; WSB's 'Autograph Diary', FM. 338/1975; *Land War*, pp. 352–7.
18 BL. 54115, 24 October 1887, WSB to J.
19 WSB, *Land War*, p. 357.
20 BL. 35958, 25 July 1887.
21 BL. 53961, 30 December 1887.
22 Lytton FM., 28 October 1887.
23 FM. 80/1977, Mrs M. Pollen to WSB. 25 October 1887.
24 FM. 344/1976, 3 November 1887, C. Walters ('Skittles') to WSB.
25 FM. 344/1976, 25 October 1887, Mrs Jane Morris to WSB.

13 *In Chains for Ireland*

1 FM. 641/1976, New Year's Day, 1888, C. Walters ('Skittles') to WSB. The main sources for this chapter are WSB, *Land War*, pp. 363–445 and Appendix D; WSB's diaries, FM. 339–340/1975, 30/1975 and 714/1977; AINB's diary, BL. 53960 and 53964–7.
2 BL. 53964, January.
3 *Ibid.*; *Land War*, pp. 365–9.
4 FM. 714/1977, 25 February 1910, p. 2.; *Land War*, p. 372 (re-written in slightly different words from Memorandum).
5 WSB, *Land War*, pp. 380–4.
6 WSB, *In Vinculis*, 'Sonnets written in an Irish Prison', published as a separate volume, 1889, and also in *PW.* I., and in *Land War*, pp. 394–7 and p. 409.
7 *Ibid.*, 'Condemned'.
8 *Ibid.*
9 BL. 53965, 11 February 1888.
10 *Ibid.*
11 Lytton FM., 13 February 1888, W. E. Gladstone to WSB.
12 WSB, *Land War*, footnote, p. 408.
13 *Ibid.*, p. 409.
14 BL. 53967, February 1888; FM. 95/1977, 28 January 1888, Margaret Pollen to WSB.; FM. 102/1977, 26 February 1888, Mrs M. Pollen to WSB.
15 Lady Gregory, *Autobiography*, p. 446; *The Times*, 29 February 1888.
16 WSB, *In Vinculis*, 'I will Smile No More'.
17 FM. 339/1975, 7 April 1888.
18 BL. 53967, 10 March 1888.
19 Lytton FM., 7 March 1888, M. Napier to WSB.
20 Hesketh Pearson, *Oscar Wilde* (second edition, London), p. 128.
21 FM., leather album containing 93 bound letters from G. Wyndham to WSB, 2 September 1887 to 16 April 1913. This letter is dated 22 December 1888.
22 Lytton FM., 10 March 1888, W. E. Gladstone to WSB.
23 FM. 339/1975, 5 April 1888.
24 WSB, *Land War*, p. 364.
25 FM. 1524/1976, 9 November 1888, Lady B. Hozier to WSB.
26 FM. 109/1977, 1 May 1888, Mrs M. Pollen to WSB.
27 FM. 340/1975, 15 June 1888.
28 Leslie, *Men Were Different*, p. 268; WSB, *Land War*, p. 445.
29 Lytton FM., 1 October 1887, H. Vivian to WSB, quoted in letter from Vivian to WSB, 29 August 1890.

14 *Disentanglement*

1 WSB, *Land War*, pp. 447–9.
2 BL. 53972, 28 May 1889.
3 FM. 30/1975, p. 4.
4 FM. 32/1975, 22 June 1892.
5 FM. 676/1976, Lady B. Hozier to WSB.
6 FM. 1027/1976, same to same.
7 FM. 30/1975, letter quoted from Lady B. Hozier to WSB, 14 April 1889; FM. 1/1975, pp. 58A to 58C.
8 J, 'Myself and Others'; notes from Tennant Papers.
9 Letters in the possession of Hon. Mrs A. H. Pollen, 14 October 1844 and 19 August 1887 J to A. Pollen; FM. 61/1977, Mrs Minnie Pollen to WSB, 25 January 1887; BL. 54115, WSB, to J, 17 September 1891.
10 BL. 53968; Tennant Papers.
11 BL. 53968, 30 October 1888.
12 FM. 341/1975.
13 J, 'Myself and Others'.
14 BL. 53969, 5 December 1888.
15 BL. 53970, 16 February 1889.
16 Tennant Papers, summer to autumn 1889.
17 FM. 1/1975, p. 58D.
18 FM. 31/1975, 7 May 1891.
19 FM. 32/1975, 11 August 1892.
20 FM. 306/1976; 1/1975, 3 November 1889; 30/1975, 24 November 1889.
21 FM. 30/1975, April, May 1890.
22 *Ibid.*, 13 July 1890.
23 *Ibid.*, July 1890, p. 316.
24 *Ibid.*, 17 August 1890, p. 332.
25 BL. 53978, 17 August and 24 September 1890; BL. 53979, 17 October 1890.

15 The Amorist

1 FM. 31/1975, 2 August 1891. The main sources for this chapter are WSB's unpublished diaries, FM. 31–2/1975 ('Alms to Oblivion' or 'Secret Memoirs'); FM. 1–3/1975 ('General Memoirs').
2 FM. 1/1975, 13 June 1890.
3 FM. 722/1977, 'The Court of Love'.
4 FM. 31/1975, 29 June 1891.
5 *Ibid.*, June, July, August, October, 1890.
6 *PW*. I., 'Later Lyrics – With Eternity Standing By'.
7 FM. 1/1975, 14 September 1891.
8 BL. 53984, 2 June 1891.
9 Harris, *Contemporary Portraits*, pp. 98–9; Lord Birkenhead, *Rudyard Kipling*, (London, 1978) pp. 106–7; FM 1044/1976, 26 August 1890, Wilde to WSB.
10 FM. 31/1975, 4 July 1891.
11 *Ibid.*, Note interpolated, p. 168.
12 Harris, *Oscar Wilde*, II., pp. 440–3.
13 FM. 3/1975, 30 June–1 July 1894.
14 J, 'Myself and Others'.
15 FM. 31/1975, 4 June 1891; FM. 1/1975, 6 November 1891.
16 *MD*. I., p. 78.
17 Tennant Papers, extract from Margot Tennant's privately printed diary, 'Christmas Eve', 1891.
18 M. Asquith, *Autobiography*, I., p. 185.
19 FM. 32/1975, 12 May 1892.
20 FM. 32/1975, 26 July 1892; FM. 1061/1976, 29 July 1892, Margot Tennant to WSB; FM. 32/1975, 1 August 1892.
21 FM. 1062/1976, 6 August 1892, Margot Tennant to WSB; FM. 32/1975, 9 August 1892.
22 FM. 32/1975, 11–12 August 1892, pp. 56–60.
23 BL. 54115, 16 August 1892, WSB to J.
24 FM. 31/1975, p. 136.
25 FM. 32/1975, 24 August 1892.
26 *Ibid.*, 5 September 1892.
27 Milner, p. 377.
28 FM. 57/1975.
29 FM. 32/1975, 15 February 1893.
30 FM. 2/1975, p. 86.
31 FM. 32/1975, 1 May 1893.
32 Meynell Papers, 14 June 1893, WSB to Mrs Alice Meynell.
33 FM. 275/1975, 12 June 1893, Lady Galloway to WSB.
34 FM. 593/1976, 20 March 1894, Same to same.
35 Lutyens, *A Blessed Girl*, 27 June 1892, Lady Emily Lytton to Rev. Whitwell Elwin; FM. 32/1975, 9 July 1892.
36 FM. 309/1975 ('Autograph Diaries'), 7 May 1893.
37 *PW*. II., 'The Bride of the Nile – An Extravaganza in Three Acts'.
38 FM. 32/1975, August 1893; Acrostic sonnet (unpublished) FM. 2/1975, 29 August 1893.
39 FM. 2/1975, 4–5 September 1893 (loose page, 240A).
40 Lutyens, *A Blessed Girl*, p. 228; FM. 33/1975, 5 September 1893; FM. 563/1976.
41 FM. 2/1975, 18 January 1894.
42 FM. 33/1975, 18 July 1894, WSB to Lady Emily Lytton.
43 *MD*. I., p. 179; FM. 33/1975, 17 July 1894.
44 BL. 54115, 11 August 1894, WSB to J; BL. 54103, 15 August 1894, WSB to AINB.
45 FM. 33/1977, 13 August 1894.

16 Grande Passion

1 FM. 342/1975, 25 October 1894.
2 FM. 34/1975, note in p. 1 ('Secret Memoirs').
3 FM. 34/1975, 9 January 1895.
4 *Ibid.*, 14 January 1895 (Diary notebook).
5 WSB, *The Golden Odes of Pre-Islamic Arabia*, 'Ántara'; also in *PW*. II.
6 FM. 34/1975, 14 January 1895.
7 *Ibid.*, 2 February 1895.
8 *Ibid.*, 6 February 1895.
9 *Ibid.*, 16 February 1895.
10 *Ibid.*, 21 February 1895.
11 Harrison, *Autobiographic Memoirs*, I., pp. 166–80.
12 WSB, Sonnets (unpubiished) 14 and 25 February 1895; FM. 34/1975, 23 February 1895.

13 FM. 34/1895, pp. 74–100. Description of Desert Journey written up on 7 May 1895.
14 FM. 34/1975, 11 April 1895, 27 April 1895.
15 *MD*. I., pp. 344–5.
16 Forster, *Abinger Harvest*, pp. 266–8.
17 FM. 34/1975, 25 August 1895.
18 FM. 568/1976, 23 August 1895; 34/1975, 5 September 1895.
19 *MD*. I., pp. 227–31; FM. 34/1975, 5 September 1895; BL. 54104, 15 October 1895, WSB to AINB.
20 FM. 35/1975, 19 August 1896; *ibid*., 15 and 20 July 1896.
21 FM. 492/1975, 27 March 1899.
22 FM. 350/1975, 22 April 1896.
23 Lutyens, *A Blessed Girl*, p. 294.
24 Lytton FM., 15 August 1896, Lady Lytton to WSB; FM. 35/1975, 14 May 1896.
25 *MD*. I., p. 267.
26 FM. 35/1975, 26 September 1896.
27 *MD*. I., p. 296.
28 J's diary, 19 November 1896; *ibid*., 9 November 1896; FM. 3/1975, 30 May 1895.

Part III

17 'Poor Wicked Century, Farewell!'

1 FM. 35/1975, 28 January 1897.
2 *MD*. I., p. 301; FM. 355/1975, 29 November 1896.
3 *MD*. I., p. 310.
4 *MD*. I., p. 340.
5 FM. 35/1975, 6 April 1897.
6 *Ibid*., 24 March 1897.
7 FM. 4/1975, 11 June 1897.
8 FM., Album of G. Wyndham's letters, 6 September 1895; FM. 35/1975, 27 April 1896.
9 FM. 36/1975, 13 August 1897.
10 *PW*. I., 'Later Lyrics – Ghost of the Beautiful Past'.
11 FM. 36/1975, 17 October 1898.
12 Lytton FM., 9 January 1900.
13 FM. 366/1975, 1 January 1900.
14 FM. 5/1975, 28 May 1898.
15 Letters in the possession of Christopher Blunt, 2 October 1907, Sir S. Cockerell to WSB.
16 *MD*. I., pp. 366–7; FM. 5/1975, 12 October 1898.
17 FM. 364/1975 and 5/1975, 20 September 1899.
18 FM. 497, 498, 500/1975.
19 BL. 54006, 8 November 1898.
20 FM. 5/1975, 2 February 1899; 37/1975, 1 January 1899; *MD*. I., p. 385.
21 *MD*. I., p. 401; FM. 363/1975; 36/1975; 5/1975; 970/1977, 2 September 1899.
22 *MD*. I., p. 423.
23 *Ibid*., pp. 434–48; FM. 37/1975; BL. 54105, 1 April 1900, WSB to AINB.
24 *MD*. I., pp. 414 and 450–1.
25 FM. 574/1976, 4 November 1895, Lady Emily Lytton to WSB.
26 Lytton FM., 23 September 1900, WSB to Cockerell.
27 *MD*. I., pp. 464–5.

18 The Shame of the Twentieth Century

1 *MD*. II., p. 2; FM. 6/1975, 23 January 1901.
2 Lytton FM., 14 February 1901, 'Ouida' to WSB.
3 *MD*. II., pp. 2, 28.
4 *Ibid*., pp. 9–10.
5 FM. 371/1975, 11 August 1901; *MD*. II., pp. 9, 15; FM. pamphlet on the fox-hunting case.
6 Stephen Gwynn, *Letters of Sir Cecil Spring-Rice*, I., p. 346. (London, 1929).
7 Fairfax-Lucy Letters, 19 January 1902.
8 Tennant Papers; BL. 54009, 17 August 1901.
10 *PW*. II., 'Fand – A Féerie in Three Acts', performed at the Abbey Theatre, Dublin, 1907; FM. 6/1975, 5 October 1903.
11 FM. 374/1975, 11 September 1902; 6/1975, 20 September 1902; 6/1975, 11 September 1903; *MD*. II., p. 74, 3 September 1903.
12 FM. 382/1975, 9 September 1904.
13 *MD*. II., p. 61; FM. 96/1975, 19 June 1903, John Redmond to WSB; Egremont, pp. 231–5.
14 *MD*. II., p. 62.

15 Egremont, p. 249 (Grosvenor Papers).
16 FM., Album of G. Wyndham's letters; FM. 7/1975, 11 February 1904.
17 FM. 378/1975, 19 September 1903.
18 FM. 529/1975, Lady Elcho to Dorothy Carleton, 1 September 1903; FM. 378/1975, 28 October 1903.
19 BL. 54116, 1 April 1904, WSB to J.
20 FM. 101/1975, 30 July 1903.
21 FM. 6/1975, 16 September 1903.
22 FM. 379/1975, 2 November 1903.
23 *Ibid.*, 9 September 1904.
24 FM. 520/1975, 1903; BL. 54115, 20 February 1903.
25 FM. 7/1975, 17 January 1905; BL. 54015, 13 March 1905; *ibid.*, 28 April 1905.
26 FM. 383/1975, 8 June 1905.
27 BL. 54017, 4 July 1905; BL. 54015, 3 July 1905; FM. 384/1975, 7/1975, 28 July 1905.
28 BL. 54097, Lord Lovelace to AINB, 7 July 1905; BL. 54015, 17 July 1905.
29 BL. 54016, 16 October 1905.
30 *Ibid.*, 28 November 1905.
31 FM. 383/1975.
32 FM. 7/1975, 7 July 1906; *MD*. II., p. 152 *et. seq.*
33 BL. 54018, 11 July 1906.

19 The Parting

1 FM. 385/1975, 11 June 1906. The main sources for this chapter are WSB's diaries in the Fitzwilliam Museum and AINB's diary in the British Library, Wentworth Bequest.
2 *Ibid.*, 19 June 1906; BL. 54107, 9 March 1906, WSB to AINB.
3 BL. 54097, 21 July 1906, Lord Lovelace to AINB.
4 BL. 54017, 9 July 1906.
5 BL. 54097, AINB to Lord Lovelace, 9 July 1906.
6 FM. 7/1975, 30 July 1906; BL. 54018, 1 August 1906.
7 FM. 565/1975, 1 August 1906; 8/1975, 14 August 1906.
8 FM. 7/1975, 9 July 1906.
9 FM. 388/1975, 17 November 1906; 7/1975, 30 July 1906.
10 BL. 54097, 31 July 1906; FM. 8/1975, 24 August 1906; BL. 54097, 6 September 1906.
11 FM. 388/1975, 15 November 1906.
12 FM. 8/1975, 31 December 1906 and 28 February 1907.
13 FM. 391/1975, 20 August 1907.
14 *MD*. II., pp. 187–96; FM. 8/1975.
15 Meynell Papers. See also V. Meynell, *Francis Thompson and Wilfrid Meynell*, pp. 178–82.
16 Lytton FM.
17 Lytton FM.; *Academy*; Meynell Papers.
18 V. Meynell, *Alice Meynell*, p. 313.
19 Lytton FM. [1894], 'Fructidor de l'An 98'; BL. 54115, 18 March 1902, WSB to J.
20 FM. 391/1975, 15 August 1907.
21 Lytton FM., G. B. Shaw to WSB, 20 September 1909.
22 *MD*. II., p. 174, 11 April 1907; FM. 392/1975, 16 November 1907.
23 FM. 8/1975, 10 March 1908 (letter sent 6 March); Lytton FM., C. P. Scott to WSB, 16 February 1908, 2 September 1908, 29 April 1910.
24 Lytton FM., 3 October 1908, H. N. Brailsford to WSB; 13 May 1908, Mrs Jane Brailsford to WSB; 9/1975, 12 March 1909.
25 FM. 11/1975, 27 January 1911; 7/1975, 10 and 28 May 1906.
26 FM. 673/1976, 20 September 1905; 398/1975, 5 March 1909.
27 FM. 7/1975, 15 April 1906; 9/1975, 27 June 1909.
28 FM. 9/1975, 4 June 1909.
29 *Ibid.*, 30 April 1909, 4 June 1909.
30 *Ibid.*, 5 March 1909, 7 February 1909; FM. 689/1976, 27 October 1910.
31 Tennant Papers, 15 March 1908, J to WSB.
32 *Ibid.*, 1 April 1908, Guy Carleton to WSB; FM. 8/1975, 2–12 April 1908; FM. 393/1975, 3–13 April 1908; Tennant Papers, 7 April 1908, Neville Lytton to WSB; *ibid.*, 10 April 1908, J to WSB.

33 FM. 394/1975, 15 April 1908; BL. 54113, 21 April 1908, AINB to J; BL. 54107, 22 April 1908, AINB to WSB (received by WSB 29 April 1908); FM. 394/1975, pp. 26–7, copy of J to AINB.
34 Tennant Papers (copy) 5 May 1908; FM. 9/1975, 2–4 May 1908; 394/1975, 4–5 May 1908.
35 FM. 394/1975, 2 May 1908; Tennant Papers, 16 May 1908, Guy Carleton to WSB.
36 FM. 584/1975, 25 December 1908, Dorothy Carleton to WSB.
37 FM. 402/1975, 15 October 1908.

20 Pilgrim of Distress

1 FM. 406/1975, 1 February 1910.
2 FM. 11/1975, 14 December 1910.
3 FM. 11/1975, 14 July 1911.
4 FM. 10/1975, 30 December 1909.
5 Lytton FM., 15 August 1909, Lord A. Douglas to WSB; 16 August 1909, WSB to Lord A. Douglas; 17 August 1909, WSB to Lord A. Douglas; 3 June 1911, Lord A. Douglas to WSB; 7 June 1911, WSB to Lord A. Douglas; 8 June 1911, Lord A. Douglas to WSB; 14 June 1911, M. Napier to WSB; FM. 9/1975, 23 August 1909; 11/1975, 7 June 1911; 408/1975, 11 June 1911.
6 FM. 13/1975, 31 December 1913; 413/1975, 17 November 1912.
7 Lytton FM., 5 February 1913, Mahmud to WSB.
8 FM. 11/1975, 21 January 1911; Lytton FM., 26 January 1909.
9 *PW.* I., 'Later Sonnets'; see also *MD.* II., FM. 12/1975, 414/1975, all in April 1913.
10 Lytton FM., 22 January 1913, John Dillon to WSB.
11 FM. 12/1975, 8 December 1912; 13/1975, 4 August 1913.
12 FM. 13/1975, 19 June 1913.
13 FM. 395/1975, 12 September 1908; 739/1976, 16 September 1908; 8/1975, 3 October 1908; 320/1977, 25 July 1910.
14 FM. 11/1975, 30 January 1911.
15 BL. 54116; *MD.* II., Appendix IV, Memorandum on Prison Reform.
16 FM. 10/1975, 3, 15, 16, 24 March 1910; 325/1977, 22 March 1910.
17 *MD.* II., pp. 414–15; FM. 10/1975, 3 March 1910.
18 FM. 9/1975, 2 October 1909.
19 FM. 12/1975, 19, 20 October 1912; *MD.* II., p. 415, 21 October 1912.
20 FM. 351/1977, 17 October 1911.
21 FM. 11/1975, 30 June 1911; *ibid.*, 1 February 1912.
22 BL. 54114, 13 January 1912, AINB to J; FM. 642/1975, 3 July 1912, Fr Lawrence to WSB; 412/1975, 4 July 1912.
23 FM. 643/1975, 3 September 1912, 645/1975, 4 September 1912, Dorothy Carleton to WSB; 662/1975, 18 April 1913; 400/1975, 17 June 1909.
24 FM. 412/1975, 26 and 27 September 1912.
25 FM. 11/1975, 14 September 1911; *ibid.*, 6 July 1913.
26 *MD.* II., pp. 431–2; FM. 13/1975, 9 June 1913.
27 FM., Album of G. Wyndham's letters, 16 April 1913; *ibid.*, 22 December 1896.
28 *PW.* II., 'To a Happy Warrior'; FM. 415/1975, 24 June 1913.

21 Peacocks and Prophets

1 FM. 13/1975, 28 December 1913.
2 Lady Gregory, *Autobiography*, p. 479.
3 FM. 13/1975, 18 January 1914.
4 Lytton FM., 'The Poets' (Peacock Dinner).
5 Christopher Blunt Letters, 23 January 1914, WSB to Sir S. Cockerell.
6 *Ibid.*, 26 January 1814, Lord Osborne Beauclerk to Sir S. Cockerell.
7 FM. 13/1975, 19 January 1914.
8 Lytton FM., 21 January 1914, E. Pound to WSB; *ibid.*, 8 January 1914 and 20 April 1914, J. Masefield to WSB; FM. 13/1975, 19 April 1914.
9 Lytton FM., 23 March 1914, E. Pound to WSB.

10 FM. 13/1975, 26 March 1914; 419/1975, 19 July 1914; Lytton FM., 21 July 1914, Mrs Dorothy Pound to WSB.
11 Lytton FM., 11 June 1915, W. B. Yeats to WSB.
12 Ezra Pound, *The Pisan Cantos*, LXXXIII and LXXXI (London, 1949).
13 FM. 134/1976, May 1914, Mrs Mary Colum to WSB; 136/1976, 12 May 1914, same to same; 135/1976, 25 May 1914, same to same; *MD.* II., Appendix VI, all four Casement letters to WSB; FM. 13/1975, 12–13 May 1914.
14 FM. 13/1975, 3 August 1914.
15 *Ibid.*, 5 August 1914; *MD.* II., p. 449.
16 FM. 1296/1976, 15 July 1917, C. Walters ('Skittles') to WSB.
17 FM. 429/1975, 7 May 1916, Margot Asquith to WSB.
18 FM. 16/1975, 29 June 1916.
19 *Ibid.*, 11 July 1916; 142/1975, 10 July 1916; 168/1975, 9 August 1916, Dorothy Carleton to WSB; Reid p. 148; 16/1975, 30 June 1916.
20 FM. 168/1975, 9 August 1916, Dorothy Carleton to WSB.
21 FM. 14/1975, 31 December 1914.
22 FM. 15/1975, 12 May 1915.
23 Lytton Papers.
24 BL. 54029, 29 September 1917; J's diary and 'Myself and Others'; FM. 16/1975, 10 July 1916.
25 BL. 54113, 29 January 1917, AINB to J; BL. 54108, 31 July and 21 September 1917, AINB to WSB.
26 BL. 54113, 2 November 1917, AINB to J. This typed copy of AINB's diary entry of 10 August 1883 is *without* the date 1883, but *with* the heading added by J, 'My Mother's last written message'.
27 FM. 15/1975, 14 August 1915.
28 *Ibid.*, 15 November 1915.
29 FM. 439/1975, 12 May 1918.
30 FM. 319/1977, 21 March 1917, Winston S. Churchill to WSB; 320/1977, 'Easter Monday' 1918, Clementine Churchill to WSB.
31 FM. 15/1975, 4 January 1916; 897/1975, 7 January 1919, Mrs Minnie Pollen to WSB; 159/1976, 23 January 1921, Rev. John Pollen to WSB.
32 FM. 16/1975, 28 December 1916; 778/1975, 18 November 1915, Lady Wemyss to WSB.

22 *The Unconquered Flame*

1 FM. 17/1975, 18 December 1917.
2 BL. 54028, 13 September 1915.
3 FM. 438/1975, 26 and 31 March 1918.
4 FM. 454/1975, 5 and 12 March 1920; 999/1975, 14 March 1920, Mrs G. Napier to WSB; 462/1975, 20 November 1920.
5 Lytton FM., 5 September 1918, H. N. Brailsford to WSB.
6 P. N. Furbank, *E. M. Forster: A Life*, pp. 142–3; FM. 1037/1977, 20 November 1919, Masood to WSB; 1044/1977, 14 September 1920 and 1036/1977, 21 November 1921, Kamel to WSB; 454/1975, 16 March 1920, Saad Zaghloul's secretary (Hamed Mahmud) to WSB; 198/1975, 5 May 1919, WSB to Lord Parmoor; 445/1975, 15 February 1919.
7 India Office Library and Records, IOR: L/P&J/8/621, Dr Syed Mahmud to the Viceroy's private secretary, 19 August 1944; see also Lytton Papers, Mahmud to 4th Earl of Lytton; FM. 201/1975, 19 November 1921, A. Rothstein to WSB; 93/1976, 16 August 1920 and 100/1976, 25 August 1920, St John Philby to WSB; 459/1975, 21 August 1920 and 460/1975, 6 September 1920, visit of T. E. Lawrence to WSB; 458/1975, 10 August 1920, Professor S. Chew in the *New Republic* (28 July 1920), and 235/1976, 24 August 1921; 244/1976, 15 September 1920, Winston S. Churchill to WSB.
8 FM. 1027/1975, 7 May 1920, Sir S. Cockerell to WSB.
9 WSB, *Love Sonnets of Proteus*, 'Gods and False Gods – Sybilline Books, LXIX'.

10 FM. 442/1975, 18 August 1918; 979/1975, 2 February 1920, Lady Wemyss to WSB.
11 FM. 469/1975, 22 October 1921; 470/1975, 13 and 16 November 1921.
12 Meynell Papers, 3 March 1922, WSB (pp. D. Carleton) to W. Meynell.
13 FM. 472/1975, 17 and 25 March 1922.
14 FM. 472/1975A, 5 August 1922; 294/1976, 14 August 1922, Fr Vincent MacNab to WSB.
15 Christopher Blunt Letters, 22 and 24 August 1922, WSB (pp. D. Carleton) to Sir S. Cockerell.
16 BL. 54116, 17 August 1922, WSB to J.
17 FM. 18/1975, copy of letter, 5 September 1922, WSB to Winston S. Churchill. (Signed.)
18 Tennant Papers, packet 21, letter from India to D. Carleton, 12 September 1922; Lytton, *WSB*, p. 356; Christopher Blunt Letters, 2 and 11 September 1922, D. Carleton to S. Cockerell; *The Times*, 13 September 1922. Edith Finch, p. 372, gives the wrong dates (12 and 15 September) for WSB's death and funeral, which were 10 and 12 September.
19 FM. 11/1975, 19 November 1911.
20 Meynell Papers, 14 June 1900, WSB to W. Meynell.
21 Lytton FM., 7 September 1886, H. Brand to WSB; *ibid.*, 27 September 1910, Riza Bey Tewfik to WSB.
22 FM. 12/1975, 17 October 1912.
23 Lytton FM., 19 November 1910, Keir Hardie to WSB; *MD*. II., p. 422.
24 FM. 166/1975, 7 July 1916, WSB to J. Dillon; 1084/1975, 15 October 1909, Hilda Guest to WSB; Lady Gregory, *Autobiography*, p. 204.
25 FM. 331/1976, 1884, Mrs Jane Morris to WSB; 383/1975, 5 December 1904.
26 FM. 722/1977, 'The Court of Love'; 30/1975, 15 May 1890 (reference Lady Carlisle).
27 Lord Lytton, *WSB*, p. 290.
28 Tschiffely, p. 354; Lord Newton, *Recollections* (London, 1941), p. 61; MacCarthy, *Portraits I*, p. 31; Forster, *Abinger Harvest*, p. 272.
29 FM. 190/1975, 28 November 1917, E. A. Chandler to WSB.
30 Lady Gregory, *The Journals I*, p. 43, 24 February 1919; FM. 183/1975, 15 January 1917, Maitland Hardyman to WSB.
31 *Catholic Herald*, 6 January 1939, Barbara Wall, review of Finch, *WSB*; FM. 16/1975, 14 November 1916.

Index

Index

A Court, Emily, 70
Abbas II, Khedive, 299–300, 301, 358
Abbey Theatre, Dublin, 349
Abd-el-Kader, 137, 169
Abdallah Minjowar, Sheykh, 327–8, 330
Abdu Dia, 359
Abdul Hamid II, Sultan, 169, 182, 183, 188, 212, 213, 218, 242, 300
Aberdeen, John Hamilton-Gordon, 5th Earl of, 33
Abu Klea, battle of (1885), 210, 214
Academy, 372, 382
Achmet Vefyk, ex-Grand Vizier, 214
Achmetaga, 25, 277
Adeane, Charles, 415
Adeane, Sibell, 420
Afghan Wars, 152–3
Agra, 156
Airlie Castle, 271
Aix-en-Provence, 14
Al-Afghani, Sayyid Jamal-al-Din, 198, 210, 212, 219, 220, 300; and nationalist movement, 167, 171; and idea of Arabian Caliphate, 167, 193
Albaro, 15, 16
Aleppo, 126–8
Alexandra, Queen, 29, 381
Alexandria, 180, 181, 182, 299; riots (1882), 183, 194; bombardment, 185, 186, 188, 189
Alfonso XII of Spain, as Prince of Asturias, 31
Algeria, 97–8
Ali Koli Khan, 143–4, 145
Ali Pasha Sherif, 316
Alice of Hesse, Princess, 29, 53
Alverstoke, 7
Anazeh tribes, 127, 128
'Angelina' – *see* Singleton, Mrs Minnie
Anita (South American mistress), 68–9, 161; death, 83
Anti-Aggression League, 181
Antonin, 213
Arab Defence Fund, 191
Arab Horse Society, 431
Arabi, Ahmed, 216, 219; deposes ministry, 171–2; meets Blunt, 173; and later nationalist movement, 173–8, 180–91, 197; Anglo-French challenge to, 174; Minister for War, 175; Blunt's reckless advice to, 175–6; Circassian Plot against, 179; and Alexandria riot, 183; war with England, 185–6; defeat at Tel-el-Kebir, 186, 198; trial and exile, 187–9, 192; spelling of name, 189n; proposed recall of, 197, 199, 210, 212; visited by Blunt, 301; return from exile, 383; confused with Mazzini by Pound, 395
Arabia: first tour of, 126–33; exploration of Nejd, 135, 136–45; secret imperial mission planned, 153–4, 163–4, 170; plan for Caliphate at Mecca, 167–8, 169
Arbitration and Peace Society, 214
Archer, R., 416n
Arcos, Zizi, 51, 368
Arran, Earl of, 228
Ashington (Sussex), 362
Ashley Combe (Somerset), 73
Asquith, Herbert Henry (later Earl of Oxford and Asquith), 260, 298, 299, 307, 409; as Prime Minister, 384, 385, 400, 402
Asquith (formerly Tennant, q.v.), Margot, 374–5, 386n, 399, 402
Astarte (Lovelace), 349
Asturias, Prince of (later Alfonso XII of Spain), 31
Athenaeum, 335
Athens, Blunt's first diplomatic posting to, 24–5
Atkinson, John (later Baron), 254, 260
Augustine, St, 30
Austin, Alfred, 38, 316, 349
Authentic Arabian, The (Wentworth), 41, 155, 407
Avignon, 12

Bactiari horses, 144, 145, 147

Baghdad, 128, 144–5
Bagnères de Bigorre, 8, 33
Baillie, Alec, 157
Baird, Ella ('Juliet'), 286; Blunt's 'great passion of the soul' for, 55–6, 57, 60, 61, 62–3, 78; temporary end of romance, 63; reunion, 65; apparent defection, 69; at Blunt's wedding, 73; renewed attachment at Ouchy, 75, 77, 83; dismisses Blunt, 83–4; brief reunion and quarrel, 100–101, 102–3; relationship 'without passion', 104; farewell sonnets to, 104, 106, 107; death, 419
Baird, Robert, 62, 63, 75
Baker, General Sir Samuel, 187
Baker Pasha, Valentine, 240
Balfour, Arthur James, Earl, 246–8, 264, 299n, 300, 307, 331, 375; friendship with Mary Elcho, 247–8, 297, 307, 310, 311–12, 313, 319; as Irish Secretary, 247; drive against Home Rule, 247, 248, 249, 255, 257, 258–9, 261, 262; Clouds conversation, 247, 257, 259, 262, 265, 266; Blunt's revised opinion of, 266–7; as Prime Minister, 349, 350
Balfour, Lady Betty, 303
Balfour, Gerald, 267, 303, 304
Ballantyne, Serjeant, 117, 119
Bannister (later Parry), Gertrude, 402, 403–4
Baring, Evelyn (later Lord Cromer, q.v.), 170; as Consul-General in Egypt, 197–9, 238, 239–40; abortive talk with Blunt, 199
Baring, Maurice, 321
Baring, Roland, 341
Barraghderin, 228
Barrie, J. M., 388
Bartlett, Sir Ellis Ashmead, 272–3, 295n
Bates (Crabbet forester), 330
Batten, Mary, 214; Blunt's romance with, 152, 156, 162, 427
Beauchamp, William Lygon, 7th Earl, 321
Beauclerk, Lord Osborne, 394, 396
Bedouin Tribes of the Euphrates, The (Anne Blunt), 132–3, 134, 151, 157
Beer, Governor (Kilmainham gaol), 263
Beer, Wilfrid Blunt, 263
Beerbohm, Max, 398
Beirut, 131
Bell, Moberly, 177, 187, 190, 383
Belloc, Elodie, 372–3
Belloc, Hilaire, 372–3, 384, 391, 394, 409, 418, 426, 431; and restoration of Blunt's faith, 420, 422
Benares, 203
Beni Laam tribe, 146, 150
Berkeley Castle, 88
Berne, Blunt's posting to, 74, 75
Bertie, Feodorowna Wellesley, Lady, 42–4
Beseys (Harabi guide), 327–9
Biarritz, 36, 39
Bidwell, John, 23
Bint Helwa (brood mare), 331
Birmingham, 217; Blunt's political ambitions, 232–3
Birmingham Oratory: three-day retreat at, 122; Anne received into Church at, 160–1
Bismarck, Otto von, 51–2, 57, 65, 79
Blessed Girl, A (Lutyens), 320
Blount, Edward, 274
Blunt, Alice Maria (twin daughter), 86, 90
Blunt (later Wheatley), Alice Mary (sister), 6, 12, 29, 66, 75, 81; received into Catholic Church, 14; at Sacred Heart, Roehampton, 20, 22; Blunt's affection for, 22, 45, 76, 243, 315; breach over desire to take veil, 27–8, 44; reunion with Blunt, 33, 34; abortive love affair, 50, 63; and Blunt's illness, 54, 55, 56; and his pursuit of Anne, 63, 64, 65, 69; as his housekeeper in South America, 65, 67; with Francis, 68, 69, 70, 71, 81, 84; marriage, 73; illness, 76, 89; death, 90
Blunt, Lady Anne (Lady Annabella King-Noel) (wife): ancestry, 57, 58, 72; meeting with Blunt in Florence, 57–60; early life, 58–9, 72; character, 59, 69, 72, 114; declines Blunt's proposal, 63–5; correspondence with, 68–9, 70–71; engagement, 71–2; marriage and honeymoon, 72–4; miscarriages, 74, 78, 97–8, 100–101, 109; and Byron scandal, 74–5, 105; agrees to Blunt leaving Diplomatic Service, 76; upset by his absence, 78; reticence, 79; in France during Franco-Prussian war, 80–81; birth of short-lived son, 81–2; riding holiday in Spain, 83; loss of twin girls, 85–6, 88; 'consoled' by Blunt, 88; birth of Judith, 92–3; love of poetry, 94; Eastern travels, 94–5, 97–8, 113–16, 123–31, 136–45; 'new honeymoon', 95; shyness with child, 96; ill health, 101, 102;

unselfishness over 'Juliet' crisis, 102–3; anguish over miscarriages, 100–101, 109, 115, 116–17; as protective wife in Blunt's affairs, 113, 117–18, 196–7; growing reticence, 118; fondness for riding, 120, 123; mildly reproachful letters, 121; facility in acquiring languages, 123, 130; publishes two-volume travelogue, 132; founds Crabbet Stud, 133–4; attacked by Bedouin, 138–9; in Persia, 145–50; finally convinced of Christianity, 148; her vision of heavens opening, 148–9, 160; determined to become Catholic, 149, 160; in India, 151–7, 200–205; received into Church, 160–1, 169, 197; equestrian portrait of Blunt, 172; reaction to loss of Blunt's physical love, 194–7, 408; and Anglo-Indian 'planters', 200; growing estrangement, 207, 212, 225, 230, 234–5, 243; overprotective of Judith, 208–9; and Blunt's electioneering, 222, 252, 261, 263; 'new pilgrimage' to Rome, 235–7; and Woodford affair, 249–52, 254–6, 260; and quarrel with Pollens, 274–6; temporary better relations with Blunt, 276, 284, 330; in Greece, 276–7; income, 331; and Judith's wedding, 340–1; her only poem and Blunt's first compliment, 347; and Blunt's malarial fever, 354–8; and nurse's ascendancy, 355–6, 357, 367n, 369; sale of lands of Sheykh Obeyd, 358, 362; parting from Blunt, 361, 362–7, 369, 378–9, 380; and partition of Stud, 362–5, 366, 369, 413; refusal to meet Blunt, 367, 380; happiness at Sheykh Obeyd, 389, 407; reconciliation, 404–5; last sight of Blunt, 405; last days and death, 407–8; her will, 412–13, 416; a great lady, 427–8

Blunt, Elizabeth Cordelia Catherine (twin daughter), 85–6, 90

Blunt, Francis Scawen (father), 5–6, 9, 74, 243

Blunt, Francis Scawen (brother), 6, 12, 14, 25, 34, 50, 70, 71, 75, 103, 391; 'his only wilful crime', 8; appearance and character, 9; at Twyford School, 10, 13; received into Catholic Church, 14; in Italy, 15–16; at Oscott, 19, 20, 21; army career, 26; and sister's desire to take veil, 27, 28; and Blunt's serious illnesses, 33, 54; illness, 68, 69, 76, 81, 84, 85; death, 86–7, 90, 121; Blunt's effigy of, 89

Blunt, Henry (great-great-uncle), 5

Blunt, Judith (later Lytton, then Lady Wentworth), *passim*; birth, 88, 92–3; beginning of real relationship with Blunt, 101; on Zouche divorce, 118–19; known as 'Beebee' or 'Bibi', 121; on Blunt's 'double lights', 123; on his 'dangerous' friendships, 155; equestrian skill, 158; brought up a Catholic, 160; source of dispute between parents, 208–9, 234–5; adoration of Blunt, 226, 319–21; companionship, 243; and Pollens' quarrel, 273–6, 278; first sight of Greece, 276–7; litigiousness, 278, 413–16; unsuccessful attachments, 312, 316, 321, 339; jealousy of Blunt's loves, 315, 319–21, 378, 407; and Blunt's wills, 317, 378, 390, 428; estrangement, 321, 322; in love with Victor Lytton, 329; loveless marriage to Neville, 339–41; birth of Anthony, 344; birth of daughters, 353; takes name Blunt-Lytton, 353; Crabbet Park settled on, 353–4; resents nurse's ascendancy over Blunt, 355, 357; and parents' separation, 363, 364, 365, 366–7; quarrel over acceptance of Dorothy, 377–9, 380, 404; success as poet, 389; and general family reconciliation, 404–5, 407; extravagance, 405, 406; further rift with Blunt, 405–7; sells part of Crabbet estate, 406, 431; inherits title of Wentworth, 412; dispute and court case over ownership of Stud, 413–16; unforgiven, 420; divorce, 420; reconciliation with Blunt, 423; and news of his death, 423–4; embittered after reading of will, 428–9

Blunt, Mary (great-grandmother), 5, 74

Blunt, Mary (mother), 6, 12, 17; character, 6, 7, 18; various homes, 6–7, 13; religious fervour, 7, 9, 13, 15, 20; frail

Blunt, Mary (mother) – *contd.*
health, 7, 9, 18–19; Continental tours, 7–9, 14–15, 16; and Blunt's early illness, 11; conversion to Catholicism, 13; censorious letters, 15; death, 19
Blunt, Robert (great-great-uncle), 5
Blunt, Samuel (great-great-grandfather), 5
Blunt, Sarah (great-great-grandmother), 5
Blunt, Wilfrid Scawen: ancestry, 4–6; birth, 6; early years, 6–9; Continental travel, 7–9; 'earliest ... piece of wickedness', 8; first religious feelings, 8–9; education, 9–14, 17–22; serious illness, 11; winters abroad, 11–12; received into Catholic Church, 14–15; early confusion of religion and love, 16; and mother's death, 19, 20; ambition to become poet, 21, 47; in Diplomatic Service, 23–32, 42, 43, 45–6, 51, 53–4, 60, 65, 66–9, 74, 76; accused of seducing tutor's wife, 23; loses faith in God as Creator, 26–8, 30; takes a mistress, 32, 34; first *grande passion*, 34–42, 43–5, 48–50; later love-life and friendships, 41, 42, 46, 51, 52, 55–7, 61–3, 65, 68–70, 75, 83–5, 87–9, 91, 96–7, 99, 100, 104–5, 109–13, 116–19, 152, 156, 159–62, 191, 271–3, 275–6, 278–84, 286, 287–9, 293, 295–8, 301–7, 309–15, 317, 320, 331–3, 337–8, 347–8, 353, 354, 362, 365–6, 368–70, 381, 386, 391, 425–7; sudden fever, 54; convalescence, 54, 55–6; courtship and marriage, 57–60, 63–5, 68–73; honeymoon, 73–4; departure from Foreign Office and freedom to write poetry, 77; thwarted paternity, 82, 85–6, 88; as country squire, 89–90, 95, 274, 353–4, 431; enters upon 'second youth', 90, 93; finds poetry in birth of Judith, 92; social life, 93–4, 106, 224, 243–4, 248, 289–93, 307, 387–8; Eastern travels, 94–5, 97–8, 113–16, 123–32, 136–57, 167–9, 198–205, 318, 327–30, 342; political interest and involvement, 99, 134, 152–5, 158–9, 163, 167–8, 172–8, 180–91, 193–4, 197–9, 201–4, 207, 209–23, 224, 225, 227–34, 237, 239–53, 254–63, 265–7, 299–301, 333, 341–2, 344, 349–52, 359, 373–4, 383–6, 399–404, 417–18, 425–6; publication of sonnets, 104–5; learns Arabic, 116; escape from divorce action, 115, 117–19; social ostracism, 119, 123, 134, 266; return to religion, 120–2, 132, 235–7; miraculous recovery from dysentery, 148–9; as journalist and letter-writer, 156–7, 158, 169, 171, 177, 180–1, 210–11, 224, 242, 300, 333–5, 345–6, 360–1, 373–4, 384; literary activities, 161–2, 169, 315–16, 348–9; and Anne's attitude to his infidelities, 194–7; Parliamentary ambitions, 197, 207, 215–23, 231, 232–4, 252, 254, 259, 261–3, 269, 270; growing breach with Anne, 207, 212, 225, 230, 234–5, 243; slide towards frivolity, 243–4, 271, 289–93; trial and imprisonment in Ireland, 251, 254–63; overcoat question, 257–8, 260, 261; decision to leave English public life, 266, 270; fiftieth birthday, 284; desire to establish desert 'hermitage', 308, 320, 327; amassing of cottages, 309; beginning of tubercular condition, 315; new wills, 317, 336, 390; break-up of family life, 319–22, 339; life of quiet content, 330–1, 336–8; income, 331; first ride in motor car, 343; malarial fever, 354–8; difficulties with Anne, 356–8; and her departure, 362–7, 369, 378–9, 380; financial windfall, 367–8; 'marriage' to Dorothy, 364, 368–70; literary 'coterie', 372–3; and gossip, 375–7, 382, 385; new domestic rupture, 377–80; beginning of terminal illness, 381; acceptance of physical second childhood, 388; homage of 'disciples', 393–8, 401, 417–18, 430; reconciliation with family, 404–5, 420, 423; rift with Judith, 405–7; as detached philosopher, 410; and Anne's will, 412–13, 416; dispute over ownership of Stud, 413–16; publication of diaries, 418–19; poignant last two years, 419–23; cry for spiritual help, 421, 422–3; reconciled with Judith,

423; death and burial, 423–4, 428; appraisal of, 424–32
WRITINGS:
Alms to Oblivion, 32n, 34, 58, 61, 94, 153, 154, 163n
'Arabic Ballads', 296 (*Golden Odes*, q.v.)
Atrocities of Justice Under British Rule in Egypt, 360–1
Bride of the Nile, 304
'Butterflies', 427n.
'Canon of Aughrim, The', 227
'Chanclebury Ring', 424, 430
'Court of Love, The', 315–16, 427
Esther, 35, 37n, 40, 47, 56
Fand of the Fair Cheek, 349
Future of Islam, The, 162, 168n, 169
'Ghost of the beautiful past', 332
'Gibraltar', 430
Golden Odes of Arabia, 425
Gordon at Khartoum, 363
Griselda, 237
'He is not a Poet', 93
'I know the spring was coming', 162
Ideas about India, 154–5, 212
'If I could live without the thought of death', 100
In Vinculis, 258, 265, 279
India under Ripon, 155n, 205
'Juliet' sonnet, 96
Land War in Ireland, The, 236n, 363
Little Left Hand, The, 282n
Love Lyrics and Songs of Proteus, 296
Love Sonnets of Proteus, The, 52, 104, 162, 163, 217, 262
'Love's Novitiate', 386
Manon sonnets, 39, 40, 41
My Diaries, 34, 316, 333, 343n, 345, 370, 382n, 418–19, 429
'My Duty Right or Wrong', 385
New Pilgrimage, A, 237, 303
'No, I will smile no more', 263
'On Reading Certain Letters', 39
'Origins of the Kehilan, The', 158
Pilgrimage to Nejd (with Anne), 137, 162
Poetical Works, 392, 401, 429
Proteus and Amadeus: A Correspondence, 122, 132
'Religion of Happiness', 150, 284, 287
'Roumeli Hissar', 95
'Sancho Sanchez', 32, 415
Satan Absolved: a Victorian Mystery, 334–5, 374, 429
'Sea Lavender', 380
Secret History of the English Occupation of Egypt, 4, 167, 191n, 299n
'Secret Memoirs', 4, 34, 191, 280, 302, 310n, 364, 423
Songs and Sonnets of Proteus, 22, 104–5, 156
'To a Dead Journalist', 384
'Two Highwaymen, The', 86, 430
Wind and the Whirlwind, The, 191–2, 204, 215n, 429
Worth Forest, 50
Blunt, Wilfrid Scawen (son), 82–3, 90
Blunt, William (great-grandfather), 5, 74
Blunt, Winifrid (great-great-grandmother), 5
Blyth, Henry, 35n, 40
Boehm, Sir Joseph Edgar, 157, 376
Boer War, 338, 341–2, 344, 345, 425
Bombay, 205
Bordeaux, 34–5
Boughzoul, 98
Boulanger, General, 276
Bourke, Hon. Algernon 'Button' (cousin; son of 6th Lord Mayo), 48, 193, 209, 210, 215, 218, 230, 333, 377n; and Egyptian nationalism, 176, 187, 188
Bourke, Hon. Charles, (son of 5th Lord Mayo), 257, 259, 268
Bourke, Charlie, 23
Bourke, Edward, 156
Bourke, Emma, 156
Bourke, Hon. Maurice (cousin; son of 6th Lord Mayo), 113, 119
Bourke, Hon. Terence (cousin; son of 6th Lord Mayo), 119, 307–8, 327
Bowen, Sir George, 300
Brailsford, H. N., 274, 417
Brailsford, Jane, 374
Brand, Sir Henry (later Viscount Hampden Speaker), 183
Brand, Harry, 112, 113, 119, 151, 154, 163, 174, 212, 215, 224, 231, 425
Brett, Hon. Reginald (later Lord Esher), 266
Bright, John, 185
Britain and Egypt (Milner), 299
British Association, 157
Broadley, A. M., 187, 188
Brown, John, 88
Browne, Professor E. G., 374, 425
Browning, Robert, 47, 162
Buckle, George, 211
Buenos Aires, Blunt posted to, 60, 65, 66–9
Bulwer, Sir Henry, 25, 121, 140n
Burke, T. H., 179
Burne-Jones, Sir Edward, 103, 241, 252, 280, 281, 283, 331, 337

Burrell, Sir Charles, 5
Burrell, Sir Percy, 73
Burrell, Lady, 29, 70, 71, 72, 91, 108, 109, 112
Burton, Sir Richard, 67, 131, 136, 147, 148
Bushire, 149, 150
Byrne, Major (magistrate), 250–1, 259–61
Byron, Lord, 6, 13, 16, 17, 24, 25, 45, 55, 56, 59, 64, 159, 173, 276, 366; revival of incest story, 74–5, 105–6, 349; letters to Lady Melbourne, 105–6; Blunt's self-identification with, 106, 164, 324, 428; lameness, 134–5, 277; his warning to Greeks, 175; his great-great-great-grandchildren, 420n
Byron, Annabella Milbanke, Lady, 57, 58, 64, 277, 366, 367, 412; influence on Anne, 59; and incest story, 74, 75, 106

Caen, 80
Caffin (Crabbet agent), 405, 406, 413, 431
Caine, Hall, 373
Cairo, 114–15, 168, 170–4, 198–9, 240, 299, 327; Judith's wedding in, 339, 340–1; Anne's death in, 408
Calcutta, 202–3
Caldwell, 76
Camargues, 102–3
Camberwell, Blunt as unsuccessful candidate for, 219–23, 224
Cambridge University Carlton Club, 225
Cameron, Julia Margaret, 18
Cameron, Captain Verney, 145
Campbell-Bannerman, Sir Henry and Lady, 270
Cape Verde Islands, 66
Carey, Father, 402
Carleton, Dorothy, 333, 385, 388, 389, 390, 403, 405, 406, 413; Blunt's romance with, 338, 347, 353, 354, 362, 364, 365–6, 368–70, 377–80, 381, 391, 407; other flirtations, 365; 'adoption' as niece, 365, 368, 370–1, 378; difficulty over acceptance by Crabbet, 377–9; on Churchill, 387; insulted and accused by Judith, 407, 428; and Blunt's last years, 419, 421, 422, 424, 428; inherits Newbuildings, 428
Carleton, Mrs Dudley (later Lady Dorchester), 105
Carleton, Guy, 363, 364, 366, 368, 369, 377, 378, 379
Carlisle, Lord (formerly George Howard, q.v.), 273, 278
Carlisle, Lady (formerly Rosalind Howard, q.v.), 282
Carlsbad, 18
Carlton Club, 216, 219n, 263
Carlyle, Thomas, 25, 121n
Carnegie, Lady Helena, 287, 301, 308
Carson, Edward, Viscount, 249, 251, 254
Cascais, 48
Casement, Sir Roger, 3; and Irish Volunteers, 399; Easter Rising, 401–2; trial and execution, 402–4
Cassel, Sir Ernest, 358, 376
Castel Solcio, 56, 65
Castle Howard, 219, 234, 282
Castle Menzies, 271, 288
Catchfrench, 74
Cathleen ni Houlihan (Yeats), 348
Catholicism, 13–14, 16; Blunt loses faith in, 26–8, 30, 168; Anne's conversion to, 160–1, 169, 197; Blunt's renewed interest in, 235–7; 'final farewell' to, 279; return to, 421–3
Cavagnari, Sir Louis, 153, 154
Cavendish, Lord Frederick, 179
Caxtons (cottage near Crabbet), 330, 405, 412
'Celtic Twilight', 349
Ceylon, 200–202; Arabi's exile in, 189, 193, 198; Blunt's illness in, 200–201, 207
Chamberlain, Dora, 244, 287
Chamberlain, Joseph, 185, 233, 247n; and Home Rule, 231–2; and Transvaal, 333, 342
Chamberlain, Richard, 244
Chanctonbury Ring, 333, 362
Chandler, Edward, 49, 367, 412, 413
Chandler, Mary, 72
Charteris, Hon. Evan, 298
Charteris, Hon. Ivo, 319, 401
Charteris, Hon. Mary, 354, 369; birth, 318–19; Blunt's delight in, 389–90, 420–1; legacy from Blunt, 390, 391, 421, 428; marriage, 411
Chatsworth House, 38, 66
Chatterton, Thomas, 370
Chenery, Thomas, 181, 187, 190
Chesney, Colonel Francis Rawdon, 126, 132
Chesterton, Cecil, 384
Chesterton, G. K., 384
Chew, Samuel C., 418
Childe Harold (Byron), 276
Christian, Princess, 334
Church, Sir Richard, 25
Churchill, Lord Randolph, 197, 209, 219, 241, 270; and Egyptian nationalism, 190, 193–4, 196; his Fourth Party and 'Tory Democracy', 215–16,

217, 218, 221, 222; resignation, 237, 240; regrets Blunt's Woodford action, 252; death, 312
Churchill, Lady Randolph, 382
Churchill, Winston, 257, 259, 263, 384, 418, 426, 430; Blunt's fascination with, 386–8, 417; marriage, 386; as Home Secretary, 387; conviviality, 387–8; and First World War, 400, 409–10, 417; Blunt's prophecy concerning, 410; on Ireland, 418; Blunt's last letter to, 423
Churchill, Mrs Winston (Clementine Hozier, q.v.), 307, 386, 388, 409, 410
Clanricarde, Hubert de Burgh, Marquess of, 228, 252, 258, 377
Clapham, spiritual retreat at, 28
Clarence, Prince Albert Victor ('Eddy'), Duke of, 288
Clarke, Sir Andrew, 256
Cleeve Hill, 318–19
Clouds (Wyndham country home), 246–8, 334, 338, 354, 369, 391; Balfour's 'coercion' remarks at, 247–8, 257, 258, 262, 266, 267
Cockerell, Sir Sydney, 344, 395, 415, 416; as Blunt's secretary, 336–7, 342, 346, 355, 356, 367, 368, 418, 423; and Blunt's death, 423, 424, 428
Coffin, Father Edmund, 14, 18, 19, 20, 23, 24, 30, 72, 91, 94, 96, 197
Cole, George, 339
Colley, Sir George, 152, 153
Colombo, 200–201
Colum, Mrs Padraic, 399
Colvin, Sir Auckland, 197, 201, 343; and Arabi's mutiny, 171–2; and later nationalist movement, 173, 174, 175, 177, 185; favours annexation, 175, 180, 183
Colvin, John Russell, 156
Confessions (Rousseau), 55
Connolly, Father Terence L., 371
Conrad, Joseph, 168
Conservative Party: Blunt as candidate, 217–23, 224; Deptford success (1888), 262–3
Constantinople, 25, 213, 300–301, 327
Coole, 365
Cordery, Mr (Hyderabad Resident), 202, 204, 206
Cordova, 67
Corinne (De Staël), 56
Covey, G. F., 405, 407
Cowie, Isabella (Anne's maid), 82, 84, 92, 201, 207, 235, 237, 249, 256, 336, 340, 341, 357; engagement of, 71; death, 354–5
Cowley, Henry Wellesley, 1st Earl, 42, 45
Cowley, Lady, 42, 43, 46
Cowper, Lady, 344
Crabbet Arabian Stud, 3, 213, 302; forerunner of, 95; founding of, 127–8, 133–4, 151; increasing fame, 157–8, 316; successes, 339; partition of, 362–5, 366, 369, 413; reorganization of, 404–5, 413; dispute between Blunt and Judith over, 412–16, 417
Crabbet Club, 228, 252, 277, 289–93; foundation, 243–4; Wilde's election to, 289–91; verses, 290–1, 292; last meeting, 292–3
Crabbet Park (ancestral home), 5–6, 100–102, 118, 162, 196, 197, 220, 224, 287, 304–5; early years at, 6; rebuilding of, 89–90; Anne's delight in, 123; Judith's romanticism over, 208; lowering of rents, 230; indebtedness, 244, 405; 'Welcome Home' after Blunt's imprisonment, 264; letting of, 316; settled upon Judith, 353–4; Judith's move to, 377; her sale of part of, 406, 431
Crawford, Mrs Donald, 375
Crawley Monastery, 50, 391; Blunt graves in, 83, 89, 90; 'Skittles' buried at, 419
Crimes Act (1887), 241–2, 245, 247, 249
Croke, Dr, Archbishop of Cashel, 245
Cromer, Lord (formerly Evelyn Baring, q.v.), 189, 299, 300, 301, 330, 343; and Judith's wedding, 340–1; Blunt's hostility to, 347, 360, 373–4; and Denshawai case, 347, 361; strong line against financial corruption, 359; Blunt's attack on, 360, 361; resignation, 373–4
Cromer, 317, 320
Cumberbatch, Dr, 92, 101, 102, 116
Cumloden, 302
Cunninghame Graham, Robert, 157, 346, 418, 429
Curragh 'Mutiny', 399
Currie, Daphne, 420
Currie, Emily (cousin), 58
Currie, Francis Gore ('Bitters') (cousin), 49, 62, 68, 78; Blunt's hedonistic existence in Paris with, 60–61; in First World War, 80–81; death, 283
Currie, George (cousin), 106, 160
Currie, Henry (great-uncle), 6, 20, 21, 27
Currie, Laurence (cousin), 420

Currie, Mary (cousin), 20, 22, 58
Currie, Philip (later Baron) (cousin), 73, 123, 134, 159, 163, 173; rivalry with Blunt over Mrs Singleton, 161, 162; views on Egypt, 310
Currie, Lady (formerly Mrs Singleton, q.v.), 318
Curzon, Darea, 72, 108n
Curzon, Edward, 112
Curzon, George (later Marquis), 292, 388; and Wilde's election to Crabbet Club, 289–90, 291
Cust, Harry, 289, 291, 293, 342, 387
Cyprus, 136, 173

D'Abernon, Edgar Vincent, Viscount, 295
Dahman Shahwan (white horse), 294
Daily Herald, 401
Daily News, 266, 341, 347, 400
Damascus, 131, 132, 136–7, 169, 354
Darling, Charles (later Lord), 262–3, 270
Darmstadt, 53
Darwin, Charles, 21, 26, 84n
Davitt, Michael, 99, 228, 242, 245, 248, 350, 402
Davitt, Mrs, 245, 246
De La Warr, Lord, 185
De La Warr, Lady, 337
De Silva, Inez, 9
De Vere, Aubrey, 16, 121–2, 132
Deane, Mrs (cousin of Dillon), 228, 269
Dechaume, Charlot Geoffroy, 387n
Delhi, 203
Denshawai case (1906), 347, 359–61, 373
Deptford, Blunt as candidate for (1888), 252, 254, 259, 261–3, 270
Dervish Pasha, 183
Desborough, Lady (formerly Ettie Grenfell, q.v.), 297, 307, 344, 382, 401, 430
Devonshire, William Cavendish, 7th Duke of, 38
Deyr, 127, 128, 130, 131
Dieppe, 81
Digby el Mesrab, Jane, 131, 137, 169
Dilke, Sir Charles, 164, 221, 375; and Egyptian nationalism, 173, 176, 183
Dillon, John, 179, 228, 259, 266, 360, 373, 374, 384, 399, 426; and 'Plan of Campaign', 237, 239, 246, 247, 248–50, 266; anti-eviction meetings, 249–50; trial, 268–9; and Irish Land Act, 350, 351
Disraeli, Benjamin, 153, 190, 216, 376
Dives, 80
Dizful, 146–7
Doctor's Dilemma, The (Shaw), 356n
Doughty, C. M., 143, 150, 329
Douglas, Lord Alfred, 22, 246, 292, 293, 307, 321, 373; clash with Blunt, 382–3; and *My Diaries*, 418
Douglas, Lady Alfred, 373
Dreyfus, Colonel Alfred, 189
'Druid, The', 12
Dublin, 244–5, 248, 249, 268; Kilmainham gaol, 259, 260, 261, 263
Duckworth, George, 339
Dueri river, 146
Dufferin, Frederick Blackwood, 1st Lord, 25, 188, 206
Duggan, Dr, Bishop of Clonfert, 227, 268
Duke, Henry, 351, 352
Dunmore, Lord, 44

Earthly Paradise, The (Morris), 87
East Grinstead, 219
East Horsley, Lovelace home at, 6, 72
Easter Rising (1916), 401–2
Edensor, 66
Edward VII, 261, 375–6, 401; death, 381; Blunt's summary of, 381–2
Edward VII (as Prince of Wales), 29, 117, 119, 217, 218; opinion of Blunt, 178, 185, 211, 222; anxiety to have him in Parliament, 222, 232; anger at his activities in Ireland, 230
Edwin and Angelina (Fane), 159
Egoist, The, 397
Egypt: tour of, 113–15; nationalist movements, 168, 169–78, 179–91, 197–200, 299–301, 358–9; Anglo-French 'Joint Note', 174; probable annexation, 175, 180, 183; Blunt's attempt to lobby, 175, 176–8; Circassian Plot, 179–81, 183; Anglo-French hostilities, 181, 182, 185–6; Blunt's proposals for, 210–11; Blunt exiled from, 212; his return to, 239–40; Wolff Convention on, 242–3; Blunt's call for evacuation, 299–301; his changed views on, 359, 383–4
Egypt's Ruin (Rothstein), 373
Egyptian Independence Committee, 431
Egypt, 373, 383, 384, 385
El Islam, Sheykh, 180
Elcho, Hugh, Lord (later Wemyss), 295, 297, 311, 312–13, 314, 315, 317, 318, 319, 386, 390
Elcho, Mary Wyndham, Lady (later Wemyss), 72, 246, 261, 295, 308, 331, 333, 347, 390, 401, 411, 421; first noticed by Blunt, 157, 310; friendship with

Balfour, 247–8, 297, 307, 310, 311–12, 313, 319, 375; as Blunt's *grande passion*, 309–20, 353; with Blunt in Egypt, 309–14, 332; confession to husband, 315, 317; ends affair, 315–16; further meetings, 317, 318–19, 368; birth of their child Mary, 318–19
Eliot, George, 104, 106
Elwin, Rev. Whitwell, 303, 305–6
Elwin, Mrs Amy, 340
English Country Gentleman, The (Lytton), 140n, 155
Ernest of Saxe-Coburg, Prince, 376
'Esther' – *see* 'Skittles'
Euboea, 277
Eugénie, Empress, 35, 36, 51
Evelyn, W. J., 190, 254, 256, 262, 343, 373

Faber, Frederick William, 18
Fakkri Pasha, 299
Farid Bey, 374
Faris (Shammar leader), 129–30
Fashoda, 334
Fernando, Don, ex-King Consort of Portugal, 46
Fernycroft (Hants), 337, 338, 369, 372
Fielding, Everard, 312, 412
Fifield, Arthur, 373
Figaro, Le, 360
Finch, Edith, 37n, 40, 330
Finlay, George, 25
First World War, 400–404, 409–11, 415, 417, 425
Fitzwilliam, George, Lord, 37
Fleming, Rev. W., 262n
Fletcher, Sir Henry, 220
Flint, F. S., 394, 395
Florence, 57–60, 64
Flower, Cyril, 232
Flower, Peter, 296
Folignano, 238
Folkestone, Lord, 220
Forbes, Lady Angela, 390
Forster, E. M., 316, 322, 330, 417, 425; on Blunt's *Diaries*, 418, 429
Forster, W. E., 247
Fortescue, Mary, 72
Fortnightly Review, 154n, 157, 163, 169, 177, 212
Fould, Achille, 49n
Fourth Party, 215, 218
Fox, Richard Lane, 21
Francisco (husband of Isabella of Spain), 31
Franco-Prussian War, 78–81, 83
Frankfurt: Blunt's posting to, 26–30; return to, 51–4
Frant, 159
Frascati, 281
Fraser, Alec, 109–10, 111, 112, 113, 114, 116, 117
Fraser, Pagan, 110, 112, 113
Frederick the Great (Carlyle), 25
Froude, James Anthony, 224
Froufrou (Sardou), 63

Gaisford, Lady Alice, 267
Galloway, Lady: Blunt's romance with, 301–2, 307, 308; death, 353
Galway, 232, 268; Blunt in gaol, 255–9
Gambetta, Leon, 172–3
Gandamak, Treaty of (1878), 153
Garibaldi, Giuseppe, 65
Gaudier-Brzeska, Henri, 394
Gebel al Ahmar, 408
Geneva, Lake of, 55
Genoa, 15, 16
George v, 399
Gerard, John, 17, 18
Gerarde's Herbal, 337
Ghafil (Beni Laam leader), 146
Ghervor, Wady, 115–16
Gibraltar, 120, 123
Gladstone, Mary, 242
Gladstone, William Ewart, 158, 214, 256, 270, 426; and Blunt's idea of Arabian Caliphate, 163–4; and Egyptian nationalism, 176–8, 180–1, 182, 184–5, 187, 189–90, 197–8, 199, 210; misleading interview with Blunt, 177–8; Blunt's open letter to, 180, 184; Blunt's disillusion with, 182, 189–90, 198; and plan to bring back Egyptian exiles, 197–8, 199, 212; rejects Blunt's offer to mediate with Mahdi, 212; apparent renewal of support, 213, 218; meetings with 'Skittles', 217, 218, 376; fall of government, 218, 219; and Home Rule, 222, 225, 228, 231; return to power, 224; praises Blunt's Woodford action, 261; attempt to use him for Liberal cause, 265–6, 269; advice to prostitute, 377n
Gladstone, Mrs, 213, 242, 262, 270
Glamis Castle, 271
Glanville, Bessie (aunt), 74
Glanville, Harry (uncle), 74
Glasgow Herald, 335, 401
Glen, The (Tennant Scottish home), 296, 297–8
Glyn's Bank, 385
Gobineau, Joseph Arthur, Comte de, 84
Godley, Arthur (later Baron Kilbracken), 180
Godson, A. F., 234
Goethe, 56
Goff, Robin, 55, 56
Golden Legend, The (Morris), 296
Goldsmid, General Sir Frederick, 175n
Gomussa tribe, 131
Gordon, General Charles George, 158–9, 333; on Arabi, 186, 189; on India, 193; and Sudan,

Gordon, General Charles George – *contd.* 209–10, 211–12; death at Khartoum, 215
Gordon, Major William 'Monkey', 341
Gorey (Co. Wexford), 245
Gorsey End (Hants), 337
Gorst, Sir Eldon, 358, 374, 383
Gorst, John, 190
Gosbrook, 370, 372
Gosse, Edmund, 105
Graham, Captain Reginald, 33
Granada, 83
Granby, Violet, 297
Grant, Dr Thomas, Catholic Bishop of Southwark, 20, 24, 27
Granville, George Leveson-Gower, 2nd Earl, 163, 299n; and Egyptian nationalism, 176, 177, 181, 185, 187, 188, 190
Granville-Barker, Harley, 387
Gray, May, 9
Greene, Graham, 168n
Gregory, Robert, 365
Gregory, Sir William, 32, 191, 201; and Egyptian nationalism, 174, 181, 190; predicts Blunt's return to faith, 422n
Gregory, Lady, 185, 186, 190, 208, 215, 228, 230, 240, 263, 295n, 398, 399n, 422n, 426, 430; Blunt's romance with, 191–3, 194, 214; her sonnet-sequence, 194; Blunt's Bible left to, 268; and Irish theatre, 349, 365; and 'Peacock Dinner', 393–4
Grenfell, Ettie – *see* Lady Desborough
Grenfell, Julian, 401
Grenfell, William, 401
Greville, Charles, 4
Grey of Fallodon, Edward Grey, 1st Viscount, 359, 360, 374, 383, 384, 400, 409, 417
Grosvenor, Mrs Algernon ('Queenie'), 288, 293
Grosvenor, Caroline, 287, 295, 297
Grosvenor, Dick, 289
Grosvenor, Sibell (wife of George Wyndham), 241, 246, 256, 336; love for Blunt, 287, 288, 293

Hadban (Indian horse), 151
Hail, 142–4, 150, 154
Hajji Batran, 328
Hajji Mahmud, 129, 328
Hajji Mohammed, 145, 146, 147, 149
Hamad tribes, 168
Hamill-Stewart, Captain J. D., 169
Hamilton, Sir Edward, 163, 176, 180, 183, 193, 209, 211, 212
Hanna (servant), 129, 137
Hannen, Sir James, 118
Harcourt, Lewis, Viscount, 429
Harcourt, Sir William, 252–3, 267, 303, 333
Hardie, Keir, 360, 426
Hardyman, Maitland, 430
Hare, Augustus, 106
Harrington, Tim, 239, 254
Harris, Frank, 289, 291
Harrison, Frederic, 191, 212, 242, 313, 425
Harrow, 13
Hartington, Lord (later 8th Duke of Devonshire): affair with 'Skittles', 37–8, 40, 377; opposes Home Rule, 231–2
Hawarden, 214
Healy, Tim, 249, 260
Heartbreak House (Shaw), 431
Heathfield, 234
Hebron, 140
Hedda Gabler (Ibsen), 287
Heinemann, William, 373
Hélène of Orléans, Princess, 288
Henley, W. E., 429
Henn, Mr Justice, 254–5, 260
Hensler, Elise, 47, 48
Herbert, Auberon, 210, 212, 271
Herbert, Lady Mary (later Baroness von Hügel), 76
Herbert, Sidney, 230
Hicks Pasha, 209
Hill, Octavia, 390
Hinton, Janey, 84
Hobhouse, John Cam, 105
Hogarth, David George, 150
Holman (groom), 413, 414
Holywell (Cheshire), 336
Homburg, 52, 53, 54
Home Rule Union, 225, 241, 248
Hope, Edward, 232, 233, 234, 254n
Horsham, 5, 182
Houghton, Richard Monckton Milnes, 1st Baron, 184, 187, 289
Howard, Cardinal, 60
Howard, George (later Earl Carlisle, q.v.), 84, 176, 215, 224
Howard, Hubert, 333, 339
Howard, Rosalind Stanley (later Lady Carlisle, q.v.), 26, 176, 184, 193, 198, 224, 234; Blunt's attachment to, 84, 87; advises Blunt to enter Parliament, 210, 233; suggests peerage, 215; objects to his Conservatism, 219; introduces him to 'frivolous life', 271
Hozier, Bill, 271
Hozier, Lady Blanche, 224, 267, 278, 289, 375; Blunt's romance with, 271–3, 295; other lovers, 271, 386; and children's paternity, 271, 386
Hozier, Clementine (later Mrs Winston Churchill, q.v.), 271
Hozier, Sir Henry, 271, 295n
Hozier, Kitty, 271, 386
Hozier, Nellie (later Mrs

Romilly), 271, 409; Blunt's flirtation with, 386
Hueffer (later Ford), Ford Madox, 398
Hugo, Victor, 52, 261
Husseyn Koli Khan, 146, 147
Hyderabad, 201–2, 203, 204–5
Hyeres, 97
Hyndman, H. M., 213, 384, 387

Iddesleigh, Stafford Northcote, Earl of, 238
Ilbert, Courtenay Peregrine (later Sir), 200, 202–3, 204
India, 151–7, 201–6; and self-government, 193, 200, 202–4; Anglo-Indian arrogance, 203–4; Islamic university, 203, 204–5
Ireland: land war, 99, 227, 228–31, 237–8, 239, 244–6, 249–52, 254–5; coercion of, 176, 241–2, 246–52, 254; Blunt's political tour of, 225, 227–31; 'Plan of Campaign', 237, 239, 242, 245, 246, 268; Blunt's thought of settling in, 263–4; effect on his poetry, 264–5; his last visits to, 267–9; 'disentanglement' from, 268, 270; rebellion, 401–4
Irish Home Rule, 217, 221, 222, 225, 227, 228, 231, 232, 233–4, 241–2, 247, 252, 350, 351, 384, 399
Irish Land Bill (1908), 349–52
Irish National League, 216, 225, 227, 228, 259–61, 384
Irish National Volunteers, 399
Isabella, Queen of Spain, 31
Islam, 26; reform movement, 167–8, 169, 193, 204–5, 212, 213; Blunt's attempt to rediscover, 327–30
Ismail Pasha, Khedive, 170, 179

James, Henry, 246, 272
Jameson Raid, 333
Jedaan (Anazeh sheykh), 127, 128, 130
Jeddah, 163, 167–8, 170
Jenkins, Minnie, 72
Jersey, Margaret, Countess of, 302
Jerusalem, 116
Joachim, Joseph, 59
Jobba, 141–2
Jof (Al Jawf), 137, 138–40
John Bull's Other Island (Shaw), 360
Julie ('Skittles's' *bonne*), 43, 44, 45, 48, 54, 60, 61, 79, 84

Kabul, 153
Kamel, Aly, 417
Kars (Arab stallion), 128, 134
Kelmscott House, 279n
Kelmscott Manor, 279, 280, 323
Kenmare, Lord, 99
Kenmare, Lady, 29, 98–9
Kensett, Alfred, 424, 428
Keppel, Mrs, 381
Kerim Khan, 146
Kerkha river, 146
Kerr, Lady Alice, 70, 84
Kerr, Brigadier-Surgeon B. C., 204
Kerr, Lord Schomberg (later 9th Marquis of Lothian, q.v.), 27, 28, 51
Kerr, Lord William, later Father William, 50, 63, 202, 278
Khalil, 167, 168
Khartoum, 159, 209, 210, 211–12, 215
Kidderminster, 249; Blunt fails to win (1886), 233–4; Home Rule meeting at, 242
Kiepert, Heinrich, 137
King, Hester, 72
King Harman, Colonel, 229, 230
Kinglake, A. W., 191
Kingscote, Nigel, 84
Kingston, Lord, 229, 230
Kipling, Rudyard, 335n, 431
Kitchener, Lord, 198, 322, 342; and Omdurman, 341; as Consul-general in Egypt, 385, 388; and First World War, 401
Knebworth, John Scawen Lytton, Viscount, 420n
Knebworth, 79, 249, 321
Knight, William, 424
Knowles, James Thomas, 157, 158, 197, 212

Labouchere, Sir George, 190
Labouchere, Henry, 42, 52, 233
Labour Monthly, 418
Lady Windermere's Fan (Wilde), 295
Lahore, 151
Lansdowne, Henry Petty-Fitzmaurice, Marquess of, 346, 388
Laprimaudaye, Annie, 15–16, 20, 24, 66
Laprimaudaye, Catherine, 16
Laprimaudaye, Rev. Charles, 13, 15
Laprimaudaye, Charlie, 230
Laprimaudaye, Lucy, 84, 99
Lascelles, Sir Frank, 34
Lausanne, 54
Lawrence, Father, 389, 407
Lawrence, D. H., 387
Lawrence, Elizabeth (nurse), 336, 337, 342, 354, 362, 371, 378, 388, 407; ascendancy of, 355–6, 357, 367, 369, 406; mischief-making, 379; and Blunt's death, 423, 424, 428
Lawrence, T. E., 3, 418, 426
Lawson, Sir Wilfrid, 190, 211, 252, 267, 294, 335
Layard, Sir Henry, 126, 127, 150n
Lecky, W. E. H., 162

Leconfield, George Wyndham, 1st Lord (uncle), 5
Leconfield, Mary Wyndham, Lady (aunt), 5, 24, 31, 62; as guardian, 20, 22, 23; furthers Blunt's career, 23, 26; disapproves of Alice's desire to become nun, 27–8; death, 33
Leigh, Augusta, 74–5, 105, 366
Leinster, Hermione, Duchess of, 309, 312, 313, 314, 317
Leo XIII, Pope, 236–7, 242, 245; Papal Rescript, 268
Leopold II of the Belgians, 344
Leslie, Sir Shane, 204, 269, 419, 422n
Lesseps, Ferdinand de, 186
Leutwein, Helen, 25
Leveson-Gower, George, 292
Lewes, George Henry, 104, 105
Liaisons Dangereuses, Les (Laclos), 61, 348
Liberal Party: Blunt's connection with, 232–4, 242, 252–3, 265–7; Blunt as liability to, 269; end of connection, 270
Limerick, 249
Lisbon, 71; Blunt's posting to, 45–8
Liverpool, 232
Lloyd George, David, 385
Loch Awe, 271
Lockhart, Father, 264, 286
Lola (Spanish mistress), 32, 34, 47
Lothian, Schomberg Kerr, 9th Marquis of, 102
Lothian, Victoria, Marchioness of, 102
Loughrea gaol, 251, 268
Louise, Princess (Duchess of Argyll), 178, 376
Louise of Schleswig-Holstein, Princess, 345
Love in a Mist (Wentworth), 389
Lovelace, Ada, 6, 57, 100, 106, 277
Lovelace, William King, 1st Earl of, 6, 20, 57, 59, 73; opposes Anne's marriage, 58, 72; and Byron incest story, 75, 106
Lovelace, Ralph Noel Milbanke, 2nd Earl of (formerly Viscount Wentworth, q.v.), 349, 357, 364; death, 367–8
Lovelace, Lady (formerly Viscountess Wentworth, q.v.), 368, 405, 414, 423
Lowe, General Drury, 186
Lowell, James Russell, 220
Lucca, 15–16, 66
Ludwig, King of Bavaria, 65
Lufti-al-Sayyid, 359
Lushington, Godfrey, 74
Lushington, Dr Stephen, 74
Lutyens, Sir Edwin, 321, 409
Lyall, Sir Alfred, 154, 215
Lynbarskaya, Alla Mihailovna, 191n
Lyttelton, Alfred, 218
Lyttelton, Laura, 218, 224
Lytton, Lady Anne (granddaughter), 149n, 379; birth, 353; beneficiary under Anne's will, 412, 416; and dispute over Stud, 413–14; reunion with Blunt, 420; and his death, 424; inherits Newbuildings from Dorothy, 428
Lytton, 'Bina' (later Lady Betty Balfour), 155
Lytton, Lady Caroline, 420n
Lytton, Lady Constance, 155, 353, 387
Lytton, Edward Robert Bulwer, 1st Earl of, 72, 79, 102, 106, 140n, 162, 208, 259; at Lisbon legation, 45–8; impressed by Blunt, 45–6, 48; literary tastes, 46; encouragement of and influence on Blunt's writing, 47–8, 50, 52, 93, 104; and Blunt's renewed affair with 'Skittles', 48; urges 'relaxations of nuptial knot', 77; as Viceroy of India, 114–15, 151–3; rejects Blunt's request to be secretary, 115; Blunt's visit to, 151–4, 155; and Afghan War, 152–3; plans secret imperial mission with Blunt, 153–4, 163; as ambassador in Paris, on Margaret Talbot, 283, 284; death, 303
Lytton, Edith, Lady, 45–8, 79, 144, 145, 151, 152, 155, 162, 300, 304, 320, 321, 389; and Judith's marriage, 339, 340, 341
Lytton, Lady Emily (later Lady Emily Lutyens), 339; Blunt's 'little love', 303–7, 308, 317–18, 319–21
Lytton, John, Viscount Knebworth, 420n
Lytton, Lady Lucy, 420n
Lytton, Lady Madeleine (daughter of Neville), 420n
Lytton, Neville, 155, 355, 357, 360, 408, 430; Judith's unromantic marriage to, 339–41; and Anne's separation from Blunt, 363, 364, 365, 366; paints Francis Thompson's portrait, 370; and acceptance of Dorothy, 378, 380; war service, 401, 411; divorce, 420; 3rd Earl of, 420n
Lytton, Noel Anthony Scawen Blunt, 4th Earl of (grandson), 353, 367n, 377, 379, 408n, 409, 430; birth, 344; involved in mother's

dispute with Blunt, 405–6, 413–14; reunion with Blunt, 420; marriage and family, 420n; and Blunt's death, 423, 424, 428; and mother's thirty-year silence, 429
Lytton, Clarissa Palmer, Lady (wife of 4th Earl), 420n
Lytton, Hon. Roland, 429n
Lytton, Lady Sarah, 420n
Lytton, Victor (later 2nd Earl of), 155, 420n; Judith's forbidden love for, 339, 340
Lytton (later Tryon), Lady Winifrid (granddaughter), 379, 389, 406; birth, 353; beneficiary under Anne's will, 412; and dispute over Stud, 413–14; reunion with Blunt, 420; marriage, 420

MacCarthy, Desmond, 429
McCarthy, Huntley, 216
McCarthy, Justin, 216
McCormack, Dr, Bishop of Galway, 256, 258
MacDermot, Hugh O'Rorke MacDermot, The, 254, 255, 260
MacDonald, Ramsay, 400, 417
Macleod, Rev. Norman, 88
Macmillan's Magazine, 74
MacNab, Father Vincent, 420, 422, 423, 424, 426
Madeira, 84–5
Madras, 201
Madrid: Blunt posted to, 30, 31–4, 39, 41–2; first mistress in, 32, 34; serious illness in, 33
Maggiore, Lake, 56, 65
Mahdi, the (Mohammed Ahmed ibn Abdullah), 198, 209–10, 216; Blunt's proposed mission to, 211–12, 214; death, 215; desecration of body, 34
Mahmud, Syed, 383, 417
Malcolm, Sir John, 57
Malet, Sir Alexander, 26, 28, 52, 54
Malet, Lady, 26, 28, 29, 31, 41–2, 53–4, 57, 61, 183
Malet, Sir Edward, 54, 137, 197; as Consul-general in Egypt, 171, 172; opposes nationalist movement, 174, 175, 179, 180, 181–2, 183, 187
Malet, Henry, 184
Malkum Khan, 163
Malmesbury, James Harris, 3rd Earl of, 23–4
Malory, Sir Thomas, 337
Manchester, 266
Manchester Guardian, 360, 374, 400
Manning, Charles, 15
Manning, Frederic, 394
Manning, Henry, Cardinal, 72, 122, 161, 219, 222, 235, 259, 375, 421; friendship with Mary Blunt, 7, 16; received into Catholic Church, 13; on reign of force in Europe, 158, 159; and papal mission to Dublin, 242, 244; accused of opposing Home Rule, 262; advice to Blunt to 'stand and wait', 264, 269
Mansfield, Peter, 360
Marconi scandal, 384, 385
Marseilles, 11
Marsh, Sir Edward, 430
Marx, Karl, 191n
Mary, Queen, 399
Mary Adelaide of Cambridge, Princess, 29
Masefield, John, 394, 395, 397
Mason, Captain (Galway prison governor), 255, 256, 258
Masood, Syed Ross, 417
Mathew, Theobald, 291
Maud (Tennyson), 22
Mayo, Dermot, Lord, 111, 112, 113, 117, 118–19, 218
Mecca, proposed Arabian Caliphate at, 167–8, 169
Medjuel of Mesrab, 131, 137, 169
Melbourne, Lady, 105
Menelik II of Abyssinia, 322
Mentone, 15, 309
Meredith, George, 230, 301, 348
Merry England, 197
Meshur-Ibn-Mershid, 131
Meynell, Alice, 226, 301, 337, 373; and Francis Thompson, 371–2
Meynell, Dr Charles, 23, 26; at Oscott, 20–21; Blunt's 'Proteus' controversy with, 120–2, 132, 256
Meynell, Everard, 370, 371
Meynell, Viola, 372
Meynell, Wilfrid, 197, 221, 222, 269, 337, 348, 373, 375, 425; and Francis Thompson, 370–2; on Churchill, 387; and Casement, 402, 403; 'a gossip', 418; and restoration of Blunt's faith, 420, 421, 422n
Michel, Louise, 276
Middleton, 'Bay', 271, 386
Midhat Pasha, 137
Milan, 64
Military Fox-hunting Case (1901), 345–7
Millais, Sir John, 94, 241
Milner, Alfred, Lord, 189, 299, 342
Miltown, Lord, 176
Minshawi (Harabi guide), 327, 328
Mischad, A. M., 417
Mitchelstown (Co. Cork), 248
Modern Egypt (Cromer), 171, 194
Modern Love (Meredith), 348

Mohammed Abdu, Sheykh, 168, 212, 300, 327, 359
Mohammed-Ibn-Aruk, 130, 131, 137, 138, 140, 143, 144, 329
Mohammed Ibn Rashid, 142–3
Molony, C., 42, 172, 214
Moloney, William, J., 360
Monaco, 102
Monte Rosa, 21
Monteviot, 100
Montgomery, Alfred, 322
Montgomery, Edith, 7, 9
Montgomery, Sybil (later Marchioness of Queensberry), 22, 246
Moore, Thomas, 75
Moore, T. Sturge, 394, 395
Moorey, Robert, 8
Morley, John, Viscount, 157, 177, 231, 259
Morris, Jane, 224, 252, 337; Blunt's romance with, 278–80, 296, 308, 323, 427; and Rossetti, 279, 280, 281, 286; death, 419
Morris, Jenny, 224, 278
Morris, May, 224, 242, 278, 323
Morris, William, 224, 225, 278–9, 283, 294, 296; death, 322; Blunt's appreciation of, 322–3; refectory table, 337, 396; lock of hair, 390; Blunt as his disciple, 430
Morte d'Arthur, 323, 337
Mortimer, Raymond, 426
Mortlake, 17, 18
Mure, Constance, 22, 92
Murray, Gilbert, 282
Murray, John, 104
Murray, Mary, Lady, 282
Mustafa Pasha Kamel, 359, 374
'Myself and Others' (Wentworth), 40, 117, 276, 316n, 317n, 320, 321, 339, 368, 406, 414

Napier, Gabrielle, 408, 416
Napier, Jack, 212
Napier, Mark, 187, 188, 211–12, 264, 293, 383, 388, 400, 409, 414
Napier, Philip, 385, 408, 412, 415
Napoleon III, 35, 36; coup d'état, 14; and 'Skittles', 36, 38; and Franco-Prussian war, 78–9, 80
Nation, 418
National Trust, 390
Natrun, Wady, 306, 329
Naworth Castle, 224, 248
Nefud ('sand passes'), 136, 138, 139, 140–1, 143, 144
Nejd: Blunt's exploration of, 136–45, 150; intended diplomatic 'Pilgrimage' to, 154
Nevinson, H. W., 403
New Witness, 384, 401
Newbuildings Place, 5, 91, 295, 332, 362–3, 386n, 417, 418, 430; let to Blunt by Francis, 76, 81, 82; furniture for, 85, 337; Pollen family at, 97, 273; Pollen exodus from, 274–5; Burne-Jones tapestries, 283n, 337; Blunt's move into, 316; Morris's table, 337; Anne's departure from, 364–5, 367; intended literary coterie, 372–3; male conviviality at, 387–8; 'child Mary's' delight in, 389–90; Jubilee Press, 392; 'Peacock Dinner', 393–8; Anne revisits, 405; banned to grandchildren, 406; grandchildren revisit, 420; Blunt's death and burial at, 423–4, 428; bequeathed to Dorothy, 428
Newman, John Henry, Cardinal, 19, 86, 132; attempt to convert Blunt, 121–2, 123; his 'miraculous' hand, 122, 213; and Anne's conversion, 160, 161
Newmarket, 157
News from Nowhere (Morris), 294
Newton, William Legh, 1st Baron, 429
Nice, 102, 103
Nîmes, 12
Nineteenth Century, 157, 158, 197
Noel, Alice, 25, 72
Noel, Edward, 25, 207
Noel (later Noel-Baker), Irene, 277, 357
Noel-Baker, Lord, 277n
Notre Dame de Paris (Hugo), 261
Nubar Pasha, 170, 187

O'Brien, Peter, 260
O'Brien, William, 266; and 'Plan of Campaign', 239, 245, 247, 248, 249; in gaol, 258; fresh arrest and trial, 266, 267–8; wedding, 270; and Irish Land Act, 350, 351
O'Connor, T. P., 242, 266, 295
O'Shea, Guillermo, 32
O'Shea, Kitty, 247n, 399
O'Shea, Captain William, 19, 232
Observer, 181, 184
Ockham, Byron Noel, Viscount, 58, 72
Olga of Denmark, Princess, 29
Omdurman, battle of (1898), 333–4, 339, 341
Origin of Species (Darwin), 21, 26
Orleans, 23
Orton, Arthur ('Tichborne Claimant'), 67
Oscott, 19, 20–21
Othman, Prince, 172
Ouchy, 55–6, 65, 75, 76, 77; disastrous visit to 'Juliet' at, 83–4
Oude, ex-king of, 129
'Ouida', 343, 345
Oxford Movement, 13, 24n
Oxford Union, 242

Paget, Walburga, Lady, 331

Palgrave, William Gifford, 136, 141, 157
Pall Mall Gazette, 118, 177, 211, 229, 252, 266, 300, 335
Palles, Christopher, 260
Pamplona, 33
Parham, 81; 'carnival of folly' at, 108, 109–12, 119, 123
Paris, 39, 50–51, 71, 101, 198, 235, 276, 287–8; Blunt's posting to, 42–5; 'hedonistic' weeks in, 60–63; semi-permanent residence in, 78–81, 83; siege of, 81; 'dear July days' in (1890), 282–3
Parmoor, Charles Cripps, Baron, 417
Parnell, Charles Stewart, 179, 215, 228, 247n, 255, 270, 350, 399; failure to use Blunt, 216, 232, 269; and Home Rule, 221, 242; Blunt's likeness to, 269, 429
Parry, Sydney, 404
Patmore, Coventry, 226n, 301
Patna, 203–4
Pau, 8, 9
Paul, Kegan, 132
'Peacock Dinner' (1914), 3, 393–8
Pearl, Cora, 51
Pease, Mr (Dublin juryman), 260, 261
Peel, George, 290, 295
Peel, Julia, 295
Peel, Willy, 295
Pembroke, George Herbert, 13th Earl of, 228, 230, 244, 295
Penetration of Arabia, The (Hogarth), 150
Persia 'campaign', 145–50
Persico, Mgr, 242, 244–5
Peter Pan (Barrie), 388
Petre, Maude, 373, 421
Petworth House, 5, 6–7, 90; Blunt born at, 6
Petworth Posie, 431
Petworth Rectory, 6, 7
Pharaoh (Arab stallion), 172, 182
Philby, H. St John, 418
Philpot, Dr, 330, 337, 356, 357, 358
Pilgrimage to Al Madinah and Mecca (Burton), 136, 147
Pioneer, 201
Piraeus, 276
Pisan Cantos (Pound), 398
Pius IX, Pope, 60, 92
Pius XI, Pope, 422
Plarr, Victor, 394, 395
Pollen, Annie (Pansy), 92n, 160, 162; Blunt's brief flirtation with, 99
Pollen, Arthur, 226, 242, 244, 245, 252, 289; misunderstood attentions to Judith, 273–5, 277–8
Pollen, Benjamin, 116, 163n
Pollen, Father John, 232, 410, 422
Pollen, John Hungerford, 13, 24, 87, 89, 94, 99, 112, 113, 118, 160, 161, 226, 254, 261, 262, 275
Pollen, Margaret, 262, 423
Pollen, Maria Margaret (Minnie), 24, 29, 70, 86, 94, 99, 100, 112, 113, 225, 237, 267, 269, 295; first kiss, 66, 87; 'longest love of my life', 87–8, 91–2, 96–7, 102, 103; mothering of Judith, 97, 145, 160, 235; miscarriage, 98; compared with Augusta Leigh, 105; fresh pregnancy, 111; birth and death of Benjamin, 116, 120, 163n; and cuts in Anne's diary, 117n; 'abandonment' of Blunt, 159–60, 161; renewed affair, 162–3; attempt to reconcile Blunt and Anne, 230; delight at Blunt's Woodford action, 252; support in Deptford campaign, 261–2; Blunt's final rupture with her and family, 273–6, 277–8; death, 410, 419
Pollen, Stephen, and Judith, 276, 312, 316, 339
Pollen, Walter, 202
Pompey (majordomo), 66, 96, 98, 110, 116, 123
Pope, Father Thomas, 161
Pope-Hennessy, Mrs, 268
Porter, Grace (nurse), 8, 11
Porter, Father Thomas, 17, 18
Portumna County Court, 254–5
Potocki, Count Roman, 172
Pound, Ezra, 52, 397–8, 401, 431; and 'Peacock Dinner', 3, 393–5, 397
Powell, Sir Douglas, 356
Prince Imperial, 36
Prinsep, Val, 162, 241
Punch, 185
Pyrenees, 8, 33

Queensberry, Sybil, Marchioness of, 22, 246

Ragonath Rao, 201
Ram Hormuz, 148
Rapley, Felix and Jack, 424
Rascall's Corner, 371
Rawlinson, Sir Henry, 177
Reading, Rufus Isaacs, 1st Marquess of, 402
Redesdale, Algernon Freeman-Mitford, 1st Baron, 386n
Redmond, John, 249, 346, 387; and Irish Land Act, 350–2
Reid, Robert (later Lord Loreburn), 260
Resurrection (Tolstoy), 342
Rhodes, Cecil, 333, 425
Rhodes, 126
Riaz Pasha, 170
Ribblesdale, Lord, 307, 401, 415
Rifaat (Arabian colt), 362, 363
Rifky, Osman, 170–1, 179

Ripon, George Robinson, Marquis of, 215, 259; as Viceroy of India, 193, 200, 202, 204, 206, 209
Ripon, Lady, 262
Roala tribe, 130–1, 138–9
Roberts, Lord, 153
Roberts, David (manservant), 181, 333, 336, 354, 371
Roberts (Twyford headmaster), 12
Robson, William Snowdon (later Baron), 260
Roehampton, Sacred Heart Convent at, 20, 22, 27
Rogers, Samuel, 162
Rome, 60, 235–8, 280–1
Romilly, Lady Arabella, 273
Ronan, Stephen, 251
Rosebery, Archibald Primrose, 5th Earl of, 180, 244, 299
Rossetti, Dante Gabriel, 24, 84; and Jane Morris, 279, 280, 281n, 286
Rothschild, Sir Nathan Meyer, Baron, 177, 183, 190
Rothstein, Andrew, 418
Rothstein, Theodore, 373, 400
Rouen, 81
Rousseau, Jean-Jacques, 55
Rowlands, James, 249
Rowlands, Mrs, 250
Royal Geographical Society, 126, 128, 144, 157, 322
Ruskin, John, 59
Russell, Sir Charles (later Baron Russell of Killowen), 260, 270
Russell, Sir Charles, 347, 348
Russell, Adeline, Blunt's romance with, 347–8, 353
Russell, Lord John, 48, 75
Russo–Japanese War, 358
Ryala (Arabian mare), 413, 414
Ryan, Frederick, 373, 384
Ryder, Father, 122, 132
Sabunji, Louis, 163, 173, 183, 184, 185
Saccara, 327
Sackville, Lady Margaret, Blunt's romance with, 337–8
Sackville-West, Amalia, 302, 308
Sadowa, Battle of (1866), 54
Saighton Grange, 288
St Fagan's Castle, 331–2
St James's Gazette, 181, 184
St John, Charles, 12
St Leonards-on-Sea, Mary Blunt's death at, 19
Saintes Maries, 103
Salar Jung, 202, 204, 206
Salisbury, Robert Cecil, 3rd Marquis of, 134, 267, 349; as Prime Minister, 218, 219, 221, 237, 238, 239–40, 346; and Egypt, 239–40, 242; and Home Rule, 221
Saltoun, Lord, 108, 113, 117
Samuel, Sir Herbert, 385
San Remo, 68, 69
Sanderson, Sir Thomas, 346
Sardou, Victorien, 63
Sassoon, Siegfried, 431
Saturday Review, 184
Saumarez, Hon. Gerald de, 37, 386n, 419
Schnadhorst, Francis, 233
Scott, C. P., 374
Selwood, Henry (valet to Blunt's father), 7, 8
Selwood, Mrs, 12, 19, 50, 73, 82, 224, 243
Senussi people, 328–30
Sermoneta, Duke and Duchess of, 238
Seymour, Sir Beauchamp, 185
Shakik, wells of, 140–1
Shammar tribe, 129
Shammar, Jebel, 138, 141, 142, 150
Shaw, George Bernard, 356n, 360, 373, 431
Shelley, Mary, 75n, 135n
Shelley, Percy Bysshe, 5, 55, 60, 74, 75, 156
Sherif Pasha, 170, 171, 172, 175, 198
Sherifa (Arab mare), 130, 134
Sheykh Obeyd, 287; purchase of, 172; cache of guns at, 200; Blunt exiled from, 212; return to, 239, 240; Anne's use as 'retreat', 241; winters at, 277, 280, 281, 284, 294–5, 299, 318, 344, 354–5; El Kheysheh house, 294, 309, 310–11, 341; *grande passion* at, 309–15; Blunt's malarial fever at, 354–5; Anne's profitable sale of, 358, 362; bequeathed to granddaughters, 412
Shipley (Sussex), 373, 384, 408, 409
Shustar, 147–9; Blunt's delirium and Anne's vision at, 148–9, 160
Sidi Khaled, 116
Silk and Scarlet ('The Druid'), 12, 127
Simla, 151–3, 155–6
Sinai, Mount, 115, 142, 308, 316, 342
Singleton, Henry, 159, 161, 162
Singleton, Mrs Minnie ('Angelina' authoress 'Violet Fane') (later Lady Currie, q.v.), 185, 225, 295; Blunt's affair with, 123, 159–60, 161–2
Siwa, 327, 328–30
Skene, James Henry, 127, 129, 131; and origin of Arabian Stud, 127–8, 130, 133, 172
'Skittles' (Catherine Walters), 47, 51, 63, 70, 228, 252, 254, 256, 261, 288; as Blunt's first *grande passion*, 34–41, 302; her past, 36–8; his first suspicions, 39; disaster, 39–41; brief renewals of affair, 43, 44–5, 48–50, 61, 65–6, 102; 'worthlessness' rediscovered, 49–50;

help for Blunt in Zouche divorce, 119; shown over Crabbet Stud, 157; political interests, 209, 211, 222, 232, 276; meetings with Gladstone, 217, 218, 376; reminiscences and gossip, 375–7, 381, 385, 399; match-making offer, 390; ultra-patriotism, 401; death, 419
Smith, F. E. (later 1st Lord Birkenhead), 403
Smith, Francis, 357, 367
Smith, W. H., 242
Smyrna, 95
Social Democratic Federation, 213
Sorrows of Werther (Goethe), 56
Souls, the, 297, 303–4, 310, 331
Southampton, Francis' death at Radley's Hotel, 86, 87
Southwater, 371
Spencer, Herbert, 334, 335
Stäel, Mme de, 56
Stamboul, 95. *See also* Constantinople
Standard, 400
Stanhope, Philip, 247, 266
Stanley, Dean, 162
Stanley, Henry Morton, 240
Stanley, Katherine (later Lady Amberley), 26
Stanley, Lyulph, 210
Stanley, Maude, 26
Stanley, Rosalind (later Howard, then Lady Carlisle, q.v.), 26
Stanley of Alderley, Henry, Lord, 26, 215
Stanway, 206–7, 307
Stead, W. T., 211, 241
Stephen, Sir Leslie, 93
Stewart, Sir Charles, 414
Stillman, Marie (Spartali), Blunt's love for, 280–1
Stonor, Mgr, 60, 92, 236
Stonyhurst College, 17–18
Storey, Mrs Waldo, 237
Stout, Mary, 313n
Stowe, Harriet Beecher, 74
Strachey, Sir John, 152, 154
Stratford upon Avon, 307
Stratford de Redcliffe, Lord, 159
Sudan, 158–9; Arab rebellion, 198, 209–12, 214–15; Blunt's proposals for, 210–11; his proposed mission to, 211–12, 214
Suez Canal, 25, 170, 184, 186, 190, 198
Suez, Gulf of, 342–3
Suleyman (servant), 329, 343
Sullivan, Sir Arthur, 216
Sullivan, T. D., 266
Sullivan, Mrs T. D., 245
Sultan Pasha, 180
Sumner, Arthur, 84, 85
Sumner, Berkeley (son of Blunt and Georgie Sumner), 88, 207, 322, 369, 389
Sumner, Georgie, 29, 87, 207–8; Blunt's romance with, 84–5, 88–9; birth of their son, 88; death, 419
Swinburne, Algernon, 376
Swinburne, Sir John, 244
Swinford, 316
'Swing, Captain', 5

Taba (Gulf of Aqaba), 359
Taj Mahal, 156
Talbot, Mgr, 92
Talbot, Lady Edmund, Blunt's romance with, 287, 288, 293
Talbot, Margaret Jane, 286, 297, 346; Blunt's romance with, 281–4, 287–8, 293, 295, 307
Tanjore, 201
Taylor, Helen, 221
Taylor, Sir Henry, 18
Tel-el-Kebir, Battle of (1882), 186, 198
Tennant, Sir Charles, 295, 298
Tennant, Eddy, 315
Tennant, Laura, 297, 298
Tennant (later Asquith, q.v.), Margot, 294–5, 303, 305, 310; romance with Blunt, 296, 297–9, 306
Tennant, Pamela, 315
Tennyson, Alfred, Lord, 47, 162
Tewfik Pasha, Khedive: and national uprising, 170–2, 174, 175, 179, 180, 185, 186; Anglo-French support for, 174, 179, 181–2, 185, 199; death, 299
Tewfik, Riza Bey, 425
Thomas, Edward, 401
Thompson, Francis, 301, 330, 337; last weeks, 370–2
Three Bridges, 365, 367
Thun, Lake, 74
Thurlow, Mrs, 123
Ticha tribe, 116
Tibb river, 146
Times, The, 174, 176, 177, 180, 184, 185, 187, 188, 190, 210–11, 220, 222, 224, 238, 242, 263, 266, 333, 334, 335, 344, 347, 383, 393, 397, 425
Tolstoy, Leo, 342
To-morrow: A Woman's Journal for Men, 303
Torquay, 76–7
'Tory Democracy', 215–16, 217, 219, 220
Travels in Arabia Deserta (Doughty), 143, 150
Trelawny, Edward John, 134–5, 162
Trevor, Lord, 119
Tricoupi, Miss, 276–7
Trivulzio, Count, 60, 64, 65
Trochu, General, 80
Tryon, Claude, 420
Tryon, Lady Winifrid – *see* Lytton, Lady Winifrid
Tudmur, 130, 131, 132
Tunis, 307–8
Tunisia, 172–3
Turco (mastiff), 67, 69
Turkey: Blunt's travels in, 94–5; landing at Taba, 359; revolution (1908), 374

Turkeycock (forerunner of Arabian Stud), 95, 109, 110
Twyford School, 10–11, 12–13, 14, 17, 67n
Tynan, Katharine, 401
Tyrrell, Father, 373

United Ireland, 268
Usedom, Count, 27, 51, 53, 57, 65
Usedom, Countess Olympia, 27, 51, 53, 56, 65; 'petting' of Blunt, 29, 57; matchmaking, 57–8, 59, 60, 63, 64
Usedom, Hildegard, 27, 56, 65

Vanity Fair, 197
Venice, 355
Vevey, 56
Victoria, Queen, 88, 185, 226, 376; Golden Jubilee, 243; Diamond Jubilee, 333; and Judith's marriage, 339, 341; Blunt's obituary of, 345
Vienna, 26
Villayat Ali Khan, Nawab, 203
Vivian, Herbert, 234n, 244, 252; as Blunt's secretary, 254; Blunt's advice to, on joining political parties, 269

Wagram, Berthe, Princess, 293, 295, 353
Walford, Edward, 23
Walsh, Dr, Archbishop of Dublin, 227
Walter, John, 177
Walters, Catherine – *see* 'Skittles'
Watts, G. F., 18, 45, 62, 335
Weatherby, James, 157, 332
Webb, Godfrey (cousin), 104, 176, 292, 294, 312
Webb, Philip, 337, 405
Webb, Sam (groom), 331, 333
Webster, Lady Fanny, 105
Weekly Register, 269
Wellesley, Lady Feodorowna (Feodore) (later Lady Bertie), Blunt's brief romance with, 42–4, 46
Wellesley, Richard Colley, Marquess, 322
Wellington, Arthur Wellesley, Duke of, 9, 42, 302
Wemyss, Lord and Lady – *see* Elcho
Wenham, Canon, 26, 27, 28, 33
Wenlock, Lady, 293
Wentworth, Ada Mary, 412
Wentworth, Fanny Herriot, Viscountess, 74, 75, 93
Wentworth, Judith, Lady – *see* Blunt, Judith
Wentworth, Mary (later Lady), 93, 94, 97, 100
Wentworth, Ralph Noel King Milbanke, Viscount (later 2nd Earl of Lovelace, q.v.), 58, 73, 75, 98, 106, 150, 161, 234, 324; engagement, 74; divorce, 93; partner in Crabbet Stud, 128, 133, 134; second marriage, 160
Wentworth, Mary Wortley, Viscountess (later Lady Lovelace, q.v.), 160, 234, 339
Wentworth, Thomas, 277n
West Grinstead Park, 91, 109
West Horsley, 6, 20, 22
Western Desert, Blunt's 'forty days' in, 327–30
Wexford, 249
Wheatley, William ('Nep'), 69, 75, 81; marriage to Alice Blunt, 73; Blunt's jealousy of, 76; and Crabbet Stud, 128
Whirlwind, The, 234n
White, Maud, 386
Wilberforce, Mrs Henry, 28
Wilberforce, Samuel, 7, 13
Wilbury (Wilts), 157
Wilde, Oscar, 225, 270, 272, 292, 293, 295, 307, 418; on effect of prison on Blunt's poetry, 264; election to Crabbet Club, 289–90, 291
William I of Prussia (later German Emperor), 79, 81
William II, German Emperor, 342, 401
Williams, Edward and Jane, 75n
Wilson, Sir Rivers, 158, 163
Windsor (later Plymouth), Gay, 391; Blunt's romance with, 331–3, 353
Winifred, St, 336, 343, 419, 421
Witley (Surrey), 6, 13, 28, 243
Wolff, Sir Henry Drummond, 23, 190, 218, 219; Convention on Egypt, 242–3, 244
Wolseley, Sir Garnet, 136, 177, 186, 188, 217
Woodford (Co. Galway), Blunt's arrest at anti-eviction meeting, 249–51, 254–5, 259–61
Worth, 19, 82–3, 220; Manor House, 404, 421
Worth Forest, 5, 63, 73, 101, 208, 406; offered to National Trust, 390; bequeathed to child Mary, 421, 428
Worth Forest Cottage, 7–8, 45, 50, 81, 364; honeymoon in, 73; Alice's death in, 89, 90; Anne's move to, 365, 367
Wyndham (later Kingscote), Caroline, 84
Wyndham (later Mure), Constance, 22, 92
Wyndham, Frank (cousin), 10
Wyndham, George (later 1st Lord Leconfield) (uncle), 5

Wyndham, George (cousin), 48, 241, 246, 247, 261, 265, 267, 287, 288, 301, 322, 368, 383, 386, 388, 426; and Crabbet Club, 292, 293; and Blunt's affair with Mary Elcho, 317, 318; his own love affairs, 331–3, 391; and policy in Africa, 333, 334; as 'Tory Jingo', 343; as Irish Secretary, 349–52; and agrarian problem, 350–2; resignation, 352; and Blunt's Fernycroft estate, 369; death, 390–2; selection of Blunt's poems edited by, 429
Wyndham, Madeline (Mrs Percy Wyndham), 29, 70, 84, 86, 94, 119, 157, 241, 246, 281, 293, 331, 338, 373, 391; Blunt's brief affair with, 62, 88; renewed romance, 88, 96, 102; and Blunt's 'adoption' of Dorothy, 365, 368, 369; death, 419
Wyndham, Mary (later Lady Leconfield, q.v.) (aunt), 5, 24; as guardian, 20, 22, 23
Wyndham, Mary (later Lady Elcho, q.v.), 72; first noticed by Blunt, 157
Wyndham, Pamela, 246, 291n
Wyndham, Percy (cousin), 50, 54, 62, 73, 113, 157, 163, 190, 212, 246, 319, 334, 338, 373; and Blunt's 'adoption' of Dorothy, 365, 368; death, 391
Wyndham, Percy (son of George and Sibell), 389, 391
Wyndham, Sibell – *see* Grosvenor, Sibell
Wynford, Lady, 184
Yeats, W. B., 52, 117, 336, 348–9, 397, 398, 430; and 'Peacock Dinner', 3, 394, 395, 397; eulogy of Blunt, 365

Zaghloul, Saad, 417, 423
Zahru, M. A., 417
Zeytoun, 341; monastery, 328
Zouche, Robert Curzon, Lord, 81, 214; marriage to Doll Fraser, 108–9; betrayal, 109–13; divorce, 115, 117–19
Zouche, Dorothea ('Doll') Fraser, Lady, 214; marriage, 108–9; romance with Blunt, 109–13; agreement to love for ten years, 111; other lovers, 111–12, 113, 117, 118–19; divorce, 115, 117–19; later marriage and death, 119

THE BEST IN BIOGRAPHY FROM GRANADA PAPERBACKS

Maurice Ashley

Charles II £1.25 ☐

John Brooke

King George III £1.95 ☐

Margaret Forster

The Rash Adventurer £1.25 ☐

Antonia Fraser

Mary Queen of Scots £3.95 ☐
Cromwell: Our Chief of Men £2.50 ☐

Elizabeth Jenkins

Elizabeth the Great 95p ☐

Eric Linklater

The Prince in the Heather £1.50 ☐

Douglas Liversidge

Prince Philip £1.00 ☐
The Queen Mother £1.95 ☐
Prince Charles £1.50 ☐

Peter Townsend

The Last Emperor £1.95 ☐

P23481

THE BEST IN BIOGRAPHY FROM GRANADA PAPERBACKS

BIOGRAPHY

MARIE CURIE   Robert Reid   £1.95
Widely acclaimed biography of the double Nobel Prize winner. Marie Curie discovered radium and her work has been the basis for much modern chemistry and nuclear physics. A rounded and readable portrait of a brilliant but troubled woman.

OSCAR WILDE   Philippe Jullian   £1.75
A fascinating account of Wilde's life and work. 'There is no better life of Wilde then this one.'
Philip Toynbee *The Observer*

VIRGINIA WOOLF Vols 1 & 2
Quentin Bell   (Vol 1 £1.95; Vol 2 £1.50)
Acclaimed as one of the outstanding literary biographies of the century, these books trace the troubled development of Virginia Woolf as a writer and as a woman. Her Bloomsbury friends are chronicled in parallel.

WELSH DYLAN   John Ackerman   £1.95
This penetrating new biography places a new light on Dylan Thomas' identity as a Welshman, showing the close relationship between his work and his Welsh background.

THE LIFE OF MILAREPA   Lobsang P Lhalungpa   £1.95
A biography of an eleventh-century Tibetan mystic, which is a personal and moving introduction to Tibetan Buddhism. It is also a powerful and graphic folk tale full of magic, disaster, deceptions and humour. Illustrated with Tibetan religious paintings.

THE LIFE AND TIMES OF CHAUCER   John Gardner   £1.95
A fascinating and lively picture of Chaucer; the man of affairs, the diplomat, the wealthy man, the hob-nobber with the nobility, the winer and diner and also the philosopher.

SOCIAL HISTORY

IN A COUNTRY CHURCHYARD Ronald Fletcher £1.50
The author has traced many life stories hidden in the country churchyards where he lives. His generously illustrated narrative recalls to life the personalities and communities of the past in a series of luminous tableaux.

SHEEP BELL & PLOUGHSHARE Marjorie Reeves £1.95
A colourful account of life in a Wiltshire village, gathered from the domestic bric-a-brac and family documents, of two Wiltshire families. It is also the wider story of changing traditions in rural and industrial England through 300 years of its history. Illustrated.

TRAVELLING BROTHERS R A Leeson £2.50
An exploration into the development of the organised craft movements from the days of the medieval guilds to those of the modern trade unions. Illustrated.

THE EDWARDIANS Paul Thompson £1.95
A marvellous collage of interviews and reminiscences of living Edwardians of all classes. This is social history at its best – a superb analysis of a misinterpreted era.

All these books are available to your local bookshop or newsagent, or can be ordered direct from the publisher. Just tick the titles you want and fill in the form below.

Name ....

Address ....

....

Write to Granada Cash Sales. PO Box 11. Falmouth. Cornwall TR10 9EN
Please enclose remittance to the value of the cover price plus:

UK: 40p for the first book. 18p for the second book plus 13p per copy for each additional book ordered to a maximum charge of £1.49.

BFPO and EIRE: 40p for the first book. 18p for the second book plus 13p per copy for the next 7 books. thereafter 7p per book.

OVERSEAS: 60p for the first book and 18p for each additional book.

Granada Publishing reserve the right to show new retail prices on covers, which may differ from those previously advertised in the text or elsewhere.

PAL 31 (SOCIAL HISTORY) 481